T0202962

Lecture Notes in Computer Science 14495

The series Lecture Notes in Computer Science (LNCS), including its subseries Lecture Notes in Artificial Intelligence (LNAI) and Lecture Notes in Bioinformatics (LNBI), has established itself as a medium for the publication of new developments in computer science and information technology research, teaching, and education.

LNCS enjoys close cooperation with the computer science R & D community, the series counts many renowned academics among its volume editors and paper authors, and collaborates with prestigious societies. Its mission is to serve this international community by providing an invaluable service, mainly focused on the publication of conference and workshop proceedings and postproceedings. LNCS commenced publication in 1973.

Bin Sheng · Lei Bi · Jinman Kim ·
Nadia Magnenat-Thalmann · Daniel Thalmann
Editors

Advances in
Computer Graphics

40th Computer Graphics International Conference, CGI 2023
Shanghai, China, August 28 – September 1, 2023
Proceedings, Part I

 Springer

Editors
Bin Sheng (ID)
Shanghai Jiao Tong University
Shanghai, China

Jinman Kim (ID)
University of Sydney
Sydney, NSW, Australia

Daniel Thalmann
Swiss Federal Institute of Technology
Lausanne, Switzerland

Lei Bi (ID)
Shanghai Jiao Tong University
Shanghai, China

Nadia Magnenat-Thalmann (ID)
MIRALab-CUI
University of Geneve
Carouge, Geneve, Switzerland

ISSN 0302-9743   ISSN 1611-3349 (electronic)
Lecture Notes in Computer Science
ISBN 978-3-031-50068-8   ISBN 978-3-031-50069-5 (eBook)
https://doi.org/10.1007/978-3-031-50069-5

This Springer imprint is published by the registered company Springer Nature Switzerland AG
The registered company address is: Gewerbestrasse 11, 6330 Cham, Switzerland

Paper in this product is recyclable.

Preface Lecture Notes in Computer Science (14495)

CGI is one of the oldest annual international conferences on Computer Graphics in the world. Researchers are invited to share their experiences and novel achievements in various fields of Computer Graphics and Virtual Reality. Previous recent CGI conferences have been held in Sydney, Australia (2014), Strasbourg, France (2015), Heraklion, Greece (2016), Yokohama, Japan (2017), Bintan, Indonesia (2018), and Calgary in Canada (2019). CGI was virtual between 2020 and 2022 due to the COVID pandemic. This year, CGI 2023 was organized by the Shanghai Jiao Tong University, with the assistance of the University of Sydney and Wuhan Textile University, and supported by the Computer Graphics Society (CGS). The conference was held during August 28 to September 1, 2023.

These CGI 2023 LNCS proceedings are composed of 149 papers from a total of 385 submissions. This includes 51 papers that were reviewed highly and were recommended to be published in the CGI Visual Computer Journal track. To ensure the high quality of the publications, each paper was reviewed by at least two experts in the field and authors of accepted papers were asked to revise their paper according to the review comments prior to publication.

The CGI 2023 LNCS proceedings also include papers from the ENGAGE (Empowering Novel Geometric Algebra for Graphics & Engineering) 2023 Workshop (11 full papers), focused specifically on important aspects of geometric algebra including surface construction, robotics, encryption, qubits and expression optimization. The workshop has been part of the CGI conferences since 2016.

We would like to express our deepest gratitude to all the PC members and external reviewers who provided timely high-quality reviews. We would also like to thank all the authors for contributing to the conference by submitting their work.

September 2023

Bin Sheng
Lei Bi
Jinman Kim
Nadia Magnenat-Thalmann
Daniel Thalmann

Organization

Honorary Conference Chairs

Enhua Wu   Chinese Academy of Sciences/University of
                              Macau, China
Dagan Feng   University of Sydney, Australia

Conference Chairs

Nadia Magnenat Thalmann   University of Geneva, Switzerland
Bin Sheng   Shanghai Jiao Tong University, China
Jinman Kim   University of Sydney, Australia

Program Chairs

Daniel Thalmann   École Polytechnique Fédérale de Lausanne,
                               Switzerland
Stephen Lin   Microsoft Research Asia, China
Lizhuang Ma   Shanghai Jiao Tong University, China
Ping Li   Hong Kong Polytechnic University, China

Contents – Part I

Image Restoration and Enhancement

Image Attention and Perception

Detection and Recognition

Leveraging Computer Vision Networks for Guitar Tablature Transcription

Charbel El Achkar[1,2]($\boxtimes$), Raphaël Couturier[2], Abdallah Makhoul[2],
and Talar Atéchian[1]

[1] TICKET Lab, Antonine University (UA), Baabda, Lebanon
{charbel.elachkar,talar.atechian}@ua.edu.lb
[2] Université de Franche-Comté, CNRS, institut FEMTO-ST, 90000 Belfort, France
{charbel.el_achkar,raphael.couturier,abdallah.makhoul}@univ-fcomte.fr

Abstract. Generating music-related notations offers assistance for musicians in the path of replicating the music using a specific instrument. In this paper, we evaluate the state-of-the-art guitar tablature transcription network named TabCNN against state-of-the-art computer vision networks. The evaluation is performed using the same dataset as well as the same evaluation metrics of TabCNN. Furthermore, we propose a new CNN-based network named TabInception to transcribe guitar-related notations, also called guitar tablatures. The network relies on a custom inception block converged by dense layers. The TabInception network outperforms the TabCNN in terms of multi-pitch precision (MP), tablature precision (TP), and tablature F-measure (TF). Moreover, the Swin Transformer achieves the best score in terms of multi-pitch recall (MR) and tablature recall (TR), while the Vision Transformer achieves the best score in terms of multi-pitch F-measure (MF). Motivated by the previous insights, we train the networks with more epochs and propose another network named Inception Transformer (InT) to surpass all the estimation metrics of TabCNN using a single network. The InT network relies on an inception block converged by a Transformer Encoder. The TabInception and the InT network outperformed all estimation metrics of TabCNN except the tablature disambiguation rate (TDR) when trained using a bigger epoch size.

Keywords: Guitar Tablature Transcription · Computer Vision · Automatic Music Transcription

1 Introduction

Over the last decade, researchers have been exploring the benefits of their innovations in music-related fields while producing tools that can facilitate musicians' daily tasks. One of the latter fields is automatic music transcription (AMT). The AMT is the task of generating a symbolic notation, and instructing a musician how to play a song using a specific instrument. Several studies have been conducted in the AMT field, but only a few of them dealt with the guitar instrument

B. Sheng et al. (Eds.): CGI 2023, LNCS 14495, pp. 3–15, 2024.
https://doi.org/10.1007/978-3-031-50069-5_2

[2,3,8]. As for automatic guitar transcription, the guitarist generally relies on both the music score and the tablature notation to play the song in question. The music score represents the distribution of pitches in time, and the tablature notation defines the guitar strings and the position of the fingers along the fretboard to produce those pitches.

This paper explores several computer vision techniques for automatic guitar transcription. Inspired by the TabCNN model published in [23], Constant-Q spectrograms are generated from each audio track and computed through Computer Vision approaches as visual representations of the audio data. Furthermore, we propose a new CNN-based network named TabInception that relies on Inception and Dense Blocks for automatic guitar transcription. Moreover, we propose another network named Inception Transformer (InT) to attempt to improve the results of TabInception and other featured networks. The Int network relies on an Inception Block converged by the Transformer Encoder Block proposed in [21]. Thus, the leading purpose of this study is to evaluate the TabCNN network against state-of-the-art computer vision networks while proposing new networks that might be capable of outperforming the latter network in the field of guitar tablature transcription. All the aforementioned networks, in addition to the TabInception and the InT network, are evaluated using the GuitarSet dataset published in [25], by the fact that TabCNN was assessed earlier against this dataset [23]. At a broader level, the aim is to explore which of the shallow networks like TabCNN or the deeper networks, such as the proposed ones, can perform better on music transcription use cases. The remainder of this paper is organized as follows: In Sect. 2, recent automatic guitar transcription studies are discussed. Section 3 presents the selected dataset in addition to the adopted preprocessing procedure. Section 4 interprets the proposed networks for automatic guitar transcription, while Sect. 5 compares the proposed networks with state-of-the-art CNNs and Transformer-based networks in terms of multi-pitch and tablature estimation metrics. Section 6 concludes the work and gives some directions for future work.

2   Related Work

The technological advances and innovations in the field of human-computer interaction were reflected in various practices. A novel method for gesture recognition was proposed in [26], emphasising the need for improved data generalisation. Another initiative extended innovation by discussing multimodal learning and its relevance in computer vision [4]. Advances in technology such as EMG signal analysis helped in the development of highly accurate recognition methods [13] after demonstrating the continuous progress in this area. Another area of recognition is automatic tablature transcription, which we are developing in this study.

Many studies are proposed for automatic tablature transcription, but only a few seek to detect the real fretting of the guitarist. One of the first approaches leverages the fundamentals and partials for candidate pitches to determine the most used string per pitch [3]. This approach is limited to detecting no more than four pitches sounding simultaneous. Two years later, a system for applying the Blind Harmonic Adaptive Decomposition Algorithm was developed to classify several performance parameters, including the detection of the note's guitar string [8]. This system is not evaluated for framewise tablature estimation. Nevertheless, it is considered an insightful approach for multi-pitch estimation and guitar tablature estimation. Additionally, several studies focused on the guitar in their pursuit of automatic transcription. For instance, A. M. Barbancho et al. [2] transcribed guitar chords and fingering using a hidden Markov Model, while Humphrey and Bello [11] took the benefit of a convolutional neural network (CNN) model to achieve chord recognition.

The results of the latter approach encouraged the researchers to take advantage of CNN for similar music-related tasks. A combination of a CNN for framewise acoustic modelling and a recurrent neural network (RNN) model is proposed for piano transcription in [17].

The use of neural networks for music-related tasks helped in providing solutions for tablature arrangement problems [20]). It tackled various music information retrieval tasks such as instrument classification [9,10], music genre classification [7], and singing voice detection [16]. It also helped in achieving the first guitar tablature estimation model using CNNs. The model was trained using solo acoustic guitar performances of the GuitarSet dataset presented in Xi et al. (2019) [25], while outperforming state-of-the-art multi-pitch estimation algorithms. This paper also introduced a set of metrics found to be specific for evaluating guitar tablature estimation models, as described in Wiggins and Kim (2019) [23]. Several attempts took place to improve the TabCNN's results presented in [23]. One of those attempts was the thesis report in Maaiveld et al. (2021) [15]. It yielded insights into the CNNs' functioning for automatic music transcription. The proposition relied on several adaptations such as data augmentation, Oracle method adaptation, and increasing the amount of training data. The latter study was not able to outperform the results of the TabCNN [23]) but presented intuitive conclusions, such as the fact that Dense layers play a major role in tablature estimation CNNs and that the size of the dataset is a key factor in the model's performance.

The fast growth of neural networks encouraged researchers to test the latest approaches in the music industry. An unsupervised pitch estimation model was reported by Wiggins and Kim (2020) [24] to analyse audio clips by estimating their pitches and amplitudes. The model was not tested through experiments but gave thoughtful ideas for further unsupervised acoustic guitar transcription attempts. Also, a method for generating note-level transcription for guitar transcription is proposed to demonstrate successful transcription using notes rather than frames [12]. This work outperformed the conventional frame-level CNN methods. Nevertheless, it did not outperform all TabCNN's estimation metrics results [23].

Last but not least, a unified model and methodology for estimating pitch contours took place to transcribe guitar tablatures [5]. It produced pitch esti-

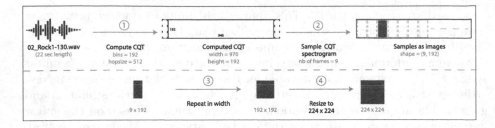

Fig. 1. Audio to Image transformation through Constant-Q Transform computation

mates with a higher resolution than modern models. However, and to the best of our knowledge, neither the approaches listed in this section nor any other associated work can outperform all TabCNN's [23] estimation metrics for guitar tablature transcription.

3   Data Selection and Preparation

The TabCNN model proposed in [23] holds the state-of-the-art record for guitar tablature transcription using CNNs. In this study, the same dataset chosen in TabCNN is used, in addition to the preprocessing procedure for computing audio features to images.

Similar to the TabCNN approach [23], the audio recordings were downsampled from 44100 to 22050 Hz to reduce the input signals' dimension. The input signals were normalized to obtain an identical range of amplitudes among all the recordings. This normalization is essential to achieve the next step: computing the convenient audio signal feature out of each recording. Inspired by previous experiences in guitar tablature transcription, the Constant-Q Transform (CQT) is adopted as the feature to compute. For this reason, and to directly compare all studied networks with TabCNN, similar CQT parameters are adopted. As shown in Fig. 1, and using the *Librosa* Python library, the CQT is computed over the audio recording in the first place. A value of 192 is selected for the bins and 512 for the hopsize parameter. The bins parameter consists of the intervals between samples in the frequency domain. It is estimated by dividing the sampling rate by the Fast Fourier Transform (FFT) size. On the other hand, the hopsize is the number of samples between each successive FFT window. It is processed by dividing the FFT size by an integer defining the overlap factor of FFT windows. As for this parameter selection validation, we plotted the chroma_cqt features using the selected bins and hopsize parameters. The chroma features captures harmonic and melodic characteristics of music while being robust to changes in timbre and instrumentation. In this case, the chroma_cqt analyses these musical features following the CQT parameter already computed. While visualizing the plots, it was found that the produced chroma features were slightly noisy and unclear. Thus, the number of bins per octave parameter was scaled from its default value (12) to 24 to clarify the computed CQT by increasing its resolution. The CQT is then computed using the new parameter values: hopsize = 512, number of bins = 192, and number of bins per octave = 24. At this stage, the computed CQT can be obtained as a visual representation of size 970 × 192, while adding zero padding on both sides of the CQT to achieve the sampling step (the initial size is 946 × 192 since the audio used in this example has a 22 s length and the hopsize used corresponds to 43 frames per seconds approximately). In addition, the sampling step (second in Fig. 1) is where the sliding context window of 9 frames takes place to generate multiple images of size 9 × 192 out of the initial computed CQT. The entire process results in multiple CQT images out of the same audio recording. Each image concerns nine successive frames of the initially computed CQT. It was essential to resize the sampled CQT images into square-shaped images to compare the proposed and the existing approaches with state-of-the-art computer vision networks. The majority of the latter networks are trained and evaluated using squared images. Thus, the need to resize the images to the smallest recurrent size, 224 × 224. Consequently, using the function of the *numpy* Python library, we repeated the same pixels of the sampled image in width to achieve a size of 192 × 192. Then, the images were resized from 192 × 192 to 224 × 224. It is important to note that this is the most convenient resizing technique, since resizing from 9 × 192 directly to 224 × 224 may distort the image content. Also, both versions were kept, the 9 × 192 sampled images and the 224 × 224 resized images for further network comparisons. Concerning the annotations, the same approach in [23] is adapted to sample the stringwise pitch features stored in the JAMS files. These features are transformed into binary matrices. Each matrix represents a frame belonging to a computed audio recording.

$$
\begin{aligned}
&[\,[1.\,0.\,0.\,0.\,0.\,0.\,0.\,0.\,0.\,0.\,0.\,0.\,0.\,0.\,0.\,0.\,0.\,0.\,0.\,0.\,0.] \\
&\ [1.\,0.\,0.\,0.\,0.\,0.\,0.\,0.\,0.\,0.\,0.\,0.\,0.\,0.\,0.\,0.\,0.\,0.\,0.\,0.\,0.] \\
&\ [1.\,0.\,0.\,0.\,0.\,0.\,0.\,0.\,0.\,0.\,0.\,0.\,0.\,0.\,0.\,0.\,0.\,0.\,0.\,0.\,0.] \\
&\ [1.\,0.\,0.\,0.\,0.\,0.\,0.\,0.\,0.\,0.\,0.\,0.\,0.\,0.\,0.\,0.\,0.\,0.\,0.\,0.\,0.] \\
&\ [0.\,0.\,0.\,0.\,0.\,0.\,0.\,1.\,0.\,0.\,0.\,0.\,0.\,0.\,0.\,0.\,0.\,0.\,0.\,0.\,0.] \\
&\ [1.\,0.\,0.\,0.\,0.\,0.\,0.\,0.\,0.\,0.\,0.\,0.\,0.\,0.\,0.\,0.\,0.\,0.\,0.\,0.\,0.]\,]
\end{aligned}
$$

Fig. 2. Label associated to the 512th frame of the 02_Rock_1_130.wav recording

Figure 2 represents a matrix associated with one of the frames in a guitar recording. The matrix is of shape 6 × 21, equal to the six strings of the guitar having 21 different fret classes. Since the GuitarSet is recorded using an acoustic guitar of 19 frets, the remaining two frets correspond to two descriptive states of a guitar string. The first fret associated with the first column (from left to right) of the matrix indicates if the string is in an open state (no frets are pressed), while the second fret (second column) indicates if the latter is in a closed state. The remaining 19 frets correspond to the remaining 19 columns of the matrix to define the pressed fret at a given frame.

4   Proposed Networks

4.1   The TabInception Network

Inspired by the insightful conclusion in [15], especially the point mentioning the essential role of Dense layers in guitar tablature transcription, a custom CNN-based network named TabInception is proposed. As shown in Fig. 3, the TabInception starts with an input layer taking images of shape (192, 9, 1). Thus, it involves swapping the axes of the computed images in the preprocessing steps to provide a proper data fitting. Consequently, we propose adding a two-dimensional convolutional layer of 32 filters adjacent to a Batch Normalization, a Relu activation, and a Max Pooling layer with a pool size equal to (4,1). The output of the latter bundle is fed into an Inception block that can be described as follows:

The proposed Inception block uses a similar architecture to the Inception v4 architecture implemented in [18], while adding Batch Normalization and Relu activation layers among adjacent Conv2D layers.

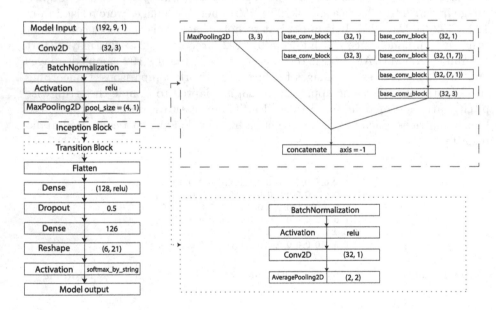

Fig. 3. Architecture of the TabInception network

Figure 3 shows a high-level visualization of the Inception block, where several base convolutional blocks (base_conv_block) are interconnected together and are concatenated at the end with a MaxPooling2D layer. Each base_conv_block consists of a Batch Normalization, a Relu activation, and a Conv2D layer with 32 filters. This technique ensures that the adopted inception approach will be less likely to over-fit. Also, the Batch Normalization improves memory optimization to backpropagation while reducing the intensive computations caused by convolutional layers. After concatenating the Inception block's calculations, the output is fed to the Transition Block. As presented in Fig. 3, the Transition block is the same as a base_conv_block with the addition of an AveragePooling2D layer after the Conv2D one. This approach is essential to downsample the huge spatial dimensions caused by the Inception block, and to converge the network into its decisive and final layers. Since TabInception concerns guitar tablature transcription, the network should be able to compute multidimensional calculations. Hence, the use of the Flatten layer to convert the sixth channelled output to a single channelled one for Dense layer calculations. Each of the sixth channels consists of a guitar string having 21 frets. The Dense calculations are dropped out with a value of 0.5 while re-iterating the Dense computations using a number of units equal to the multiplication of the number of strings and frets ($6 \times 21 = 126$ units). The output of the concluding layer is reshaped back to (6, 21) to compute the activation of each guitar string separately. Finally, the softmax_by_string activation function proposed in [23] is used to concatenate the separately computed six softmax calculations and to unify the output.

4.2   The Inception Transformer Network

Inspired by the precision of the TabInception network and the recall and the F-measure of the Transformer-based models, the InT proposes a fusion between the Inception block of the TabInception network and the Transformer Encoder proposed in [21] and adopted in the Vision Transformer (ViT) model [6].

Similar to TabInception, The InT network relies on similar Input layers except using a number of filters equal to 64 instead of 32, as well as adding 4 strides to the initial Conv2D layer. The increased number of filters is adapted into the Inception Block of the InT network. The latter Block is identical to the one used in TabInception except for the number of filters. Furthermore, the computed calculations are concatenated and reshaped to (96, 64) to match the input shape needed for the Transformer Encoder. The Transformer Encoder adopted in [6] expects a sequence of embeddings vector that serves as input. These vectors consist of positional embeddings in addition to those of previously generated patches. As for the Transformer Encoder of the InT network, it expects a sequence of positional embedding along with the reshaped tensors produced out of the previously mentioned Inception block. Thus, the idea of generating patches and feeding them to the encoder is replaced by loading the encoder with convolutional-based tensors. The Transformer Encoder is responsible for alternating multihead self-attention blocks with MLP blocks. A LayerNormalization layer is applied before every block in addition to a residual connection after every block inside the encoder [1,22]. The Transformer Encoder used in the proposed InT network relies on six transformer layers, an MLP dimension of 128, and a patch size equal to 4. The output of the latter encoder is fed to a ReduceMean layer to reduce the dimension of the tensor for the succeeding Dense layer. The Dense layer of shape 126 is then fed to the same concluding layers as TabInception to compute the activation of each guitar string separately. The same activation function and optimizer are adopted for both, the TabInception and the Inception Transformer networks.

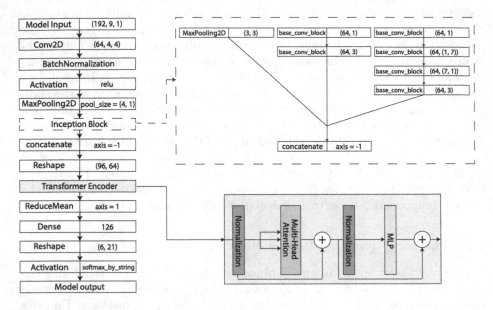

Fig. 4. Architecture of the Inception Transformer (InT) network

5 Experiments

In this section, the TabCNN network is compared to the TabInception and InT networks, in addition to state-of-the-art computer vision (CV) networks such as [6,14,19]. The CV networks were modified slightly by reshaping their decisive layers to provide a unified output across all networks (shape of $(6, 21)$ as a matrix of 6 strings with 21 frets each). The implementation took place using the official version of the CV networks or its equivalent in *Keras*. The same parameters and hyperparameters are used across all the networks for better comparison with TabCNN. A batch size of 128 and a 6-fold cross-validation training method were selected while relying on the preprocessed CQT as input images to the network. The images were divided using an 85% training and 15% testing ratio for all networks.

The Swin Transformer (SwinTF) [14] and the EfficientNetB0 [19] [1] networks perform their best when trained using squared images since they rely on patch-based architectural structures. Therefore, it was favourable to experiment with

---

[1] The B0 base model of EfficientNet is the only selected model for this experiment since it is the only compatible model for computing 224×224-sized images. As for the SwinTF, we use the base architecture for this experiment, also known as swin_b.

Table 1. Comparative table for guitar tablature transcription using computer vision networks. The best score per metric is highlighted in **black**, the second best in **green**, and the third best in **red**.

Image Size	Epochs	Network	MP	MR	MF	TP	TR	TF	TDR
192 × 9	8	TabCNN	0.9 ±0.016	0.764 ±0.043	0.826 ±0.025	0.809 ±0.029	0.696 ±0.061	0.748 ±0.047	0.899 ±0.033
192 × 9	16	TabCNN	0.927 ±0.008	0.7805 ±0.003	0.8474 ±0.0176	0.8101 ±0.0115	0.711 ±0.0268	0.757 ±0.0151	0.873 ±0.006
192 × 9	300 with ES	TabCNN	0.8549 ±0.013	0.722 ±0.021	0.782 ±0.0172	0.815 ±0.0185	0.697 ±0.0346	0.751 ±0.0237	**0.953** ±0.0136
192 × 9	8	TabInception	0.941 ±0.008	0.7189 ±0.031	0.815 ±0.0176	0.7973 ±0.0115	0.6455 ±0.0268	0.7134 ±0.0151	0.8473 ±0.006
192 × 9	16	TabInception	**0.9688** ±0.0192	0.7454 ±0.0518	0.8425 ±0.0317	**0.8519** ±0.0199	0.6911 ±0.0608	**0.7631** ±0.0443	0.8793 ±0.0244
192 × 9	300 with ES	TabInception	0.9533 ±0.0147	0.7834 ±0.0339	0.86 ±0.0187	**0.8639** ±0.0158	0.739 ±0.0356	**0.7965** ±0.0221	0.906 ±0.0104
192 × 9	8	ViT	0.908 ±0.0165	0.8209 ±0.0373	0.8622 ±0.0204	0.7291 ±0.0329	0.7144 ±0.0444	0.7216 ±0.0349	0.802 ±0.0313
192 × 9	16	ViT	0.882 ±0.0066	0.8 ±0.0155	0.839 ±0.0056	0.7043 ±0.0074	0.6901 ±0.0183	0.6971 ±0.0099	0.798 ±0.0093
192 × 9	300 with ES	ViT	0.937 ±0.0115	**0.8524** ±0.0264	**0.8927** ±0.013	0.7586 ±0.0201	**0.7441** ±0.0313	0.7512 ±0.0224	0.8096 ±0.0203
192 × 9	8	InT	0.8785 ±0.0083	0.8213 ±0.0092	0.8489 ±0.0056	0.7202 ±0.0128	0.7206 ±0.0132	0.7203 ±0.0117	0.8198 ±0.0089
192 × 9	16	InT	0.891 ±0.0031	0.82 ±0.0062	0.854 ±0.0031	0.7134 ±0.0356	0.7019 ±0.0738	0.7076 ±0.0473	0.8 ±0.0034
192 × 9	300 with ES	InT	**0.9481** ±0.0057	**0.914** ±0.0077	**0.9307** ±0.0043	**0.8551** ±0.0242	**0.8041** ±0.0435	**0.828** ±0.0295	**0.901** ±0.00615
224 × 224	8	SwinTF	0.8875 ±0.0146	0.8034 ±0.0374	0.843 ±0.0146	0.709 ±0.0226	0.693 ±0.0212	0.7 ±0.041	0.798 ±0.031
224 × 224	16	SwinTF	0.9035 ±0.0075	0.8421 ±0.0034	0.8717 ±0.0024	0.7331 ±0.0019	0.726 ±0.0069	0.729 ±0.002	0.8114 ±0.007
224 × 224	300 with ES	SwinTF	0.9259 ±0.011	**0.8531** ±0.0204	**0.888** ±0.0085	0.7307 ±0.0122	0.7191 ±0.014	0.7248 ±0.0215	0.789 ±0.019
224 × 224	8	EfficientNetB0	0.839 ±0.0176	0.7691 ±0.0071	0.8025 ±0.016	0.6739 ±0.026	0.6406 ±0.048	0.656 ±0.034	0.803 ±0.031
224 × 224	16	EfficientNetB0	0.861 ±0.006	0.691 ±0.067	0.766 ±0.0386	0.733 ±0.0359	0.615 ±0.0695	0.668 ±0.0475	0.851 ±0.0401
224 × 224	300 with ES	EfficientNetB0	0.8947 ±0.0118	0.7747 ±0.037	0.83 ±0.0273	0.748 ±0.0309	0.6723 ±0.0587	0.708 ±0.0407	0.836 ±0.0355

both networks using a squared image format instead of performing architecture changes for fitting non-squared images. Hence, the resized 224 × 224 CQT images are used for these approaches. In contrast, the 192 × 9 CQT images are adopted to train the TabCNN, the TabInception, The InT, and the Vision Transformer (VIT) networks [6]) by the fact that they are not image size dependent. Thus, the proposed networks can be directly compared with the TabCNN network [23], while presenting other approaches where an image resizing may impact the training results.

It is important to mention that the VIT network relies on a patch-based structure. Nevertheless, it can be fed with non-squared images by its ability to transform each image into patches of equal width and height size. Thus, the input images are transformed into patches before being fed to the VIT encoder. In this experiment, and for the VIT network exclusively, we adopt a patch size of 4 and a hidden size of 64 after performing several empirical tests where both parameters were varied to maximize the evaluation results. Consequently, each of the 192×9 input images is transformed into 64 patches, having a size of 64×64 for each patch. The latter is conducted using the patch generation function proposed in the original code of the VIT [6] for rescaling and transforming the input images into patches. Table 1 presents all the networks that we compare with TabCNN. The first training of TabCNN is written in *italic* to indicate that its results are shown as they appear in the official contribution. Contrarily, the remaining training is performed in our test environment. The table header presents seven different multi-pitch and tablature estimation metrics. Each metric manifests an essential role already proposed in [23]. The metrics referenced in Table 1 are the following: Multi-pitch Precision (MP), Multi-pitch Recall (MR), Multi-pitch F-measure (MF), Tablature Precision (TP), Tablature Recall (TR), Tablature F-measure (TF), and Tablature Disambiguation Rate (TDR). As shown in Table 1, the networks were trained using two different epoch sizes. An epoch size of 8 is used to compare the results with the official TabCNN results. Furthermore, an epoch size of 16 is adopted to identify the behaviour of each network using longer iterations. At an epoch size of 8, the TabInception outperformed the TabCNN by 4.1% points (*pp* in terms of multi-pitch precision (MP). On the other hand, the InT network and the transformer-based networks (ViT and SwinTF) can either outperform or obtain the same results as the TabCNN in terms of multi-pitch recall (MR) and F-measure (MF). The VIT exceeded the TabCNN by 3.62 *pp* in terms of MF and 5.69 *pp* in terms of MR. Also, the SwinTF exceeded TabCNN's MF by 1.7 *pp*, and TabCNN's MR by 3.94 *pp*. As for the InT network, it exceeded TabCNN's MF by 2.29 *pp* and TabCNN's MR by 5.73 *pp*. These results show that the TabInception network is a good solution for better pitch detection, while both, the proposed InT network and the transformer-based networks are better options when the comparison concerns the MR and MF metrics. The TabInception network outperformed the TabCNN network in terms of MP, TP, and TF metrics when increasing the epoch size to 16. It achieved the greatest results concerning the multi-pitch precision metric. It outperformed TabCNN's MP by 4.18 *pp*, the TP by 4.17 *pp*, and the TF by 0.61 *pp*. As for the proposed InT network, it surpassed the TabCNN network in terms of MR and MF. Moreover, among the remaining networks, the SwinTF improved its results using an increased epoch size. Contrarily, the EfficientNetB0 could not exceed TabCNN's results in either epochs variations.

Motivated by the increase in metrics when raising the epochs size, we configured an epochs size of 300 while establishing the early stopping mechanism with a patience value equal to 5. Thus, the models will keep training until they reach a safe point to stop without overfitting. All the tests produced using the latter configuration are highlighted in a dashed outline in Table 1 to discriminate the latter from the legacy configuration (8–16 epochs without an early stopping mechanism). **green** Also, we highlight the best score per metric with a **black** bold color, the second best with a **green** bold color, and the third best with a **red** bold color. The results show that the TabInception network achieved the best result in terms of TP, and the InT network achieved the best results for MR, MF, TR, and TF. Both proposed networks were able to surpass all of TabCNN's results except the TDR metric. The TabCNN preserved the best result in terms of TDR in that case. The significant TDR value of TabCNN is due to the closer MP and TP values compared to the remaining networks. As for the SwinTF, the ViT, and the EfficientNetB0, some of their metrics' results increased but could not considerably surpass TabCNN's values at all times.

6   Conclusion and Future Work

In this paper, two networks were proposed for guitar tablature transcription. The first network, TabInception, relies on a custom inception block converged by dense layers. The second network, Inception Transformer (InT), relies on a similar inception block of TabInception converged by a Transformer Encoder. Both networks were compared against the state-of-the-art guitar tablature transcription network named TabCNN and other recent computer vision networks. The experiment results showed that the proposed networks can outperform the TabCNN in terms of multi-pitch precision (MP), multi-pitch recall (MR), multi-pitch F-measure (MF), tablature precision (TP), tablature recall (TR), and tablature F-measure (TF). Our future work should focus on exploring the performance and the usability of both proposed networks for transcribing tablatures of other string instruments such as the violin, cello, and harp. Furthermore, it would be essential to test the proposed networks on computer vision use cases beyond the tablature transcription or even the music field to better evaluate and explore the importance of such contribution. The source code for implementing the discussed networks is publicly available on the following repository: https://github.com/elachkarcharbel/Guitar-Tablature-Transcription

Acknowledgments. This work was performed using HPC resources from GENCI-IDRIS (Grant 2021-AD011013289). It is funded by the "Agence Universitaire de la Francophonie" (AUF) and supported by the EIPHI Graduate School (contract ANR-17-EURE-0002).

References

1. Baevski, A., Auli, M.: Adaptive input representations for neural language modeling. arXiv preprint arXiv:1809.10853 (2018)
2. Barbancho, A.M., Klapuri, A., Tardon, L.J., Barbancho, I.: Automatic transcription of guitar chords and fingering from audio. IEEE Trans. Audio Speech Lang. Process. **20**(3), 915–921 (2012). https://doi.org/10.1109/TASL.2011.2174227
3. Barbancho, I., Tardon, L.J., Sammartino, S., Barbancho, A.M.: Inharmonicity-based method for the automatic generation of guitar tablature. IEEE Trans. Audio Speech Lang. Process. **20**(6), 1857–1868 (2012). https://doi.org/10.1109/TASL.2012.2191281

4. Bayoudh, K., Knani, R., Hamdaoui, F., Mtibaa, A.: A survey on deep multimodal learning for computer vision: advances, trends, applications, and datasets. The Visual Computer, pp. 1–32 (2021)
5. Cwitkowitz, F., Hirvonen, T., Klapuri, A.: Fretnet: Continuous-valued pitch contour streaming for polyphonic guitar tablature transcription. arXiv preprint arXiv:2212.03023 (2022)
6. Dosovitskiy, A., et al.: An image is worth 16x16 words: Transformers for image recognition at scale. arXiv preprint arXiv:2010.11929 (2020)
7. El Achkar, C., Couturier, R., Atéchian, T., Makhoul, A.: Combining reduction and dense blocks for music genre classification. In: Mantoro, T., Lee, M., Ayu, M.A., Wong, K.W., Hidayanto, A.N. (eds.) Neural Information Processing, pp. 752–760. Springer, Cham (2021)
8. Fuentes, B., Badeau, R., Richard, G.: Blind harmonic adaptive decomposition applied to supervised source separation. In: 2012 Proceedings of the 20th European Signal Processing Conference (EUSIPCO), pp. 2654–2658 (2012)
9. Gómez, J.S., Abeßer, J., Cano, E.: Jazz Solo Instrument classification with convolutional neural networks, source separation, and transfer learning. In: Proceedings of the 19th International Society for Music Information Retrieval Conference, pp. 577–584. ISMIR, Paris, France, September 2018. https://doi.org/10.5281/zenodo.1492481
10. Han, Y., Kim, J., Lee, K.: Deep convolutional neural networks for predominant instrument recognition in polyphonic music. IEEE/ACM Trans. Audio Speech Lang. Process. **25**(1), 208–221 (2017). https://doi.org/10.1109/TASLP.2016.2632307
11. Humphrey, E.J., Bello, J.P.: From music audio to chord tablature: Teaching deep convolutional networks toplay guitar. In: 2014 IEEE International Conference on Acoustics, Speech and Signal Processing (ICASSP), pp. 6974–6978 (2014). https://doi.org/10.1109/ICASSP.2014.6854952
12. Kim, S., Hayashi, T., Toda, T.: Note-level automatic guitar transcription using attention mechanism. In: 2022 30th European Signal Processing Conference (EUSIPCO), pp. 229–233. IEEE (2022)
13. Li, J., Wei, L., Wen, Y., Liu, X., Wang, H.: An approach to continuous hand movement recognition using semg based on features fusion. Vis. Comput. **39**(5), 2065–2079 (2023)
14. Liu, Z., et al.: Swin transformer: hierarchical vision transformer using shifted windows. In: Proceedings of the IEEE/CVF International Conference on Computer Vision, pp. 10012–10022 (2021)
15. Maaiveld, T., Driedger, J., Yela, D., Meroño-Peñuela, A.: Automatic tablature estimation with convolutional neural networks: Approaches and limitations (04 2021). https://doi.org/10.13140/RG.2.2.13906.48320
16. Schlüter, J., Lehner, B.: Zero-mean convolutions for level-invariant singing voice detection, September 2018
17. Sigtia, S., Benetos, E., Dixon, S.: An end-to-end neural network for polyphonic piano music transcription. IEEE/ACM Trans. Audio Speech Lang. Process. **24**(5), 927–939 (2016). https://doi.org/10.1109/TASLP.2016.2533858
18. Szegedy, C., Ioffe, S., Vanhoucke, V., Alemi, A.: Inception-v4, inception-resnet and the impact of residual connections on learning. In: Proceedings of the AAAI Conference on Artificial Intelligence, vol. 31 (2017)
19. Tan, M., Le, Q.: Efficientnet: Rethinking model scaling for convolutional neural networks. In: International Conference on Machine Learning, pp. 6105–6114. PMLR (2019)

20. Tuohy, D.R., Potter, W.D.: An evolved neural network/hc hybrid for tablature creation in ga-based guitar arranging. In: International Conference on Mathematics and Computing (2006)
21. Vaswani, A., et al.: Attention is all you need. Advances in neural information processing systems 30 (2017)
22. Wang, Q., et al.: Learning deep transformer models for machine translation. arXiv preprint arXiv:1906.01787 (2019)
23. Wiggins, A., Kim, Y.: Guitar Tablature Estimation with a Convolutional Neural Network. In: Proceedings of the 20th International Society for Music Information Retrieval Conference, pp. 284–291. ISMIR, Delft, The Netherlands, November 2019. https://doi.org/10.5281/zenodo.3527800
24. Wiggins, A., Kim, Y.: Towards unsupervised acoustic guitar transcription. J. **7**(2), 43–55 (2020)
25. Xi, Q., Bittner, R.M., Pauwels, J., Ye, X., Bello, J.P.: Guitarset, August 2019. https://doi.org/10.5281/zenodo.3371780
26. Zeghoud, S., et al.: Real-time spatial normalization for dynamic gesture classification. The Visual Computer, pp. 1–13 (2022)

Serial Spatial and Temporal Transformer for Point Cloud Sequences Recognition

Shiqi Zou and Jingqiao Zhang[(✉)]

School of Computer Engineering and Science, Shanghai University, Shanghai 200444,
China
{sitchzou,jqzhang}@shu.edu.cn

Abstract. Point cloud sequences are unordered and irregular, which means extracting spatial and temporal features from them is challenging. This paper presents a novel network named Serial Spatial and Temporal Transformer (SerialSTTR) for point cloud sequences recognition. Specifically, point-based self-attention is used to gather global information on each point at the spatial level, and frame-based self-attention is used to reconstruct the sequences with motion features at the temporal level. In addition, an orderly local module is proposed to supplement the local feature learning ability that spatial transformer lacks. And relative position encoding is adopted to complete the order information for temporal transformer. Extensive experiments demonstrate that the SerialSTTR achieves the state-of-the-art performance on 3D human action recognition with the challenging dataset MSR-Action3D. And to show its generalizability, experiments on gesture recognition with SHREC'17 dataset are performed, which also present competitive results.

Keywords: point cloud sequences · transformer · point-based network · 3D action recognition

1 Introduction

Perception of 3D world is becoming increasingly important as the fields of autonomous driving and robotic manipulation rapidly develop [1,16]. Point cloud sequence is classic 3D data format that provides rich information about dynamic environment. With geometry structures and motion features presented, point cloud sequences are used for various applications, such as human action recognition and gesture recognition.

Since point cloud sequences consist of unordered and irregular point sets, it is challenging to extract spatial and temporal features by traditional operations. For the intra-frame learning, operations should be symmetric to keep consistency across different input orders of points, which means traditional convolution is not suitable. For the inter-frame learning, there is no correspondence between points in different frames, which makes it difficult to learn motion features.

One workaround is to transform the point cloud sequences into regular format frame by frame. For example, 3DV-PointNet [30] voxelized point cloud and

© The Author(s), under exclusive license to Springer Nature Switzerland AG 2024
B. Sheng et al. (Eds.): CGI 2023, LNCS 14495, pp. 16–27, 2024.
https://doi.org/10.1007/978-3-031-50069-5_3

represented motion information by dynamic voxels. FaF [21] tried to convert 3D structure into bird's eye view and apply 3D convolutions on it. However, voxelization not only costs a lot of memories and computation, but also introduces quantization errors. Another solution is to apply position-independent operations. For example, PointNet [23] used multi-layer perceptron (MLP), PCT [10] employed self-attention. However, they could not handle dynamic sequence data. To this end, MeteorNet [19] tried to track points across frames, and P4Transformer [8] used spatial-temporal attention to find related structures across time. Nevertheless, tracking points and structures across frames is difficult, like the optical flow problem in image processing [26].

In this paper, to overcome the above problems, we propose the Serial Spatial and Temporal Transformer (SerialSTTR) network to model spatial and temporal features separately, which constructs two transformer modules serially.

The first one is Spatial Transformer Module (STR), which gathers related information at each point from their relevant points, so that global spatial features can be encoded at each point. The second is Temporal Transformer Module (TTR), where each frame is treated as a word in a sentence, and frame-level self-attention is used to gather motion features at each frame. Moreover, we construct a learnable relative position encoding in temporal dimension to enhance the order information across frames.

Although transformer can extract most of the features by self-attention, it lacks local learning ability, which is important for representing point cloud [24]. Therefore, we construct two kinds of Orderly Local Module (OL) to learn local features: Gaussian OL and adaptive OL. The former method reasonably treats the local area as a Gaussian structure to represent the influences of neighbors, which are gradually diminishes based on distances. The latter method constructs a learnable kernel to model influences adaptively. In addition, by merging neighbor frames, OL modules are able to capture spatial-temporal local structures.

With the above methods, the SerialSTTR has the ability to model point cloud sequences. We evaluate our model on 3D human action recognition with MSR-Action3D [14] dataset, which achieves state-of-the-art result. Moreover, we perform experiments on gesture recognition with SHREC'17 [5] dataset to demonstrate the generalizability of the model. The contributions of this paper are threefold:

- We propose a dual transformer based network, named SerialSTTR, which constructs transformer modules in space and time serially, to extract intra-frame and inter-frame global features for point cloud sequence recognition.
- We propose a local learning module named OL to represent the influences of neighbor points in local structures, which makes it more effective to extract local features.
- Extensive experiments of the proposed SerialSTTR are performed on 3D action recognition and gesture recognition, which demonstrate the application potential in 3D fields.

2   Related Work

2.1   Static Point Cloud Learning

Recently, more and more works have been devoted to solving 3D tasks, such as model classification, posture recognition and semantic segmentation. PointNet [23] is the pioneering work that applied deep learning on point cloud directly, which was proposed as a symmetric MLP network for model classification and segmentation. To enhance local representation, Lu et al. [20] used hierarchical mini-PointNet to capture the local features, while PCEDNet [12] constructed scale-space matrix to capture local descriptors. As convolution has shown strong local learning ability, works [2,9,25] such as DDGCN [2] defined custom 3D convolution to model point cloud. However, most of these works do not pay attention to aggregating local features with meaningful and explainable weights. Therefore, we introduce the orderly local module, which provides a reasonable and effective solution to the local learning problem.

2.2   Point Cloud Sequences Learning

Considering the dynamics of frames, point cloud sequences learning is a new field about 3D understanding. Due to the irregularity of point cloud sequences, FaF [21], 3DV [30] converted point cloud sequences into videos of voxels. To avoid the loss of voxelization, some works chose to construct temporal structures on point cloud sequence directly. MeteorNet [19] proposed two methods to group points' temporal neighbors at each frame and then processed them with intra-frame model. PSTNet [9] constructed point tube to model temporal local structure. GeometryMotion-Net [18] and VirtualActionNet [15] proposed two-stream frameworks to extract the geometry information and motion information respectively. Considering the advantages of recurrent neural networks on sequence problems, PointRNN [7] and PointLSTM [22] construct recurrent neural networks to learn the inter-frame relations. Point transformer networks [8,31] used transformer to learn the relations across spatial-temporal structures. He et al. [11] constructed recurrent cost volume to save temporal information. To model sequence features, most of these works are constructing spatial-temporal structures in each point cloud. Subsequently, spatial processing methods, such as transformer and convolution, are used to learn features. In our work, instead of converting the temporal learning problem into a spatial one, we treat the task as a sequence task. The members of the sequence are independent frame-level features encoded from each point cloud. And based on it, we then construct a temporal transformer to learn sequence connections. In addition, we also construct temporal local module to capture local motion information.

3   Method

3.1   Overall Architecture

Figure 1 presents an overview of the SerialSTTR architecture and the specific input and output of each module. To begin with, we use a two-layer fully connected MLP to transform each frame $P_{raw} \in \mathbb{R}^{N \times 3}$ of original sequence S_{raw} into a preliminary feature space $P \in \mathbb{R}^{N \times C_{pre}}$, where N is the number of points and C_{pre} is the feature dimension. Then, each frame will be processed by OL and STR. In order to provide a clear motivation of our approach, we choose to introduce the STR first, since the OL module is designed to complement the local learning ability of STR.

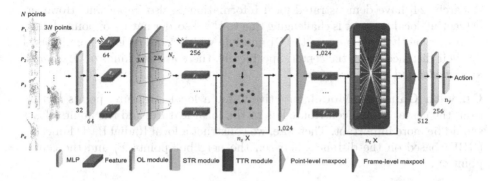

Fig. 1. Overall architecture of the SerialSTTR. Each MLP module is followed by batch normalization and ReLU. The numbers below Features and MLP modules represent the dimensions of features.

3.2 Spatial Transformer Module (STR)

The STR serves as a fundamental module in our approach, providing essential spatial encoding for each frame. Different from P4Transformer [8] which leveraged structure-level attention to identify connections across areas in space and time simultaneously, our STR is based on point-level self-attention to gather global point features, which is inspired by the previous works such as Transformer [17, 27] and PCT [10].

Let $S = (P_1, P_2 ..., P_k)$ is the input sequence, STR takes each frame $P \in \mathbb{R}^{N \times C}$ as input. Self-attention first transforms the input feature P into Q, K, V by linear module respectively, which means *query*, *key* and *value*. Then, scaled dot-product is performed to calculate the attention map $A \in \mathbb{R}^{N \times N}$,

$$A = \frac{Q \times K^T}{\sqrt{C_{qk}}} \tag{1}$$

where $Q, K \in \mathbb{R}^{N \times C_{qk}}$ and C_{qk} is the feature dimension. Finally, we use the points' attention map to calculate the weighted average for each point:

$$O_s = \mathrm{softmax}(A) \times V \tag{2}$$

where $V \in \mathbb{R}^{N \times C_v}$ and C_v is the output dimension, $O_s \in \mathbb{R}^{N \times C_v}$ is the final output frame of STR layer. Note that, the position encoding method is not used in STR, since it will lose its meaning due to the disorder attribute of point clouds. Through the STR, relevant points of each point are able to be found, and the related information is gathered to complement the features of each point.

3.3   Orderly Local Module (OL)

STR is able to integrate global information on each point. Nevertheless, prior research [24] have demonstrated local information is also important. However, extracting local features is challenging due to the disorder nature of point clouds. To overcome that, we propose the OL module which reorders local points based on their distances from the center. Specifically, there are two kinds of OL: *Gaussian model* and *adaptive model*.

OL with Gaussian Model. Intuitively, for a local structure, points farther from the center should contribute less to the local feature, and the points closer should be more important. Therefore, we construct a local Radial Basis Function (RBF) based on the distances between the neighbor points x_j and the center point x_i,

$$F(L_i) = \text{MLP}(\sum_{j=1}^{k} W_i^j F(x_j)) = \text{MLP}(\sum_{j=1}^{k} e^{-\frac{\|x_i - x_j\|^2}{2\sigma^2}} F(x_j)) \qquad (3)$$

where W_i^j is the Gaussian weight of x_j with respect to the local structure L_i. σ is related to how smooth the Gaussian model is. $F(x)$ represents the feature of point x. In this way, local information of all neighbor points can be gathered to the center point reasonably.

OL with Adaptive Model. Gaussian model is an effective and reasonable way to present the neighbor weights. Additionally, leveraging the reordering of local points, we can also construct a trainable kernel,

$$F(L_i) = \text{MLP}(\sum_{j=1}^{k} W_j F(x_j)) \qquad (4)$$

where W is the adaptive kernel with k learnable parameters. In this sense, the adaptive local model can also be considered as a form of local position encoding. Note as mentioned in Sect. 3.2, original position encoding is not applicable for point cloud due to the disorder. But after reordering points based on local distances, this kind of position encoding can be used in the local space of point cloud.

Different from the Gaussian model, the adaptive method is susceptible to the uneven distribution of point clouds. Therefore, we implement OL layers in the form of hierarchical pyramid as shown in Fig. 1, which can reduce the influence of uneven distribution. After the OL layers, each input frame $P \in \mathbb{R}^{N \times C_{pre}}$ has transformed into $P_c \in \mathbb{R}^{N_c \times C_{ol}}$ and received by STR, where N_c is the number of center points and C_{ol} is the feature dimension.

3.4   Temporal Transformer Module (TTR)

After being encoded by OL and STR modules, each point cloud P_{raw} of the original sequence S_{raw} has been transformed into feature representation $P_s \in \mathbb{R}^{N_c \times C_v}$. Then, a layer of MLP and max-pooling is applied to convert each P_s into representative frame-level feature $F_i \in \mathbb{R}^{d_s}$, which constitutes the input sequence $S \in \mathbb{R}^{k \times d_s}$ of TTR. Similar to STR, each TTR layer reconstructs the input feature sequence into the output $S' \in \mathbb{R}^{k \times d_v}$ with $Q', K' \in \mathbb{R}^{k \times d_{qk}}$ and $V' \in \mathbb{R}^{k \times d_v}$, where d_s, d_{qk}, d_v are the feature dimensions and k is the length of sequence. Meanwhile, relative position encoding and temporal OL are proposed to enhance frame order information. After TTR layers, max-pooling is applied to select one representative feature to processed later.

Frame Order Encoding with Relative Position. In the original transformer [27], a triangular encoding method is adopted to remember the absolute positions of words, which is simple and suitable for the sentences of varying length. However, point cloud sequences are always of fixed length, which makes triangular method lose its advantages. Therefore, we draw upon the ideas of [6] to construct a learnable relative position encoding.

Specifically, for the sequence S with length k, a relative position cell $E \in \mathbb{R}^{k \times k}$ is constructed to encode all possible relative positions for each frame. Different from the original transformer, we incorporate the position encoding into attention weights, which represents the relations between each pair of relative positions. Thus the new weighted sum sequence S' is,

$$S' = \text{softmax}\left(\frac{Q' \times K'^T}{\sqrt{C'_{qk}}} + E\right) \times V' \tag{5}$$

Temporal OL. The TTR learns the relation between frame-level features. However, same as the spatial processing, the learning of local structures is also important in temporal dimension, which is lacking in the TTR. Inspired by [18], we construct spatial-temporal local structure by merging neighbor frames within frame radius of 1, which avoids point tracking. Specifically, for point cloud sequence is S, the new merged sequence $S_m = (P_{1,2,3}, P_{2,3,4}..., P_{k-2,k-1,k})$. And the new local structure with spatial radius r is,

$$L_m(x_i; t) = \{x_j^{\Delta t} \| \|x_j^{\Delta t} - x_i^t\| \leq r, \Delta t \in [t-1, t+1]\} \tag{6}$$

where $L_m(x_i; t)$ means the merged local structure of point x_i of frame t. After the local structures are constructed at the beginning, the subsequent OL and STR modules can extract local features with motion information.

4   Experiments

In this section, firstly we perform experiments on the challenging 3D action recognition dataset, MSR-Action3D [14], with 5 different sequence lengths. Secondly, in order to demonstrate the generalizability of our SerialSTTR, additional experiments are performed on 3D gesture recognition dataset, SHREC'17 [5]. Finally, detailed ablation study is performed to demonstrate the contribution of each module in the network.

4.1 Dataset

MSR-Action3D [14]. MSR-Action3D is a classical human action dataset, which consists of 567 depth map sequences and 23,797 frames in total. All sequences are divided into 20 kinds of actions. For a fair comparison, we use the same partition of training/test set as previous works [8,9,19], and follow the same preprocessing methods to convert the depth data into point cloud.

SHREC'17 [5]. SHREC'17 is a dynamic human gesture dataset, which consists of 2800 depth map sequences and skeleton sequences. Specifically, the dataset is divided into 28 classes (i.e., 14 meanings are represented by 2 different ways). We also follow the previous works [3,4,32] to set the dataset, where the training set has 1960 sequences and the test set has 840 sequences. Each sequence is sampled to 32 frames, and each frame is converted to point cloud from depth map.

4.2 Implementation Details

For all experiments, we use the Furthest Point Sampling (FPS) [23] to sample 1024 points at each frame for a fair comparison with other works. And the same data augmentation strategies as previous work [8] are used. The hyperparameters of our SerialSTTR are set as follows. For the general level, both STR and TTR are set to 4 layers, where the self-attention is implemented with 8 heads. For the intra-frame level, the number of center points sampled after the last OL layer is 64. For the inter-frame level, all temporal self-attentions share the same position encoding. The learning rate is managed by stochastic gradient descent (SGD) optimizer and MultiStepLR scheduler with a warm up strategy. The initial learning rate is 0.0001, and the SGD is performed with momentum of 0.9 and weight decay of 0.0001. The batch size is always set as 6.

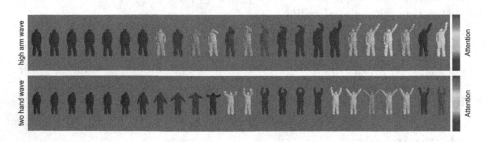

Fig. 2. Visualization of TTR weights on MSR-Action3D. Frames with brighter colors indicate a higher level of importance.

Table 1. Action recognition results on MSR-Action3D with different sequence length k.

Method	Input	Accuracy (%)				
		k = 8	k = 12	k = 16	k = 20	k = 24
Klaser [28]	depth	81.43 (k = 18)				
Actionlet [29]	skeleton	88.21 (k = all)				
PointNet++ [24]	point	61.61 (k = 1)				
MeteorNet [19]	point	–	86.53	88.21	–	88.50
PSTNet [9]	point	83.50	87.88	89.90	–	91.20
P4Transformer [8]	point	83.17	87.54	89.56	90.24	90.94
SerialSTTR (ours)	point	81.82	88.89	90.57	92.15	**95.12**

Table 2. Gesture recognition results on SHREC'17.

Method	Input	Accuracy (%)	
		14 classes	28 classes
SoCJ+HoHD+HoWR [4]	skeleton	88.2	81.9
Res-TCN [13]	skeleton	91.1	87.3
STA-Res-TCN [13]	skeleton	93.6	90.7
ST-GCN [32]	skeleton	92.7	97.7
DG-STA [3]	skeleton	**94.4**	**90.7**
KeyFrames [5]	depth	82.9	71.9
PointBaseline	point	89.6	76.7
SerialSTTR (ours)	point	**93.8**	**90.2**

4.3 Results

In Table 1, the results of 3D action recognition on MSR-Action3D are reported. At the most common frame rate of 24, the proposed SerialSTTR outperforms the state-of-the-art methods and achieves the best accuracy of 95.12%. In addition, as more and more frames are encoded, our model shows more superior performance, which demonstrates our model can extract temporal features more effectively. For the 24 frames setup, our model achieves the greatest improvement by 3.92% comparing with the other works in table. On the other hand, our best model achieves the precision of 95.59% and the recall rate of 95.31% under macro-average, which indicates the ability to avoid false recognition.

Table 2 shows the performances on gesture recognition with SHREC'17 dataset. Skeleton-based methods used skeleton data from dataset as input. Point-based methods used point clouds converted from depth data. In order to compare with the other point-based methods and enhance the persuasiveness of the contrast, we implement the P4Transformer [8] with source code and original parameters settings as the PointBaseline model in Table 2. The proposed SerialSTTR outperforms the depth-based method by a clear improvement, and has certain advantages over the PointBaseline model. As skeleton-based methods can make full use of the precise skeleton data in SHREC'17, most of previous works with great performance used skeleton-based model. Without skeleton features, our model still achieve a comparable result to the best skeleton-based model, which demonstrates the generalizability of our model.

To help understand the result and investigate what SerialSTTR learns, we visualize some TTR's attention weights in Fig. 2. As expected, the first several frames with less variation are less important to the model. And on the other hand, the model is capable of identifying frames with distinctive features in action sequences, and utilizing the contextual information for action recognition.

Table 3. Comparisons of computational efficiency on MSR-Action3D. Sequence length is 24.

Method	FLOPs (G)	Parameters (M)	Inference time (ms)	Accuracy (%)
MeteorNet [19]	–	17.60	80.11	88.50
PSTNet [9]	–	8.44	43.88	91.20
SerialSTTR (ours)	5.81	6.42	50.46	95.12

We also provide a computational efficiency comparison in Table 3, experiments are conducted with 1 Nvidia RTX 3080 GPU. As a result, our method has less parameters than others, and the efficiency is sufficient to support real-time recognition (24 fps/50.46 ms). Furthermore, the complete model training on MSR-Action3D takes only about 2.6 h. These results demonstrate the effectiveness and generalizability of our approach for real-time applications.

4.4 Ablation Study

In order to demonstrate the contributions of each component, we take the MSR-Action3D dataset with 24 frame rate to perform related ablation studies. For each experiment, the implementation details follow the above, except for the ablation modules.

Table 4. Influence of each module in the SerialSTTR.

Models	Component	Accuracy (%)
Baseline	STR+local max+time max	85.02
Local	STR+OL+time max	87.21
STTR	STR+local max+TTR	92.68
SerialSTTR	STR+OL+TTR	95.12

Main Modules. Firstly, we investigate the influence of three main modules: STR, OL, and TTR, and all results are reported in Table 4. Specifically, the Baseline model only use the STR to process point clouds frame by frame, and then max-pool operations are performed on local areas and the entire sequence. In the Local model, the OL is attached to the local processing instead of max-pool. In the STTR model, the TTR is used for extracting motion information instead of temporal max-pool. Finally, in the proposed SerialSTTR model, complete components are used.

Since the Baseline model uses only the intra-frame global information, it achieves the basic accuracy of 85.02%. In the Local model, the OL module improves accuracy by +2.19%, which indicates its superior ability of local learning. However, temporal information is the most important feature of sequence learning, which is lacking in above models. Therefore, the STTR model achieves a great improvement by 7.66% comparing with the Baseline, which demonstrates our TTR module has a strong ability of learning temporal features. After the STTR model introduces spatial-temporal local structures, the OL module is able to extend its local learning ability to the temporal dimension. Therefore, the complete SerialSTTR has a significant performance improvement by 10.10% comparing with the Baseline, and by 2.44% comparing with the STTR.

Gaussian Model and Adaptive Model of OL. We conduct the ablation study on the two methods we proposed for OL. As shown in Table 5, the adaptive model achieves the better performance than others. Gaussian model also yields comparable results, and it has good interpretability, which models the local area as a Gaussian structure. Compared to the traditional maxpool method, both the two OL models have significant advantages.

Table 5. Comparisons of different submodules.

Submodules	Local method			Position encoding		
	Maxpool	Gaussian OL	Adaptive OL	None	Traditional	Relative
Accuracy (%)	92.68	94.43	95.12	93.16	94.54	95.12

Different Position Encoding. Table 5 shows the relative method has better performance than the traditional encoding in the original Transformer. For the traditional method, positions are encoded into fixed features by sine and cosine functions. Thus, the traditional method is focused on order feature extracting, which means the same position always get the same order feature. On the contrary, the relative method that we adopt is focused on the relative influence across frames. With the learnable weight kernel for relative positions, this method can capture the temporal relations between action frames, which is more suitable and reasonable for our sequence recognition tasks.

5   Conclusions

In this paper, we propose Serial Spatial and Temporal Transformer (SerialSTTR) network for extracting motion features from point cloud sequences, which can be applied in 3D recognition. In the network, point-based and frame-based transformer are used to extract spatial and temporal global information respectively. And an orderly local module is proposed to convert the unordered local structure of point clouds into orderly array, which facilitates the ability of extracting local features. Extensive experiments demonstrate the performance and generalizability of the proposed model for 3D action recognition and gesture recognition.

References

1. Aouaidjia, K., Sheng, B., Li, P., Kim, J., Feng, D.D.: Efficient body motion quantification and similarity evaluation using 3-d joints skeleton coordinates. IEEE Trans. Syst. Man Cybern. Syst. **51**(5), 2774–2788 (2019)

2. Chen, L., Zhang, Q.: Ddgcn: graph convolution network based on direction and distance for point cloud learning. Vis. Comput. **39**(3), 863–873 (2023)

3. Chen, Y., Zhao, L., Peng, X., Yuan, J., Metaxas, D.: Construct dynamic graphs for hand gesture recognition via spatial-temporal attention. In: Proceedings of the British Machine Vision Conference (BMVC), pp. 48.1-48.13 (2019)

4. De Smedt, Q., Wannous, H., Vandeborre, J.P.: Skeleton-based dynamic hand gesture recognition. In: Proceedings of the IEEE Conference on Computer Vision and Pattern Recognition Workshops, pp. 1–9 (2016)

5. De Smedt, Q., Wannous, H., Vandeborre, J.P., Guerry, J., Le Saux, B., Filliat, D.: Shrec'17 track: 3d hand gesture recognition using a depth and skeletal dataset. In: 3DOR-10th Eurographics Workshop on 3D Object Retrieval, pp. 1–6 (2017)

6. Dosovitskiy, A., et al.: An image is worth 16x16 words: transformers for image recognition at scale. arXiv preprint arXiv:2010.11929 (2020)

7. Fan, H., Yang, Y.: Pointrnn: point recurrent neural network for moving point cloud processing. arXiv preprint arXiv:1910.08287 (2019)

8. Fan, H., Yang, Y., Kankanhalli, M.: Point 4d transformer networks for spatio-temporal modeling in point cloud videos. In: Proceedings of the IEEE/CVF Conference on Computer Vision and Pattern Recognition, pp. 14204–14213 (2021)

9. Fan, H., Yu, X., Ding, Y., Yang, Y., Kankanhalli, M.: Pstnet: point spatio-temporal convolution on point cloud sequences. arXiv preprint arXiv:2205.13713 (2022)

10. Guo, M.H., Cai, J.X., Liu, Z.N., Mu, T.J., Martin, R.R., Hu, S.M.: Pct: point cloud transformer. Comput. Visual Media **7**, 187–199 (2021)

11. He, P., Emami, P., Ranka, S., Rangarajan, A.: Learning scene dynamics from point cloud sequences. Int. J. Comput. Vision **130**(3), 669–695 (2022)

12. Himeur, C.E., Lejemble, T., Pellegrini, T., Paulin, M., Barthe, L., Mellado, N.: Pcednet: a lightweight neural network for fast and interactive edge detection in 3d point clouds. ACM Trans. Graph. (TOG) **41**(1), 1–21 (2021)

13. Hou, J., Wang, G., Chen, X., Xue, J.H., Zhu, R., Yang, H.: Spatial-temporal attention res-tcn for skeleton-based dynamic hand gesture recognition. In: Computer Vision - ECCV 2018 Workshops, pp. 273–286 (2019)

14. Li, W., Zhang, Z., Liu, Z.: Action recognition based on a bag of 3d points. In: 2010 IEEE Computer Society Conference on Computer Vision and Pattern Recognition-Workshops, pp. 9–14. IEEE (2010)

15. Li, X., Huang, Q., Wang, Z., Yang, T.: Virtualactionnet: a strong two-stream point cloud sequence network for human action recognition. J. Vis. Commun. Image Represent. **89**, 103641 (2022)

16. Lin, L., Huang, P., Fu, C.W., Xu, K., Zhang, H., Huang, H.: On learning the right attention point for feature enhancement. Sci. China Inf. Sci. **66**(1), 1–13 (2023)
17. Lin, X., Sun, S., Huang, W., Sheng, B., Li, P., Feng, D.D.: Eapt: efficient attention pyramid transformer for image processing. IEEE Trans. Multimed., 50–61 (2021)
18. Liu, J., Xu, D.: Geometrymotion-net: a strong two-stream baseline for 3d action recognition. IEEE Trans. Circuits Syst. Video Technol. **31**(12), 4711–4721 (2021)
19. Liu, X., Yan, M., Bohg, J.: Meteornet: deep learning on dynamic 3d point cloud sequences. In: Proceedings of the IEEE/CVF International Conference on Computer Vision, pp. 9246–9255 (2019)
20. Lu, H., Nie, J.: Coarse registration of point cloud base on deep local extremum detection and attentive description. Available at SSRN 4106324
21. Luo, W., Yang, B., Urtasun, R.: Fast and furious: Real time end-to-end 3d detection, tracking and motion forecasting with a single convolutional net. In: Proceedings of the IEEE conference on Computer Vision and Pattern Recognition, pp. 3569–3577 (2018)
22. Min, Y., Zhang, Y., Chai, X., Chen, X.: An efficient pointlstm for point clouds based gesture recognition. In: Proceedings of the IEEE/CVF Conference on Computer Vision and Pattern Recognition, pp. 5761–5770 (2020)
23. Qi, C.R., Su, H., Mo, K., Guibas, L.J.: Pointnet: deep learning on point sets for 3d classification and segmentation. In: Proceedings of the IEEE Conference on Computer Vision and Pattern Recognition, pp. 652–660 (2017)
24. Qi, C.R., Yi, L., Su, H., Guibas, L.J.: Pointnet++: deep hierarchical feature learning on point sets in a metric space. Adv. Neural. Inf. Process. Syst. **30**, 5099–5108 (2017)
25. Riegler, G., Osman Ulusoy, A., Geiger, A.: Octnet: learning deep 3d representations at high resolutions. In: Proceedings of the IEEE Conference on Computer Vision and Pattern Recognition, pp. 3577–3586 (2017)
26. Tu, Z., et al.: A survey of variational and cnn-based optical flow techniques. Sig. Process. Image Commun. **72**, 9–24 (2019)
27. Vaswani, A., Shazeer, N., Parmar, N., Uszkoreit, J., Jones, L., Gomez, A.N., Kaiser, Ł, Polosukhin, I.: Attention is all you need. Adv. Neural. Inf. Process. Syst. **30**, 6000–6010 (2017)
28. Vieira, A.W., Nascimento, E.R., Oliveira, G.L., Liu, Z., Campos, M.F.M.: STOP: space-time occupancy patterns for 3D action recognition from depth map sequences. In: Alvarez, L., Mejail, M., Gomez, L., Jacobo, J. (eds.) CIARP 2012. LNCS, vol. 7441, pp. 252–259. Springer, Heidelberg (2012). https://doi.org/10.1007/978-3-642-33275-3_31
29. Wang, J., Liu, Z., Wu, Y., Yuan, J.: Mining actionlet ensemble for action recognition with depth cameras. In: 2012 IEEE Conference on Computer Vision and Pattern Recognition, pp. 1290–1297. IEEE (2012)
30. Wang, Y., et al.: 3dv: 3D dynamic voxel for action recognition in depth video. In: Proceedings of the IEEE/CVF Conference on Computer Vision and Pattern Recognition, pp. 511–520 (2020)
31. Wei, Y., Liu, H., Xie, T., Ke, Q., Guo, Y.: Spatial-temporal transformer for 3d point cloud sequences. In: Proceedings of the IEEE/CVF Winter Conference on Applications of Computer Vision, pp. 1171–1180 (2022)
32. Yan, S., Xiong, Y., Lin, D.: Spatial temporal graph convolutional networks for skeleton-based action recognition. In: Proceedings of the AAAI Conference on Artificial Intelligence, vol. 32, pp. 7444–7452 (2018)

TadML: A Fast Temporal Action Detection with Mechanics-MLP

Bowen Deng[1,2], Shuangliang Zhao[2(✉)], and Dongchang Liu[1(✉)]

[1] Institute of Automation, Chinese Academy of Sciences, Beijing 100190, China
dongchang.liu@ia.ac.cn
[2] Guangxi University, Nanning 69121, China
szhao@gxu.edu.cn

Abstract. Temporal Action Detection (TAD) involves identifying action categories and their respective start and end frames in lengthy untrimmed videos, with current models utilizing both RGB and optical flow streams that require manual intervention, add computational complexity, and consume time. Moreover, two-stage approaches prioritizing proposal generation in the ini-tial stage result in a substantial reduction in inference speed. To address this, we propose a single-stage anchor-free method that solely utilizes the RGB stream and incorporates a novel Newtonian Mechanics-MLP architecture. Our model achieves comparable accuracy to existing state-of-the-art models but with significantly faster inference speeds, clocking in at an av-erage of 4.44 videos per second on THUMOS14. Our approach showcases the potential of MLP in downstream tasks like TAD. The source code is available at https://github.com/BonedDeng/TadML.

Keywords: Temporal action detection · MLP-like · RGB and optical flow · Real time · Anchor free

1 Introduction

As videos become ubiquitous in the wake of advances in mobile communication and the internet, video understanding has become increasingly important in both academia and industry [1]. In particular, temporal action detection, detecting categories, start and end timestamps of human actions in untrimmed footage, has diverse applications in areas such as human-computer interaction, video surveillance, and intelligent security [2]. In the past, numerous TAD frameworks employed complex pipelines. Some earlier methods even utilized manually crafted features, including color and texture features of each frame, for video action classification and detection [3]. Currently, research on temporal action detection (TAD) has shifted towards utilizing deep models that combine raw RGB streams and optical flow, emerging as the mainstream and potential approach. RGB frames contain vital shape and spatial information of videos, which are necessary for Temporal Action Detection (TAD). Most TAD research also use optical flow, a two-dimensional velocity field that captures action information and three-dimensional scene structure of the observed object [4,5]. However, fusing RGB and optical flow data requires time-consuming conversion, computations, and resources. TAD has two objectives: predicting action categories based on available information and their corresponding timestamps in the video. While TAD shares similarities with object detection, it is focused on detecting actions in the time domain, unlike object detection that identifies positions in the spatial domain, leading TAD methods to draw inspiration from object detection research. TAD models can be categorized into one-stage and two-stage models based on their network structure. Two-stage frameworks generate proposals with high recall, which are then classified to predict corresponding labels, but their inference speed is slower and incurs higher computing costs than one-stage frameworks. One-stage frameworks simultaneously generate the start and end frames of each action and their corresponding labels in a single step, making them more efficient for real-time applications.

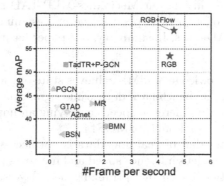

Fig. 1. Comparing to the performance (average chart) and speed of the latest time action detection model on THUMOS 14. Our method shows advanced performance and very fast speed when using RGB stream.

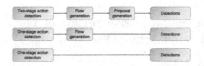

Fig. 2. The image showcases three mainstream methods. The traditional two stream method, the two stream one stage method and the RGB only one stage method.

Based on the anchor structure, previous research can be categorized into three groups: (a) action-guided methods, such as BSN [6], (b) anchor-based methods, such as BMN [7], and (c) anchor-free methods, such as AFSD [8].

Methods that employ anchors not only exhibit high time complexities, namely (T^2) and $(c * t)$, but also require numerous hyperparameters to be fine-tuned, including the scale and quantity of anchors, as well as the computational cost of IOU thresholds [9]. Drawing inspiration from anchor-free models in target detection research, anchor-free methods have emerged as the mainstream approach and demonstrated significant potential in TAD. In this paper, we present a novel TAD model called Mechanics-MLP, which employs a one-stage anchor-free framework and considers each token as a force. The Newtonian Mechanics-MLP unit inspired by MLP's success in computer vision backbones, achieved promising results using the $\beta - GloU$ loss for TAD, with our Tad-ML model achieving a maximum average precision (mAP) of 69.73% (RGB and optical flow streams at tIoU = 0.4) on THUMOS14 while exhibiting rapid processing speeds and superior accuracy compared to other methods, as demonstrated in Fig. 1a. As shown in Fig. 2, illustrating that B represents a two-stage method, C represents a one-stage method, and D represents an end-to-end one-stage method. Our pro-posed method eliminates the need for the optical flow conversion pipeline, leading to faster processing. In conclusion, our Mechanics-MLP TAD model demonstrates promising results and offers a fresh perspective on designing one-stage anchor-free frameworks for TAD tasks. In summary, our paper has the following contributions:

- To the best of our knowledge, TadML achieves state-of-the-art or highly competitive performance on benchmark data while significantly surpassing previous methods in terms of inference speed, achieving an impressive 4.44 videos per second inference speed on THUMOS14.
- TadML demonstrates that optical flow data is not necessary for TAD tasks, thus improving the model's inference speed and improves performance in both RGB stream and two-stream by optimizing neck layers, while also finding $\beta - Giou$ to be a more appropriate metric for TAD.
- Our Newtonian mechanics-based MLP model confirms the applicability of MLP for TAD and achieves highly competitive results using both RGB and optical flow data.

2 Related Works

This section provides a comprehensive review of previous studies related to Action Recognition, Temporal Action Detection, and MLP.

Temporal Action Recognition. Action recognition in video clips, which involves identifying human actions in 2D frame sequences, has traditionally relied on manual feature extraction and classification through methods such as HOG, HOF, Dense Trajectories, SVM, and RF [10], but deep learning methods like Lrcns, R(2+1), and I3D have since become dominant in the field. These models use CNNs to extract spatial features, while RNNs like LSTM [11] and 3D convolutions enable temporal feature extraction and improved re-mote loss and long-distance time modeling [12]. The goal of sequential action detection is to identify action instances, time boundaries, and categories in videos, with two-stage methods dividing videos into proposals before assigning them to specific categories and one-stage models directly localizing and classifying actions for improved efficiency. The BMN model simplifies the BSN process and improves efficiency through a boundary matching mechanism, while PGCN [13] employs graph convolutional networks to facilitate context and background information exchange. In contrast to two-stage models, one-stage models directly localize and classify actions, resulting in improved efficiency. For instance, SSAD simultaneously performs category prediction, time series offset correction, and IOU prediction, bypassing the requirement of initially predicting candidate time intervals. AFSD [12] maximizes the utilization of boundary characteristics and extracts essential boundary features through boundary pooling.

MLP. Various new computer vision architectures, including transformers and MLP, have recently demonstrated superior performance compared to CNN in several upstream tasks. Visual MLP-Like methods exhibit simplistic stacked MLP architectures, as exemplified by MLP-Mixer, which applies MLP independently and across image patches and has achieved comparable performance to SOTA models on the ImageNet dataset. The MorphMLP [14] architecture emphasizes local information in the low-level layer and gradually transitions to a long-term model in the high-level layer. The WaveMLP [15] introduce quantum mechanics into MLP. Both of these architectures have demonstrat-ed competitive performance in image classification tasks. Motivated by these findings, our objective is to investigate the potential of MLP-Like architectures in TAD, showcasing their applicability in visual downstream tasks as well.

3   Method

3.1   Overview

TadML architecture features three elements, including a backbone module for feature extraction and down-sampling in time, a time fusion pyramid network (TFPN) as the neck, and action and time prediction branches acting as the head. Representing the untrimmed video datasets as $D = \{D_{train}, D_{test}\}$, each video in set as $V \in \mathbb{R}^{T \times C \times H \times W}$, where T,C,H,W represent time step, channel, height and width respectively. In most TAD tasks, V will be converted into (V_{rgb}, V_{opt}) first, where V_{rgb} contains RGB streams, and V_{opt} contains optical flow. This conversion takes a lot of time and calculation resources. Our model only takes RGB data as input. We obtain the output via the module, where output $Y = (d_{i,s}, d_{i,e}, c_i)$. Here, $d_{i,s}$, $d_{i,e}$ are the distances between the current time step and the start and end of this action. A moment is either part of one action category or part of the background category, denoted with c_i.

3.2 Architecture

Mechanics token mixing block. Compared with the time complexity of the multi-head attention mechanism in Transformer, we aim to develop a similar approach that is relatively simple for rapid application in video understanding tasks. The MLP-like model is a neural architecture that is primarily made up of fully-connected layers and non-linear activation functions. We enhance token aggregation by dynamically adjusting the relationship between tokens and fixed weights in MLP through the application of Newtonian mechanics principles. In this work, given $D^0 \in \{X_1, X_2..., X_n\}$ with n time steps. z^0 is projected by F_a and F_b with FC layer, where the angle between F_a and F_B is θ and W^i and W^j are the weight with learnable parameters. According to the laws of mechanics, their resultant force is A_f, which is calculated by summing the vectors of F_a and F_b.

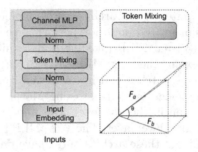

Fig. 3. Left the diagram of a block in the Mechanics-MLP architecture, right is token mixing.

$$Token_{mechanics} = \{X_1, X_2..., X_n\}$$
$$F_a = FC(Token_{mechanics}, W^i)$$
$$F_b = FC(Token_{mechanics}, W^j) \tag{1}$$
$$A_f = \sqrt{F_a + F_b + 2F_a F_b \cos\theta}$$

The inputs (embedding) in a basic mechanics unit undergo sequential processing through a mechanics token mixing block and a channel mixing block. Both two mixing block operation capture spatial information by blending features from multiple tokens. Furthermore, a layer normalization step is performed before each mixing operation, as depicted in Fig. 3. The mechanics token mixing MLP consists of one MTM module, which aggregates various tokens by considering both F_1 and F_2, and applies the ReLU activation function. The channel mixing MLP extracts features for each token.

$$X = Norm(X)$$
$$Z = A_f(X)$$
$$Z = Norm(Z) \tag{2}$$
$$Z = Channel - FC(Z)$$

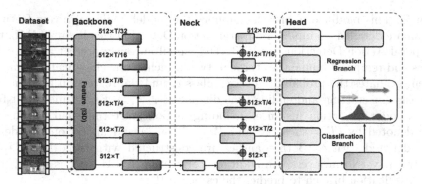

Fig. 4. The architecture consists of three main parts: a backbone module for feature extraction and downsampling in time, a time fusion pyramid network (TFPN) serving as the neck, and action and time prediction branches operating as the head.

Backbone. To begin with, we generate video clips with a constant time window from the input video and reshape each clip to (T, C, H, W). Feature extraction converts the video into a sequence of feature vectors corresponding to the RGB visual modality. Current TAD methods struggle to achieve fast detection due to their reliance on optical flow, which consumes computing resources and introduces time-consuming conversion processes. The conversion process is bypassed in our model's backbone module, eliminating the need for cumbersome operations. The backbone network utilizes a pre-trained I3D model on the Kinetics datasets to extract 3D features. The videos are segmented into short, overlapping 8-frame chunks. Finally, we obtain $Y_{I3D} = (Y_{rgb}, Y_{opt})$, where both of them are 1024-dim features. Different from previous, our method only needs Y_{rgb}. We also tried Y_{I3D} as our input, and it also played a good effect, indicating the superiority of our method. The feature is flattened along the last four dimensions to form a two-dimensional feature sequence encompassing both temporal and spatial information from the entire video. The feature sequence is then passed through a multi-layer semantic module (MSM) consisting of six down-sample layers. Each layer, composed of mechanics units, has an output dimension of 512. The outputs of the layers are $(512, t/2)$, $(512, t/4)$, $(512, t/8)$, $(512, t/16)$, $(512, t/32)$, and $(512, t/64)$, as shown in Fig. 4. This module produces multi-coarse texture basic features as its output. Temporal Feature Pyramid Network. The TAD architecture incorporates the concept of object detection, making the utilization of complex adaptive attention modules in AFFPN and the repeated superposition method in BIFPN impractical. The neck is designed to establish connections between semantically strong, low-temporal-resolution features and semantically weak, high-temporal-resolution features. This is achieved through a six-layer pathway comprising $((T,512), (T/2,512), (T/4,512), (T/8,512), (T/16,512), (T/32,512))$. The six-layer design proves highly effective in extracting temporal content. The high-resolution features extracted by the backbone are sequentially up-sampled to each of the six layers. The up-sampling operation involves bi-linear interpolation and simultaneous combination with the high-resolution features. This modified approach simplifies the model while capturing features from more detailed examples. Temporal Action Detection Heads. In TadML, the Temporal Action Detection Heads (TADH) simultaneously predict action categories and temporal boundaries through two branches: the classification branch, which estimates the probability of each class c_i and the regression branch that forecasts the starting and ending time distance $(t_{i,s}, t_{i,e})$. Each time step t further decodes an action instance, including: action start time and action end time denoted by $(T_s = T - T^e$ and $T_e = T + T^s)$ and an action confidence score denoted with c_i. Both branches are constructed with three MLP layers and two LayerNorm layers. An additional activation ReLU layer is included in the classification branch to predict the category ID.

Loss Construction. $\mathcal{L}_{cls}$ is Focal loss that employed as the classification loss, effectively mitigating class imbalance by adjusting the weights of positive and negative samples based on their classification difficulty levels, thereby enhancing overall detection accuracy. $\mathcal{L}_{reg}$ is the regression loss that defined to differentiate the regression of instance time boundaries. For the regression loss, we define it to distinguish the instance time boundary regression. We propose an improvement of GIoU, called $\beta - GIoU$, to constructed the regression loss. In $\beta - GIoU$, the hyper-parameter β is defined to detect shapes sensitively in the error term of the predicted value and position, A is candidate object, the B represents the object ground-truth and C is minimum bounding box area. To accomplish this, the total loss is defined by two super parameters λ_{cls} and λ_{reg} are set up for classification loss and regression loss separately. T_{at} is an indicator function indicating to determine whether there is an action in the time step. while T_+ represents the total number of positive samples.

$$\mathcal{L}_{reg} = \mathcal{L}_{\beta- \text{GIoU}} = 1 - IoU + \left(\frac{|C\backslash(A \cup B^{gt})|}{|C|}\right)^{\beta}$$

$$\mathcal{L}_{cls}(\{\hat{y}_i\}) = \frac{1}{N}\sum_i \ell_{\text{focal}}(\hat{y}_i, y_i) \tag{3}$$

$$\mathcal{L} = \sum_{k=1}^{N}(\frac{\mathcal{L}_{cls}}{T}\ell_{cls} + \frac{\lambda_{reg}}{T_+}\mathbb{T}_{at}\mathcal{L}_{reg})$$

Train and Inference. We implement our network using the pytorch framework. All experiments were run on a workstation equipped a single Tesla P100 GPU, and Intel(R) Xeon(R) CPU (E5-2690 v4 @ 2.90 GHz). The models were trained for 80 epochs using Adam with warm-up for training, which is crucial for achieving model convergence and optimal performance. The base learning rate is set to 10^{-5} and the batch size was set to 4. The weights of the loss terms, λ_{cls} and λ_{reg} were both set to 1. The parameter β, in $\beta - Giou$, was set to 3. Input sequences were cropped or padded to the maximum length 2304. During the inference process, only the action predictions from the last lightweight MLP layer are considered, while the full sequences are fed into the model. Our model takes the input video X and outputs $(t_{i,s}, t_{i,e}, c_i)$ for each time step T across all neck levels. The final TAD results are generated by processing action candidates with Non-maximum Suppression (Soft-NMS) to remove highly overlapping instances.

4 Experiments and Results

We evaluated the effectiveness of our proposed approach through benchmark evalua-tions on THUMOS14 [16] and ActivityNet1.3 [17], as well as extensive ablation stud-ies to analyze model performance.

4.1 Evaluation

For all datasets, we report the standard mean average precision (mAP) at different temporal intersection over union (tIoU) thresholds, which is widely used to evaluate TAD models. For the THUMOS14, the tIoU threshold is selected from 0.3, 0.4, 0.5, 0.6, 0.7. For ActivityNe-t1.3, the tIoU threshold is 0.5, 0.75, 0.95. We also report the average graph with fine-scale tIoU threshold ([0.5, 0.95] step is 0.05). THUMOS14 is comprised of 413 untrimmed videos spanning 20 action categories. Each video contains 15 action instances on average, each instance has an average of 8% overlapping with others. The datasets are divided into two subsets: a verification set and a test set. The verification set contains 200 videos and the test set contains 213 videos. Following the standard setup, we use validation sets for training and the testing videos for evaluation. The experimental results on THUMOS14 are shown in Table 1. The results are presented in Table 1. Without optical flow input, our method achieves an average mAP of 53.46% ([0.3: 0.1: 0.7]), with a mAP of 56.61% at tIoU = 0.5 and a mAP of 31.88% at tIoU = 0.7. This result exceeds those of most methods of TAD, even including models with additional optical flow input. This suggests that our model is not only achieves comparable in accuracy but also faster than most methods in practice. This is because our model skips the step of conversion (from raw RGB to optical flow), which is especially time-consuming. In order to further prove the superiority of our model, we also conducted experiments using optical flow input. The results show that our model achieves an average mAP of 59.7% ([0.3 : 0.1 : 0.7]), with a mAP of 62.53% at tIoU = 0.5 and a mAP of 39.6% at tIoU = 0.7. ActivityNet1.3 is a large-scale action dataset that comprises 200 action classes and approximately 2k untrimmed videos. And it's total video length exceeds 600 h. The dataset has been split into three subsets, with 10,024 videos for training, 4,926 videos for validation, and 5,044 videos for testing. In line with the established methodology, we trained TadML on the training set and test, the performance on the validation set. The experiment results on ActivityNet v1.3 are presents in Table 2. The results are presented in Table 2. Using I3D features, our method achieves an average mAP of 34.94% ([0.5 : 0.05 : 0.95]), this outperforms all previous methods that use the same features by at least 0.6%. This improvement is significant as it is averaged across multiple tIoU thresholds, including those tight ones e.g. 0.95. Furthermore, by employing the pre-training method from TSP, we slightly improve our results, achieving an 36.0% average mAP. Our model thus outperforms the best method with the same features by a small margin. Again, our method largely outperforms TadTR. Our results are only inferior to TCANet-a latest two-stage method using stronger SlowFast features. We conjecture that our method will also benefit from better features. Nevertheless, our simple model clearly demonstrates state-of-the-art results on this challenging dataset.

Table 1. Performance comparison with methods on THUMOS14, measured by mAP at different IoU thresholds, and average mAP in [0.3 : 0.1 : 0.7] on THUMOS14.

Type	Method	RGB stream	0.3	0.4	0.5	0.6	0.7	Avg
Two-stage	CDC [18]	✗	40.10	29.40	23.30	13.10	7.90	20.76
	TCN [19]	✗	–	33.30	25.60	15.90	9.00	–
	TURN-TAP [20]	✗	44.10	34.90	25.60	–	–	–
	R-C3D [21]	✗	44.80	35.60	28.90	–	–	–
	MGG [22]	✗	53.9	46.8	37.4	29.5	21.3	37.78
	BMN [7]	✗	56	47.4	38.8	29.7	20.5	38.48
	DBG [23]	✗	57.8	49.4	39.8	30.2	21.7	39.78
	BSN++ [24]	✗	59.90	45.90	41.30	31.90	22.80	40.36
	GCN [15]	✗	63.6	57.8	49.1	–	–	–
	TAL-Net [25]	✗	53.2	48.5	42.8	33.8	20.8	39.8
	G-TAD [26]	✗	58.7	52.7	44.9	33.6	23.8	42.7
	MR [27]	✗	53.9	50.7	45.4	38.0	28.5	43.3
	ContextLoc [28]	✗	68.3	63.8	54.3	41.8	26.2	50.88
One-stage	PBRNet[?]	✗	58.5	54.6	51.3	41.8	29.5	–
	A2Net [30]	✗	58.6	54.1	45.5	32.5	17.2	41.6
	A2Net	✗	58.6	54.1	45.5	32.5	17.2	41.6
	G-TAD [31]	✓	57.8	47.2	38.8	–	–	–
	TadTR [5]	✗	62.4	57.4	49.2	37.8	26.3	46.6
	TadML	✓	68.78	64.66	56.61	45.40	31.88	53.46
	TadML	✗	73.29	69.73	62.53	53.36	39.60	59.70

Table 2. Performance comparison with methods on ActivityNetv1.3, measured by mAP at different IoU thresholds, and average mAP in [0.5 : 0.75 : 0.95] on ActivityNetv1.3.

Method	Single-stage	0.5	0.75	0.95	Avg
R-C3D [21]	✗	26.80	–	–	–
TAL-Net [25]	✗	38.23	18.30	1.30	20.22
BSN [6]	✗	56.45	29.96	8.02	30.03
BMN [7]	✗	50.07	34.78	8.29	33.85
P-GCN [13]	✗	42.90	28.14	2.47	26.99
Contextloc [28]	✗	51.24	31.40	2.83	30.59
TadTR+BMN [5]	✗	50.51	35.35	8.18	34.55
A2Net [31]	✓	43.55	28.69	3.70	27.75
SSN [32]	✓	43.26	28.70	5.63	28.28
TadTR [5]	✓	49.08	32.58	8.49	32.27
G-TAD [31]	✓	50.36	34.60	9.02	34.09
AFSD [8]	✓	52.4	35.3	6.5	34.4
Ours	✓	53.15	35.75	7.47	34.94

4.2 Ablation Study

In this section, we conducted several ablation studies on THUMOS14 to further verify the efficacy of our model. Our experiments examined the efficacy of key components and recommended hyper-parameters settings. For all experiments, we kept the evaluation settings constant and only made changes to the corresponding components. Neck layers play a crucial role in temporal action detection, as evidenced by our comparison of different neck layers and RGB streams presented in Table 3. The number of neck layers ranges from 1 to 7, and as the number of neck layers increases, the average mAP also increased from 36.03% to 53.46%, and reach its peak at 6th neck layer. At this point, when the neck layer added again, the performance stars to decline. Furthermore, our method also exhibits great performance in two-streams. with the number of layers are set to 7, achieving an average mAP is 59.7%. We have also conducted comparisons using different MLP-Like blocks. While keeping other parameter settings keep unchanged. The results are presented in Table 4, when only RGB streams are used, the average MAP achieved with Waveblock is 51.64%, with MorphMLP it is 52.09%, and with TadML it is 53.46%. To further evaluate our model, we have also included optical flow for comparison. Our model achieved an average MAP as high as 59.70%. These results are shown in Table 5. When the weight of classification and regression loss is set at 1, the best performance is achieved by β, which achieves a MAP of 53.46% when the value of β is 3.

Table 3. Study of different number of frozen stages of backbone on THUMOS14 in terms of mAP(%)@tIoU.

Neck Stages	RGB	0.3	0.4	0.5	0.6	0.7
1	✗	56.09	49.11	38.35	24.92	12.03
2	✗	61.74	55.6	44.81	29.39	14.29
3	✗	65.74	60.16	49.91	36.09	19.78
4	✗	66.82	62.32	53.82	43.26	28.96
5	✗	66.98	62.77	55.42	44.81	31.82
6	✗	68.7	64.66	56.61	45.40	31.88
7	✗	68.7	64.66	56.61	45.40	–
1	✓	62.7	57.06	46.64	30.73	14.52
2	✓	68.04	62.6	52.37	35.65	18.52
3	✓	70.78	66.1	57.6	44.36	27.41
4	✓	68.7	64.66	56.61	45.40	–
5	✓	73.32	68.91	62.28	52.81	39.04
6	✓	72.79	69.49	62.72	52.29	38.94
7	✓	73.59	69.69	62.79	53.13	40.22

Table 4. Study of three different backbone (WaveMLP, MorphMLP, Mechaincs-MLP) on THUMOS14 in terms of mAP(%)@tIoU.

Neck Stages	RGB	0.3	0.4	0.5	0.6	0.7	Avg
WaveMLP [15]	✗	66.87	62.46	54.33	44.00	30.53	51.64
WaveMLP [15]	✓	72.01	68.02	61.51	52.01	38.28	58.36
MorphMLP [14]	✗	66.91	62.83	54.93	44.57	31.20	52.09
MorphMLP [14]	✓	72.21	69.12	62.87	52.55	38.47	59.04
Ours	✗	68.78	64.66	56.61	45.40	31.88	53.46
Ours	✓	73.29	69.73	62.53	53.36	39.60	59.70

Table 5. Study of different β ($\beta - Giou$) on THUMOS14 in terms of mAP(%)@tIoU.

β	0.3	0.4	0.5	0.6	0.7	Avg
1	66.68	63.60	56.55	43.77	31.24	52.57
2	67.95	63.55	56.68	45.12	31.97	53.05
3	68.78	64.66	56.61	45.40	31.88	53.46
4	67.75	64.03	56.47	43.74	31.34	52.67
5	67.64	63.82	56.43	44.06	31.17	52.63
10	67.44	63.80	56.42	44.15	30.81	52.52

5   Conclusion

In this work, we introduce TadML, an anchor-free one-stage MLP method designed for TAD using RGB stream input. Our method simplifies the traditional TAD pipe-line by eliminating the need for manual conversion of optical flow data. Additionally, we propose $\beta - GloU$ for the framework. To the best of our knowledge, TadML is the first MLP-like model suitable for TAD. We leverage Newtonian Mechanics to address the token mixing problem. TadML showcases the potential of MLP-like methods in downstream visual tasks, surpassing many recent methods (including those using optical flow input) and offering twice the inference speed of BMN. Due to its independence from optical flow conversion, our method holds promise for practical applications in the field of TAD. Moreover, it achieves impressive performance when both RGB and flow data are utilized. Our goal is to promote the development of efficient models for temporal action detection and facilitate their adoption in industrial set-tings. The source code is available at https://github.com/BonedDeng/TadML.

Acknowledgements. Supported by the National Key Research and Development Program of China (Nos. E2M2010801).

References

1. Liu, X., Bai, S., Bai, X.: An empirical study of end-to-end temporal action detection. In: Proceedings of the IEEE/CVF Conference on Computer Vision and Pattern Recognition, pp. 658–666. IEEE, Long Beach (2019)
2. Ali, S.G., Ali, R.: Experimental protocol designed to employ Nd: YAG laser surgery for anterior chamber glaucoma detection via UBM. IET Image Proc. **16**(8), 2171–2179 (2020)
3. Li, J., Chen, J., Sheng, B., et al.: Automatic detection and classification system of domestic waste via multimodel cascaded convolutional neural network. IEEE Trans. Industr. Inf. **18**(1), 163–173 (2021)
4. Bahroun, S., Abed, R., Zagrouba, E.: Deep 3D-LBP: CNN-based fusion of shape modeling and texture descriptors for accurate face recognition. Vis. Comput. 1–16 (2021)
5. Hu, X., Zheng, C., Huang, J., et al.: Cloth texture preserving image-based 3D virtual try-on. Vis. Comput. **39**(8), 3347–3357 (2023)
6. Lin, T., Zhao, X., Su, H., Wang, C., Yang, M.: BSN: boundary sensitive network for temporal action proposal generation. In: Ferrari, V., Hebert, M., Sminchisescu, C., Weiss, Y. (eds.) ECCV 2018. LNCS, vol. 11208, pp. 3–21. Springer, Cham (2018). https://doi.org/10.1007/978-3-030-01225-0_1
7. Lin, T., Liu, X., Li, X., Ding, E., Wen, S.: BMN: boundary-matching network for temporal action proposal generation. In: 2019 IEEE/CVF International Conference on Computer Vision (ICCV), pp. 3888–3897. IEEE, Seoul (2019)
8. Lin, C., et al.: Learning salient boundary feature for anchor-free temporal action localization. In: 2021 IEEE/CVF Conference on Computer Vision and Pattern Recognition (CVPR), pp. 3319–3328. IEEE, Nashville (2021)
9. Rezatofighi, H., Tsoi, N., Gwak, J., Sadeghian, A., Reid, I., Savarese, S.: Generalized intersection over union: a metric and a loss for bounding box regression. In: 2019 IEEE/CVF Conference on Computer Vision and Pattern Recognition (CVPR), pp. 658–666. IEEE, Long Beach (2019)
10. Uijlings, J.R.R., Duta, I.C., Rostamzadeh, N., Sebe, N.: Realtime video classification using dense HOF/HOG. In: Proceedings of International Conference on Multimedia Retrieval, pp. 145–152. Association for Computing Machinery, New York (2014)
11. Graves, A.: Long short-term memory. In: Graves, A. (ed.) Supervised Sequence Labelling with Recurrent Neural Networks, pp. 37–45. Springer, Heidelberg (2012). https://doi.org/10.1007/978-3-642-24797-2_4
12. Dai, C., Wei, Y., Xu, Z., Chen, M., Liu, Y., Fan, J.: An investigation into performance factors of two-stream I3D networks. In: 2021 26th International Conference on Automation and Computing (ICAC), pp. 1–6 (2021)
13. Zeng, R., et al.: Graph convolutional networks for tmporal action localization. In: Proceedings of the IEEE/CVF International Conference on Computer Vision, pp. 4560–4570. IEEE, Seoul (2019)
14. Zhang, D.J., et al.: MorphMLP: an efficient MLP-Like backbone for spatial-temporal representation learning. In: Avidan, S., Brostow, G., Cissé, M., Farinella, G.M., Hassner, T. (eds.) ECCV 2022. LNCS, vol. 13695, pp. 230–248. Springer, Cham (2022). https://doi.org/10.1007/978-3-031-19833-5_14
15. Tang, Y., et al.: An image patch is a wave: phase-aware vision MLP. In: 2022 IEEE/CVF Conference on Computer Vision and Pattern Recognition (CVPR), pp. 10925–10934. IEEE, New Orleans (2022)

16. Idrees, H., et al.: The THUMOS challenge on action recognition for videos "in the wild.". Comput. Vis. Image Underst. **155**, 1–23 (2017)
17. Heilbron, F.C., Escorcia, V., Ghanem, B., Niebles, J.C.: ActivityNet: a large-scale video benchmark for human activity understanding. In: 2015 IEEE Conference on Computer Vision and Pattern Recognition (CVPR), pp. 961–970 (2015)
18. Yang, K., Qiao, P., Li, D., Lv, S., Dou, Y.: Exploring temporal preservation networks for precise temporal action localization. In: Proceedings of the Thirty-Second AAAI Conference on Artificial Intelligence, pp. 7477–7484. AAAI Press, New Orleans (2018)
19. Dai, X., Singh, B., Zhang, G., Davis, L.S., Chen, Y.Q.: Temporal context network for activity localization in videos. In: 2017 IEEE International Conference on Computer Vision (ICCV), pp. 5727–5736. IEEE, Venice (2017)
20. Gao, J., Yang, Z., Sun, C., Chen, K., Nevatia, R.: TURN TAP: temporal unit regression network for temporal action proposals. In: 2017 IEEE International Conference on Computer Vision (ICCV), pp. 3648–3656. IEEE, Venice (2017)
21. Xu, H., Das, A., Saenko, K.: R-C3D: region convolutional 3D network for temporal activity detection. In: 2017 IEEE International Conference on Computer Vision (ICCV), pp. 5794–5803. IEEE, Venice (2017)
22. Liu, Y., Ma, L., Zhang, Y., Liu, W., Chang, S.-F.: Multi-granularity generator for temporal action proposal. In: 2019 IEEE/CVF Conference on Computer Vision and Pattern Recognition (CVPR), pp. 3599–3608. IEEE, Long Beach (2019)
23. Song, Q., Zhou, Y., Hu, M., Liu, C.: Faster learning of temporal action proposal via sparse multilevel boundary generator. Multim. Tools Appl. (2023)
24. Sooksatra, S., Watcharapinchai, S.: A comprehensive review on temporal-action proposal generation. J. Imaging **8**, 207 (2022)
25. Chao, Y.-W., Vijayanarasimhan, S., Seybold, B., Ross, D.A., Deng, J., Sukthankar, R.: Rethinking the faster R-CNN architecture for temporal action localization. In: 2018 IEEE/CVF Conference on Computer Vision and Pattern Recognition, pp. 1130–1139. IEEE, Salt Lake (2018)
26. Xu, M., Zhao, C., Rojas, D.S., Thabet, A., Ghanem, B.: G-TAD: sub-graph localization for temporal action detection. In: 2020 IEEE/CVF Conference on Computer Vision and Pattern Recognition (CVPR), pp. 10153–10162. IEEE, Seattle (2020)
27. Zhao, P., Xie, L., Ju, C., Zhang, Y., Wang, Y., Tian, Q.: Bottom-up temporal action lcalization with mutual regularization. In: Vedaldi, A., Bischof, H., Brox, T., Frahm, J.-M. (eds.) ECCV 2020. LNCS, vol. 12353, pp. 539–555. Springer, Cham (2020). https://doi.org/10.1007/978-3-030-58598-3_32
28. Zhu, Z., Tang, W., Wang, L., Zheng, N., Hua, G.: Enriching local and global contexts for temporal action localization. In: 2021 IEEE/CVF International Conference on Computer Vision (ICCV), pp. 13496–13505. IEEE, Montreal (2021)
29. Dai, P., Li, Z., Zhang, Y., Liu, S., Zeng, B.: PBR-Net: imitating physically based rndering using deep neural network. IEEE Trans. Image Process. **29**, 5980–5992 (2020)
30. Yang, L., Peng, H., Zhang, D., Fu, J., Han, J.: Revisiting anchor mechanisms for temporal action localization. IEEE Trans. Image Process. **29**, 8535–8548 (2020)
31. Long, F., Yao, T., Qiu, Z., Tian, X., Luo, J., Mei, T.: Gaussian temporal awareness networks for action localization. In: 2019 IEEE/CVF Conference on Computer Vision and Pattern Recognition (CVPR), pp. 344–353 (2019)
32. Zhao, Y., Xiong, Y., Wang, L., Wu, Z., Tang, X., Lin, D.: Temporal action detection with structured segment networks. Int. J. Comput. Vis. **128**, 74–95 (2020)

Image Analysis and Processing

A Multi-label Privacy-Preserving Image Retrieval Scheme Based on Object Detection for Efficient and Secure Cloud Retrieval

Ruizhong Du[1], Jing Cui[1,2(✉)], and Mingyue Li[1]

[1] Hebei Province Key Laboratory of High Confdence Information System,
Hebei University, Baoding, China
[2] School of Cyber Security and Compute, Hebei University, Baoding, China
cuijing20171227@163.com

Abstract. With the development of self-media, encrypted image retrieval faces a challenge of striking a balance between security and efficiency. To address this issue, a Multi-label Privacy-preserving Image Retrieval scheme based on Object Detection (MPIR-OD) is proposed. Firstly, image labels are extracted using object detection techniques. Then, frequent itemsets of labels are discovered through mining label association rules, and they are matched and classified with the previously extracted image labels to construct an index. Lastly, the Asymmetric Scalar-product Preserving Encryption (ASPE) is employed to encrypt image feature vectors, ensuring the privacy of the images, and enabling secure K-Nearest Neighbor (KNN) operations using the ASPE algorithm. Compared to existing schemes, the MPIR-OD scheme achieves a reduction in retrieval time of approximately 6 times and an improvement in retrieval accuracy of around 15%.

Keywords: Searchable Encryption · Encrypted Image Retrieval · Object Detection · Association Rule

1 Introduction

Amidst the exponential growth in image quantities, Content-Based Image Retrieval (CBIR) stands out as a promising technology for swift image retrieval [11]. Cloud services have emerged as a convenient and cost-effective solution for image storage and sharing, but they come with security risks when transmitting data to unfamiliar third parties. To address data leakage risks, existing searchable encryption methods encrypt data before outsourcing it to the cloud

This work was supported by National Natural Science Foundation of China (No. 61572170), the Key R&D Program of Hebei Province (22340701D), the Natural Science Foundation of Hebei Province (F2022201005) and Hebei Province Postgraduate Innovation Funding Project (CXZZSS2023005).

B. Sheng et al. (Eds.): CGI 2023, LNCS 14495, pp. 43–55, 2024.
https://doi.org/10.1007/978-3-031-50069-5_5

server, enabling the retrieval and sharing of encrypted images [19]. However, the complexity of the encryption search mechanism can lead to significant computational burdens for data owners and query users. As a remedy, researchers propose outsourcing computationally intensive steps to the cloud server to alleviate the computational burden experienced by data owners and query users.

In reference [13], a feature adaptive fusion encrypted image retrieval method is proposed, where encrypted images are uploaded to a cloud server, and a fine-tuned convolutional neural network extracts semantic and low-level features. Reference [2] introduces an S-HashMap indexing structure that enables fuzzy ciphertext retrieval with multiple keywords, utilizing the KNN algorithm to calculate vector and index similarity. Additionally, reference [6] utilizes a fine-tuned convolutional neural network to extract image features, which are encrypted using the KNN algorithm to construct a hierarchical index graph. However, since the number of images users need to retrieve is much smaller than the total number of images stored in the database, which leads to linearly increasing retrieval time. Anju et al. applied clustering techniques in a cloud environment, using MPEG-7 visual descriptors to perform indexing through clustering [1]. Liu et al. utilized the k-means algorithm to construct a tree-based index structure with XOR similarity for parent nodes [12]. However, challenges arise with the k-means algorithm, as seen in literature [8,16], where recursive k-means clustering is used to achieve data privacy and search speed acceleration. Nonetheless, the k-means algorithm's effectiveness diminishes as data volume increases. Wang et al. proposed the EPIRM protection framework, which differs from traditional vector index encryption retrieval schemes by achieving KNN retrieval without randomly splitting vectors, resulting in cost savings [17]. Prioritizing retrieval security over efficiency is not suitable for the current big data privacy environment.

In the field of computer vision, to enhance the accuracy of encrypted image retrieval, target detection techniques are commonly employed to locate and identify image content [3,4,10] Tan et al. introduces a method based on polarized image fusion and the Grouped Convolutional Attention Network (GCAnet) to improve the detection of vehicles and pedestrians in foggy street scenes [15]. Ruyi et al. presents an automatic image orientation detection method that combines attention features (AF) and rotation features (RF) to accurately determine image orientation by capturing advanced semantics and directional characteristics [14]. Jiang et al. proposes a novel PhotoHelper system that enhances image quality by integrating aesthetic rules, machine learning, and deep neural networks [7]. Li et al. introduces a multi-modal cascaded convolutional neural network (MCCNN) for the detection and classification of domestic waste images, combining three subnetworks (DSSD, YOLOv4, and Faster-RCNN) to enhance detection precision [9].

Based on these contributions, this paper presents an encrypted image retrieval solution based on target detection techniques. This solution utilizes object detection technology to recognize image content and label the identified results, thus enabling precise image classification based on the correlations among these labels. During the retrieval process, it effectively mitigates the "needle in a haystack" problem within the database. The contributions of the program are as follows:

1. In order to reduce retrieval time, the proposed scheme employs object detection methods to achieve fine-grained image classification.
2. To enhance retrieval accuracy, we adopted data mining techniques and designed a two-tiered index, encompassing both image labels and feature vectors. By mining association rules, frequent itemsets of labels can be discovered. These frequent itemsets are then matched with corresponding image vectors to construct the index. This dual-layer index design helps improve the accuracy of image retrieval.
3. The privacy of the images is safeguarded by incorporating encryption mechanisms, yielding promising experimental results. The research findings demonstrate the security of the MPIR-OD scheme.

2   Model Definition

2.1   System Model

The multi-label privacy-preserving image retrieval system based on object detection involves three entities: the data owner responsible for encrypting and uploading preprocessed images, the cloud server handling storage, similarity calculations, and search result delivery to authorized requesting users, and the requesting user category comprising all users authorized by the data owner with search needs. Figure 1 illustrates the relationship between these entities.

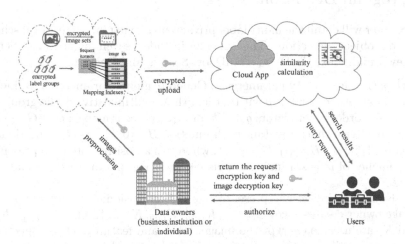

Fig. 1. The system model

2.2   Threat Model

The multi-label encrypted image retrieval model assumes that the cloud environment is "honest and curious". According to the available information on the cloud server, the scheme considers the following two threat models. Level-1 Attack: The attacker only knows the encrypted ciphertext information, such as encrypted images, encrypted multi-labels, etc., and the plaintext information is unknown. Therefore, an attacker can deduce the plaintext or key by analyzing one or more ciphertext encrypted with the same key. Level-2 Attack: The attacker will obtain some additional plaintext information, such as statistics, in addition to the ciphertext. Therefore, attackers can infer more plaintext information through background knowledge.

2.3   Design Goals

To achieve secure and efficient multi-label encrypted image retrieval, the design goals of the scheme are as follows: (1) Data privacy. Corresponding encryption mechanisms are used to protect the privacy of various image data after image preprocessing. (2) Security. Trapdoor indistinguishability: Using indistinguishability ensures that two queries are indistinguishable from the trapdoor to an attacker. Indistinguishability of searchable ciphertext: The searchable ciphertext formed by two queries is guaranteed to be indistinguishable to an attacker. (3) High retrieval accuracy. Image preprocessing and search are more in line with human vision, and retrieval accuracy is higher. (4) High retrieval efficiency. Narrow the search space to improve the search efficiency.

3   Program Definition

This chapter will detail the multi-label privacy-preserving image retrieval scheme based on object detection. The scheme includes seven algorithms: SetUp, GenKey, BuildIndex, EncData, TradDoor, Search, and DecData.

1. SetUp: Obtain security parameter λ. Generate global parameters G_P, including a large prime number p with bit length λ, multiplicative cyclic groups G_1 and G_T of order p, generators g and h for G_1, a bilinear map $e : G_1 \times G_1 \rightarrow G_T$, and a one-term shock-resistant hash function $H : \{0,1\}^* \rightarrow G_1$. Additionally, create a label set $L = \{l_1, l_2, \ldots, l_i\}$, where i is a positive integer representing the number of labels. Finally, announce the global parameters G_P and label set L.

2. GenKey: Each image is represented by a d-dimensional feature vector. The image owner creates a key $SK = \{K_{Img}, K_{Lab}, K_v, M\}$, where K_{Img}, K_{Lab}, and K_v are used to encrypt the image, label, and feature vector respectively. M is an invertible matrix with dimensions $(d+1)*(d+1)$. The image owner shares the encryption key with authorized requesting users.

3. BuildIndex: Given an image set and extracted image labels, create an encrypted index of images according to Algorithm 1. The specific process is as follows:

(a) For the n images in the image dataset DataSet=$\{Img_1, ..., Img_n\}$, extract the image features $F_V = \{f_{v1}, ...f_{vn}\}$ and each label.
(b) Extend the extracted image feature vector f_{vi} $(1 \leq i \leq n)$ from the d-dimension to the $(d+1)$-dimension according to (1):

$$f_{vi} = (f_{vi}^T, -0.5\,||f_{vi}||)^T (1 \leq i \leq n) \tag{1}$$

Encrypt the expanded feature vector according to (2):

$$f_{Evi} = M^T * f_{vi}(1 \leq i \leq n) \tag{2}$$

(c) Based on data miningtechnology [5], the Image_label_Association algorithm is proposed to train frequent label combinations. The specific process is described in Algorithm 2.
(d) Encrypt the labels extracted from the image.
(e) Upload each index to the cloud server.
Figure 2 illustrates an example of generating frequent itemsets. P1 {people, dog, bike}, P2 {people, bike, cat, traffic light}, P3 {dog, bike, traffic light}, and P4 {people, bike, traffic light}. During each iteration, only the item sets that meet the minimum support threshold are retained as frequent item sets. The support of an itemset is represented by the probability of both tags A and B occurring together, denoted as $P(A \cap B)$. For instance, {people} and {dog} co-occur only once in P1, so the probability is calculated as $P = 1/4 = 0.25$.

4. EncData: Image encryption uses ASE. Image feature encryption uses ASPE [18].
5. TradDoor: After authentication, the user extracts multiple labels representing the image content from the query image $L\{l_1, l_2, l_3.....\}$ and d-dimensional image features f_q. Then, the feature vector is extended, and f_q is extended from the d-dimension to the $(d+1)$-dimension according to (3):

$$f_q = r * (f_q^T, 1)^T \tag{3}$$

r is a random number, the first d-dimension is the original f_q, and the $(d+1)$-th dimension is 1. The user is requested to encrypt the feature vector and the extracted multi-labels. The feature vector is encrypted according to (4):

$$f_{Eq} = M^{-1}f_q \tag{4}$$

Finally, request the user to send the processed search trapdoor to the cloud server for subsequent search operations.
6. Search: the cloud server runs the Search algorithm and returns similar results to the requesting user. According to (5):

$$(f_{Ev1} - f_{Ev2}) \cdot f_{Eq} = 0.5r(d(f_{v2}, f_q) - d(f_{v1}, f_q)) \tag{5}$$

Using Eqs. (3) and (4), we calculate the Euclidean distance between each image's feature vector and the query image's feature vector as specified in (5). The top-k results are then retrieved and returned to the user. The inequality

$0.5r(d(f_{v2}, f_q) - d(f_{v1}, f_q)) > 0$ correctly determines if $d(f_{v2}, f_q)$ is greater than $d(f_{v1}, f_q)$, where r is a random number. If there is no matching label set, a direct search is performed among unrelated label combinations.

During the search phase, encrypted feature vectors and image labels are input to the cloud server, which generates the top-k most similar result sets as output. The process is as follows: (1) Submit the encrypted image label set and feature vectors to the cloud server. (2) The cloud server matches the encrypted label set with pre-stored frequent label item sets. If a successful match is found, it retrieves the index of the corresponding image IDs and extracts the corresponding feature vectors. (3) Calculate the Euclidean distance between the query image vector and the image vectors in the frequent label item set using the K-nearest neighbors (KNN) rule. (4) Output the top-k result sets containing the most similar images.

7. DecData: the users decrypt the search results obtained from the cloud server using the DecData algorithm, implemented based on the decryption module described in ASPE, to obtain the ciphertext images.

Algorithm 1 : BuildIndex Algorithm.

Input: DataSet()
Output: LabelIndexTree
 1: association_label_map = {}
 2: model = YOLOv5()
 3: **for** each image in DataSet **do**
 4:     $detected\_objects$ = model.detect($image$)
 5:     image_labels = extract_labels($detected\_objects$)
 6:     feature_vector = extract_features($image$)
 7: **end for**
 8: loading Image_label_Association algorithm
 9: association_label_map{} .add ($feature\_vector$)
10: association_label_map{} .add ($image.ID$)
11: encrypted labels, feature vectors and corresponding images
12: LabelIndexTree = {}
13: **for** associated_label_set, mapping in association_label_map.items() **do**
14:     LabelIndexTree[$associated\_label\_set$] = {"$feature\_vectors$" : $mapping$ ["$feature\_vectors$"] , "$image\_ids$" : $mapping$ ["$image\_ids$"]}
15: **end for**
16: **return** LabelIndexTree

Algorithm 2 : Image_label_Association.

Input: A DataSet of images with labels
Output: Association rules between labels
 1: transactionList={}
 2: **for** each image in the DataSet **do**
 3:     itemList={}

4:      **for** each label associated with the image **do**
5:          itemList.add{*label*}
6:          transactionList.add{*itemList*}
7:      **end for**
8: **end for**
9: Apply the rules in Fig. 2 on transaction List to find frequent itemsets
10: **return** the frequent itemsets

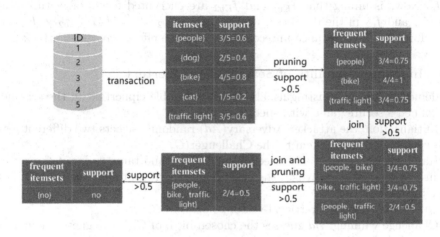

Fig. 2. Example of label association rule

4 Security Analysis

4.1 Data Privacy

The image data contains the image itself, labels, and index vectors. Using AES to encrypt the image and index, the cloud server cannot obtain the data of the original image based on the encrypted information without the key. The ASPE encrypts the index vectors in a known ciphertext attack context. As long as the key of ASPE is unknown, the attacker cannot obtain the plaintext information.

4.2 ASPE Can Effectively Resist Two Types of Attacks

Theorem 1: Encryption of feature vectors is distance non-recoverable

Prove: High-level attack schemes are resistant to low-level attacks. In order to resist Level-2 attack, we must use an encryption function that cannot reveal any information. Now, assume that the distance is recoverable. Let f_{EV1} and f_{EV2} be encrypted forms of f_{V1} and f_{V2}. There is an operation process f such that $f(f_{EV1}, f_{EV2}) = \sqrt{f_{EV1} \cdot f_{EV1} - 2(f_{EV1} \cdot f_{EV2}) + f_{EV2} \cdot f_{EV2}}$. And because the encryption process preserves the scalar product, the distance can be expressed as $\sqrt{f_{V1} \cdot f_{V1} - 2(f_{V1} \cdot f_{V2}) + f_{V2} \cdot f_{V2}}$. Let E be an encryption function, $E(f_{V1}, K_V)$ be the encrypted value of the feature vector f_{V1} encrypted with the key K_V.

In this definition, different encryption methods are used to deal with the encryption operation of database feature vector and query feature vector, namely $E_T()$ and $E_Q()$. Assumption $f_{Ev} = E_T(f_v, K_v) = M^T \cdot f_v$, $f_{Eq} = E_Q(f_q, K_v) = M^{-1} \cdot f_q$. Obviously, it is impossible to deduce the values of f_v and f_q from f_{Ev} and f_{Eq} without knowing the matrix M. Similarly, $f_{Ev}^T f_{Eq} = f_v^T M M^{-1} f_q = f_v^T f_q$. Now, assuming that f_{Ev1} and f_{Ev2} are encrypted forms of feature vectors f_{v1} and f_{v2} in the database, we have $f_{Ev1}^T f_{Ev2} = f_{v1}^T M M^{-1} f_{v2} \neq f_{v1}^T f_{v2}$. Therefore, ASPE is distance unrecoverable and can effectively resist attack 2.

4.3   Indistinguishability of Searchable Ciphertext

To demonstrate the indistinguishability of searchable ciphertext in the scheme, we defined a secure game with specific steps:

Initialization: the attacker Adversary(Ad) randomly selects two different feature vectors and sends them to the Challenger(C).

Randomness: C randomly selects a bit $b \in 0, 1$ and takes as input the set of feature vectors f_{vb} and invokes the encryption algorithm to get the image C' of the ciphertext.

Query: Ad chooses a retrieval vector to send to C.

Challenge winning: Ad guesses the chosen bit b of C. If the guess is equal to the actual choice of C, the challenge is won.

Safety requirements stipulate that: the probability of winning for any polynomial-time Ad in the game, and is comparable to that of a random guess.

Construct a simulator that demonstrates the above security. The simulator can simulate behavior that is almost indistinguishable from that of a real challenger. The steps of the simulation are as follows:

Initialization: Simulator receives the set of vectors f_{v0} and f_{v1} sent by Ad.

Randomness: Simulator chooses a random bit $b \in \{0, 1\}$. Simulated encryption: The simulator invokes the encryption algorithm using the vector set f_{vb} as input to obtain a simulated ciphertext image C'.

Query: Simulator receives the search vector sent by Ad.

Simulated search: The simulator uses the search algorithm and gives a simulated search result R'.

Output: Simulator sends C' and R' to Ad.

The complete trustworthiness of the data owners' environment and the semantic security inherent in the cryptographic framework pose a challenge to Ad in ensuring that their returned results match those generated by the simulator. This requirement indicates that the adversary is unable to differentiate between results obtained in the real-world and the ideal-world scenario. Consequently, the scheme successfully achieves searchable ciphertext indistinguishability.

$$Adv_{MPIR-OD}^{IDG-SC}, A^\lambda = \left| Pr\lfloor A^{b=0} wins \rfloor - Pr\lfloor A^{b=1} wins \rfloor \right| \tag{6}$$

4.4   The Unlinkability of Trapdoors

During the search the trapdoor was encrypted as: $F_{Eq} = M^{-1}r^*(f_q^T, 1)^T$. The comparison of two trapdoors generated from the same extended f_q presents a challenge for the cloud server due to the introduction of random noise, denoted as r, during trapdoor generation. Consequently, instances arise where different trapdoors are produced from identical search queries, and even the same image yields distinct encryption results. Consequently, the cloud server faces considerable difficulty in directly extracting the relationship between two trapdoors.

5   Performance Analysis

5.1   Experiment Analysis

To analyze the performance of the MPIR-OD scheme, we collectively refer to the CBIR-based encrypted image retrieval schemes [2,13] as CBIR-KNN, and compare it with both CBIR-KNN and the EPIR/EPIRM scheme [17] for comparative analysis.

Experiments were conducted using the YOLO v5 model on the Caltech 256 dataset. The experimental setup was deployed on the Alibaba Cloud environment with an Ubuntu 20.04 64-bit operating system and a server configuration featuring four cores (vCPU) @ 8 GiB.

Indexes Creation and Memory Overhead. Although the MPIR-OD scheme sacrifices additional index creation time and memory overhead to improve retrieval performance, as shown in Table 1 and Table 2, the extra index creation time is minimal. Furthermore, considering the significant storage capabilities of cloud servers, the memory costs associated with index creation fall within an acceptable range for cloud server infrastructure.

Table 1. Index Creation overhead

	d	single index	multi-label index	full indexs
Indexes	32	0.0002/s	0.0369/s	0.0371/s
	64	0.0006/s	0.0359/s	0.0365/s
	128	0.0007/s	0.0342/s	0.0349/s

Table 2. Memory overhead

	d	single index	multi-label index	full indexs
Memory	32	5.0/MB	355.6/MB	360.6/MB
	64	19.4/MB	1331.2/MB	1350.6/MB
	128	77.2/MB	5324.8/MB	5402.0/MB

Privacy of Images. To verify the privacy of the images, Fig. 3(a) illustrates the visual appearance of the test image before and after encryption. It is evident that the encrypted image is visually indistinguishable. Figure 3(b) and Fig. 3(c) displays the histogram distributions of the test image before and after encryption. As depicted in Fig. 3(c), the histogram distribution of the encrypted image is more uniform, thus ensuring the privacy of the image.

Search Performance. As shown in Fig. 4, the query image is always the first-ranked image, indicating that MPIR-OD can ensure query accuracy. In addition, for the sake of ensuring data security and retrieval privacy, all operations must be carried out in an encrypted environment. Nevertheless, in order to enhance comprehensibility and better showcase experimental outcomes, the results verifying retrieval performance are presented as decrypted outputs.

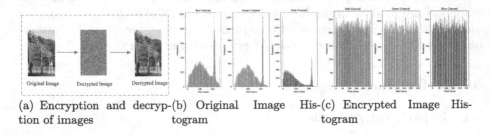

(a) Encryption and decryption of images (b) Original Image Histogram (c) Encrypted Image Histogram

Fig. 3. Privacy of images

Fig. 4. Retrieval results

Search Accuracy. We used a 512-dimensional feature vector. Figure 5(a) shows that MPIR-OD significantly improves retrieval accuracy. As K increases, the accuracy decreases to 80% and stabilizes around 70%. In contrast, CBIR-KNN's retrieval accuracy sharply declines below 50% with increasing K. In Fig. 5(b), MPIR-OD maintains approximately 70% retrieval accuracy across different K values, while other schemes remain below 30%. Figure 5(c) compares retrieval accuracy with the same K value and dimensions. Lower dimensionality leads to reduced retrieval accuracy, but MPIR-OD outperforms the other schemes. This advantage arises from MPIR-OD's detailed retrieval range division based on multiple labels, which ensures stable retrieval accuracy within the desired range.

Search Time. Figure 5(d) shows, when the number of images is set to 20000, the search time of MPIR-OD is 7.28 ms, which is about 8 times, 3 times, and

6 times faster than that of CBIR-KNN, EPIR, and EPIRM. When the number of images is 100,000, the search time of CBIR-KNN is ten times that of MPIR-OD. The reason is that the mapping between tag item set and image ID can effectively remove irrelevant images and improve the retrieval precision and efficiency. In Fig. 5(e), when the number of images is 10,000, The larger the dimension, the higher the search accuracy, but the more time-consuming the search. However, in this scheme, the influence of the increase in dimension on the search time is minimal, which means that the search precision and the search time can be balanced, and the performance of both can be significantly improved simultaneously.

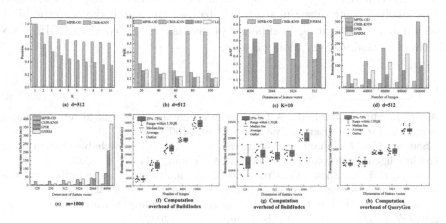

Fig. 5. Algorithm Performances

Figure 5(a) and (b) show the accuracy of k from 0–10 and the change of $P@K$ from 10 to 100, respectively, for a feature vector dimension of 512. In (c), the average retrieval accuracy is depicted for $k = 10$, with the feature vector dimension reduced from 4096 to 512. Figure 5(d) illustrates the change in search time as the number of search images increases from 20,000 to 100,000 with a dimension of 512. In (e), the change in search time is presented for 10,000 images, as the number of images increases from 128 to 4,096. Figure 5(f) displays the relationship between the number of images and the time consumption for index creation when using the MPIR-OD dimension of 512. Furthermore, (g) and (h) depict the relationship between the difference in vector dimension and the time consumption of index creation and query request generation when the number of MPIR-OD images in this scheme is 10,000.

These experiments compare the performance of multi-label searchable encryption algorithms, using feature vectors of dimension 512 and 10,000 images. Figure 5(f), (g), and (h) show the performance indicators for each algorithm. Although this scheme requires two additional steps compared to CBIR-KNN during encrypted image retrieval, namely label extraction and frequent label itemset detection, the retrieval time increases. However, considering the benefits for retrieving users, sacrificing data preprocessing cost for enhanced retrieval performance is a feasible approach.

6 Conclusion

This paper introduces MPIR-OD, a secure and efficient multi-label searchable encrypted image retrieval framework based on object detection. The scheme utilizes the YOLO v5x model to detect objects and extract image labels, establishing a label association rule to link frequent label itemsets. To ensure image retrieval security and content privacy, two encryption methods are employed, tailored to different data types (images, labels, and feature vectors). The retrieval process involves using query image labels to directly match the corresponding frequent label set, resulting in superior performance compared to CBIR-KNN and other searchable encryption schemes.

References

1. Anju, J., Shreelekshmi, R.: A faster secure content-based image retrieval using clustering for cloud. Expert Syst. Appl. **189**, 116070 (2022)
2. Chen, Q., Fan, K., Zhang, K.: Wang: privacy-preserving searchable encryption in the intelligent edge computing. Comput. Commun. **164**, 31–41 (2020)
3. Gao, Y., Dai, M., Zhang, Q.: Cross-modal and multi-level feature refinement network for rgb-d salient object detection. Vis. Comput. 1–16 (2022)
4. Guo, Z., Shuai, H., Liu, G., Zhu, Y., Wang, W.: Multi-level feature fusion pyramid network for object detection. Vis. Comput. 1–11 (2022)
5. Hamdi, A., Shaban, K., Erradi, A., Mohamed, A., Rumi, S.K., Salim, F.D.: Spatiotemporal data mining: a survey on challenges and open problems. Artif. Intell. Rev. **55**(2), 1441–1488 (2022)
6. Huang, Z., Zhang, M., Zhang, Y.: Toward efficient encrypted image retrieval in cloud environment. IEEE Access **7**, 174541–174550 (2019)
7. Jiang, N., Sheng, B., Li, P., Lee, T.Y.: Photohelper: portrait photographing guidance via deep feature retrieval and fusion. IEEE Trans. Multim. (2022)
8. Lafta, A.L.: Privacy-preserve content-based image retrieval using aggregated local features. Iraqi J. Electric. Electron. Eng. **18**(2) (2022)
9. Li, J., et al.: Automatic detection and classification system of domestic waste via multimodel cascaded convolutional neural network. IEEE Trans. Indust. Inf. **18**(1), 163–173 (2021)
10. Li, R., Shen, Y.: Yolosr-IST: a deep learning method for small target detection in infrared remote sensing images based on super-resolution and yolo. Sig. Process. **208**, 108962 (2023)
11. Li, X., Yang, J., Ma, J.: Recent developments of content-based image retrieval (CBIR). Neurocomputing **452**, 675–689 (2021)
12. Liu, H., Zhang, Y., Xiang, Y., Liu, B., Guo, E.: Multi-user image retrieval with suppression of search pattern leakage. Inf. Sci. **607**, 1041–1060 (2022)
13. Ma, W., Qin, J., Xiang, X., Tan, Y., He, Z.: Searchable encrypted image retrieval based on multi-feature adaptive late-fusion. Mathematics **8**(6), 1019 (2020)
14. Ruyi, B.: A general image orientation detection method by feature fusion. Vis. Comput. 1–16 (2023)

15. Tan, A., Guo, T., Zhao, Y., Wang, Y., Li, X.: Object detection based on polarization image fusion and grouped convolutional attention network. Vis. Comput. 1–17 (2023)
16. Wang, Q., Feng, C., Xu, Y.: Zhong: a novel privacy-preserving speech recognition framework using bidirectional LSTM. J. Cloud Comput. **9**, 1–13 (2020)
17. Wang, X., Ma, J., Liu, X., Miao, Y.: Search in my way: practical outsourced image retrieval framework supporting unshared key. In: IEEE INFOCOM 2019-IEEE Conference on Computer Communications, pp. 2485–2493. IEEE (2019)
18. Wong, W.K., Cheung, D.W.l., Kao, B., Mamoulis, N.: Secure KNN computation on encrypted databases. In: Proceedings of the 2009 ACM SIGMOD International Conference on Management of Data, pp. 139–152 (2009)
19. Xia, Z., Ji, Q., Gu, Q., Yuan, C., Xiao, F.: A format-compatible searchable encryption scheme for jpeg images using bag-of-words. ACM Trans. Multim. Comput. Commun. Appl. **18**(3), 1–18 (2022)

AMCNet: Adaptive Matching Constraint for Unsupervised Point Cloud Registration

Feng Yu, Zhuohan Xiao, Zhaoxiang Chen, Li Liu, Minghua Jiang$^{(\boxtimes)}$,
Xiaoxiao Liu, Xinrong Hu, and Tao Peng

Wuhan Textile University, Wuhan 430200, China
Minghuajiang@wtu.edu.cn

Abstract. The registration of 3D point cloud with numerous applications in robotics, medical imaging and other industries. However, due to the lack of accurate data annotation, the performance of unsupervised point cloud registration networks is often unsatisfactory. In this paper, we propose an unsupervised method based on generating corresponding points and utilizing structural constraints for rigid point cloud registration. The key components in our approach are similarity optimization module and structure variation checking module. In the similarity optimization module, we improve the similarity matrix by adaptively weighting the matching scores of neighbors. Through this method, the spatial information of matching point pairs can be fully utilized, resulting in high-quality corresponding estimations. We observe that predicted point cloud is crucial for constructing accurate correspondences. Therefore, we developed a structure variation checking module to constrain the predicted point cloud and the source point cloud to have similar structural information. Based on the constraints, the extraction network is continuously optimized and adjusted to obtain even better features. The extensive experimental results show that our method achieves state-of-the-art performance when compared with other supervised and unsupervised tasks on the ModelNet40 data set, and significantly outperforms previous methods on the real-world indoor 7Scenes data set.

Keywords: Point cloud · Deep learning · Adaptive registration · Point cloud registration

1 Introduction

Point cloud registration involves identifying the matching relationship between the points in a source point cloud and a target point cloud, and then using a rigid transformation matrix to align the two point clouds precisely. Currently, with the decreasing price of depth camera devices, point cloud data has become increasingly common in the real world. Registration quality directly affects subsequent tasks, including robotics [2], 3D reconstruction [6,18], autonomous driving [4,23,28] and other fields [13,14]. However, challenges related to point cloud

© The Author(s), under exclusive license to Springer Nature Switzerland AG 2024
B. Sheng et al. (Eds.): CGI 2023, LNCS 14495, pp. 56–68, 2024.
https://doi.org/10.1007/978-3-031-50069-5_6

registration still persist, due to significant pose changes, partial views, and variations in point density.

The registration problem exists in many computer graphics tasks. For 2D images, common methods involve extracting feature [12] and finding matching pixels between multiple images [1]. This approach enables the establishment of accurate correspondence between pixels in different images. Similarly, for 3D point cloud registration, many networks are designed to find correspondence pairs in point clouds. In the past several years, deep learning has demonstrated powerful learning capabilities, and scholars have been focused on employing deep learning networks for completing point cloud registration tasks [5,7,21]. Many methods among them use supervised approach to learning the rigid transformation matrix. However, in complicated cases, due to the inevitable limitations of unsupervised learning network, the performance of point cloud registration networks is less impressive than that of supervised networks.

In this paper, we propose a novel network that solves the point cloud registration problem in an unsupervised manner by utilizing the neighborhood information of correspondence pairs for computing a more precise rigid transformation matrix. Specifically, our network is divided into similarity optimization, structure variation checking and inlier evaluation modules. Firstly, given two point clouds with unknown correspondence, according to the neighborhood distance of each point in point cloud, different weights are adaptively assigned to reflect the influence of various neighborhood points, the neighborhood matching scores are then aggregated to the center point to optimize the score matrix for generate a high-quality predicted point cloud. After constructing the predicted point cloud, both the source point cloud and predicted point cloud are sent to the structure variation checking module. We aim for have one-to-one correspondence between the predicted point cloud and the points in the source point cloud, while also having the same pose as the target point cloud. Therefore, we leverage the structural differences between the two point clouds to constrain the feature extraction network and capture better features. Meanwhile, based on the learned predicted point cloud, the inlier evaluation module inspired by RIENet [20] evaluates the reliability of the source point cloud neighborhood and the corresponding target point cloud neighborhood through geometric differences to calculate confidence value used to SVD.

To summarize, the significant contribution of this study are as follows:

- We propose a novel correspondence search method for unsupervised point cloud registration, which integrates spatial distance information to provide more excellent correspondence of points.
- In the similarity optimization module, we use matching pair weights to adaptively clarify fuzzy scores in the similarity matrix.
- According to the structural differences between predicted point cloud and source point cloud, we design a structure variation checking module to constrain extractor for obtaining more robust features.

- Extensive experimental results on indoor 7Scenes and ModelNet40 data sets demonstrate that our network can achieve state-of-the-art registration precision.

2   Related Works

2.1   Traditional Model-Free Point Cloud Registration

For point cloud registration, traditional registration methods have been used for a long time. ICP [3] iteratively estimates the correspondence of the matching points and solves an optimal rigid transformation by minimizing the distances between the coordinates of the corresponding points. However, if the ICP algorithm is initialized with an inappropriate pose, it may easily fall into a local optimal solution. The Fast ICP [9] improves the previous algorithms and optimizes the accuracy and speed of ICP. Segal [19] comprehensively considers the relationship between points and planes in variety of cases, which accuracy and robustness are both improved for the previous single algorithms. FPFH [16] reduces the computational requirements based on PFS, resulting in significant improvement in computational efficiency. None of above methods require training, they use hand-crafted features to solve point cloud registration problems.

2.2   Supervised Point Cloud Registration Method

Recent research has demonstrated the advantages of using deep learning for point cloud classification, segmentation, and registration. DGCNN [25] is a commonly used backbone for extracting single-point features. PCRNet [17] adopts a Point-Net [15] for fast point cloud registration. DCP [24] employs DGCNN for extract features and sends them to Transformer [22] to learn transformation matrix. RPMNet [26] uses differentiable sinkhorn layers and annealing techniques to achieve point pairs soft allocation using a mixture of spatial coordinates and local geometry information. In the process of identifying matching point pairs, IDAM [11] integrates Euclidean spatial information and point cloud features to identify matching point pairs and eliminate incorrectly matched pairs. Most of these works use a detect-then-match approach to identify matching point pairs. However, supervised point cloud registration networks have limitations such as laborious data labeling and noisy points, which restrict their real-world application.

2.3   Unsupervised Point Cloud Registration Method

Unsupervised point cloud registration networks rely on appropriate evaluation methods to determine alignment, in contrast to supervised networks. Based on the idea of PointNetLK, FMR [8] solves the rigid transformation matrix iteratively by taking the difference of point cloud features under different poses as the objective function. Inspired by the PointHop classification method, R-Pointhop

[10] innovatively uses local reference frames and hierarchical features to compute the rigid transformation matrix. CorrNet3D [27] uses a permutation module to learn point clouds when the correspondence between two groups is unknown. The model then measures the difference between the reconstructed result and the target value to achieve unsupervised learning.

3 Methodology

Figure 1 shows an illustration of our method. At each iteration, the computed rigid transformation matrix $\{R^{i-1}, t^{i-1}\}$ is combined with the source point cloud X^{i-1} as a new input X. We simply name our adaptive matching constraint (AMC) based Registration Network as AMCNet.

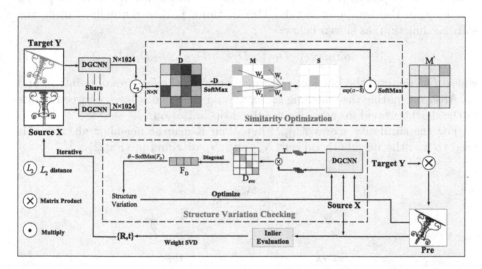

Fig. 1. Pipeline of our proposed method. We first extract the single point features by DGCNN. Generate similarity matrix D according to features. Then, the similarity scores are further adaptive adjusted through the similarity optimization module to construct the prediction point cloud *Pre*. Based on the structure difference between *Pre* and *Source* , we use structure variation checking module to constraint feature extractor to capture better correspondence pairs. Meanwhile, inlier evaluation module output confidence w and is used to weighted SVD to calculate the rigid transformation matrix. The framework is iteratively optimized.

3.1 Similarity Optimization Module

Most single-point feature distance-based point cloud registration methods can be affected by the similarity of features between points, potentially leading to inaccurate matching scores. To address this, we can optimize the scores of similar points by considering the neighborhood of matching points. Correct correspondences tend to have high neighborhood similarity scores, while incorrect correspondences have low scores. This method can accurately avoid errors resulting from the feature extraction network. However, simply averaging neighboring scores is insufficient, as closer neighborhoods should be given greater weight. Therefore, we use adaptive weighting to optimize similarity scores in consideration of spatial proximity.

Given the source point cloud $X = \{x_i \in \mathbb{R}^3 | i = 1, 2, 3, ..., N\}$ and the target point cloud $Y = \{y_j \in \mathbb{R}^3 | j = 1, 2, 3, ..., M\}$, where X and Y have unknown correspondence. In the first step of the method, we input the unaligned point cloud X ,Y and use the dynamic graph convolution (DGCNN) as the feature extractor to extract the features $\mathcal{F}_X \in \mathbb{R}^{N \times d}$ and $\mathcal{F}_Y \in \mathbb{R}^{M \times d}$. According to the feature of each point, we calculate the negative feature distance between points x_i and y_j in the two point clouds. This distance is then normalized using the softmax function, as shown below:

$$M = \text{softmax}\left(\left[-D_{i,1}, -D_{i,2}, -D_{i,3}, ..., -D_{i,M}\right]\right)_j \qquad (1)$$

where $D_{i,j}$ denotes the Euclidean distance between the features of points x_i and y_j. After estimating the matching score, we can use the distances between points in the neighborhood for adaptive weighted optimization.

For the similarity scores $M_{i,j}$. First, The K-nearest neighbor algorithm is used to find the neighborhood sets N_{x_i} and N_{y_j} of x_i and y_j (Fig. 2).

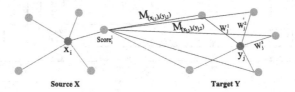

Fig. 2. Example of Eq. (2).

For a neighborhood point $x_{i,1}$ of x_i:

$$Score_i^1 = W_j^1 M_{(x_{i,1}),(y_{j,1})} + ... + W_j^k M_{(x_{i,1}),(y_{j,k})} \qquad (2)$$

$$W_j = \text{softmax}(d(y_j, y_{(j,1)}), ..., d(y_j, y_{(j,k)})) \qquad (3)$$

where $Score_i^1$ represents the similarity score after adaptive aggregation of point $x_{i,1}$ with y_j neighborhood points, W denotes adaptive weight, N_{x_i} denotes the neighbor points around point x_i, $M_{(,)}$ denotes the similar score, $d(,)$ denotes spatial distance. Similarly, we can get the score of all the neighbors of x_i with the neighborhood of y_j, where we also add weights to adjust the impact of different distances on the points.

$$S_{i,j} = W_i^1 Score_i^1 + W_i^2 Score_i^2 + ... + W_i^k Score_i^k \qquad (4)$$

$$W_i = \text{softmax}(d(x_i, x_{(i,1)}), ..., d(x_i, x_{(i,k)})) \tag{5}$$

In general, our formula can be expressed as follows:

$$S_{i,j} = W_i \sum_{x_{(i,k)} \in N_{x_i}} W_j \sum_{y_{(j,k)} \in N_{y_j}} M_{(i,k),(j,k)} \tag{6}$$

We use the matching scores of the neighborhood to perform adaptive optimization of the matching point pairs centered around each point.

Finally, the optimized point similarity matrix can be formulated as:

$$D'_{i,j} = \exp(\alpha - S_{i,j}) * D_{i,j} \tag{7}$$

$$M'_{i,j} = \text{softmax}\left([-D'_{i,1}, -D'_{i,2}, ..., -D'_{i,N}]\right)_j \tag{8}$$

where α is a hyper-parameter to control the influence of neighborhood on optimal matching points. Based on the optimized point similarity matrix, we can generate a predicting point cloud Pre as follows:

$$pre_i = \sum_{j=1}^{N} M'_{i,j} \cdot y_j \in \mathbb{R}^3 \tag{9}$$

3.2 Inlier Evaluation Module

Inspired by RIENet, we use an inlier evaluation module to optimize the network. Pairs of matched points whose neighborhoods are the same called inlier points, and pairs that are different called outlier points. The inlier evaluation module evaluates the confidence coefficient of the matching point pair (x_i, pre_i) based on the geometric difference in their neighborhoods. According to geometric difference of correspondence pairs, the confidence score is assigned to perform the weighted SVD algorithm.

Firstly, the graph structure is constructed in the neighborhood of matching point pairs (x_i, pre_i). The neighborhood edge features of x_i and pre_i can be defined as:

$$e_{i,k}^x = x_i - x_k, e_{i,k}^{pre} = pre_i - pre_k \tag{10}$$

where x_k, pre_k are points in the neighborhood of x_i and pre_i. Then we use an EdgeConv with convolution kernel of (1×3) to fuse the edge features of its neighboring points. Subtraction is applied to the fused edge features to represent the difference between the neighborhoods of the matched point pairs. Using the neighborhood space difference $e_{i,k}$, the attention weight of each edge is obtained by a softmax function:

$$\gamma_{i,k} = \text{softmax}\left([\delta(e_{i,1}), \delta(e_{i,2}), ..., \delta(e_{i,k})]\right)_k \tag{11}$$

where k is the number of neighborhoods, and δ is another Edge convolution operation. Finally, multiply the attention weight and the neighborhood difference

$e_{i,k}$ and sum the weighted w_i to get the reliability weight of the matching point pair (x_i, pre_i):

$$w_i = 1 - \tanh\left(\left|g\left(\sum_{k=1}^{K} \gamma_{i,k} * e_{i,k}\right)\right|\right) \tag{12}$$

where g is a unary function. In each iteration, we can get the matching point pairs and their initial confidence w. Last, we use weighted SVD to calculate the rigid transformation R, t.

The precision of the neighborhood difference is crucial for determining the final confidence value, and obtaining an outstanding neighborhood local feature extractor is crucial for solving the neighborhood difference. Therefore, we designed a structure variation checking module to restrict feature extraction network.

3.3   Structure Variation Checking Module

The correspondence points in predicted and source point cloud should have identical spatial features. Inspired by this idea, we design a structure variation checking module to obtain better feature extractor.

The feature extractor aims to generate feature $\mathcal{F}_X$ and $\mathcal{F}_{Pre}$ from source point cloud and predicted point cloud respectively. For convenience, we use DGCNN which shares the weight with the previous layers to extract the respective features. Then, we build distance matrix according to $\mathcal{F}_X \in \mathbb{R}^{N \times d}$ and $\mathcal{F}_{Pre} \in \mathbb{R}^{M \times d}$:

$$D_{svc} = (\mathcal{F}_X)^T \times \mathcal{F}_{Pre} \tag{13}$$

Ideally, we aim to set the diagonal values of matrix D_{svc} to be equal or close to 1.0, but due to the uncertainty of the feature extractor network, errors may occur. Firstly, we select the diagonal values of matrix D_{svc} and then flatten to F_D. Then as follows:

$$Constraint_{svc} = \Theta - SoftMax(F_D) \tag{14}$$

where hyper-parmeter Θ controls the influence of F_D. In complex scenes, F_D will be selected to avoid the influence of noise on the result. At each iteration, $Constraint_{svc}$ will constraints feature extractor to capture better features.

4   Experiment

4.1   Implementation Details

For confirm the effectiveness of our method, extensive experiments are conducted following the hyper-parameter and data set settings in RIENet. k is set to 5. The training batch size is set to 8 and testing batch size set to 1. The number of iterations is set to 3. α is set to 0.7. All networks are implemented in PyTorch using Nvidia RTX 2080Ti GPU.

Different from supervised point cloud registration networks, we refrain from utilizing the ground truth transformations, and instead, devise a suitable loss function for optimizing the model. During the operation of our network, we use loss function $Loss_{RIE}$ from RIENet and $Constraint_{svc}$. RIENet proved that $Loss_{RIE}$ is a useful loss function. In particular, our loss function is as follows:

$$Loss = Constraint_{svc} + Loss_{RIE} \tag{15}$$

The judging criterion are the rotation mean square error (MAE(R)) and the translation mean square error (MAE(t)) of the rigid transformation matrix.

4.2   Comparison Evaluation on ModelNet40

The ModelNet40 data set contains 12311 models,9843 models for training, 2468 models for testing. We follow the data set Setting in RIENet, which downsampled each point cloud to 1024 points and then selected 768 simulated partial overlaps. The source point cloud is randomly sampled in the rotation angle $[0°,45°]$ and translation $[-0.5,0.5]$ to generate a transformation matrix and transform into the target point cloud. For convenience, we will MAE(R) $(\times 10^2)$ write to MAE(R), MAE(t) $(\times 10^4)$ write to MAE(t).

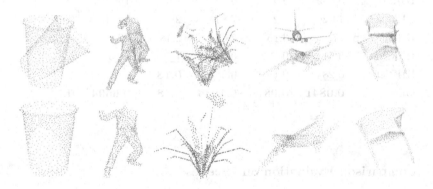

Fig. 3. ModelNet40 partial data set registration visualization. Red: source point cloud. Blue: target point cloud. All data sets have been preprocessed to remove 25%(256) points.

Partial Overlapping Clean Point Cloud. From the left of Table 1, our approach achieves the lowest error in comparison to traditional learning-free methods and unsupervised networks, and even outperforms supervised point cloud registration networks. The best experimental result is bolded and the second best is underlined. some visualization results are shown in Fig. 3.

Partial Overlapping Unseen Categories. In order to verify the generalization of our network, we train our model on 20 categories and test on other 20. The testing category is not visible during the network training. As can be seen from the middle of Table 1, compared to other methods, our method can extract better context information and maintain good generalization ability.

Partial Overlapping Gaussioan Noise. To test the anti-noise ability of our method, we train the model on the noise-free ModelNet40 data set, and then added Gaussian noise to all the test sets. Following the results presented in Table 1 right, it is evident that even in the presence of noise, the neighborhood adaptive score method can effectively modify the similarity matrix.

Table 1. Registration Performance on ModelNet40.

Model	Clean		Unseen		Noise	
	MAE(R)	MAE(t)	MAE(R)	MAE(t)	MAE(R)	MAE(t)
ICP	473	174	375.39	145	448.37	179
FMR	373.69	237	374.92	97	277.91	103
DCP	243.67	163	232.96	223	324.53	457.3
IDAM	52.39	27	62.33	43	106.323	79
CEMNet	14.26	1.2	7.84	2	40.19	9
R-PointHop	27	3.15	23.5	2.48	27	18.3
RPMNet	0.51	0.73	0.64	<u>1.7</u>	<u>0.75</u>	<u>0.85</u>
RIENet	<u>0.2844</u>	<u>0.15</u>	<u>0.3614</u>	**0.18**	1.034	0.93
Ours	**0.0841**	**0.08**	**0.1836**	**0.18**	**0.6594**	**0.51**

4.3   Comparison Evaluation on 7Scenes

We performed experiments on the 7Scenes indoor data set to further confirm the effectiveness of our method in real-world scenarios. The 7Scenes data set is more complex data set and consists of 7 scenes, making it more suitable for evaluating the practical application of our network. Similar to the previous experiment, we removed some points to simulate partial overlapping scenarios. Table 2 shows that our method achieves satisfactory performance.

Table 2. Registration Performance on 7Scenes.

Model	MAE(R) ($\times 10^{-2}$)	MAE(t) ($\times 10^{-4}$)
ICP	675	304
FMR	356.75	87
DCP	532.37	231
IDAM	543.94	296
RPMNet	32.767	125
CEMNet	4.96	4
RIENet	0.9779	0.49
Ours	**0.0625**	**0.06**

4.4 Ablation Study

In the ablation study, we conduct an analysis of two key components of our network, similarity optimization module (SO) and structure variation checking module (SVC). Then, different values of the hyper-parameter θ are set to adjust and obtain an optimal result. We use the original RIENet (including all components) as the baseline (Base). Ablation experiments are respectively performed on the ModelNet40-Clean data set and 7Scenes data set, which are downsampled to 768 points and 1536 points.

Effect of Module. Table 3 shows that using the SO module alone can improve performance compared to the Base network, and the best results can be obtained by combining the two modules. Incorporating spatial information between the point clouds can clarify fuzzy boundaries and improve the feature extractor's ability to distinguish similar points.

Table 3. Module Ablation Study on ModelNet40-Clean.

Method	MAE(R) ($\times 10^{-2}$)	MAE(t) ($\times 10^{-4}$)
Base	0.2971	0.17
Base+SO	0.178	0.13
Base+SO+SVC	**0.085**	**0.08**

Effect of Hyper-parmeter. In our research, a hyper-parmeter θ is designed to control influence of F_D. To examine the influence of various values of θ on the final experimental outcomes, we present the statistical registration results of the 7Scenes data set in Table 4. It can be observed that the point cloud registration network achieves the optimal rotation and displacement errors when the value of theta is set to 0.4.

Table 4. θ Ablation Study on 7Scenes.

θ	MAE(R) ($\times 10^{-2}$)	MAE(t) ($\times 10^{-4}$)
0.3	0.66	0.47
0.4	**0.0862**	**0.09**
0.5	0.3848	0.36
0.6	0.5709	0.43

5   Conclusion

In this paper, we propose a novel unsupervised method that uses neighborhood spatial distance information to add adaptive weights and design a similarity optimization module for constructing more accurate matching matrices and generating prediction point clouds. We also use a structure variation checking module to constrain the spatial structure feature difference between the source point cloud and predicted point cloud, thereby obtaining a better point cloud feature extractor. Experimental results on the ModelNet40,7Scenes demonstrate that our method outperforms the latest unsupervised and supervised networks, as well as traditional registration methods.

Acknowledgements. This work was supported by national natural science foundation of China (No. 62202346), Hubei key research and development program (No. 2021BAA042), open project of engineering research center of Hubei province for clothing information (No. 2022HBCI01), Wuhan applied basic frontier research project (No. 2022013988065212).

References

1. Bay, H., Tuytelaars, T., Van Gool, L.: SURF: speeded up robust features. In: Leonardis, A., Bischof, H., Pinz, A. (eds.) ECCV 2006. LNCS, vol. 3951, pp. 404–417. Springer, Heidelberg (2006). https://doi.org/10.1007/11744023_32
2. Ben-Shabat, Y., Lindenbaum, M., Fischer, A.: 3dmfv: three-dimensional point cloud classification in real-time using convolutional neural networks. IEEE Robot. Automat. Lett. **3**(4), 3145–3152 (2018)
3. Besl, P.J., McKay, N.D.: Method for registration of 3-d shapes. In: Sensor Fusion IV: Control Paradigms and Data Structures, vol. 1611, pp. 586–606. SPIE (1992)
4. Deschaud, J.E.: IMLS-slam: scan-to-model matching based on 3d data. In: 2018 IEEE International Conference on Robotics and Automation (ICRA), pp. 2480–2485. IEEE (2018)
5. Groß, J., Ošep, A., Leibe, B.: Alignnet-3d: fast point cloud registration of partially observed objects. In: 2019 International Conference on 3d Vision (3DV), pp. 623–632. IEEE (2019)
6. Handa, A., Whelan, T., McDonald, J., Davison, A.J.: A benchmark for rgb-d visual odometry, 3d reconstruction and slam. In: 2014 IEEE International Conference on Robotics and Automation (ICRA), pp. 1524–1531. IEEE (2014)

7. Huang, S., Gojcic, Z., Usvyatsov, M., Wieser, A., Schindler, K.: Predator: registration of 3d point clouds with low overlap. In: Proceedings of the IEEE/CVF Conference on Computer Vision and Pattern Recognition, pp. 4267–4276 (2021)
8. Huang, X., Mei, G., Zhang, J.: Feature-metric registration: a fast semi-supervised approach for robust point cloud registration without correspondences. In: Proceedings of the IEEE/CVF Conference on Computer Vision and Pattern Recognition, pp. 11366–11374 (2020)
9. Jost, T., Hügli, H.: Fast ICP algorithms for shape registration. In: Van Gool, L. (ed.) DAGM 2002. LNCS, vol. 2449, pp. 91–99. Springer, Heidelberg (2002). https://doi.org/10.1007/3-540-45783-6_12
10. Kadam, P., Zhang, M., Liu, S., Kuo, C.C.J.: R-pointhop: a green, accurate, and unsupervised point cloud registration method. IEEE Trans. Image Process. **31**, 2710–2725 (2022)
11. Li, J., Zhang, C., Xu, Z., Zhou, H., Zhang, C.: Iterative distance-aware similarity matrix convolution with mutual-supervised point elimination for efficient point cloud registration. In: Vedaldi, A., Bischof, H., Brox, T., Frahm, J.-M. (eds.) ECCV 2020. LNCS, vol. 12369, pp. 378–394. Springer, Cham (2020). https://doi.org/10.1007/978-3-030-58586-0_23
12. Lin, X., Sun, S., Huang, W., Sheng, B., Li, P., Feng, D.D.: EAPT: efficient attention pyramid transformer for image processing. IEEE Trans. Multim. (2021)
13. Liu, Y., Cong, Y., Sun, G., Zhang, T., Dong, J., Liu, H.: L3doc: lifelong 3d object classification. IEEE Trans. Image Process. **30**, 7486–7498 (2021)
14. Pan, X., Xia, Z., Song, S., Li, L.E., Huang, G.: 3d object detection with pointformer. In: Proceedings of the IEEE/CVF Conference on Computer Vision and Pattern Recognition, pp. 7463–7472 (2021)
15. Qi, C.R., Su, H., Mo, K., Guibas, L.J.: Pointnet: deep learning on point sets for 3d classification and segmentation. In: Proceedings of the IEEE Conference on Computer Vision and Pattern Recognition, pp. 652–660 (2017)
16. Rusu, R.B., Blodow, N., Beetz, M.: Fast point feature histograms (FPFH) for 3d registration. In: 2009 IEEE International Conference on Robotics and Automation, pp. 3212–3217. IEEE (2009)
17. Sarode, V., et al.: Pcrnet: point cloud registration network using pointnet encoding. arXiv preprint arXiv:1908.07906 (2019)
18. Schonberger, J.L., Frahm, J.M.: Structure-from-motion revisited. In: Proceedings of the IEEE Conference on Computer Vision and Pattern Recognition, pp. 4104–4113 (2016)
19. Segal, A., Haehnel, D., Thrun, S.: Generalized-ICP. In: Robotics: Science and Systems, vol. 2, p. 435. Seattle (2009)
20. Shen, Y., Hui, L., Jiang, H., Xie, J., Yang, J.: Reliable inlier evaluation for unsupervised point cloud registration. In: Proceedings of the AAAI Conference on Artificial Intelligence, vol. 36, pp. 2198–2206 (2022)
21. Song, Y., Shen, W., Peng, K.: A novel partial point cloud registration method based on graph attention network. Vis. Comput. **39**(3), 1109–1120 (2023)
22. Vaswani, A., et al.: Attention is all you need. Adv. Neural Inf. Process. Syst. **30** (2017)
23. Wang, Y., et al.: Pillar-based object detection for autonomous driving. In: Vedaldi, A., Bischof, H., Brox, T., Frahm, J.-M. (eds.) ECCV 2020. LNCS, vol. 12367, pp. 18–34. Springer, Cham (2020). https://doi.org/10.1007/978-3-030-58542-6_2
24. Wang, Y., Solomon, J.M.: Deep closest point: Learning representations for point cloud registration. In: Proceedings of the IEEE/CVF International Conference on Computer Vision, pp. 3523–3532 (2019)

25. Wang, Y., Sun, Y., Liu, Z., Sarma, S.E., Bronstein, M.M., Solomon, J.M.: Dynamic graph CNN for learning on point clouds. ACM Trans. Graph. **38**(5), 1–12 (2019)
26. Yew, Z.J., Lee, G.H.: Rpm-net: robust point matching using learned features. In: Proceedings of the IEEE/CVF Conference on Computer Vision and Pattern Recognition, pp. 11824–11833 (2020)
27. Zeng, Y., Qian, Y., Zhu, Z., Hou, J., Yuan, H., He, Y.: Corrnet3d: unsupervised end-to-end learning of dense correspondence for 3d point clouds. In: Proceedings of the IEEE/CVF Conference on Computer Vision and Pattern Recognition, pp. 6052–6061 (2021)
28. Zhang, J., Singh, S.: Loam: lidar odometry and mapping in real-time. In: Robotics: Science and Systems, vol. 2, pp. 1–9. Berkeley (2014)

COCCI: Context-Driven Clothing Classification Network

Minghua Jiang[1,2], Shuqing Liu[1], Yankang Shi[1], Chenghu Du[1],
Guangyu Tang[1], Li Liu[1,2], Tao Peng[1,2], Xinrong Hu[1,2], and Feng Yu[1,2(✉)]

[1] School of Computer Science and Artificial Intelligence, Wuhan Textile University,
Wuhan 430200, China
{minghuajiang,l_liu,pt,hxr,yufeng}@wtu.edu.cn
[2] Engineering Research Center of Hubei Province for Clothing Information, Wuhan
430200, China

Abstract. Clothing classification serves as a fundamental task for clothing retrieval, clothing recommendation, etc. In this task, there are two
inherent challenges: suppressing complex backgrounds outside the clothing region and disentangling the feature entanglement of shape-similar
clothing samples. These challenges arise from insufficient attention to
key distinctions of clothing, which hinders the accuracy of clothing classification. Also, the high computational resource requirement of some
complex and large-scale models also decreases the inference efficiency.
To tackle these challenges, we propose a new **CO**ntext-driven **C**lothing
Class**I**fication network (COCCI), which improves inference accuracy
while reducing model complexity. First, we design a self-adaptive attention fusion (SAAF) module to enhance category-exclusive clothing features and prevent misclassification by suppressing ineffective features
with confused image contexts. Second, we propose a novel multi-scale
feature aggregation (MSFA) module to establish spatial context correlations by using multi-scale clothing features. This helps disentangle
feature entanglement among shape-similar clothing samples. Finally, we
introduce knowledge distillation to extract reliable teacher knowledge
from complex datasets, which helps student models learn clothing features with rich representation information, thereby improving generalization while reducing model complexity. In comparison to state-of-the-art
networks trained with one single model, our method achieves SOTA performance on the widely-used clothing classification benchmark.

Keywords: Clothing classification · Knowledge distillation · Attention
mechanism · Apparel parsing and understanding

1 Introduction

With the rise of e-commerce, online shopping has become a major method
of purchasing for people. In this context, platforms that accurately categorize, retrieve, and recommend clothing among a diverse range of products

© The Author(s), under exclusive license to Springer Nature Switzerland AG 2024
B. Sheng et al. (Eds.): CGI 2023, LNCS 14495, pp. 69–80, 2024.
https://doi.org/10.1007/978-3-031-50069-5_7

have become essential. At the core of these technologies lies clothing classification, which involves parsing the feature of a given clothing item. In recent years, machine learning-based clothing classification, particularly deep learning approaches [5,6,10,13,18–22], has gradually taken over the field. Previous methods have been capable of swiftly surpassing manual accuracy in providing class labels for in-shop clothing images. However, these methods have encountered three inherent challenges due to their insufficient focus on key clothing features: 1) effectively suppressing complex backgrounds outside the clothing region, 2) accurately distinguishing between shape-similar clothing samples, and 3) effectively reducing high computational resource requirements. These challenges hinder the accuracy of clothing classification.

Regarding complex backgrounds outside the clothing region, several research works have focused on directing the network's attention to clothing in order to classify fine-grained attributes. Yu et al. [19] introduced the capsule network, which aims to capture detailed spatial information. Shajini et al. [10] utilized a module similar to the convolutional block attention module (CBAM) [15] to activate clothing features. However, these methods do not comprehensively analyze the category-exclusive features of clothing, thereby limiting the improvement in classification accuracy. For shape-similar clothing samples, Wang et al. [13], Zhang et al. [21], and Shajini et al. [10] have all estimated additional landmarks of the clothing as the shape representation of clothing. However, these approaches introduce computational overhead due to the additional task branch, and the improvements in classification accuracy for shape-similar clothing are limited due to irresponsible landmarks. Moreover, Wang et al. [13] proposed a bidirectional convolutional recurrent neural network that effectively captures the rich features of clothing. Zhang et al. [21] divided clothing features into two streams: shape and texture. However, the shape feature is learned based on broad landmarks, which makes it challenging to classify clothing with subtle shape differences. Furthermore, to reduce the computational resource requirements, some classification networks incorporate residual structures as alternatives to deep convolutional structures. Yu et al. [19] utilized smaller-scale convolution layers to decrease computational complexity, but it proved ineffective in improving classification accuracy.

To address the challenges mentioned above, we propose a context-driven clothing classification network (COCCI). The main contributions can be summarized as follows:

- We propose COCCI, a novel clothing classification network that improves inference accuracy while reducing model complexity, offering a new perspective for clothing classification tasks.
- We propose a new SAAF module that boosts the clothing representation of image features, emphasizing their category-exclusive features. This module effectively suppresses irrelevant background features, preventing misclassification caused by ineffective features that have confused image contexts.
- We propose a new MSFA module to help the model to comprehend multiscale clothing features. By establishing spatial context correlation between

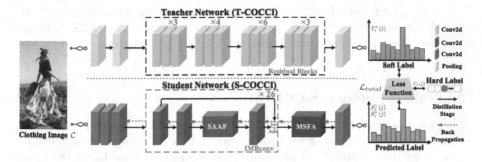

Fig. 1. Overview of our proposed COCCI. First, the teacher network T-COCCI is pre-trained to generate soft labels $T_i^\tau(j)$. After that, hard labels $C_i(j)$ and soft labels $T_i^\tau(j)$ are used to train the student network to predict desired labels $S_i^1(j)$ and $S_i^\tau(j)$.

global and fine-grained aspects of clothing, this module effectively disentangles feature entanglement among clothing samples with similar shapes.

– We employ knowledge distillation to extract responsible teacher knowledge, which helps the student model to learn rich class relationship information, thereby improving generalization and accuracy while reducing complexity.

– Extensive experiments on popular benchmarks show that our framework outperforms state-of-the-art methods.

2 Method and Methodology

Overview. In clothing classification tasks, the objective is to accurately predict labels for given clothing images C. As shown in Fig. 1, our framework for this task consists of two sub-networks: a teacher classification network (T-COCCI) represented as $\mathbf{T}_c$, and a student classification network (S-COCCI) represented as $\mathbf{S}_c$. The details of the COCCI framework are described in the following.

2.1 Teacher Network (T-COCCI)

In the knowledge distillation architecture, the teacher network $\mathbf{T}_c$ is a pre-trained model that exhibits complex structure and high performance in the task and is used to guide the learning of the student network $\mathbf{S}_c$ by using generated soft labels $T_i^\tau(j)$. The characteristic of the teacher network lies in obtaining a comprehensive and rich knowledge representation from a large-scale dataset to reflect the correlations between categories.

Soft labels $T_i^\tau(j)$ are a type of probability distribution used to describe the probabilities or confidences of each category. Compared to hard labels $C_i(j)$ (i.e. real labels), soft labels provide more abundant class correlation information.

By conducting preliminary experiments and considering the time and computational cost required for training, we employ ResNet50 [2] as the teacher network in this architecture. Finally, we optimize T-COCCI by using cross-entropy loss $\mathcal{L}_{teach}$.

2.2   Student Network (S-COCCI)

The student network is a lightweight model that learns and trains by leveraging the knowledge of the teacher network to reduce its complexity and enhance its performance. It accomplishes this by utilizing hard labels from the dataset and soft labels $T_i^\tau(j)$ from the teacher network, as the training targets and learning the mapping from input samples to labels.

In this work, we have found that many samples in the dataset have complex backgrounds, with some background colors even resembling the colors of the clothing, making it difficult for the network to effectively focus on the correct clothing regions to determine the type of clothing. Previous methods [16] employed a semantic segmentation model as a pre-processing step to segment the clothing from the image, aiming to avoid the interference of the background. However, if irresponsible and erroneous segmentations exist in semantic maps corresponding to clothing, the network is forced to learn incorrect clothing representations, thereby reducing the classification accuracy of the network. Other methods [19,21] introduced attention modules to compel the network to focus on the clothing regions. Although this approach has shown considerable performance improvement, the complex structure and low efficiency of some modules limit the gains achieved by the network and increase the model's complexity. To solve the above problem, we propose a self-adaptive attention fusion module that guarantees low model complexity while forcing the network to focus on the target clothing region.

Self-adaptive Attention Fusion Module. As shown in Fig. 2, we design a new improved mobile inverted residual bottleneck convolution (IMBConv) module. It consists of two 1×1 convolutional layers, a 3×3 depthwise convolutional layer, and a self-adaptive attention fusion (SAAF) module. More lightweight and efficient channel attention can focus on fine-grained features of clothing, while spatial attention can establish correlations between fine-grained local features and spatial features. Inspired by [15], in SAAF (see Fig. 2), we first introduce the efficient channel attention (ECA) [12] to learn the channel weights of the input image feature map F_I, the channel attention mechanism dynamically adjusts the importance of each feature channel, focusing more attention on the channels that contain relevant clothing features and reducing attention to irrelevant background information, expressed as:

$$F_m = \text{ECA}(F_I) \cdot F_I, \tag{1}$$

where F_m is the feature map processed by ECA, and $\cdot$ denotes element-wise multiplication. Afterward, we design a spatial attention block that adapts the

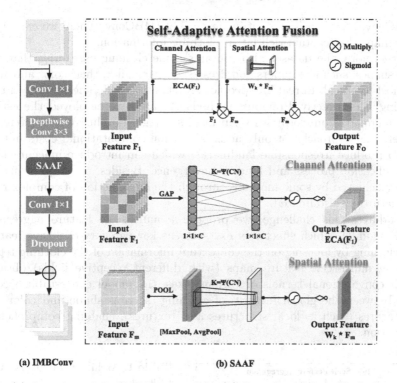

(a) IMBConv   **(b) SAAF**

Fig. 2. (a) Overview of the IMBConv module. (b) Overview of the self-adaptive attention fusion module.

convolution kernel size according to the number of feature channels, to adjust the importance of clothing features in the global spatial features of F_m. It automatically focuses on features with category-exclusive parts while further suppressing interference from irrelevant background regions. It can be expressed as:

$$K = \Psi\,(CN) = \left\lceil \frac{\log_2\,(CN) + b}{\gamma} \right\rceil, \qquad (2)$$

where K represents the kernel size, and CN denotes the number of channels. b and γ are the constants that control the linear relationship, $b = 1$ and $\gamma = 2$. We then process F_m by a convolution kernel of size K, and output the final feature F_O:

$$F_O = (W_K * F_m) \cdot F_m, \qquad (3)$$

where W_K denotes the corresponding parameters of convolution, and $*$ represents the convolution operation. Overall, the process of IMBConv can be expressed as:

$$F_{out} = f_p\left(f^{1 \times 1}\left(\mathrm{SF}\left(f_d^{3 \times 3}\left(f^{1 \times 1}\left(F_{in}\right)\right)\right)\right)\right) + F_{in}, \qquad (4)$$

where f denotes the convolution operation, f_p denotes the dropout operation, and f_d represents the depthwise convolution operation. F_{in} is the input feature of IMBConv, and F_{out} is the output feature of IMBConv. Then, we can obtain feature maps that contain rich latent clothing information.

Furthermore, the dataset also contains some clothing categories that have similar shapes, such as rompers and dresses. In particular, their color and shape are almost identical. In real life, people rely on subtle differences between them to distinguish correctly. Previous methods [13,21] have employed the estimation of landmarks on clothing to capture its category-exclusive characteristics. However, this approach not only adds additional computational costs but also tends to produce irresponsible landmarks, which can introduce inaccuracies in the classification process and hinder convergence. Besides, the improvement in accuracy achieved by some methods through the introduction of complex residual structures is also limited.

To address this challenge, we propose a multi-scale feature aggregation (MSFA) module, which effectively extracts the key category-exclusive features of the clothing by focusing on the contextual information of the clothing region. By fusing multi-scale feature maps (with different receptive fields) obtained through convolutional kernels of various sizes, the model can establish correlations between the global features of clothing (such as shape and color) and local features (such as local structures and textures), enabling comprehensive classification.

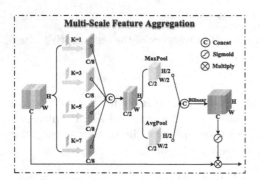

Fig. 3. Overview of the multi-scale feature aggregation module.

Table 1. Architectural Overview of COCCI.

Operator	Stride	Kernel	Channel	Layer
Conv3×3	1	3	24	1
Conv3×3	2	3	24	2
IMBConv4	2	3	48	4
IMBConv4	2	3	64	4
IMBConv4	2	3	128	3
IMBConv6	1	3	160	6
IMBConv6	2	7	256	9
MSFA	–	–	256	1
Conv1×1	1	1	1280	1
FC	–	–	10\14	1

Multi-scale Feature Aggregation Module. As shown in Fig. 3, we first utilize convolutions with four scales to extract global-to-local clothing context feature maps with different receptive fields. This is done to establish the spatial correlation of clothing features F_{out}, which can be represented as follows:

$$F_g = f^{1\times1}\left(F_{out}\right); f^{3\times3}\left(F_{out}\right); f^{5\times5}\left(F_{out}\right); f^{7\times7}\left(F_{out}\right), \tag{5}$$

where ; represents the concatenation in the channel direction. At this stage, although the fused features F_g contain global and fine-grained clothing information, the cluttered features still struggle to systematically perceive and integrate the contextual features of complete clothing. Therefore, we further refine the spatial correlation of clothing features by employing max pooling and average pooling operations. Additionally, we leverage bilinear interpolation (BI) to expand the features within the domain and propagate the relevant vectors. This process can be represented as follows:

$$F_f = \text{BI}\left[Maxp\left(F_g\right); Avgp\left(F_g\right)\right]. \tag{6}$$

Thus, we obtain a gated feature vector F_f that suppresses irrelevant noise in the clothing feature map F_f from the perspective of spatial contextual relevance. This can enhance the category-exclusive clothing features, effectively disentangling the feature entanglement between similarly shaped clothing and achieving more precise classification. This process can be represented as follows:

$$F_g' = \sigma\left(F_f\right) \cdot F_g, \tag{7}$$

where σ is *softmax* activation function, and F_g' is optimized feature map F_g.

2.3 Training Strategy

Figure 1 shows the construction of our proposed COCCI. We predict a label $C_i(j)$ for a given clothing image. To do this, we first pre-trained the T-COCCI to provide the soft label $T_i^\tau(j)$ for subsequent training of the S-COCCI.

Objective Functions. We further illustrate the loss functions during training, the first is loss $\mathcal{L}_{stu}$ used to train S-COCCI, represented as:

$$\mathcal{L}_{stu} = -\sum_{i=1}^{M}\sum_{j=1}^{N}\left(C_i(j) \cdot \log\left(S_i^1(j)\right)\right), \tag{8}$$

where $C_i(j)$ represents the true label of the jth class for the ith sample in the S-COCCI, and $S_i^1(j)$ represents the predicted result of the jth class for the ith sample in the S-COCCI. 1 is assigned to positive labels and 0 is assigned to negative labels. M represents the number of samples, and N represents the number of classes.

The second is the loss $\mathcal{L}_{dis}$ used in the knowledge distillation structure for learning responsible teacher knowledge, represented as:

$$\mathcal{L}_{dis} = \sum_{i=1}^{M}\sum_{j=1}^{N}\left(T_i^\tau(j) \cdot \log\left(\frac{T_i^\tau(j)}{S_i^\tau(j)}\right)\right), \tag{9}$$

where $T_i^\tau(j)$ represents the predicted result of the jth class for the ith sample of the T-COCCI, $S_i^\tau(j)$ represents the predicted result of the jth class for the ith sample in the S-COCCI, and τ denotes temperature.

Our objective loss can be expressed as follows:

$$\mathcal{L}_{total} = \alpha \cdot \tau^2 \cdot \mathcal{L}_{dis} + (1 - \alpha) \cdot \mathcal{L}_{stu}, \tag{10}$$

where τ denotes the temperature factor, and α is the hyperparameter used to balance the sub-losses.

3   Experiments

3.1   Dataset

Deepfashion dataset [9] is further screened out for use in our experiments, which consist of 5,000 images in 10 categories. Each category contains 500 images of the corresponding clothing. The resolution of each image in the dataset is 224×224. 4,500 images are used for training, and another 500 images are used for testing.

Clothing 1M dataset [17] comprises 1 million clothing images categorized into 14 classes. The resolution of each image in the dataset is 224×224. The dataset is characterized by having noisy labels, but it also includes subsets of images with clean labels that can be used for training, validation, and testing. Specifically, there are 47,570, 14,313, and 10,526 images with clean labels allocated for training, validation, and testing, respectively.

3.2   Implementation Details

The COCCI is implemented using PyTorch and trained on a single Nvidia Tesla V100 GPU running Ubuntu 16.04. The training process involves using a batch size of 16 for 100 epochs. The optimizer used is the Adam optimizer with parameters $\beta_1 = 0.9$ and $\beta_2 = 0.999$, in which the initial learning is $1e^{-4}$, after every 20 epochs, the learning rate is reduced by a factor of 0.6. In Eq. 10, the temperature parameter τ is set to 4, and the hyperparameter α is set to 0.4. Table 1 illustrates the architecture of COCCI. Notably, In ablation experiments, SAAF is replaced by the SE [3] in the IMBconv to verify the validity of SAAF.

Baselines and Evaluation Metrics. We perform comparative evaluations of our model's performance by benchmarking it against publicly available state-of-the-art methods. To achieve this, we utilize eight popular methods, including ResNet [2], DenseNet [4], Efficientnet [11], ConvNext [8], Vision Transformer [1], EnCaps [19], Swin Transformer [7], and ConvNextV2-tiny [14], as baseline methods for quantitative evaluation. Accuracy, mean accuracy (m-Acc.), top-1 accuracy (top-1 Acc.), F_1, and mean F_1 (m-F_1) are used to evaluate the performance of the classification models.

3.3   Quantitative Analysis

Results of Deepfashion. Table 2 lists the accuracy scores of baselines and our proposed method on the DeepFashion dataset. The mean accuracy results indicate that our COCCI outperforms the SOTA classification model ConvNextV2-tiny [14] by 0.8. These results show the effectiveness of our proposed method. Table 2 lists the F_1 scores of baselines and our proposed method. The mean F_1 results indicate that our COCCI outperforms the SOTA ConvNextV2-tiny by 4.3. These results show the robustness of our method in distinguishing clothing samples with similar shapes.

Table 2. Quantitative evaluation results between baselines and ours on the DeepFashion dataset. The best result is in **bold**.

Model	top-1 Accuracy (%) ↑	Size (M) ↓	Params (M) ↓	FLOPs (G) ↓	m-Acc. (%)↑	m-F$_1$ (%) ↑
ResNet50 [2]	88.4	90.09	25.557	4.133	97.7	88.6
ResNet101 [2]	88.0	162.81	44.549	7.866	97.6	88.1
DenseNet169 [4]	80.4	48.67	14.149	3.436	96.1	80.4
DenseNet201 [4]	80.8	70.41	20.014	4.390	96.2	81.0
EfficientnetV2-S [11]	91.6	77.91	21.458	2.899	98.3	91.6
Vit-base [1]	51.8	327.38	86.416	16.864	90.4	51.6
Swin-tiny [7]	72.6	105.30	28.265	4.372	94.5	72.5
EnCaps [19]	/	/	/	/	96.3	81.1
ConvNext-small [8]	88.0	188.80	49.420	8.683	97.6	88.3
ConvNext-tiny [8]	88.8	106.22	27.806	4.455	97.8	88.8
ConvNextV2-base [14]	88.0	334.69	88.535	15.355	97.6	88.1
ConvNextV2-tiny [14]	90.8	106.40	28.568	4.456	98.2	90.9
COCCI (ours)	**95.2**	**45.93**	**13.156**	**1.649**	**99.0**	**95.2**

Table 3. Quantitative evaluation results in accuracy and F$_1$ score between baselines and ours on the Clothing 1M dataset. The best result is in **bold**.

Model	Publication	top-1 Accuracy (%) ↑	Size (M) ↓	m-Accuracy (%) ↑	m-F$_1$ (%) ↑
ResNet50 [2]	CVPR 2016	73.80	90.09	96.3	70.8
ResNet101 [2]	CVPR 2016	74.14	162.84	96.3	72.1
DenseNet169 [4]	CVPR 2017	72.31	48.69	96.0	70.0
DenseNet201 [4]	CVPR 2017	72.10	70.44	96.0	70.1
EfficientnetV2-S [11]	PMLR 2019	76.50	77.91	96.6	74.5
Vit-base [1]	ICLR 2021	44.95	327.39	92.1	41.3
Swin-tiny [7]	ICCV 2021	68.25	105.31	95.5	65.4
ConvNext-small [8]	CVPR 2022	72.00	188.81	96.0	69.5
ConvNext-tiny [8]	CVPR 2022	73.10	106.23	96.2	71.1
ConvNextV2-base [14]	CVPR 2023	72.92	334.71	96.1	70.7
ConvNextV2-tiny [14]	CVPR 2023	72.58	106.41	96.1	70.4
COCCI (ours)	**This Work**	**78.57**	**45.95**	**96.9**	**76.7**

Results of Clothing 1M. Table 3 lists the accuracy and F$_1$ scores of baselines and our proposed method on the Clothing 1M dataset. The top-1 accuracy results indicate that our COCCI outperforms the ConvNextV2-tiny by 5.99. In the mean accuracy metric, our COCCI surpasses ConvNextV2-tiny by 0.8. In the mean F$_1$ metric, our COCCI surpasses ConvNextV2-tiny by 6.3. These results show the effectiveness of our method in tackling the challenge of complex image backgrounds outside the clothing region.

Computational Complexity Analysis. Under the same dataset (DeepFashion) and hardware configurations (1 Nvidia Tesla V100 GPU). As shown in Table 2, we show the computational costs of baselines and COCCI. It can be observed that compared to the SOTA ConvNextV2-tiny [14] model, our proposed model achieves a 4.4% increase in top-1 accuracy. Remarkably, the weight size of our model is smaller than half of ConvNextV2-tiny's. Furthermore, we analyze the parameters and FLOPs of the baselines and find that COCCI achieves

Table 4. Ablation studies of COCCI on the DeepFashion dataset.

KD	SAAF	MSFA	SE	top-1 Acc. (%) ↑	Params (M) ↓
			✓	92.4	13.60
✓			✓	93.8	13.60
✓	✓			94.4	**12.47**
✓	✓	✓		**95.2**	13.16

Table 5. Ablation studies of knowledge distillation on the DeepFashion dataset.

Model	top-1 Acc. (%)	Size (M)	Params (M)	FLOPs (G)
T-COCCI	88.4	90.09	25.557	4.133
S-COCCI	93.2	45.93	13.156	1.649
COCCI	**95.2**	45.93	13.156	1.649

the highest accuracy while having fewer parameters and FLOPs. This makes it well-suited for real-time prediction, particularly for mobile devices or online services.

3.4 Ablation Studies

We perform ablation experiments to evaluate the effectiveness of the proposed modules. In these experiments, we remove each module individually and retrain our model thoroughly. The results are presented in Tables 4. We initially remove all the parts, which demonstrate a significant decrease in accuracy without the help of the KD, the SAAF module, and the MSFA module, highlighting the crucial role of all the proposed improvements. When we remove the SAAF module and MSFA module, i.e. only the knowledge distillation architecture is retained, our method only achieves a limited improvement in accuracy without the help of the SAAF module, and the MSFA module. When we remove the MSFA module only, our method achieves a 2.0% increase in accuracy without the help of the MSFA module. When all modules are added in COCCI, it achieves the highest accuracy.

Furthermore, we conduct additional validation of the knowledge distillation framework employed in our model. As depicted in Table 5, we initially utilize the teacher network alone (ResNet50 [2]), referred to as T-COCCI. As observed in the table, the teacher model exhibited high complexity but low accuracy. Subsequently, we employ the student network alone, referred to as S-COCCI, which demonstrated lower complexity and limited accuracy. When we leverage teacher knowledge to train the student network, referred to as COCCI, its performance is optimal in terms of both accuracy and complexity.

To summarize, the quantitative results presented in the tables mentioned above provide additional evidence to support the effectiveness of our proposed modules.

4   Conclusion

In this paper, we present a novel lightweight clothing classification network called COCCI, which is capable of quickly predicting the corresponding category of any given clothing image. To achieve this, we propose several innovative modules for COCCI. Firstly, the self-adaptive attention fusion module enhances clothing features by focusing on category-exclusive features. This module effectively suppresses irrelevant background features, thereby mitigating misclassification caused by background interference. Secondly, we propose the multi-scale feature aggregation module, which is designed to extract clothing context features. This module establishes spatial context correlations between global and fine-grained aspects of clothing, enabling the network to capture both global clothing characteristics and detailed information. This is for disentangling feature entanglement among clothing samples with similar shapes, further enhancing the discriminative power of the network. Additionally, we introduce knowledge distillation in our framework. It enables the student model (COCCI) to learn clothing features with rich representation information by extracting reliable teacher knowledge from complex datasets. This process improves the generalization capability and classification accuracy of COCCI while reducing model complexity. Extensive experiments demonstrate that our proposed network achieves significant improvements in both generalization and classification accuracy compared to state-of-the-art methods, making it a promising solution for clothing classification tasks.

Acknowledgements. This work was supported by the national natural science foundation of China (No. 62202346), Hubei key research and development program (No.2021BAA042), open project of engineering research center of Hubei province for clothing information (No. 2022HBCI01), Wuhan applied basic frontier research project (No. 2022013988065212), MIIT's AI Industry Innovation Task unveils flagship projects (Key technologies, equipment, and systems for flexible customized and intelligent manufacturing in the clothing industry), and Hubei science and technology project of safe production special fund (Scene control platform based on proprioception information computing of artificial intelligence).

References

1. Dosovitskiy, A., et al.: An image is worth 16 × 16 words: transformers for image recognition at scale. In: ICLR, pp. 1–12 (2021)
2. He, K., Zhang, X., Ren, S., Sun, J.: Deep residual learning for image recognition. In: Proceedings of the IEEE Conference on Computer Vision and Pattern Recognition, pp. 770–778 (2016)
3. Hu, J., Shen, L., Sun, G.: Squeeze-and-excitation networks. In: Proceedings of the IEEE Conference on Computer Vision and Pattern Recognition, pp. 7132–7141 (2018)
4. Huang, G., Liu, Z., Van Der Maaten, L., Weinberger, K.Q.: Densely connected convolutional networks. In: Proceedings of the IEEE Conference on Computer Vision and Pattern Recognition, pp. 4700–4708 (2017)
5. Lan, S., Li, J., Hu, S., Fan, H., Pan, Z.: A neighbourhood feature-based local binary pattern for texture classification. Vis. Comput. 1–25 (2023)
6. Liu, Y., Dou, Y., Jin, R., Li, R., Qiao, P.: Hierarchical learning with backtracking algorithm based on the visual confusion label tree for large-scale image classification. Vis. Comput. **38**(3), 897–917 (2022)

7. Liu, Z., et al.: Swin transformer: hierarchical vision transformer using shifted windows. In: Proceedings of the IEEE/CVF International Conference on Computer Vision (ICCV), pp. 10012–10022, October 2021
8. Liu, Z., Mao, H., Wu, C.Y., Feichtenhofer, C., Darrell, T., Xie, S.: A ConvNet for the 2020s. In: Proceedings of the IEEE/CVF Conference on Computer Vision and Pattern Recognition, pp. 11976–11986 (2022)
9. Liu, Z., Luo, P., Qiu, S., Wang, X., Tang, X.: DeepFashion: powering robust clothes recognition and retrieval with rich annotations. In: Proceedings of the IEEE Conference on Computer Vision and Pattern Recognition, pp. 1096–1104 (2016)
10. Shajini, M., Ramanan, A.: A knowledge-sharing semi-supervised approach for fashion clothes classification and attribute prediction. Vis. Comput. **38**(11), 3551–3561 (2022)
11. Tan, M., Le, Q.: EfficientNet: rethinking model scaling for convolutional neural networks. In: International Conference on Machine Learning, pp. 6105–6114. PMLR (2019)
12. Wang, Q., Wu, B., Zhu, P., Li, P., Zuo, W., Hu, Q.: ECA-Net: efficient channel attention for deep convolutional neural networks. In: Proceedings of the IEEE/CVF Conference on Computer Vision and Pattern Recognition, pp. 11534–11542 (2020)
13. Wang, W., Xu, Y., Shen, J., Zhu, S.C.: Attentive fashion grammar network for fashion landmark detection and clothing category classification. In: Proceedings of the IEEE Conference on Computer Vision and Pattern Recognition, pp. 4271–4280 (2018)
14. Woo, S., et al.: ConvNeXt V2: co-designing and scaling ConvNets with masked autoencoders. In: Proceedings of the IEEE/CVF Conference on Computer Vision and Pattern Recognition (CVPR), pp. 16133–16142, June 2023
15. Woo, S., Park, J., Lee, J.-Y., Kweon, I.S.: CBAM: convolutional block attention module. In: Ferrari, V., Hebert, M., Sminchisescu, C., Weiss, Y. (eds.) ECCV 2018. LNCS, vol. 11211, pp. 3–19. Springer, Cham (2018). https://doi.org/10.1007/978-3-030-01234-2_1
16. Xia, T.E., Zhang, J.Y.: Clothing classification using transfer learning with squeeze and excitation block. Multimedia Tools Appl. **82**(2), 2839–2856 (2023)
17. Xiao, T., Xia, T., Yang, Y., Huang, C., Wang, X.: Learning from massive noisy labeled data for image classification. In: Proceedings of the IEEE Conference on Computer Vision and Pattern Recognition, pp. 2691–2699 (2015)
18. Xu, J., Wei, Y., Wang, A., Zhao, H., Lefloch, D.: Analysis of clothing image classification models: a comparison study between traditional machine learning and deep learning models. Fibres Text. East. Eur. **30**(5), 66–78 (2022)
19. Yu, F., et al.: EnCaps: clothing image classification based on enhanced capsule network. Appl. Sci. **11**(22), 11024 (2021)
20. Zeghoud, S., et al.: Real-time spatial normalization for dynamic gesture classification. Vis. Comput. 1–13 (2022)
21. Zhang, Y., Zhang, P., Yuan, C., Wang, Z.: Texture and shape biased two-stream networks for clothing classification and attribute recognition. In: Proceedings of the IEEE/CVF Conference on Computer Vision and Pattern Recognition, pp. 13538–13547 (2020)
22. Zhou, Z., Liu, M., Deng, W., Wang, Y., Zhu, Z.: Clothing image classification with DenseNet201 network and optimized regularized random vector functional link. J. Nat. Fibers **20**(1), 2190188 (2023)

Hierarchical Edge Aware Learning for 3D Point Cloud

Lei Li$^{(\boxtimes)}$

Department of Computer Science, University of Copenhagen,
2100 Copenhagen, Denmark
lilei@di.ku.dk

Abstract. This paper proposes an innovative approach to **H**ierarchical **E**dge **A**ware 3D Point Cloud Learning (HEA-Net) that seeks to address the challenges of noise in point cloud data, and improve object recognition and segmentation by focusing on edge features. In this study, we present an innovative edge-aware learning methodology, specifically designed to enhance point cloud classification and segmentation. Drawing inspiration from the human visual system, the concept of edge-awareness has been incorporated into this methodology, contributing to improved object recognition while simultaneously reducing computational time. Our research has led to the development of an advanced 3D point cloud learning framework that effectively manages object classification and segmentation tasks. A unique fusion of local and global network learning paradigms has been employed, enriched by edge-focused local and global embeddings, thereby significantly augmenting the model's interpretative prowess. Further, we have applied a hierarchical transformer architecture to boost point cloud processing efficiency, thus providing nuanced insights into structural understanding. Our approach demonstrates significant promise in managing noisy point cloud data and highlights the potential of edge-aware strategies in 3D point cloud learning. The proposed approach is shown to outperform existing techniques in object classification and segmentation tasks, as demonstrated by experiments on ModelNet40 and ShapeNet datasets.

Keywords: 3D Point Cloud · Edge Learning · Classification · Segmentation

1 Introduction

Point clouds, a versatile data representation format, are central to numerous fields such as autonomous driving, augmented reality, and robotics. With the rise of advanced 3D sensing technologies, the acquisition of 3D data has become notably accessible, leading to the creation of an array of online data repositories, including ModelNet [26] and ShapeNet [1]. Amidst the variety of 3D shape representations, including voxel, mesh, and multi-view images, point clouds stand out as the preliminary data captured by LiDAR or depth cameras, like Kinect.

B. Sheng et al. (Eds.): CGI 2023, LNCS 14495, pp. 81–92, 2024.
https://doi.org/10.1007/978-3-031-50069-5_8

The robust utility of point cloud data, underpinned by the critical task of representative point sampling, is evidenced in its broad applications, from scene reconstruction and autonomous driving navigation to virtual reality. As such, the development of efficient point cloud learning algorithms remains a significant focus in contemporary scientific and technological research (Fig. 1).

Within the realm of 3D data processing, point cloud sampling methodologies, such as random sampling (RS), grid sampling, uniform sampling, farthest point sampling (FPS) [4], and geometric sampling, are foundational. RS, while boasting efficiency, tends to overlook sparser regions, and FPS, despite its wide coverage, is hindered by latency issues during parallel operations. The application of grid sampling, through its use of regular grids, lacks the ability to accurately control the number of sampled points. Geometric sampling strategies that focus on local geometric properties, like shape curvature, along with techniques like Inverse Density Importance Sampling (IDIS) that favor points with lower cumulative distances to neighbors, call for high-density point clouds for maximum efficacy.

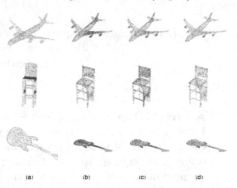

Fig. 1. Our study applies edge-aware sampling to point cloud data at varying complexities-1024, 512, and 256 points-demonstrating consistent preservation of critical object geometry and topology information, irrespective of the reduction in point complexity. (a) Original point cloud; (b, c, d) edge-aware sampling.

Yet, in spite of the advancements brought about by these traditional methodologies, the preservation of geometric information during the sampling process, particularly for complex objects with nuanced topology structures and irregular surface morphology, remains a daunting challenge. This obstacle has led to the emergence of cutting-edge learn-to-sample methods that concurrently optimize both the sampling process and specific downstream tasks. Such innovations have made substantial contributions to domains such as point cloud classification and reconstruction. Nonetheless, the challenge of maintaining geometric integrity within complex objects is still a largely unexplored area in academic research. In light of the vast diversity of object topological structures, defining a consistent category-agnostic edge at the semantic level poses a significant non-trivial challenge. Current datasets typically encompass only singular or a limited range of known object categories. Additionally, topological methods, which are ordinarily category-agnostic, concentrate predominantly on the geometric and topological attributes of the shape, such as its connectivity, topology, length, direction, and width.

With the advancement of deep learning techniques, several neural network-based sampling methods, such as S-Net [3], SampleNet [7], and DA-Net [12], have emerged. These approaches leverage multi-layer perceptrons (MLPs) to produce resampled point cloud sets of prescribed sizes, with MOPS-Net offering an innovation of generating a sampling transformation matrix. Despite their novelty, these methods lean toward a generative approach, bypassing direct point selection. Meanwhile, research has grown around creating neural network-based local feature aggregation operators for point clouds. However, these techniques, while reducing point numbers during latent feature learning, don't strictly qualify as sampling methods as they lack real spatial points during processing. Furthermore, the complex task of skeleton extraction adds another layer of complexity due to the inherent diversity of object topological structures and sensitivity to surface noise.

The concept of edge-awareness is inspired by the human visual system that profoundly relies on edge or part information for object recognition. The integration of such edge-aware strategies into point cloud learning can augment recognition capacities and concurrently decrease computational time. In this study, we introduce an edge-aware learning methodology that significantly bolsters point cloud classification and segmentation, contributing in three keypoints:

- We propose an innovative, edge-aware 3D point cloud learning framework handling object classification and segmentation.
- The fusion of local and global network learning paradigms, further supplemented by corresponding edge-focused local and global embeddings that enrich the model's interpretive abilities.
- The application of a hierarchical, transformer architecture that enhances point cloud processing efficiency, offering sophisticated insight into structural understanding.

2   Related Work

Point Cloud Sampling. The paramountcy of point cloud sampling in processing high-resolution dense point clouds is undeniable, and this recognition has precipitated the development of an array of innovative methods. Some techniques, for instance, harness K-means clustering to highlight representative points, concurrently removing redundancy. Others combine the power of clustering with a coarse-to-fine methodology to enhance point cloud processing efficiency. Intrinsic point cloud algorithms, providing a guarantee of density, further contribute to this field, facilitating uniform and feature-sensitive resampling. However, these strategies tend to concentrate on subset identification based on geometric or topological criteria, often overlooking the downstream task implications during sampling. In recent years, the advent of learn-to-sample approaches has heralded a new era in this domain. These methodologies introduce learning-based [7,9,24,32], task-oriented sampling strategies [20,30] explicitly designed to cater to downstream tasks like point cloud classification, retrieval, and reconstruction. These learning-based techniques often outperform the traditional non-learning-based sampling methods, such as the well-known FPS, emphasizing the continued evolution in this field.

Point Cloud Representation Learning. Deep learning methodologies have become integral to point cloud analysis, exhibiting pervasive influence across a spectrum of areas such as point cloud classification/segmentation [1,7,8,13,16,21,28,29], object detection/tracking [5], point cloud autoencoders [20], generation, completion, regression [14,18], and registration. The inherent complexity associated with the unstructured nature of point clouds, where the points are not positioned on a regular grid and exhibit varying degrees of mutual independence and inconsistent distances to neighboring points, presents significant challenges to the application of deep learning techniques.

Edge Learning. The incorporation of edge or skeleton learning has emerged as a fundamental aspect for capturing crucial properties such as geometry, topology [31], and symmetry [10,30,34] in objects, providing a concise and intuitive representation. This representation has demonstrated its efficacy across diverse computer vision tasks, encompassing shape recognition, reconstruction, segmentation, and point cloud completion. For instance, deep learning techniques have been proposed to leverage edge-awareness in generating mesh reconstructions of object surfaces from single RGB images. In the realm of image processing, the detection of edges typically relies on well-established techniques such as the Canny edge detector, which involves a multi-stage algorithm encompassing Gaussian filtering, intensity gradient computation, gradient magnitude thresholding, double thresholding, and edge suppression. These techniques enable the identification and extraction of salient edges while effectively suppressing weaker and disconnected ones, thereby enhancing the edge-aware analysis and interpretation capabilities.

3   Methods

We introduce our **H**ierarchical **E**dge **A**ware 3D Point Cloud Learning (HEA-Net) framework, which incorporates global and local learning for capturing edge information effectively. The framework uses deep tier learning, which processes the point cloud at different tiers to learn hierarchical features, similar to the workings of a human visual system. A detailed discussion of the architecture, layers, and algorithms involved is provided.

3.1   Overview of Framework.

The Fig. 2 illustrates our proposed Hierarchical Edge-Aware Network (HEA-net), which is specifically designed to adeptly execute classification and segmentation tasks for point clouds. A key aspect to note is the consistent application of the downsampling process across both classification and segmentation tasks. Subsequent to the application of local and global embeddings, the resultant data is fused and then fed into a multi-level network, specifically the Global-Local Downsampling (GLD) module. Evidently, from the classification tasks, it is apparent that the multi-layer downsampling accentuates the contours and

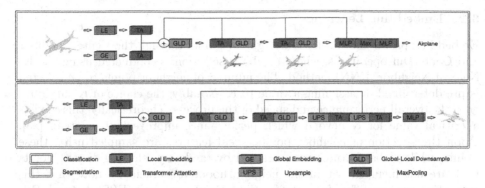

Fig. 2. The Hierarchical Edge-Aware network (HEA-Net) architectures employ distinctive strategies for classification (above) and segmentation (below) tasks. For classification and segmentation, the architecture combines local and global embeddings to effectively learn edge features, followed by an innovative global-local downsampling process that reduces a point cloud's complexity from N to M points. On the other hand, in the context of segmentation, an upsample layer is introduced to augment the point cloud's complexity back from M to N points. Integral to the HEA network's process is the use of transformer-based attention mechanisms which enable the architecture to focus on and learn critical sampling features.

edges of the object (in this case, an airplane). This approach efficiently discards superfluous information, thereby enhancing the pipeline's accuracy and speed, making the HEA-net an effective tool for processing and interpreting point cloud data.

Within the scope of the classification task, the point cloud's maximal feature is ultimately classified via the max pooling module. Conversely, in the context of segmentation tasks, a sequence of downsampling followed by upsampling is executed prior to conducting the segmentation. It is worth noting that two skip connections have been incorporated within the entire network structure. These skip connections significantly enhance the network's ability to learn hierarchical features. Subsequently, we will delve into a detailed exposition of the embedding, downsampling, and transformer

Fig. 3. Hierarchical deep downsampling. The visual representation from top to bottom depicts the evolution of point cloud information following three stages of downsampling. The elements depicted in red symbolize the point cloud post-sampling. (Color figure online)

attention modules, further elucidating their pivotal roles in the overall architecture of the Hierarchical Edge-Aware Network.

3.2   Embedding Learning

Embedding process obtain local and global points through the CenterNeighbor and CenterDiff operations, where neighbor selection is conducted using the K-Nearest Neighbor (KNN) method. The number of neighbor points to be selected is pre-determined by assigning a value to K. Notably, the choice of K can influence the overall performance and speed of the process. Theoretically, there exists a critical value for K beyond which performance improvements plateau [23]. Upon the selection of neighbor points, local features are sampled using these points, while global features are extracted by randomly selecting distant points that are not included within the neighborhood. It's crucial to note that this extraction process differs from the Farthest Point Sampling (FPS) method. Following the embedding of these points, multi-level feature learning is then applied, thus facilitating a more nuanced understanding of the data at various scales.

As shown in the associated figure, point cloud data from the multi-scale fused embedding is integrated through local and global attention operations. After this fusion, the output point cloud's dimension is N * D. This process enables the effective learning of global and local features from the fused embeddings. This output is then subjected to a downsampling procedure, yielding M*D data. So, combined with Embedding layers, we can use hierarchical global and local feature to downsampling the point cloud.

3.3   Global and Local Learning for the Edge

The GlobalDownsample process, using a transformer-based approach, derives Q, K, and V parameters and learns global correspondences. Meanwhile, the Local-Downsample process uses KNN to acquire neighbor points, then employs attention mechanisms to understand their relationship with feature points (Fig. 4).

As shown in the associated figure, point cloud data from the multi-scale fused embedding is integrated through local and global attention operations. After this fusion, the output point cloud's dimension is N * D. This process enables the effective learning of global and local features from the fused embeddings. This output is then subjected to a downsampling procedure, yielding M * D data. So, combined with Embedding layers, we can use hierarchical global and

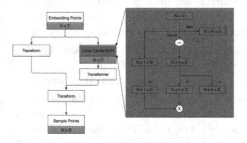

Fig. 4. Hierarchical downsampling combined with global feature and local feature for the edge.

local feature to downsampling the point cloud.

The global and local correlation maps, denoted as $MgM^g and MlM^l$, are combined into a single $N \times 2N N \times 2N$ correlation matrix MM:

$$M = \begin{bmatrix} - m_1^{g\top} - & - m_1^{l\top} - \\ - m_2^{g\top} - & - m_2^{l\top} - \\ \vdots & \vdots \\ - m_N^{g\top} - & - m_N^{l\top} - \end{bmatrix} \tag{1}$$

As demonstrated in Fig. 3, the feature information of the object post three hierarchical downsamplings and the final point cloud backcalculation is distinctly evident. Upon completion of the final sampling process, the M-dimensional information manifests as an effective representation of the object's information, highlighting the efficacy of the Hierarchical Global-Local Downsample algorithm in preserving essential data attributes. As we traverse from left to right, we observe the varying feature information expressed by different objects, underlining the capacity of this methodology to capture and illustrate a wide array of object-specific characteristics in an efficient and concise manner.

3.4 Loss Function

In the field of 3D point cloud analysis, the CrossEntropyLoss function is frequently used to quantify the discrepancy between predicted class probabilities and the actual labels. This loss function is vital for training models involved in semantic segmentation or classification tasks on 3D point cloud data. For a single point within the point cloud, the CrossEntropyLoss is defined as:

$$L(y, \hat{y}) = - \sum_{c=1}^{C} y_c \cdot \log(\hat{y}_c) \tag{2}$$

Here, $L(y, \hat{y})$ represents the CrossEntropyLoss between the true labels y and the predicted labels $\hat{y}$. The notation y_c stands for the true label of class c, and $\hat{y}_c$ denotes the predicted probability of class c. The logarithmic term intensifies the penalty for incorrect predictions, aiding the model to enhance its prediction accuracy.

4 Experiments

4.1 Evaluation Metric

For Classification task, we use Accuracy to present the performance of the methods.

$$Acc = \frac{1}{N} \sum_{i=1}^{N} 1(y_i = \hat{y}_i) \tag{3}$$

Cat.mIoU is utilized to assess the performance of semantic segmentation models. It quantifies the intersection-over-union (IoU) for each category or class and computes the average over all categories.

$$Cat.mIoU = \frac{1}{C} \sum_{i=1}^{C} \frac{TP_i}{TP_i + FP_i + FN_i} \tag{4}$$

4.2 Data Setting and Results

To validate our method, we carry out a series of experiments using ModelNet40 and ShapeNet datasets. During the training phase, we employed the `AdamW` optimizer with an initial learning rate of 1×10^{-4} and utilized a cosine annealing schedule to gradually decay the learning rate to 1×10^{-8} over the course of 400 epochs, while maintaining a batch size of 16. Additionally, we incorporated a weight decay hyperparameter of 1×10^{-5} to regulate the network weights, and introduced dropout with a probability of 0.5 in the last two fully connected layers.

Table 1. Segmentation results on ShapeNet Part.

Method	Cat. mIoU	Ins. mIoU
PointNet [15]	80.4%	83.7%
PointNet++ [16]	81.9%	85.1%
SpiderCNN [28]	82.4%	85.3%
DGCNN [21]	82.3%	85.2%
SPLATNet [19]	83.7%	85.4%
PointCNN [11]	84.6%	86.1%
PointConv [25]	82.8%	85.7%
KPConv [20]	85.0%	86.2%
PT [1] [5]	–	85.9%
PT [2] [33]	83.7%	86.6%
PRA-Net [2]	83.7%	86.3%
PAConv [27]	84.6%	86.1%
CurveNet [13]	–	86.6%
StratifiedT [6]	85.1%	86.6%
HEA-Net	83.9%	85.9%

Table 2. Classification performance on ModelNet40.

Method	Overall Accuracy
PointNet [15]	89.2%
PointNet++ [16]	91.9%
SpiderCNN [28]	92.4%
DGCNN [21]	92.9%
PointCNN [11]	92.2%
PointConv [25]	92.5%
KPConv [20]	92.9%
PointASNL [29]	93.2%
PT[1] [5]	92.8%
PT[2] [33]	93.7%
PRA-Net [2]	93.7%
PAConv [27]	93.6%
CurveNet [13]	93.8%
DeltaConv [22]	93.8%
HEA-Net	93.8

A thorough quantitative analysis was conducted to evaluate the performance of our proposed methodology in both classification and segmentation tasks, utilizing the ModelNet40 and ShapeNet Part datasets respectively in Table 2 and Table 1. Despite operating with a reduced number of sample points, our method consistently exhibited superior performance, as substantiated by the empirical results. In essence, our approach demonstrated an exceptional capability to succinctly capture the intricate patterns inherent in the sampled point cloud outlines.

These specific choices of hyperparameters and regularization techniques were carefully selected to optimize the training process, ensure model convergence, and enhance the overall performance and generalization capability of the network.

5   Discussion

In our current research focus on indoor object analysis, we have applied our edge-aware learning method. However, extending this approach to outdoor objects presents unique challenges due to the complex and diverse nature of outdoor scenes. Outdoor environments encompass a wide range of factors, including varying lighting conditions, occlusions from natural elements, and intricate background structures, which complicate edge analysis. Effectively capturing hierarchical edge information becomes crucial for accurate outdoor object analysis. Nonetheless, addressing these challenges and extending edge-aware learning to outdoor contexts offers promising opportunities to enhance computer vision systems in real-world applications such as autonomous driving, surveillance, and environmental monitoring.

Additionally, striking a balance between achieving high accuracy and managing computational complexity is a key consideration. Future work involves outdoor scenarios, and exploring potential enhancements to our proposed framework. Acknowledging the possible implications of noise on our method allows us to consider more comprehensive strategies for method improvement and sets the stage for more robust and reliable 3D point cloud processing in noisy environments. This entails investigating novel strategies to address the unique characteristics and challenges of outdoor scenes, as well as optimizing the trade-off between accuracy and computational efficiency. Our proposed sampling technique is systematically evaluated alongside established methodologies, including Random Sampling (RS), Farthest Point Sampling (FPS), and recent learning-based approaches such as S-Net and SampleNet as shown in Table 3.

Table 3. Our method is assessed against other prevalent sampling techniques, utilizing diverse sampling sizes within the ModelNet40 classification benchmark for a comprehensive comparison.

Method	M = 512	M = 256	M = 128
Voxel	73.82	73.50	68.15
RS	87.52	77.09	56.44
FPS [4]	88.34	83.64	70.34
S-NET [3]	87.80	82.38	77.53
SampleNet [7]	88.16	84.27	80.75
MOPS-Net [17]	86.67	86.63	86.06
DA-Net [12]	89.01	86.24	85.67
APES [23]	90.81	90.40	89.77
HEA-Net	93.75	92.26	90.24

In order to conduct a rigorous comparative analysis, our proposed sampling technique is systematically evaluated alongside established methodologies, including Random Sampling (RS), Farthest Point Sampling (FPS), and recent learning-based approaches such as S-Net and SampleNet. The primary objective of this study is to assess the classification performance on the ModelNet40 dataset (Figs. 5 and 6).

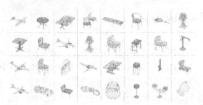

Fig. 5. Visualization of varied shape sampling results are generated by HEA-Net with all shapes being drawn from the test set.

Fig. 6. We provide a visualization of segmentation results as the point clouds of different shapes undergo downsampling. All shapes are from test set.

6 Conclusion

The human visual system relies extensively on edge and part information for object recognition, serving as inspiration for edge-awareness in computer vision. In this paper, we propose a novel framework for learning from 3D point cloud data, specifically addressing object classification and segmentation tasks. Our approach integrates the strengths of both local and global network learning paradigms, complemented by edge-focused local and global embeddings that enhance the model's interpretive capacities. Furthermore, we leverage a hierarchical, transformer-based architecture to improve the efficiency of point cloud processing and enable deeper structural comprehension. Through extensive experiments, we validate the efficacy of our proposed framework, demonstrating superior performance in object classification and segmentation compared to state-of-the-art methods. Our work paves the way for further exploration of edge-awareness in 3D point cloud analysis, advancing the frontiers of computer vision research.

References

1. Chang, A.X., et al.: ShapeNet: an information-rich 3D model repository. arXiv preprint arXiv:1512.03012 (2015)
2. Cheng, S., Chen, X., He, X., Liu, Z., Bai, X.: PRA-Net: point relation-aware network for 3D point cloud analysis. IEEE Trans. Image Process. **30**, 4436–4448 (2021)
3. Dovrat, O., Lang, I., Avidan, S.: Learning to sample. In: Proceedings of the IEEE/CVF Conference on Computer Vision and Pattern Recognition, pp. 2760–2769 (2019)
4. Eldar, Y., Lindenbaum, M., Porat, M., Zeevi, Y.Y.: The farthest point strategy for progressive image sampling. IEEE Trans. Image Process. **6**(9), 1305–1315 (1997)
5. Engel, N., Belagiannis, V., Dietmayer, K.: Point transformer. IEEE Access **9**, 134826–134840 (2021)
6. Lai, X., et al.: Stratified transformer for 3D point cloud segmentation. In: Proceedings of the IEEE/CVF Conference on Computer Vision and Pattern Recognition, pp. 8500–8509 (2022)

7. Lang, I., Manor, A., Avidan, S.: SampleNet: differentiable point cloud sampling. In: Proceedings of the IEEE/CVF Conference on Computer Vision and Pattern Recognition, pp. 7578–7588 (2020)
8. Li, J., et al.: Automatic detection and classification system of domestic waste via multimodel cascaded convolutional neural network. IEEE Trans. Industr. Inf. **18**(1), 163–173 (2021)
9. Li, L., Zhang, T., Kang, Z., Jiang, X.: Mask-FPAN: semi-supervised face parsing in the wild with de-occlusion and UV GAN. Comput. Graph. **116**, 185–193 (2023)
10. Li, L., Zhang, T., Oehmcke, S., Gieseke, F., Igel, C.: BuildSeg: a general framework for the segmentation of buildings. Nordic Mach. Intell. **2**(3) (2022)
11. Li, Y., Bu, R., Sun, M., Wu, W., Di, X., Chen, B.: PointCNN: convolution on X-transformed points. In: Advances in Neural Information Processing Systems, vol. 31 (2018)
12. Lin, Y., Huang, Y., Zhou, S., Jiang, M., Wang, T., Lei, Y.: DA-Net: density-adaptive downsampling network for point cloud classification via end-to-end learning. In: 2021 4th International Conference on Pattern Recognition and Artificial Intelligence (PRAI), pp. 13–18. IEEE (2021)
13. Muzahid, A., Wan, W., Sohel, F., Wu, L., Hou, L.: CurveNet: curvature-based multitask learning deep networks for 3D object recognition. IEEE/CAA J. Automatica Sinica **8**(6), 1177–1187 (2020)
14. Oehmcke, S., et al.: Deep learning based 3D point cloud regression for estimating forest biomass. In: Proceedings of the 30th International Conference on Advances in Geographic Information Systems (SIGSPATIAL), pp. 1–4. ACM (2022)
15. Qi, C.R., Su, H., Mo, K., Guibas, L.J.: PointNet: deep learning on point sets for 3D classification and segmentation. In: Proceedings of the IEEE Conference on Computer Vision and Pattern Recognition, pp. 652–660 (2017)
16. Qi, C.R., Yi, L., Su, H., Guibas, L.J.: PointNet++: deep hierarchical feature learning on point sets in a metric space. In: Advances in Neural Information Processing Systems, vol. 30 (2017)
17. Qian, Y., Hou, J., Zhang, Q., Zeng, Y., Kwong, S., He, Y.: MOPS-Net: a matrix optimization-driven network for task-oriented 3D point cloud downsampling. arXiv preprint arXiv:2005.00383 (2020)
18. Revenga, J.C., et al.: Above-ground biomass prediction for croplands at a sub-meter resolution using UAV-LiDAR and machine learning methods. Remote Sens. **14**(16), 3912 (2022)
19. Su, H., et al.: SPLATNet: sparse lattice networks for point cloud processing. In: Proceedings of the IEEE Conference on Computer Vision and Pattern Recognition, pp. 2530–2539 (2018)
20. Thomas, H., Qi, C.R., Deschaud, J.E., Marcotegui, B., Goulette, F., Guibas, L.J.: KPConv: flexible and deformable convolution for point clouds. In: Proceedings of the IEEE/CVF International Conference on Computer Vision, pp. 6411–6420 (2019)
21. Wang, Y., Sun, Y., Liu, Z., Sarma, S.E., Bronstein, M.M., Solomon, J.M.: Dynamic graph CNN for learning on point clouds. ACM Trans. Graph. (TOG) **38**(5), 1–12 (2019)
22. Wiersma, R., Nasikun, A., Eisemann, E., Hildebrandt, K.: DeltaConv: anisotropic point cloud learning with exterior calculus. arXiv preprint arXiv:2111.08799 (2021)
23. Wu, C., Zheng, J., Pfrommer, J., Beyerer, J.: Attention-based point cloud edge sampling. In: Proceedings of the IEEE/CVF Conference on Computer Vision and Pattern Recognition, pp. 5333–5343 (2023)

24. Wu, M., Li, L., Li, H.: FASE: feature-based similarity search on ECG data. In: 2019 IEEE International Conference on Big Knowledge (ICBK), pp. 273–280. IEEE (2019)
25. Wu, W., Qi, Z., Fuxin, L.: PointConv: deep convolutional networks on 3D point clouds. In: Proceedings of the IEEE/CVF Conference on Computer Vision and Pattern Recognition, pp. 9621–9630 (2019)
26. Wu, Z., et al.: 3D ShapeNets: a deep representation for volumetric shapes. In: Proceedings of the IEEE Conference on Computer Vision and Pattern Recognition, pp. 1912–1920 (2015)
27. Xu, M., Ding, R., Zhao, H., Qi, X.: PAConv: position adaptive convolution with dynamic kernel assembling on point clouds. In: Proceedings of the IEEE/CVF Conference on Computer Vision and Pattern Recognition, pp. 3173–3182 (2021)
28. Xu, Y., Fan, T., Xu, M., Zeng, L., Qiao, Yu.: SpiderCNN: deep learning on point sets with parameterized convolutional filters. In: Ferrari, V., Hebert, M., Sminchisescu, C., Weiss, Y. (eds.) ECCV 2018. LNCS, vol. 11212, pp. 90–105. Springer, Cham (2018). https://doi.org/10.1007/978-3-030-01237-3_6
29. Yan, X., Zheng, C., Li, Z., Wang, S., Cui, S.: PointASNL: robust point clouds processing using nonlocal neural networks with adaptive sampling. In: Proceedings of the IEEE/CVF Conference on Computer Vision and Pattern Recognition, pp. 5589–5598 (2020)
30. Zhang, T., Li, L., Cao, S., Pu, T., Peng, Z.: Attention-guided pyramid context networks for detecting infrared small target under complex background. IEEE Trans. Aerosp. Electron. Syst. **59**(4), 4250–4261 (2023). https://doi.org/10.1109/TAES.2023.3238703
31. Zhang, T., Li, L., Igel, C., Oehmcke, S., Gieseke, F., Peng, Z.: LR-CSNet: low-rank deep unfolding network for image compressive sensing. In: 2022 IEEE 8th International Conference on Computer and Communications (ICCC), pp. 1951–1957. IEEE (2022)
32. Zhang, Y., Li, L., Song, L., Xie, R., Zhang, W.: FACT: fused attention for clothing transfer with generative adversarial networks. In: Proceedings of the AAAI Conference on Artificial Intelligence, vol. 34, pp. 12894–12901 (2020)
33. Zhao, H., Jiang, L., Jia, J., Torr, P.H., Koltun, V.: Point transformer. In: Proceedings of the IEEE/CVF International Conference on Computer Vision, pp. 16259–16268 (2021)
34. Zhou, C., et al.: Multi-scale pseudo labeling for unsupervised deep edge detection (2023). Available at SSRN 4425635

Neural Differential Radiance Field: Learning the Differential Space Using a Neural Network

Saeed Hadadan$^{(\boxtimes)}$ and Matthias Zwicker

University of Maryland, College Park, USA
{saeedhd,zwicker}@cs.umd.edu

Abstract. We introduce an adjoint-based inverse rendering method using a Neural Differential Radiance Field, i.e. a neural network representation of the solution of the differential rendering equation. Inspired by neural radiosity techniques, we minimize the norm of the residual of the differential rendering equation to directly optimize our network. The network is capable of outputting continuous, view-independent gradients of the radiance field w.r.t scene parameters, taking into account differential global illumination effects while keeping memory and time complexity constant in path length. To solve inverse rendering problems, we simultaneously train networks to represent radiance and differential radiance, and optimize the unknown scene parameters. Our method is not scalable to millions of scene parameters, but we propose future work directions that could make that happen in the future.

Keywords: Neural radiance fields · physically-based differentiable rendering · inverse rendering

1 Introduction

Differentiable rendering is the problem of computing derivatives of a rendering process w.r.t scene parameters such as BRDFs, geometry, illumination, or camera parameters. Differentiable rendering is attractive because it enables gradient-based optimization in inverse rendering problems, where scene parameters are optimized such that the rendering process produces a target image (or multiple target images from different viewpoints).

Here we are focusing on differentiable rendering for algorithms that solve the rendering equation, with the ultimate goal to eventually enable inverse rendering based on real world photographs under large numbers of unknown scene parameters. In the scope of this paper, we are only focused on a set of algorithms that use a neural network approximation of the radiance function. Such methods account for global illumination by querying a radiance cache instead of building complete Monte Carlo path integrals which could be very costly. Despite being

B. Sheng et al. (Eds.): CGI 2023, LNCS 14495, pp. 93–104, 2024.
https://doi.org/10.1007/978-3-031-50069-5_9

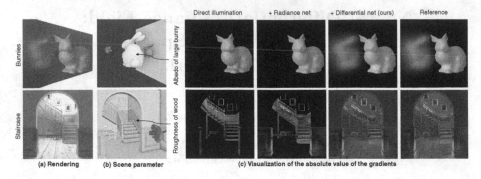

Fig. 1. Our differential radiance network can account for primary and secondary gradients. In (a) we showcase bunny scene where the reflection of bunnies in the mirror creates indirect effects, and staircase scene with significant levels of global illumination. (b) We pick a scalar non-spatially varying material parameter in each scene, and (c) visualize the gradient space for each method. The largest bias expectedly appears in the direct illumination solver; we observe improvement in gradients when we use a radiance cache on top of it. However, the inter-reflection of gradients in the scene is still totally missing. Next, our differential radiance network gives us the full differential solution, despite bouncing light only once, see Fig. 3a.

computationally simpler than path integrals, these methods tend to miss *indirect gradients* as a result of not differentiating the radiance cache w.r.t scene parameters. This could result in considerable bias in gradients (see the missing indirect effects in Fig. 1 under 'radiance net').

In this paper, we propose a novel technique to account for the missing indirect gradients. Our key idea is to represent the entire *differential radiance field*, that is, the derivative of the radiance field w.r.t a set of scene parameters, using a neural network, in addition to the radiance cache proposed by state-of-the-art. We then train this network to satisfy the *differential rendering equation* introduced by Nimier-David et al. [8]. Our method is inspired by the Neural Radiosity approach by Hadadan et al. [3] to solve the rendering equation; here we use the same training scheme to train our differential network as well. We show that we can account for indirect gradients more accurately than neural-network based methods that learn radiance caches such as [4,12]. In addition, our approach is the first that produces continuous view-independent differential radiance fields for given scene parameters, instead of only sampling derivatives for a discrete set of rays.

On the other hand, we can only optimize a limited number of parameters using our approach as the size of the output layer of our differential radiance network is equal to the number of parameters being optimized. Finally, even with the correction of indirect gradients using our differential radiance network, our gradients would not be perfectly unbiased due to the fact that they are approximated by a neural network.

2   Related Work

2.1   Neural Network Techniques for Realistic Rendering.

Neural networks can be leveraged in various ways for realistic rendering, from computational photography to medical imaging [10]. In particular, we are interested in the case where neural networks can directly represent the solution of the rendering equation as proposed in Neural Radiosity [3] and Neural Radiance Caching [7], where the radiance function is represented by neural networks as a form of a *radiance cache*.

This paper aims at leveraging neural networks to learn view-independent, continuous *differential* radiance fields, which is to the best of our knowledge unprecedented. We use a single neural network to represent the *differential radiance function* w.r.t arbitrary scene parameters. In a similar approach to Neural Radiosity, we optimize our network parameters directly by minimizing the norm of the residual of the *differential* rendering equation. We benefit from the re-renderability of the radiance network as in Neural Radiosity.

2.2   Differentiable Rendering with Indirect Effects

Inverse rendering problems in computer vision and graphics heavily rely on differentiable rendering to reconstruct a set of scene parameters (geometry [1], reflectance properties, camera positions, etc.) from images. Most computer vision techniques on differentiable rendering simply ignore indirect illumination effects [5,6], but if we want to account for them, we require a full solution of the rendering equation. Techniques to differentiate the rendering equation while accounting for indirect effects have been proposed in prior work. The most naive approach would be to differentiate a path tracer using Automatic Differentiation (AD), which requires a transcription of the whole rendering process, thus suffering from prohibitive memory requirement. Instead, adjoint-based techniques take advantage of differential light properties to avoid the enormous transcript of AD. Specifically, *Radiative Backpropagation* (RB) [8] differentiates the rendering equation to obtain a *differential rendering equation*, which describes scattering and emission of *differential light*. The equation reveals that *differential light* travels through a scene similarly as regular light does. RB proposes an adjoint approach for differentiable rendering, which is more efficient than naive Automatic Differentiation of a Monte Carlo path tracer. RB's main shortcoming is that its time complexity is quadratic in path length, since at every scattering event during the adjoint phase, it requires to estimate incident radiance by building another complete light path. Although follow up works [11] have solved this issue, these algorithms still needs to build complete path integrals.

As opposed to the above methods that require building path integrals of arbitrary length, recent works such as Hadadan et al. [4] and Zhang et al. [12] propose to use a neural network to approximate the radiance function and query it during inverse rendering to account for global illumination effects. This approximation requires less computation memory and significantly less computation time than path tracing with arbitrary bounces. We will show that although this approximation can correctly account for global illumination in *primal* radiance space, it cannot account for global illumination effects in the *differential* radiance space. In other words, it misses the indirect gradients. Instead, in this paper we will propose a few alterations to the radiance-cache-based methods to correctly compute indirect gradients as well, with the help of a differential radiance network. Additionally, Hadadan et al. [4] and Zhang et al. [12] use automatic differentiation to compute the gradients of the whole process, while we propose to use an adjoint-based method. We validate our gradients compared to RB in Fig. 2.

3   Background

3.1   (Differential) Rendering Equation

Realistic rendering algorithms compute a set of measurements I_k where k corresponds to a pixel, given by the measurement equation

$$I_k = \int_{\mathcal{A}} \int_{\mathcal{H}^2} W_k(x, \omega) L(x, \omega) dx d\omega_i^{\perp}, \qquad (1)$$

where L is the incident radiance at location x and direction ω on the pixel, and W_k is the importance of pixel k. As radiance L remains constant along unoccluded rays, incident radiance at a pixel location and direction is equal to the outgoing radiance from the nearest surface along the ray. The outgoing radiance at surfaces can be computed using the rendering equation,

$$L(x, \omega_o) = E(x, \omega_o) + \int_{\mathcal{H}^2} f(x, \omega_i, \omega_o) L(x'(x, \omega_i), -\omega_i), d\omega_i^{\perp}. \qquad (2)$$

Nimier-David et al. [8] differentiate the above equations w.r.t an arbitrary set of scene parameters $p = (p_1, ..., p_n)$. For simplicity, we use ∂_p to represent ∂ / ∂_p. Note that variables preceded by ∂_p imply a vectorized gradient w.r.t each parameter. By assuming a static camera where $\partial_p W_k = 0$, we can differentiate Eq. 1 as,

$$\partial_p I_k = \int_{\mathcal{A}} \int_{\mathcal{H}^2} W_k(x, \omega) \partial_p L(x, \omega) dx d\omega_i^{\perp}, \qquad (3)$$

which describes the relationship between *differential measurement* $\partial_p I_k$ and *differential radiance* $\partial_p L$. Differential radiance $\partial_p L$ in turn can be found by differentiating Eq. 2,

$$\partial_p L(x, \omega_o) = \partial_p E(x, \omega_o) + \int_{\mathcal{H}^2} f(x, \omega_i, \omega_o) \partial_p L(x'(x, \omega_i), -\omega_i) d\omega_i^{\perp}$$

$$+ \int_{\mathcal{H}^2} \partial_p f(x, \omega_i, \omega_o) L(x'(x, \omega_i), -\omega_i) d\omega_i^{\perp}, \qquad (4)$$

which is referred to as *differential rendering equation*. This equation explains the scattering of differential radiance in a similar manner to regular radiance. More

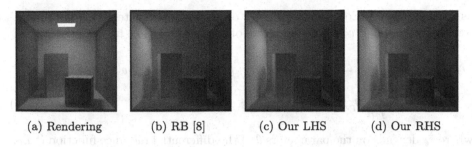

(a) Rendering   (b) RB [8]   (c) Our LHS   (d) Our RHS

Fig. 2. Validation of our gradients compared to Radiative Backpropagation [8]. (a), (b) and (c) are the gradient images with respect to the red wall albedo.

specifically, the first term describes how differential radiance is *emitted* from surfaces whose emission is dependent on the scene parameters p. The second term means differential radiance *scatters* on surfaces based on their BRDFs, similar to regular radiance in the rendering equation. The new third term represents additional differential *emission* from the surface if its BRDF function changes with perturbations of scene parameters p. This term is dependent on the incident radiance L at (x, ω_i), which implies computing $\partial_p L$ depends on computing L also.

3.2   Neural Radiosity

Neural Radiosity [3] is an algorithm to find a solution of the rendering equation (Eq. 2) using a single neural network. More formally, the radiance function $L(x, \omega_o)$ in Eq. 2 is represented by a neural network with a set of parameters ϕ (such as geometry, lighting, and material properties), as $L_\phi(x, \omega_o)$. The parameters ϕ of this network can be directly optimized in a self-training approach by minimizing the norm of the *residual* of the rendering equation. The residual $r_\phi(x, \omega_o)$ is

$$r_\phi(x, \omega_o) = L_\phi(x, \omega_o) - E(x, \omega_o)$$
$$- \int_{\mathcal{H}^2} f(x, \omega_i, \omega_o) L_\phi(x'(x, \omega_i), -\omega_i) d\omega_i^\perp, \qquad (5)$$

which is simply the difference of the left and right-hand sides of Eq. 2 when the radiance function L is substituted by L_ϕ. This neural network takes a location x and outgoing direction ω_o as input and returns the outgoing radiance. Such a pre-trained network serves as a compact, re-renderable, and view-independent solution of the rendering equation.

4   Solving the Differential Rendering Equation

Similar to Neural Radiosity, we propose to use neural network-based solvers to find the solution of the *differential rendering equation*. We call this Differentiable Neural Radiosity. Let us denote a differential radiance distribution $\partial_p L_\theta(x, \omega_o)$

as the unknown in Eq. 4, given by a set of network parameters θ. Additionally, we define a *residual* r_θ as the difference of the left and right hand side of Eq. 4,

$$r_\theta(x, \omega_o) = \partial_p L_\theta(x, \omega_o) - \partial_p E(x, \omega_o) - \int_{\mathcal{H}^2} f(x, \omega_i, \omega_o) \partial_p L_\theta(x'(x, \omega_i), -\omega_i) d\omega_i^\perp$$

$$- \int_{\mathcal{H}^2} \partial_p f(x, \omega_i, \omega_o) L_\phi(x'(x, \omega_i), -\omega_i) d\omega_i^\perp, \tag{6}$$

where r_θ depends on the parameters θ of the differential radiance function $\partial_p L_\theta$. Also, the primal radiance can be represented by a constant parameter set ϕ in L_ϕ which is independent of θ.

We define our loss as the L2 norm of the residual,

$$\mathcal{L}(\theta) = \|r_\theta(x, \omega_o)\|_2^2$$

$$= \int_{\mathcal{M}} \int_{\mathcal{H}^2} r_\theta(x, \omega_o)^2 dx d\omega_o, \tag{7}$$

where $\mathcal{M}$ means integration over all scene surfaces. We propose to minimize $\mathcal{L}(\theta)$ using stochastic gradient descent.

4.1 Monte Carlo Estimation

The Monte Carlo estimation of the residual norm is

$$\mathcal{L}(\theta) \approx \frac{1}{N} \sum_{j=1}^N \frac{r_\theta(x_j, \omega_{o,j})^2}{p(x_j, \omega_{o,j})}, \tag{8}$$

where N is the number of samples, x_j and $\omega_{o,j}$ are the surface location and the outgoing direction samples, taken from a distribution with density $p(x, \omega)$.

The Monte Carlo estimation of the incident integral for any $r_\theta(x_j, \omega_{o,j})$ is

$$r_\theta(x_j, \omega_{o,j}) = \partial_p L_\theta(x_j, \omega_{o,j}) - \partial_p E(x_j, \omega_{o,j})$$

$$- \frac{1}{M} \sum_{k=1}^M \frac{f(x_j, \omega_{i,j,k}, \omega_{o,j}) \partial_p L_\theta(x'(x_j, \omega_{i,j,k}), -\omega_{i,j,k})}{p(\omega_{i,j,k})}$$

$$- \frac{1}{Z} \sum_{l=1}^Z \frac{\partial_p f(x_j, \omega_{i,j,l}, \omega_{o,j}) L_\phi(x'(x_j, \omega_{i,j,l}), -\omega_{i,j,l})}{p(\omega_{i,j,l})}. \tag{9}$$

The notation $\omega_{i,j,k}$ and $\omega_{i,j,l}$ indicates that each sample $x_j, \omega_{o,j}$ has its own set of samples of M and Z incident directions $\omega_{i,j,k}$ and $\omega_{i,j,l}$ (i stands for "incident", it is not an index).

5   Inverse Rendering Using Our Method

For inverse rendering, the goal is to optimize a set of scene parameters p using an objective function $z(.)$, which denotes the distance between a candidate image to the reference, and a rendering function $g(.)$. To minimize $z(g(p))$, we need the gradient $\frac{\partial z}{\partial p}$,

$$\frac{\partial z}{\partial p} = \frac{\partial z}{\partial y} \cdot \frac{\partial y}{\partial p}, \tag{10}$$

where y is a rendered image $y = g(p)$. The term $\frac{\partial z}{\partial y}$ can be interpreted as the gradient of the loss w.r.t pixel values of the candidate image. In most cases, computing this gradient is easy either manually (e.g. if it is $L2$ or $L1$) or using AD (e.g. if it is a neural network). The more challenging part is $\frac{\partial y}{\partial p}$, which is equivalent to the differential measurement vector $[\partial_p I_0...\partial_p I_n]$, since we need to differentiate the rendering algorithm. Recall from Eq. 3 that $\partial_p I_k$ is the result of integrating the incident *differential radiance* $\partial_p L$ over locations x and directions ω on the hemisphere at pixel k. Therefore, the task breaks down to finding $\partial_p L(x, w)$. In our approach we query our neural network $\partial_p L_\theta(x, w)$ for the differential radiance, as it represents the entire differential radiance distribution in the scene.

   With the use of our network, inverse rendering breaks down into an iteration over the following steps:

1. Train (or fine-tune) our networks $\partial_p L_\theta$ and L_ϕ with the current state of the scene parameters (minimize Eqs. 5 and 7).
2. Compute a non-differentiable candidate primal rendering and its distance to the reference ($L2, L1$, etc.). In case of multi-view optimization, the losses are summed.
3. Find the derivatives of the loss w.r.t the pixels of the primal image (to get $\frac{\partial z}{\partial y}$).
4. Compute $\frac{\partial y}{\partial p}$, which is equivalent to the measurement vector $[\partial_p I_0...\partial_p I_n]$. To do so, we trace rays from the sensor to find the first hit point and at that point, query our differential radiance network $\partial_p L_\theta$. More formally,

$$\partial_p I_{k,\theta} = \int_{\mathcal{A}} \int_{\mathcal{H}^2} W_k(x, \omega) \partial_p L_\theta(x'(x, \omega)) dx d\omega_i^\perp. \tag{11}$$

5. Compute the gradient of the loss w.r.t the parameters $\frac{\partial z}{\partial p}$ by multiplying the gradients from Step (2) and (3) as in Eq. 10.
6. Update the scene parameters using the computed gradient using an optimizer such as Adam).

   Figure 3b summarizes the steps of our pipeline.

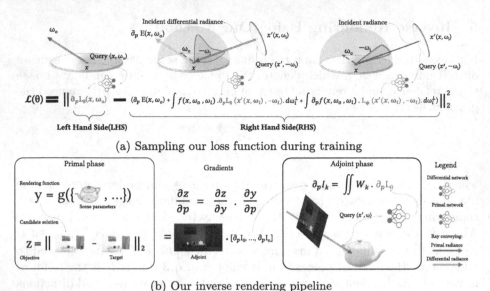

(a) Sampling our loss function during training

(b) Our inverse rendering pipeline

Fig. 3. Pipeline schematics illustrating our training scheme and inverse optimizations steps.

6   Implementation

6.1   Training

The training process for our networks is end-to-end and it occurs simultaneously with the parameter optimization, i.e., during every optimization step, we take a certain number of training steps for our networks to adapt to the most recent changes in the scene parameters. In each training step, we minimize the norm of the residual of the rendering equation and the differential rendering equation simultaneously as

$$\mathcal{L}(\theta, \phi) = \|r_\phi(x, \omega_o)\|_2^2 + \|r_\theta(x, \omega_o)\|_2^2,$$

using a separate set of samples for location and direction in each residual term. Please note that the network L_ϕ is also present in the differential residual term r_θ (see the loss function Eq. 7). In practice, we use a $sg(.)$ to prevent our primal network from adapting itself to the differential loss.

Similar to Neural Radiosity, our training scheme is a *self-training* approach, that is, instead of providing noisy estimated data to our network as ground truth regression data, we compute both sides of the differential rendering equation using the same network and minimize the difference (residual) during training (Fig. 3a).

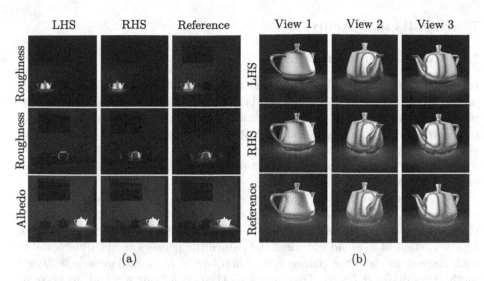

(a)   (b)

Fig. 4. (a) Separate renderings of our differential network w.r.t to the BRDF parameters of each teapot in the Fig. 3b. Our network is capable of learning non-diffuse gradients and global illumination effects in differential space. Using 8 spp for LHS and 2048 for RHS and reference (b) Multi-view renderings of our view-independent solution of the differential rendering equation compared to reference. We show the derivative with respect to the copper teapot's roughness (the first row in Fig. 4a).

6.2   Sampling and Architecture

To sample the norm of the residual, we uniformly sample locations x_i and directions $w_{o,i}$ in Eq. 8. The incident direction samples are taken using MIS of emitter and BSDF. Each of our networks is an MLP with 3 fully-connected layers with 256 neurons per hidden layer, preceded by multi-resolution sparse grid encoding of location x.

6.3   LHS Vs. RHS for Differential Radiance

As stated in Sect. 5, Step (4) of inverse rendering requires a query to $\partial_p L_\theta$ to compute gradients of pixels w.r.t. scene parameters. Equivalently, one could query our RHS to compute these gradients. Ideally, if the residual is zero everywhere, there should be no difference between the LHS and RHS; in practice, however, the is always a nonzero residual. We find that our RHS more quickly adapts to scene parameter changes, as computing the RHS requires one extra ray-tracing step using the updated parameters. Hence, we use the RHS to query the gradients in the experiments in this paper.

7   Results and Analysis

7.1   Comparison to Previous Work

In Sect. 2.2, we mentioned that automatic differentiation of multi-bounce path integrals could be memory intensive and time-consuming when dealing with complex scenes. A solution to alleviate the memory and time complexity of building path integrals is to use a radiance cache; it can provide global illumination effects while removing the need to trace further bounces. Such a radiance cache can be solely trained from input images [12], and/or using a global illumination solver [4] based on Neural Radiosity [3].

More formally, in Eq. (4), a radiance cache would provide an approximation of the term L in the second integral term which would make it more accurate than a direct illumination solver (see Fig. 1). The issue is, having a network representation of L would not yield $\partial_p L$, since the network is not differentiable with respect to the scene parameters. Therefore, using a radiance-cache-based method results in $\partial_p L = 0$. That is the motivation for our method, to account for the term $\partial_p L$ and L at the same time using separate networks; Fig. 1 shows that our method yields the least biased gradients, accounting for the global illumination effects in both primal and differential spaces, needless of tracing further bounces.

Here we provide an analysis of our method:

- **Smooth gradients:** All path integral based methods compute gradients using Monte Carlo sampling which results in noisy gradients. Instead, our networks $\partial_p L_\theta$ and L_ϕ produce smooth gradients that could enable a faster and more robust optimization process.
- **Constant time complexity:** Our time complexity is *constant* in path length, similar to other radiance-cache-based methods that avoid computing path integrals. Our method requires tracing only one bounce to compute a full global illumination solution in both differential and primal space.
- **View-independence:** Our method provides view-independent solutions to the differential rendering equation (Fig. 4b). This means our solutions need not be recomputed/updated under changes of sensor parameters – except if sensor parameters are in the set of parameters that are being optimized. This property can be helpful for multi-view optimization tasks.
- **Memory complexity** The inference and training memory complexity of our differential network (LHS) with batch size of k samples is $O(k * n)$ where n is the number of the parameters of our networks; for the RHS with N surface samples and M samples for the hemispherical integral, the complexity would be $O(N * M * l)$. As our differential network requires an output channel for each scene parameter included in the gradient, assuming a fixed network size except the last layer, the number of network parameters l grows linearly with the number of scene parameters in gradient.

7.2 Inverse Rendering Experiments

We conduct an inverse rendering using our method to find the albedo of the small bunny in Fig. 1 from a single view; the bunny is not directly visible by the camera, but only the reflection off the camera can provide information about its albedo. Results in Fig. 5 show that radiance-cache based methods completely fail to account for indirect gradients, while our method can successfully optimize for the parameter using the differential radiance field.

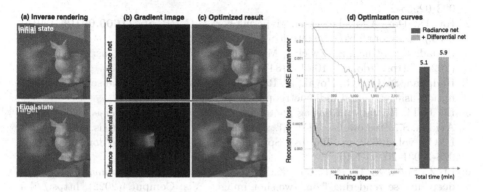

Fig. 5. Inverse rendering using our method compared to when a radiance cache was trained based on the input images similar in spirit to [4,12]. The parameter being optimized for is the albedo of the small bunny.

8 Limitation and Future Work

Our method has a key limitation: our differential network requires an output channel for each scene parameter included in the gradient. As we use fully-connected layers, the number of connections in the last layer grows linearly with the number of outputs (assuming fixed-sized network except the output layer) and this generates a memory constraint for differentiable rendering tasks that require optimizing w.r.t millions of parameters. One could use techniques such as low rank factorization [9] to reduce the output dimension of the neural network; another approach could be using hypernetworks [2] to have a neural network learn the weights of a small network $\partial_p L$ with millions of outputs.

9 Conclusion

In this paper, we introduced a new method to solve the differential rendering equation using a single neural network. Our network parameters are optimized directly by minimizing the norm of the residual of the differential rendering equation. Our learnable network architecture is capable of representing the full continuous, view-independent differential radiance distribution and accounts for global differential illumination. Such a network can be utilized on top of a radiance-cache based method to fix the bias issue of missing indirect gradients.

Acknowledgments. We would like to thank professor Ming C. Lin from the University of Maryland, College Park for the insightful discussion, as the idea of this project formed during her Differentiable Programming course.

References

1. An, H., Lee, W., Moon, B.: Adaptively weighted discrete Laplacian for inverse rendering. Vis. Comput. **39**(8), 3211–3220 (2023). https://doi.org/10.1007/s00371-023-02955-2
2. Ha, D., Dai, A.M., Le, Q.V.: Hypernetworks. CoRR **abs/1609.09106** (2016). http://arxiv.org/abs/1609.09106
3. Hadadan, S., Chen, S., Zwicker, M.: Neural radiosity. ACM Trans. Graph. **40**(6) (2021). https://doi.org/10.1145/3478513.3480569
4. Hadadan, S., Lin, G., Novák, J., Rousselle, F., Zwicker, M.: Inverse global illumination using a neural radiometric prior (2023)
5. Li, J., Li, H.: Self-calibrating photometric stereo by neural inverse rendering. In: Avidan, S., Brostow, G., Cissé, M., Farinella, G.M., Hassner, T. (eds.) ECCV 2022. LNCS, vol. 13662, pp. 166–183. Springer, Cham (2022). https://doi.org/10.1007/978-3-031-20086-1_10
6. Li, Z., Shen, X., Hu, Y., Zhou, X.: High-resolution SVBRDF estimation based on deep inverse rendering from two-shot images. Vis. Comput. (2022). https://doi.org/10.1007/s00371-022-02612-0
7. Müller, T., Rousselle, F., Novák, J., Keller, A.: Real-time neural radiance caching for path tracing **40**(4) (2021). https://doi.org/10.1145/3450626.3459812
8. Nimier-David, M., Speierer, S., Ruiz, B., Jakob, W.: Radiative backpropagation: an adjoint method for lightning-fast differentiable rendering. ACM Trans. Graph. **39**(4) (2020). https://doi.org/10.1145/3386569.3392406
9. Sainath, T.N., Kingsbury, B., Sindhwani, V., Arisoy, E., Ramabhadran, B.: Low-rank matrix factorization for deep neural network training with high-dimensional output targets. In: 2013 IEEE International Conference on Acoustics, Speech and Signal Processing, pp. 6655–6659 (2013). https://doi.org/10.1109/ICASSP.2013.6638949
10. Shetty, K., et al.: Deep learning compatible differentiable x-ray projections for inverse rendering (2021)
11. Vicini, D., Speierer, S., Jakob, W.: Path replay backpropagation: differentiating light paths using constant memory and linear time. ACM Trans. Graph. **40**(4) (2021). https://doi.org/10.1145/3450626.3459804
12. Zhang, Y., Sun, J., He, X., Fu, H., Jia, R., Zhou, X.: Modeling indirect illumination for inverse rendering. In: Proceedings of the IEEE/CVF Conference on Computer Vision and Pattern Recognition (CVPR), pp. 18643–18652 (2022)

Aware-Transformer: A Novel Pure Transformer-Based Model for Remote Sensing Image Captioning

Yukun Cao[1], Jialuo Yan[1(✉)], Yijia Tang[2], Zhenyi He[1], Kangle Xu[1], and Yu Cheng[1]

[1] Shanghai University of Electric Power, Shanghai 201306, China
yanjialuo@mail.shiep.edu.cn
[2] Nanjing University of Aeronautics and Astronautics, Nanjing 211106, China

Abstract. Remote sensing image captioning (RSIC) is the task of generating accurate and coherent descriptions of the visual content in remote sensing images. While recent progress has been made in developing CNN-Transformer based models for this task, given the significant scale differences in the visual objects within these images, many existing methods still have some deficiencies in effectively capturing the multiscale visual features of these images. Additionally, applying these visual features directly to a vanilla Transformer architecture may result in the loss of important visual information. To address these challenges, we propose a novel pure Transformer-based model that first utilizes a fine-tuned Swin-Transformer as the encoder to extract multiscale visual features from remote sensing images. Then it introduces an Aware-Transformer as the decoder, which enhances multiscale and multiobject visual information to help generate accurate and detailed captions. To assess the performance of our proposed method, we conducted ablation and comparison experiments on three publicly available RSIC datasets: Sydney-Captions, UCM-Captions, and NWPU-Captions. The results demonstrate that our method outperforms state-of-the-art RSIC models in captioning quality.

Keywords: Remote sensing image captioning · Multiscale and multiobject · Transformer · Awareness

1 Introduction

With the advancements in aerial remote sensing systems, researchers are able to obtain an increasing number of high spatial resolution remote sensing images. These images can be used to observe changes in the surface environment and have various applications, including geological disaster monitoring, geographic mapping, and military surveillance. In order to understand remote sensing images at the semantic level, remote sensing image captioning (RSIC) has gained attention. RSIC is a multi-modal learning task that connects Computer Vision (CV) and

Natural Language Processing (NLP). It aims to generate accurate and detailed sentences that comprehensively describe the content of remote sensing images.

Remote sensing images from aerial or satellite platforms present significant scale variations among depicted objects, as illustrated in Fig. 1. These images introduce multiscale challenges due to the presence of objects of different sizes and the intricate relationships between them. Extracting and effectively leveraging this multiscale and multiobject information for RSIC represents a challenging task.

Miniature   Multiscale   Multiobject

Fig. 1. The characteristic of remote sensing images.

Nevertheless, prior research has frequently utilized CNNs pre-trained on natural images (i.e., models trained on ImageNet [4]) as the encoder for RSIC models to extract visual features. This approach may result in the encoder being unable to capture the unique visual features of remote sensing images well. Furthermore, recent studies have demonstrated the outstanding potential of Transformer architecture in CV tasks [6,9,10]. This innovation offers a fresh possibility for encoding images into vector features and enables the exploration of more efficient and sophisticated designs for RSIC.

In recent years, the use of a decoder comprising LSTM with attention has been a prevalent approach. While LSTM addresses the issues of gradient vanishing and exploding, it still operates on the concept of time series and lacks the capability of efficient parallel computation. Drawing inspiration from the triumph of Transformer architecture in NLP tasks [7,11,14], that implement Transformer as the decoder for RSIC models. However, the majority of studies have utilized the vanilla Transformer [14] as the decoder. Generating automatic captions for remote sensing images requires a higher degree of accuracy. Achieving effective RSIC necessitates an investigation of the multiscale and multiobject visual information. Thus, effective and efficient ways should be explored to combine visual features with Transformer for RSIC.

Considering the above two limitations, we develop a novel pure Transformer-based model and present it in Fig. 2. To address the first shortcoming, we employ the fine-tuned Swin-Transformer (Swin-T) [10] backbone network in the encoder to fully capture the proprietary visual features of remote sensing images. In the decoder, we develop an Aware-Transformer to generate descriptive sentences with multilevel awareness module (MAM) to enhance the multiscale and multiobject visual information.

Our contributions are summarized as follows:

- We present a novel pure Transformer-based model, an emerging research architecture, that combined the strengths of vision and language Transformers to enhance multimodal interactions and provide a reliable solution for RSIC.
- We employ a fine-tuned Swin-T backbone network as the encoder to bridge the visual gap between natural images and remote sensing images, and to effectively extract multiscale visual features.
- We design an Aware-Transformer, incorporating the multilevel awareness module, to serve as the decoder. It can enhance multiscale and multiobject visual information in visual features, leading to the generation of superior caption sentences.
- We conduct ablation and comparison experiments on three publicly available RSIC datasets. The results demonstrate that our method outperforms other state-of-the-art models.

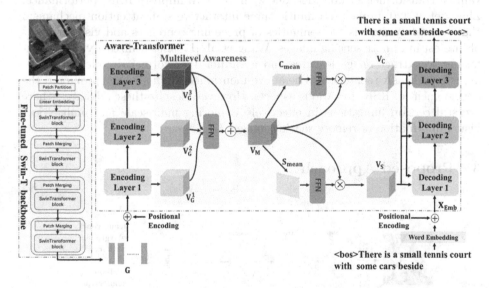

Fig. 2. The overview of our pure Transformer-based captioning model. Its encoder is composed of fine-tuned Swin-T, and its decoder is Aware-Transformer. FFN refers to the feed-forward network.

2   Related Work

RSIC is largely influenced by the natural image captioning (NIC) task, which has made great progress through years of work. Vinyals et al. [16] first applied the encoder-decoder method based on deep learning to the image captioning task, which CNN as the encoder to extract visual features, and LSTM as the decoder to generate descriptive sentences. Since then, the encoder-decoder methods have become the mainstream pattern. Recent NIC research has introduced various pure Transformer-based models, with the encoder and decoder composed entirely of Transformer, that significantly improve the performance of NIC. However, in the field of RSIC, research is still in its early stages.

The development of RSIC is not as rapid as that of NIC, but the same as NIC, the encoder-decoder framework is adopted as the mainstream pattern of research work. Qu et al. [13] first used an encoder-decoder framework (CNN + RNN/LSTM) for RSIC and released two RSIC datasets of UCM-captions and Sydney-captions. Considering the huge difference between low-level features and high-level semantics in remote sensing images, Zhang et al. [21] proposed an attribute attention mechanism, which utilizes the visual features of different layers of CNN to guide the attention computation of RSIC model. Wang et al. [18] proposed a word-sentence framework consisting of a word extractor and a sentence generator, which better explained the encoder-decoder architecture and was in line with human intuitive understanding. Zhang et al. [23] combined vanilla Transformer encoder-decoder with CNN to improve RSIC performance. Zhang et al. [20] proposed a multi-source interactive stair attention mechanism that separately models the semantics of preceding sentences and visual regions of interest in remote sensing images. Wang et al. [17] first utilizes a vision transformer to extract image features and a vanilla Transformer decoder to generate comprehensive sentences. The above-mentioned methods have promoted the development of RSIC in various aspects. However, despite these advances, there are still certain limitations in effectively exploring multiscale and multiobject visual information of remote sensing images.

3   Proposed Approach

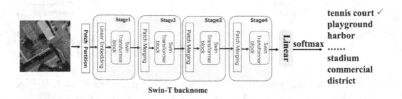

Fig. 3. The remote sensing image classification task using the Swin-T backbone pretrained on ImageNet-1k for feature awareness.

3.1   Classification-Based Feature Awareness

Inspired by the vision Transformers on CV tasks, we adopt the Swin-T pretrained on ImageNet-1k [4] as our backbone encoding network. Furthermore, considering the multiscale features specific to remote sensing images, we fine-tune the Swin-T on the remote sensing image classification task for better feature awareness. We can learn the specific characteristics of the unique data distribution by training the Swin-T on the remote sensing image classification task, as shown in Fig. 3, further improving Swin-T's ability to extract relevant visual features for the RSIC. We respectively fine-tune the Swin-T on two remote sensing image classification datasets: the UC Merced Land Usedataset (UCM) [19] and the Remote Sensing Image Scene Classification dataset created by Northwestern Polytechnical University (NWPU) [2]. Due to experimental device limitations, we randomly select a subset of images from each category in NWPU for fine-tuning. Table 1 provides the information of two datasets.

Table 1. General information about the datasets for the finetuning task.

Dataset	Number of categories	Total number of images	Image size
UCM [19]	21	2100	256×256
NWPU [2]	45	4500	256×256

3.2   Image Feature Representation

Effective image feature representation is critical for generating high-quality image captions. We then use the fine-tuned Swin-T as the image encoder to bridge the visual gap between natural and remote sensing images and learn the specific characteristics of remote sensing images to obtain multiscale features of remote sensing images. Specifically, we extract grid features $\mathbf{G}$ from images I at the last stage of the fine-tuned Swin-T as the multiscale visual features representation, where $\mathbf{G} \in \mathbb{R}^{m \times D}$, m is the number of gird features, and D is the embedding dimension of each gird feature.

3.3   Aware-Transformer-Based Caption Generation

The Aware-Transformer is based on a vanilla Transformer architecture, and has N identical encoding layers composed of multi-head self-attention (MSA) [14] and feed-forward network, which is consistent with the vanilla Transformer's encoder without any modifications. The encoding layers aim to enhance the visual features $\mathbf{G}$ by capturing the internal correlations among them:

$$\mathbf{V}_{\mathbf{G}}^1, \mathbf{V}_{\mathbf{G}}^2, ..., \mathbf{V}_{\mathbf{G}}^N = EncodingLayers\,(\mathbf{G}) \tag{1}$$

Note: Internal calculation processes such as positional encoding, residual operations, and layer normalization are omitted for brevity.

Unlike general Transformer-based models, which obtain encoded features from the top encoding layer and feed them directly to the decoder. Our proposed

MAM will first explore low- and high-level encoded features, and then apply spatial and channel attention to optimize it to obtain spatial-aware features $\mathbf{V_S}$ and channel-aware features $\mathbf{V_C}$ with the rich multiscale and multiobject visual information:

$$\mathbf{V_S}, \mathbf{V_C} = MAM\left(\mathbf{V_G^1}, \mathbf{V_G^2}, ..., \mathbf{V_G^N}\right) \qquad (2)$$

We then input $\mathbf{V_S}$ and $\mathbf{V_C}$ into the decoding layers, respectively. The decoding layers generates descriptive sentences by interacting with visual and linguistic features. We add positional encoding to the word embedding features as the linguistic features $\mathbf{X_{Emb}} \in \mathbb{R}^{(L-1) \times D}$ input to the first decoding layer, where L is the maximum word length in the training caption set.

$$S = DecodingLayers\left(\mathbf{V_S}, \mathbf{V_C}, \mathbf{X_{Emb}}\right) \qquad (3)$$

The decoding layer is also the same as the vanilla Transformer's decoder, which consists of two main components: Masked MSA and Cross MSA. So for the sake of brevity, we omit the internal calculation process. The detail of our MAM is described in the next subsection.

3.4   Multilevel Awareness Module (MAM)

To address the ignorance of multiscale and multiobject visual information, we propose a multilevel awareness module (MAM) that connects the Aware-Transformer encoding and decoding layers. The MAM aggregates encoded features from each encoding layer, addresses the loss of underlying visual information, and parallel employs spatial and channel attention mechanisms [1] to obtain spatial-aware and channel-aware features with the rich object and region visual information. Specifically, we concatenate the encoded features from each encoder layer and use a feed-forward network (FFN) with an adjustable weighting factor η to adaptively integrate low- and high-level encoded features. We then employ residual connections to add the encoded features from the top encoding layer and to obtain multiscale-aware features $\mathbf{V_M}$, which helps to retain the important visual information from the top encoding layer while incorporating the underlying visual information from the bottom layers.

$$\mathbf{V_G^{all}} = \left[\mathbf{V_G^1}; \mathbf{V_G^2}; ...; \mathbf{V_G^N}\right], \mathbf{V_M} = \mathbf{V_G^N} + \eta FFN\left(\mathbf{V_G^{all}}\right) \qquad (4)$$

Next, we parallel utilize the spatial and channel attention mechanism to obtain spatial-aware features and channel-aware features based on $\mathbf{V_M}$. Firstly, we spatially aggregate $\mathbf{V_M}$ to obtain a single feature $\mathbf{S_{mean}}$ that retains complete spatial information. Then, spatial attentive weights for $\mathbf{S_{mean}}$ are generated by the feed-forward network to enhance $\mathbf{V_M}$ and obtain spatial-aware features $\mathbf{V_S}$ that are aware of crucial objects in the image. Similarly, we aggregate the channel attention mechanism on the channel to obtain the channel descriptor $\mathbf{C_{mean}}$ to represent the channel-wise mean of $\mathbf{V_M}$. $\mathbf{C_{mean}}$ generates channel attentive weights through another feed-forward network to further enhance $\mathbf{V_M}$

and obtain channel-aware features $\mathbf{V_C}$ that are aware of overall image regions.

$$\mathbf{S_{mean}} = \frac{1}{D} \sum_{k=1}^{D} \mathbf{V_M(i,j,k)}, \mathbf{V_S} = \mathbf{V_M} \odot \mathrm{FFN}(\mathbf{S_{mean}}) \qquad (5)$$

$$\mathbf{C_{mean}} = \frac{1}{H \times W} \sum_{i=1}^{H} \sum_{j=1}^{W} \mathbf{V_M(i,j,k)}, \mathbf{V_C} = \mathbf{V_M} \odot \mathrm{FFN}(\mathbf{C_{mean}}) \qquad (6)$$

where $\mathbf{S_{mean}} \in \mathbb{R}^{H \times W \times 1}$, $\mathbf{C_{mean}} \in \mathbb{R}^{1 \times 1 \times D}$, and $H \times W = m$, $\odot$ represents the multiplication.

3.5 Captioning Training Algorithm

We optimize our pure Transformer captioning model by using cross-entropy loss function (XE):

$$L_{XE}(\theta) = - \sum_{t=1}^{T} \log(p_\theta(s_t \mid (s_1, \ldots s_{t-1}))) \qquad (7)$$

where θ denotes the parameters, $(s_1 \ldots s_T)$ is the ground-truth image sentence, and T is the length of the sentence.

4 Experiments and Results

4.1 Datasets Introductions and Evaluation Metrics

To validate the effectiveness of our proposed model, we conduct experiments on three publicly available RSIC datasets: Sydney-Captions [13], UCM-Captions [13], NWPU-Captions [3]. From these datasets, we used 80% of the data for training, 10% for evaluation, and 10% for testing.

To ensure a fair evaluation, we employ four widely-used metrics to assess the quality of the generated captions: BLEU [12], ROUGE-L [8], METEOR [5], and CIDEr [15]. A higher evaluation score indicates a better quality of the generated descriptions by the model.

Table 2. Ablation studies on the UCM-Captions dataset.

	Encoder-Decoder	BLEU-1	BLEU-2	BLEU-3	BLEU-4	METEOR	ROUGE-L	CIDEr
1	VGG16+Aware-T	82.0	75.8	70.7	66.4	42.7	77.6	305.1
2	VGG19+Aware-T	82.4	76.4	71.9	68.2	43.6	77.0	320.8
3	ResNet101+Aware-T	83.9	78.4	73.7	69.4	44.2	78.2	327.3
4	Swin-T+Aware-T w/o MAM	85.4	79.7	74.8	70.3	45.3	81.1	329.1
5	Swin-T+Aware-T	87.1	81.9	77.4	73.3	47.9	83.1	336.1
6	Swin-T(UCM)+Aware-T	**90.1**	**85.5**	**81.5**	**78.1**	**51.1**	**86.5**	**377.9**
7	Swin-T(NWPU)+Aware-T	89.9	84.9	80.6	76.8	49.9	85.4	371.5

4.2   Experimental Settings

Our method adopts a two-stage training scheme.

During the backbone fine-tuning stage, we set the output dimension to be the total number of categories in the two remote sensing image classification datasets. We employ the Adam optimizer with alpha and beta values of 0.9 and 0.999, respectively, with an initial learning rate of 1e-3, and train the model for 20 epochs. The fine-tuning process is considered complete when the classification accuracy of remote sensing images reaches and stabilizes at around 95%.

During the entire caption model training stage, we set the model embedding dimension D to 512, the number of MSA heads to 8, the hyper-parameter η = 0.2 in Eq. (4), and the number N of layers for both the Aware-Transformer encoding and decoding layers to 3. We train our model for 20 epochs using the cross-entropy loss L_{XE}, and set the batch size to 10. Note that the parameters in the Swin-T backbone network are kept fixed, and we use the Adam optimizer with default values of alpha and beta for other parameters. In the validation and evaluation process, we set the beam size to 5.

4.3   Ablation Study

We found our method behaves similarly on three datasets. For brevity, we only report the results on the UCM-Captions in Table 2.

Influence of Multilevel Awareness Module (MAM). Swin-T is a backbone network without fine-tuning. Aware-T represents the proposed Aware-Transformer. Aware-T w/o MAM denotes Aware-Transformer without the MAM. The results are presented in rows 4 and 5. It is observed that the MAM improves the accuracy of all evaluation metrics. (+1.7% on BLEU-1, +3.0% on BLEU-4, +2.6% on METEOR, +2.0% on ROUGE-L, +7.0% on CIDEr).

Table 3. Evaluation Scores (%) of our method and other State-of-the-Art methods on the UCM-Captions dataset. † represents retrieved from the original papers. '-' means not reported.

Methods	BLEU-1	BLEU-2	BLEU-3	BLEU-4	METEOR	ROUGE-L	CIDEr
CNN-LSTM based models							
Structured Attention [22] †	85.4	80.4	75.7	71.5	46.3	81.4	334.9
MLCA-Net [3] †	82.6	77.0	71.7	66.8	43.5	77.2	324.0
Multi-Source Attention [20] †	87.2	81.0	75.5	70.4	46.5	82.6	371.3
CNN-Transformer based models							
Word-Sentence [18] †	79.3	72.4	66.7	62.0	44.0	71.3	278.7
Grid Features [23] †	83.4	77.6	72.3	67.6	-	76.0	336.0
Transformer-Transformer based models							
Capformer [17]	83.3	76.8	71.7	67.2	44.3	78.4	324.8
Swin-T +Aware-T(our)	87.1	81.9	77.4	73.3	47.9	83.1	336.1
Swin-T (NWPU)+Aware-T (our)	89.9	84.9	80.6	76.8	49.9	85.4	371.5
Swin-T (UCM)+Aware-T (our)	**90.1**	**85.5**	**81.5**	**78.1**	**51.1**	**86.5**	**377.9**

Influence of Different Backbone Network. To evaluate the impact of different backbone networks on the quality of extracted features, we conduct experiments with different backbone configurations. The results are presented in rows 1, 2, 3, and 5, where we use VGG16, VGG19, ResNet101, and Swin-T as the backbone networks. VGG and ResNet are CNN-based architectures widely used in RSIC. Our results demonstrate that Swin-T achieves the best performance. Specifically, Swin-T outperforms ResNet101, VGG16, and VGG19 in extracting visual features for RSIC, which highlights the advantages of Swin-T in feature extraction for remote sensing images.

Influence of Feature Awareness. We conduct experiments to evaluate the impact of the fine-tuned Swin-T. Specifically, we use the fine-tuned Swin-T (i.e., Swin-T (UCM) and Swin-T (NWPU)) instead of the original pre-trained Swin-T (i.e., Swin-T), while keeping other configurations unchanged. The results are presented in rows 5, 6, and 7, where Swin-T (UCM) and Swin-T (NWPU) refer to Swin-T fine-tuned on the UCM dataset and NWPU dataset, respectively. Compared to Swin-T without fine-tuning, using either Swin-T (UCM) or Swin-T (NWPU) shows significant performance improvement. This indicates that using feature awareness through fine-tuning can help alleviate the visual gap between natural images and remote sensing images, leading to improved captioning accuracy of the entire model.

Table 4. Evaluation scores (%) of our method and other State-of-the-Art methods on Sydney-Captions. † represents retrieved from the original papers. '-' means not reported.

Methods	BLEU-1	BLEU-2	BLEU-3	BLEU-4	METEOR	ROUGE-L	CIDEr
CNN-LSTM based models							
Structured Attention [22] †	77.9	70.2	63.9	58.6	39.5	73.0	237.9
MLCA-Net [3] †	83.1	74.2	65.9	58.0	39.0	71.1	232.4
Multi-Source Attention [20] †	76.4	69.2	62.8	57.3	39.5	71.7	281.2
CNN-Transformer based models							
Word-Sentence [18] †	78.9	70.9	63.2	56.3	41.8	69.2	204.1
Grid Features [23] †	81.0	73.2	65.0	57.1	-	74.9	256.7
Transformer-Transformer based models							
Capformer [17]	82.3	74.0	65.6	57.9	42.0	74.9	258.8
Swin-T +Aware-T(our)	84.2	76.9	68.6	60.7	43.3	76.6	261.7
Swin-T (NWPU)+Aware-T (our)	**85.4**	**78.0**	**71.2**	**65.1**	**45.1**	**78.3**	283.2
Swin-T (UCM)+Aware-T (our)	84.7	77.3	69.9	62.9	44.5	77.1	**292.2**

4.4 Comparison with State-of-the-Art Methods

We compare the proposed method with some state-of-the-art methods on the Sydney-Captions, UCM-Captions and NWPU-Captions datasets, and the results

114   Y. Cao et al.

are shown in Table 3, Table 4 and Table 5. The best scores are marked as bold. Notably, the pure Transformer architecture outperforms most CNN-Transformer and CNN-LSTM methods on three RSIC datasets. Additionally, our model achieves the highest scores on all datasets without fine-tuning the Swin-T. When we do fine-tune the Swin-T on remote sensing images, the accuracy of our model is further improved. We believe that our novel pure Transformer architecture is particularly well-suited for training on large datasets. For instance, our approach demonstrates a remarkable improvement in the NWPU-Captions dataset. Even without the fine-tuned Swin-T, we achieve an average improvement of 11.2% on BLEU-1, 8.9% on METEOR, 13.5% on ROUGE-L, and 57.0% on CIDEr compared to other methods.

(a): There is a church with a blue circular roof next to the road. (b): The lake lies in farmland and the water is dark blue. (c): There are many buildings next to the ground track field. (d): The river goes through yellow bare land. (e): There are many buildings next to the thermal power station.

Fig. 4. Heat-map visualization of the MAM's channel and spatial attention preferences. The brighter regions in the heat maps indicate the channel and spatial attention preferences of the models, showcasing the visual content that they focus on during the caption generation process.

4.5   Qualitative Results Analysis

Figure 4 shows channel-attentive and spatial-attentive heat maps along with captions generated by our model from the NWPU-Captions dataset. The captions generated by our method are grammatically correct, logically sound, and capture the main object attributes in the image, such as church, road, lake, river, buildings, power station. The heat maps demonstrate the respective attention mechanisms' ability to focus on visual content for caption generation. The brighter regions in the spatial and channel heat maps exhibit their focusing capability. Specifically, the spatial attention mechanism focuses on significant geospatial

Table 5. Evaluation Scores (%) of our method and other State-of-the-Art methods on the NWPU-Captions dataset. † represents retrieved from the original papers.

Methods	BLEU-1	BLEU-2	BLEU-3	BLEU-4	METEOR	ROUGE-L	CIDEr
CNN-LSTM based models							
FC-Att+LSTM [21] †	73.6	61.5	53.2	46.9	33.8	60.0	123.1
SM-Att+LSTM [21] †	73.9	61.7	53.2	46.8	33.0	59.3	123.6
MLCA-Net [3] †	74.5	62.4	54.1	47.8	33.7	60.1	126.4
CNN-Transformer based models							
Grid Features [23]	88.1	80.3	73.9	68.8	44.3	77.4	197.0
Transformer-Transformer based models							
Capformer [17]	89.0	81.1	74.5	69.2	45.4	78.4	201.9
Swin-T+Aware-T(our)	91.0	84.2	78.1	73.1	46.9	80.5	211.4
Swin-T (NWPU)+Aware-T(our)	**91.5**	**85.2**	**79.6**	**75.0**	**47.7**	**81.1**	**214.7**
Swin-T(UCM)+Aware-T(our)	91.2	84.5	78.9	74.3	47.5	80.8	212.7

objects. On the other hand, the channel attention mechanism disperses throughout the visual region to collect scale, positional, directional, and relational information. This demonstrates the effectiveness of our MAM in enhancing multiscale and multiobject information in remote sensing images.

5   Conclusion

In this paper, we propose a novel pure Transformer-based model with a feature awareness strategy to address the challenge of efficiently capturing multiscale and multiobject visual information in remote sensing images. Specifically, we first fine-tune the Swin-Transformer and extract visual features as the multiscale feature representation. Then, we introduce an Aware-Transformer to enhance multiscale and multiobject visual information and explore the interaction with linguistic features to generate accurate and detailed captions. The experimental results demonstrate the effectiveness of our method. Moreover, our method offers a reliable solution for RSIC, bringing significant performance improvements. We anticipate that the pure Transformer architecture will emerge as a significant research direction in the field of remote sensing image captioning in the future.

References

1. Chen, L., et al.: SCA-CNN: spatial and channel-wise attention in convolutional networks for image captioning. In: Proceedings of the IEEE Conference on Computer Vision and Pattern Recognition, pp. 5659–5667 (2017)
2. Cheng, G., Han, J., Lu, X.: Remote sensing image scene classification: benchmark and state of the art. Proc. IEEE **105**(10), 1865–1883 (2017)
3. Cheng, Q., Huang, H., Xu, Y., Zhou, Y., Li, H., Wang, Z.: NWPU-captions dataset and MLCA-net for remote sensing image captioning. IEEE Trans. Geosci. Remote Sens. **60**, 1–19 (2022)

4. Deng, J., Dong, W., Socher, R., Li, L.J., Li, K., Fei-Fei, L.: Imagenet: a large-scale hierarchical image database. In: 2009 IEEE Conference on Computer Vision and Pattern Recognition, pp. 248–255. IEEE (2009)
5. Denkowski, M., Lavie, A.: Meteor universal: language specific translation evaluation for any target language. In: Proceedings of the Ninth Workshop on Statistical Machine Translation, pp. 376–380 (2014)
6. Huang, S., et al.: TransMRSR: transformer-based self-distilled generative prior for brain MRI super-resolution. Vis. Comput. **39**(8), 3647–3659 (2023)
7. Jain, D., Kumar, A., Beniwal, R.: Personality BERT: a transformer-based model for personality detection from textual data. In: Proceedings of International Conference on Computing and Communication Networks: ICCCN, pp. 515–522 (2022)
8. Lin, C.Y.: Rouge: a package for automatic evaluation of summaries. In: Text summarization branches out, pp. 74–81 (2004)
9. Lin, X., Sun, S., Huang, W., Sheng, B., Li, P., Feng, D.D.: EAPT: efficient attention pyramid transformer for image processing. IEEE Trans. Multimedia **25**, 50–61 (2023)
10. Liu, Z., et al.: Swin transformer: hierarchical vision transformer using shifted windows. In: Proceedings of the IEEE/CVF International Conference on Computer Vision, pp. 10012–10022 (2021)
11. Miao, Y., Liu, K., Yang, W., Yang, C.: A novel transformer-based model for dialog state tracking. In: International Conference on Human-Computer Interaction, pp. 148–156 (2022)
12. Papineni, K., Roukos, S., Ward, T., Zhu, W.J.: Bleu: a method for automatic evaluation of machine translation. In: Proceedings of the 40th annual meeting of the Association for Computational Linguistics, pp. 311–318 (2002)
13. Qu, B., Li, X., Tao, D., Lu, X.: Deep semantic understanding of high resolution remote sensing image. In: 2016 International Conference on Computer, Information and Telecommunication Systems (CITS), pp. 1–5 (2016)
14. Vaswani, A., et al.: Attention is all you need. In: Advances in Neural Information Processing Systems, vol. 30 (2017)
15. Vedantam, R., Lawrence Zitnick, C., Parikh, D.: Cider: consensus-based image description evaluation. In: Proceedings of the IEEE Conference on Computer Vision and Pattern Recognition, pp. 4566–4575 (2015)
16. Vinyals, O., Toshev, A., Bengio, S., Erhan, D.: Show and tell: a neural image caption generator. In: 2015 IEEE Conference on Computer Vision and Pattern Recognition (CVPR), pp. 3156–3164 (2015)
17. Wang, J., Chen, Z., Ma, A., Zhong, Y.: Capformer: pure transformer for remote sensing image caption. In: IGARSS 2022–2022 IEEE International Geoscience and Remote Sensing Symposium, pp. 7996–7999. IEEE (2022)
18. Wang, Q., Huang, W., Zhang, X., Li, X.: Word-sentence framework for remote sensing image captioning. IEEE Trans. Geosci. Remote Sens. **59**(12), 10532–10543 (2021)
19. Yang, Y., Newsam, S.: Bag-of-visual-words and spatial extensions for land-use classification. In: Proceedings of the 18th SIGSPATIAL International Conference on Advances in Geographic Information Systems, pp. 270–279 (2010)
20. Zhang, X., et al.: Multi-source interactive stair attention for remote sensing image captioning. Remote Sens. **15**(3), 579 (2023)
21. Zhang, X., Wang, X., Tang, X., Zhou, H., Li, C.: Description generation for remote sensing images using attribute attention mechanism. Remote Sens. **11**(6), 612 (2019)

22. Zhao, R., Shi, Z., Zou, Z.: High-resolution remote sensing image captioning based on structured attention. IEEE Trans. Geosci. Remote Sens. **60**, 1–14 (2021)

23. Zhuang, S., Wang, P., Wang, G., Wang, D., Chen, J., Gao, F.: Improving remote sensing image captioning by combining grid features and transformer. IEEE Geosci. Remote Sens. Lett. **19**, 1–5 (2022)

Blind Image Quality Assessment Method Based on DeepSA-Net

Haobing Tian$^{(\boxtimes)}$, Jingyi Li, Qi Yan, Yang Zhong, Lang Zhang,
and Pengju Jiao

China Mobile (Suzhou) Software Technology Company Limited,
Suzhou 215163, China
tianhaobing@cmss.chinamobile.com

Abstract. Blind image quality assessment refers to the accurate prediction of the visual quality of any input image without a reference image. With the rapid growth of the number of images and increasing requirements for image quality, how to assess image quality has become an urgent problem. Complex images are difficult to consider professionally from a single perspective. A blind image quality assessment algorithm based on a deep semantic adaptation network (DeepSA-Net) is proposed. Based on the end-to-end deep learning model, the semantic pre-trained models and multi-resolution adaptive module are added. The adaptive factor α is proposed to better capture global and local quality information and fuse multi-resolution features to improve the convergence ability and speed of the network. Finally, the quality assessment results of images are obtained by regression. The experiment used the Spearman correlation coefficient and Pearson correlation coefficient as assessment indicators. The results showed that DeepSA-Net outperformed most current methods in real distortion scene databases and had excellent assessment ability in synthetic distortion databases. In addition, ablation study and different distortion studies were designed to fully validate the effectiveness and feasibility of the algorithm.

Keywords: Blind image quality assessment · Deep neural network · Self-supervised semantic learning · Multi-resolution fusion

1 Introduction

With the development of society and technology, digital imaging and communication technologies are rapidly gaining popularity in daily life. But images introduce a variety of distortions during acquisition, compression, transmission and storage, resulting in degradation of image quality [1–5]. To assess the performance of image compression algorithms, the design of image quality assessment methods has become an important task in the field of image processing [6,7]. As

Supported by organization China Mobile (Suzhou) Software Technology Company Limited.

B. Sheng et al. (Eds.): CGI 2023, LNCS 14495, pp. 118–129, 2024.
https://doi.org/10.1007/978-3-031-50069-5_11

the original images are difficult to obtain, the blind image has become a research hotspot in the field of image quality assessment [8–11].

The current blind image quality assessment methods can be divided into two categories, one is to first extract image features, and then use machine learning methods to train a mapping model between image features and quality assessment results, such as NIQE, BRISQUE, PGF-BIQA, CoDIQE3D; the other is an assessment model based on an end-to-end framework that uses deep learning methods to train the quality assessment model, such as HOSA, BIECON, DBCNN, SCIs-IQA [12,13]. Mittal et al. [14] proposed a natural image quality evaluator (NIQE), which was based on a spatial domain natural image statistical model. Moorthy et al. [15] proposed a blind referenceless image spatial quality evaluator (BRISQUE), which used linear least squares to train the model. Liu et al. [16] proposed a blind image quality assessment algorithm via probability gcForest (PGF-BIQA), it used five qualitative labels to replace the specific quality score, and extracted image color and textured features to represent image quality. Poreddy et al. [17] proposed a stereoscopic image quality estimator named CoDIQE3D, which utilizes the color and depth of stereoscopic images for modeling, and then estimates the overall perceived quality of stereoscopic images. Xu et al. [18] proposed a blind image quality assessment method based on high order statistics aggregation (HOSA), it supported vector regression to learn the mapping between perceptual features and subjective opinion scores. Kim et al. [19] proposed a blind image evaluator based on a convolutional neural network (BIECON), which added a pooling layer to regress the features extracted from convolutional neural network (CNN). Zhang et al. [20] proposed a deep bilinear CNN (DBCNN) model, which consisted of two deep CNNs that dealt with synthetic distortion and real distortion, respectively. Ji et al. [21] proposed a no-reference image quality assessment named SCVS, which using visual saliency and Gaussian function to consider the quality of different blocks.

Since most of the traditional image quality assessment metrics are assessed from a single perspective such as structure and noise, they cannot adequately reflect the image quality of multiple scenes and features [22–24]. In this paper, we propose an image quality assessment algorithm based on semantic understanding and multi-resolution feature adaption called DeepSA-Net. The main contributions of this work can be summarized as follows:

1. We propose multi-resolution adaptive module and factor α to better capture global and local quality information and fuse multi-resolution features.
2. We design a novel the semantic pre-trained models to better capture the content information embedded in the images.
3. DeepSA-Net outperforms most current methods in real distortion scene databases and has great assessment ability in synthetic distortion databases.

2 Image Quality Assessment Algorithm Based on DeepSA-Net

2.1 Overview

The pipeline of the image quality assessment algorithm based on the deep semantic adaptation network (DeepSA-Net) is shown in Fig. 1, which mainly consists of the following five parts. A pre-trained model for learning semantic features, a quality assessment dataset, a backbone network for extracting features, a multi-resolution adaptive regression module, and predicting image quality assessment scores.

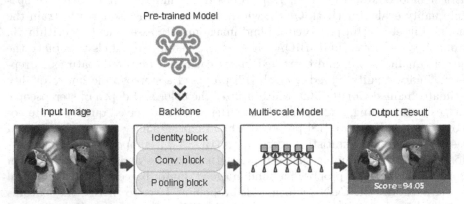

Fig. 1. The pipeline of the image quality assessment method proposed.

2.2 Self-supervised Semantic Learning Models

In this paper, we proposed the self-supervised random swapping and contrasting views (RSCV) algorithm based on pooling block deep ResNet (PBDResNet), which performed contrastive learning on the unlabeled image dataset to capture potential semantic features. The model performed random data enhancement on the original image, such as brightness, contrast, saturation, random rotation, random cropping, random scaling, which ensured the generalization ability of the model. Contrastive learning by learning similar or dissimilar features of two images, was ensured that the similar samples were made as close to each other as possible, and the different samples were increasingly distant. The RSCV algorithm architecture is shown in Fig. 2.

The specific objective formula of the RSCV algorithm is shown in Eq. 1, Where x is the given data, and x^+ is a positive sample with similar features to x, x^- is a negative sample with dissimilar features to x, $Sim()$ is a measurement function to measure the similarity of the sample features. $Sim(*)$ is generally chosen as Euclidean distance or cosine similarity. To better optimize the model encoder f, the loss function use a modified SimCVLoss is shown in Eq. 2.

$$Sim(f(x), f(x^+)) \gg Sim(f(x), f(x^-)) \tag{1}$$

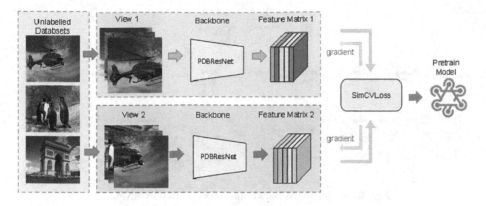

Fig. 2. RSCV algorithm architecture.

$$L_{SimCV} = -\frac{log[exp(Sim(f(x), f(x^+))) * exp(Sim(f(x), f(x_j)))]}{exp(Sim(f(x), f(x^+))) + \sum_{i=0}^{n-1} exp(Sim(f(x), f(x_j)))} \quad (2)$$

This loss function trained the model by maximizing the positive sample similarity and minimizing the negative sample similarity. It is more consistent with the goal of image-level comparative learning of different views, and more suitable for image quality assessment tasks.

2.3   Backbone Network Architecture

DeepSA-Net was proposed based on the PBDResNet with a multi-resolution feature fusion module. The weights of the pre-trained model in the previous subsection were loaded and supervised training was performed using multiple image quality evaluation datasets. The pooling deep residual network PBDResNet was used as the backbone network for extracting the semantic feature in the images. Due to the problems of excessive parameters and complexity of the aforementioned model, the deep neural network might suffer from severe overfitting during the training process. PBDResNet not only used convolutional block and identity block, but also added a pooling strategy. Max pooling focused excessively on foreground information and average pooling highlighted background information, but for the foreground and background information of an image were equally important. Stochastic pooling was chosen to calculate the value according to the feature values and the probability. It was not only can reduce the feature dimensionality of the convolutional layer output, but also can reduce the network parameters with lower computational cost and avoid overfitting. This study took advantage of pooling to reduce unnecessary redundant parameters, and further improved the training speed and the accuracy of quality assessment.

Each residue block consisted of three convolutional layers with convolutional kernels of different sizes (1×1, 3×3 and 1×1 in size) and different numbers of filters (64, 128, 256 or 512) to generate a multi-resolution feature matrix. The

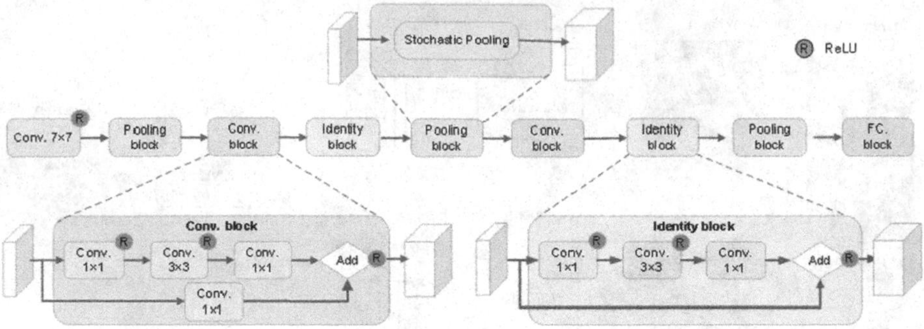

Fig. 3. Structure of backbone network PBDResNet.

backbone network structure is shown in Fig. 3. Conv. block represents a set of convolutional layers.

In addition, each block used a residual network structure, and a shortcut was used in each residual block to splice and fuse the input and output features, which was used to compensate for the detailed information lost in the semantic feature extraction process. The feature mapping process is shown in Eq. 3. Where $F(*)$ represents the activation function and W_i denotes the weight of the convolution learned in the ith block ($1 \leq i \leq 33$). $W_{1\times1}$ represents the weight of the convolution layer with a convolution kernel size of 1×1. Better extraction of original image features while deepening the number of network layers helped to solve the gradient disappearance and gradient explosion. The last convolutional layer in PBDResNet output a feature matrix that contained rich information.

$$y = \begin{cases} F(y, W_i) + y, & i = 1, 4, 8, 31 \\ F(y, W_i) + yW_{1\times1}, & others \end{cases} \tag{3}$$

2.4   Adaptive Perception Image Assessment Algorithm

This study was based on an improved image quality assessment model based on a multi-resolution quality assessment (MR-QA) network. The coding part used four multi-resolution dilation convolutional layers and a global pooling layer. The multi-resolution convolution layer rate was set as 1, α, 2α, 3α, α was an adaptive factor according to the size of images, when α was 1, it was a traditional convolution layer, when α was an integer greater than 1, it was a multi-resolution convolution layer, and the α was dynamically adjusted during the backpropagation process and ranges from $[1, image\_size^{1/2}]$. Adding adaptive factors to expand the perceptual field was helpful to improve the convergence ability and convergence speed of the network, which was used to capture multi-resolution visual features and global-local information. The upsampling in the multi-resolution convolutional network was improved by upsampling the outputs of the convolutional layers with different step expansions separately to minimize the loss of semantic information. The multi-resolution feature matrix after upsampling was stitched through a 1×1 convolutional layer. In the quality assessment network, the advanced feature matrix after multi-resolution convolution was bilinearly upsampled with the original input features, using the Sigmoid function as the activation function. Finally, it was fed into the fully connected layer, and the quality assessment score corresponding to each input image was weighted by the ensemble algorithm. The network architecture of MR-QA is shown in Fig. 4.

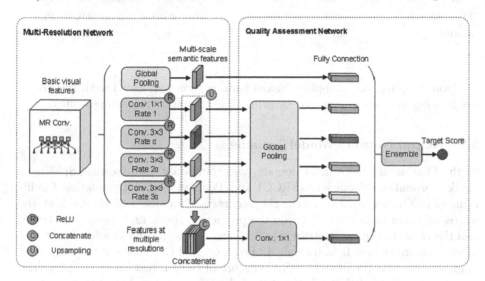

Fig. 4. Deep learning MR-QA network architecture.

3   Results and Analysis

3.1   Data Collection and Processing

In this study, four public databases commonly used for image quality assessment were used, namely, LIVE [25], CSIQ [26], TID2013 [27] and KonIQ-10k [28]. The basic information of the above databases are listed in Table 1, containing common synthetic and real distortions, where the LIVE into distortions including JPEG, JPEG2000 compression (JP2K), Gaussian white noise (WN), Gaussian blur (GB) and fast fading signal distortion (FF). MOS and DMOS were used as image quality assessment metrics. The three databases, LIVE, CSIQ, and TID2013, are based on a set of original images with multiple synthetic distortions, and the KonIQ-10k database contains 10,073 real distorted images. The above datasets can verify the generalization performance of the model under a variety of distortion scenarios.

To avoid overestimation of model performance, this study used a ten-fold cross-validation to assess model performance, with 80% for the training set and 20% for the testing set. The training was repeatedly executed until all parts had served as the training set and testing set. The number of datasets was expanded to ten times the original size using data augmentation such as random

Table 1. Overview of database.

Database	Number of raw images	Number of distorted images	Number of distortion types	Distortion Type	Score type and range
LIVE	29	779	5	synthetic distortions	DMOS[0,100]
CSIQ	30	866	6	synthetic distortions	DMOS[0,1]
TID2013	25	3000	24	synthetic distortions	MOS[0,9]
KonIQ	–	10773	–	real distortions	MOS[0,5]

rotation, flipping, and cropping. Model training was performed until the loss of the training set was minimized, ensuring that the model was more robust.

3.2   Neural Network Model Training

In the blind image assessment domain, two commonly used metrics, Spearman Rank Correlation Coefficient (SRCC) and Pearson Linear Correlation Coefficient (PLCC), are used to assess the accuracy of model, and they reflect the degree of linear correlation between the prediction result and the ground truth, and the range of the two metrics is $[-1, 1]$, and the larger the absolute value, the more accurate the prediction result. In Eq. 4, Q_s^i and Q_o^i represent the subjective opinion score and the model prediction score of the ith test image, respectively. σ_X and σ_Y represent the variance of the subjective score and the variance of the test image prediction score, respectively. In Eq. 5, N is the total number of test images, and Q_o^i and Q_s^i indicate the subjective opinion score and model prediction score of the ith test image, respectively. Subjective scoring of image quality by the observer is usually done using MOS, or DOM, which is the difference between human eye assessment scores for distortion-free and distorted images.

$$PLCC = \frac{\sum_i^N (Q_s^i - Q_s^{mean})(Q_o^i - Q_o^{mean})}{(N-1) \times \sigma_X \times \sigma_Y} \tag{4}$$

$$SRCC = 1 - \frac{6 \sum_i^N ((Q_o^i - Q_s^i)^2)}{N(N^2 - 1)} \tag{5}$$

Subjective scoring of image quality by the observer is usually done using mean opinion score (MOS), or differential mean opinion score (DMOS), which is the difference between human eye assessment scores for distortion-free and distorted images. The calculation formula for MOS is shown in, Eq. 6, where P is the total number of participants in the rating and $S(i)$ is the score of the ith person. The calculation formula for DMOS is shown in Eq. 7, where MOS_{src} stands for the assessment score for distortion-free images and MOS_{dst} stands for the assessment score for distorted images.

$$MOS = \frac{\sum_{i=1}^{P} S(i)}{P} \qquad (6)$$

$$DOMS = MOS_{src} - MOS_{dst} \qquad (7)$$

Smooth L1 is used as the loss function for training, and it is shows in Eq. 8. Where Q is the batch size for training, M_i is the MOS of the ith sample of this batch, and P_i is the predicted MOS of the ith sample of this batch. The training process used an Adam optimizer with a weight decay of 5×10^{-4} and a maximum training round of 20. The learning rate was set to 1×10^{-3} and will go to the original value 0.1 times after every 5 iterations.

$$L = \frac{1}{Q} \sum_{i}^{Q} \begin{cases} 0.5(P_i - M_i)^2, & |P_i - M_i| < 1 \\ |P_i - M_i| - \frac{1}{2}, & others \end{cases} \qquad (8)$$

3.3 Model Performance Comparison

Comparison of Algorithms of the Same Type. To assess the methods proposed, five state-of-the-art image quality assessment methods were selected for the experiments, including traditional machine learning-based regression methods and end-to-end deep learning-based methods. The experiments were based on the LIVE, CSIQ, TID2013 and KonIQ datasets assessed, trained and tested on each dataset and compared to multiple methods, the results of which are shown in Table 2. The prediction results on the four datasets outperformed all state-of-the-art methods, indicating that the incorporation of multi-resolution semantic information contributes to the prediction of image quality.

Table 2. Performance comparison of DeepSA-Net and classical similar algorithms on image assessment databases.

Dataset	LIVE		CSIQ		TID2013		KonIQ	
Method	SRCC	PLCC	SRCC	PLCC	SRCC	PLCC	SRCC	PLCC
NIQE [14]	0.921	0.916	0.803	0.807	0.513	0.553	0.531	0.568
BRISQUE [15]	0.938	0.935	0.935	0.929	0.568	0.641	0.675	0.691
HOSA [18]	0.945	0.947	0.936	0.901	0.689	0.761	0.759	0.768
BIECON [19]	0.961	0.962	0.815	0.820	0.713	0.759	0.606	0.613
DBCNN [20]	0.963	0.966	0.936	0.949	0.800	0.831	0.865	0.884
DeepSA-Net	**0.970**	**0.974**	**0.939**	**0.955**	**0.845**	**0.857**	**0.870**	**0.886**

The prediction results for each method were plotted as scatter plots and non-linear curves were fitted using a logistic function. This provided a visual representation of the ability of model to assess image quality, as shown in Fig. 5. Each point in the scatter plot represented a test image, the X-axis represented

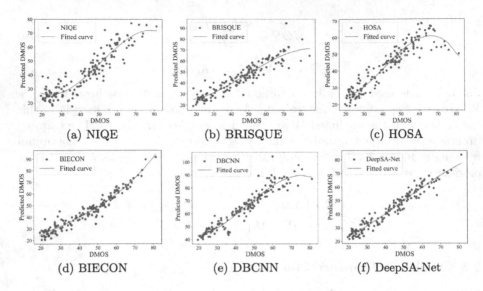

Fig. 5. Comparison of scatter plots and fitted curves using different IQA tools based on LIVE database.

the ground truth DMOS of the image as scored by multiple people, and the Y-axis represented the predicted DMOS of the image quality. It can be seen from the images that there was a higher correlation between the predicted scores and ground truth, and there were fewer outliers. It indicated that the model performed better and was more consistent with the subjective scores.

Comparison of Distortion Type Results. To verify the generalization ability of the model, the experimental compared the performance of image quality assessment under different distortion scenarios. The precision was significantly reduced in the case of severe image distortion, especially in the case of both WN and FF distortion scenarios. As shown in Table 3, each method has a strong prediction capability for images in one or both distortion scenarios, and our method has a strong advantage over other algorithms in the three distortion scenarios JP2K, JPEG and GB, and the model performance is also competitive in both WN and FF distortion conditions.

Optimization of Training Parameters. The current datasets on the field of image quality assessment were small in size, and there was a problem of inconsistent image size in multiple datasets, and scaling the images to the same size will affect the image quality. Therefore, to ensure the uniformity of the training data and the adequacy of the training process, the image resolution was randomly cropped from the original 1280×720 and 512×384 to 224×224 image patches, and the scores of the image patches inherited the scores of the original images. To further investigate the effect of the number of image patches

Table 3. SRCC and PLCC comparison of different distortion types on LIVE datasets.

Distortion Type	JP2K		JPEG		WN		GB		FF	
Method	SRCC	PLCC	SRCC	PLCC	SRCC	PLCC	SRCC	PLCC	SRCC	PLCC
NIQE [14]	0.917	0.937	0.938	0.956	0.967	0.977	0.934	0.952	0.859	0.913
BRISQUE [15]	0.914	0.923	0.965	0.973	0.977	0.985	0.951	0.951	0.877	0.903
HOSA [18]	0.932	0.940	0.950	0.961	0.975	0.978	0.944	0.951	0.936	0.953
BIECON [19]	0.942	0.955	0.964	0.977	0.970	0.970	0.946	0.945	0.923	0.931
DBCNN [20]	0.969	0.962	0.955	0.978	0.976	0.975	0.925	0.946	0.920	0.948
DeepSA-Net	**0.971**	**0.975**	**0.974**	**0.979**	0.970	0.977	**0.953**	**0.959**	0.930	0.951

on the image quality assessment, the number of image patches was set to 5, 10, 15, 20, 25 and 30 for training and testing on the LIVE and TID2013 datasets respectively, and the experimental result are shown in Fig. 6. On both LIVE and TID2013 datasets, the performance of the model reached the optimum when the number of image patches was 25.

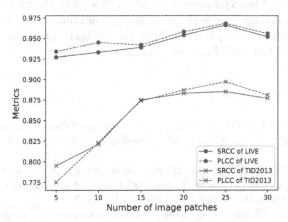

Fig. 6. The impact of the number of image patches on model performance.

Ablation Study. In this paper, we analyzed the impact of the semantic pre-trained model and adaptive network module on image quality assessment through ablation experiments. DeepSA-Net w/o AD and DeepSA-Net w/o SE represent the removal of adaptive module and removal of semantic pre-trained model respectively. The experiments were trained and tested on the LIVE dataset, and the experimental results are shown in Table 4. The performance of the image quality assessment model was enhanced considerably due to the addition of the convolutional adaptive factor, which increased the image perceptual field. Also adding the adaptive network module with semantic pre-trained of the model eventually achieved a great performance improvement and outperforms the same type of methods.

Table 4. Results of the ablation study.

Dataset	LIVE	
Module	SRCC	PLCC
DeepSA-Net w/o AD+SE	0.923	0.927
DeepSA-Net w/o AD	0.936	0.938
DeepSA-Net w/o SE	0.953	0.956
DeepSA-Net	**0.975**	**0.979**

4   Conclusion

This paper propose a DeepSA-Net-based blind image quality assessment algorithm to overcome the loss of information at different scales and lack of semantic understanding. The network introduce semantic pre-trained model to capture the content information embedded in the images, while a multi-resolution adaptive factor is added to expand the perceptual field and reduce unnecessary missing image information. The experimental results reveal that DeepSA-Net has better performance and stronger generalization ability, and has certain advantages and strong competitiveness compared with similar methods, providing novel idea for subsequent applications of blind image quality assessment.

References

1. Niu, Y., Huang, D., Shi, Y., et al.: Siamese-network-based learning to rank for no-reference 2D and 3D image quality assessment. IEEE Access **7**, 101583–101595 (2019)
2. Su, S., Yan, Q., Zhu, Y., et al.: Blindly assess image quality in the wild guided by a self-adaptive hyper network. In: 2020 IEEE/CVF Conference on Computer Vision and Pattern Recognition (CVPR). IEEE (2020)
3. Feng, Y., Li, S., Chang, Y.: Multi-scale feature-guided stereoscopic video quality assessment based on 3D convolutional neural network. In: ICASSP 2021–2021 IEEE International Conference on Acoustics, Speech and Signal Processing (ICASSP), Toronto, ON, Canada. IEEE (2021)
4. He, L., Zhong, Y., Lu, W., et al.: A visual residual perception optimized network for blind image quality assessment. IEEE Access **7**, 176087–176098 (2019)
5. Ma, J., Wu, J., Li, L., et al.: Active inference of GAN for no-reference image quality assessment. In: 2020 IEEE International Conference on Multimedia and Expo (ICME). IEEE (2020)
6. Varga, D., Szirányi, T.: No-reference video quality assessment via pretrained CNN and LSTM networks. Sig. Imgage Video Process. **13**, 1569–1576 (2019)
7. Moorthy, A., Bovik, A.: Visual importance pooling for image quality assessment. IEEE J. Sel. Topics Sig. Process. **3**(2), 193–201 (2009)
8. Suresh, S., Babu, R., Kim, H.: No-reference image quality assessment using modified extreme learning machine classifier. Appl. Soft Comput. **9**(2), 541–552 (2009)

9. Javier, G., Sébastien, M., Julian, F.: Image quality assessment for fake biometric detection: application to iris, fingerprint, and face recognition. IEEE Trans. Image Process. **23**(2), 710–24 (2015)
10. Babu, R., Suresh, S., Perkis, A.: No-reference JPEG-image quality assessment using GAP-RBF. Sig. Process. **87**(6), 1493–1503 (2007)
11. Cai, R., Fang, M.: Blind image quality assessment by simulating the visual cortex. Vis. Comput. 1–18 (2022)
12. Mittal, A., Muralidhar, G., Ghosh, J., et al.: Blind image quality assessment without human training using latent quality factors. IEEE Sig. Process. Lett. **19**(2), 75–78 (2012)
13. Tang, H., Joshi, N., Kapoor, A.: Blind image quality assessment using semi-supervised rectifier networks. In: IEEE Conference on Computer Vision and Pattern Recognition. IEEE Computer Society, CVPR (2014)
14. Mittal, A.: Making a 'completely blind' image quality analyzer. IEEE Sig. Process. Lett. **20**(3), 209–212 (2013)
15. Mittal, A., Moorthy, A.K., Bovik, A.C.: No-reference image quality assessment in the spatial domain. IEEE Trans. Image Process. **21**(12), 4695–4708 (2012)
16. Liu, H., Li, C., Jin, S., et al.: PGF-BIQA: blind image quality assessment via probability multi-grained cascade forest. Comput. Vis. Image Und. **232**, 103695 (2023)
17. Poreddy, A., Kara, P., Tamboli, R., et al.: CoDIQE3D: a completely blind, no-reference stereoscopic image quality estimator using joint color and depth statistics. Vis. Comput. (2023)
18. Xu, J., Ye, P., Li, Q., et al.: Blind image quality assessment based on high order statistics aggregation. IEEE Trans. Image Process. 4444–4457 (2016)
19. Kim, J., Lee, S.: Fully deep blind image quality predictor. IEEE J. Sel. Top. Sig. Process. **11**(1), 206–220 (2017)
20. Zhang, W., Ma, K., Yan, J., et al.: Blind image quality assessment using a deep bilinear convolutional neural network. IEEE Trans. Circuits Syst. 1 (2019)
21. Ji, J., Xiang, K., Wang, X.: SCVS: blind image quality assessment based on spatial correlation and visual saliency. Vis. Comput. **39**, 443–458 (2023)
22. Saad, M., Bovik, A., Charrier, C.: Blind image quality assessment: a natural scene statistics approach in the DCT domain. IEEE Trans. Image Process. **21**(8), 3339–3352 (2012)
23. Zhang, C., Huang, Z., Liu, S., et al.: Dual-channel multi-task CNN for no-reference screen content image quality assessment. IEEE T. Syst. Video **32**(8), 5011–5025 (2022)
24. Varga, D., Saupe, D., Sziranyi, T.: DeepRN: a content preserving deep architecture for blind image quality assessment. In: 2018 IEEE International Conference on Multimedia and Expo (ICME). IEEE (2018)
25. Bovik, A., Sabir, M., Sheikh, H.: A statistical evaluation of recent full reference image quality assessment algorithms. IEEE Trans. Image Process. **15**(11), 3440–3451 (2006)
26. Chandler, L.: Most apparent distortion: full-reference image quality assessment and the role of strategy. J. Elecron. Imaging **19**(1), 011006 (2010)
27. Ponomarenko, N., Ieremeiev, O., Lukin, V., et al.: Color image database TID2013: peculiarities and preliminary results. In: European Workshop on Visual Information Processing. IEEE (2013)
28. Hosu, V., Lin, H., Sziranyi, T., et al.: KonIQ-10k: an ecologically valid database for deep learning of blind image quality assessment. IEEE Trans. Image Process. **29**, 4041–4056 (2020)

Deep Feature Learning for Image-Based Kinship Verification

Shuhuan Zhao[1,2], Chunrong Wang[1,2], Shuaiqi Liu[1,2,3(✉)], and Hongfang Cheng[1,2]

[1] College of Electronic and Information Engineering, Hebei University, Baoding 071002, China
shdkj-1918@163.com
[2] Machine Vision Technological Innovation Center of Hebei, Baoding 071002, China
[3] National Laboratory of Pattern Recognition (NLPR), Institute of Automation, Chinese Academy of Sciences, Beijing 100190, China

Abstract. Facial image-based kinship verification is one of the challenging tasks in computer vision. It has many potential applications, such as human trafficking, studying human genetics, generating family maps, family photo albums, etc. Therefore, we propose a deep feature learning method (DFLKV) which can extract more discriminative features for kinship verification. For a pair of facial images, we firstly design a network with multi-scale channel attention for the features extraction; then, select four methods for feature fusion; finally, infer kinship based on the fused features. We jointly adopt the contrastive loss and the binary cross-entropy loss to compute matching degree for paired samples. The experimental results on four widely used datasets KinFaceW-I, KinFaceW-II, Cornell KinFace and TS KinFace to validate the effectiveness of our approach.

Keywords: Kinship verification · Deep feature learning · Channel attention

1 Introduction

The purpose of facial image-based kinship verification is to determine whether two persons have kinship through face images [1]. It has various potential applications, such as finding missing children, smart family photo album generation [2], etc. At present, kinship verification based on facial images still faces many challenges. Firstly, compared with other datasets related to face recognition, there are fewer samples, usually only a few hundred pairs. Secondly, genetic and environmental factors can result in similar facial features despite no kinship. Lastly, image quality and redundant information pose additional challenges in this research. Therefore, it is particularly important to be able to overcome the influence of unfavorable factors such.as genetics, environment, and image redundant information in a limited number of samples, and to extract discriminative features that are helpful for kinship verification. In order to address these issues, some methods for facial image-based kinship verification have been proposed [3]. Initially, most researchers adopt traditional feature extraction methods, including hand-crafted feature method and another group is metric learning method. Methods based on hand-crafted features mainly include the Histogram of Gradients (HOG) [4], LBP [5], Gabor

Gradient Orientation Pyramid [2], self-similarity [6], etc. Later, methods based on metric learning achieved superior results in kinship verification, such as MNRML [7] proposed by Lu et al. aim to learn a distance metric under which facial images with kinship are projected as close as possible and those without kinship are pulled as far as possible. However, traditional methods often struggle to extract discriminative hidden facial features, limiting their performance in kinship verification. In recent years, deep learning technology has been applied for kinship verification based on facial images. While some methods have advanced kinship verification research, the aggregation of global and local genetic information in facial images has not received sufficient attention. To better use of the global and local genetic information of facial images to make the features more discriminative, we propose a new kinship verification method DFLKV, which composed mainly of feature learning module and feature fusion module. By combining local channel attention and global channel attention, the kinship feature learning module can better extract the hidden information in facial images, and reduce the difference between facial images with kinship relations. Then, the extracted image features are fused using four methods to enhance the similarity and difference between features according to different fusion methods; Finally, kin relationships are inferred based on the fused features. The main contributions of this paper are as follows: (1) A novel deep feature learning kinship verification DFLKV method based on facial images is proposed. In the backbone network, a method combining multi-scale local channel attention and global channel attention is designed, which can better extract and fuse the local and global information, and improve the discriminability of features. (2) In order to reduce the intra-class difference of positive sample pairs and increase the inter-class difference of negative sample pairs, the network is trained by combining contrastive loss function and binary cross-entropy loss function. (3) Extensive experiments are conducted on publicly available kinship datasets, and the results demonstrate that this method outperforms the current state-of-the-art methods.

2 Related Work

2.1 Kinship Verification Method Based on Deep Learning

Biometrics recognizes individuals on the basis of unique physiological [30] and kinship verification based on facial image is a type of biometric recognition. Deep learning has already become one of the most significant branches in the field of machine learning, that can extract discriminative middle-level or high-level representations from original data [31], and has demonstrated superior performance in areas such as computer vision, object detection [32] and autonomous driving. Some researchers have attempted to use deep learning method to tackle kinship verification problem. Zhang et al. [8] proposed a deep learning-based convolutional neural network method which mainly according to the key points in the facial image. Zhou et al. [9] produced a kinship metric learning (KML) method coupled with deep neural networks (DNNs) to reduce the impact of insufficient kinship data.

2.2 Attention Mechanism

The attention mechanism is essentially similar to the human attention for external things, which makes the network focus on more important information [33]. With the application of attention mechanism in deep learning, some researchers have developed many deep learning networks with attention for kinship verification. Li [10] et al. used GNN to reason relationship and selected the self-attention mechanism to extract more discriminative original features. Compared with simple pooling operation, the accuracy increasing after adding self-attention.

3 Proposed Method

3.1 Overview of Network Structure

For improve the network's ability to extract discriminative features, this paper proposes a method with multi-scale channel attention. Figure 1 shows the whole structure of the network. Firstly, the image pair is fed into the feature learning module. The module consists of three multiscale channel attention residual blocks, each of which combines the local channel attention with global channel attention to extract discriminative features f_x and f_y respectively. Then, fuse f_x and f_y with 4 methods to obtain 4 fused features f_1, f_2, f_3 and f_4. After that concatenating the 4 features to get the feature $f_{Kin} = [f_1, f_2, f_3, f_4]$. Finally, we sent f_{Kin} to the classifier which mainly consists of fully connected (FC) layers. The loss function is constructed by contrastive loss and binary cross-entropy loss with different weights to improve the network's ability to discriminate features.

3.2 Feature Learning Module

The feature learning module consists of three multi-scale channel attention residual blocks with same structure, where the third residual block removes the last max-pooling layer. The multi-scale channel attention residual block mainly consists of a local channel attention structure, a global channel attention structure and a convolution. Taking the first residual block as an example, the first convolutional layer Conv has 32 convolution kernels with a size of 5×5, and then a feature matrix x_1 with size of $32 \times 60 \times 60$ is obtained. The feature matrix x_1 through the global channel attention and the local channel attention structure get the matrices size of $32 \times 1 \times 1$ and $32 \times 60 \times 60$ respectively. Add these two matrices and pass through Sigmoid to get x_2, the size is $32 \times 60 \times 60$. Multiply x_1 by x_2 and then added by x_1 to get x_3, the size is $32 \times 60 \times 60$, as shown in Eq. 1. Finally, x_3 goes through batch normalization (BN), Relu and max pooling layers in sequence to obtain a feature matrix with size $32 \times 30 \times 30$. The details of the multi-scale channel attention residual block structure are shown in Fig. 1 The multi-scale channel attention residual block increases the weight of important information in the feature map and reduces the weight of irrelevant information through the fusion of local channel attention and global channel attention, so as to extract more useful facial information for kinship verification.

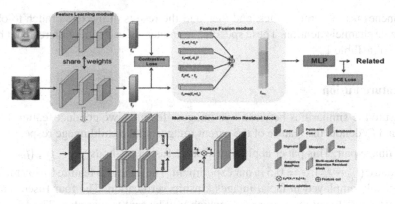

Fig. 1. DFLKV model structure.

3.3 Multi-scale Channel Attention Fusion

Table 1. Network structure of multi-scale channel attention residual blocks.

Block 1		Block 2		Block 3	
conv 5×5, 32		conv 5×5, 64		conv 5×5, 128	
(60,60)		(26,26)		(9,9)	
Global	Local	Global	Local	Global	Local
Adaptive		Adaptive		Adaptive	
MaxPool	conv 1×1, 8	MaxPool	conv 1×1, 16	MaxPool	conv 1×1,32
1×1	BN+ReLU	1×1	BN+ReLU	1×1	BN+ReLU
conv 1×1, 8	conv 1×1, 32	conv 1×1, 16	conv 1×1, 64	conv 1×1, 32	conv 1×1, 128
BN+ReLU	BN	BN+ReLU	BN	BN+ReLU	BN
conv 1×1, 32	(60,60)	conv 1×1, 64	(26,26)	conv 1×1,128	(9,9)
BN		BN		BN	
(1×1)		(1×1)		(1,1)	
Sigmoid		Sigmoid		Sigmoid	
BN+ReLU		BN+ReLU		BN+ReLU	
MaxPool 2×2, stride=2		MaxPool 2×2, stride=2		(9,9)	
(30,30)		(13,13)			

Inspired by related research on channel attention feature fusion [11], this paper applies related methods in the multi-scale channel attention residual block. The multi-scale channel attention is to extract the channel attention weights of different scales through two branches, one is global channel attention branch, local channel attention branch is the other one. These two branches are mainly composed of point wise convolution, adaptive max pooling, batch normalization and Relu layers. The global channel attention branch uses adaptive max pooling to extract global channel attention and global texture information, while retaining and highlighting the main features; the local channel attention branch employs point convolution to extract local feature attention. These two branches use different scales, and then add the results of the two branch to obtain multi-scale channel attention. These specific parameters of each attention residual block are shown in Table 1.

3.4 Feature Fusion

To measure the similarities between two images' features, we conduct feature fusion. Let f_{ip} and f_{ic} denote the feature of the parent image and the child image respectively in the i-th image pair. This paper apply four feature fusion methods: $f_{ip}^2 - f_{ic}^2$, $(f_{ip} - f_{ic})^2$, $f_{ip} - f_{ic}$, and $\alpha(f_{ip} + f_{ic})$, $\alpha = 0.5$ in our experiment. These several feature fusion methods are frequently employed in facial images kinship verification. The four fused features are concatenated to get the feature f_{Kin}, which will be sent to classifier. The FC layers, activation function and dropout layers make up the classifier.

3.5 Loss Function

Y_i represent the true kinship label of the i-th pair of images, if the i-th pair of images have no kinship, then $y_i = 0$, otherwise $y_i = 1$. $\hat{y}_i$ is the predicted kinship label of the i-th pair of images, if the network predicts the i-th pair of images have kinship then $\hat{y}_i = 1$, otherwise $\hat{y}_i = 0$. $Loss_{BCE}$ and $Loss_{Contrastive}$ represent the binary cross-entropy loss function and the contrastive loss function respectively.

Binary Cross Entropy Loss Function. In fact, kinship verification by facial image is a binary classification issue and the widely used loss function is $Loss_{BCE}$.

$$Loss_{BCE} = -\frac{1}{n} \sum_{i=0}^{n} \left[y_i \log \hat{y}_i + (1 - y_i) \log \left(1 - \hat{y}_i\right) \right] \tag{1}$$

Contrastive Loss. The contrastive loss function, shown in Eq. 2, is applied in this paper to reject the negative sample pairs as much as possible while maintaining positive sample pairs as similar as possible.

$$Loss_{Contrastive} = -\frac{1}{2n} \sum_{i=1}^{n} y_i d_i^2 + (1 - y_i) \max(margin - d_i, 0)^2 \tag{2}$$

$$\begin{aligned} Loss = &\ Loss_{BCE} + \lambda Loss_{Contrastive} \\ &- \frac{1}{n} \sum_{n}^{i=1} \left[y_i \log(y_i) + (1 - y_i) \log \left(1 - \hat{y}_i\right) \right] \\ &- \frac{\lambda}{2n} \left[\sum_{i=1}^{n} y_i d_i^2 + (1 - y_i) \max(margin - d_i, 0)^2 \right] \end{aligned} \tag{3}$$

In this paper, binary cross-entropy loss and contrastive loss are combined for training. The overall design of the loss function is shown in Eq. 3, where λ is a weight coefficient used to measure the proportion of the two losses. The two losses are combined with different weights to minimize the distance between the same class and maximize the distance between different classes.

4 Experiment

4.1 Datasets

We conduct extensive experiments on four publicly available datasets: KinFaceW-I, KinFaceW-II, Conell KinFace, and TS KinFace. KinFaceW Dataset proposed by Lu et al. [7] consists of two datasets, KinFaceW-I and KinFaceW-II, encompassing four kin relationships: mother and daughter (MD), mother and son (MS), father and daughter (FD) and father and son (FS). The dataset contains image pairs for each relationship, consisting of one parent face image and one child face image, both with a size of 64×64 pixels. There are 127, 116, 134 and 156 image pairs for each relationship in KinFaceW-I and 250 image pairs for each relationship in KinFaceW-II dataset. Unlike the images in KinFaceW-I, which were cropped from different photographs, the images in KinFaceW-II were cropped from the same photograph. Cornell KinFace Dataset proposed by Fang et al. [12] has 143 pairs of four relationships (MD, MS, FD, FS) in the dataset with size of 100×100. This dataset is extreme imbalance in four relationships, for example the FS has 67 pairs, while the MS has only 16 pairs. We no longer divided into specific kinship categories, but mixed the four relationships together for training and testing. TS KinFace Dataset introduced by Qin et al. [13] comprises 2589 images and includes two kin relationships: father-mother-daughter (FM-D) and father-mother-son (FM-S). The two relationships consist of 502 and 513 triplet kinship image pairs respectively. To evaluate the performance of DFLKV on the TS KinFace dataset, we re-divided the data into four relationships (MD, MS, FD, FS) with pair numbers of 502, 513, 502, and 513, respectively. Samples selected from the above datasets are shown in Fig. 2.

Fig. 2. Images from the KinFaceW-I, KinFaceW-II, Cornell KinFace and TS KinFace datasets.

4.2 Experimental Settings

Following the training and testing protocols of most relevant researchers [7], we use the five-fold cross validation for each relationship and the number of positive and negative pairs in each fold is the same. The average precision is used as the final result for each relationship. In original KinFaceW dataset, positive and negative pairs for each relationship have already been divided. However, the Cornell KinFace and TS KinFace datasets only provide positive sample pairs, and the number of negative sample pairs is inherently much larger than the number of positive pairs.

Table 2. Total number of samples and index for each fold after random sampling of negative samples for Cornell KinFace and TS KinFace datasets.

fold	TS KinFace				Cornell KinFace
	FS	FD	MS	MD	All Kinship
1	[1,204]	[1,200]	[1,204]	[1,200]	[1,56]
2	[205,408]	[201.400]	[205,408]	[201,400]	[57,112]
3	[409,614]	[401,600]	[409,614]	[401,600]	[113,170]
4	[615,820]	[601,802]	[615,820]	[601,802]	[171,228]
5	[821,1026]	[803,1004]	[821,1026]	[803,1004]	[229,286]
All	1026	1004	1026	1004	286

Therefore, we choose the same method as most researchers do, randomly selects negative sample pairs with the same number of positive sample pairs in the dataset. Table 2 lists the number of samples and the index of each fold after randomly sampling negative samples for the Cornell KinFace and TS KinFace datasets. Since the data volume of the Cornell KinFace dataset is much smaller than other datasets, we do not distinguish specific relationships, but mixes sample pairs of four relationships in train and test together. In addition, considering that the images in the Cornell KinFace dataset have many backgrounds, which may have a negative impact on the results, we use the method of RetinaFace [14] to re-detect and then extract the facial image. These obtained facial images are cropped into 64 × 64.

Experiment Details. Our network is deployed on Pytorch framework and runs on a computer equipment with a NVIDIA GeForce RTX 3080 GPU. To alleviate the effect of overfitting, we first resize images to 73 × 73, and then center crop them to 64 × 64. In the end, a random horizontal flip is performed with probability of 50%. In the experiment, the lr and Batchsize are set to 2.5×10^{-4} and 32 respectively. The values of λ in various datasets are shown in Table 3. We used the Adam optimizer and set the number of epochs to 120 for all datasets. Figure 3 shows the performance various with (λ) on KinFaceW-I and KinFaceW-II.

Table 3. Parameters of different datasets.

Datasets	KinFaceW-I	KinFaceW-II	TS KinFace	Cornell KinFace
λ	0.2	0.8	0.3	1.0

4.3 Compared with State-of-the-Art Methods

We present the experimental results of the DFLKV on four kinship datasets and compare it with other approaches including traditional methods such as MNRML [7], DMML

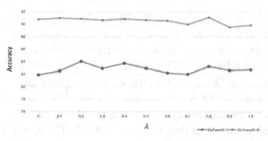

Fig. 3. Accuracy on KinFaceW-I and KinFaceW-II with different values.

[15], LMNN [16], MPDFL [17], BSIF [18], GMP [19], MKSM [20] and deep learning methods such as GA [21], DKV [22], SMCNN [23], FSP [24], WGEML [25], Advkin [26], NESN-KVN [27], DSMM [3], H-GRN [10], K-BDPCA [28], and DDMML [29]. Table 4 and Tabel 5 show the experiment's results on KinFaceW-I and KinFaceW-II respectively, and Table 6 and Tabel 7 show the result on TS KinFace and Cornell KinFace datasets respectively, where bold fonts indicate the best result and the underlined fonts indicate the sub-optimal result.To ensure the fairness of the results comparison, we adopts same experimental strategy as most related researches.

Table 4. Accuracy on KinFaceW-I dataset.

Method	FS	FD	MS	MD	Mean
MNRML(2014) [7]	72.5	66.5	66.2	72	69.3
DMML(2014) [15]	74.5	69.5	69.5	75.5	72.3
MPDFL(2015) [17]	73.5	67.5	66.1	73.1	70.1
LMNN(2017) [16]	69.5	63	63	59.4	63.7
GA(2014) [21]	72.5	76.4	77.3	71.9	74.5
DKV(2015) [22]	71.8	62.7	66.4	66.6	66.9
SMCNN(2016) [23]	75	75	68.7	72.2	72.7
FSP(2018) [24]	74.6	74.9	78.3	86	76.8
WGEML(2019) [25]	73.9	78.5	81.9	80.6	78.7
AdvKin(2020) [26]	75.7	78.3	77.6	83.1	78.7
NESN-KVN(2020) [27]	77	76.5	75.8	85.2	78.6
DSMM(2021) [3]	81.7	76.7	**82.3**	**89**	82.4
H-GRN(2021) [10]	<u>81.7</u>	<u>78.8</u>	<u>81.4</u>	<u>88.6</u>	<u>82.6</u>
DFLKV	**86.2**	**82.5**	79.3	88.2	**84**

In Table 4, DFLKV achieves the best performance on the KinFaceW-I dataset, with an average accuracy of 84%, outperforming the sub-optimal result by 1.4%. In terms of FS and FD, the accuracy is increased by 4.5% and 3.7% than the sub-optimal method H-GRN [13] respectively. But in MS and MD, the accuracy is decreased by 3% and

0.8% respectively. The possible reason is H-GRN [13] focuses on the graph-based face matching stage, and more research is done on the face matching stage to better utilize the genetic relationship of the two features. On the KinFaceW-II dataset, the average accuracy of DFLKV is 91.1%, which is lower than the best results DSMM [34] by 1.9%. The possible reason is that DSMM fully utilize more negative pairs. DFLKV achieves the best performance on the TS KinFace dataset, with an average accuracy of 92.9%, outperforming the sub-optimal result by 0.2%. On the Cornell KinFace dataset, DFLKV achieves sub-optimal result, lower than DSMM by 9.8%. The possible reason is that the Cornell KinFace dataset has the smallest data size compared with other three datasets, and the DSMM method uses more negative samples to increase the amount of data.

Table 5. Accuracy on KinFaceW-II dataset.

Method	FS	FD	MS	MD	Mean
MNRML(2014) [7]	76.9	74.3	77.4	77.6	76.6
DMML(2014) [15]	78.5	76.5	78.5	79.5	78.3
MPDFL(2015) [17]	77.3	74.7	77.8	78	77
LMNN(2017) [16]	74.8	71.1	75.8	76	74.4
GA(2014) [21]	76.7	83.9	84.8	83.4	82.2
DKV(2015) [22]	73.4	68.2	71	72.8	71.3
SMCNN(2016) [23]	75	79	78	85	79.3
FSP(2018) [24]	92.3	84.5	80.3	94.8	90.2
WGEML(2019) [25]	77.4	88.6	81.6	83.4	82.8
AdvKin(2020) [26]	88.4	85.8	88	89.8	88
NESN-KVN(2020) [27]	88.7	86.7	89.1	91.6	89
DSMM(2021) [3]	**92.6**	**89.8**	**95.8**	93.6	**93**
H-GRN(2021) [10]	90.6	86.8	93	**96**	91.6
DFLKV	91.6	86.6	91.6	94.6	91.1

Table 6. Accuracy on TS KinFace dataset.

Method	FS	FD	MS	MD	Mean
BSIF(2016) [18]	81.4	81.5	79.9	82	81.2
DDMML(2017) [29]	86.6	82.5	83.2	84.3	84.2
GMP(2015) [19]	88.5	87	87.9	87.8	87.8
MKSM(2018) [20]	82	81.4	82.3	81.9	81.9
DSMM(2021) [3]	91.4	**92.4**	**93.9**	**93.2**	92.7
DFLKV	**93.8**	91.9	93.5	92.3	**92.9**

According to the results in Table 4 and Table 5, we easily can see that most of the deep learning-based methods obtain higher accuracy on KinFaceW-II than that on KinFaceW-I. The possible reason is that KinFaceW-II has 1000 pairs of samples which is almost twice that of KinFaceW-I with 533 pairs. Deep learning methods usually require large amount of data to learn high-level information, so the performance of most methods on KinFaceW-II is better than that on KinFaceW-I. In addition, the images of KinFaceW-II are all cut from same photo, and similar image backgrounds may increase the accuracy of discrimination. According to the results in Table 5 and Table 7, it can conclude that most methods have lower accuracy on the Cornell KinFace. The possible reason is Cornell KinFace dataset does not have specific relationships. When the relationships are mixed together, it will be more difficult for model to distinguish. Furthermore, the Cornell KinFace dataset has only 143 pairs of samples, which is the smallest compared with the other three datasets. There is a little difficult for network to learn more discriminative information from few samples.

Table 7. Accuracy on Cornell KinFace dataset.

Method	All
DMML(2014) [15]	73.8
MNRML(2014) [7]	71.6
MPDFL(2015) [17]	71.9
FSP(2018) [24]	76.7
K-BDPCA(2019) [28]	71.9
AdvKin(2020) [26]	80.4
DSMM(2021) [3]	**90.5**
DFLKV	80.8

4.4 Comparison of the Number of Parameters

The number of parameters is a crucial metric in deep learning, as it reflects computational complexity, model size, and running speed to a certain extent.

Table 8. The number of parameters for different methods.

Method	WGEML (2019) [25]	FSP (2018) [24]	NESN-KVN (2020) [27]	DSMM (2021) [3]	DFLKV
Parameters	138357544	6422784	5519200	11180617	**4999476**

We compared the parameter count of the DFLKV method with other deep learning-based approaches. However, since many methods do not public the source code and detailed model parameter settings in their papers, the number of parameters of these models cannot be calculated. Table 8 shows the number of parameters of our method DFLKV compared to some computable methods. According to the results in Table 8, it can be seen that our method DFLKV has fewer number of model parameters in cases where the overall performance shows better results or is competitive with other advanced deep learning methods. These advanced deep learning methods include FSP [24], WGEML [25], NESN-KVN [27] and DSMM [3].

5 Conclusion

In this paper, a dual-stream structure of deep feature learning kinship verification (DFLKV) is proposed, and The experiment results on datasets KinFaceW-I, KinFaceW-II, Cornell KinFace, TS KinFace prove that DFLKV is superior to many advanced algorithms. This paper uses balanced data of negative and positive sample pairs in training, but in practical applications, the number of sample pairs without kinship is far great than the number of sample pairs with kinship. When there are N pairs of positive samples, there will naturally be N(N-1) for negative samples, how to find the negative samples that contribute more to the network among the many negative samples and still retain a high discrimination accuracy in the case of unbalanced samples, requires further research.

Acknowledgement. This work was supported in part by National Natural Science Foundation of China under Grant 62172139, Natural Science Foundation of Hebei Province under Grant F2022201055, Project Funded by China Postdoctoral under Grant 2022M713361, Natural Science Interdisciplinary Research Program of Hebei University under Grant DXK202102, Hebei University Research and Innovation Team Support Project under Grant IT2023B05, Open Project Program of the National Laboratory of Pattern Recognition (NLPR) under Grant 202200007. This work was also supported by the High-Performance Computing Center of Hebei University.

References

1. Wang, S., Robinson, J.P., Fu, Y.: Kinship verification on families in the wild with marginalized denoising metric learning. In: IEEE International Conference on Automatic Face & Gesture Recognition, pp. 216–221 (2017)
2. Zhou, X., Lu, J., Hu, J., Shang, Y.: Gabor-based gradient orientation pyramid for kinship verification under uncontrolled environments. In: ACM International Conference on Multimedia, pp. 725–728 (2012)
3. Li, W., Wang, S., Lu, J., Feng, J., Zhou, J.: Meta-mining discriminative samples for kinship verification. In: IEEE/CVF Conference on Computer Vision and Pattern Recognition, pp. 16135–16144 (2021)
4. Dalal, N., Triggs, B.: Histograms of oriented gradients for human detection. In: IEEE Computer Society Conference on Computer Vision and Pattern Recognition, pp. 886–893 (2005)
5. Ahonen, T., Hadid, A., Pietikainen, M.: Face description with local binary patterns: application to face recognition. IEEE Trans. Pattern Anal. Mach. Intell. **28**(12), 2037–2041 (2006)
6. Kohli, N., Singh, R., Vatsa, M.: Self-similarity representation of weber faces for kinship classification. In: IEEE Fifth International Conference on Biometrics: Theory, Applications and Systems (BTAS), pp. 245–250. IEEE (2012)

7. Lu, J., Zhou, X., Tan, Y.-P., Shang, Y., Zhou, J.: Neighborhood repulsed metric learning for kinship verification. IEEE Trans. Pattern Anal. Mach. Intell. **36**(2), 331–345 (2013)
8. Zhang, K., Huang, Y., Song, C., Wu, H., Wang, L., Statistical Machine Intelligence: Kinship verification with deep convolutional neural networks. In: British Machine Vision Conference. BMVA Press (2015)
9. Zhou, X., Jin, K., Min, X., Guo, G.: Learning deep compact similarity metric for kinship verification from face images. Inf. Fus. **48**, 84–94 (2019)
10. Li, W., Lu, J., Wuerkaixi, A., Feng, J., Zhou, J.: Reasoning graph networks for kinship verification: from star-shaped to hierarchical. IEEE Trans. Image Process. **30**, 4947–4961 (2021)
11. Dai, Y., Gieseke, F., Oehmcke, S., Wu, Y., Barnard, K.: Attentional feature fusion. In: IEEE/CVF Winter Conference on Applications of Computer Vision, pp. 3560–3569 (2021)
12. Fang, R., Tang, K.D., Snavely, N., Chen, T.: Towards computational models of kinship verification. In: IEEE International Conference on Image Processing, pp. 1577–1580 (2010)
13. Qin, X., Tan, X., Chen, S.: Tri-subject kinship verification: understanding the core of a family. IEEE Trans. Multimedia **17**(10), 1855–1867 (2015)
14. Deng, J., Guo, J., Ververas, E., Kotsia, I., Zafeiriou, S.: RetinaFace: single-shot multi-level face localisation in the wild. In: Proceedings of the IEEE/CVF Conference on Computer Vision and Pattern Recognition, pp. 5203–5212 (2020)
15. Yan, H., Lu, J., Deng, W., Zhou, X.: Discriminative multimetric learning for kinship verification. IEEE Trans. Inf. Forensics Secur. **9**(7), 1169–1178 (2014)
16. Yan, H.: Kinship verification using neighborhood repulsed correlation metriclearning. Image Vis. Comput. **60**, 91–97 (2017)
17. Yan, H., Lu, J., Zhou, X.: Prototype-based discriminativefeature learning for kinship verification. IEEE Trans. Cybern. **45**(11), 2535–2545 (2014)
18. Wu, X., Boutellaa, E., López, M.B., Feng, X., Hadid, A.: On the usefulness of color for kinship verification from face images. In: IEEE International Workshop on Information Forensics and Security, pp. 1–6 (2016)
19. Zhang, Z., Chen, Y., Saligrama, V.: Group membership prediction. In: IEEE International Conference on Computer Vision, pp. 3916–3924 (2015)
20. Zhao, Y.-G., Song, Z., Zheng, F., Shao, L.: Learning a multiple kernel similarity metric for kinship verification. Inf. Sci. **430**, 247–260 (2018)
21. Dehghan, A., Ortiz, E.G., Villegas, R., Shah, M.: Who do i look like? Determining parent-offspring resemblance via gated autoencoders. In: IEEE Conference on Computer Vision and Pattern Recognition, pp. 1757–1764 (2014)
22. Wang, M., Li, Z., Shu, X., Wang, J., Tang, J.: Deep kinship verification. In: IEEE International Workshop on Multimedia Signal Processing, pp. 1–6 (2015)
23. Li, L., Feng, X., Wu, X., Xia, Z., Hadid, A.: Kinship verification from faces via similarity metric based convolutional neural network. In: International Conference on Image Analysis and Recognition, pp. 539–548 (2016)
24. Dawson, M., Zisserman, A., Nellåker, C.: From same photo: cheating on visual kinship challenges. In: Asian Conference on Computer Vision, pp. 654–668 (2018)
25. Liang, J., Hu, Q., Dang, C., Zuo, W.: Weighted graph embedding-based metric learning for kinship verification. IEEE Trans. Image Process. **28**(3), 1149–1162 (2018)
26. Zhang, L., Duan, Q., Zhang, D., Jia, W., Wang, X.: AdvKin: adversarial convolutional network for kinship verification. IEEE Trans. Cybern. **51**(12), 5883–5896 (2020)
27. Wang, S., Yan, H.: Discriminative sampling via deep reinforcement learning for kinship verification. Pattern Recognit. Lett. **138**, 38–43 (2020)
28. Dehshibi, M.M., Shanbehzadeh, J.: Cubic norm and kernel based bi-directional PCA: toward age-aware facial kinship verification. Vis. Comput. **35**(1), 23–40 (2019)

29. Lu, J., Hu, J., Tan, Y.-P.: Discriminative deep metric learning for face and kinship verification. IEEE Trans. Image Process. **26**(9), 4269–4282 (2017)
30. Chai, T., Prasad, S., Yan, J., et al.: Contactless palmprint biometrics using DeepNet with dedicated assistant layers. Vis. Comput. **39**, 4029–4047 (2023)
31. Pan, S., Wang, R., Lin, C.: Bio-inspired feature cascade network for edge detection. Vis. Comput. **39**, 4149–4164 (2023)
32. Gao, Y., Dai, M., Zhang, Q.: Cross-modal and multi-level feature refinement network for RGB-D salient object detection. Vis. Comput. **39**, 3979–3994 (2023)
33. Xie, Z., Zhang, W., Sheng, B., Li, P., Philip Chen, C.L.: BaGFN: broad attentive graph fusion network for high-order feature interactions. IEEE Trans. Neural Netw. Learn. Syst. **34**(8), 4499–4513 (2023)

Efficient Semantic-Guidance High-Resolution Video Matting

Yue Yu$^{(\boxtimes)}$, Ding Li, and Yulin Yang

Beijing Institute of Technology, Beijing, China
yuyue@bit.edu.cn

Abstract. Video matting has made significant progress in trimap-based field. However, researchers are increasingly interested in auxiliary-free matting because it is more useful in real-world applications. We propose a new efficient semantic-guidance high-resolution video matting network for human body. We apply the convolutional network as the backbone while also employing the transformer in the encoder, which is used to utilize semantic features, while ensuring that the network is not overly bloated. In addition, a channel-wise attention mechanism is introduced in the decoder to improve the representation of semantic feature. In comparison to the current state-of-the-art methods, the method proposed in this paper achieves better results while maintaining the speed and efficiency of prediction. We can complete the real-time auxiliary-free matting for high-resolution video (4K or HD).

Keywords: Video Matting · Transformer · Auxiliary-Free Video Matting Network · Attention Mechanism

1 Introduction

Matting aims to predict alpha matte and foreground from the input image or video. A linear formula can reveal the core of the matting issue:

$$I = \alpha F + (1 - \alpha)B$$

The goal of matting is to recover foreground F and α from I, and then replace the original background B with the arbitrary background $B^{'}$. Matting has become a hot topic in computer vision due to its wide range of applications, such as video conferencing, video content creation, etc.

Current matting methods can be broadly classified into three categories. Trimap-based matting algorithms [22,23,25] are all based on additional input trimap to manually mark unknown regions. Background-based matting algorithms [11,20] only require a pre-captured background image as an additional input. However, once the background changes, it must be recaptured again.

Supported by National Natural Science Foundation of China (61807002).

Therefore, such methods can only handle scenes with fixed lens, such as video conferencing. Auxiliary-free matting [2,12,16] requires no additional input images or video. Compared with the first two methods, it is more difficult but has a wider range of applications, such as movie and short video production.

Semantic information is uniquely important in understanding the content of an image. Li et al. [9] used a semantic guidance mechanism that can adaptively reconstruct edges and improve image details. The current application of semantic information in auxiliary-free matting tasks can be broadly divided into two directions. Taking into account the similarity between the semantic segmentation task and the matting task, one direction is to utilize the semantic segmentation network to assist the matting task [2,12]. The second direction tries to exploit the unique advantage of the transformer for extracting semantic information [15]. We are compatible with the benefits of both directions.

This paper proposes a new efficient semantic-guidance auxiliary-free matting network for human body. By enhancing the network's ability to extract and utilize semantic feature, we improve the prediction performance in regions where the background and foreground low-level convolutional features are close. We use convolutional network as the backbone and use part of transformer's module to extract semantic feature. This allows the network to balance speed with effectiveness. Lightweight cross-attention is used to fuse convolutional features and global tokens to enable optimization of semantic features and guidance for convolutional feature maps. In addition, a channel-wise attention module is added to the decoder to improve the expression of semantic information. Experiments show that the results of this network outperform current state-of-the-art matting algorithms and can guarantee real-time prediction of high-resolution videos. We publicly release the source code of our project, which can be accessed at https://github.com/JuanMaoHSQ/Efficient-Semantic-Guidance-High-resolution-Video-Matting.

2   Related Works

2.1   Auxiliary-Free Matting

To obtain auxiliary-free matte, many methods tried to use the features of the images and videos themselves to help implement the matting process. RVM [12] exploited temporal information by learning what information to keep and forget in a continuous video stream through a recurrent network decoder. Li et al. [10] added an attention module to this recurrent network to correct the temporal information of misaligned video frames. Inspired by these works, which demonstrated the effectiveness of temporal information in matting tasks, we added the ConvGRU [1] module to maintain temporal consistency. SGHM [2] directly introduced a lightweight matting decoder module in a human semantic segmentation network, using semantic masks to guide the matting. Yao et al. [26] achieved high quality image matting effect through a lightweight cascaded network structure. And we adopt MobileNet as the network backbone, which makes our model more lightweight and efficient for real-time high-resolution video matting. These methods have achieved good results in image matting, but it is highly dependent on the accuracy of the segmentation network. At the same time, the number of parameters is very large and there are obvious problems with speed.

2.2 Vision Transformers

ViT [5] and its successors have achieved excellent performance on several vision tasks. Park et al. [15] proposed a trimap-based image matting method based on transformer encoding. They viewed trimap as a global prior token to partici-pate in the transformer's self-attention mechanism. Transformer-only networks are more computationally expensive than convolutional networks on small-scale data, and less capable of handling local convolutional features. Recent works [7,21] have shown that combining convolutional network with transformer has unique advantages, but most works chose to use the two encoders serially. This makes the network lose some of the advantages of a complete convolutional net-work in local awareness. Chen et al. [3] used MobileNet and Transformer in parallel and performed bidirectional attention exchange between the two. This algorithm maintained the unique advantages of a complete convolutional net-work and transformer to the greatest extent. Our proposed auxiliary-free mat-ting method extends this design from two dimensions to three dimensions. The transformer's ability to understand semantic feature is exploited in video tasks while ensuring the speed of runtime. Lin et al. proposed a transformer-based image processing network, EAPT [14], which efficiently models global depen-dencies using a self-attention mechanism. We used a convolutional network as the backbone of the U-net network,and use part of the module of the trans-former. Compared with direct use of the transformer, the network combines the advantages of both localization ability and global dependency modeling through the fusion with the convolutional network.

3 Method

Our model adopts U-net [18] architecture. The encoder backbone is a MobileNet convolutional network. It adds transformer block to extract semantic informa-tion, and additionally adds Semantic Feature Adjustment Module (SAM) and Semantic Feature Guidance Module (SGM). The decoder adds attention mech-anisms to improve the representation of semantic feature. A Depth-Guided Fil-ter (DGF) module is used for high-resolution upsampling. The specific network design is shown in Fig. 1.

3.1 Semantic Guidance Encoder

The encoder has two inputs for each layer, local feature maps X and learnable global tokens Z. The downsampled low-resolution image is first fed through a stem block (inverted bottleneck block [19]), which generates the local feature

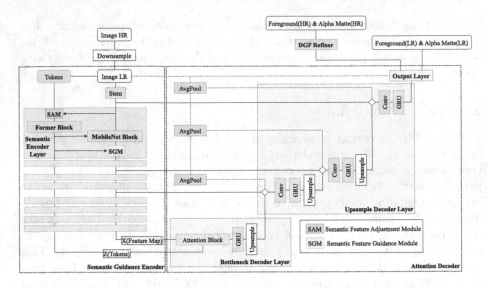

Fig. 1. Our network consists of Semantic Guidance Encoder, Attention Decoder and Deep Guided Filter module.

map (the number of channels will increase from 3 to 16, while the resolution will be reduced to $\frac{1}{2}$ of the original input) and randomly initializes the learnable global tokens Z in $R^{M \times d}$. M and d are the number and size of the tokens, and each M represents a global prior for that frame. The numbers of M and d do not vary with encoding. The structure of each module in the encoder layer is shown in the Fig. 2.

MobileNet Block. The backbone of each layer of our encoder adopts a MobileNet [19] convolutional network because it is good at extracting foreground edge contours. In MobileNet block dynamic-ReLU [4] replaces the standard ReLU. Dynamic-ReLU gets the parameters by applying two MLP layers to the average pool layer, while we feed Z output from the form block through two MLP layers to obtain the required parameters.

Former Block. A transformer block is also used in the encoder layer because the transformer is good at extracting semantic feature, and we call it a Former block for short. Former block includes a multi-headed attention (MHA) and a feed-forward network (FFN).

SAM and SGM. Semantic Feature Guidance Module(SGM) and Semantic Feature Guidance Module(SGM) are adopted in each layer of the encoder. Both modules adopt the cross-attention mechanism. SAM uses X to add attention to Z before the Former block to optimize the semantic feature. SGM uses Z to add attention to X to achieve the guidance of semantic feature to convolutional features.

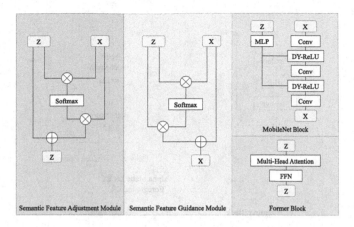

Fig. 2. The semantic guidance encoder layer consists of four parts, MobileNet Block (convolutional network module), Former Block (transformer module), SAM (Semantic Feature Adjustment Module) and SGM (Semantic Feature Guidance Module).

3.2 Attention Decoder

Our decoder architecture consists of five layers, including a bottleneck attention layer, three upsample layers and an output layer. The specific structure of the attention block and output layer is shown in Fig. 3.

The high-level convolutional feature map has a large receptive field. It contains semantic information, layout information, and other global information. We want to enhance the representation of semantic features in the high-level convolutional feature map, so we use a channel-wise attention module to enhance the representation of semantic feature. The inputs of the attention block are convolutional feature map and global tokens output from the top layer of the encoder. Channel-wise attention utilizes global pooling to generalize global tokens, employs a shared MLP and uses a sigmoid layer, and finally multiplies them with upsampled pyramid local features for semantic distillation.

3.3 Deep Guided Filter

Note that the Deep Guided Filter (DGF) [24] module is not completely necessary, which is also reflected in our training strategy. The DGF module is only used for high-resolution prediction. It outputs high-resolution alpha and foreground using the low-resolution alpha, foreground, and final hidden features output from the decoder output block, as well as the high-resolution input frame.

3.4 Loss Function

The loss for the matting task consists of two parts, alpha loss and foreground loss. When $t \in [1, T]$, to learn alpha α_t (ground-truth α_t^*), we use L1 loss $\mathcal{L}_{l1}^{\alpha}$ and pyramid Laplacian loss $\mathcal{L}_{lap}^{\alpha}$, we also adopt temporal coherence loss $\mathcal{L}_{tc}^{\alpha}$ to

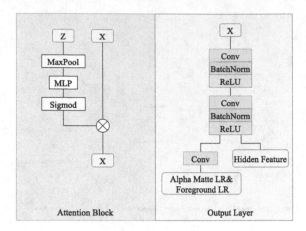

Fig. 3. The channel-wise attention module and the architecture of the decoder output layer.

reduce flicker. To learn foreground F_t (ground-truth F_t^*), we apply pixel-wise L1 loss $\mathcal{L}_{l1}^F$ and temporal coherence loss $\mathcal{L}_{tc}^F$ on pixels where $\alpha_t > 0$ to avoid being disturbed by background pixels.

$$\mathcal{L}_{l1}^{\alpha} = \|\alpha_t - \alpha_t^*\|_1 \quad (1) \qquad \mathcal{L}_{l1}^F = \|(a_t^* > 0) * (F_t - F_t^*)\|_1 \quad (4)$$

$$\mathcal{L}_{tc}^{\alpha} = \left\|\frac{d\alpha_t}{dt} - \frac{d\alpha_t^*}{dt}\right\|_2 \quad (2) \qquad \mathcal{L}_{tc}^F = \left\|(a_t^* > 0) * \left(\frac{dF_t}{dt} - \frac{dF_t^*}{dt}\right)\right\|_2 \quad (5)$$

$$\mathcal{L}_{\text{lap}}^{\alpha} = \sum_{s=1}^{5} \frac{2^{s-1}}{5} \left\|L_{pyr}^s(\alpha_t) - L_{pyr}^s(\alpha_t^*)\right\|_1 \tag{3}$$

The loss for the semantic segmentation task can be represented as a simple binary cross entropy loss.

4   Evaluation

In our experiments, we perform fair comparisons with several state-of-the-art auxiliary-free methods(RVM [12], ModNet [8] and SGHM [2]) and a background-based method (BGMv2 [11]) under similar conditions on one Nvidia RTX 2080Ti GPU. We retrained RVM [12] to be fair. We changed the maximum input frame length when it was trained to match the device memory constraints. ModNet [8] and SGHM [2] are image matting algorithms. Both of them do not have open source code, but provide image and video matting demos. BGMv2 [11] requires an additional first frame of background as input.

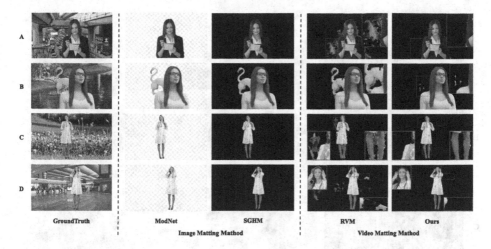

Fig. 4. High-resolution qualitative comparison in the test dataset.

4.1 Training Strategy

We used the same training method as RVM [12], where the matting and semantic segmentation objectives are jointly used to train network. During the training process, the two objectives are served alternately. Firstly, compared to most traditional matting algorithms, auxiliary-free matting methods require a higher level of understanding of scene semantics. There is also a high similarity between semantic segmentation tasks and matting tasks. This rationale has been demonstrated in the work by RVM. Second, semantic segmentation tasks have more mature and robust datasets available, while in recent years, there has been a lack of better datasets for matting tasks. Using datasets for both tasks prevents our model from overfitting the synthetic distribution.

4.2 Datasets

We use one video matting dataset VideoMatte240K (VM) [11], and two image matting datasets, Adobe Image Matting (AIM) [16] and Distinctions-646 (D646) [25], while only segments containing human bodies are selected. The background dataset consists of two parts: the dynamic background is provided by the dataset of [23] to provide high-resolution background videos suitable for matting composition, containing a variety of motions such as passing cars, shaking leaves, and camera movements; the static background is collected by ourselves.

We use one video semantic segmentation dataset YouTubeVIS, and two image semantic segmentation datasets COCO [13] and SPD, while only segments containing human bodies are selected.

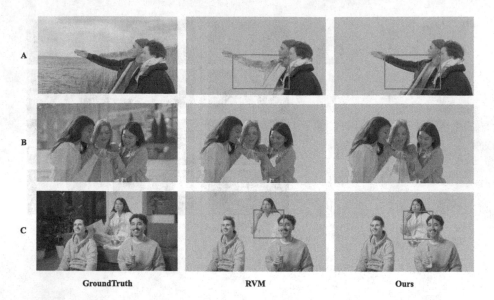

Fig. 5. High-resolution qualitative comparison in the real web videos. All stock footage provided by Freepik, downloaded from videvo.net.

4.3   Qualitative Comparison

Figure 4 shows the results of our high-resolution qualitative comparison in the test dataset. The dataset used for testing is from VideoMatte240K [11]. In Fig. 4-A, the traffic in the background is moving and the roads have a similar color to the human body. In Fig. 4-B, the flamingos in the background have a similar color to the clothes in the foreground. In Fig. 4-C, the colors of the plants in the background interfere with the prediction. In Fig. 4-D, the edges and colors of the roof area in the background are similar to those in the foreground. In all these regions, our prediction results are better than those of RVM. Compared to the two image matting algorithms, our results in the three images of Fig. 4-A C D are similar to their results. However, our method makes better semantic estimates in Fig. 4-B.

Figure 5 shows the results of our high-resolution qualitative comparison with video matting algorithm on real web videos. In the multi-foreground videos, our method can show each foreground figure better. For example, the arm of the man in Fig. 5-A, the breast of the lady on the right side of Fig. 5-B, and the lady in the back of Fig. 5-C, all of these parts are correctly predicted by our method. It can be seen that our method performs better semantic estimation assisted matting in the parts where colors and backgrounds are similar.

4.4   Quantitative Comparison

We employ MAD (Mean Absolute Difference), MSE (Mean Squared Error), Grad (spatial gradient), and Conn (connectivity) [17] to evaluate α, and dtSSD [6] to

Table 1. Quantitative Comparison

Method	Dataset	Low-resolution					High-resolution			
		MAD	MSE	Grad	Conn	dtSSD	MAD	MSE	Grad	dtSSD
BGMv2 [11]	Video	25.19	19.63	2.28	3.26	2.74	–	–	–	–
SGHM [2]		6.12	1.08	0.57	0.45	3.89	5.58	1.14	14.97	3.85
ModNet [8]		14.65	7.03	8.57	1.65	7.01	13.82	6.79	21.47	4.21
RVM [12]		9.61	4.02	1.94	0.93	1.66	11.07	3.91	17.89	2.38
Ours		8.01	2.18	1.73	0.71	1.81	9.51	3.44	16.77	2.43
SGHM [2]	Image	6.87	1.47	0.66	0.72	5.63	6.45	4.69	19.18	4.92
ModNet [8]		12.39	6.85	7.46	1.86	4.46	14.28	8.12	32.21	2.28
RVM [12]		8.97	3.46	1.28	0.74	1.42	11.78	6.73	31.51	1.68
Ours		7.03	1.21	1.18	0.62	1.59	8.25	5.41	25.38	1.73

evaluate temporal coherence. MAD and MSE are enlarged by $1e^3$, and dtSSD is enlarged by $1e^2$ for better readability.

Table 1 shows results with low-resolution inputs and high-resolution inputs. The Conn metric is no longer used because computing connectivity for high-resolution images is too expensive. BGMv2 is a background-based method that requires an additional frame of background input, but the results are still poorer. Although the quantitative results of SGHM are mostly better than all other methods, they have great troubles in terms of size and speed (shown in Table 2). ModNet produces less accurate and coherent results than ours. The processing effect of RVM on regions with similar textures is less clear than ours. There is a very minor difference between the performance of our network and RVM on the dtSSD metric–which is because ConvGRU receives the feature map weighted by the attention mechanism in our method. In high resolution input comparison, our method still outperforms ModNet and RVM on all metrics except dtSSD. In particular, it achieves a large improvement in the Grad metric, proving that our method can obtain better alpha matte results.

4.5   Size and Speed Comparison

Table 2 shows the results of our size and speed comparison. We compare with the three state-of-the-art auxiliary-free matting methods and perform experiments at each of the three resolutions. The results show that we can process 4K (3840 × 2160) at 62 FPS and HD (1920 × 1080) at 75 FPS on one Nvidia RTX 2080Ti GPU. This allows our method to achieve real-time high-resolution video matting. Neither SGHM [2] nor ModNet [8] can do real-time or high frame rate prediction. Although RVM can do higher frame rate prediction, its prediction results are not as good as ours.

4.6   Ablation Studies

Table 3 shows the results of our ablation experiments for high-resolution video input. We conduct experiments on three ablation scenarios: encoder that only

Table 2. Size and Speed Comparison

Method	Resolution	FPS	Parm/M
ModNet [8]	512 × 288	73	6.487
	1920 × 1080	18.8	
	3840 × 2160	12.6	
SGHM [2]	512 × 288	15.4	69.92
	1920 × 1080	8.4	
	3840 × 2160	3.5	
RVM [12]	512 × 288	131.9	3.749
	1920 × 1080	104.2	
	3840 × 2160	76.5	
Ours	512 × 288	83.6	2.97
	1920 × 1080	75.1	
	3840 × 2160	62.4	

Table 3. Ablation studies on encoder and decoder

Method	Alpha			
	MAD	MSE	Grad	dtSSD
Ours	9.50	3.44	16.77	2.43
Encoder w/o Semantic	12.26	4.81	18.01	2.79
Decoder w/o Attention	10.83	3.65	17.29	2.41
Decoder w/ Attention in every layer	11.83	4.16	17.55	2.58

uses MobileNet [19], decoder that does not include an attention mechanism, and decoder that has an attention mechanism in every layer.

In the ablation experiment where the encoder only uses MobileNet [19], the channel-wise attention of the decoder is changed to a self-attention module that adds attention to itself using the convolutional feature map. The results in this case are worse than those of baseline, proving that our semantically guided encoder works more clearly. Ablation experiment with decoders that do not use attention show that attention has a benign effect on all other metrics, while it makes the dtSSD metric worse. When we are using the attention mechanism in each layer of the decoder, it becomes worse, proving that it is not reasonable to boost the semantic feature representation in shallow convolutional feature maps.

5   Conclusion

We propose a new auxiliary-free video matting network. We use a new efficient semantic-guided encoder architecture with a channel-based attention decoder. Compared with the current state-of-the-art methods, the method proposed in this paper achieves better results, while maintaining speed and performance. We believe that architectures based on transformer or leveraging both transformer and convolutional network still have great potential in video matting tasks. Our method has a wider range of applications; however, a limitation lies in the difficulty for users to edit the results. To increase controllability, our future research will also focus on exploring whether the use of prompt paradigms can enhance the controllability and interactivity of video matting.

References

1. Ballas, N., Yao, L., Pal, C., Courville, A.: Delving deeper into convolutional networks for learning video representations. arXiv preprint arXiv:1511.06432 (2015)
2. Chen, X., et al.: Robust human matting via semantic guidance. In: Wang, L., Gall, J., Chin, T.J., Sato, I., Chellappa, R. (eds.) ACCV 2022. LNCS, vol. 13842, pp. 2984–2999. Springer, Cham (2022). https://doi.org/10.1007/978-3-031-26284-5_37
3. Chen, Y., et al.: Mobile-former: bridging mobilenet and transformer. In: Proceedings of the IEEE/CVF Conference on Computer Vision and Pattern Recognition, pp. 5270–5279 (2022)
4. Chen, Y., Dai, X., Liu, M., Chen, D., Yuan, L., Liu, Z.: Dynamic ReLU. In: Vedaldi, A., Bischof, H., Brox, T., Frahm, J.-M. (eds.) ECCV 2020. LNCS, vol. 12364, pp. 351–367. Springer, Cham (2020). https://doi.org/10.1007/978-3-030-58529-7_21
5. Dosovitskiy, A., et al.: An image is worth 16x16 words: transformers for image recognition at scale. arXiv preprint arXiv:2010.11929 (2020)
6. Erofeev, M., Gitman, Y., Vatolin, D.S., Fedorov, A., Wang, J.: Perceptually motivated benchmark for video matting. In: British Machine Vision Conference, pp. 1–12 (2015)
7. Graham, B., et al.: Levit: a vision transformer in convnet's clothing for faster inference. In: Proceedings of the IEEE/CVF International Conference on Computer Vision, pp. 12259–12269 (2021)
8. Ke, Z., et al.: Is a green screen really necessary for real-time portrait matting? arXiv preprint arXiv:2011.11961 (2020)
9. Li, L., Tang, J., Ye, Z., Sheng, B., Mao, L., Ma, L.: Unsupervised face super-resolution via gradient enhancement and semantic guidance. Vis. Comput. (2021)
10. Li, Y., Fang, L., Ye, L., Yang, X.: Deep video matting with temporal consistency. In: International Forum on Digital TV and Wireless Multimedia Communications, pp. 339–352 (2022)
11. Lin, S., Ryabtsev, A., Sengupta, S., Curless, B.L., Seitz, S.M., Kemelmacher-Shlizerman, I.: Real-time high-resolution background matting. In: Proceedings of the IEEE/CVF Conference on Computer Vision and Pattern Recognition, pp. 8762–8771 (2021)
12. Lin, S., Yang, L., Saleemi, I., Sengupta, S.: Robust high-resolution video matting with temporal guidance. In: Proceedings of the IEEE/CVF Winter Conference on Applications of Computer Vision, pp. 238–247 (2022)
13. Lin, T.-Y., et al.: Microsoft COCO: common objects in context. In: Fleet, D., Pajdla, T., Schiele, B., Tuytelaars, T. (eds.) ECCV 2014. LNCS, vol. 8693, pp. 740–755. Springer, Cham (2014). https://doi.org/10.1007/978-3-319-10602-1_48
14. Lin, X., Sun, S., Huang, W., Sheng, B., Li, P., Feng, D.D.: EAPT: efficient attention pyramid transformer for image processing. IEEE Trans. Multimedia (2021)
15. Park, G., Son, S., Yoo, J., Kim, S., Kwak, N.: Matteformer: transformer-based image matting via prior-tokens. In: Proceedings of the IEEE/CVF Conference on Computer Vision and Pattern Recognition, pp. 11696–11706 (2022)
16. Qiao, Y., et al.: Attention-guided hierarchical structure aggregation for image matting. In: Proceedings of the IEEE/CVF Conference on Computer Vision and Pattern Recognition, pp. 13676–13685 (2020)
17. Rhemann, C., Rother, C., Wang, J., Gelautz, M., Kohli, P., Rott, P.: A perceptually motivated online benchmark for image matting. In: Proceedings of the IEEE/CVF Conference on Computer Vision and Pattern Recognition, pp. 1826–1833 (2009)

18. Ronneberger, O., Fischer, P., Brox, T.: U-net: convolutional networks for biomedical image segmentation. In: International Conference on Medical Image Computing and Computer-assisted Intervention, pp. 234–241 (2015)
19. Sandler, M., Howard, A., Zhu, M., Zhmoginov, A., Chen, L.C.: Mobilenetv 2: inverted residuals and linear bottlenecks. In: Proceedings of the IEEE/CVF Conference on Computer Vision and Pattern Recognition, pp. 4510–4520 (2018)
20. Sengupta, S., Jayaram, V., Curless, B., Seitz, S.M., Kemelmacher-Shlizerman, I.: background matting: the world is your green screen. Proceedings of the IEEE/CVF Conference on Computer Vision and Pattern Recognition, pp. 2291–2300 (2020)
21. Srinivas, A., Lin, T.Y., Parmar, N., Shlens, J., Abbeel, P., Vaswani, A.: Bottleneck transformers for visual recognition. In: Proceedings of the IEEE/CVF Conference on Computer Vision and Pattern Recognition, pp. 16519–16529 (2021)
22. Sun, Y., Tang, C.K., Tai, Y.W.: Semantic image matting. In: Proceedings of the IEEE/CVF Conference on Computer Vision and Pattern Recognition, pp. 11120–11129 (2021)
23. Sun, Y., Wang, G., Gu, Q., Tang, C.K., Tai, Y.W.: Deep video matting via spatio-temporal alignment and aggregation. In: Proceedings of the IEEE/CVF Conference on Computer Vision and Pattern Recognition, pp. 6975–6984 (2021)
24. Wu, H., Zheng, S., Zhang, J., Huang, K.: Fast end-to-end trainable guided filter. In: Proceedings of the IEEE/CVF Conference on Computer Vision and Pattern Recognition, pp. 1838–1847 (2018)
25. Xu, N., Price, B., Cohen, S., Huang, T.: Deep image matting. In: Proceedings of the IEEE/CVF Conference on Computer Vision and Pattern Recognition, pp. 2970–2979 (2017)
26. Yao, G., Huang, R.: An image matting algorithm based on inception-resnet-v2 network. In: International conference on Variability of the Sun and Sun-Like Stars: From Asteroseismology to Space Weather, pp. 323–334 (2022)

Segment Any Building

Lei Li[✉]

Department of Computer Science, University of Copenhagen,
2100 Copenhagen, Denmark
lilei@di.ku.dk

Abstract. The identification and segmentation of buildings in remote sensing imagery has consistently been a important point of academic research. This work highlights the effectiveness of using diverse datasets and advanced representation learning models for the purpose of building segmentation in remote sensing images. By fusing various datasets, we have broadened the scope of our learning resources and achieved exemplary performance across several datasets. Our innovative joint training process demonstrates the value of our methodology in various critical areas such as urban planning, disaster management, and environmental monitoring. Our approach, which involves combining dataset fusion techniques and prompts from pre-trained models, sets a new precedent for building segmentation tasks. The results of this study provide a foundation for future exploration and indicate promising potential for novel applications in building segmentation field.

Keywords: Image Segmentation · Remote Sensing

1 Introduction

The building environment, constituting a diverse spectrum of structures, remains a crucial facet of our urban and rural landscapes. Structures, ranging from residential and commercial spaces to industrial facilities, play instrumental roles in shaping economic dynamics, facilitating societal interactions, and influencing environmental outcomes. Consequently, the task of building segmentation and subsequent analysis holds paramount significance across an array of disciplines, including but not limited to urban planning, real estate, and disaster management [22]. These analytical processes provide indispensable insights and contribute to both the theoretical understanding and practical applications within these domains, affirming the necessity of building segmentation in contemporary academic research and industry practice.

Building segmentation significantly depends on data derived from an array of imaging sources, chiefly encompassing high-resolution aerial photography and remote sensing imagery. Each of these sources offers unique vantage points and insights, which collectively contribute to a holistic understanding of built environments and forest management [3,21,23]. High-resolution aerial photography, for instance, is instrumental in providing intricately detailed depictions of buildings and their immediate surroundings. These close-up views are invaluable for conducting fine-grained analyses that delve into the minutiae of individual structures and their architectural features. Together, these data sources, each with its own strengths, enrich the process of building segmentation by offering different layers of information, ultimately allowing researchers to unearth nuanced understandings of the built environment from multiple scales and perspectives.

Despite the valuable insights provided by high-resolution aerial photography and satellite imagery [20], these data sources do present inherent challenges that must be acknowledged. The primary limitation of aerial photography lies in its restricted spatial coverage, rendering it less applicable for expansive geographical analyses. In contrast, satellite imagery, while boasting extensive coverage, often suffers from a relatively lower resolution, potentially compromising the detail of analytical outputs.

Acknowledging the challenges inherent to the differing data sources, and building upon the recent advancements in the field of general segmentation, particularly the Segment Anything (SA) [12], Semantic Segment Anything (SSA) [4] method, we adopt a nuanced approach. Our strategy involves the amalgamation of multiple datasets processed through pretrained models, thereby addressing data discrepancies and facilitating mutual learning across various data domains.

Our research contributions within the realm of building segmentation are manifold:

Firstly, we harness the robust framework of the SSA method, utilizing its capacity for extensive data processing within large models. This aids in augmenting the precision and efficiency of building segmentation tasks, illustrating the value of integrating sophisticated algorithms within such expansive data processes.

Secondly, we confront the issue of inter-data discrepancies through the individual processing of various datasets, thereby encouraging cross-domain learning. This approach not only serves to alleviate the constraints tied to individual data sources but also amplifies the overall learning process through the incorporation of diverse and extensive information.

Lastly, our adapted method exhibits commendable results across an array of datasets, thereby underlining its efficacy and flexibility. This superior performance, regardless of dataset variability, reinforces the potential of our approach in providing general insights within the field of building segmentation.

2   Related Work

Image Segmentation. Image Segmentation, as an essential step in image analysis and interpretation, has received considerable attention in academic research over the past few years. Such as Unet [10], Segformer [19,26], Deeplab [5], ConNext [16]. The body of work spans various techniques and methods, ranging from traditional threshold-based and region-growing methods to more advanced machine learning and deep learning techniques. Some work [14] in particular, the U-Net architecture, first introduced by Ronneberger et al. [24]. In 2015, has been widely adopted for biomedical image segmentation due to its impressive performance and then been utilized to other different data domains. However, despite the strides made in this field, segmentation remains a challenging task due to issues such as the variability of object shapes and sizes, background clutter, and imaging conditions, thus, necessitating continued exploration and innovation in this area.

Image Data fusion. Image data fusion has emerged as a critical process in numerous image segmentation tasks [9,13,27], including building segmentation, due to its capacity to combine complementary information from multiple data sources, thereby enhancing the quality and utility of the resulting data. Extensive literature exists concerning the methods and techniques utilized for this purpose. Conventional methods often incorporate mathematical transformations such as Principle Component Analysis (PCA) [1,15,27,28] and Intensity Hue Saturation (IHS) for fusing low-resolution multispectral data with high-resolution panchromatic data. Recent years have witnessed a surge in research exploring machine learning and deep learning techniques for image fusion. Channel fusion [29], particularly Convolutional Neural Networks (CNNs), have been employed for their ability to learn complex and high-level features from multi-source data with similarity [25]. Despite the significant advancements in this domain, the fusion of image data remains a nontrivial task due to issues like preserving spectral and spatial information and mitigating artifacts in fused images. This ongoing challenge underscores the need for continued research and development of sophisticated fusion techniques tailored to specific segmentation tasks.

Pre-trained model. The use of large pre-trained models [2] as the basis for various specialized tasks is a prevalent strategy in the contemporary machine learning landscape. This approach leverages the broad feature learning capabilities of these models, which have been trained on extensive and diverse datasets, thus providing a robust starting point for a variety of specialized tasks. Models such as BERT [8], GPT, and SA [12], for instance, have shown significant efficacy when fine-tuned for specific tasks like text classification, object detection, and semantic segmentation, amongst others. These models offer the advantage of leveraging transfer learning, which allows the application of learned features to new tasks, thereby reducing the need for extensive data and computational resources.

3   Methods

3.1   Problem Formulation

In the Fig. 1, The four datasets highlighted in this research, namely MapAI Building [11], Inria Aerial Image Labeling Benchmark [18], WHU Building Dataset [10], and FloodNet [22], each bring their unique strengths and nuances to building segmentation tasks. The MapAI Building dataset stands out for its incorporation of laser data and ground truth masks, along with aerial images.

It covers diverse building types and environments spanning Denmark and Norway, and the real-world derived data poses unique challenges and authenticity. The Inria Aerial Image Labeling Benchmark excels in its wide geographical coverage and high-resolution aerial imagery. The segmentation task is further complicated by the presence of diverse remote sensing platforms. Lastly, the FloodNet dataset is specialized for disaster management with its UAS-based high-resolution imageries. The dataset uniquely categorizes building and road structures based on their flood status, thus bringing a novel dimension to building segmentation tasks. Each dataset's idiosyncrasies underscore the need for adaptable segmentation methods capable of handling different data types, resolutions, and scenario-specific complexities.

3.2   Data

MapAI Building [11]. The dataset employed in this research amalgamates aerial images, laser data, and ground truth masks corresponding to building structures, catering to a diverse range of environmental and building types. The training dataset is composed of data derived from multiple locations across Denmark, thereby ensuring considerable variability and diversity in the nature of the data. Conversely, the test dataset consists of seven distinct locations in Norway, encompassing both urban and rural environments. It's worth noting that the data originates from real-world scenarios, leading to certain instances where buildings in the aerial images do not align with the corresponding ground truth masks.

(a) MapAI Building   (b) Inria Aerial Image

(c) WHU Building   (4) FloodNet

Fig. 1. This study utilizes four distinct datasets, each embodying unique areas and scenes.

Inria Aerial Image Labeling Benchmark [18]. The dataset under investigation is characterized by extensive coverage, spanning 810 km², which is equally divided for training and testing purposes. It utilizes high-resolution (0.3 m) aerial orthorectified color imagery, which encompasses varied urban landscapes, from densely populated areas like San Francisco's financial district to less dense regions like Lienz in Austrian Tyrol. The ground truth data comprises two semantic classes: "building" and "not building", publicly accessible only for the training subset. Unique to this dataset is its geographical division across training and testing subsets; training employs imagery from cities like Chicago, while testing uses data from different regions. This structure tests the techniques' generalization capabilities under diverse conditions including varied illumination, urban landscape, and seasons. The dataset's assembly involved merging public domain imagery and official building footprints, providing a comprehensive depiction of building structures.

WHU Building Dataset [10]. The WHU building dataset, meticulously curated for this study, incorporates both aerial and satellite imagery of building samples. The aerial component of the dataset comprises over 220,000 distinct building structures, gleaned from aerial images with a fine spatial resolution of 0.075 m, and spans an area of 450 km^2 in Christchurch, New Zealand. The satellite imagery dataset is bifurcated into two subsets: one encompasses images from diverse cities globally, sourced from multiple remote sensing platforms including QuickBird, Worldview series, IKONOS, ZY-3, among others, encapsulating a broad range of geographic and urban contexts. The second subset consists of six contiguous satellite images covering an expanse of 550 km^2 in East Asia with a ground resolution of 2.7 m. Collectively, the WHU building dataset offers a comprehensive and varied collection of images, affording the opportunity to explore building segmentation across different scales, geographical locations, and imaging sources.

Floodnet [22]. The FloodNet dataset is a meticulously curated resource aimed at revolutionizing disaster management through the provision of high-resolution and semantically detailed unmanned aerial system (UAS) imagery, specifically in the context of natural disasters such as hurricanes. It leverages the flexible and efficient data collection capabilities of small UAS platforms, namely DJI Mavic Pro quadcopters, which are especially valuable for rapid response and recovery in large-scale and difficult-to-access areas. The dataset was collated in the aftermath of Hurricane Harvey and comprises 2343 images, apportioned into training (approximately 60%), validation (around 20%), and testing (roughly 20%) subsets. The semantic segmentation labels within the dataset are notably comprehensive, covering categories such as background, flooded and non-flooded buildings, flooded and non-flooded roads, water bodies, trees, vehicles, pools, and grass.

3.3 Overview

In our comprehensive methodology, we integrate four distinct datasets: MapAI Building, Inria Aerial Image Labeling Benchmark, WHU Building Dataset, and Floodnet. Irrespective of the original pixel resolution disparities, all data are reformatted into a standardized size of 256 × 256 pixels. Correspondingly, we apply similar alterations to the associated masks, enabling the generation of uniformly dimensioned image-mask patches.

We employ Segformer-B5 [26] as our backbone, a decision underpinned by its robust performance in diverse segmentation tasks. To augment the model's initial capabilities, we incorporate pre-trained parameters, which are instrumental in defining the initial weights of our network, thereby optimizing our model's learning trajectory.

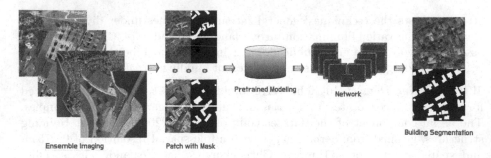

Fig. 2. The propose SegAnyBuild framework. Initially, we align the architectural structures and corresponding images as per the utilized dataset. Subsequently, the entire dataset is homogenized into a uniform 256*256 patch accompanied by a mask. Feature pre-learning is performed utilizing the pretrained model of Semantic Segmentation Anything (SSA) [4]. Ultimately, the architectural structure is delineated via a segmentation network. The entire procedure is executed in an end-to-end manner.

The culmination of our pipeline involves an up-sampling procedure, through which we transform the processed data into a style compatible with the target results. This rigorous, systematic approach bolsters our segmentation efficacy, contributing to efficient output production.

3.4   Network

In this paragraph, we briefly introduce the more popular U-Net structure and the SegFormer network architecture. For more details about ConvNext, refer to ConvNext [16].

The U-Net architecture is a widely recognized model for biomedical image segmentation, characterized by its symmetric expansive and contracting structure. The architecture mathematically operates as a series of nonlinear mappings that progressively transform the input image into the output segmentation. Incorporating sequences of convolution operations, max-pooling, upsampling, and a softmax layer, this model is recognized for its effectiveness in detail retention and accurate segmentation.

The SegFormer architecture is an innovative blend of transformer and U-Net components, offering a novel approach to semantic segmentation tasks. A core component of the transformer section of the architecture is the self-attention mechanism, which can be represented mathematically as:

$$\text{Attention}(Q, K, V) = \text{softmax}\left(\frac{QK^T}{\sqrt{d_k}}\right) V \tag{1}$$

In this formula, Q, K, and V respectively represent the query, key, and value derived from the input feature maps. The term d_k signifies the dimension of the key vectors. The softmax operation guarantees that the aggregate of all input feature weights is 1, while the division by $\sqrt{d_k}$ is a scaling factor which contributes to a stable learning process.

The SegFormer employs the self-attention mechanism across various scales, also known as multi-head attention. This approach ensures the assimilation of diverse feature information and can be defined mathematically as:

$$\text{MultiHead}(Q, K, V) = \text{Concat}(\text{head}_1, \text{head}_2, ..., \text{head}_n)W_O \tag{2}$$

In this equation, the output from the multi-head attention is subsequently integrated into a feature map, which is processed by a segmentation head to yield the final semantic segmentation output. $\text{head}_i = \text{Attention}(QW_{Qi}, KW_{Ki}, VW_{Vi})$, with W_{Qi}, W_{Ki}, and W_{Vi} being parameter matrices. W_O serves as the output transformation matrix, while "Concat" represents the concatenation operation.

3.5 Loss Function

CrossEntropyLoss function is crucial for training the segmentation models as it encourages the accurate prediction of the class of each pixel in the image, for a single pixel, the cross entropy loss is defined as:

$$L(y, \hat{y}) = - \sum_{c=1}^{C} y_c \cdot \log(\hat{y}_c) \tag{3}$$

Here, C is the total number of classes, y_c represents the ground truth (which would be 1 for the true class, and 0 for all other classes), and $\hat{y}_c$ denotes the predicted probability of the pixel belonging to class c.

4 Experiments

4.1 Metrics

IOU Intersection over Union (IoU), also known as the Jaccard index, is a commonly utilized metric for the quantitative evaluation of segmentation tasks.

$$\text{IoU} = \frac{\text{Area of Intersection}}{\text{Area of Union}} = \frac{|A \cap B|}{|A \cup B|} \tag{4}$$

BIOU We also use The Boundary Intersection over Union (BIoU) [6] as a important metric.

$$\text{BIoU} = \frac{\text{Length of Intersection of Boundaries}}{\text{Length of Union of Boundaries}} = \frac{|B_A \cap B_B|}{|B_A \cup B_B|} \tag{5}$$

In this equation, B_A denotes the set of boundary pixels in the predicted segmentation and B_B represents the set of boundary pixels in the ground truth. A higher BIoU signifies that the predicted and actual boundaries align more closely, signifying a more accurate delineation of the object's contours.

4.2   Setting and Results

In the empirical analysis, we utilized the robust MMsegmentation [7] framework, conducting experiments on an advanced NVIDIA A100 Tensor Core GPU machine. We chose the SegFormer model for our examination, applying the AdamW optimizer. The initial learning rate was set to 0.0006, betas were in the range of 0.9 to 0.999, and the weight decay was adjusted to 0.01. We used a dynamic learning rate strategy, following a polynomial updating policy with a linear warmup phase of 1500 iterations. The warmup ratio was a minute 1e-6, and the power for the policy was set at 1.0, with a minimum learning rate of 0.0. These adjustments occurred within

Fig. 3. The effectiveness of our pipeline in performing quantitative segmentation across various scenes and regions is presented in our study. Red mask is the building prediction. (Color figure online)

each iteration rather than at the epoch level. We carried out the experiments with a batch size of 3232.

Table 1. Performance of different models on the MapAIcompetition image test set (without post-processing). As baseline we show a standard U-Net [17], ConvNext [16], SegFormer [26]. And Last row is our SegAnyBuild performance.

Model	IOU	BIOU
U-Net	0.7611	0.5823
ConvNext	0.7841	0.6105
SegFormer-B0	0.7632	0.5901
SegFormer-B4	0.7844	0.6116
SegFormer-B5	0.7902	0.6185
SegAnyBuild	0.8012	0.6213

Table 1 presents compelling evidence of a substantial improvement in results when incorporating these techniques. Notably, in the fifth row of the table, a notable distinction is observed between SegFormer-B5 and SegAnyBuild, solely based on the inclusion or exclusion of pre-trained models. In our analysis, we established U-net, ConvNext, and SegFormer as baseline models for comparative purposes.

we conducted a comprehensive quantitative analysis by testing the dataset in various locations. The results, as depicted in Figure 3, clearly illustrate the effectiveness of our approach in performing building recognition and segmentation across diverse scenes in both urban and rural areas. This quantitative analysis further reinforces the robustness and generalizability of our framework in different geographical contexts. The ability to accurately identify and segment buildings in various settings, including towns and villages, highlights the versatility and practical applicability of our proposed methodology. These findings contribute to the growing body of evidence supporting the efficacy of our approach in addressing real-world challenges in the field of building recognition and segmentation.

Our study involved a thorough data analysis of the MapAI dataset, where we examined the impact of data fusion and pre-trained models on performance.

Table 2. Performance of SegAny-Build model on the different Dataset.

Dataset	IOU	BIOU
MapAI	0.8012	0.6213
INRIA Aerial Image	0.8265	0.6424
WHU Building	0.8452	0.6165
Floodnet	0.5031	0.4012

The findings unequivocally demonstrate that our proposed framework outperforms these baseline models, thus establishing its superiority on the MapAI dataset.

Our investigation also encompassed testing our approach on various datasets, as demonstrated in Table 2. The results unequivocally substantiate the efficacy of joint training through data fusion, coupled with the utilization of pre-trained large models. Notably, our approach consistently achieved favorable outcomes across multiple datasets, thereby showcasing its robustness and generalizability. This ability to achieve impressive results on diverse datasets using a single model highlights the superiority and practicality of our proposed methodology. These findings contribute to the body of knowledge, providing empirical evidence of the effectiveness of our approach in addressing the challenges associated with multiple datasets, while emphasizing its potential for broader applications in the field.

Table 3. The result is for using self data and fusion data on MapAI dataset.

Method	self	fusion	IOUIOU($\uparrow\uparrow$)	BIOU($\uparrow\uparrow$)
SegAnyBuild-self	$\checkmark$		0.7642	0.6024
SegAnyBuild-fusion		$\checkmark$	0.8012	0.6213

4.3 Ablation Study

In Table 3. there is significant potential for enhancing performance by learning deep features that capture these similarities. This approach offers a promising avenue for improving performance in building recognition and segmentation tasks. The results of our study provide empirical evidence supporting the notion that joint learning, driven by the fusion of multiple datasets, can effectively enhance performance by leveraging deep, similar features. These findings contribute to advancing our understanding of how to leverage shared knowledge across datasets for improved performance in building-related tasks.

4.4   Discussion

More diverse data source. Our study successfully conducted effective building segmentation on multiple datasets by combining dataset fusion and prompts from pretrained models. In Figure 4, the efficacy of segmentation diminishes in scenarios characterized by intricate corner details or limited illumination, such as in dark environments. This can primarily be attributed to two contributing factors. Firstly, the limitation of available

Fig. 4. The segmentation results illustrate two distinct night scenes: on the left, a scenario featuring illuminated street lights, and on the right, a comparatively darker setting devoid of prominent light sources.

data can impose constraints on the segmentation performance under these challenging conditions. Secondly, the task of learning texture features of buildings becomes increasingly arduous in dark or blurry scenes due to the decreased visibility and clarity of the distinguishing attributes. These complexities underscore the challenges associated with performing segmentation in less than optimal conditions and highlight the need for advanced models capable of overcoming such limitations.

3D Knowledge learning. Furthermore, certain datasets may provide valuable depth information, such as the MapAI dataset, which can be leveraged to enhance the uniform segmentation of buildings. By incorporating depth data, the segmentation process can benefit from additional cues, leading to more accurate and consistent delineation of building boundaries.

Self-supervising learning. further exploration and integration of diverse datasets in self-supervised learning [22, 29, 30], including those with depth information, offer promising avenues for advancing building segmentation performance across a broader range of scenarios. These insights contribute to the ongoing research in the field, highlighting the potential of incorporating additional datasets and depth information to improve building segmentation techniques.

4.5   Conclusion

The study presented elucidates the pivotal role of diversely sourced datasets and the application of sophisticated representation learning models in the context of building segmentation in remote sensing imagery. Our methodology, which strategically amalgamates multiple datasets, has not only broadened the informational landscape available for learning but also displayed unparalleled performance across all the datasets employed. This study serves as a robust stepping stone for future investigations, creating an avenue for potentially transformative breakthroughs and applications in this building segmentation field.

Acknowledgments. This work was supported by the DeepCrop project and PerformLCA project (UCPH Strategic plan 2023 Data+ Pool).

References

1. Arbelaez, P., Maire, M., Fowlkes, C., Malik, J.: Contour detection and hierarchical image segmentation. IEEE Trans. Pattern Anal. Mach. Intell. **33**(5), 898–916 (2010)
2. Bao, H., Dong, L., Piao, S., Wei, F.: BEiT: BERT pre-training of image transformers. arXiv preprint arXiv:2106.08254 (2021)
3. Boguszewski, A., Batorski, D., Ziemba-Jankowska, N., Dziedzic, T., Zambrzycka, A.: Landcover. AI: dataset for automatic mapping of buildings, woodlands, water and roads from aerial imagery. In: Proceedings of the IEEE/CVF Conference on Computer Vision and Pattern Recognition, pp. 1102–1110 (2021)
4. Chen, J., Yang, Z., Zhang, L.: Semantic segment anything. https://github.com/fudan-zvg/Semantic-Segment-Anything (2023)
5. Chen, L.C., Papandreou, G., Kokkinos, I., Murphy, K., Yuille, A.L.: DeepLab: Semantic image segmentation with deep convolutional nets, atrous convolution, and fully connected CRFs. IEEE Trans. Pattern Anal. Mach. Intell. **40**(4), 834–848 (2017)
6. Cheng, B., Girshick, R., Dollár, P., Berg, A.C., Kirillov, A.: Boundary IoU: Improving object-centric image segmentation evaluation. In: Proceedings of the IEEE/CVF Conference on Computer Vision and Pattern Recognition, pp. 15334–15342 (2021)
7. Contributors, M.: MMSegmentation: OpenMMLab semantic segmentation toolbox and benchmark. https://github.com/open-mmlab/mmsegmentation (2020)
8. Devlin, J., Chang, M.W., Lee, K., Toutanova, K.: BERT: pre-training of deep bidirectional transformers for language understanding. arXiv preprint arXiv:1810.04805 (2018)
9. He, K., Gkioxari, G., Dollár, P., Girshick, R.: Mask R-CNN. In: Proceedings of the IEEE International Conference on Computer Vision, pp. 2961–2969 (2017)
10. Ji, S., Wei, S., Lu, M.: Fully convolutional networks for multisource building extraction from an open aerial and satellite imagery data set. IEEE Trans. Geosci. Remote Sens. **57**(1), 574–586 (2018)
11. Jyhne, S., et al.: Mapai: precision in buildingsegmentation (2022)
12. Kirillov, A., et al.: Segment anything. arXiv preprint arXiv:2304.02643 (2023)
13. Li, L., Zhang, T., Kang, Z., Jiang, X.: Mask-FPAN: semi-supervised face parsing in the wild with de-occlusion and UV GAN. Comput. Graph. **116**, 185–193 (2023)
14. Li, L., Zhang, T., Oehmcke, S., Gieseke, F., Igel, C.: BuildSeg: a general framework for the segmentation of buildings. Nordic Mach. Intell. **2**(3) (2022)
15. Li, Z., Wang, H., Liu, Y.: Semantic segmentation of remote sensing image based on bilateral branch network. Vis. Comput., 1–22 (2023)
16. Liu, Z., Mao, H., Wu, C.Y., Feichtenhofer, C., Darrell, T., Xie, S.: A convnet for the 2020s. In: Proceedings of the IEEE/CVF Conference on Computer Vision and Pattern Recognition (CVPR) (2022)
17. Long, J., Shelhamer, E., Darrell, T.: Fully convolutional networks for semantic segmentation. In: Proceedings of the IEEE Conference on Computer Vision and Pattern Recognition, pp. 3431–3440 (2015)

18. Maggiori, E., Tarabalka, Y., Charpiat, G., Alliez, P.: Can semantic labeling methods generalize to any city? the inria aerial image labeling benchmark. In: IEEE International Geoscience and Remote Sensing Symposium (IGARSS). IEEE (2017)
19. Nazir, A., et al.: ECSU-Net: an embedded clustering sliced u-net coupled with fusing strategy for efficient intervertebral disc segmentation and classification. IEEE Trans. Image Process. **31**, 880–893 (2021)
20. Oehmcke, S., et al.: Deep learning based 3D point cloud regression for estimating forest biomass. In: International Conference on Advances in Geographic Information Systems (SIGSPATIAL). ACM (2022)
21. Oehmcke, S., et al.: Deep learning based 3D point cloud regression for estimating forest biomass. In: Proceedings of the 30th International Conference on Advances in Geographic Information Systems, pp. 1–4 (2022)
22. Rahnemoonfar, M., Chowdhury, T., Sarkar, A., Varshney, D., Yari, M., Murphy, R.R.: FloodNet: a high resolution aerial imagery dataset for post flood scene understanding. IEEE Access **9**, 89644–89654 (2021)
23. Revenga, J.C., et al.: Above-ground biomass prediction for croplands at a submeter resolution using UAV-lidar and machine learning methods. Remote Sensing **14**(16), 3912 (2022)
24. Ronneberger, O., Fischer, P., Brox, T.: U-Net: convolutional networks for biomedical image segmentation. In: Navab, N., Hornegger, J., Wells, W.M., Frangi, A.F. (eds.) MICCAI 2015. LNCS, vol. 9351, pp. 234–241. Springer, Cham (2015). https://doi.org/10.1007/978-3-319-24574-4_28
25. Wu, M., Li, L., Li, H.: FASE: feature-based similarity search on ECG data. In: 2019 IEEE International Conference on Big Knowledge (ICBK), pp. 273–280. IEEE (2019)
26. Xie, E., Wang, W., Yu, Z., Anandkumar, A., Alvarez, J.M., Luo, P.: SegFormer: simple and efficient design for semantic segmentation with transformers. Adv. Neural. Inf. Process. Syst. **34**, 12077–12090 (2021)
27. Zhang, T., Li, L., Cao, S., Pu, T., Peng, Z.: Attention-guided pyramid context networks for detecting infrared small target under complex background. IEEE Trans. Aerospace Electron. Syst. (2023)
28. Zhang, T., Li, L., Igel, C., Oehmcke, S., Gieseke, F., Peng, Z.: LR-CSNet: low-rank deep unfolding network for image compressive sensing. In: 2022 IEEE 8th International Conference on Computer and Communications (ICCC), pp. 1951–1957. IEEE (2022)
29. Zhang, Y., Li, L., Song, L., Xie, R., Zhang, W.: FACT: fused attention for clothing transfer with generative adversarial networks. In: Proceedings of the AAAI Conference on Artificial Intelligence, vol. 34, pp. 12894–12901 (2020)
30. Zhou, C., et al.: Multi-scale pseudo labeling for unsupervised deep edge detection. Available at SSRN 4425635

A Novel Zero-Watermarking Algorithm Based on Texture Complexity Analysis

Xiaochao Wang[1], Qianqian Du[1], Xiaodong Tan[1], Jianping Hu[2], Ling Du[3], and Huayan Zhang[4]($\boxtimes$)

[1] School of Mathematical Sciences, Tiangong University, Tianjin, China
[2] School of Sciences, Northeast Electric Power University, Jilin, China
[3] School of Software, Tiangong University, Tianjin, China
[4] School of Computer Science and Technology, Tiangong University, Tianjin, China
zhanghy307@163.com

Abstract. Aiming at the problem of existing watermarking algorithms cannot effectively resist complex attacks, a novel zero-watermarking algorithm based on texture complexity analysis is proposed. First, we calculate the standard deviation map of the host image by the spatially selective texture method and achieve the optimal target regions (OTRs) by clustering the binary standard deviation map. To improve the robustness of the proposed algorithm, we use singular value decomposition (SVD) to extract multiple feature sequences from the OTRs. Then, these robust feature sequences are binarized to generate multiple feature images. For the watermark image, we apply the chaotic mapping to encrypt it and ensure the security of the watermark image. Finally, we perform an exclusive-or (XOR) operation on each of the extracted multiple feature images with the encrypted watermark image to construct multiple zero watermarks, which will be saved at the Copyright Certification Center to protect the copyright of the image. A large number of experimental results show that the newly-proposed algorithm not only has good distinguishability, but also has high robustness to complex attacks. Compared with existing watermarking algorithms, our proposed algorithm has advantages in invisibility, robustness and security.

Keywords: zero-watermarking · texture complexity

1 Introduction and Motivation

With the high-speed development of networks, images can be easily obtained and spread over the world, which inevitably brings about copyright problems. How to protect the copyright of images has become an urgent problem. In order to ensure the security and legality of images, image watermarking technologies have been extensively researched.

Supported by Natural Science Foundation of Jilin Province (No. 20210101472JC).

Traditional watermarking algorithms focus on how to embed information in the host image. However, when the watermark information is embedded into a image, the pixels of the image will be modified more or less, which can cause certain damage to the quality of the image. In order to solve the problems of traditional watermarking algorithms, zero-watermarking algorithms are developed, which do not damage the host image and effectively balances the relationship between robustness and invisibility.

However, the existing zero-watermark algorithms still have the following problems. (1) They usually extract global feature information from the host image, which may lead to inaccurate copyright detection if significant parts of the image are cropped. (2) They can only construct a single zero watermark, which reduces the ability to resist complex attacks and leads to lower reliability.

To address the aforementioned issues, we propose a novel zero-watermarking algorithm based on texture complexity analysis. Texture analysis is used to extract important information from images by computing and modeling textures, and they are often used to describe and compare different features. The following are the primary contributions of our work.

- Local texture features of the image are extracted from the optimal target region of the host image using texture complexity analysis, which improves the robustness of the proposed algorithm to resist various attacks.
- We utilize a majority voting strategy on the constructed multiple zero watermark images, which effectively resists different complex attacks and enhances the reliability of our algorithm.
- We construct features with high distinguishability for different images, which not only improve the security of the zero-watermarking algorithm, but also facilitate its practical application.

2 Related Work

2.1 Zero-Watermarking Algorithms

In the past few years, frequency domain based zero-watermarking algorithms have attracted extensive researches. Wen et al. [17] first proposed a zero-watermarking algorithm using DCT to extract features. Wang et al. [16] proposed a robust zero-watermarking algorithm by combining discrete cosine transform (DCT) and singular value decomposition (SVD) for natural images. Vaidya [13] proposed a medical image watermarking method based on lifting wavelet transform (LWT) and discrete wavelet transform (DWT). This is a non-blind method, the original host image should be used in watermark extraction. Hu et al. [5] proposed a zero-watermarking algorithm based on Bi-dimensional empirical mode decomposition (BEMD) and SVD, which has good robustness. At the same time, they have obtained good results in medical image tampering detection.

Due to the low complexity of the spatial domain-based zero-watermarking algorithms, they have also received extensive attention. A zero-watermarking algorithm based on the spatial domain was proposed by Chang and Lin [3]. In [4],

Hosny et al. used orthogonal multichannel fractional-order bias Gegenbauer moments to construct the zero watermark. The algorithm has better resistance to conventional and combinatorial attacks.

2.2 Texture-Based Watermarking Algorithms

Textures is a visual feature with uniformity in an image, which reflects the arrangement characteristics of the structure of an object that changes slowly or periodically [12]. Combined with the visual properties of textures, Palak et al. [6] designed a watermarking algorithm using gradient histogram and Log Gabor filter to match the watermark with the texture of the host image. Andalibi et al. [1] proposed an image watermark algorithm with adaptive mark texturing. Wang et al. [14] proposed an image texture analysis-based neural network watermarking algorithm, which can successfully improve the quality of watermark image without sacrificing its robustness.

Sangeetha et al. [10] proposed a texture watermarking algorithm based on entropy and DWT. Varsha and Virendra [11] proposed an algorithm based on local texture information to achieve optimal embedding. To discover the most textured blocks, Taha et al. [2] proposed a low-texture hiding model utilizing the lifted wavelet transform (LWT). In summary, textures combine the properties of human visual masking to improve the robustness and invisibility of the algorithm and are widely considered in zero-watermarking algorithms.

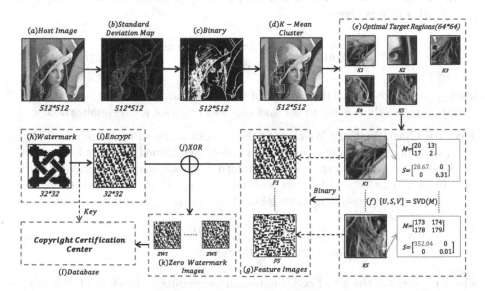

Fig. 1. The flowchart of watermark construction. (a) Host image. (b) Standard deviation map. (c) Binary. (d) K-Mean cluster. (e) Optimal target regions. (f) SVD. (g) Feature images. (h) Watermark. (i) Encrypt. (l) Database. (k) Zero watermark images.

3 Proposed Zero-Watermarking Algorithm

3.1 Texture Complexity

Texture features are not pixel-based features, which require statistical computations in regions containing multiple pixel points. To improve the robustness of the algorithm to against various attacks, stable regions are selected from the host image for feature construction. In this subsection, we adopt the spatially selective texturization technique [1] to identify the texture regions of the image. The process of texture analysis is described as follows.

Texture Extraction: Computing the features of a digital image means to describe its texture properties numerically. Texture extraction is mainly based on the standard deviation map R (Fig. 1(b)) to measure the texture regions in the host image. It is mathematically represented as follows:

$$R(x,y) = \sqrt{\frac{\sum_{i=x-1}^{x+1} \sum_{j=y-1}^{y+1} (H(i,j) - H_{xy})^2}{8}}, \tag{1}$$

where H_{xy} is the average value of pixels in local blocks. Experimental results show that the block size of 3×3 is sufficient to capture the changing trend of pixel values while remaining small enough to enable adequate spatial location in the standard deviation map.

After that, set thresholds for generating binary standard deviation map BR (Fig. 1(c)), which is given by:

$$BR(x,y) = \begin{cases} 1, if\, R\,(x,y) \geq \alpha \cdot max(R), \\ 0, otherwise, \end{cases} \tag{2}$$

where α is used to control the number of zeros and ones in the binarized standard deviation map, which is set to 0.1 and can well ensure a good equalization.

Texture Classification: We classify the texture image into textured and low-textured regions. Then determine which one of the defined region it belongs to. To this end, we search on the binary standard deviation map to identify whether each block of size $m \times m$ belongs to a texture region or a low-texture region. Here, we let S_k represent the class label of blocks l_k:

$$S_k = \begin{cases} texture, if \frac{1}{m^2} \sum_{x,y \epsilon C_k} BR(x,y) > 0.5, \\ low-texture, otherwise, \end{cases} \tag{3}$$

where C_k denotes the set of coordinates corresponding to block l_k ($1 \leq k \leq p$). After that, we perform K-means clustering (Fig. 1(d)) of the texture regions in S_k to obtain the optimal target regions (OTRs) (Fig. 1(e)), denoted as K_i, which are saved as location index $key1$.

3.2 Singular Value Decomposition

Singular value decomposition is a powerful transformation technique and the singular values maintain good stability under small perturbations [7,8]. Benefit from the desirable property, we use singular value decomposition to construct robust image features. We first divide K_i into $P \times Q$ blocks with size of $b \times b$, with $P = m/b, Q = m/b$. Then, we perform SVD for each $b \times b$ sized block and use the first singular value after decomposition to construct the feature images F_i (Fig. 1(g)), defined as follows:

$$F_i = \begin{cases} 1, if \ S_i(x,y) > T_i, (1 \leq i \leq r), \\ 0, otherwise, \end{cases} \tag{4}$$

where T_i is the mean value of $S_i(x,y)$, which represents the singular value matrix of the $i-$th block.

3.3 Zero Watermark Construction and Extraction

Zero Watermark Construction: The construction of a zero watermark is achieved by first identifying stable features in the host image. These features are then used to perform XOR operations with the watermark to create the zero watermark. The basic flow of this algorithm is summarized as follows.

Step1: Calculate the optimal target regions of the host image $H(x,y)$ (Fig. 1(a)) according to the texturing process in Subsect. 3.1.

Step2: Perform SVD on the selected OTRs (Fig. 1(e)) to obtain the feature image F_i (Fig. 1(g)).

Step3: Encrypt the binary watermark image W (Fig. 1(h)) using chaotic mapping to improve the security of the algorithm and obtain the encrypted watermark image W' (Fig. 1(i)). The second-degree polynomial chaotic mapping is given as follows:

$$R_{i+1} = \mu R_i(1 - R_i) \ (0 < R_i < 1), \tag{5}$$

where system parameter $\mu \in [0,4]$ and initial condition $R_0 \in (0,1)$, when $3.5699456... < \mu \leq 4$, the mapping enters the chaos state.

Step4: Perform the XOR operation between F_i and W' to obtain multiple zero watermark images ZW_i (Fig. 1(k)) by Eq. 6, which are stored in the Copyright Certification Center for further copyright protection:

$$ZW_i = XOR(F_i, W'). \tag{6}$$

Zero Watermark Extraction: In order to verify the copyright ownership of the image, the watermark image needs to be extracted from the potentially compromised host image. This extraction process is similar to the zero watermark construction, and the extraction flowchart is shown in Fig. 2.

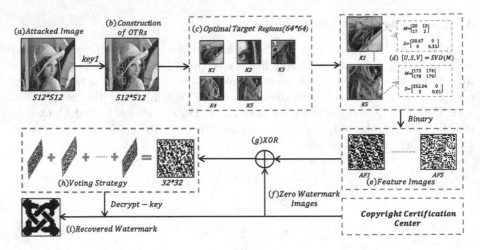

Fig. 2. The flowchart of watermark extraction. (a) Attacked image. (b) Construction of OTRs. (c) Optimal target regions. (d) SVD. (e) Feature images. (f) Zero watermark images. (g) XOR. (h) Voting strategy. (i) Recovered watermark.

Step1: We use the *key*1 saved from the zero watermark construction process to locate the optimal target region (Fig. 2(c)) of the attacked host image.

Step2: Then, we apply SVD to select the optimal target regions. The feature images $\boldsymbol{AF}_i$ (Fig. 2(e)) are obtained by the rules defined in Eq. 4.

Step3: We perform XOR operation on $\boldsymbol{AF}_i$ and $\boldsymbol{ZW}_i$ saved by the Copyright Certification Center to obtain an encrypted watermark image $\boldsymbol{EW}_i$

$$EW_i = XOR(\boldsymbol{AF}_i, \boldsymbol{ZW}_i), \tag{7}$$

where $\boldsymbol{AF}_i$ denotes the feature image of the $i-$th OTR and $\boldsymbol{ZW}_i$ denotes the $i-$th zero watermark image.

Step4: We constructs multiple zero watermarks, so we decrypt the extracted multiple watermark images $\boldsymbol{EW}_i$, denoted as $\boldsymbol{SW}_i$. To this end, a voting strategy (Fig. 2(h)) is used to obtain the accurate watermark image $\boldsymbol{DW}$ (Fig. 2(i)), the formula is as follows:

$$DW = \begin{cases} 1, if \ SW_i(x,y) \geq \lceil r/2 \rceil, \\ 0, otherwise, \end{cases} \tag{8}$$

where $\boldsymbol{SW}_i(x,y)$ is the sum of the elements corresponding to the decrypted multiple watermark images, and r is the number of extracted watermark images.

4   Experimental Results

In this section, we perform extensive experiments to test the performance of the proposed zero-watermarking algorithm, including robustness, distinguishability.

Fig. 3. Selected images. (a) Lena. (b) Placard. (c) Female. (d) Splash. (e) Helicopter. (f) Cover. (g) Butterfly. (h) Starfish. (i) Unity. (j) Coin. (k) Sun. (l) Game.

4.1 Experimental Settings

Experimental Data Set: Figure 3 shows the selected host images with the size of 512×512, which can be found in (https://github.com/txd2021/Test_tl/tree/main). All the different types of watermark images of size 32×32 are shown in Fig. 3(i-l) for evaluation and comparison.

Parameter Setting: The initial value of chaotic encryption $x_0 = 0.1, \mu = 4$, iterate 500 times to make it reach a fully chaotic state. Considering that fewer OTRs will affect the accuracy of the voting strategy, which in turn will reduce the robustness of the algorithm, and on the other hand more OTRs will increase the complexity of the algorithm. Through extensive experimental verification, we can achieve much better results by selecting five OTRs from the host images.

Evaluation Metrics: Robustness is a key indicator to measure the resistance of zero-watermarking algorithms to attacks. Table 1 lists the abbreviations for attacks. The commonly used bit error rate (BER) and normalized cross-correlation (NC) [15] are adopted to assess the robustness of our approach by comparing the extracted watermark image with the original watermark image.

4.2 Evaluation of Similarity and Equalization

Since the construction of zero watermark is dependent on the features of the host image, the zero watermark image is inextricably linked to the host image. The zero watermark images generated by different host images should be dissimilar. Table 2 evaluates the similarity of the zero watermark images generated by eight different host images (as shown in Fig. 3(a-h)). As shown in Table 2, the maximum and minimum similarity between the zero watermark images generated from eight significantly dissimilar host images are 0.5648 and 0.3874, respectively. This indicates that our algorithm has low similarity and good distinguishability for different kinds of images.

Table 1. The abbreviations for 13 kinds of attacks.

Classes	Full name of attack type	Abbreviation
Noise Attacks	Pepper & salt Noise	PN
	Speckle Noise	SN
	Gaussian Noise	GN
Filtering Attacks	Median Filtering	MF
	Average Filtering	AF
	Wiener Filtering	WF
	Gaussian low pass Filtering	GF
Image Enhancement Attacks	Sharpening	SH
	Histogram Equalization	HE
	JPEG Compression	JC
Geometric Attacks	Resizing	RS
	Cropping attack	CA
	Rotation	RT

Table 2. Similarities between the zero-watermark generated from eight Host images.

Host Image	Lena	Placard	Female	Splash	Helicopter	Cover	Butterfly	Starfish
Lena	1.0000	0.5116	0.4456	0.4869	0.4954	0.4798	0.5617	0.5061
Placard	0.5116	1.0000	0.5207	0.5002	0.5293	0.5456	0.4731	0.5029
Female	0.4456	0.5207	1.0000	0.5283	0.4404	0.5010	0.3874	0.5315
Splash	0.4869	0.5002	0.5283	1.0000	0.4994	0.5648	0.4898	0.4640
Helicopter	0.4954	0.5293	0.4404	0.4994	1.0000	0.5250	0.5230	0.5132
Cover	0.4798	0.5456	0.5010	0.5648	0.5250	1.0000	0.4941	0.4787
Butterfly	0.5617	0.4731	0.3874	0.4898	0.5230	0.4941	1.0000	0.4943
Starfish	0.5061	0.5029	0.5315	0.4640	0.5132	0.4787	0.4943	1.0000

4.3   Robustness Resist on Various Attacks

To assess the robustness of the algorithm, 13 different types of attacks are executed on the host image, including filtering, noise, image enhancement, geometric transformation and combination attacks.

Noise Attacks. Since noise is random in nature, it causes some distortion in the image. Therefore, we evaluate the resistance of the algorithm to noise attacks of different strengths, such as Pepper & salt, Gaussian and Speckle noise. Because the singular value decomposition is more resistant to noise attacks, its perturbation range will be small even if the attack intensity increases. As shown in Table 3, the three different noise attacks have a small impact on the algorithm.

Filter Attacks. Filtering inevitably leads to a loss of image details. Since we optimize the target regions using multiple mechanisms, we can maintain good

Table 3. Robustness results of watermark images extracted from eight different host images and watermark image unity under thirteen attacks.

Attck&Host	Lena	Placard	Female	Splash	Helicopter	Cover	Butterfly	Starfish
PN-0.01	1.0000	1.0000	1.0000	1.0000	1.0000	1.0000	1.0000	1.0000
SN-0.01	1.0000	1.0000	0.9992	0.9992	1.0000	0.9995	1.0000	0.9993
GN-0.01	0.9979	0.9995	0.9982	0.9984	0.9944	0.9966	1.0000	0.9969
MF-[3,3]	1.0000	1.0000	1.0000	1.0000	1.0000	1.0000	1.0000	1.0000
AF-[3,3]	0.9990	0.9990	1.0000	1.0000	1.0000	1.0000	1.0000	1.0000
WF-[3,3]	1.0000	1.0000	1.0000	1.0000	1.0000	1.0000	1.0000	1.0000
GF-[3,3]	1.0000	0.9990	1.0000	1.0000	1.0000	1.0000	1.0000	1.0000
SH-3	0.9990	1.0000	1.0000	1.0000	0.9990	1.0000	1.0000	0.9990
HE-64	0.9990	0.9979	1.0000	0.9990	0.9969	0.9979	1.0000	0.9990
JC-40	1.0000	1.0000	1.0000	1.0000	1.0000	1.0000	1.0000	1.0000
RS-4-0.25	1.0000	1.0000	1.0000	1.0000	1.0000	1.0000	1.0000	1.0000
CA-1/16	1.0000	1.0000	1.0000	1.0000	1.0000	1.0000	1.0000	0.9979
RT-45°	1.0000	1.0000	1.0000	1.0000	1.0000	1.0000	1.0000	1.0000

stability even when the pixel values fluctuate at the same time. Table 3 gives the NC values for the four types of filtering attacks with a window size of 3×3. It can be seen from the results that the NC values of different types of filtering attacks are all greater than 0.99.

Enhancement Attacks. Enhancement can also cause loss of image pixels, which directly affects the visual quality of the image. As can be seen in Table 3, the NC values of the extracted images for eight images under different types of enhancement attacks are almost close to 1, which intuitively reflects the ability of the algorithm to resist the enhancement attacks.

Geometric Attacks. Geometric attacks usually cause the watermarks unsynchronized. Since we construct multiple zero watermark images by localizing stable regions instead of a single zero watermark for the whole image, even when the image is massively cropped or scaled, the impact on the image quality is minimal, which largely eliminates the impact of such attacks. Table 3 shows the impact of geometric attacks on the robustness at different intensities, which indicates that the algorithm has a strong resistance to geometric attacks.

To further verify the generalization performance of the algorithm, we tested different types of images, which include Sensing noise images, Computer-synthesis images and Untexture images. From Fig. 4, it can be seen that the proposed algorithm has good robustness on both real images with sensor noise and computer-generated images, with NC values above 0.98. However, our algorithm does not perform well for texture-frees images. The reason is that such images cannot extract rich texture features to construct zero watermark information. In addition, for the effect of image resolution on the algorithm, we

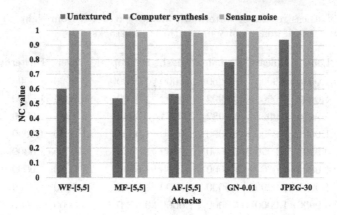

Fig. 4. NC value results for three different types of images under various attacks.

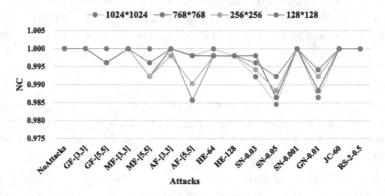

Fig. 5. NC values for images at different resolutions under multiple types of attacks.

tested the robustness experiments for four resolutions of 1024×1024, 768×768, 256×256, and 128×128. As can be seen from Fig. 5, the NC values at different resolutions are above 0.98, which illustrates our algorithm is not sensitive to different resolutions.

4.4   Comparison with Previous Algorithms

Comparison with Zero-watermarking Algorithms. Table 4 gives the NC values of our algorithm compared with the three zero-watermarking algorithms. From Table 4, it can be seen that the NC value of our algorithm outperforms the other zero-watermarking algorithms. Therefore, the proposed algorithm has stronger robustness compared with other zero-watermarking algorithms.

Comparison with Texture-based Algorithms. Algorithm [18] designs a texture-based watermarking algorithm. As shown in Table 5, although Algorithm [18] is slightly more robust to Gaussian noise than our algorithm. However,

Table 4. NC of the extracted watermark images compared with zero-watermarking algorithms. The best results in each row are marked in bold.

Attacks	Intensity	[7]	[9]	[4]	Proposed
PN	0.01	NAN	0.9629	0.9917	**1.0000**
GN	0.01	NAN	0.9462	0.9886	**0.9990**
MF	[3,3]	0.9954	0.9676	0.9916	**1.0000**
	[5,5]	0.9911	0.9022	0.9891	**1.0000**
GF	[3,3]	0.9978	**1.0000**	0.9940	**1.0000**
	[5,5]	0.9942	0.9963	0.9936	**1.0000**
AF	[3,3]	0.9927	0.9718	0.9919	**0.9990**
	[5,5]	0.9864	0.9200	NAN	**0.9979**
JC	30	0.9872	0.9951	0.9943	**1.0000**
	50	0.9899	**1.0000**	0.9924	**1.0000**
RT	5°	0.8123	0.9061	0.9917	**1.0000**

Table 5. NC results compared with the algorithm [18].

Attacks	Intensity	[18]	Proposed
MF	[3,3]	0.9993	**1.0000**
GF	[3,3]	0.9761	**1.0000**
AF	[3,3]	0.9963	**0.9990**
GN	0.01	**0.9967**	0.9945
PN	0.01	0.9990	**1.0000**
SN	0.01	0.9996	**1.0000**
CA	1/4	0.9904	**1.0000**
RA	45°	0.9942	**1.0000**
JC	30	0.9962	**1.0000**
JC	50	0.9964	**1.0000**
SH	2	0.9873	**0.9979**

our algorithm outperforms it in terms of filtering, sharpening, JPEG compression, and rotation attacks.

5   Conclusion and Future Work

In this paper, we have presented a multiple zero-watermarking algorithm based on the texture complexity and the SVD for copyright protection. The experimental results show that the algorithm not only has good distinguishability, but also has high robustness to complex attacks. Although our algorithm achieves much better results on different types of images and various attacks, there are still some some limitations. First, we found that high-intensity noise can cause significant changes in image pixel values, which can lead to larger image distortion. Second, our algorithm perform not well for texture-free images due to less texture features can be extracted to construct robust feature image. In the near future, we will focus on improving the proposed algorithm to resist high-intensity noise attacks and texture-free images.

References

1. Andalibi, M., Chandler, D.M.: Digital image watermarking via adaptive logo texturization. IEEE Trans. Image Process. **24**(12), 5060–5073 (2015)
2. Basheer Taha, T.: Digital image watermarking algorithm based on texture masking model. J. Eng. Sci. Technol. **14**(6), 3347–3360 (2019)
3. Chang, C.C., Lin, P.Y.: Adaptive watermark mechanism for rightful ownership protection. J. Syst. Softw. **81**(7), 1118–1129 (2008)
4. Hosny, K.M., Darwish, M.M.: New geometrically invariant multiple zero-watermarking algorithm for color medical images. Biomed. Signal Process. Control **70**, 1–16 (2021)
5. Hu, K., Wang, X., Hu, J., Wang, H., Qin, H.: A novel robust zero-watermarking algorithm for medical images. Vis. Comput. **37**(9), 2841–2853 (2021)
6. Jain, P., Ghanekar, U.: Robust watermarking technique for textured images. Procedia Comput. Sci. **125**, 179–186 (2018)
7. Kang, X.B., Lin, G.F., Chen, Y.J., Zhao, F., Zhang, E.H., Jing, C.N.: Robust and secure zero-watermarking algorithm for color images based on majority voting pattern and hyper-chaotic encryption. Multimedia Tools Appl. **79**(1), 1169–1202 (2020)
8. Liu, R., Tan, T.: An SVD-based watermarking scheme for protecting rightful ownership. IEEE Trans. Multimedia **4**(1), 121–128 (2002)
9. Ma, B., Chang, L., Wang, C., Li, J., Li, G., Xia, Z., Wang, X.: Double medical images zero-watermarking algorithm based on the chaotic system and ternary accurate polar complex exponential transform. J. Math. Imaging Vis. **63**(9), 1160–1178 (2021)
10. Sangeetha, N., Anita, X.: Entropy based texture watermarking using discrete wavelet transform. Optik **160**, 380–388 (2018)
11. Sisaudia, V., Vishwakarma, V.P.: Copyright protection using KELM-PSO based multi-spectral image watermarking in DCT domain with local texture information based selection. Multimedia Tools Appl. **80**(6), 8667–8688 (2021)
12. Suen, P.H., Healey, G.: The analysis and recognition of real-world textures in three dimensions. IEEE Trans. Pattern Anal. Mach. Intell. **22**(5), 491–503 (2000)
13. Vaidya, S.P.: Fingerprint-based robust medical image watermarking in hybrid transform. Vis. Comput. **39**(6), 2245–2260 (2023)
14. Wang, K., Li, L., Luo, T., Chang, C.-C.: Deep neural network watermarking based on texture analysis. In: Sun, X., Wang, J., Bertino, E. (eds.) ICAIS 2020. CCIS, vol. 1252, pp. 558–569. Springer, Singapore (2020). https://doi.org/10.1007/978-981-15-8083-3_50
15. Wang, X., Ma, D., Hu, K., Hu, J., Du, L.: Mapping based residual convolution neural network for non-embedding and blind image watermarking. J. Inf. Secur. Appl. **59**, 1–10 (2021)

16. Wang, X., Wen, M., Tan, X., Zhang, H., Hu, J., Qin, H.: A novel zero-watermarking algorithm based on robust statistical features for natural images. Vis. Comput. **38**(9–10), 3175–3188 (2022)
17. Wen, Q., Sun, T., Wang, S.: Based zero-watermark digital watermarking technology. In: Proceedings of 3rd China Information Hiding Multimedia Security Workshop (CIHW), pp. 102–109 (2001)
18. Yang, X., Liu, Y., Zhu, T.: Adaptive robust watermarking algorithm based on image texture. In: 2020 2nd Symposium on Signal Processing Systems, pp. 7–12 (2020)

Video-Based Self-supervised Human Depth Estimation

Qianlin Li and Xiaoyan Zhang$^{(\boxtimes)}$

School of Computer Science and Software Engineering,
Shenzhen University, Shenzhen 518060, China
xyzhang15@szu.edu.cn

Abstract. In this paper, we propose a video-besed method for self-supervised human depth estimation, aiming at the problem of joint point distortion in human depth and insufficient utilization of 3D information in video-based depth estimation. We use the relative ordinal relations between human joint point pairs to deal with the problem of joint point distortion. Meanwhile, a temporal correlation module is proposed to focus on the temporal correlation between past and present frames, taking into account the influence of temporal characteristics in the video sequence. A hierarchical structure is adopted to fuse adjacent features, thus fully mine the 3D information based on the video. The experimental results show that this model significantly improves the human depth estimation performance, especially at the joints.

Keywords: Human · Video · Depth estimation

1 Introduction

Nowadays, obtaining the corresponding depth map through the RGB image has always been a basic problem in computer vision. Depth capture devices are not only expensive, but also their depth systems are always affected by natural environments, resulting in certain defects, such as holes. To estimate depth only from a picture, many deep learning-based methods have been proposed, such as DPT [6] and MiDaS [7], which have large training datasets that combine various types of labeled data. As one of the important components of society, it is an inevitable trend to acquire human depth. When performing depth estimation on human images in the 'wild', it is difficult to estimate the local geometric details and clothing texture details of the image. At the same time, the lack of ground truth dense depth and labeled data has always been a real problem. At this point, we propose to perform human depth estimation from videos and using self-supervised between frames in the video to constrain the depth estimation.

Supplementary Information The online version contains supplementary material available at https://doi.org/10.1007/978-3-031-50069-5_16.

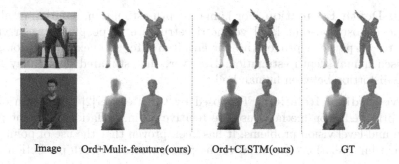

Fig. 1. Examples of estimated depth and reconstructed 3D mesh. The first image is from Tang et al. dataset [11] and the second image is from THuman2.0 dataset [15].

As shown in Fig. 1, the depth map predicted by our method is not only full of details but also the shape of the reconstructed 3D mesh character is complete. For accurate human depth estimation, it is necessary to consider not only the shape of the complete person and global geometric details, but also the local details of the person and the order correctness of the body parts. The methods proposed by Jafarian et al. [3], Saito et al. [8,9], Xiu et al. [14], Wang et al. [13] respectively, use normal to enhance the local geometric details of the human and confirm that normal is effective for restoring local geometric details. However, observation of the 3D human mesh constructed based on the estimated depth by recent work in Jafarian et al. [3] found that the relative order between human body parts may be distorted. To solve this problem, we use the relative depth ordinal relations between human joint points to correct the depth error of predicted human joint points. Instead of relying solely on static features of frames, we propose a joint spatio-temporal feature extraction strategy to fully mine the 3D information between consecutive frames in the video.

Our contributions are summarized as follows:

- We use the human joint ordinal relation to correct the distortion of the joints in the predicted depth.
- Propose a temporal correlation module to predict human depth jointly with spatio-temporal features, rather than being dominated by static features alone.
- The experiments demonstrate the importance of relative depth ordinal relations and fully exploiting spatio-temporal features across videos in human depth estimation.

2   Related Works

Accurately obtaining image depth is a widely discussed topic in computer vision. Deep learning-based methods for depth estimation [4,5,17] offer a practical and precise approach.

Human Depth Estimation. For human depth estimation, Jafarian et al. [3] used the almost constant local geometric structure of people between video frames to warp the depth of the current frame to the next frame for self-supervised human depth estimation. However, the estimated depth may have relative distortion between human body.

Relative Ordinal Relations. Proposed by Chen et al. [2] and Zoran et al. [19], depth prediction methods use the relative ordinal relations of point pairs to solve mid-level vision problems. It has been proven that the use of point pair relative ordinal relations can improve the performance of depth prediction.

Spatio-temporal Feature Extraction. Convolutional Long Short Term Memory (CLSTM) [16] adds a convolutional structure to LSTM to better extract spatio-temporal features. However, when the number of input frames is small, it may not be able to take advantage of the structure.

3   Method

In this section, we detail our proposed network structure for video-based self-supervised human depth estimation. As shown in Fig. 2, in our method, after using the stacked hourglass network to extract spatial features, the main modules are the Order Network that generates relative depth ordinal relations and the temporal correlation module. In order to obtain sufficient 3D information from the video, we propose two different strategies for the temporal correlation module, namely multi-feature fusion and CLSTM.

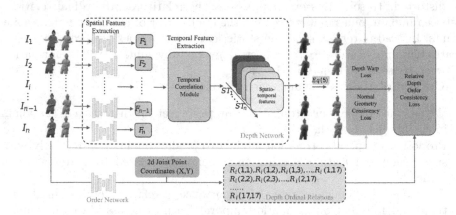

Fig. 2. Depth Estimation Network, including Order Network and Depth Network. In the Order Network, our main task is to obtain the relative depth ordinal relations of the input image. Subsequently, the obtained depth ordinal relations are added to the Depth Network to constrain the relative depth between human body parts. R_i represents the relative depth ordinal relations between joint points in frame i. 2D Joint Point Coordinates (X, Y) is a set of human joint point coordinates. In Depth Network, it consists of two stages: extracting spatial features and obtaining temporal correlation.

3.1   Joint Relative Ordinal Relations

In order to correct misordering of depths between body joints, we use the SUR-REAL dataset [12] to train the Order Network as the pre-training model, and its backbone network is a stacked hourglass network. According to the 2D joint point coordinates of the human obtained by learning the Mask R-CNN [1], the relative depth ordinal relations between the corresponding joint points is extracted. In order to prevent the distortion of joint points, we design a depth order loss function L_{order} to constrain the prediction of depth order. There are three types of depth order r_k (i_k, j_k) for each pair of joint points, namely '$<$' means the former is closer, '$>$' means the former is farther away, and '$=$' means the distance between the two is equal. The depth order loss function can be expressed as:

$$L(i_k, j_k) = \begin{cases} \log(1 + \exp(-D_{i_k} + D_{j_k})), & r_k \text{ is } "<" \\ \log(1 + \exp(D_{i_k} - D_{j_k})), & r_k \text{ is } ">" \\ (D_{i_k} - D_{j_k})^2, & r_k \text{ is } "=" \end{cases} \tag{1}$$

where D_{i_k} and D_{j_k} are the predicted depth values of joint i and j. We then get relative depth order consistency loss L_{order} of frame t, namely:

$$L_{order}(t) = \sum_{k=1}^{K} L(i_k, j_k), \tag{2}$$

3.2   Temporal Correlation Module

To better explore the features of different poses exhibited by characters, we introduce a temporal correlation module that delves into the 3D information between videos by considering both time distance and content relevance. We design the module in a way that considers the influence of frames on the current frame by layering the connection between the current frame and adjacent frames as shown in Fig. 3(a). This connection strategy aids in assigning varying feature weights to each frame based on its distance from the current frame. The farther away a frame is, the smaller its impact on the current frame, and the lower its feature weight. We propose two potential strategies, multi-feature fusion and CLSTM, for extracting 3D information in the temporal correlation module, both of which are shown in Fig. 3(b). Overall, our temporal correlation module is designed to align with human perception and extract meaningful 3D features in a way that minimizes depth errors.

Extracting Temporal Features Based on Multi-feature Fusion. When using the multi-feature fusion strategy to extract spatio-temporal features, we focus on the spatial features of the current frame and connect the temporal features of other adjacent frames. This ensures that the spatio-temporal features of the current frame account for the largest proportion of the fused features. The spatio-temporal ST features between adjacent frames can be calculated, as shown in Fig. 3(b). Its process can be expressed as:

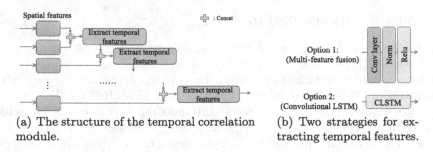

(a) The structure of the temporal correlation module.

(b) Two strategies for extracting temporal features.

Fig. 3. Details of the temporal correlation module.

$$ST_n = F_n,$$
$$ST_{n-1} = relu\left(C\left[ST_n, F_n - 1\right] * W_{n-1} + b_{n-1}\right)),$$
$$......$$
$$ST_t = relu\left(C\left[ST_{t+1}, F_t\right] * W_t + b_t\right)),$$

$$(3)$$

where F_t represents the spatial feature of the t_{th} frame, and $t = (1, 2, \ldots, n)$, n is the number of frames input by the network. In the formula, $relu$ is the rectified linear units activation function, and $*$ represents the convolution operation. C stands for connecting the fusion information of the next frame with the spatial features of the current frame and compressing it to 64 channels. W_t and b_t are the kernel and bias in the corresponding convolutional layer, respectively.

Extract Temporal Features Based on CLSTM. As the number of frames increases, the combination of adjacent frame spatial features may result in the inclusion of a large amount of irrelevant or redundant information in the final spatio-temporal features, leading to a decrease in the performance of the method. To address this issue, we propose the use of CLSTM to extract spatio-temporal features (see Fig. 3(b)). In each frame, the relevant characteristic information is selectively retained, and subsequent characteristic information is not obtained.

3.3 Self-supervised Learning

We adopt a self-supervised learning method similar to HDNet [3] to generate sparse warped depth by distorting the 3D geometry of people between two frames in a video sequence. The self-supervised process is only used between frames of the video sequence. First, we use the densepose method [10] to obtain the UV map corresponding to the input RGB image. Based on the UV map, we can warp the predicted depth of the previous frame to obtain the warp depth of the next frame. Since the geometry is almost constant before the local transformation between successive frames of the video, we use the nearest neighbor algorithm to correspond the points in each part in the current frame t to the same part in the next frame to generate sparse warped depth. We use a depth warp loss L_{warp} to measure the geometric difference between two consecutive frames. L_{warp} is expressed as:

$$L_{warp}(t+1) = \sum_{q} \sum_{m \in U_q} ||p_{t+1}(m) - p_{t \to (t+1)}(m)||^2, \qquad (4)$$

where q refers to the q_{th} body part of the human body, and U_q is the set of UV corresponding point coordinates corresponding to q_{th} body part in previous frame. We parametrize a 3D point $p \in \mathbb{R}^3$ reconstructed by the depth prediction using the UV coordinate. $p_{t+1}(m)$ and $p_{t \to (t+1)}(m)$ are the 3D points constructed from the predicted depth in the depth estimation network and the warped depth from the previous frame to the current frame, respectively.

Because we use normal maps in the depth estimation network to obtain details such as human local geometry and clothing folds, we estimate the corresponding normal map $\hat{n}$ from the predicted depth by:

$$\hat{n}(X) = \frac{\partial p(X)}{\partial x} \times \frac{\partial p(X)}{\partial y} / \left\| \frac{\partial p(X)}{\partial x} \right\| \left\| \frac{\partial p(X)}{\partial y} \right\|. \qquad (5)$$

We combine it with the input normal map n of our depth estimation network to minimize the normal geometry consistency loss:

$$L_n = \sum_{X \in R(t)} \cos^{-1} \left(\frac{n^T(X)\hat{n}(X)}{\|n(X)\| \|\hat{n}(X)\|} \right), \qquad (6)$$

where $R(t)$ is the coordinate range of frame t. When training Depth Network, we minimize the following overall loss:

$$L = \lambda_o L_{order} + \lambda_w L_{warp} + \lambda_n L_n + L_d, \qquad (7)$$

where λ_o, λ_w, λ_n are the relative weight coefficients between losses. L_d is the loss between the calculated ground truth depth G and the predicted depth D from the Depth Network. It is calculated as follows:

$$L_d = \sum_{X \in R(t)} \|D(X) - G(X)\|^2, \qquad (8)$$

4   Experiments

To demonstrate the effectiveness of our method for predicting human depth, we evaluate it using three indicators: mean error, RMSE, and weighted human disagreement rate between predicted relative depth ordinal relations and ground truth relative depth ordinal relations (WHDR).

During training, we use RGB images and corresponding normal maps, and the image size is 256×256. The input normal maps are predicted by using the normal pre-trained model in HDNet [3]. We use the stacked hourglass network as the backbone network to extract spatial features, and train the model using the Adam optimizer for 50 epochs with a learning rate of 0.001. The GPU model used is an NVIDIA V100.

4.1 Datasets

During our model training process, we used both the TikTok dataset [3] and the SURREAL dataset [12]. After serializing the videos in the TikTok dataset [3], we selected about 60000 images as our training data. To enhance our training data, we extracted a subset of 50,000 images from the SURREAL dataset [12] and capitalized on the supervised depth estimation training benefits due to the availability of genuine dense depth in this particular dataset subset.

For fair comparison, all the compared methods are tested in a third dataset that is not used for training. We evaluate model performance on two datasets: Tang et al. dataset [11] and THuman2.0 dataset [15]. We randomly selected about 1300 images from the Tang et al. dataset [11] as our evaluation data. In the THuman dataset [15], 260 3D meshes are selected and rendered from 5 angles to form 1300 images with ground truth dense depth.

4.2 Comparisons with State-of-the-Art Methods

We compared our human depth prediction model to six state-of-the-art models including PIFU [8], PIFUHD [9], PaMIR [18], ICON [14], ST-CLSTM [16], and HDNet [3]. As we can see in Table 1, our model outperforms other models in global human depth estimation and relative depth ordering between human body parts. It reduces overall depth errors and improves distortion issues between human joints. Figure 4 presents a visualization of the depth maps predicted by each model on the Tang et al. dataset [11] and THuman2.0 Dataset [15], with areas of significant error differences highlighted in green boxes. Our method generated depth maps that were notably closer to the ground truth, emphasizing its improved accuracy and reliability.

Table 1. Performance comparison of our model with other state-of-the-art methods. The numbers in red are optimal results, the numbers in blue are suboptimal results.

Tang et al. Dataset [11]				THuman2.0 Dataset [15]		
Method	Mean Error (↓)	RMSE (↓)	WHDR (↓)	Mean Error (↓)	RMSE (↓)	WHDR (↓)
PIFU [8]	14.49	28.64	18.80	13.76	24.30	22.38
PIFUHD [9]	32.35	49.68	43.04	28.14	44.71	35.99
PaMIR [18]	16.78	32.95	20.47	15.85	28.95	25.35
ICON [14]	17.42	34.02	20.81	18.36	33.39	25.19
ST-CLSTM [16]	16.63	22.73	29.88	15.98	21.04	27.57
HDNet [3]	8.09	10.54	12.90	8.53	11.43	**14.72**
Ord+Multi-feature(ours)	**5.71**	**8.01**	**12.72**	**7.96**	10.90	14.74
Ord+CLSTM (ours)	5.64	7.99	10.91	7.90	**10.98**	13.46

To further analyze our model, we conducted various types of comparative analysis with advanced models. We focused on the global human depth prediction capabilities of ST- CLSTM [16] and HDNet [3], and evaluated the relative depth ordering between different body parts of PIFU [8], PIFUHD [9], PaMIR [18],

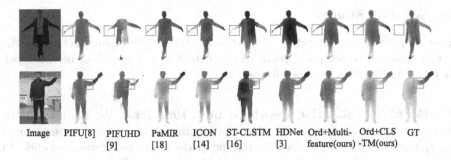

Image   PIFU[8]   PIFUHD   PaMIR   ICON   ST-CLSTM   HDNet   Ord+Multi-   Ord+CLS   GT
                      [9]   [18]   [14]   [16]   [3]   feature(ours) -TM(ours)

Fig. 4. Examples of estimated depth for comparison with state-of-the-art methods.

and ICON [14] models. In Fig. 5(a), we show the normalized predicted depth error distribution results of our method and compared with those of ST-CLSTM [16] and HDNet [3]. It is found that compared with the depth errors predicted by the ST-CLSTM [16] and HDNet [3] methods, the pixel depth errors predicted by our two methods are generally smaller. In Fig. 5(b), we show the 3D meshes reconstructed based on the predicted depths of our method, PIFU [8], PIFUHD [9], PaMIR [18], and ICON [14] respectively. Obviously, these advanced human depth prediction methods PIFU [8], PIFUHD [9], PaMIR [18], and ICON [14], do not focus on the relative depth ordinal relations of human, and do not make full of the 3D information between consecutive frames in the video. In this way, their estimated depth maps may have local distortion of body parts.

Therefore, from the experimental results, it is effective to use the relative depth ordinal relations and fully mine the 3D information in the video proposed by us. **Our predicted depth video can be found in the supplementary video.**

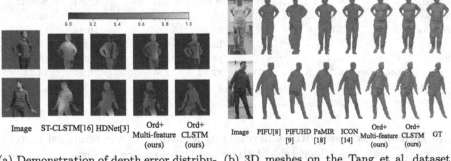

Image   ST-CLSTM[16] HDNet[3]   Ord+   Ord+   Image   PIFU[8] PIFUHD PaMIR ICON   Ord+   Ord+   GT
                               Multi-feature CLSTM   [9]   [18]   [14] Multi-feature CLSTM
                                 (ours)   (ours)   (ours)   (ours)

(a) Demonstration of depth error distribu- (b) 3D meshes on the Tang et al. dataset
tion on the THuman2.0 dataset [15].   [11].

Fig. 5. Our method compares with other state-of-the-art methods on predicted depth maps and reconstructed 3D meshes.

4.3   Ablation Studies

In our approach, we separately verify the relative depth ordinal relations, the effectiveness of two temporal correlation strategies, and the effect of the depth warp loss and number of input frames.

The Benefits of Relative Depth Ordinal Relations. We pre-trained the Order Network to predict the relative depth ordinal relationships among human joints, and used it to supervise the training of the depth estimation network. In Table 2, without the supervision of the relative depth ordinal relationships, the model performed poorly, but when we added them, the WHDR decreases. However, there is no significant improvement in the depth error, because the relative depth ordinal relation is only for the joint points in the human body rather than the whole character, which may cause the predicted depth distribution to be discrete. However, combining the relative depth order relationship with the temporal correlation module improved the depth error prediction, reducing the predicted depth error while correcting for body distortion. This demonstrates that relative depth ordinal relationships provide reasonable supervision and adjustment in the depth estimation network.

In Fig. 6, we show the 3D meshes reconstructed from the predicted depth information by both the baseline method [3] and our method. We can clearly see that under the supervision of relative depth ordinal relationships, joint deformations between arms and legs (green and red boxes) have been corrected.

Table 2. The first three rows are based on experiments performed without relative depth ordinal relations (Ord), and the last three rows represent the cases with Ord. At the same time, we compare the performance of two temporal correlation strategies (Multi-feature fusion and CLSTM) under the same conditions.

Tang et.al Dataset [11]				THuman2.0 Dataset [15]		
Method	Mean Error (↓)	RMSE (↓)	WHDR (↓)	Mean Error (↓)	RMSE (↓)	WHDR (↓)
Baseline	5.97	8.20	13.17	8.13	11.02	15.23
Multi-feature	5.73	8.05	13.36	7.98	**10.94**	14.86
CLSTM	5.86	8.35	13.25	**7.93**	11.39	14.91
Ord	6.07	8.33	12.87	8.33	11.22	15.08
Ord+Multi-feature(Ours)	**5.71**	**8.01**	**12.72**	7.96	10.90	**14.74**
Ord+CLSTM(Ours)	5.64	7.99	10.91	7.90	10.98	13.46

The Benefits of Temporal Correlation Module. In the temporal correlation module, we use a hierarchical structure to fuse pairwise features between adjacent frames in chronological order. We provide two strategies, multi-feature fusion and CLSTM, to extract the temporal features. As shown in Table 2, under the blessing of temporal feature extraction strategy, the performance of the model reaches the best. To validate the effectiveness of the hierarchical structure of fusing features in the temporal correlation module, we designed an All-feature

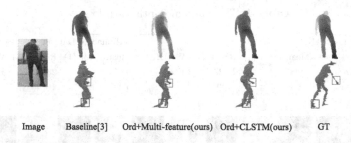

Image   Baseline[3]   Ord+Multi-feature(ours)   Ord+CLSTM(ours)   GT

Fig. 6. The visualization of the 3D meshes reconstructed from the depth map (only the side is shown).

fusion method that unifiedly fused all input frame features. However, this weakened the impact of the temporal order of input frames on the current frame, resulting in higher error rates for depth and relative depth order prediction (see Table 3). This indicates that the hierarchical structure is more reasonable for feature fusion in the temporal correlation module to maintain consistency with human perception.

According to the performance comparison of these two different temporal feature extraction strategies on the evaluation datasets, we finally adopt the CLSTM strategy as part of the final depth estimation model. Because it is better in reducing the depth error and correcting the distortion of the human body.

Table 3. The effect of different feature fusion methods.

Tang et al. Dataset [11]				THuman2.0 Dataset [15]		
Method	Mean Error ($\downarrow$)	RMSE ($\downarrow$)	WHDR ($\downarrow$)	Mean Error ($\downarrow$)	RMSE ($\downarrow$)	WHDR ($\downarrow$)
Baseline	5.97	8.20	13.17	8.13	11.02	15.23
Ord+All-feature fusion	5.72	8.02	13.08	8.18	11.11	15.25
Ord+Hierarchical-feature fusion	5.71	8.01	12.72	7.96	10.90	14.74

The Influence of Depth Warp Loss. To verify the impact of depth warp loss in the self-supervised process, we compared the models trained under the CLSTM strategy with and without depth warp loss, and the results are shown in the Table 4. It shows that the model with depth warp loss (i.e. combining temporal and spatial consistency) performs significantly better. In Fig. 7, we show the depth map and reconstructed 3D mesh for inference based on a single image and multiple images, respectively. The transformation of body parts between depth maps estimated based on multiple images is more reasonable and also conforms to human perception. Thus, exploiting spatio-temporal consistency between consecutive frames has a positive impact on model performance.

The Influence of the Number of Input Frames. In our method, the temporal correlation module is sensitive to the number of input frames. Because the evaluation pictures are randomly selected in the evaluation dataset, the time difference between successive frames is not equal. It can be seen from Fig. 8 that the

Table 4. The effect of depth warp loss.

Tang et al. Dataset [11]				THuman2.0 Dataset [15]		
Method	Mean Error (↓)	RMSE (↓)	WHDR (↓)	Mean Error (↓)	RMSE (↓)	WHDR (↓)
W/O depth warp loss	11.06	14.27	13.65	18.07	23.77	15.75
W depth warp loss	5.64	7.99	10.91	7.90	10.98	13.46

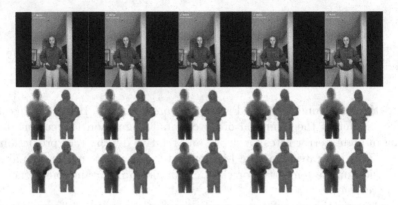

Fig. 7. Depth maps and reconstructed 3D meshes based on single-frame and multi-frame predictions. The first row is the continuous RGB image from the TikTok dataset [3], the second row is the depth map based on single-frame prediction, and the last row is the depth map based on multi-frame prediction.

multi-feature fusion strategy performs better when the number of input frames is 1, 3, and 7, respectively. When the number of input frames is 5, the advantage of CLSTM is turned on. At 7 frames, the performance starts to drop a bit. In order to save cost and reduce model complexity, we use 5 consecutive frames as input for experiments.

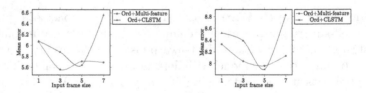

Fig. 8. The effect of the number of input frames on the mean error of predicted depth. The left is the result on the Tang et al. dataset [11], and the right is on the THuman2.0 dataset [15].

4.4   Extra Experimental Results

To verify the generalization of our proposed model, we conducted depth estimation on web images. In Fig. 9, we show the results of depth estimation and its reconstructed 3D mesh using only a single web image. Our model provides

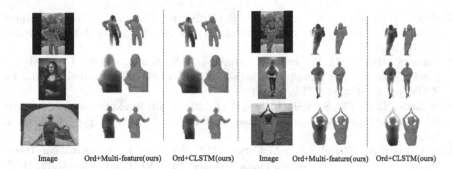

Image   Ord+Multi-feature(ours)   Ord+CLSTM(ours)   Image   Ord+Multi-feature(ours)   Ord+CLSTM(ours)

Fig. 9. Examples of some depth maps predicted by our method and 3D meshes reconstructed from the depth maps in web images.

a clear distribution of human depth levels closely related to human perception. Additionally, the relative ordinal of predicted body parts is seldom distorted.

5 Conclusion

To obtain human depth information in images we propose a novel depth estimation framework that combines relative depth ordinal relationships and temporal correlation modules. Judging from the effect in experimental results, our proposed method can effectively correct the distortion of some body parts and reduce the error rate of the overall depth of the person.

Acknowledgements. The authors wish to acknowledge the financial support in part by Guangdong Basic and Applied Basic Research Foundation under Grant 2020B1515120047, in part by Guangdong Natural Science Foundation under Grant 2021A1515011632 and 2021A1515012014.

References

1. Mask R-CNN for object detection and instance segmentation on Keras and TensorFlow. https://github.com/matterport/Mask_RCNN. Accessed 11 Jun 2023
2. Chen, W., Fu, Z., Yang, D., Deng, J.: Single-image depth perception in the wild. Adv. Neural. Inf. Process. Syst. **29**(1), 730–738 (2016)
3. Jafarian, Y., Park, H.S.: Self-supervised 3D representation learning of dressed humans from social media videos. PAMI (2022)
4. Li, C., et al.: RADepthNet: reflectance-aware monocular depth estimation. Virtual Reality Intell. Hardware **4**(5), 418–431 (2022)
5. Li, Y., Luo, F., Li, W., Zheng, S., Wu, H.H., Xiao, C.: Self-supervised monocular depth estimation based on image texture detail enhancement. Vis. Comput. **37**(9–11), 2567–2580 (2021)
6. Ranftl, R., Bochkovskiy, A., Koltun, V.: Vision transformers for dense prediction. In: ICCV, pp. 12179–12188. IEEE Computer Society (2021)

7. Ranftl, R., Lasinger, K., Hafner, D., Schindler, K., Koltun, V.: Towards robust monocular depth estimation: mixing datasets for zero-shot cross-dataset transfer. PAMI (2020)
8. Saito, S., Huang, Z., Natsume, R., Morishima, S., Kanazawa, A., Li, H.: PIFu: pixel-aligned implicit function for high-resolution clothed human digitization. In: ICCV, pp. 2304–2314. IEEE (2019)
9. Saito, S., Simon, T., Saragih, J., Joo, H.: Pifuhd: Multi-level pixel-aligned implicit function for high-resolution 3D human digitization. In: CVPR, pp. 84–93. IEEE (2020)
10. Sanakoyeu, A., Khalidov, V., McCarthy, M.S., Vedaldi, A., Neverova, N.: Transferring dense pose to proximal animal classes. In: CVPR, pp. 5233–5242. IEEE (2020)
11. Tang, S., Tan, F., Cheng, K., Li, Z., Zhu, S., Tan, P.: A neural network for detailed human depth estimation from a single image. In: ICCV, pp. 7750–7759. IEEE (2019)
12. Varol, G., et al.: Learning from synthetic humans. In: CVPR, pp. 109–117. IEEE (2017)
13. Wang, L., Zhao, X., Yu, T., Wang, S., Liu, Y.: NormalGAN: learning detailed 3D human from a single RGB-D image. In: Vedaldi, A., Bischof, H., Brox, T., Frahm, J.-M. (eds.) ECCV 2020. LNCS, vol. 12365, pp. 430–446. Springer, Cham (2020). https://doi.org/10.1007/978-3-030-58565-5_26
14. Xiu, Y., Yang, J., Tzionas, D., Black, M.J.: Icon: Implicit clothed humans obtained from normals. In: CVPR, pp. 13286–13296. IEEE (2022)
15. Yu, T., Zheng, Z., Guo, K., Liu, P., Dai, Q., Liu, Y.: Function4D: real-time human volumetric capture from very sparse consumer RGBD sensors. In: CVPR, pp. 5746–5756. IEEE (2021)
16. Zhang, H., Shen, C., Li, Y., Cao, Y., Liu, Y., Yan, Y.: Exploiting temporal consistency for real-time video depth estimation. In: ICCV, pp. 1725–1734. IEEE (2019)
17. Zhao, T., Pan, S., Gao, W., Sheng, C., Sun, Y., Wei, J.: Attention UNet++ for lightweight depth estimation from sparse depth samples and a single RGB image. Vis. Comput. **38**(5), 1619–1630 (2022)
18. Zheng, Z., Yu, T., Liu, Y., Dai, Q.: PaMIR: parametric model-conditioned implicit representation for image-based human reconstruction. PAMI **44**(6), 3170–3184 (2021)
19. Zoran, D., Isola, P., Krishnan, D., Freeman, W.T.: Learning ordinal relationships for mid-level vision. In: ICCV, pp. 388–396. IEEE (2015)

TSC-Net: Theme-Style-Color Guided Artistic Image Aesthetics Assessment Network

Yin Wang[1], Wenjing Cao[1], Nan Sheng[1], Huiying Shi[1], Congwei Guo[1], and Yongzhen Ke[1,2(✉)]

[1] School of Computer Science and Technology, Tiangong University, No. 399 Binshui Road, Tianjin 300387, China
keyongzhen@tiangong.edu.cn
[2] Tianjin Key Laboratory of Autonomous Intelligence Technology and Systems, Tianjin 300387, China

Abstract. Image aesthetic assessment is a hot issue in current research, but less research has been done in the art image aesthetic assessment field, mainly due to the lack of large-scale artwork datasets. The recently proposed BAID dataset fills this gap and allows us to delve into the aesthetic assessment methods of artworks, and this research will contribute to the study of artworks and can also be applied to real-life scenarios, such as art exams, to assist in judging. In this paper, we propose a new method, TSC-Net (Theme-Style-Color guided Artistic Image Aesthetics Assessment Network), which extracts image theme information, image style information, and color information and fuses general aesthetic information to assess art images. Experiments show that our proposed method outperforms existing methods using the BAID dataset.

Keywords: Artistic Image Aesthetics Assessment · BAID · Theme · Style · Color

1 Introduction

Image aesthetic assessment aims to automatically determine aesthetic quality qualitatively or quantitatively and can be widely used in many downstream applications such as assisted photo editing, web-scale image retrieval, and smart album management. Image aesthetic assessment is a particular challenge because of the highly subjective and complex nature of human aesthetic preferences. In recent years assisted scoring of artworks and AI painting have become hot research areas, and the study of computational aesthetics of art has important applied and scientific values. BAID [1] compensates for the lack of a dataset of art images, which collects 60,408 artworks with different styles, themes, and contents and contributes to the automated analysis of large-scale art images to provide auxiliary information for art appreciation.

In fact, art images have diverse themes, and most of the aesthetic scores given by the human subconscious are related to themes, which are different for different art images, but existing methods do not take this into account or utilize this point; moreover, art

B. Sheng et al. (Eds.): CGI 2023, LNCS 14495, pp. 193–203, 2024.
https://doi.org/10.1007/978-3-031-50069-5_17

images are extremely sensitive to colors, and in the art world, color is a unique artistic language, as artists will express the style and ideas of their work through color. We add an information-entropy method to perceive the color of art images in our model. Art images are significantly different from common images in terms of visual features such as color, texture, and composition; compared with real photographs, art images also have extremely strong artistic features and unique artistic styles, which include pastel, watercolor, ink, and others. Observing the style of an artwork is crucial in assessing its aesthetic value. In the aesthetic assessment of art images, our identification and judgment of artistic style will effectively improve the aesthetic assessment of art images.

In order to solve the above problems, this paper takes art images as the research object. Combined with the unique attributes of art images, we propose an art image assessment network TSC-Net based on theme, style, and color. It can effectively utilize the theme, style, color, and general aesthetic features of a given artwork. Our model consists of four parts: 1) Theme feature extraction sub-network: theme is an extremely important factor in appreciating and assessing art images. Art images with different themes need to extract different theme-related features. We propose a theme feature extraction sub-network incorporating theme information into the model to deal with the distraction problem effectively. 2) Style feature extraction sub-network: inspired by the study [**Error! Reference source not found.**], observing the style of an artwork is crucial in assessing its aesthetic value, and different styles require the extraction of different style-related aesthetic features. We propose a style-specific aesthetic branch that incorporates the style information into the aesthetic features and extracts the style-specific aesthetic features via an adaptive instance normalization module. 3) Color feature extraction sub-network: art images are extremely sensitive to color. We incorporate an information-entropy guided color distributed feature extraction module to extract color features in art images. 4) General aesthetic feature extraction sub-network: we train the general aesthetic feature extraction sub-network to extract aesthetic perceptual features, which allows the model to learn the aesthetic quality of different artworks better.

The main contributions of our work:

1. Exploring the problem of aesthetic assessment of art images from the dimension of theme and proposing a theme-specific art image assessment network that incorporates theme features into the aesthetic model.
2. Based on the unique attributes of art images: color, and style, we design the style feature extraction module and information-entropy guided color extraction module in the model, which enables the aesthetic model to extract more fine-grained art features.

2   Related Work

Generic Image Aesthetic Assessment (IAA).   Since 2014, research on aesthetic classification and scoring of images has fully entered the deep learning era. Lu *et al.* [2] proposed RAPID for binary aesthetic classification using an architecture similar to AlexNet [3]. In 2017, NIMA [4], based on MobileNet [5], VGG [6] and Inception [7], performed image preprocessing for better accuracy. NIMA also scores the image for errors and other problems and optimizes the image by selecting the best parameters based on the given scores, which outperforms the existing methods. In 2016, Kong *et al.* [8] created an AADB dataset with multiple aesthetic labels where each image has an aesthetic score and an attribute score. Gao *et al.* [9] converted a classifier into an SVM and used ResNet [10] to categorize the attributes and extract the image feature layer. The model achieved on the AVA dataset [11] with advanced performance.

Multiple-theme Image Aesthetic Assessment. Generalized aesthetic assessment studies have also pointed out that the subject matter or style of an image can also have a direct impact on aesthetic scores. However, early studies did not explicitly propose a solution for the impact of subject matter variation on aesthetic assessment models. Earlier researchers assisted the aesthetic assessment task through image classification and scene recognition methods, Cui *et al.* [12] proposed an improvement based on VGG-16 to develop a hybrid fully convolutional network that utilizes semantic cues of objects and image scenes to predict their perceived aesthetic quality; in the most recent study, He *et al.* [13] pointed out that the existing labels of the IAA dataset generally do not consider that different themes have different scoring criteria, created a theme-oriented aesthetic dataset TAD66K, and established a baseline model TANet, which can effectively extract theme information and adaptively build perceptual rules to assess images with different themes. The article demonstrates that TANet achieves state-of-the-art performance through large-scale testing.

Artistic Image Aesthetic Assessment (AIAA). Computational aesthetic assessment of artworks has become popular research in recent years. Hosu *et al.* [14] proposed the first AIAA method, which efficiently supports full-resolution images as inputs and can be trained on variable input sizes. Yi *et al.* [1] proposed the first large-scale art image dataset BAID and designed the style-specific Network SAAN to assess art images. The AIAA method has yet to be fully investigated. Theme and style are the most important features in a collection of artworks, and different works have different themes and styles, so we combine stylistic features, thematic features, color features, and generalized aesthetic features to evaluate artworks.

3 Methodology

3.1 Theme Understanding Network

The BAID dataset contains various themes, such as people, animals, and landscapes. Learning aesthetics directly from images will ignore the effect of theme changes on human visual perception. As shown in Fig. 1, we add a theme information extraction module to the model, which can effectively extract theme information and adaptively build perceptual rules to assess images with different themes.

We use ResNet-18 [10], trained on the scene dataset [24], as the backbone network. The scene dataset contains 10 million images, labeled with more than 400 unique topic semantic categories and environments, thus the backbone network can learn thematic information. In addition, in order to enable topic features to build perceptual rules adaptively, we refer to TANet [13] and process the output of the backbone into two streams, one to adaptively generate weights and biases via a parameter generator, and the other

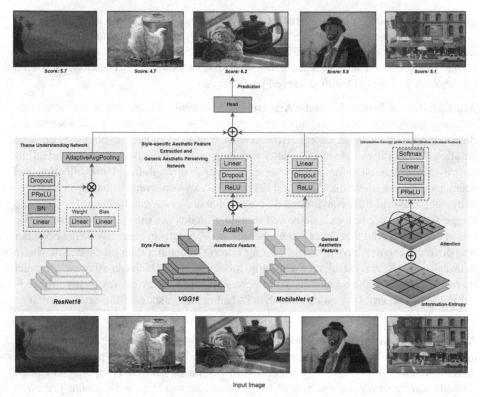

Fig. 1. The overall pipeline of our TSC-Net for artistic image aesthetic assessment.

stream to pass through a feature preprocessor to reduce spatial redundancy in the potential representations. The final output is obtained by multiplying the two streams with a linear layer. This module's output features thus contain basic topic and perceptual rule information. For the artwork dataset BAID, most of the artworks have scene themes that are basically the same as the daily environments in the scene dataset [24], but some artworks may have scenes that are different from the normal daily scenes, such as some abstract works, which should be taken into account in future research. For this paper, the model can perceive the thematic scenes of most art pictures and enhance the results with other aesthetic features.

3.2 Style Feature Extraction

The art paintings in the BAID dataset contain many painting styles, such as Expressionism, Cubism, Fauvism, and Surrealism. From the perspective of human perception, different styles bring different feelings to people. For example, the lines of Expressionism are more twisted, and Cubism contains many geometric shapes, and these features determine the differences in the underlying characteristics of the images. Style is important in research in the field of images, such as the study of style in the field of image generation

[25–27]. Therefore, the goal of the style feature extraction branch is to extract the aesthetic characteristics of artworks that are compatible with their artistic style. Drawing on mainstream style migration methods [16–19], we use VGG-19 [6], which has been pre-trained by ImageNet [15], as the backbone network to extract the style feature f_{sty}, while obtaining the generic aesthetic feature (Sect. 3.4) f_{aes}, and then fusing the style feature into the generic aesthetic feature via the AdaIN [16] layer to obtain f_{style}. Given the content feature mapping f_{aes} and the style feature mapping f_{sty}, AdaIN encodes the content and style information in the feature space by aligning the mean and variance of the channel direction of f_{aes} to match the mean and variance of the channel direction of f_{sty}. The AdaIN layer encodes the content and style information in the feature space:

$$f_{style} = AdaIN\left(f_{aes}, f_{sty}\right)$$

$$= \sigma\left(f_{sty}\right) * \frac{f_{aes} - \mu(f_{aes})}{\sigma(f_{aes})} + \mu\left(f_{sty}\right) \tag{1}$$

3.3 Information-Entropy Guided Color Distribution Attention Network

Fig. 2. Information-entropy of different kinds of images.

The color perception module extracts high-level color features from RGB space to perceive features such as color distribution and harmony of art images to improve the understanding of the artistic aesthetics of images. The color distribution is important information in aesthetics, and it is especially important in art images. From the point of view of human aesthetic perception, the single or strong color of an image and whether the hue is harmonious and rhythmic will visually leave different impressions, affecting the aesthetic rating of the whole image. There have been a number of recent articles examining images through color [26, 27]. In order to explore the characteristics of the color in the image, we introduce the information-entropy [20] into the image. The information-entropy can quantify the amount of information contained in a signal, the entropy is large to indicate that the system is more chaotic and has more information, and the entropy is small to contain less information. For the image, the entropy is large to indicate that the image is rich in color. As shown in Fig. 2, compared to the second image, the first image has only one object, so the information-entropy is low; while the second image contains more content, so the information-entropy is high; compared to the fourth image, the third image has monotonous colors, so the information-entropy is low; while the fourth image has rich colors and high information-entropy.

Specifically, computing the information-entropy of a region in an image can be expressed as:

$$H(C) = -\sum_{c\in C} P(c) log_2 P(c) \tag{2}$$

where $P(C) = S_c/S$, S_c denotes the number of pixels of color c, and S denotes the total number of pixels in the image. We partition the input into non-overlapping patches, and for each patch, we compute the information-entropy values of the three channels and the average of the original pixel RGB values. For an image of size 224×224, the patch space consists of k*k (k = 8) centroids, and the information-entropy value of each patch is summed with the average RGB value and input to the Attention module. f_{ab}, f_{uv} represent the two centroids, and the output of the color perception module f_{color}, can be described as:

$$f_{color} = ||_{l=1}^N \left(Softmax\left(\frac{(Q^l f_{ab})^T (K^l f_{uv})}{\sqrt{d}} \right) \right) \tag{3}$$

where $||_{l=1}^N$ is the splicing of RGB channels, Q^l, K^l, and d are the query, key, and dimension generated by the standard self-attentive input, respectively. After extracting such relational features, they are sent to the final Softmax layer of the color perception module to get the result f_{color}.

3.4 Generic Aesthetic Perceiving Network

In addition to the theme feature understanding network, the style feature extraction network, and the color perception module, we used a generic aesthetic branch to extract aesthetic features common to artworks. Given an image, we use MobileNetV2 [21] as the backbone to extract the aesthetic feature map f_{aes} of shape $W \times H \times C$, where W and H denote width and height, and C denotes channel-wise. Finally, four features are fused, and ReLu, Dropout, Linear, and Sigmiod are added to the outputs of the four feature fusions. Get the predicted aesthetic score, and the whole process is described as:

$$p = head \left(f_{theme} \oplus f_{style} \oplus f_{color} \oplus f_{aes} \right) \tag{4}$$

4   Experiments and Discussions

4.1   Datasets

We use the art image dataset BAID [1], which aims to fill a research gap in the aesthetic assessment of art images. The source of the BAID dataset is the Boldbrush website, which hosts a monthly artwork contest in which certified artists upload their artwork and receive public votes from online users. Voters can click on the detail page of the artwork and vote, with the number of votes reflecting the aesthetics and popularity of the artwork.

The selection of the BAID dataset has the following advantages: first, the contest does not restrict the subject matter, style, or medium of the works, so the dataset contains works in a wide range of artistic styles and content. Second, the voters consisted mainly of artists and art collectors, so the results of the dataset have a high degree of credibility and authority. The BAID dataset employs a sigmoid-like method to generate scores. The number of votes was converted into an image score, where the higher the number of votes, the higher the aesthetic value of the image. The scoring range was the common [0, 10] interval, where 0 means the worst and 10 means the best. The introduction of the BAID dataset provides insights for further research in the field of AIAA and improves the accuracy and universality of assessing the aesthetic quality of art images.

4.2 Experimental Setup

Evaluation Metric. We employ three commonly used metrics to evaluate IAA tasks. Accuracy is reported for binary aesthetic quality classification. For the regression task of aesthetic scores, we used Spearman's rank correlation coefficient (SRCC) and linear correlation coefficient (PCC). PCC and SRCC are computed between predicted scores and ground truth mean scores and standard deviation of scores. These metrics can verify the gap between the model prediction and ground truth in various aspects.

The PCC linear correlation coefficient describes the linear correlation between the subjective and objective assessments and is defined as follows:

$$PCC = \frac{\sum_{i=1}^{N}(y_i-\bar{y})(\hat{y}_i-\bar{y})}{\sqrt{\sum_{i=1}^{N}(y_i-\bar{y})^2}\sqrt{\sum_{i=1}^{N}(\hat{y}_i-\bar{y})^2}} \tag{5}$$

where N represents the number of distorted images, y, $\hat{y}_i$ denote the true aesthetic value and the predicted aesthetic score of the ith image, respectively, and $\bar{y}$, $\breve{y}$ represent the aesthetic true mean value and the algorithm predicted mean value, respectively.

SRCC is used to measure the monotonicity and order correlation of the algorithm predictions and is the best nonlinear correlation metric in aesthetic assessment, calculated as:

$$SRCC = 1 - \frac{6\sum_{i=1}^{N}(v_i-p_i)^2}{N(N^2-1)} \tag{6}$$

where v_i, p_i denote the ranking positions of y_i, $\hat{y}_i$ in the sequence of true and predicted values, respectively.

Loss Function. In BAID, since each image has only one score label s, $s \in [0,10]$. Therefore, the mean square error (MSE) loss between the predicted and true aesthetic scores is used to train the whole network. The loss function formula is as follows:

$$L(p, \hat{p}) = \frac{1}{n} \times \sum_{i=1}^{n}(p_i - \hat{p}_i)^2 \tag{7}$$

where n is the size of a batch during training, p is the true value, and p is the predicted value.

Implementation Details. We use ResNet-18 and VGG-19 pre-trained on ImageNet as the backbone of our feature extraction module. During training, we scaled the images to 224 × 224 size. We train the network on an NVIDIA RTX A5000 machine, set the batch_size to 64, and run it for 20 epochs. The initial learning rate is set to 0.0003. We implemented our proposed framework using the deep learning platform PyTorch.

Table 1. Performance of different methods on the BAID dataset.

Methods	Backbone Network	Image size	Classification	Score Regression	
			Accuracy↑	SRCC ↑	PCC ↑
M P_{ada} [22]	ResNet-18	224 × 224	74.33%	0.437	0.425
MLSP [14]	InceptionResNet	Full resolution	74.92%	0.441	0.430
NIMA [4]	Inception-v2	299 × 299	71.01%	0.393	0.382
BIAA [23]	Inception-v3	299 × 299	71.61%	0.389	0.376
TANet [13]	MobileNet-V2 ResNet-18	224 × 224	75.45%	0.453	0.437
SAAN [1]	VGG-19 ResNet-50	224 × 224	76.80%	0.473	0.467
ours	MobileNet-V2 VGG-19	224 × 224	**76.97%**	**0.480**	**0.479**

4.3 Comparison with Generic Aesthetic Models

Table 1 shows the performance of M P_{ada} [22], MLSP [14], NIMA [4], BIAA [23], TANet [13], SAAN [1] and our method on the BAID dataset. Compared to these methods, our model uses MobileNet-V2 and VGG-19 as the backbone network with input images scaled to 224 × 224 and achieves the best performance on all metrics. Figure 3 shows some of the prediction results of our model, TANet, and NIMA on the BAID dataset.

4.4 Ablation Study

Table 2 demonstrates the results of the ablation experiments: 1) We first verified the effectiveness of the theme-aware module. When the theme-aware module was removed, SRCC decreased by 7.3%, PCC decreased by 6.5%, and Accuracy decreased by 0.36%, and this discrepancy suggests that the theme-aware module has a greater impact on the evaluation of artworks. 2) We then verified the effectiveness of the style-specific feature extraction module. When this module was removed, SRCC decreased by 3.5%, PCC decreased by 6.7%, and Accuracy decreased by 1.52%. 3) When the Information-Entropy guided Color distribution Attention Network was removed, SRCC decreased by 3.1%, PCC by 1.5%, and Accuracy by 0.91%. 4) When the Generic Aesthetic Prediction Module was removed, SRCC decreased by 10.8%, PCC decreased by 18.2%, and

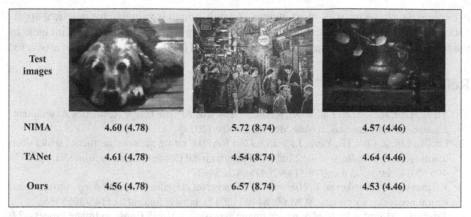

Fig. 3. Selected predictions on the BAID dataset. Black font indicates the predicted value, green font indicates the true value.

Accuracy decreased by 0.35%, It can be seen that the general aesthetic perception network improves the model results a lot, indicating that ordinary photographic images and artworks have some commonalities, but the general aesthetic model also has potential limitations. For example, the general aesthetic perception network may not obtain the correct aesthetic information for artworks with abstract styles, so this should be considered in future research to further improve the assessment of artworks. This discrepancy suggests that the combination of the image's subject matter, style, color information, and generic aesthetic information can impact the most in assessing the artwork.

Table 2. Ablation studies of different components in our model.

Method	SRCC↑	PCC↑	Accuracy↑
w/o Theme Understanding Network	0.445	0.448	76.61%
w/o Style-specific Aesthetic Feature Extraction	0.463	0.447	75.45%
w/o Information-Entropy guided Color distribution Attention Network	0.465	0.472	76.06%
w/o Generic Aesthetic Perceiving Network	0.428	0.392	76.62%
Ours	**0.480**	**0.479**	**76.97%**

5   Conclusion

In this paper, we focus on the challenging problem of AIAA. Benefiting from the emergence of the BAID large-scale art image assessment dataset, we construct a model that fuses image subject-aware and stylistic feature-aware networks to achieve state-of-the-art performance on the BAID dataset. The emergence of the BAID has allowed researchers to explore the characteristics of art images in depth, which is valuable for practical applications such as fine art examination assistance in judging and generating art images. In the future, different network models can be developed for the characteristics of artworks.

References

1. Yi, R., Tian, H., Gu, Z., Lai, Y.-K., Rosin, P.: Towards Artistic Image Aesthetics Assessment: a Large-scale Dataset and a New Method. ArXiv. (2023)
2. Lu, X., Lin, Z., Jin, H., Yang, J., Wang, J.Z.: RAPID: rating pictorial aesthetics using deep learning. In: Proceedings of the 22nd ACM International Conference on Multimedia, pp. 457–466 (2014). https://doi.org/10.1145/2647868.2654927
3. Krizhevsky, A., Sutskever, I., Hinton, G.E.: ImageNet classification with deep convolutional neural networks. Commun. ACM 60, 84–90 (2017). https://doi.org/10.1145/3065386
4. Talebi, H., Milanfar, P.: NIMA: neural image assessment. IEEE Trans. on Image Process. 27, 3998–4011 (2018). https://doi.org/10.1109/TIP.2018.2831899
5. Howard, A.G., et al.: MobileNets: efficient convolutional neural networks for mobile vision applications. ArXiv. (2017)
6. Simonyan, K., Zisserman, A.: Very deep convolutional networks for large-scale image recognition. CoRR. (2014)
7. Szegedy, C., et al.: Going deeper with convolutions. In: 2015 IEEE Conference on Computer Vision and Pattern Recognition (CVPR), pp. 1–9 (2015). https://doi.org/10.1109/CVPR.2015.7298594
8. Kong, S., Shen, X., Lin, Z., Mech, R., Fowlkes, C.: Photo Aesthetics Ranking Network with Attributes and Content Adaptation. 9905, 662–679 (2016).https://doi.org/10.1007/978-3-319-46448-0_40
9. Gao, F., Li, Z., Jun, Y., Junze, Y., Huang, Q., Tian, Q.: Style-adaptive photo aesthetic rating via convolutional neural networks and multi-task learning. Neurocomputing 395, 247–254 (2020). https://doi.org/10.1016/j.neucom.2018.06.099
10. He, K., Zhang, X., Ren, S., Sun, J.: Deep residual learning for image recognition. In: 2016 IEEE Conference on Computer Vision and Pattern Recognition (CVPR), pp. 770–778 (2016). https://doi.org/10.1109/CVPR.2016.90
11. Murray, N., Marchesotti, L., Perronnin, F.: AVA: A large-scale database for aesthetic visual analysis. In: 2012 IEEE Conference on Computer Vision and Pattern Recognition, pp. 2408–2415 (2012). https://doi.org/10.1109/CVPR.2012.6247954
12. Cui, C., Liu, H., Lian, T., Nie, L., Zhu, L., Yin, Y.: Distribution-Oriented aesthetics assessment with Semantic-aware hybrid network. IEEE Trans. Multimedia 21(5), 1209–1220 (2019). https://doi.org/10.1109/TMM.2018.2875357
13. He, S., Zhang, Y., Xie, R., Jiang, D., Ming, A.: Rethinking image aesthetics assessment: models, datasets and benchmarks. In: Proceedings of the Thirty-First International Joint Conference on Artificial Intelligence, pp. 942–948. International Joint Conferences on Artificial Intelligence Organization, Vienna, Austria (2022). https://doi.org/10.24963/ijcai.2022/132
14. Hosu, V., Goldlucke, B., Saupe, D.: Effective aesthetics prediction with multi-level spatially pooled features. In: 2019 IEEE/CVF Conference on Computer Vision and Pattern Recognition (CVPR), pp. 9367–9375 (2019). https://doi.org/10.1109/CVPR.2019.00960
15. Deng, J., Dong, W., Socher, R., Li, L.-J., Kai Li, Li Fei-Fei: ImageNet: a large-scale hierarchical image database. In: 2009 IEEE Conference on Computer Vision and Pattern Recognition, pp. 248–255 (2009). https://doi.org/10.1109/CVPR.2009.5206848
16. Huang, X., Belongie, S.: Arbitrary Style Transfer in Real-Time with Adaptive Instance Normalization. In: 2017 IEEE International Conference on Computer Vision (ICCV), pp. 1510–1519 (2017). https://doi.org/10.1109/ICCV.2017.167

17. Li, Y., Fang, C., Yang, J., Wang, Z., Lu, X., Yang, M.-H.: Universal style transfer via feature transforms. Presented at the NIPS May 23 (2017)
18. Liu, S., et al.: AdaAttN: revisit attention mechanism in arbitrary neural style transfer. In: 2021 IEEE/CVF International Conference on Computer Vision (ICCV), pp. 6629–6638 (2021). https://doi.org/10.1109/ICCV48922.2021.00658
19. Park, D.Y., Lee, K.H.: Arbitrary style transfer with style-attentional networks. In: 2019 IEEE/CVF Conference on Computer Vision and Pattern Recognition (CVPR), pp. 5873–5881 (2019). https://doi.org/10.1109/CVPR.2019.00603
20. Lee, B., et al.: Dissecting landscape art history with information theory. Proc. Natl. Acad. Sci. U.S.A. **117**, 26580–26590 (2020). https://doi.org/10.1073/pnas.2011927117
21. Sandler, M., Howard, A., Zhu, M., Zhmoginov, A., Chen, L.-C.: MobileNetV2: inverted residuals and linear bottlenecks. 2018 IEEE/CVF Conference on Computer Vision and Pattern Recognition, pp. 4510–4520 (2018). https://doi.org/10.1109/CVPR.2018.00474
22. Sheng, K., Dong, W., Ma, C., Mei, X., Huang, F., Hu, B.-G.: Attention-based multi-patch aggregation for image aesthetic assessment. In: Proceedings of the 26th ACM International Conference on Multimedia, pp. 879–886 (2018). https://doi.org/10.1145/3240508.3240554
23. Zhu, H., Li, L., Wu, J., Zhao, S., Ding, G., Shi, G.: Personalized image aesthetics assessment via Meta-Learning with bilevel gradient optimization. IEEE Trans. Cybern. **52**, 1798–1811 (2022). https://doi.org/10.1109/TCYB.2020.2984670
24. Zhou, B., Lapedriza, A., Khosla, A., Oliva, A., Torralba, A.: Places: A 10 million image database for scene recognition. IEEE Trans. Pattern Anal. Mach. Intell. **40**, 1452–1464 (2018). https://doi.org/10.1109/TPAMI.2017.2723009
25. Yu, Y., Li, D., Li, B., Li, N.: Multi-style image generation based on semantic image. Vis. Comput. (2023). https://doi.org/10.1007/s00371-023-03042-2
26. Li, H., Sheng, B., Li, P., Ali, R., Chen, C.L.P.: Globally and locally semantic colorization via exemplar-based Broad-GAN. IEEE Trans. Image Process. **30**, 8526–8539 (2021). https://doi.org/10.1109/TIP.2021.3117061
27. Sun, Q., et al.: A GAN-based approach toward architectural line drawing colorization prototyping. Vis. Comput.Comput. **38**, 1283–1300 (2022). https://doi.org/10.1007/s00371-021-02219-x

Weakly Supervised Method for Domain Adaptation in Instance Segmentation

Jie Sun[1], Yan Tian[1(✉)], Jialei Wang[2], Zhaocheng Xu[3], Hao Wang[1], Zhaoyi Jiang[1], and Xun Wang[1]

[1] School of Computer Science and Technology, Zhejiang Gongshang University, Hangzhou 310018, China
tianyan@zjgsu.edu.cn
[2] Shining 3D Tech Co., Ltd., Hangzhou 311258, China
[3] School of Mathematical and Computational Sciences, Massey University, Auckland 0632, New Zealand

Abstract. The domain adaptation of an instance segmentation model has gained much attention. However, manual annotation is tedious and self-training contains too much pseudolabel noise. Inspired by weakly supervised methods, we propose a method to handle these challenges by limited verification signals and label propagation. Semantic trees are constructed to explore the relation between samples by using a clustering method; Then, reliable pseudolabels are verified and propagated to unreliable labels, which improves instance segmentation model by employing the updated samples. Experiments on public datasets demonstrate that the proposed approach is competitive with state-of-the-art approaches.

Keywords: Visual Computing · Deep Learning · Instance Segmentation · Domain Adaptation

1 Introduction

Instance segmentation, which discovers different regions belonging to individual objects, has been applied in multiple visual computing fields, such as autonomous driving [34]. With the rapid development of deep convolutional neural networks (DCNNs) [26,28,29], instance segmentation have achieved satisfactory effectiveness. However, for domain adaptation, where models learning from a source domain are applied in a target domain, performance drops rapidly because of data drift between the source and target domains. Pixel-level annotations on a large number of samples in the target domain are time consuming [24], which is illustrated in Fig. 1. Unsupervised methods minimize the task-specific loss, which is restricted by the overlap of the distribution between the source and target domains, for the source domain and domain adversarial loss [11,14,15]. Alternatively, a self-training strategy is employed to fine tune the segmentation model by using target-specific pseudolabels [7,23]. However, the model only

---

J. Sun and Y. Tian— Equal contribution.

experiences limited improvement owing to pseudolabel noise or the introduction of strong assumptions, which is illustrated in Fig. 1.

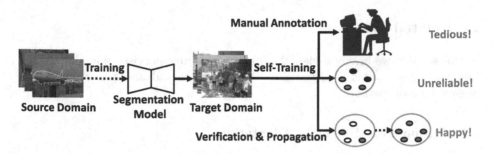

Fig. 1. Illustration of problems in domain adaptation. Supervised learning requires a large amount of annotations, while unsupervised learning is restricted by pseudolabel noise. Our approach verifies partial samples and obtains supervision signals by label propagation. The solid arrows represent the flow of data, and the dotted arrows indicate the results obtained from the input.

Weakly supervised learning improves the effectiveness such as cascaded detection tasks (CDT) [6] and cross-domain images and weak labels (CDIWL) [33]. However, both the bounding box in CDT and the object center in CDIWL provide relatively coarse supervision signals for fine tasks such as instance segmentation. We argue that the domain adaptation of instance segmentation can be improved by using limited verification signals in the target domain and that these limited verification signals can be propagated to the remaining samples through some kind of relations between all the samples, which is illustrated in Fig. 1.

We decide to construct semantic trees to explore the relation among test samples in the target domain because a tree has a naturally hierarchical characteristic and the semantic plays an important role in instance distinguishing. Given a pretrained instance segmentation model, features and semantic scores of the samples in a target domain are obtained, and these features and semantic scores are hierarchically clustered to generate a semantic tree for each class, where the corresponding features and semantic scores of the parent node (generated node after fusion) are a linear combination of those of corresponding child nodes. To decrease the labeling cost and increase the annotation efficiency, we verify the pseudolabels of the sampled data on semantic trees rather than labeling them. After that, the unreliable samples on a semantic tree are revised by label propagation and the structure of this semantic tree.

The contributions of this paper are as follows:

- We develop a weakly supervised method for domain adaptation based on semantic trees to handle the tedious annotation challenge by verifying predicted masks in the target domain.

– We design a simple mechanism to propagate reliable pseudolabels in semantic trees to the corresponding unreliable pseudolabels to improve the instance segmentation model by utilizing the revised samples.

2   Related Work

In this section, we briefly review the literature on unsupervised domain adaptation and weakly supervised learning. We present the advantages or drawbacks of each kind of method.

2.1   Unsupervised Domain Adaptation

Domain adaptation [1,5,8,9,22,30] transfers the knowledge learned from the source domain to the target domain to reduce the domain gap. Unsupervised domain adaptation (UDA) [7,11,14,15,23] shows potential value in deployment because only unlabeled samples in the target domain are needed.

Adversarial learning based methods focus on minimizing task-specific loss for the source domain and domain adversarial loss. In panoptic domain adaptive mask R-CNN (PDAM) [15], feature alignment is designed to learn domain-invariant features; However, redundant background has negative effects on model transfer. Therefore, the cycle-consistent PDAM (CyC-PDAM) [14] is proposed to add an inpainting mechanism to remove the auxiliary generated objects. Later, the spatial attention pyramid network (SAPNet) [11] and mutual information maximization (MIM) [21] are explored to capture multiscale context information. Nevertheless, inaccurate segmentation masks are obtained in most cases owing to the difficulty in distribution alignment.

Self-training-based methods retrain the model with generated target-specific pseudolabels. The domain adaptive region-based CNN (DARCNN) [7] refines segmentation masks in image-level and category-aware feature alignment and pseudo-labeling network (CAPL-Net) [10] generates pseudolabels in nuclei-level. AdaptOR [23] exploits explicit geometric constraints to generate accurate pseudolabels. However, the model only experiences limited improvement owing to pseudolabel noise or the introduction of strong assumptions.

2.2   Weakly Supervised Learning

Weakly supervised methods in domain adaptation (WDA) does not consider domain distribution alignment and thus cannot make full use of the labeled data from different domains. The CDT [6] leverages 2D bounding boxes as weak labels in both domains to explain the domain shift. Cross-domain images and weak labels (CDIWL) [33] combines the UDA and WDA methods, in which an adversarial domain discriminator is used to align local features and cyclic adaptation is adopted to work with pseudolabels. However, both the bounding box in CDT and the object center in CDIWL provide relatively coarse supervision signals for fine tasks such as instance segmentation.

3   Materials and Methods

We design a domain adaptation method for instance segmentation by using only limited annotations. This principle is illustrated in Fig. 2.

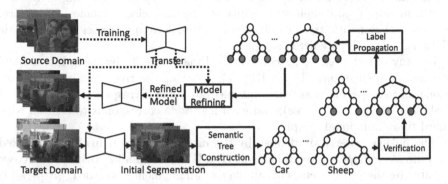

Fig. 2. Illustration of the framework. Obtaining an initial model learned from the source domain, we construct semantic trees, and then the model is refined according to the supervision information. Then, we verify and propagate partial samples and finetune the segmentation model by employing the updated supervision signals. The solid arrows represent the flow of data, and the dotted arrows indicate results obtained from the input.

3.1   Training and Mask Inference

The initial instance segmentation model based on a swin transformer [16] is learned on a source dataset $\{\mathbf{X}_s, \mathbf{Y}_s\}_{s=1}^S$ comprising an input image $\mathbf{X}_s \in \mathbb{R}^{W \times H \times 3}$ and corresponding mask image $\mathbf{Y}_s \in \mathbb{R}^{W \times H}$ with sample index s, image height H, and image width W. In an unlabeled target dataset, only input images $\{\mathbf{X}_t\}_{t=1}^T$ with sample index t are included. The target image $\mathbf{X}_t$ goes through an initial instance segmentation model and obtains backbone feature maps $\mathbf{bf}_t \in \mathbb{R}^{w \times h \times d}$ and semantic score maps $\mathbf{sl}_t \in \mathbb{R}^{W \times H \times K}$, where w, h, and d are the height, width, and channel number of feature maps, respectively, and K is the number of classes including the background. The segmented mask map $\mathbf{m}_t \in \mathbb{R}^{W \times H}$ is obtained via the argmax operation on semantic score maps $\mathbf{sl}_t$. Backbone feature maps $\mathbf{bf}_t$ are upsampled to be $\widetilde{\mathbf{bf}_t} \in \mathbb{R}^{W \times H \times d}$ and the mask map $\mathbf{m}_t$ is permuted to be $\mathbf{md}_t \in \mathbb{R}^{W \times H \times d}$ and $\mathbf{mk}_t \in \mathbb{R}^{W \times H \times K}$. Masked feature maps $\mathbf{f}_t \in \mathbb{R}^{W \times H \times d}$ and masked semantic score maps $\mathbf{s}_t \in \mathbb{R}^{W \times H \times K}$ are calculated by $\mathbf{f}_t = \widetilde{\mathbf{bf}_t} \odot \mathbf{md}_t$ and $\mathbf{s}_t = \mathbf{sl}_t \odot \mathbf{md}_K$, respectively, where $\odot$ is the elementwise dot product.

3.2   Construction of Semantic Trees

To explore the relation among the instance segmentation results, it is natural to consider hierarchical clustering/grouping. However, the metric measuring the similarity between samples remains a challenge because instances that belong to the same category may have large variances in appearance owing to the difference in object pose, lighting condition, and intraclass variance. Therefore, we construct semantic trees to hierarchically explore appearance and semantic relations among the predicted samples.

For any object class k, we construct a binary tree T_k by using hierarchical agglomerative clustering (HAC) [12]. The root of the tree contains all masks belonging to a specific class, each intermediate node corresponds to a cluster of masks (as a root of a subtree), and each leaf node corresponds to a mask with regard to an individual sample.

The linkage criteria are defined by the masked feature maps $\mathbf{f}_t$ and masked semantic score maps $\mathbf{s}_t$. Assuming that $D = W \times H \times d$ and $E = W \times H \times K$, we concatenate these two vectors of sample t as an augmented vector $\mathbf{f}_t^+ = [\mathbf{f}_t; \mathbf{s}_t] \in \mathbb{R}^{D+E}$, and then the Euclidean distance $||\mathbf{f}_t^+ - \mathbf{f}_o^+||$ between samples t and o works as a linkage metric to determine the merging order of masks. We assume that samples t and o merge are an intermediate tree node that is represented as n_j (the corresponding cluster is C_j) with index j; then, the feature and semantic score of the intermediate node are linear combinations of the child nodes

$$\mathbf{f}_j^+ = w_t \mathbf{f}_t^+ + w_o \mathbf{f}_o^+, \tag{1}$$

$$\mathbf{s}_j = w_t \mathbf{s}_t + w_o \mathbf{s}_o, \tag{2}$$

where $\mathbf{f}_t^+$ and $\mathbf{f}_o^+$ are augmented vectors of child nodes t and o, respectively, and $\mathbf{s}_t$ and $\mathbf{s}_o$ are corresponding masked semantic score maps. Weights w_t and w_o relate to the size of child nodes t and s, respectively.

$$w_t = \frac{|\mathcal{P}_t|}{|\mathcal{P}_t| + |\mathcal{P}_o|}, w_o = \frac{|\mathcal{P}_o|}{|\mathcal{P}_t| + |\mathcal{P}_o|}, \tag{3}$$

where $\mathcal{P}_t$ and $\mathcal{P}_o$ are sample sets in child nodes t and s, respectively, and $|.|$ is the sample number in the set.

By recurrently merging the intermediate nodes, a semantic tree can be constructed, and an example of the class "car" is illustrated in Fig. 3. We assume the root node is represented as n_0, and the remaining intermediate nodes in white are represented as $\{n_j\}_{j=1}^{J_k}$, where J_k is the number of intermediate nodes of class k. Leaves $\{p_i\}_{i=1}^{I_k}$ in orange represent instances segmented by the initial segmentation model in the target domain, where I_k is the number of instances of class k.

Our approach has several advantages. The constructed trees are semantic mask trees (SMTs) because the merging metric is based on features augmented by the semantic score, considering class and confidence.

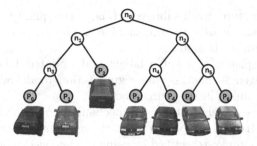

Fig. 3. Illustration of the semantic tree construction with respect to "car" class. White nodes represent intermediate nodes and orange nodes represent leaves. The segmented mask of an instance corresponding a specific leaf is illustrated under the leaf. (Color figure online)

3.3   Verification and Label Propagation

Fine-tuning is an effective method to improve accuracy in domain adaptation at the cost of tedious and time-consuming labeling stages. To address this problem, we propose a method to quickly locate and supervise limited samples and propagate these valuable supervision signals to relevant samples.

Manual Annotation. We are inspired by the fact that the annotation for dense prediction tasks is complex, tedious, and time consuming, but annotation verification is easy and fast. For instance, a person may spend several minutes annotating a segmented mask for an image, while the verification process only costs one second [25]. Therefore, we design a method to quickly verify whether the predicted mask is correct. For any class k (semantic tree T_k), we randomly select R ratio samples with inferred masks $\{\mathbf{m}_t\}_{t=k_1}^{k_N}$, where $\{k_1, ..., k_N\}$ are indexes of samples to be verified according to the selection ratio R. Then, we verify each selected sample regarding whether the inferred mask is consistent with the ground truth according to the annotator's intuition and record the conclusion that the predicted mask $\mathbf{m}_t$ correctly outlines the target object, which is represented by the symbol $l_t = 1$, or the predicted mask $\mathbf{m}_t$ is fault ($l_t = 0$).

Label Propagation. We estimate the quality Q_k for class k as

$$Q_k = \frac{1}{k_N} \sum_{t=k_1}^{k_N} l_t, \tag{4}$$

and compare the class quality with a fixed threshold K_a. In each semantic tree, neighboring leaves have both similar semantics and appearance because the tree is constructed according to the hierarchy relation in these terms. If the class quality $Q_k \geq K_a$, it means that the corresponding class k is well predicted, and the unsatisfied masks $\{\mathbf{m}_t\}$ with $l_t = 0$ in this class are revised by their neighbors with similar semantics and appearance with satisfactory masks $\{\mathbf{m}_t\}$ with $l_t = 1$ by using label propagation [35]. If class quality $Q_k \leq K_a$, the corresponding class k is unreliable, and the semantic tree T_k is split into two subtrees according to its constructed structure. Each subtree estimates the quality by using a similar method and compares it with the threshold K_a. The division continues until at least one reliable cluster is found.

After label propagation, reliable labels and updated labels in the target domain are employed to finetune the segmentation model which is originally learned by using samples in the source domain.

Our approach uses a relatively simple mechanism to discover reliable samples and employs these trustful samples to adapt the segmentator. In addition, partial noise in unreliable samples is rectified by using the knowledge of reliable samples, which is also helpful in domain adaptation.

4   Results

4.1   Datasets and Evaluation Criterion

The experiments are performed from the BBBC [18] to TNBC [20] dataset and from the Pascal VOC 2012 [4] to COCO 2017 dataset [13].

The BBBC dataset includes 200 images with a resolution of 520×696 for U2OS cells under a high-throughput chemical screen. A total of 10,000 patches of BBBC of size 256×256 are randomly cropped from the training images. The TNBC dataset includes 50 annotated 512×512 patches from 11 different patients. We use the aggregated Jaccard index (AJI) and pixel-level F1 score as the evaluation criteria.

The Pascal VOC 2012 dataset consists of 1464 training images and 1449 validation images with segmentation ground truth. There are 20 classes in the Pascal VOC 2012 dataset. The COCO 2017 dataset consists of 118k training images, 5k validation and 20k test images in 80 classes, and images containing the common 20 classes with Pascal VOC 2012 are selected for evaluation. The evaluation criteria are AP_{box} and AP_{mask}. We also report AP_{50}, AP_{75} (AP at different IoU thresholds) for AP_{mask}.

4.2   Implementation Details

The initial instance segmentation model is based on the swin transformer [16]. During inference, all predictions are kept with a confidence score above 0.5.

In the training stage, data augmentation includes horizontal/vertical flipping, translation with offsets (-3, 0, 3), and scale variance with ratios (0.9, 1.0, 1.1) to expand the data to $4 \times 3 \times 3 = 12$ times the original size. The initial network is trained by using the AdamW optimizer [19]. The initial learning rate is 1e-3, and then a polynomial decay policy is followed, where the weight decay is 1e-2 to train 110 epochs in the Pascal VOC 2012 dataset and 130 epochs in the BBBC dataset. The batch size is 4 in the Pascal VOC 2012 dataset and 8 in the BBBC dataset.

The annotator is trained to manually verify inferred masks with IoU $\geqslant$ 0.80 with the ground truth as correct and negative otherwise. We provide some instructions with examples; after that, the annotator must pass a qualification test to start the annotation stage; and finally, we monitor performance via hidden quality control images. Although different persons have their own judgments, we find that the judgment threshold of different persons is in the interval [0.75, 0.85]. We sample test images in the COCO 2017 dataset (with 20 classes) and TNBC dataset with ratio $R = 0.15$ for verification, and the number of verified images is approximately 750 in the COCO 2017 dataset and 15 in the TNBC dataset, respectively, which only costs the annotator 15 min for verification.

4.3 Ablation Study

Features for Semantic Tree Construction. We choose features combined with semantic scores to construct trees, including mask logits, backbone features, and mask features, and the details are listed in Table 1. We choose to use the mask features in the following experiments for their advantage in accuracy.

Table 1. Comparison of different features in clustering on COCO test set.

Approach	COCO 2017 Dataset			
	AP_{box}	AP_{mask}	AP_{50}	AP_{75}
Mask Logits	42.5	37.4	60.6	42.1
Backbone Features	45.3	39.0	63.0	43.9
Mask Features	**48.7**	**41.1**	**65.2**	**45.8**

Clustering. The comparison of different clustering methods is reported in Table 2, including hierarchical fuzzy clustering (HFC) [31], hierarchical linkage clustering (HLC) [3], and HAC [12]. Clustering methods effectively increase the information utilization and improve the segmentation performance, among which the HAC achieves maximum performance improvement.

Table 2. Comparison of different clustering methods on COCO test set.

Approach	COCO 2017 Dataset			
	AP_{box}	AP_{mask}	AP_{50}	AP_{75}
No Clustering	42.2	36.5	59.5	39.7
HLC [3]	45.9	39.1	62.9	42.8
HFC [31]	46.4	39.5	63.4	43.3
HAC [12]	**48.7**	**41.1**	**65.2**	**45.8**

Segmentation Model. The comparison of different segmentation models is reported in Table 3. Swin Transformer V2 obtains the optimum performance and hence is selected as the segmentation model in the experiment. We also compare the performance of different approaches using or not using our approach in this table. It shows that our approach improves the AP_{mask} by approximately 1.8%.

Table 3. Effectiveness comparison of different segmentation models on the COCO 2017 test set. Note that */* means the approach using or not using our semantic tree construction and label propagation methods.

Approach	COCO 2017 Dataset		
	AP_{mask}	AP_{50}	AP_{75}
Mask2Former [2]	38.3/36.6	62.1/60.3	42.4/40.5
SwinTrans.V1 [17]	39.6/37.7	63.4/61.8	43.8/41.7
FocalSelf-att. [32]	40.5/38.9	64.5/62.9	44.6/42.7
SwinTrans.V2 [16]	**41.1/39.9**	**65.2/63.8**	**45.8/43.9**

Table 4. Performance comparison of different methods under the setting (source: BBBC, target: TNBC) and the setting (source: Pascal VOC 2012, target: COCO 2017); '*' denotes that the approach is reimplemented.

Approach	TNBC		COCO 2017	
	AJI	Pixel-F1	AP_{box}	AP_{mask}
MIM [21]	56.5	75.6	42.1	36.5
PDAM [15]	57.2	77.4	42.3	36.6
CyC-PDAM [14]	56.7	75.9	42.4	36.7
SAPNet [11]*	57.3	77.5	42.5	36.9
DARCNN [7]*	51.2	71.7	42.7	37.4
CAPL-Net [10]*	54.4	74.6	42.9	37.7
AdaptOR [23]	57.7	77.8	43.2	38.0
CDT [6]*	58.0	78.0	45.4	39.0
CDIWL [33]*	58.8	78.4	46.3	39.1
Ours	**59.9**	**79.3**	**48.7**	**41.1**

4.4 Evaluation on the TNBC Dataset

We compare our approach to other domain adaptation approaches, and the experimental results are shown in Table 4. Methods based on adversarial learning such as MIM, focusing on fooling the discriminator to confuse the feature distributions of the source and target, still suffer from domain bias between the source and target images due to imperfect translations. For instance, CyC-PDAM [14] experiences relatively weak improvement (less than 0.2 in AJI or 0.3 in Pixel-F1 on the TNBC dataset) because there is no guarantee on the alignment of class conditional distributions. Methods based on self-training, such as DARCNN [7] and AdaptOR [23], retrain the model with generated target-specific pseudolabels. Nevertheless, self-training methods such as CAPL-Net also receive limited performance (less than 1.2 in AJI or 2.2 in Pixel-F1 on the TNBC dataset) owing to the lack of real supervision signals. The pseudolabels stem from the information of the supervision signal of the source domain.

The weakly supervised methods closest to our method are CDT [6] and CDIWL [33]. However, both the bounding box in CDT and the object center in CDIWL provide relatively coarse supervision signals for fine tasks such as instance segmentation. Fine tasks need information at the pixel level, and we have described in implementation details that humans can judge accurate segmentation results (IoU $\geqslant 0.80$) in an image by approximately 1 s. As a result, our method achieves competitive performance on the TNBC dataset by incorporating fast and accurate evaluation signals.

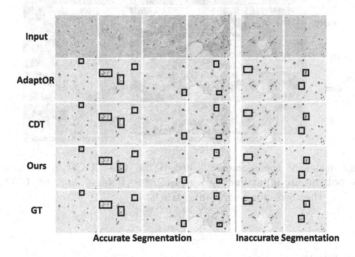

Fig. 4. Illustrations of the segmented outputs on the TNBC dataset. Rows from top to bottom are input images, outputs of AdaptOR, CDT, and our approaches, and the corresponding ground truth (GT).

Comparisons between AdaptOR, CDT, and our method are illustrated in Fig. 4. The AdaptOR achieves limited improvement in all classes, partially because noises that are contained in pseudolabels confuse the model refinement. Failure cases in our method are also provided in Fig. 4. Information about the fine parts of objects, is missing owing to downsampling in multiple layers of the network. Moreover, in the evaluation stage, if fine parts of the sample are lost, the accuracy only drops slightly and the sample is regarded as the positive sample for information propagation.

4.5   Evaluation on the COCO 2017 Dataset

Our approach also obtains competitive results on the COCO 2017 dataset, and it achieves 48.7 in AP_{box} and 41.1 in AP_{mask}. Note that we spend approximately 4 h verifying 14k instances, while we only manually annotate 180 instances in the same amount of time.

Some segmented results obtained from AdaptOR, SAPNet, CDT, and our approach are illustrated in Fig. 5. The discrepancy among segmented masks demonstrates that our approach is not sensitive to the object category, camera pose, or scene environment. Although our approach performs well in most cases, sometimes it outputs inaccurate results, as illustrated in the right part of Fig. 5. Interactions such as two zebras close to each other and objects of small size are easily omitted owing to missing information that may confuse the model.

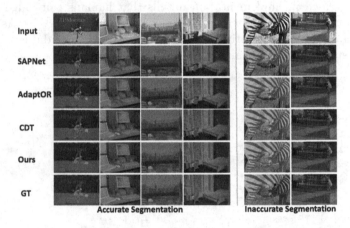

Fig. 5. Illustrations of the segmented outputs on the COCO 2017 dataset. Rows from top to bottom are input images, outputs of SAPNet, AdaptOR, CDT, and our approaches, and the corresponding ground truth.

5   Discussion

Weakly supervised learning methods based on adversarial learning and self-training for domain adaptation explore the relation of features between domains or reliabilities of inference in the target domain; however, they ignore the relation among samples in target domains for knowledge transfer. In contrast, our approach uses semantic trees to model dependency among samples in the target domain and designs a human-in-the-loop for sample evaluation and model learning.

Information about the fine parts of objects is missing owing to downsampling in multiple layers of the network. For example, our approach has limited capability to discover the fine parts such as nuclei masks in Fig. 4, because hollow layers in the deep network are rich in detail information but lack semantic knowledge.

The capability of human perception varies in different individuals, hence, we provide standard templates and corresponding masks for each annotator to learn before experiments. These templates are from the third-party dataset which is similar to target domains, and their number is approximately 100 images. The judgement threshold of different annotators is between the interval [0.75, 0.85] when these templates are provided and prior knowledge is learned.

In the future, we will employ multiscale analysis [27] to handle missing information by combining semantic information from deep layers and detailed information from hollow layers via a residual learning framework. This method can be employed in swin transformers to fuse information from multiple perception fields to decrease errors in fine parts.

6 Conclusions

We propose a weakly supervised method for domain adaptation in instance segmentation. Our work requires limited human resources for label verification and gains a mask AP of 41.1 on the COCO 2017 dataset, which obtains an effectiveness close to that of the supervised learning method.

Acknowledgments. This work was supported by the National Natural Science Foundation of China (61976188, 61972351, 62111530300). The authors declare no conflicts of interest.

References

1. Ali, R., et al.: Optic disk and cup segmentation through fuzzy broad learning system for glaucoma screening. IEEE Trans. Industr. Inf. **17**(4), 2476–2487 (2020)
2. Cheng, B., Misra, I., Schwing, A.G., Kirillov, A.: Masked-attention mask transformer for universal image segmentation. In: Proceedings of the IEEE/CVF in Proceedings on Computer Vision and Pattern Recognition, pp. 1290–1299 (2022)
3. Dogan, A., Birant, D.: K-centroid link: a novel hierarchical clustering linkage method. Appl. Intell. **52**(5), 5537–5560 (2021). https://doi.org/10.1007/s10489-021-02624-8
4. Everingham, M., Van Gool, L., Williams, C.K., Winn, J., Zisserman, A.: The pascal visual object classes (VOC) challenge. Int. J. Comput. Vis. **88**(2), 303–338 (2010)
5. Ganin, Y., Lempitsky, V.: Unsupervised domain adaptation by backpropagation. In: International in Proceedings on Machine Learning, pp. 1180–1189 (2015)
6. Hanselmann, N., Schneider, N., Ortelt, B., Geiger, A.: Learning cascaded detection tasks with weakly-supervised domain adaptation. In: IEEE Intelligent Vehicles Symposium, pp. 532–539 (2021)
7. Hsu, J., Chiu, W., Yeung, S.: DARCNN: domain adaptive region-based convolutional neural network for unsupervised instance segmentation in biomedical images. In: Proceedings of the IEEE/CVF in Proceedings on Computer Vision and Pattern Recognition, pp. 1003–1012 (2021)
8. Jia, Z., Li, Y., Tan, Z., Wang, W., Wang, Z., Yin, G.: Domain-invariant feature extraction and fusion for cross-domain person re-identification. Vis. Comput. **39**(3), 1205–1216 (2023)

9. Kong, X., Xia, S., Liu, N., Wei, M.: GADA-SegNet: gated attentive domain adaptation network for semantic segmentation of lidar point clouds. Vis. Comput., 1–11 (2023). https://doi.org/10.1007/s00371-023-02799-w

10. Li, C., et al.: Domain adaptive nuclei instance segmentation and classification via category-aware feature alignment and pseudo-labelling. In: Proceedings of the Medical Image Computing and Computer Assisted Intervention, pp. 715–724 (2022)

11. Li, C., et al.: Spatial attention pyramid network for unsupervised domain adaptation. In: Proceedings of the European in Proceedings on Computer Vision, pp. 481–497 (2020)

12. Li, T., Rezaeipanah, A., El Din, E.M.T.: An ensemble agglomerative hierarchical clustering algorithm based on clusters clustering technique and the novel similarity measurement. J. King Saud Univ.-Comput. Inf. Sci. **34**(6), 3828–3842 (2022)

13. Lin, T.-Y., et al.: Microsoft COCO: common objects in context. In: Fleet, D., Pajdla, T., Schiele, B., Tuytelaars, T. (eds.) ECCV 2014. LNCS, vol. 8693, pp. 740–755. Springer, Cham (2014). https://doi.org/10.1007/978-3-319-10602-1_48

14. Liu, D., Zhang, D., Song, Y.: Unsupervised instance segmentation in microscopy images via panoptic domain adaptation and task re-weighting. In: Proceedings of the IEEE/CVF in Proceedings on Computer Vision and Pattern Recognition, pp. 4243–4252 (2020)

15. Liu, D., et al.: PDAM: a panoptic-level feature alignment framework for unsupervised domain adaptive instance segmentation in microscopy images. IEEE Trans. Med. Imaging **40**(1), 154–165 (2020)

16. Liu, Z., Hu, H., Lin, Y., Yao, Z., Xie, Z., Wei, Y.: Swin transformer v2: scaling up capacity and resolution. In: Proceedings of the IEEE/CVF Conference on Computer Vision and Pattern Recognition, pp. 12009–12019 (2022)

17. Liu, Z., Lin, Y., Cao, Y., Hu, H., Wei, Y., Zhang, Z.: Swin transformer: hierarchical vision transformer using shifted windows. In: Proceedings of the IEEE/CVF International Conference on Computer Vision, pp. 10012–10022 (2021)

18. Ljosa, V., Sokolnicki, K.L., Carpenter, A.E.: Annotated high-throughput microscopy image sets for validation. Nat. Methods **9**(7), 637–637 (2012)

19. Loshchilov, I., Hutter, F.: Decoupled weight decay regularization. In: International in Proceedings on Learning Representations, pp. 1526–1537 (2019)

20. Naylor, P., Laé, M., Reyal, F., Walter, T.: Segmentation of nuclei in histopathology images by deep regression of the distance map. IEEE Trans. Med. Imaging **38**(2), 448–459 (2018)

21. Sharma, Y., Syed, S., Brown, D.E.: MaNi: Maximizing mutual information for nuclei cross-domain unsupervised segmentation. In: Proceedings of the Medical Image Computing and Computer Assisted Intervention, pp. 345–355 (2022). https://doi.org/10.1007/978-3-031-16434-7_34

22. Shen, Y.: Domain-invariant interpretable fundus image quality assessment. Med. Image Anal. **61**, 101654 (2020)

23. Srivastav, V., Gangi, A., Padoy, N.: Unsupervised domain adaptation for clinician pose estimation and instance segmentation in the operating room. Med. Image Anal. **80**, 102525 (2022)

24. Tian, Y., et al.: Global context assisted structure-aware vehicle retrieval. IEEE Trans. Intell. Transp. Syst. **21**(10), 1–10 (2021)

25. Tian, Y., Cheng, G., Gelernter, J., Yu, S., Song, C., Yang, B.: Joint temporal context exploitation and active learning for video segmentation. Pattern Recogn. **100**, 107158 (2020)

26. Tian, Y., Gelernter, J., Wang, X., Li, J., Yu, Y.: Traffic sign detection using a multi-scale recurrent attention network. IEEE Trans. Intell. Transp. Syst. **20**(12), 4466–4475 (2019)
27. Tian, Y., Wang, X., Wu, J., Wang, R.: Multi-scale hierarchical residual network for dense captioning. J. Artif. Intell. Res. **64**, 181–196 (2019)
28. Tian, Y., et al.: 3D tooth instance segmentation learning objectness and affinity in point cloud. ACM Trans. Multimed. Comput. Commun. Appl. **18**, 202–211 (2022)
29. Tian, Y., Zhang, Y., Zhou, D., Cheng, G., Chen, W.G., Wang, R.: Triple attention network for video segmentation. Neurocomputing **417**, 202–211 (2020)
30. Tzeng, E., Hoffman, J., Saenko, K., Darrell, T.: Adversarial discriminative domain adaptation. In: Proceedings of the IEEE in Proceedings on Computer Vision and Pattern Recognition, pp. 7167–7176 (2017)
31. Varshney, A.K., Muhuri, P.K.: PIFHC: the probabilistic intuitionistic fuzzy hierarchical clustering algorithm. Appl. Soft Comput. **120**, 108584 (2022)
32. Yang, J., Li, C., Zhang, P., Dai, X., Xiao, B.: Focal self-attention for local-global interactions in vision transformers. arXiv preprint arXiv:2107.00641 (2021)
33. Yang, S., Zhang, J., Huang, J., Lovell, B.C., Han, X.: Minimizing labeling cost for nuclei instance segmentation and classification with cross-domain images and weak labels. In: Proceedings of the AAAI in Proceedings on Artificial Intelligence, pp. 697–705 (2021)
34. Zhou, D., Tian, Y., Chen, W.G.: Self-supervised saliency estimation for pixel embedding in road detection. IEEE Signal Process. Lett. **28**, 1325–1329 (2021)
35. Zhu, Y., et al.: Improving semantic segmentation via video propagation and label relaxation. In: Proceedings of the IEEE/CVF in Proceedings on Computer Vision and Pattern Recognition, pp. 8856–8865 (2019)

Op-PSA: An Instance Segmentation Model for Occlusion of Garbage

Sheng Yu[1(✉)] and Fei Ye[2]

[1] Beijing University of Technology, 100 Pingleyuan, Beijing, China
`falseYuu_Sheng@163.com`

[2] Jingyue Development Zone, Jilin Jianzhu University, 5088 Xincheng Street, Changchun, Jilin, China

Abstract. With the increasing emphasis on green development, garbage classification has become one of the important elements of green development. However, in scenarios where garbage stacking occurs, the task of segmenting highly overlapping objects is difficult because the bottom garbage is in an obscured state and its contours and obscured boundaries are usually difficult to distinguish. In this paper, we propose an Op-PSA model, which uses the HTC model as the baseline model and improves the modeling method of backbone network and model interest region using attention model and occlusion perception model. The Op-PSA model constructs the image as two overlapping layers and uses the two-layer structure to explicitly model the occluded and occluded objects, so that the boundaries of the occluded and occluded objects are naturally decoupled, and their interactions are considered in the mask regression. It is experimentally verified that the model can effectively detect the masked garbage and improve the detection accuracy of the masked garbage.

Keywords: Instance segmentation · Garbage detection · Attention model · Occlusion recognition

1 Introduction

Nowadays, garbage detection on urban streets often relies on manual sorting and recycling, which makes this task time-consuming and laborious [1]. Because garbage is often stacked together in the real world, which leads to the phenomenon of garbage being blocked, and the accuracy of detection and recognition of blocked garbage is seriously affected by the problem of incomplete information and fuzzy boundary information [2, 3]. How to accurately detect and recognize blocked garbage is an important problem of Waste sorting, which has important research significance [4].

Therefore, this study investigates high-precision image segmentation for garbage with difficult feature extraction in the presence of occlusion, and provides a new solution for the optimization of domestic garbage detection methods.

In this paper, we use an instance segmentation technique based on the attention model and the occlusion perception model to solve the above problem. First, the attention model

B. Sheng et al. (Eds.): CGI 2023, LNCS 14495, pp. 218–229, 2024.
https://doi.org/10.1007/978-3-031-50069-5_19

enables the neural network model to give different attention to different parts of the input data by simulating the attention allocation of the human brain, which in turn improves the detection quality of spam instance segmentation. Secondly, occlusion perception refers to modeling the region of interest in an image as two overlapping layers, with the upper layer detecting the occluder object and the lower layer inferring the partially occludee target object, thus deconstructing the boundary between the occluder object and the occludee object, and facilitating subsequent instance segmentation detection. Finally, we implement an instance segmentation model that can effectively improve the accuracy of spam detection.

2 Related Work

2.1 Garbage Detection Algorithm

Recently, the study of intelligent classification, detection, and segmentation of garbage using computer vision techniques has attracted a great deal of interest from researchers. The research of the garbage detection method based on instance segmentation is presented below. Cheng [5] optimized the CenterNet model through feature fusion to better extract the subtle features of garbage. The garbage detection adopts YOLO model and the original CenterNet model, and optimizes the backbone of YOLO using VGG and DenseNet. Kan [6] proposed a real-time garbage detection model based on the improved YOLOv5 algorithm, which introduces embedded data augmentation to enrich the background of the detected objects and improve the robustness of the network.

The aforementioned studies have been conducted to improve the detection speed of garbage, enhance the detection of garbage in the water context, and increase the utilization of spatial prior information on garbage. Existing research methods have improved the garbage detection model from different perspectives, but have not addressed the difficulty of detection in the case of occlusion caused by garbage accumulation.

2.2 Occlusion Recognition

The detection of occluded objects has always been a hot and difficult research area in computer vision. In the detection of garbage, the garbage to be detected is often occluded or mutually occluded, and solving the problem of garbage occlusion can effectively improve the detection of garbage ground.

Rajaei [7] demonstrated the important role of the repetitive process of object recognition under occlusion conditions. Tian [8] et al. proposed the DeepParts model to improve the detector's detection for occluded pedestrian performance. Chu [9] et al. changed the proposed frame of the network based on the FPN network through modules such as EMD Loss to be able to predict multiple targets. To address the limitation problem of the current loss function for the occluded population, Wang [10] et al. proposed a bounding box regression loss function Repulsion Loss for the occluded population.

It is difficult to segment instances of unnatural garbage shapes or occluded garbage due to occlusion when garbage is stacked in occurrence and there is no significant difference between object contours and occlusion boundaries.

3 Op-PSA Model

To address the problem that obscured garbage is not easy to detect, this paper carries out research on the segmentation of obscured garbage instances based on the attention model.

3.1 Network Overview

Firstly, to solve the feature extraction problem, the relationship between channels is studied on the above basis, and the pyramidal squeezed attention to structure is introduced in the feature extraction network of the hybrid task cascade model; secondly, according to the occlusion relationship of the occlusion garbage, two overlapping layers are introduced to increase the occlusion relationship between objects for the construction process of the region of interest of the hybrid task cascade model. The general architecture of the model is shown in Fig. 1.

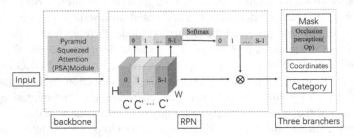

Fig. 1. Model Architecture diagram.

3.2 Pyramid Squeezed Attention (PSA)Module

Since the shape features of garbage are not easily extracted, this paper improves the feature extraction network of the hybrid task cascade model by considering the intrinsic connection between channels through the pyramid-squeezed attention structure Pyramid Squeezed Attention and automatically generates the weight of each feature channel according to the importance of the features using deep learning methods. On top of this, features with higher weights are enhanced, and conversely suppressed for features with lower weights.

The motivation for conducting this work is to build more efficient and effective channel attention mechanisms. To this end, a new Pyramid Squeezed Attention Module is proposed. As shown in Fig. 2, the module is implemented in four main steps. First, the channel-level multiscale feature maps are obtained by implementing the proposed Pyramid Squeezed Attention Module. Second, the attention of the feature maps at different scales is extracted using the channel attention module to obtain the attention vector in the channel direction. Third, the channel attention vectors are recalibrated using Softmax to obtain the recalibration weights of the multi-scale channels. Fourth, the element-by-element product operation is applied to the recalibrated weights and the corresponding feature maps. Finally, as an output, a fine feature map containing richer multi-scale feature information is obtained.

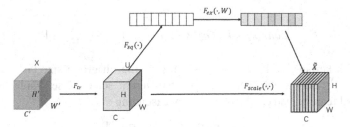

Fig. 2. Pyramid Squeezed Attention (PSA)Module.

As shown in Fig. 3, the basic operator that implements multiscale feature extraction in the proposed pyramidal squeezed attention model is the adaptive depth module, and the model extracts the spatial information of the input feature map in a multi-branch manner, with each branch having an input channel dimension of C.

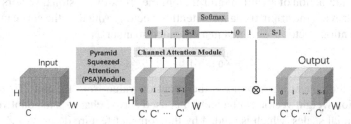

Fig. 3. Structure diagram of the pyramid squeeze attention module.

By doing so, the model can obtain richer information about the location of the input tensor and process it in a parallel manner at multiple scales. As a result, feature maps containing a single type of kernel can be obtained. Accordingly, different spatial resolutions and depths can be generated by using multi-scale convolutional kernels in a pyramidal structure. By compressing the channel dimensions of the input tensor, the spatial information at different scales on each channel feature map can be efficiently extracted. Finally, each feature map of different scales F_i has a common channel dimension $C' = \frac{C}{S}$ and $i = 0, 1, ..., S - 1$. At this point C should be divisible by S. For each branch, it learns multi-scale spatial information independently and builds cross-channel interactions in a local way. However, as the kernel size increases, the number of parameters increases significantly. In order to handle the input tensor at different kernel scales without increasing the computational effort, a group convolution method is introduced and applied to the convolution kernel. In addition, a new criterion is designed in this paper to select the group size without increasing the number of parameters. The relationship between multi-scale kernel size and group size can be written as

$$G = 2^{\frac{K-1}{2}}, \tag{1}$$

where the quantity k is the nuclear size and G is the group size. The above equations have been confirmed by ablation experiments, especially when k × k = 3 × 3 and G = 1. Finally, the multi-scale feature map generation function is given by the following eqution:

$$F_i = Conv(k_i \times k_i, G_i)(X) \quad i = 0, 1, 2, \cdots, S - 1, \tag{2}$$

where the ith kernel size $k_i = 2 \times (i + 1) + 1$, the ith group size $G_i = 2^{\frac{k_i-1}{2}}$, and $F_i \in R^{C' \times H \times W}$ denote the feature maps at different scales. The whole multi-scale preprocessed feature map can be obtained by cascading as

$$F = Cat([F_0, F_1, \cdots, F_{S-1}]). \tag{3}$$

$F \in R^{C \times H \times W}$ is the obtained multiscale feature map. The attention weight vectors at different scales are obtained by extracting the channel attention weight information from the multi-scale preprocessed feature maps. The adaptive depth module is used to obtain the attention weights from the input feature maps at different scales. By doing so, the pyramid-squeezed attention module in this paper can fuse contextual information at different scales and generate better pixel-level attention for high-level feature maps. To achieve the interaction of attention information, the cross-dimensional vectors are fused without destroying the original channel attention vectors. And thus the entire multi-scale channel attention vector is obtained in a cascaded manner as

$$Z = Z_0 \oplus Z_1 \oplus \cdots \oplus Z_{S-1}, \tag{4}$$

where $\oplus$ is the concat operator, Z_i is the attention value from F_i, and Z is the multi-scale attention weight vector. Soft attention is used across channels to adaptively select different spatial scales, which is guided by the compact feature descriptor Z_i. The soft assignment weights are given by the following equation:

$$att_i = Softmax(Z_i) = \frac{\exp(Z_i)}{\sum_{i=0}^{S-1} \exp(Z_i)}, \tag{5}$$

where Softmax is used to obtain a rescaled weight att_i of the multiscale channel that contains all the location information on the space and the attention weights in the channel. By doing so, the interaction of local and global channel attention is achieved. Next, the feature recalibrated channel attentions are fused and stitched together to obtain the whole channel attention vector as

$$att = att_0 \oplus att_1 \oplus \cdots \oplus att_{S-1}, \tag{6}$$

where att denotes the multi-scale channel weights after the attention interaction. Then, in this paper, the recalibrated weights of the multi-scale channel attention att_i are multiplied with the feature maps of the corresponding scales F_i as

$$Y_i = F_i \odot att_i \quad i = 1, 2, 3, \cdots, S - 1, \tag{7}$$

where $\odot$ denotes the channel multiplication and Y_i denotes the feature map after obtaining the multi-scale channel attention weights. The splicing operator is more efficient than the summation operator because it can keep the feature representation intact without destroying the information of the original feature map. In summary, the process of obtaining the refinement output can be written as

$$Out = Cat\left(\left[Y_0, Y_1, \cdots, Y_{S-1}\right]\right). \tag{8}$$

As shown in the above analysis, the pyramid-squeezed attention module proposed in this paper can integrate multi-scale spatial information and cross-channel attention into blocks of each feature group. Therefore, the model implemented in this paper can obtain better information interaction between local and global channel attention.

3.3 Occlusion Perception (Op)Module

Distinguishing from previous top-down instance segmentation methods, this paper proposes a two-layer decoupling model based on Occlusion perception models the region of interest in an image as two overlapping layers, with the upper layer detecting the occluded target and the bottom layer reasoning about the occluded tar-get. The explicit modeling method of the dual-layer structure separates the boundary between the occluder object and the occludee object, and achieves the consideration of the interaction between the occluder object and the target through the prediction of the occludee object and the boundary, thus improving the processing capability of the image instance segmentation model for complex occluded objects, as shown in Fig. 4. The top GCN layer detects the occluder object and the bottom GCN layer infers the instance of the occluded garbage.

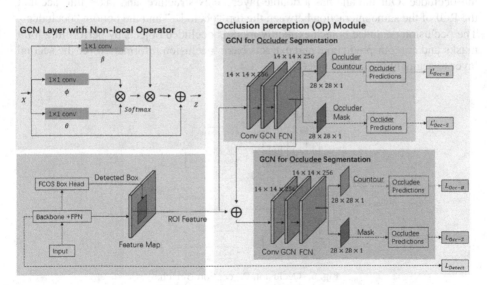

Fig. 4. Double decoupled structure.

Figure 5 shows a schematic diagram of the two-layer decoupling structure, including the top layer as well as the bottom layer. The overlapping part of the two is the invisible region of the occludee object, which is displayed and modeled by the two-layer decoupling model. The first layer, GCN, provides a large amount of occlusion information such as the shape and position of the occludee object, and guides the instance segmentation process of the occluded image.

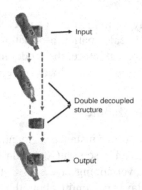

Fig. 5. Invisible Occluded Region.

The input x denotes the CNN feature after ROI extraction. Conv has 3×3 core convolution layer, FC is the full connection layer, and SAM is the spatial attention module. Bt and Mt refer to the box and mask head at t-th stage. Different from the previous occlusion perception mask head, it regress both modal and amodal masks from the occludee. Our module has a double-layer GCN structure, and takes into account the ROI of the same interaction between the top "occluder" and the bottom "occludee". The occlusion occludee branch explicitly models occluded objects by performing joint masks and contour prediction, and extracts basic occlusion information for the second layer to segment the target object Fig. 6.

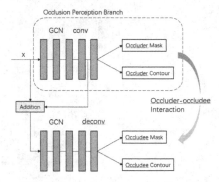

Fig. 6. Occlusion Perception Branch.

The system consists of a garbage detection part and a garbage segmentation part. Where the segmentation network can be represented as

$$Z = \sigma\left(AXW_g\right) + X, \tag{9}$$

where $X \in R^{N \times K}$ is the input feature, $N = H \times W$ is the number of pixel grids in the RoI region, K is the feature dimension of each node, $A \in R^{N \times N}$ is the adjacency matrix used to define the adjacency of graph nodes by feature similarity, and $W_g \in R^{K \times K'}$ is the learnable weight matrix of the output transformation, where in the case of this paper $K' = K$. The output feature $Z \in R^{N \times K'}$ consists of the node features that are updated by propagating them through the node features updated by global information propagation within the whole layer, which are obtained after a nonlinear function $\sigma(\cdot)$ including layer normalization and ReLU function. In this paper, a residual connection is added after the GCN layer.

To construct the adjacency matrix A, the pairwise similarity between every two graph nodes x_i, x_j is defined in this paper by dot product similarity as.

$$A_{ij} = softmax\left(F\left(x_i, x_j\right)\right); \tag{10}$$

$$F\left(x_i, x_j\right) = \theta(x_i)^T \phi\left(x_j\right)^T, \tag{11}$$

where θ and φ are two trainable transform functions implemented by a 1×1 convolution of the nonlocal operator part, making the high confidence edges between two nodes correspond to greater feature similarity.

The two-layer decoupling structure will input the extracted ROI features X_{roi} to the first GCN layer to get the updated features Z^0 and derive the contours and masks of the occluder objects. The updated feature Z^0 is then added to the ROI feature as the input to the second GCN layer ($X_f = X_{roi} + Z^0$). The second GCN layer will further derive the contours and masks of the occludee objects.

For the example of occlusion prediction in the presence of occlusion, using the occlusion-aware model would encode the occluded and occluder layers using two separate occlusion prediction layers, and later fuse the results of the two layers to obtain the final result.

4   Experiments

4.1   Datasets

In this paper, we use the publicly available Taco garbage image dataset [11] and Huawei Cloud's household garbage dataset [12] to build the garbage image dataset used in this paper for model training and testing. The constructed dataset includes different lighting conditions (e.g., strong, weak, nighttime, etc.) and different backgrounds (e.g., beach, road, grassland, etc.). The collected images were labeled using Labelme, and the labeled images were classified into 60 categories: Battery, Food Can, Paper cup, etc.

4.2   Main Results

Quantitative Evaluation.   In this paper, the proposed algorithm is compared with seven typical instance segmentation detection methods, including YOLACT [13], Contrast-Mask [14], Mask R-CNN [15], PANet [16], SOLO [17], Cascade R-CNN [18], and HTC [19].

Table 1. Quantitative evaluation

Method	mAP	AP0.5	AP0.75
YOLACT	51.3	70.7	49.8
ContrastMask	54.6	78.6	54.1
Mask R-CNN	55.2	80.2	57.6
PANet	57.3	81.4	59.4
SOLO	58.0	81.7	60.8
Cascade R-CNN	58.4	82.1	61.3
HTC	58.5	82.3	61.5
Op-PSA	59.0	83.1	62.9

As can be seen from Table 1, the Op-PSA model studied in this paper achieves the highest detection accuracy with 83.1% of garbage detection accuracy. The Op-PSA model can obtain higher accuracy and recall compared with the comparison method, which is attributed to the fact that the Op-PSA model can more accurately separate the masked objects from the masked garbage and solve the low detection rate in the case of masking in the data set. The model can solve the occlusion problem in the accuracy of the pyramidal squeezed attention model and improve the model's resistance to occlusion.

Qualitative Evaluation. In order to compare subjectively, this article extracted and tested garbage images under occlusion from the dataset, and arranged the garbage images detected by various algorithms as follows. It can be seen that the Op-PSA model has better detection performance for garbage under occlusion, and has higher detection accuracy in terms of human perception Fig. 7.

From the above, the Op-PSA model can give better detection results for the dataset used in this paper, even in the case of small-scale occlusion. And by visualizing the front and back layers separately and modeling the boundary and mask of the occluded and masked objects, the detection of occlusion situations can be better grasped, with better recognition of the occluded garbage.

4.3   Ablation Study

Effectiveness of the Pyramid Squeezed Attention (PSA) Module. In this paper, an ablation study is conducted to evaluate the impact of location when integrating the pyramid squeeze attention module into an existing architecture. In addition to the proposed design, three variants are considered in this paper: (1) a front position, where the PSA module is moved before the residual unit; (2) a back position, where the PSA module is after the residual unit; and (3) a parallel position, where the PSA module is placed on a sign connection parallel to the residual unit. These variants are shown in Fig. 8, and the detection results of each variant are shown in Table 2.

From the above table, it can be observed that the modules for the front module, the parallel module, and the proposed position are detected well, while the model using the

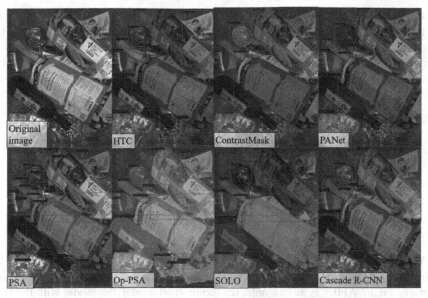

Fig. 7. A large number of occluded garbage maps.

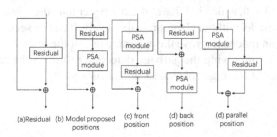

Fig. 8. Comparison diagram of ResNet and module position.

Table 2. Ablation Experiments with Adaptive PSA Module

PSA module	mAP	AP0.5	AP0.75
Front position	58.5	82.3	61.5
Back position	57.2	81.2	59.8
Parallel position	58.7	82.5	62.0
Proposed position	58.7	82.8	62.0

back module leads to performance degradation. This experiment shows that the adaptive pyramid squeezes attention module produces performance improvements that are stable for each location as long as they are applied before branch aggregation.

Effectiveness of the Two GCN Layers. A second GCN layer is added to the model and the final occlusion prediction of the effect of the second GCN on detecting the occlusion contours is guided by the output of the first GCN. That is, in the form of cascade optimization, the second level of optimization is performed on top of the first level after the prediction of the occlusion layer is completed.

Table 3. Ablation experiments with two GCN layers

First GCN layer guidance	Contour	Mask	mAP	AP0.5	AP0.75
—	—	√	52.8	78.4	57.1
√	—	√	56.3	80.3	60.4
√	√	√	59.0	83.1	62.9

As can be seen from Table 3, the model is guided by the first GCN output for the occlusion prediction of the second GCN layer to obtain a more accurate detection structure. Taking AP0.5 as an example, for the original model, the model with the two-layer decoupled structure is more accurate for garbage detection under occlusion, with a 1.7% increase in accuracy. With the addition of Contour, the model achieves the optimal detection result of 83.1%, which is 1.7% and 2.6% better than the model without the first GCN layer and the model without Contour, respectively. It can be seen that the two-layer decoupled model can indeed improve the accuracy rate of the improved HTC model for garbage detection by improving the garbage detection results in the case of occlusion, proving that this model has high robustness and accuracy.

5 Conclusion

In general, this paper proposes an attention model-based garbage instance segmentation detection method for obscured garbage based on the problems of difficult feature extraction, low feature information utilization, and more occlusion cases in the instance segmentation garbage detection method. The experimental results show that the improved network model can better extract the features of garbage information and can effectively improve the accuracy of garbage detection.

References

1. Bashkirova, D., Abdelfattah, M., Zhu, Z.: Zerowaste dataset: towards deformable object segmentation in cluttered scenes. In: Rama Chellappa(John Hopkins Univ.) Proceedings of the IEEE/CVF Conference on Computer Vision and Pattern Recognition, New Orleans, June 19–20, pp .21147–21157. IEEE, New York City (2022)
2. Zhang, C., Liu, X.:Feature extraction of ancient Chinese characters based on deep convolution neural network and big data analysis. Comput. Intell. Neurosci.-**31**(24), 249–256(2021)
3. Guo, C., Fan, B., Zhang, Q.: Augfpn: Improving multi-scale feature learning for object detection. In: Terry Boult, Proceedings of the IEEE/CVF Conference On Computer Vision and Pattern Recognition, Seattle, Jun 13- 19, pp .12595–12604. IEEE, New York City (2020)

4. Fulton, M., Hong, J., Islam, M J.: Robotic detection of marine litter using deep visual detection models. In: Yoshua Bengio. 2019 International Conference on Robotics and Automation (ICRA),Canada, May 20–24, pp .5752–5758. IEEE, New York City (2019)

5. Cheng, X., Hu, F., Song, L., et al.: A novel recyclable garbage detection system for waste-to-energy based on optimized centernet with feature fusion. J. Signal Process. Syst. Springer **95**(1), 67–76 (2023)

6. Kan, Shengqi, et al.: Real-Time domestic garbage detection method based on improved YOLOv5. International Conference on Artificial Intelligence and Security. Cham: Springer International Publishing, pp .62–74 (2022)

7. Rajaei, K., Mohsenzadeh, Y., Ebrahimpour, R.: Beyond core object recognition: Recurrent processes account for object recognition under occlusion. PLoS comput. Biol.-15(5),1007–1008(2019)

8. Tian, Y.L., Luo, P., Wang, X.G.: Deep learning strong parts for pedestrian detection. In: Sawada, T. (ed.) Proceedings of the 2015 IEEE International Conference on Computer Vision, Santiago, 11–18 December, pp. 1904–1912. IEEE Computer Society, Washington (2015)

9. Chu, X.G., Zheng, A.L., Zhang, X.Y.: Detection incrowded scenes: one proposal, multiple predictions. In: Boult, T. (ed.) Proceedings of the 2020 IEEE/CVF Conference on Computer Vision and Pattern Recognition, Seattle, 13–19 Jun, pp. 12211–12220. IEEE, Piscataway (2020)

10. Wang, X.L., Xiao, T.T., Jiang. Y.N.: Repulsion loss: detecting pedestrians in a crowd. In: Brown, M. (ed.) Proceedings of the IEEE Conference on Computer Vision and Pattern Recognition, Salt Lake City, 19–21 Jun, pp. 7774–7783. IEEE Computer Society, Washington (2018)

11. Wang T, Cai Y, Liang L: A multi-level approach to waste object segmentation. Sensors, 20(14),3816(2020)

12. 2019 Huawei Cloud AI Competition. Garbage sorting data, https://aistudio.baidu.com/aistudio/datasetdetail/ 16284.html, Accessed 20 June 2019

13. Bolya, D., Zhou, C., Xiao, F.: Yolact: Real-time instance segmentation. In: Larry Davis, Proceedings of the IEEE/CVF International Conference on Computer Vision. CA, June16–209157–9166. IEEE, New York City (2019)

14. Wang, X., Zhao, K., Zhang, R.: Contrastmask: Contrastive learning to segment everything. In: Rama Chellappa (John Hopkins Univ.) Proceedings of the IEEE/CVF Conference on Computer Vision and Pattern Recognition, New Orleans, June 19–20, pp. 11604–11613. IEEE, New York City (2022)

15. He, K., Gkioxari, G., Dollár, P.: Mask R-CNN. In: Katsushi Ikeuchi (Microsoft Research Asia) Proceedings of the IEEE International Conference on Computer Vision, Venice, October 22–29, pp .2961–2969. IEEE, New York City (2017)

16. Wang, K., Liew, J H., Zou, Y.: Panet: Few-shot image semantic segmentation with prototype alignment. In: Larry Davis Proceedings of the IEEE/CVF International Conference on Computer Vision, CA, June16–20, pp .9197–9206. IEEE, New York City (2019)

17. Wang, X., Kong, T., Shen, C.: Solo: segmenting objects by locations. In: Vittorio Ferrari Computer Vision–ECCV 2020: 16th European Conference Glasgow, UK, August 23–28, pp .649–665. Springer International Publishing, (2020)

18. Cai, Z., Vasconcelos, N.: Cascade R-CNN: delving into high quality object detection. In: Michael Brown ,Proceedings of the IEEE Conference on Computer Vision and Pattern Recognition, Salt lake city, Jun 19–21, pp .6154–6162. IEEE, New York City (2018)

19. Chen, K., Pang, J., Wang, J.: Hybrid task cascade for instance segmentation. In: Larry Davis Proceedings of the IEEE/CVF Conference on Computer Vision and Pattern Recognition, CA, June16–20, pp .4974–4983. IEEE, New York City (2019)

SPC-Net: Structure-Aware Pixel-Level Contrastive Learning Network for OCTA A/V Segmentation and Differentiation

Hanlin Liu[1,2], Huaying Hao[1], Yuhui Ma[1], Lijun Guo[2], Jiong Zhang[1], and Yitian Zhao[1(✉)]

[1] Cixi Institute of Biomedical Engineering, Ningbo Institute of Materials Technology and Engineering, Chinese Academy of Sciences, Ningbo, China
`yitian.zhao@nimte.ac.cn`
[2] Faculty of Electrical Engineering and Computer Science, Ningbo University, Ningbo, China

Abstract. Recent studies have indicated that morphological changes in retinal vessels are associated with many ophthalmic diseases, which have different impacts on arteries and veins (A/V) respectively. To this end, retinal vessel segmentation and further A/V classification are essential for quantitative analysis of related diseases. OCTA is a newly non-invasive vascular imaging technique that provides visualization of microvasculatures with higher resolution than traditional fundus imaging modality. Recently, the task of A/V classification has attracted a lot of attention in the field of OCTA imaging. However, there exist two main challenges in this task. On one hand, there is a lack of intensity information in OCTA images to differentiate between arteries and veins. On the other hand, signal fluctuations during OCTA imaging could also bring about vessel discontinuity. In this paper, we propose a novel **S**tructure-aware **P**ixel-level **C**ontrastive learning network (SPC-Net) for A/V classification. In the proposed SPC-Net, a latent alignment-based network is first utilized to produce a vessel segmentation map in the original OCTA images. Then a pixel-level contrast learning-based network is used to further differentiate between arteries and veins according to the topology of vessels. This network adopts a novel pixel-level contrast learning topology loss to accurately classify the vessel pixels into arteries and veins by taking full account of global semantic similarity. The experimental results demonstrate the superiority of our method compared with the existing state-of-the-art methods respectively on one public OCTA dataset and one in-house OCTA dataset.

Keywords: OCTA · A/V classification · latent alignment · contrast learning

1 Introduction

Extensive clinical studies have shown that structural changes in retinal arteries and veins are closely associated with a range of systemic diseases [1, 9, 31, 36, 49],

B. Sheng et al. (Eds.): CGI 2023, LNCS 14495, pp. 230–245, 2024.
https://doi.org/10.1007/978-3-031-50069-5_20

including diabetic retinopathy [36] and stroke [49]. These diseases have different effects on arteries and veins. For example, diabetic retinopathy and hypertension are respectively accompanied by the appearance of widened veins and narrowed arteries. So it is crucial to accurately distinguish between arteries and veins for analyzing their quantitative characteristics (e.g. vascular curvature, arteriolar to venular diameter ratio, etc.) and the assessment of related diseases.

Ophthalmologists usually make manual annotations on the arteries and veins in clinical practice. However, this process is time-consuming and prone to human errors [15]. Therefore, it is of great value to develop a fully automatic and accurate method to segment vessels from the images and further classify them into arteries and veins. Meanwhile, A/V segmentation and differentiation in OCTA suffer from inherent imaging properties, with challenges such as lack of discrimination between arteries and veins in terms of color and intensity [45].

To address these, we propose a structure-aware pixel-level contrastive learning network (SPC-Net) for A/V segmentation and differentiation in OCTA images, with the capability to differentiate arteries and veins only based on OCTA images. Firstly, a latent alignment-based network is adopted to segment an accurate vascular structure. In addition, we propose a topology loss based on pixel-level contrast learning to learn the relationship among vascular pixels and thus capture the topological differences between arteries and veins for A/V differentiation. Experimental results indicate that our framework outperforms other advanced methods for A/V segmentation and differentiation on public and private OCTA datasets.

2 Related Work

Over the past decade, significant efforts have been devoted to A/V classification in color fundus images [2]. These A/V classification methods can be categorized into two types: deep learning-based and graph-based approaches. For deep learning-based methods [3,21,23,25,26,32,35,48], the color fundus images are fed into a well-designed network, which automatically extracts the features of vessels and performs segmentation and differentiation of arteries and veins. All these methods rely on color and intensity information, as arteries with oxygenated blood are brighter than veins with deoxygenated blood [42]. Additionally, some researchers have found that there exist differences in topological structure between arteriole and venule. To this end, they have developed some graph-based methods [10,38,47,50] based on the finding. These methods generally segment the vessels and disconnect them from the junctions to obtain vascular segments. Vascular segments are then clustered into vessel branches by connectivity analysis. Finally, the structure and intensity features of vessels are utilized to classify the vessel branches into arteries or veins. The topological analysis of the vascular tree alleviates the dependence on local characteristics such as color or intensity features and thus improves the continuity of segmentation results.

Optical Coherence Tomography Angiography (OCTA) is a non-invasive blood flow imaging technology. Compared to color fundus images, it provides capillary-level visualization of retinal vessels with higher resolution [11]. Clinicians can observe more subtle morphological changes in retinal vessels by using the OCTA imaging technique. Thus, OCTA has been widely accepted for retinal vascular analysis and clinical disease diagnosis [33]. Recently, A/V segmentation and differentiation in OCTA have attracted the attention of many researchers.

However, there are some challenges for A/V segmentation and differentiation in OCTA. Subject to the inherent imaging properties of OCTA, lack of discrimination between arteries and veins in terms of color and intensity brings about significant difficulties for A/V classification [45]. At present, several efforts have been developed to address this issue, which can be divided into two major categories: OCT-assisted and pure OCTA methods. The former methods take full advantage of structure information in OCTA images and intensity information in OCT images through a fusion strategy to differentiate arteries and veins. The latter methods aim at accurately identifying arteries and veins only based on OCTA images, which can alleviate the dependence on additional OCT images [16,22,46]. In addition, clinical researches demonstrate that arteries in the superficial capillary plexus have adjacent capillary-free zones [4], and the vortices in the deep capillary plexus drain into veins. This finding makes it possible to classify arterioles only using OCTA images. In this paper, we aim to propose an end-to-end deep learning-based method for A/V segmentation and differentiation only based on OCTA images. Considering the lack of color and intensity features in OCTA images, A/V classification approaches only based on OCTA images require mining the relationship among pixels to effectively capture differences in topographical features between arteries and veins. However, there has been a lack of a canonical representation of the relationship among pixels [51].

Recently, unsupervised contrastive learning [20,37,44] has been one of the most effective methods for mining relationships among samples without labels, which performs significantly better than other pretext task-based methods [13,17,28]. In general, contrastive learning consists of two main components. One is setting a pretext task to discriminate between similar (positive pairs) and different (negative pairs) samples. The other is constructing an objective function that aims at reducing the distance between positive pairs and increasing the distance between negative pairs. However, these methods typically focus on exploring the relationships among image-level rather than pixel-level samples. In contrast, pixel-level contrastive learning methods [43] aim to make pixel embeddings belonging to the same category more similar than those from different categories. This method extends contrast learning from the image level to the pixel level to enhance the segmentation performance of the network by learning the semantic relationship among pixels. Inspired by pixel-level contrast learning, we introduce this strategy into the A/V classification network to mine the relationship among vascular pixels in OCTA images, which aims at learning the topological differences between arteries and veins.

Our contributions can be summarized into the following three aspects:

- We propose a structure-aware pixel-level contrastive learning network (SPC-Net) for A/V segmentation and differentiation in OCTA images. It is verified

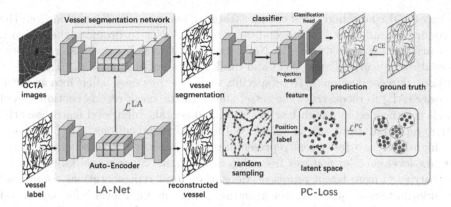

Fig. 1. The pipeline of the proposed structure-aware pixel-level contrastive learning network.

that A/V in OCTA images can be identified only using topological information, without additional color or intensity features.

- We propose a latent alignment-based vessel segmentation network, which mitigates the shortage of contextual information caused by skip connections. In this approach, the high-level feature encoder is fully trained by the consistency constraint of the latent representations.
- We introduce a pixel-level contrast learning-based topology loss to differentiate between arteries and veins. This loss helps the network learn well-structured latent representations by fully accounting for global semantic similarity.

3 Method

The proposed SPC-Net consists of two steps: **Latent alignment-based vessel segmentation network** and **Pixel-level contrast learning-based topology loss**, as shown in Fig. 1. In the first step, we develop a Latent Alignment-based Network (LA-Net) for vessel segmentation in the original image. In the second step, a pixel-level contrast learning-based topology loss is introduced into another network for further differentiation between arteries and veins based on vessel segmentation.

3.1 Latent Alignment-Based Vessel Segmentation Network

In the first step, we propose LA-Net segment the vessel pixels from the original image. The proposed network adopts the TransUNet [7] as the backbone, considering its excellent performance in medical image segmentation. However, the mechanism of the U-shaped architectures has limitations [27]. Skip connection can cause features from low-level encoder layers to be reused, resulting in information redundancy. Even worse, as the network tends to use low-level encoder features and ignore high-level encoder features, contextual information from the encoder is insufficient. To this end, we design LA-Net to promote the network to learn high-level features. LA-Net consists of two sub-networks: vessel segmentation network (TransUNet) and mask reconstruction network (TransUNet without skip connections). To be specific, we input the vessel labels into an autoencoder (AE) to reconstruct the vessel labels. In the mask reconstruction, vessel labels are encoded into high-level features, and we take high-level features as the latent representations of the vessel. Without skip connections, AE has to use the high-level features (latent representations) to reconstruct vessels rather than the low-level encoder features from skip connections. Since vessel labels can be reconstructed from latent representations, the latent representations contain all the information about the vessel structure. Thus, the high-level information can provide additional supervision for vessel segmentation. It can help alleviate the problem of insufficient contextual information due to excessive focus on low-level features.

During training, the original image x is input into the vessel segmentation network, and the label y is input into the AE. Then, Binary Cross Entropy (BCE) loss is applied to supervise the output of two networks $f_{Seg}(x)$ and $f_{AE}(y)$, which can be formulated as:

$$\mathcal{L}_{S1} = \mathcal{L}_{bce}(f_{Seg}(x), y) + \mathcal{L}_{bce}(f_{AE}(y), y). \tag{1}$$

Meanwhile, The latent representations of two networks are denoted by z_{Seg} and z_{AE}. And we introduce an auxiliary Mean Square Error (MSE) loss to train the latent representations, which is given by:

$$\mathcal{L}_{LA} = \| z_{Seg} - z_{AE} \|^2. \tag{2}$$

The MSE loss aligns the latent representations between the vessel segmentation network and AE. In summary, the first step training objective for segmentation is given by:

$$\mathcal{L}_{SEG} = \mathcal{L}_{S1} + \gamma_1 \mathcal{L}_{LA}, \tag{3}$$

where γ_1 is a tunable hyperparameter that moderates the effect of the MSE loss.

3.2 Pixel-Level Contrast Learning-Based Topology Loss

In the second step, we propose a pixel-level contrast learning-based topology loss to differentiate between arteries and veins from the vessels segmentation results in the first step. The network includes a U-shape structure (TransUNet) with a projection head and pixel-level contrast learning-based topology loss (PC-Loss). In this step, the segmented map is first fed into a U-shape structure for obtaining A/V prediction and pixel-level representation. In addition, we proposed a new PC-Loss to increase the feature difference between arteries and veins. The PC-Loss is designed based on a simple premise that only two different vessels will cross in a two-dimensional fundus image [24]. Therefore, a good A/V classification result should follow two graphic rules: 1. All pixels on the one vascular

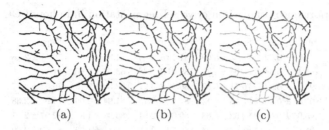

Fig. 2. (a) Vascular segmentation label; (b) A/V classification label (Red: arteries, Blue: veins, green: crossing point); (c) Vascular topology label (Each vessel is assigned a unique label). (Color figure online)

segment should be the same. 2. Two crossed vascular segments belong to different classes. We aim to turn these two rules into a supervisory loss function.

However, since there is no canonical representation for graphic feature [51], it is difficult for deep networks to learn these rules. Here, we set up a proxy task instead of graphic analysis, aiming to distinguish each vessel in the structure.

The specific process is as follows: firstly, we convert the A/V classification label Fig. 2 (b) to the vascular topology label Fig. 2 (c). We then search all connected domains in the A/V classification label. Each connected domain (vessel) is assigned a unique label. Due to the computing power cost, it is impossible to calculate the relative relationship between all pixels. Thus, we random uniform sample pixels from each batch and category to obtain representative pixels i. We define the pixels from the same vessel (pixels with the same color in Fig. 2(c)) as positive samples $\mathcal{P}_i$, and those from different vessels as negative samples $\mathcal{N}_i$. Additionally, L2 regularization is applied to guarantee that the modulus of any latent representation vector is equal to 1. To this end, we can use cosine similarity to measure the distance between the two sample vectors by calculating the inner product of the two vectors. The PC-loss can be described as:

$$\mathcal{L}_{\mathrm{PC}} = \frac{1}{|\mathcal{P}_i|}$$
$$\sum_{i^+ \in \mathcal{P}_i} -\log \frac{\exp\left(\boldsymbol{i} \cdot \boldsymbol{i}^+/\tau\right)}{\exp\left(\boldsymbol{i} \cdot \boldsymbol{i}^+/\tau\right) + \sum_{i^- \in \mathcal{N}_i} \exp\left(\boldsymbol{i} \cdot \boldsymbol{i}^-/\tau\right)}, \tag{4}$$

where $\tau > 0$ is a temperature hyper-parameter and $\cdot$ denotes the inner (dot) product. As shown in Eq. 4, the PC-loss is designed to learn a latent space with structure by pulling the pixel samples from the same vessel close and by pushing the samples from different vessels apart. Meanwhile, the pixel-level cross-entropy (CE) loss is also adopted for the classification:

$$\mathcal{L}_{S2} = \mathcal{L}_{CE}(f(x), y), \tag{5}$$

where $f(x)$ is the prediction of the model, y denotes label. Considering that CE-loss and PC-loss are complementary to each other. The training target in

Table 1. Performance comparison of vessel segmentation in in-house OCTA dataset

Methods	Acc	Se	G-mean	Dice	Kappa	IoU
U-Net [39]	95.03 ± 0.72	77.45 ± 5.00	87.12 ± 2.64	81.97 ± 1.90	79.11 ± 2.18	69.50 ± 2.68
ResUNet [12]	95.42 ± 0.64	80.94 ± 4.71	89.01 ± 2.38	83.77 ± 1.60	81.11 ± 1.86	72.11 ± 2.35
CS-Net [34]	95.21 ± 0.93	76.11 ± 5.87	86.56 ± 3.21	82.30 ± 2.72	79.57 ± 3.17	70.02 ± 3.89
CE-Net [18]	95.01 ± 0.76	77.65 ± 5.14	87.21 ± 2.73	81.94 ± 2.06	79.06 ± 2.38	69.45 ± 2.94
OCTA-Net [33]	95.95 ± 0.69	80.53 ± 5.68	89.09 ± 2.91	85.30 ± 1.89	82.97 ± 2.21	74.42 ± 2.83
TransUNet [7]	95.82 ± 0.62	81.97 ± 5.24	89.72 ± 2.62	85.11 ± 1.73	82.69 ± 2.00	74.12 ± 2.61
OCT2Former [41]	94.94 ± 1.60	89.76 ± 3.41	92.54 ± 1.70	76.58 ± 4.49	73.84 ± 5.13	62.25 ± 5.35
Swin-Unet [5,6]	95.57 ± 1.10	**92.85 ± 2.40**	**94.30 ± 1.28**	75.34 ± 4.44	73.02 ± 4.85	60.63 ± 5.36
Ours	**96.19 ± 0.71**	88.69 ± 4.64	92.98 ± 2.17	**87.08 ± 2.55**	**84.85 ± 2.88**	**77.20 ± 3.89**

Table 2. Performance comparison of A/V classification in in-house OCTA dataset

Methods	Acc	Se	G-mean	Dice	Kappa	IoU
U-Net [39]	96.08 ± 0.62	79.86 ± 3.72	84.61 ± 3.11	82.27 ± 2.59	75.88 ± 2.97	71.44 ± 3.30
ResUNet [12]	96.40 ± 0.56	82.54 ± 3.38	86.86 ± 2.70	84.06 ± 2.42	78.29 ± 2.64	73.82 ± 3.26
CS-Net [34]	96.20 ± 0.66	78.87 ± 4.05	83.77 ± 3.50	82.19 ± 2.89	76.11 ± 3.48	71.41 ± 3.68
CE-Net [18]	96.25 ± 0.60	81.24 ± 3.72	85.53 ± 3.05	83.54 ± 2.49	76.96 ± 2.92	73.09 ± 3.31
OCTA-Net [33]	96.84 ± 0.52	83.02 ± 3.49	87.14 ± 2.85	85.67 ± 2.74	80.48 ± 2.84	76.09 ± 3.69
TransUNet [7]	96.77 ± 0.55	84.10 ± 4.04	87.99 ± 3.14	85.77 ± 2.59	80.41 ± 2.81	76.20 ± 3.60
OCT2Former [41]	95.98 ± 1.25	84.28 ± 4.03	89.07 ± 2.74	77.11 ± 4.60	69.39 ± 5.96	65.40 ± 5.06
Swin-Unet [5,6]	96.73 ± 0.93	**89.23 ± 3.87**	**92.48 ± 2.48**	78.98 ± 4.75	70.61 ± 5.95	67.69 ± 5.28
Ours	**96.90 ± 0.55**	86.74 ± 3.24	90.34 ± 2.51	**86.47 ± 2.81**	**81.80 ± 3.30**	**77.23 ± 3.92**

the second step is given by:

$$\mathcal{L}_{CLS} = \mathcal{L}_{S2} + \gamma_2 \mathcal{L}_{PC}, \tag{6}$$

where $\gamma_2 > 0$ is the coefficient. Combined with the loss function in the first step, the total training objective can be expressed as:

$$\mathcal{L}_{total} = \mathcal{L}_{SEG} + \mathcal{L}_{CLS} = \mathcal{L}_{S1} + \gamma_1 \mathcal{L}_{LA} + \mathcal{L}_{S2} + \gamma_2 \mathcal{L}_{PC}, \tag{7}$$

4   Experimental Settings

4.1   Datasets

In this paper, we verify the effectiveness of the proposed method on a publicly available dataset **OCTA-500** [29,30] and an **in-house OCTA dataset**.

- **OCTA-500** contains OCTA imaging under two fields of view from 500 subjects captured by RTVue-XR (Optovue Inc., Fremont CA). The OCTA-500 dataset consists of two subsets: OCTA_3M and OCTA_6M. In this paper, 300 ILM_OPL 2D projection maps with a resolution of 400×400 pixels from the

Table 3. Performance comparison of vessel segmentation in OCTA-500 dataset

Methods	Acc	Se	G-mean	Dice	Kappa	IoU
U-Net [39]	97.66 ± 0.38	84.17 ± 3.95	91.27 ± 2.16	86.66 ± 2.58	85.38 ± 2.72	76.55 ± 3.87
ResUNet [12]	97.76 ± 0.46	84.04 ± 5.29	91.23 ± 2.95	87.10 ± 3.20	85.87 ± 3.38	77.27 ± 4.71
CS-Net [34]	97.54 ± 0.45	82.75 ± 3.11	90.50 ± 1.75	85.89 ± 2.70	84.54 ± 2.88	75.36 ± 3.98
CE-Net [18]	97.55 ± 0.42	82.54 ± 4.19	90.39 ± 2.35	85.87 ± 2.78	84.53 ± 2.94	75.34 ± 4.07
OCTA-Net [33]	97.74 ± 0.44	84.32 ± 3.93	91.37 ± 2.16	87.05 ± 2.83	85.81 ± 3.01	77.17 ± 4.22
TransUNet [7]	97.74 ± 0.42	83.48 ± 4.74	90.95 ± 2.62	86.96 ± 2.81	85.73 ± 2.96	77.03 ± 4.17
OCT2Former [41]	97.79 ± 0.44	84.29 ± 4.53	91.38 ± 2.49	87.28 ± 2.90	86.07 ± 3.08	77.54 ± 4.40
Swin-Unet [5,6]	**98.00 ± 0.34**	81.83 ± 3.68	90.11 ± **2.06**	85.49 ± 2.65	84.42 ± 2.77	74.75 ± 3.88
Ours	97.89 ± 0.41	**85.84 ± 3.83**	**92.20 ± 2.07**	**87.99 ± 2.53**	**86.84 ± 2.70**	**78.65 ± 3.87**

Table 4. Performance comparison of A/V classification in OCTA-500 dataset

Methods	Acc	Se	G-mean	Dice	Kappa	IoU
U-Net [39]	98.32 ± 0.35	87.55 ± 3.45	90.47 ± 2.66	89.04 ± 2.74	84.38 ± 3.39	81.11 ± 3.95
ResUNet [12]	98.35 ± 0.42	87.12 ± 4.43	90.18 ± 3.56	89.02 ± 3.33	84.60 ± 4.15	81.15 ± 4.70
CS-Net [34]	98.13 ± 0.48	85.30 ± 3.78	88.91 ± 2.76	87.27 ± 3.68	82.61 ± 4.12	78.62 ± 5.00
CE-Net [18]	98.27 ± 0.34	86.78 ± 3.42	89.77 ± 2.76	88.81 ± 2.70	83.79 ± 3.50	80.75 ± 3.77
OCTA-Net [33]	98.35 ± 0.42	87.57 ± 3.62	90.52 ± 2.76	89.24 ± 3.16	84.74 ± 3.84	81.45 ± 4.45
TransUNet [7]	98.41 ± 0.34	87.63 ± 3.54	90.42 ± 2.88	89.77 ± 2.46	85.11 ± 3.30	82.19 ± 3.60
OCT2Former [41]	98.21 ± 0.51	85.40 ± 5.02	89.20 ± 3.75	87.19 ± 4.41	83.24 ± 4.79	78.61 ± 5.92
Swin-Unet [5,6]	**98.50 ± 0.33**	85.17 ± 3.56	88.74 ± 2.73	87.40 ± 3.13	82.64 ± 3.69	78.78 ± 4.26
Ours	98.45 ± 0.37	**88.55 ± 3.29**	**91.26 ± 2.50**	**89.97 ± 2.73**	**85.70 ± 3.30**	**82.54 ± 3.98**

OCTA_6M subset were employed for our experimental evaluation. Consistent with the standards in paper [30], we divide all data into a training set (NO. 10001-NO. 10240), a validation set(NO. 10241-NO. 10250), and a test set (NO. 10251-NO. 10300).

- **In-house OCTA dataset** contains 118 images with a resolution of 400×400 pixels. Each OCTA image is accompanied by a matched color fundus photograph with a resolution of 2124×2056 pixels. Three clinicians were invited to manually label all the vessels in the OCTA images into arteries and veins according to the color-carrying information of the corresponding vessel in the color fundus photograph. Their consensus was used as ground truth. The dataset is partitioned into three subsets, with 70 images for training, 24 for validation, and 24 for testing.

4.2 Implementation Details

The experiments were conducted on two NVIDIA GPUs (GeForce RTX 3090), with the PyTorch library. We adopted Adam as our optimizer, with an initial learning rate of 0.0001 and weight decay of 0.00005. The number of training iterations was set to 500 epochs, and the batch size to 4. For data augmentation, all

Table 5. Ablation study of the proposed method

	two step	LA loss	PC loss	Acc	Se	G-mean	Dice	Kappa	IoU
1				96.77 ± 0.55	84.10 ± 4.04	87.99 ± 3.14	85.77 ± 2.59	80.41 ± 2.81	76.20 ± 3.60
2	✓			96.89 ± 0.55	83.85 ± 3.79	87.99 ± 2.96	85.79 ± 3.01	81.07 ± 3.00	76.30 ± 4.07
3	✓	✓		96.93 ± 0.51	84.15 ± 3.78	88.19 ± 3.05	86.06 ± 2.49	81.32 ± 2.64	76.63 ± 3.40
4	✓		✓	96.66 ± 0.60	84.57 ± 3.57	88.62 ± 2.89	85.16 ± 2.78	80.11 ± 3.47	75.38 ± 3.78
5	✓	✓	✓	**96.90 ± 0.55**	**86.74 ± 3.24**	**90.34 ± 2.51**	**86.47 ± 2.81**	**81.80 ± 3.30**	**77.23 ± 3.92**

the training images were augmented by random online transformations, including random rotation of $[-45°, 45°]$ around the image center, random scaling with a factor in $[0.8, 1.2]$, and vertical/horizontal flipping randomly.

We adopted the TransUNet as the backbone. All backbones were initialized using corresponding weights (imagenet21k_R50+ViT-B_16') pre-trained on ImageNet [40]. In pixel-level contrast learning-based topology loss, we sampled 1600 pixel points per batch, and the projection head has 128 channels. It is noteworthy that the intersection points present in the supervised labels (green pixels in Fig. 2(b)) were not utilized in the training process. As for the hyperparameter weights, the weight parameters γ_1 and γ_2 in the final objective function $\mathcal{L}_{total}$ were set to 0.5 and 0.3, respectively.

4.3   Evaluation Metrics

The evaluation was conducted including vessel segmentation and A/V classification following the paper [47]. On the one hand, the performance of vessel segmentation was evaluated by counting the number of correctly classified vessel pixels in the expert labels. The metrics used include accuracy (Acc), sensitivity (Se), G-mean score (G-mean) [14], Dice coefficient (Dice) [19], Kappa [8] and Intersection over Union (IoU).

$$\text{Acc} = \frac{\text{TP+TN}}{\text{TP+TN+FP+FN}}, \quad \text{Se} = \frac{\text{TP}}{\text{TP+FN}}, \tag{8}$$

$$\text{G-mean} = \sqrt{\frac{\text{TP}}{\text{TP+FN}} * \frac{\text{TN}}{\text{TN+FP}}}, \tag{9}$$

$$\text{Dice} = \frac{2*\text{TP}}{\text{FP+2*TP+FN}}, \quad \text{IoU} = \frac{\text{TP}}{\text{TP+FP+FN}}, \tag{10}$$

where TP, TN, FP, and FN stand for true positives, true negatives, false positives, and false negatives of the vessel segmentation. The Kappa coefficient can be described as follows:

$$\text{Kappa} = \frac{P_o - P_e}{1 - P_e}, P_o = \frac{\sum_{i=1}^{n} a_{ii}}{N}, P_e = \frac{\sum_{i=1}^{n} a_{i+} * a_{+i}}{N^2}, \tag{11}$$

with P_o representing the observed agreement between raters, P_e representing the expected agreement by chance, a_{ij} representing the number of instances where the true class is identified as i and the predicted class is identified as j, and N represents the overall number of instances. On the other hand, A/V differentiation was evaluated using the same metrics. This process can be treated as a multi-class segmentation task. Metrics are calculated using all pixels, excluding the junction of arteries and veins, which are ignored. And the reported results are macro averages of all metrics within each category.

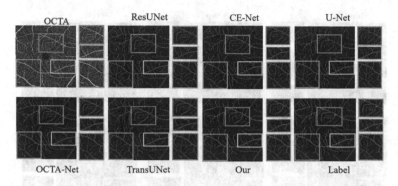

Fig. 3. Visualization results of the comparison experiment in in-house dataset.

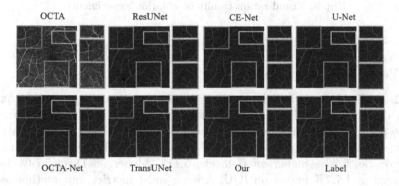

Fig. 4. Visualization results of the comparison experiment in OCTA-500 dataset.

5   Experimental Results

In order to demonstrate the effectiveness of the proposed two-step method, we evaluated the performance of vessel segmentation and A/V classification, respectively. The following methods were compared: U-Net [39], ResU-Net [12], CE-Net [18], CS-Net [34], OCTA-Net [33], OCT2Former [41], Swin-Unet [5,6] and TransU-Net [7]. Since the comparison methods are end-to-end, only A/V classification results are provided. It is worth noting that we combine arteries and veins predicted results from comparisons as vessel segmentation results for evaluation. For the comparison experiment, we determine the metrics on each image and calculate their mean and standard deviation. In all tables, each metric contains the mean (the first value) and the standard deviation (the second value). In the visualization of the prediction results, red pixels indicate arteries, blue pixels indicate veins and green pixels indicate their junctions.

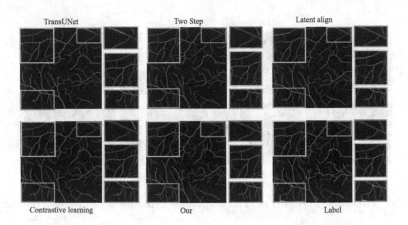

Fig. 5. Visualization results of ablation experiments.

5.1   Vessel Segmentation

Table 1 and Table 3 present the performance of the vessel segmentation on two OCTA datasets. Overall, the proposed method demonstrates superior comprehensive performance compared to the other comparisons on both two datasets. In Table 1, our method surpasses the U-Net by 1.14% higher on Acc, 11.24% higher on Se, 5.86% higher on G-mean, 5.11% higher on Dice, 5.74% higher on Kappa, and 7.7% higher on IOU. Among most metrics, our method is significantly higher in Se, Dice, and IoU, which demonstrates that our method has higher sensitivity and accuracy on vessel segmentation. Meanwhile, OCTA-Net and TransUNet perform better among all comparison methods, which is consistent with the visualization results in Fig. 3. The pure transformer-based methods OCT2Former and Swin-Unet achieve high performance on both Se and G-mean but perform poorly on the other metrics. Even though pre-training parameters have been used, both pure transformer methods still show significant over-segmentation, with poor performance on Dice and IoU. It is noteworthy that our method also yields the best results in visualization, displaying stronger continuity of the vessels and more accurate segmentation of vessel ends. Our approach enhances the model's context awareness through optimization of the latent space representation, which in turn improves the accuracy and continuity of vessel segmentation.

A similar trend is reflected in the comparative experiments conducted on the OCTA-500 dataset. As shown in Table 3, our approach's Se, Dice, and IoU significantly outperform those of the other methods. The proposed method is ahead of the second-place TransUNdongj et by 2.36%, 1.03%, and 1.62% on Se, Dice, and IoU, respectively. This further confirms the exceptional performance of the proposed method. From the visualization results in Fig. 4, we can find that our proposed method exhibits improved vessel continuity and reduced missed vessels. In comparison to the other methods, the proposed method exhibits a significant improvement in performance, particularly at the termination of the microvessels. The visualization results obtained from our experiments also demonstrate the superiority of the proposed method.

5.2 A/V Classification

On the other hand, our approach also achieves the best comprehensive performance on A/V classification in both two datasets, as shown in Table 2 and Table 4. In keeping with other A/V segmentation experiments, all metrics in this experiment were computed over all pixels, including the background. Obviously, models that have improved segmentation performance tend to perform better in classification tasks. That is why we focus on enhancing the segmentation method in the first step. The results of the experiments conducted on our in-house dataset, as depicted in Table 2, demonstrate that the proposed method has a clear advantage over OCTA-Net, the best representative in CNNs, and TransUNet, the best representative in Transformer architectures. Our method outperforms OCTA-Net by 3.72% in terms of Se, 3.2% in terms of G-mean, 0.8% in terms of Dice, 1.32% in terms of Kappa and 1.14% in terms of IOU. Compared to TransUNet, our method is 2.64% higher on Se, 2.35% higher on G-mean, 0.7% higher on Dice, 1.39% higher on Kappa, and 1.03% higher on IOU.

A comparable situation was observed in the comparison experiments of the OCTA-500 dataset. As shown in Table 4, the proposed method also achieves the best performance. Compared with our backbone TransUNet, the proposed method demonstrates an improvement of 0.84%, 0.2%, and 0.35% points in terms of Se, Dice, and IoU, respectively. These evaluations demonstrate that the proposed method outperforms other comparable methods and achieves state-of-the-art results. Meanwhile, The results also highlight the potential value of the two-step approach on the A/V segmentation of OCTA, thereby validating the hypothesis that it is possible to differentiate A/V using only the topology of the vessel.

5.3 Ablation Experiments

To confirm the efficiency of each module, we conducted ablation experiments in our in-house dataset, as depicted in Table 5 and Fig. 5.

- **Ablation for two-step structure.** After incorporating the two-step strategy, the model transforms into a tandem of two TransUNet models. Comparing experiment 1 with experiment 2, it can be observed that the performance of the two-step strategy approach is almost identical to that of the baseline (TransUNet). This implies that classifying arteries and veins can be achieved by utilizing segmentation results without intensity features.

- **Ablation for latent space alignment.** Make a comparison between experiment 2 and experiment 3. We can observe a notable improvement in metrics, such as a 0.3% increase in Se and a 0.27% increase in Dice. As mentioned above, these improvements may result from advancements in latent space representation, which leads to better vessel segmentation and subsequently results in an improvement in classification performance.
- **Ablation for pixel-level contrast learning-based topology loss.** Comparing the results of experiment 2 with those of experiment 4, a more pronounced improvement is observed, especially in Se (0.72% higher) and G-mean (0.63% higher). Frustratingly, other metrics show a decline. Observe the visualization results in Fig. 5. This may be due to contrast learning that divides some capillaries in the background into arteries or veins.
- **Ablation for the combination of all components.** In the above, we verify the effect of each component independently. Experiments show that each module plays a significant role in improving the performance of the model. In this section, we also evaluate the impact of combining them. Experiment 5 has the highest performance, indicating that combining all components achieves the best performance.

6   Conclusion

In this paper, we propose a two-step framework for A/V classification in OCTA images. The main significance of this work is that we have verified that there are topological differences between arteries and veins. We differentiate arteries and veins with vessel topology, which is free from the reliance on additional OCT images for brightness information. Moreover, since the topology of vessel segmentation eliminates the effect of image style factors, it shows greater potential for applications on various imaging devices with different styles. We have confirmed the effectiveness of our proposed components through both comparison and ablation experiments. In the first step, the latent space alignment is utilized to overcome the limitation of insufficient contextual information caused by skipping connections, resulting in increased continuity in segmented vessels. In the second step, we adopt pixel-level contrast learning to learn a well-structured latent representation by taking full account of global semantic similarity. All these components assist our proposed method to improve the segmentation and differentiation of arteries and veins in OCTA images.

In our future work, we expect to extend our work to the semi-supervised field by incorporating more unlabeled samples to improve the generalization ability of the model. We believe that learning a more diverse and comprehensive distribution of vessel topology could further facilitate the accuracy of A/V classification. Furthermore, considering the characteristic that A/V classification is not influenced by image style factors, we will extend this approach to application in the domain adaptation tasks.

References

1. Abràmoff, M.D., Garvin, M.K., Sonka, M.: Retinal imaging and image analysis. IEEE Rev. Biomed. Eng. **3**, 169–208 (2010)
2. Alam, M.N., Le, D., Yao, X.: Differential artery-vein analysis in quantitative retinal imaging: a review. Quant. Imaging Med. Surg. **11**(3), 1102 (2021)
3. Ali, S.G., et al.: Cost-effective broad learning-based ultrasound biomicroscopy with 3D reconstruction for ocular anterior segmentation. Multimedia Tools Appl. **80**, 35105–35122 (2021)
4. Balaratnasingam, C., et al.: Comparisons between histology and optical coherence tomography angiography of the periarterial capillary-free zone. Am. J. Ophthalmol. **189**, 55–64 (2018)
5. Cao, H., Wang, Y., Chen, J., Jiang, D., Zhang, X., Tian, Q., Wang, M.: Swin-unet: Unet-like pure transformer for medical image segmentation (2021)
6. Cao, H., et al.: Swin-unet: Unet-like pure transformer for medical image segmentation. In: Proceedings of the European Conference on Computer Vision Workshops(ECCVW) (2022)
7. Chen, J., Lu, Y., Yu, Q., Luo, X., Adeli, E., Wang, Y., Lu, L., Yuille, A.L., Zhou, Y.: Transunet: Transformers make strong encoders for medical image segmentation. arXiv preprint arXiv:2102.04306 (2021)
8. Chmura Kraemer, H., Periyakoil, V.S., Noda, A.: Kappa coefficients in medical research. Stat. Med. **21**(14), 2109–2129 (2002)
9. Dai, L., et al.: A deep learning system for detecting diabetic retinopathy across the disease spectrum. Nat. Commun. **12**(1), 1–11 (2021)
10. Dashtbozorg, B., Mendonça, A.M., Campilho, A.: An automatic graph-based approach for artery/vein classification in retinal images. IEEE Trans. Image Process. **23**(3), 1073–1083 (2013)
11. De Carlo, T.E., Romano, A., Waheed, N.K., Duker, J.S.: A review of optical coherence tomography angiography (OCTA). Int. J. Retina Vitreous **1**(1), 1–15 (2015)
12. Diakogiannis, F.I., Waldner, F., Caccetta, P., Wu, C.: ResUNet-a: a deep learning framework for semantic segmentation of remotely sensed data. ISPRS J. Photogramm. Remote. Sens. **162**, 94–114 (2020)
13. Doersch, C., Gupta, A., Efros, A.A.: Unsupervised visual representation learning by context prediction. In: Proceedings of the IEEE International Conference on Computer vision, pp. 1422–1430 (2015)
14. Espíndola, R.P., Ebecken, N.F.: On extending F-measure and G-mean metrics to multi-class problems. WIT Trans. Inf. Commun. Technol. **35**, 25–34 (2005)
15. Estrada, R., Allingham, M.J., Mettu, P.S., Cousins, S.W., Tomasi, C., Farsiu, S.: Retinal artery-vein classification via topology estimation. IEEE Trans. Med. Imaging **34**(12), 2518–2534 (2015)
16. Gao, M., et al.: A deep learning network for classifying arteries and veins in montaged widefield oct angiograms. Ophthalmol. Sci. **2**(2), 100149 (2022)
17. Gidaris, S., Singh, P., Komodakis, N.: Unsupervised representation learning by predicting image rotations. arXiv preprint arXiv:1803.07728 (2018)
18. Gu, Z., et al.: CE-Net: Context encoder network for 2D medical image segmentation. IEEE Trans. Med. Imaging **38**(10), 2281–2292 (2019)
19. Guindon, B., Zhang, Y.: Application of the dice coefficient to accuracy assessment of object-based image classification. Can. J. Remote. Sens. **43**(1), 48–61 (2017)
20. Hjelm, R.D., et al.: Learning deep representations by mutual information estimation and maximization. arXiv preprint arXiv:1808.06670 (2018)

21. Hu, J., et al.: Automatic artery/vein classification using a vessel-constraint network for multicenter fundus images. Front. Cell Dev. Biol. **9**, 659941 (2021)
22. Ishibazawa, A., et al.: Accuracy and reliability in differentiating retinal arteries and veins using widefield En face oct angiography. Transl. Vis. Sci. Technol. **8**(3), 60–60 (2019)
23. Jiqing, C., Depeng, W., Teng, L., Tian, L., Huabin, W.: All-weather road drivable area segmentation method based on cycleGAN. Vis. Comput. **39**(12), 1–17 (2022)
24. Joshi, V.S., Reinhardt, J.M., Garvin, M.K., Abramoff, M.D.: Automated method for identification and artery-venous classification of vessel trees in retinal vessel networks. PLoS ONE **9**(2), e88061 (2014)
25. Kang, H., Gao, Y., Guo, S., Xu, X., Li, T., Wang, K.: AVNet: a retinal artery/vein classification network with category-attention weighted fusion. Comput. Methods Programs Biomed. **195**, 105629 (2020)
26. Karlsson, R.A., Hardarson, S.H.: Artery vein classification in fundus images using serially connected U-Nets. Comput. Methods Programs Biomed. **216**, 106650 (2022)
27. Khanh, T.L.B., et al.: Enhancing U-Net with spatial-channel attention gate for abnormal tissue segmentation in medical imaging. Appl. Sci. **10**(17), 5729 (2020)
28. Larsson, G., Maire, M., Shakhnarovich, G.: Learning representations for automatic colorization. In: Leibe, B., Matas, J., Sebe, N., Welling, M. (eds.) ECCV 2016. LNCS, vol. 9908, pp. 577–593. Springer, Cham (2016). https://doi.org/10.1007/978-3-319-46493-0_35
29. Li, M., et al.: Image projection network: 3D to 2D image segmentation in octa images. IEEE Trans. Med. Imaging **39**(11), 3343–3354 (2020)
30. Li, M., et al.: IPN-V2 and OCTA-500: Methodology and dataset for retinal image segmentation. arXiv preprint arXiv:2012.07261 (2020)
31. Liu, R., et al.: DeepDRiD: diabetic retinopathy–grading and image quality estimation challenge. Patterns **3**(6), 100512 (2022)
32. Ma, W., Yu, S., Ma, K., Wang, J., Ding, X., Zheng, Y.: Multi-task neural networks with spatial activation for retinal vessel segmentation and artery/vein classification. In: Shen, D., et al. (eds.) MICCAI 2019. LNCS, vol. 11764, pp. 769–778. Springer, Cham (2019). https://doi.org/10.1007/978-3-030-32239-7_85
33. Ma, Y., et al.: Rose: a retinal OCT-angiography vessel segmentation dataset and new model. IEEE Trans. Med. Imaging **40**(3), 928–939 (2020)
34. Mou, L., et al.: CS-Net: channel and spatial attention network for curvilinear structure segmentation. In: Shen, D., et al. (eds.) MICCAI 2019. LNCS, vol. 11764, pp. 721–730. Springer, Cham (2019). https://doi.org/10.1007/978-3-030-32239-7_80
35. Nazir, A., et al.: ECSU-Net: an embedded clustering sliced U-Net coupled with fusing strategy for efficient intervertebral disc segmentation and classification. IEEE Trans. Image Process. **31**, 880–893 (2021)
36. Nguyen, T.T., Wong, T.Y.: Retinal vascular changes and diabetic retinopathy. Curr. Diab.Rep. **9**(4), 277–283 (2009)
37. Oord, A.V.D., Li, Y., Vinyals, O.: Representation learning with contrastive predictive coding. arXiv preprint arXiv:1807.03748 (2018)
38. Relan, D., MacGillivray, T., Ballerini, L., Trucco, E.: Automatic retinal vessel classification using a least square-support vector machine in vampire. In: 2014 36th Annual International Conference of the IEEE Engineering in Medicine and Biology Society, pp. 142–145. IEEE (2014)
39. Ronneberger, O., Fischer, P., Brox, T.: U-Net: convolutional networks for biomedical image segmentation. In: Navab, N., Hornegger, J., Wells, W.M., Frangi, A.F.

(eds.) MICCAI 2015. LNCS, vol. 9351, pp. 234–241. Springer, Cham (2015). https://doi.org/10.1007/978-3-319-24574-4_28

40. Russakovsky, O., et al.: ImageNet large scale visual recognition challenge. Int. J. Comput. Vision **115**(3), 211–252 (2015)

41. Tan, X., et al.: OCT2Former: a retinal oct-angiography vessel segmentation transformer. Comput. Methods Programs Biomed. **233**, 107454 (2023)

42. Vázquez, S., Barreira, N., Penedo, M.G., Ortega, M., Pose-Reino, A.: Improvements in retinal vessel clustering techniques: towards the automatic computation of the Arterio venous ratio. Computing **90**(3), 197–217 (2010)

43. Wang, W., Zhou, T., Yu, F., Dai, J., Konukoglu, E., Van Gool, L.: Exploring cross-image pixel contrast for semantic segmentation. In: Proceedings of the IEEE/CVF International Conference on Computer Vision, pp. 7303–7313 (2021)

44. Wu, Z., Xiong, Y., Yu, S.X., Lin, D.: Unsupervised feature learning via non-parametric instance discrimination. In: Proceedings of the IEEE Conference on Computer Vision and Pattern Recognition, pp. 3733–3742 (2018)

45. Xie, J., et al.: Classification of retinal vessels into Artery-Vein in OCT angiography guided by fundus images. In: Martel, A.L., et al. (eds.) MICCAI 2020. LNCS, vol. 12266, pp. 117–127. Springer, Cham (2020). https://doi.org/10.1007/978-3-030-59725-2_12

46. Xu, X., et al.: Differentiating veins from arteries on optical coherence tomography angiography by identifying deep capillary plexus vortices. Am. J. Ophthalmol. **207**, 363–372 (2019)

47. Xu, X., et al.: AV-casNet: fully automatic arteriole-venule segmentation and differentiation in OCT angiography. IEEE Trans. Med. Imaging **42**(2), 481–492 (2022)

48. Yan, G., Zhengyan, Z., Zhihua, C., Chuang, Z., Jin, Z.: CGAN: lightweight and feature aggregation network for high-performance interactive image segmentation. Vis. Comput. 1–15 (2023)

49. Yatsuya, H., Folsom, A.R., Wong, T.Y., Klein, R., Klein, B.E., Sharrett, A.R.: Retinal microvascular abnormalities and risk of lacunar stroke: atherosclerosis risk in communities study. Stroke **41**(7), 1349–1355 (2010)

50. Yin, B., et al.: Vessel extraction from non-fluorescein fundus images using orientation-aware detector. Med. Image Anal. **26**(1), 232–242 (2015)

51. Zhang, S., Yin, B., Zhang, W., Cheng, Y.: Topology aware deep learning for wireless network optimization. IEEE Trans. Wireless Commun. **21**(11), 9791–9805 (2022)

MRI-GAN: Generative Adversarial Network for Brain Segmentation

Afifa Khaled[1][(✉)] and Taher A. Ghaleb[2]

[1] School of Computer Science and Technology, Huazhong University of Science and Technology, Wuhan, China
afifakhaied@tju.edu.cn
[2] School of Electrical Engineering and Computer Science, University of Ottawa, Ottawa, Canada
tghaleb@uottawa.ca

Abstract. Segmentation is an important step in medical imaging. In particular, machine learning, especially deep learning, has been widely used to efficiently improve and speed up the segmentation process in clinical practices of MRI brain images. Despite the acceptable segmentation results of multi-stage models, little attention was paid to the use of deep learning algorithms for brain image segmentation, which could be due to the lack of training data. Therefore, in this paper, we propose $MRI-GAN$, a Generative Adversarial Network (GAN) model that performs segmentation MRI brain images. Our model enables the generation of more labeled brain images from existing labeled and unlabeled images. Our segmentation targets brain tissue images, including white matter (WM), gray matter (GM), and cerebrospinal fluid (CSF). We evaluate the performance of the $MRI-GAN$ model using a commonly used evaluation metric, which is the Dice Coefficient (DC). Our experimental results reveal that our proposed model significantly improves segmentation results compared to the standard GAN model while taking shorter training time.

1 Introduction

The significant growth of medical imaging applications in the last decade has witnessed a matching increase in image segmentation and classification. Such growth has encouraged researchers in clinical fields to develop models that make segmentation work similar to the human process in clinical practices [1,2,28, 30]. To this end, machine learning-based brain segmentation, in which brain images are divided into multiple tissues, has emerged as it makes brain image segmentation more accurate [3,4].

Many brain image segmentation models have been proposed in the literature. A common technique is to use two-stage models, which involves fusing global information with local information generated in two subsequent stages, to achieve acceptable segmentation results. The design of multi-stage models, in general, allows achieving better results, since it helps solve the information loss problem [5–8].

There have been many studies [10–12,15,26,27] proposing techniques to improve the accuracy of brain image segmentation to reach results that are close enough to manual reference. Recently, the use of deep learning algorithms for brain image segmentation started to emerge. However, there is still a lack of available data to train deep learning models. To address such an issue, adversarial learning and few-shot learning techniques have been developed to perform well in cases where only a few labeled images are available [9,13]. For example, Mondal et al. [9] proposed a few-shot 3D multi-modal image segmentation using a GAN model, which consists of U-net, a generator, and an encoder [9]. Fake images were first generated using the generator, then used along with labeled and unlabeled data to train the discriminator, which in turn distinguishes between generated and true data. The encoder was used to compute the predicted noise mean and log-variance. Despite the merits of such a model, its achieved results were not significantly higher than previous state-of-the-art models.

While previous techniques enabled neural networks to produce acceptable segmentation output, there were very few models that address the segmentation of infant brain images into White Matter (WM), Grey Matter (GM), and Cerebrospinal Fluid (CSF). As an example, Dolz et al. [14] proposed a model to segment infant brain images, which was evaluated using the iSEG Grand MIC-CAI challenge dataset. The model utilized the direct connections between layers from the same and different paths, which were used to improve the learning process. However, that model did not take into consideration deeper networks with fewer filters per layer. Moreover, individual weights from dense connections were not investigated.

Therefore, in this paper, we propose $MRI-GAN$, a novel Generative Adversarial Network (GAN) model that performs segmentation of MRI brain images, particularly WM, GM, and CSF. Our model enables the generation of more labeled data from existing labeled and unlabeled data. To do this, we employ an MRI encoder with a ground truth encoder to compress the features and convert them into low-dimensional MRI and tissues vectors. Each encoder is capable of compressing one or more inputs. In summary, this paper makes the following contributions:

- Novel MRI-GAN Model: Introduces a new GAN model for segmenting brain MRI images into WM, GM, and CSF tissues.
- Data Augmentation: Enables data modeling from labeled and unlabeled data, addressing limited annotated datasets.
- Integrated Encoders: Uses MRI and ground truth encoders for efficient feature compression and vector conversion.
- Improved Accuracy: Outperforms existing methods in accurate tissue segmentation.

The remainder of this paper is organized as follows. Section 2 reviews related work. Section 3 presents the $MRI-GAN$ model. Section 4 presents our setup materials and methods. Section 5 presents and discusses our experimental results. Finally, Sect. 6 concludes the paper and suggests possible future work.

2   Related Work

This section reviews the work related to our study.

2.1   Generative Adversarial Network for Brain Segmentation

GANs have shown promising results in both medical image diagnostics [20] and brain image segmentation [19,23]. The standard GAN has two parts: The generator is to generate the data and the discriminator is to distinguish between the generated data and real data. Much research on brain image segmentation has been conducted using GANs. For example, Cirillo et al. [21] proposed a 3D volume-to-volume (GAN) to segment the images of brain tumors. Their model achieved 94% result when the generator loss was weighted five times higher than the discriminator loss. The proposed model was evaluated on the $BraTS\ 2013$ dataset. Their model outperformed previous models with an overall accuracy of 66%. Delannoy et al. [22] proposed a super-resolution and segmentation framework using GANs to neonatal brain MRI images. The framework composed of (a) a training of a generating network that estimates the corresponding high resolution (HR) image for a given input image and (b) a discriminator network D to distinguish real HR and segmentation images. Their model outperformed previous models with an overall accuracy of 83%.

2.2   Encoder/Decoder

The encoder/decoder model emerged more than a decade ago as a concept to describe an image [5]. A well-known study of encoder/decoder was the auto encoder/decoder [17], which has investigated the encoder and decoder model based on pixel-wise classification. In addition, this model enabled the use of nonlinear upsampling and a smaller number of parameters for training, which requires higher computational power than any other deep learning architectures. However, many studies that performed encoding/decoding considered mapping a dense block into a standard encoder/decoder model. We expect that applying encoder/decoder models in a GAN model will provide more accurate segmentation results for brain images. To achieve this, we first develop a new encoder-decoder model that compresses the feature of the inputs and also maps the tissues' information to the decoder. Results show that our $MRI - GAN$ model exhibits results that are fairly close to the manual reference, and a significant reduction in training time compared to the state-of-the-art models. Furthermore, the Dice coefficient is applied to better demonstrate the significance of the $MRI - GAN$ model.

3   Proposed Model

This section describes the structure of our proposed GAN model.

3.1   Encoder/Decoder

Our $MRI-GAN$ model consists of generator and discriminator. Fig. 1 shows our proposed GAN model. All the MRI encoder, ground truth encoder, tissues mapping, boundary detection network, and decoder together represent the generator of the $MRI-GAN$ model. MRI encoder and ground truth encoder take MRI image and ground truth then convert them to MRI and ground truth vectors. The detection network provides more information about the boundary. The output of the decoder is a GT image where GT denotes the image generated from the generator.

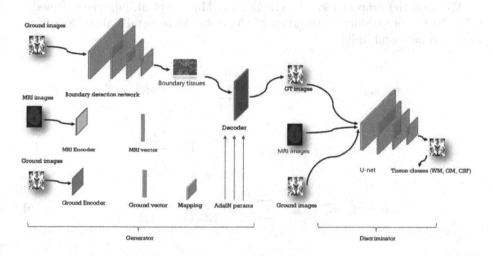

Fig. 1. Illustration of our proposed GAN model

3.2   Mapping

The decoder upscales the MRI code into a 3D geometry using SpiralBlocks that are conditioned by the ground code using Adaptive Instance normalization ($AdaIN$) [29]. Given a sample x that is passing through the network, $AdaIN$ first normalizes the activations in each channel of x to a zero μ and unit σ. The activations are then scaled on a per-channel basis. We use a mapping function R that maps a ground code y into (μ, σ) parameters for every channel of each $AdaIN$ layer. Hence the following equation:

$$AdaIN(x,y) = R_\sigma(y)\frac{x-\mu(x)}{\sigma(x)} + R_\mu(y) \tag{1}$$

where R is a learned affine function composed of multiple fully connected layers, taking the ground latent code as input. Since the AdaIN transformation operates on whole channels, the ground code alters global appearance information while the local features are determined by the MRI code.

3.3   Loss Function

Discriminator Loss Function. The discriminator in the $MRI - GAN$ model has labeled data loss, unlabeled data loss, and GT images loss (fake loss). We formulate the overall loss function of $MRI - GAN$ as follows:

$$l_{discriminator} = \lambda_{labeled} l_{labeled} + \lambda_{unlabeled} l_{unlabeled} + \lambda_{fake} l_{fake}, \tag{2}$$

where $\lambda_{labeled}$, $\lambda_{unlabeled}$, and λ_{fake} are hyper-parameters. We set the hyper-parameters in Equation (2) to $\lambda_{labeled} = 1.0$, $\lambda_{unlabeled} = 1.0$, and $\lambda_{fake} = 2.0$.

We used the proposed loss functions from Mondal et al. [9], where $Pmodel$ refers to the probability distribution of the data. More details about loss functions can be found in [9].

$$l_{labeled} = -E_{x,y \sim pdata(x,y)} \sum_{i=1}^{H \times W \times D} \log Pmodel(y_i | x) \tag{3}$$

$$l_{unlabeled} = -E_{x \sim pdata(x)} \sum_{i=1}^{H \times W \times D} \log \frac{Z_i(x)}{Z_i(x) + 1} \tag{4}$$

$$l_{fake} = -E_{z \sim noise} \sum_{i=1}^{H \times W \times D} \log \frac{1}{(Z_i(G_{\Theta G})(z)) + 1} \tag{5}$$

$$Z_i(x) = \sum_{k=1}^{K} exp[l_{i,k}(x)] \tag{6}$$

Generator Loss Function. We propose a novel generated loss to induce G to generate real data. Let x and z denote real data and noise, respectively.

$$C = E_{x \sim pdata(x)} f(x) - log(1 - D(G(z))), \tag{7}$$

In our paper, we consider $f(x)$ to contain the activation of the last layer.

$$L(G) = \| C - x \|_2^2, \tag{8}$$

By minimizing this loss, we force the generator to generate real data in order to match our data and the corresponding K classes of real data, which are defined as $classes = 1, ..., K$.

4 Setup Materials and Methods

This section describes the setup materials and methods used in our paper.

4.1 Datasets

MICCAI iSEG Dataset. The $MICCAIiSEG$ organizers[1] introduced a publicly available evaluation framework to allow comparing different segmentation models of WM, GM, and CSF on T1-weighted ($T1$) and T2-weighted ($T2$). The MICCAI iSEG dataset contains: 10 images (i.e., subject-1 up to subject-10), subject $T1$: $T1$-weighted image, subject $T2$: $T2$-weighted, and a manual segmentation label. All these images are used as a training set. The dataset also contains 13 images (i.e., subject-11 up to subject-23), which are used as a testing set. An example of the MICCAI iSEG dataset ($T1$, $T2$, and manual reference contour) is shown in Fig. 2.

Table 1 shows the parameters used to generate $T1$ and $T2$. The dataset has two different times: the longitudinal relaxation time and the transverse relaxation time, which are used to generate $T1$ and $T2$. The dataset has been interpolated, registered, and the images are skull-removed by the MICCAI iSEG organizers.

Table 1. Parameters used to generate $T1$ and $T2$

Parameter	TR/TE	Flip angle	Resolution
$T1$	1,900/4.38 ms	7	1×1×1
$T2$	7,380/119 ms	150	1.25×1.25×1.25

MRBrains Dataset. The $MRBrains$ dataset contains 20 adult images for the segmentation of (a) cortical gray matter, (b) basal ganglia, (c) white matter, (d) white matter lesions, (e) peripheral cerebrospinal fluid, (f) lateral ventricles, (g) cerebellum, and (h) brain stem on $T1$, $T2$, and FLAIR. Five images (i.e., 2

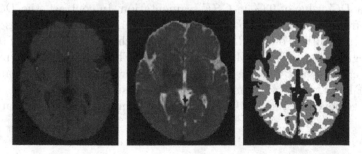

Fig. 2. An example of the MICCAI iSEG dataset ($T1$, $T2$, and manual reference contour)

---

[1] http://iseg2017.web.unc.edu.

male and 3 female) are provided as a training set and 15 images are provided as a testing set. For segmentation evaluation, these structures merged into gray matter $(a-b)$, white matter $(c-d)$, and cerebrospinal fluid $(e-f)$. The cerebellum and brainstem were excluded from the evaluation.

4.2 Experimental Setup

The experiments of the proposed model were conducted using *Python* on a *PC* with *NVIDIAGPU* running *Ubuntu 16.04*. Training *MRI−GAN* took 30 hours in total, whereas testing took 5 minutes.

4.3 Segmentation Evaluation

Dice Coefficient (*DC*). To better highlight the significance of our proposed *MRI − GAN* model, we use the Dice Coefficient (*DC*) metric to evaluate the performance of the *MRI − GAN* model. Dice Coefficient (*DC*) has been used to compare state-of-the-art segmentation models. We use V_{ref} for reference segmentation and V_{auto} for automated segmentation. The *DC* is given by the following equation:

$$DC(V_{ref}, V_{auto}) = \frac{2V_{ref} \bigcap V_{auto}|}{|V_{ref}| + |V_{auto}|}[18],$$ (9)

where *DC* values range between [0, 1], where 1 indicates a perfect overlap and 0 indicates a complete mismatch.

5   Result and Discussion

We train and test the *MRI−GAN* model on two datasets of different ages: adults and infants. Table 2 presents the results of the *MRI − GAN* model to segment *CSF*, *GM*, and *WM* using the MICCAI iSEG dataset. Our *MRI−GAN* model achieves a *DC* value of 93% in *CSF* segmentation. In contrast, the *DC* values achieved from segmenting *CSF* by Standard *GAN* is 86%, which is 7% less accurate. In addition, our *MRI − GAN* model achieves *DC* values of 94% and 92% in segmenting *GM* and *WM*, respectively. The Standard *GAN* model, in contrast, achieves a *DC* value of 80% (14% lower) for *GM* segmentation and 81% (11% lower) for *WM* segmentation. These results highlight the remarkable efficiency achieved by the *MRI − GAN* model compared to the standard *GAN*.

Table 2. Dice Coefficient (*DC*) results of the segmentation achieved on the MICCAI-iSEG dataset. The best performance for each tissue class is highlighted in bold.

Model	Dice Coefficient (DC) Accuracy		
	CSF	GM	WM
Standard *GAN*	86%	80%	81%
3D, FCN + MIL+G+K [15]	94.1%	90.2%	89.7%
Multi-stage [24]	**95%**	94%	92%
Our MRI-GAN	93%	**94%**	**92%**

Table 3 presents the results achieved using the MRBrains dataset. We observe that our $MRI-GAN$ model achieves a DC value of 91% on CSF segmentation, 90% on GM segmentation, and 95% on WM segmentation. Such results are superior to the results achieved by the Standard GAN model.

Figure 3 shows a sample visualized result of our $MRI-GAN$ model on a subject used as part of the validation set. As the images show, we observe that the segmentation achieved by the $MRI-GAN$ model is fairly close to the manual reference (ground truth) contour provided by the MICCAI iSEG organizers.

Table 3. Dice Coefficient (*DC*) results of the segmentation achieved on the MRBrains dataset. The best performance for each tissue class is highlighted in bold.

Model	Dice Coefficient (DC) Accuracy		
	CSF	GM	WM
Standard GAN	87%	87%	85%
3D, FCN + MIL+G+K [15]	87.4%	90.6%	90.1%
Multi-stage [24]	**93%**	**93%**	88%
Our MRI-GAN	91%	90%	**95%**

Our evaluation results show that the proposed model not only outperforms two baselines (Standard GAN and 3D, FCN + MIL+G+K [15]) on the three tissues, but also attempts to outperform Multi-stage [24] on two tissues. The proposed $MRI-GAN$ model improved the results in GM and WM on the MICCAIiSEG dataset and WM on the MRBrains dataset compared with Multi-stage [24]. We acknowledge that our model may not perform well for all cases and still has limitations due to the small number of images available, which we aim to improve further in the future.

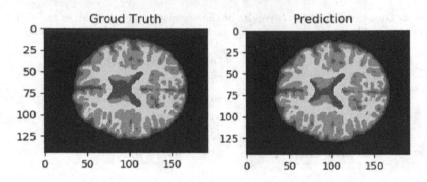

Fig. 3. A sample visualized result from the MICCAI iSEG dataset

6 Conclusion

In this paper, we proposed $MRI - GAN$, a novel Generative Adversarial Network (GAN) model that performs segmentation of MRI brain images. Our model makes segmentation more accurate by applying encoder and decoder algorithms separately, which demonstrated a significant increase in the accuracy of brain image segmentation results. We first extracted and compressed the features of the MRI encoder and ground truth encoder inputs, and then mapped the information to the decoder. Our experimental results show that the $MRI - GAN$ model is a viable solution for brain segmentation as it achieves a significant improvement in the accuracy of brain segmentation compared to the standard GAN model while taking a shorter training time.

Directions for Future Work. Based on our model, we have a number of possible directions for future work. We aim to investigate our model performance in segmenting more brain tissues and consider pathological brain images, such as with tumours or edema. Pathological brain images are not included in this study due to the lack of data.

7 Declarations

7.1 Competing Interests

The authors declare that they have no known competing financial interests.

7.2 Consent for Publication

Not applicable.

7.3   Availability of Data and Materials

The data that support the findings of this study are available from MICCAI grand challenge on 6-month infant brain MRI segmentation [1] and MRBrainS and are publicly available (see Footnote 1).

References

1. Liyan, S., Jiexiang, W., Yue, H., Xinghao, D., Hayit, G., John, P.: An adversarial learning approach to medical image synthesis for lesion detection. IEEE J. Biomed. Health Inform. **24**(8), 2303–2314 (2020)
2. Xin, Y., Ekta, W., Paul, B.: Generative adversarial network in medical imaging: a review. Med. Image Anal. **58**, 101552 (2019)
3. Hadeer, H., Mahmoud, B., Amira, H.: Toward deep MRI segmentation for Alzheimer's disease detection. Neural Comput. Appl. **34**(2), 1047–1063 (2021)
4. Salome, K., et al.: GANs for medical image analysis (2020)
5. Talha, I., Hazrat, A.: Generative adversarial network for medical images (MI-GAN). J. Med. Syst. **42**, 1–11 (2018)
6. Dinggang, S., Guorong, W., Heung-Il, S.: Deep learning in medical image analysis. Annu. Rev. Biomed. Eng. **19**, 221–248 (2017)
7. Muralikrishna, P., Ravi, S.: Medical image analysis based on deep learning approach. Multimedia Tools Appl. **80** 24365–24398 (2021)
8. Min, C., Xiaobo, S., Yin, Z., Di, W., Mohsen, G.: Deep feature learning for medical image analysis with convolutional autoencoder neural network. IEEE Trans. Big Data **7**(4), 750–758 (2021)
9. Mondal, A., Jose, D., Christian, D.: Few-shot 3D Multi-modal Medical Image Segmentation using Generative Adversarial Learning (2018). arXiv:1810.12241v1
10. Yanmei, L., et al.: Edge-preserving MRI image synthesis via adversarial network with iterative multi-scale fusion. Neurocomputing **452**, 63–77 (2021)
11. Yandi, G., Yang, P. Hongjun, L.: AIDS Brain MRIs synthesis via generative adversarial networks based on attention-encoder. In: 2020 IEEE 6th International Conference on Computer and Communications (2020)
12. Emami, H., Dong, M., Nejad-Davarani, S.P., Glide-Hurst, C.K.: SA-GAN: structure-aware GAN for organ-preserving synthetic CT generation. In: de Bruijne, M., et al. (eds.) MICCAI 2021. LNCS, vol. 12906, pp. 471–481. Springer, Cham (2021). https://doi.org/10.1007/978-3-030-87231-1_46
13. Rishav, S., Vandana, B., Vishal, P., Abhinav, K., Amit, Kumar K.: MetaMed: few-shot medical image Classification using gradient-based meta-learning. Pattern Recogn. **120**, 108111 (2021)
14. Dolz, J., Ismail, A., Jing, Y., Christian, D.: Isointense infant brain segmentation with a hyper-dense connected convolutional neural network. In: International Symposium on Biomedical Imaging (ISBI) (2018)
15. Afifa, K., chungming, O., Wenyuan, T, Taher, G.: Improved brain segmentation using pixel separation and additional segmentation features. In: The 4th APWeb-WAIM International Joint Conference on Web and Big Data (2020)
16. Vijay, B., Alex, K., Roberto, C.: SegNet: A Deep Convolutional Encoder-Decoder Architecture for Image Segmentation (2016). ArXiv:1511.00561v3
17. Arshia, R., Saeeda, N., Usman, N., Imran, R., Ibrahim, H.: Deep auto encoder-decoder framework for semantic segmentation of brain tumor. In: ICONIP (2019)

18. Wang, L., et al.: Benchmark on automatic six-month-old InfantBrain segmentation algorithms: TheiSeg-2017 challenge. IEEE Trans. Med. Imaging **38**(9), 2219–2230 (2019)
19. Cirillo, M.D., Abramian, D., Eklund, A.: Vox2Vox: 3D-GAN for brain tumour segmentation. In: Crimi, A., Bakas, S. (eds.) BrainLes 2020. LNCS, vol. 12658, pp. 274–284. Springer, Cham (2021). https://doi.org/10.1007/978-3-030-72084-1_25
20. Niyaz, U., Sambyal, S.: Advances in deep learning techniques for medical image analysis. In: 2018 Fifth International Conference on Parallel, Distributed and Grid Computing (PDGC), pp. 271–277 (2018)
21. Yi, S., Chengfeng, Z., Yanwei, F., Xiangyang, X.: Parasitic GAN for semi-supervised brain tumor segmentation. In: IEEE International Conference on Image Processing (ICIP) (2019)
22. Quentin, D., et al.: SegSRGAN: Super-resolution and segmentation using generative adversarial networks - Application to neonatal brain MRI (2020)
23. Yi, D., Fujuan, C., Yang, Z., Zhixing, W., Chao, Z., Dongyuan, W.: A stacked multi-connection simple reducing net for brain tumor segmentation. IEEE Access **7**, 104011–104024 (2019)
24. Afifa, K., Han, H., Taher, G.: Multi-model medical image segmentation using multi-stage generative adversarial networks. IEEE Access **10**, 28590–28599 (2022)
25. Jonas, W., Marcelo, L., Jos, N.: Transfer Learning for Brain Tumor Segmentation. arXiv preprint arXiv:1912.12452
26. Afifa, K., Ahmed, A.M., Kun, H.: Two Independent Teachers are Better Role Mode. arXiv preprint arXiv: 2306.05745
27. Afifa, K., Jian, J.H., Taher, A.G.: Learning to detect boundary information for brain image segmentation. BMC Bioinform. **23**(1), 332 (2022)
28. Afifa, K., Jian, J.H., Taher, A.G., Radman, M.: Fully convolutional neural network for improved brain segmentation. Arab. J. Sci. Eng. **48**(2), 2133–2146 (2023)
29. Xun H., Serge B.: Arbitrary style transfer in real-time with adaptive instance normalization. In: 2017 IEEE International Conference on Computer Vision (ICCV) (2017)
30. Hazrat, A., et al.: Correction: The role of generative adversarial networks in brain MRI: a scoping review. Insights Imaging **13**(1), 98 (2022)

Fast Prediction of Ternary Tree Partition for Efficient VVC Intra Coding

Jiamin Sun[1,2] (ID), Zhongjie Zhu[1,2(✉)] (ID), Yongqiang Bai[2] (ID), Yuer Wang[2] (ID), and Rong Zhang[2] (ID)

[1] Faculty of Information Science and Engineering,
Ocean University of China, Qingdao, China
zhongjiezhu@hotmail.com
[2] Ningbo Key Lab of DSP, Zhejiang Wanli University, Ningbo, China

Abstract. In versatile video coding (VVC) intra coding, the partition pattern depends on the rate-distortion optimization process, which is time-consuming and has a great impact on the overall coding efficiency. Hence, in this paper, a fast decision mechanism is proposed for ternary tree partition based on the LightGBM model aiming to improve the decision-making efficiency by skipping the calculation process of rate-distortion cost. Firstly, five features of each coding unit (CU) are selected based on their importance to the optimal partition pattern. Secondly, the selected five features are employed to train the LightGBM models and optimize the parameters. Finally, the trained models are embedded into the VTM 4.0 platform to predict whether to use or skip the ternary tree partition pattern for each CU. Theoretically, the proposed mechanism can effectively reduce the VVC intra coding complexity. Experiments are conducted and the results show that the proposed scheme can save 46.46% encoding time with only 0.56% BDBR increase and 0.03% BD-PSNR decrease compared with VTM4.0, out forming most of the existing major methods.

Keywords: VVC · Video coding · LightGBM · CU partition · Ternary tree

1 Introduction

With the explosive growth of visualization data, the high efficiency video coding (HEVC) gradually fails to meet the needs of the future video market, versatile video coding (VVC) has become the mainstream platform and supports multiple late-model video formats such as ultra-high definition video, high dynamic range video, virtual reality video, and 360-degree panoramic video [10, 21].

In HEVC, the coding tree unit (CTU) structure is one of the major contributions [4]. CTU can either contain a single coding unit (CU) or be recursively split into multiple smaller CUs, based on the quadtree (QT) structure. The sizes of the CUs vary from 64×64 to 8×8 [19].

B. Sheng et al. (Eds.): CGI 2023, LNCS 14495, pp. 257–269, 2024.
https://doi.org/10.1007/978-3-031-50069-5_22

Compared with HEVC, the structure of CU in VVC is further improved. The sizes of the CUs vary from 128×128 to 4×4. Based on the QT structure, multi-type tree (MTT) structure (including binary tree (BT) and ternary tree (TT)) is further developed in VVC, i.e. quadtree plus multi-type tree (QTMT) structure, in which the rectangular blocks can be used in the partitioning process [17]. Specifically, larger and square blocks are employed in smooth areas, and smaller and rectangular blocks are in complex textured areas. It makes CU partition more flexible and efficient, and effectively improves the coding efficiency. The partition patterns in VVC are No Split, binary tree horizontal (BT_H), binary tree vertical (BT_V), QT, ternary tree horizontal (TT_H), and ternary tree vertical (TT_V).

In the process of intra coding, the partition pattern depends on the rate-distortion optimization (RDO) process. The rate-distortion (RD) cost of each partition pattern needs to be calculated. The one with the lowest RD cost is selected as the optimal partition pattern. So this process consumes much encoding time. The time complexity of RDO is related to the number of blocks generated after the CU partition and the depth of the current CU. The more the number of blocks and the deeper the depth, the higher the time complexity.

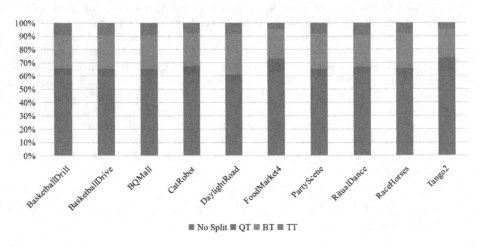

Fig. 1. The proportion of partition patterns in the coding process of each video.

In this paper, the optimal partition patterns of 10 videos after coding are counted, covering different types of video sequences in the common test conditions (CTC). It can be seen from Fig. 1 that the proportion of partition patterns from large to small is No Split, BT, TT, and QT. QT structure will produce the largest number of sub-blocks, while QT is mainly used for CU with sizes of 128×128 and 64×64, i.e. shallow partition, and the QT partition can no longer be carried out after MTT partition. TT partition not only produces more sub-blocks but also can be partitioned after any partition pattern, resulting in high time complexity for calculating the RD cost. However, in the optimal partition patterns of videos, the proportion of TT is low, which means that TT not only requires a large time complexity but also the probability of CU being partitioned by TT is low. Therefore, a fast decision mechanism is proposed based on the LightGBM model for TT partition. In the LightGBM model, the histogram algorithm and the limitation of num_leaves can effectively prevent over-fitting compared to other decision trees. The main contributions of this work can be summarized as follows:

1. We extract some features of CU from video sequences in CTC and select features by calculating the correlation between features and the importance of features.
2. We select the appropriate dataset according to the features, and two Light-GBM models are trained and optimized with the dataset to predict the TT_H and TT_V partition patterns, respectively.
3. The trained models are embedded into the VTM4.0. A threshold is set for comparison with the predicted result and decide whether the TT_H or TT_V partition pattern should be skipped in the current CU partitioning process.

2   Related Work

Compared with HEVC, nearly a 50% bit rate can be saved when encoding the same quality video in VVC. However, the coding complexity is increased by more than 10 times. MTT structure greatly increases the coding complexity of VVC in theory. According to statistics, the CU partition occupies 97% of the encoding time in the coding process [8]. To speed up the partition in VVC, a series of methods are proposed to predict CU partition patterns, inspired by improved HEVC encoder methods [11,12]. The following methods are applied to 2D video, and there is a lack of coding methods for 3D video [1].

Tang et al. [15] proposed a method that makes full use of the pooling layers in the convolutional neural network (CNN) for different CU shapes. He et al. [5] proposed a random forest-based algorithm to classify CUs into three categories (simple, fuzzy, and complex). Chen et al. [2] select the QT partition based on the gradient extracted by the Sobel operator. Yang et al. [20] proposed a fast decision framework to determine QTMT partitioning. The above methods [2,5, 20] are easy to over-fitting and [2] is for CUs of size 32×32. Both Cui et al. [3] and Liu et al. [9] proposed the method based on the directional gradient to guide the skipping of unnecessary partition patterns. But these two methods are required precomputing the gradient, which may increase the complexity. Tissier et al. [16] analyze the texture of CUs to skip impossible partition patterns, but their database consists mainly of 4K images. Wu et al. [18] proposed a fully convolutional network, which obtains the entire partition information of the current CU and sub-CUs at once, and directly predicts the specific hierarchical partition structure, but it predicts only the 32×32 CU blocks and their sub-blocks at present. Li et al. [8] established a database and proposed a multi-stage exit CNN to determine CU partition, but there are some factors to be considered, such as whether the partition pattern can be accurately predicted, the efficiency of CNN, etc. Saldanha et al. [14] proposed a fast block partition decision using a light gradient boosting machine (LightGBM), and five classifiers were trained to predict each of the five partition patterns by texture, coding, and context information, and the Bjontegaard delta bit rate (BDBR) increased by 2.43%. Park et al. [13] developed two types of features, explicit features, and derived features, and proposed a lightweight neural network (LNN) to decide whether to terminate the TT partition. The structure of the LNN model is simple, which reduces the complexity of the network but leads to a reduction in the prediction accuracy, with an accuracy of 75%.

3   Motivation and Decision Mechanism

As shown in Fig. 2, the decision mechanism is roughly divided into three modules, which are feature extraction, model training, and model embedding and intra coding.

3.1   Feature Extraction

The optimal partition pattern is related to features of the CU. Therefore, the partition pattern for each CU can be predicted by features. In Fig. 2, some features are extracted from the first frame of 21 video sequences in CTC, including directly extracted features, and further calculated features, as shown in Table 1.

In general, the larger number of features, the more accurate the predicted pattern, but the longer the encoding time. So, the effect and complexity of the features should be optimized. Here Fig. 3 shows the importance of the above features for the prediction results calculated with the feature selector [7]. The extracted features of CU are input into the feature selector, which can find features with missing values or unique values, and these two features will be discarded. The feature selector can also calculate the correlation between features based on the Pearson correlation coefficient, and discard features with high correlation (such as CuWidth, CuHeight, and BSR). The feature selector uses the extracted features to train the LightGBM model. According to the total number of splits and the total information gain, the importance of the features is calculated and sorted. The sorting results are shown in Fig. 3.

As shown in Fig. 3, the feature with the highest importance is the CurrCost, because the optimal partition pattern of CU relies on the process of RDO. The partition pattern with the smallest RD cost is selected as the optimal partition pattern. In VVC intra coding, RDO is the result of a combination of the bit rate and the peak signal to noise ratio. The ultimate goal of video coding is to achieve the maximum signal to noise ratio with the minimum possible bit rate. This problem can be described as the formula (1):

$$\min \sum D_{i,j} \quad s.t. \sum R_{i,j} < R_c \qquad (1)$$

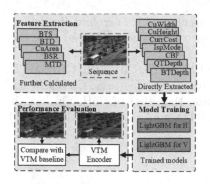

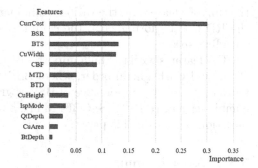

Fig. 2. Early feature extraction and decision mechanism.

Fig. 3. Feature importance for prediction results.

Table 1. Features to be selected and their description.

Category	Feature	Description
Directly extracted features	CuWidth	The width of the current CU
	CuHeight	The height of the current CU
	CurrCost	The RD cost of the current partition pattern
	IspMode	Intra sub-partition mode: if using ISP mode, taken as 1, otherwise taken as 0
	CBF	The coding block flag: when the residual coefficient after CU coding is very small, i.e. the residual can be considered to be 0, then CBF = 0, if there is a significant residual coefficient then CBF = 1
	QtDepth	The depth of the current QT partition
	BtDepth	The depth of the current BT partition.
Further calculated features	CuArea	The area of the current CU: CuArea = CuWidth × CuHeight
	BTS	BT's superiority: taken as 0.5 when there are BTs with lower RD cost than other BTs, and 1 otherwise
	BSR	Block shape ratio: $BSR = l_h/(l_h + l_w)$ if divided by TT_H or $BSR = l_w/(l_h + l_w)$ if divided by TT_V, l_h indicates the CuHeight and l_w indicates the CuWidth
	BTD	BT's direction: when the optimal BT's direction of two BTs on RD cost is the same as the TT's direction to be tested, take 1; otherwise, take 0
	MTD	MTT's depth: one-half of the depth of the BT or TT

R_c is the limited bit rate of CTU, $D_{i,j}$ and $R_{i,j}$ represent the distortion and bit rate caused by the ith CU using the jth group of coding parameters in a CU partition pattern combination, respectively. The constrained problem is transformed into an unconstrained problem using the Lagrange optimization method, namely the formula (2):

$$\min J, J = \sum D_{i,j} + \lambda \sum R_{i,j} \qquad (2)$$

The calculation methods of D include sum of squared error, mean squared error, sum of absolute difference, and so on. Most of these methods need to calculate the sum of squares and the various combinations of i and j. Therefore, if calculate the RD cost by formula (2), the complexity of computation will lead to slower encoding speed.

The features with the high importance are BSR, BTS, CuWidth, CBF, MTD, BTD, and CuHeight in order, where BSR contains two features, CuWidth and CuHeight, and the importance of BSR is greater than that of CuHeight. So, the combination of BSR, BTS, CBF, MTD, and BTD is adopted to predict the TT partition pattern in this paper.

3.2   Model Training

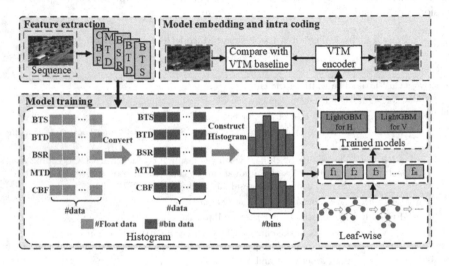

Fig. 4. Proposed fast decision mechanism.

The VTM uses a violent search approach to examine all possible CU partition patterns in a bottom-up manner. In this paper, CU partition is predicted by LightGBM, which combines N weak classifiers $(f_1, f_2, f_3, ..., f_N)$ to obtain a strong classifier F, i.e. $F = \sum_{i=1}^{N} f_i$. The TT partition is predicted by the classifier based on the current CU features. According to the prediction results, the decide whether to skip the partition. If the partition is skipped, the RD cost of this partition pattern is avoided in the RDO process, which accelerates the encoding process.

As shown in Fig. 4, a histogram algorithm is used by LightGBM to first discretize the continuous values into K integers and construct a histogram with a width of K. The histogram method not only improves the computational efficiency, but also increases a regularization process. Decision tree is a weak learner, and regularization can effectively prevent the model from over-fitting [6].

LightGBM further optimizes the histogram algorithm through max_depth, and limits the depth of the tree by leaf-wise (Fig. 4, where the red node indicates leaf nodes that will divide next time round, and the green node indicates nodes that will not divide) growth strategy. To maximize the accuracy of the LightGBM model, hyperparameter optimization is required. Firstly, a higher learning rate is chosen to speed up the convergence, the basic parameters are tuned (e.g. n_estimators), then the regularisation parameters are tuned (e.g. num_leaves), and finally the learning rate is reduced to improve the accuracy of the model.

3.3   Model Embedding and Intra Coding

In the VTM 4.0 platform, the decision-making process of the TT partition pattern depends on the RDO process. The partition pattern is selected with the smallest RD cost among all the partition patterns. Figure 5 shows the flowchart of decision mechanism. The modified process includes feature extraction, model prediction, and simplified RDO process.

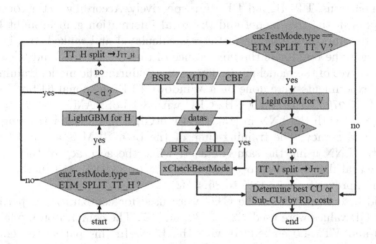

Fig. 5. Flowchart of TT partition by the VTM platform embedded with LightGBM model.

In Fig. 5, α is the threshold value to determine whether the current CU should be partitioned with the TT_H or TT_V. Since the predicted value of the model is a floating point number in [0, 1], the intermediate value 0.5 is taken as the value of α.

The five features (BTS, BTD, BSR, MTD, and CBF) of the current CU are first extracted. In the RDO process, the RD cost is calculated in the order of TT_H, and TT_V. If it is the TT_H partition pattern (ETM_SPLIT_TT_H) then the extracted features are input into the LightGBM model corresponding to the TT_H for prediction, and the predicted value y is obtained and compared with the threshold α. If $y < \alpha(\alpha = 0.5)$, it is considered that the current CU will not select the TT_H partition pattern and enter the judgment process of the TT_V. If $y >= \alpha(\alpha = 0.5)$, it is believed that the current CU may select the TT_H partition pattern, calculate the RD cost (J_{TT_H}) when the current partition pattern is TT_H, and then enter the judgment process of the TT_V. If it is the TT_V partition pattern (ETM_SPLIT_TT_V) then the extracted features are input into the LightGBM model corresponding to the TT_V for prediction, and the predicted value y is obtained and compared with the threshold α. If $y < \alpha(\alpha = 0.5)$, it is considered that the current CU will not select the TT_V partition pattern, and then return to determine the optimal partition pattern based on the RD cost of the remaining partition patterns. If $y >= \alpha(\alpha = 0.5)$ then calculate the RD cost (J_{TT_V}) when the current partition pattern is TT_V and compare it with the RD cost of the other partition patterns to determine the optimal partition pattern.

4   Experimental Results and Analysis

Two LightGBM models are trained with the datasets in [13] to predict the two partition patterns, TT_H, and TT_V, respectively. According to the total number of splits in the tree model and the total information gain brought by the features, the importance of the features is calculated and ranked. In Fig. 6, (a) and (b) show the ranking of the importance of the five features, and (c) and (d) show the curves of the model prediction accuracy during the model training process. All experiments were done on a Windows 10 Professional 64-bit, Intel(R) Core(TM) i7-9700 CPU @ 3.00GHz CPU with 8GB of RAM.

Compared with the LNN in [13], the LightGBM has a faster training speed and higher accuracy. The training time of the LightGBM is about 10.58% of that of the LNN using the same dataset, while the accuracy of the model in the horizontal direction improves from 75.17% to 83.94%, and in the vertical direction improves from 77.18% to 85.41%.

21 video sequences from the CTC were used for comparative experiments, and four QP values were used: 22, 27, 32, and 37. The comparison models were VTM4.0 and VTM4.0 embedded with the LNN. In this paper, the encoding quality and encoding efficiency are evaluated using BD peak signal-to-noise ratio (BD-PSNR), BDBR, and time-saving (TS) as recommended in CTC. The BDBR weighted average of YUV $(BDBR_{YUV})$ is represented by Eq. (3):

$$BD\dot{B}R_{YUV} = \frac{6BDBR_Y + BDBR_U + BDBR_V}{8} \tag{3}$$

$BDBR_Y$, $BDBR_U$ and $BDBR_V$ denote BDBRs for Y, U, and V respectively.

TS_{VTM} and TS_{LNN} denote the percentage of encoding time saved by the decision mechanism compared to the VTM4.0 and LNN, when encoding the same video. TS_{VTM} and TS_{LNN} are calculated by equations Eqs. (4) and (5):

$$TS_{VTM} = \frac{1}{4} \sum_{QP_i \in \{22,27,32,37\}} \frac{T_{VTM}(QP_i) - T_{LightGBM}(QP_i)}{T_{VTM}(QP_i)} \times 100\% \tag{4}$$

$$TS_{LNN} = \frac{1}{4} \sum_{QP_i \in \{22,27,32,37\}} \frac{T_{LNN}(QP_i) - T_{LightGBM}(QP_i)}{T_{LNN}(QP_i)} \times 100\% \tag{5}$$

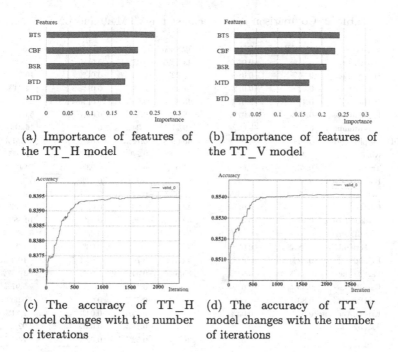

(a) Importance of features of the TT_H model

(b) Importance of features of the TT_V model

(c) The accuracy of TT_H model changes with the number of iterations

(d) The accuracy of TT_V model changes with the number of iterations

Fig. 6. Features importance and training accuracy curves of the LightGBM model.

T_{VTM}, T_{LNN} and $T_{LightGBM}$ denote the time taken to encode the video by VTM4.0, LNN and LightGBM respectively. QP_i represents the different QP values used for encoding.

Table 2 shows the experimental results. BD-$PSNR_{VTM}$, BD-$PSNR_{LNN}$, $BDBR_{VTM}$, and $BDBR_{LNN}$ indicate the percentage change in $BDBR_{YUV}$ and BD-$PSNR_Y$ of the LightGBM compared to VTM4.0 and LNN respectively, when encoding the same video. TS_{VTM} and TS_{LNN} indicate the percentage of encoding time saved by the LightGBM compared to VTM4.0 and LNN, when encoding the same video. The Average represents the average of BDBR, $BD - PSNR$, or TS per column.

According to TS_{VTM} and TS_{LNN}, the encoding time of the decision mechanism is reduced by 46.6% and 1.74% on average compared with that of the VTM4.0 and LNN. According to $BDBR_{VTM}$, BD-$PSNR_{VTM}$, $BDBR_{LNN}$, and BD-$PSNR_{LNN}$ in Table 2, the BDBR of the decision mechanism increased by only 0.56% and the BD-PSNR decreased by only 0.03% compared to that of the VTM4.0 and decreased by 0.52% and increased by 0.02% compared to that of the LNN. The changes of BDBR and BD-PSNR caused by the decision

Table 2. Comparison results against the VTM4.0 and LNN.

Class	Sequence	$BDBR_{VTM}$	BD-$PSNR_{VTM}$	TS_{VTM}	$BDBR_{LNN}$	BD-$PSNR_{LNN}$	TS_{LNN}
A1	Campfire	0.41%	−0.01%	43.48%	−0.37%	0.01%	2.36%
	FoodMarket4	0.36%	−0.01%	49.92%	−0.27%	0.01%	10.70%
	Tango2	0.32%	−0.01%	51.29%	−0.28%	0.01%	12.94%
A2	CatRobot	0.45%	−0.01%	45.83%	−0.58%	0.02%	2.58%
	DaylightRoad2	0.53%	−0.02%	48.36%	−0.51%	0.01%	5.04%
	ParkRunning3	0.28%	−0.02%	49.27%	−0.24%	0.02%	16.31%
ADD	PeopleOnStreet	0.74%	−0.05%	46.69%	−0.72%	0.04%	−1.51%
	Kimono	0.39%	−0.02%	58.79%	−0.27%	0.01%	17.50%
	Traffic	0.83%	−0.05%	44.61%	−0.63%	0.03%	0.91%
B	BasketballDrive	0.65%	−0.02%	48.12%	−0.55%	0.02%	5.35%
	BQTerrace	0.57%	−0.03%	38.55%	−0.57%	0.02%	−4.78%
	Cactus	0.59%	−0.02%	43.68%	−0.50%	0.02%	−3.42%
	MarketPlace	0.37%	−0.02%	52.96%	−0.26%	0.01%	10.68%
	RitualDance	0.60%	−0.01%	50.07%	−0.53%	0.03%	6.38%
C	BasketballDrill	0.88%	−0.05%	42.70%	−0.96%	0.03%	−7.35%
	BQMall	0.72%	−0.04%	42.33%	−0.70%	0.04%	−10.32%
	PartyScene	0.44%	−0.03%	35.88%	−0.34%	0.03%	−19.57%
D	RaceHorses	0.35%	−0.02%	42.78%	−0.41%	0.02%	−5.97%
E	FourPeople	0.83%	−0.05%	45.93%	−0.75%	0.05%	−0.90%
	KristenAndSara	0.64%	−0.03%	46.34%	−0.69%	0.04%	−2.31%
	Johnny	0.75%	−0.03%	48.17%	−0.75%	0.03%	2.02%
Average		0.56%	−0.03%	46.46%	−0.52%	0.02%	1.74%

mechanism are within a reasonable range, and the compression efficiency or the encoded video quality will not be significantly reduced. Compared with the LNN, the decision mechanism not only improves the speed of video coding but also improved the compression efficiency and video quality.

Some of the videos in Table 2 take more encoding time than the LNN (e.g., Class C videos), and these videos have non-homogeneous and complex texture characteristics. In videos with more complex texture features, CU is partitioned by TT more frequently. It means that fewer CUs are judged to skip TT partition pattern, and therefore the amount of computation that can be saved in terms of the RD cost is reduced, and the amount of coding time that can be saved by the decision mechanism is reduced accordingly.

Table 3 shows the complexity analysis for LightGBM and a comparison of prediction time with total encoding time, where PT represents the total time (in seconds) spend on TT prediction. The Ratio represents the percentage of PT to the total encoding time, the Average represents the average of the Ratio at the corresponding QP, and the Total Average denotes the total average of the Average for the four QPs. PT only accounted for 5.84% of the total encoding time on average, indicating that the complexity of the model is low.

Table 3. Complexity analysis of the proposed decision mechanism.

Class	Sequence	QP							
		22		27		32		37	
		PT(s)	Ratio	PT(s)	Ratio	PT(s)	Ratio	PT(s)	Ratio
A1	Campfire	1043.23	3.01%	798.14	4.20%	775.22	8.13%	318.40	8.24%
	FoodMarket4	937.90	5.26%	491.20	6.91%	367.17	7.17%	131.61	5.15%
	Tango2	1231.47	4.45%	642.66	10.28%	279.35	9.82%	52.23	3.41%
A2	CatRobot	1021.75	2.95%	818.42	5.16%	538.45	7.75%	302.14	7.99%
	DaylightRoad2	1285.20	2.89%	1451.28	6.79%	630.02	7.23%	316.83	7.33%
	ParkRunning3	1451.81	4.65%	910.87	4.47%	737.85	5.17%	482.50	4.95%
ADD	PeopleOnStreet	369.64	3.99%	313.60	5.24%	228.71	5.73%	212.42	7.91%
	Kimono	233.78	4.87%	194.71	8.77%	156.27	12.48%	60.72	9.10%
	Traffic	326.12	3.70%	318.14	5.42%	233.54	6.17%	173.70	7.83%
B	BasketballDrive	656.62	4.12%	461.50	5.44%	360.85	8.69%	203.64	8.68%
	BQTerrace	311.09	1.84%	466.76	3.11%	376.14	3.97%	333.75	6.10%
	Cactus	444.37	2.31%	577.83	4.85%	465.42	7.06%	334.04	9.07%
	MarketPlace	588.44	3.68%	548.42	6.64%	385.21	8.23%	253.03	9.69%
	RitualDance	459.65	4.40%	440.81	7.21%	328.77	8.64%	178.27	8.53%
C	BasketballDrill	89.87	2.65%	91.94	3.78%	99.10	6.36%	60.75	7.72%
	BQMall	110.42	2.76%	100.93	3.78%	110.37	5.88%	74.34	6.15%
	PartyScene	72.87	1.73%	82.64	2.22%	89.27	3.21%	87.42	4.32%
D	RaceHorses	17.66	2.85%	17.43	3.57%	17.58	4.71%	18.28	7.34%
E	FourPeople	309.06	4.80%	194.18	5.07%	153.44	5.85%	142.06	8.43%
	KristenAndSara	200.92	4.64%	190.14	6.70%	139.78	7.41%	77.81	6.41%
	Johnny	179.02	4.26%	149.48	5.53%	130.77	7.65%	79.33	8.07%
Average		–	3.61%	–	5.48%	–	7.01%	–	7.26%
Total Average		5.84%							

5 Conclusion

A fast prediction of TT is proposed, which can decrease the complexity of CU partition in VVC by skipping the calculation process of RD cost of TT. Firstly, five features are reselected and then are employed to train the LightGBM model. Secondly, the trained model is utilized to predict whether to skip the TT_H or TT_V based on the features. Experimental results show that the proposed mechanism is better than that of the VTM4.0 and the LNN.

The subsequent research direction is to extend the dataset, and mine more CU features for the prediction of CU partition. Meanwhile, explore the multi-threshold decision-making approach to achieve better results based on the existing ones.

Acknowledgements. This work was supported by Zhejiang Provincial Natural Science Foundation of China(LY21F010014), Natural Science Foundation of Ningbo, China(202003N4323), School-level Research and Innovation Team of Zhejiang Wanli University, and Science and Technology Innovation 2025 Major Project of Ningbo(2022Z076).

References

1. Cammarasana, S., Patanè, G.: Spatio-temporal analysis and comparison of 3D videos. Vis. Comput. **39**, 1335–1350 (2023). https://doi.org/10.1007/s00371-022-02409-1
2. Chen, J., Sun, H., Katto, J., Zeng, X., Fan, Y.: Fast QTMT partition decision algorithm in VVC intra coding based on variance and gradient. In: 2019 IEEE Visual Communications and Image Processing (VCIP), pp. 1–4 (2019)
3. Cui, J., Zhang, T., Gu, C., Zhang, X., Ma, S.: Gradient-based early termination of CU partition in VVC intra coding. In: 2020 Data Compression Conference (DCC), pp. 103–112 (2020)
4. Hannuksela, M.M., Yan, Y., Huang, X., Li, H.: Overview of the multiview high efficiency video coding (MV-HEVC) standard. In: 2015 IEEE International Conference on Image Processing (ICIP), pp. 2154–2158 (2015)
5. He, Q., Wu, W., Luo, L., Zhu, C., Guo, H.: Random forest based fast CU partition for VVC intra coding. In: 2021 IEEE International Symposium on Broadband Multimedia Systems and Broadcasting (BMSB), pp. 1–4 (2021)
6. Ke, G., et al.: LightGBM: a highly efficient gradient boosting decision tree. In: Advances in Neural Information Processing Systems. vol. 30. Curran Associates, Inc. (2017)
7. Koehrsen, W.: Feature selector. https://github.com/WillKoehrsen/feature-selector. Accessed May 2021
8. Li, T., Xu, M., Tang, R., Chen, Y., Xing, Q.: DeepQTMT: a deep learning approach for fast QTMT-based CU partition of intra-mode VVC. IEEE Trans. Image Process. **30**, 5377–5390 (2021)
9. Liu, H., Zhu, S., Xiong, R., Liu, G., Zeng, B.: Cross-block difference guided fast CU partition for VVC intra coding. In: 2021 International Conference on Visual Communications and Image Processing (VCIP), pp. 1–5 (2021)
10. Liu, J., Xia, Y., Tang, Z.: Privacy-preserving video fall detection using visual shielding information. Vis. Comput. **23**, 359–370 (2021). https://doi.org/10.1007/s00371-020-01804-w
11. Munagala, V., Kodati, S.P.: Enhanced holoentropy-based encoding via whale optimization for highly efficient video coding. Vis. Comput. **37**(8), 2173–2194 (2020). https://doi.org/10.1007/s00371-020-01978-3
12. Parihar, A.S., Varshney, D., Pandya, K., Aggarwal, A.: A comprehensive survey on video frame interpolation techniques. Vis. Comput. **38**, 295–319 (2022). https://doi.org/10.1007/s00371-020-02016-y
13. Park, S.H., Kang, J.W.: Fast multi-type tree partitioning for versatile video coding using a lightweight neural network. IEEE Trans. Multimedia **23**, 4388–4399 (2021)
14. Saldanha, M., Sanchez, G., Marcon, C., Agostini, L.: Configurable fast block partitioning for VVC intra coding using light gradient boosting machine. IEEE Trans. Circuits Syst. Video Technol. **32**(6), 3947–3960 (2022)
15. Tang, G., Jing, M., Zeng, X., Fan, Y.: Adaptive CU split decision with pooling-variable CNN for VVC intra encoding. In: 2019 IEEE Visual Communications and Image Processing (VCIP), pp. 1–4 (2019)
16. Tissier, A., Hamidouche, W., Vanne, J., Galpin, F., Menard, D.: CNN oriented complexity reduction of VVC intra encoder. In: 2020 IEEE International Conference on Image Processing (ICIP), pp. 3139–3143 (2020)
17. Viitanen, M., Sainio, J., Mercat, A., Lemmetti, A., Vanne, J.: From HEVC to VVC: the first development steps of a practical intra video encoder. IEEE Trans. Consum. Electron. **68**(2), 139–148 (2022)

18. Wu, S., Shi, J., Chen, Z.: HG-FCN: hierarchical grid fully convolutional network for fast VVC intra coding. IEEE Trans. Circuits Syst. Video Technol. **32**(8), 5638–5649 (2022)
19. Xu, M., Li, T., Wang, Z., Deng, X., Yang, R., Guan, Z.: Reducing complexity of HEVC: a deep learning approach. IEEE Trans. Image Process. **27**(10), 5044–5059 (2018)
20. Yang, H., Shen, L., Dong, X., Ding, Q., An, P., Jiang, G.: Low-complexity CTU partition structure decision and fast intra mode decision for versatile video coding. IEEE Trans. Circuits Syst. Video Technol. **30**(6), 1668–1682 (2020)
21. Zhao, X., et al.: Transform coding in the VVC standard. IEEE Trans. Circuits Syst. Video Technol. **31**(10), 3878–3890 (2021)

Large GAN Is All You Need

Kai Liu$^{(\boxtimes)}$ (iD), Qingyang Wu, and Mengkun Xie

Shanghai Jiao Tong University, Shanghai 200240, China
{kai_liu,alkalisoda}@sjtu.edu.cn

Abstract. Sketch-to-portrait conversion is an emerging research area
that aims to transform rough facial line sketches into highly detailed and
realistic portrait images. This paper presents a comprehensive study on
the impact of different loss functions and data augmentation techniques
in achieving superior results using the U-Net256 network architecture.
The study explores the effects of Mean Squared Error (MSE) loss, L1
loss, Generative Adversarial Network (GAN) loss, and the number of
parameters on the quality of the generated portrait images. Experimental results demonstrate that the choice of loss function significantly influences the perceptual quality and accuracy of the converted portraits.
While both MSE and L1 loss contribute to capturing the overall structure, GAN loss excels in generating fine-grained details. Moreover, a
trade-off is observed between the number of parameters and image quality, with higher parameter counts resulting in more intricate outputs but
increased computational complexity. In conclusion, this paper offers valuable insights into the sketch to portrait conversion task, shedding light on
the effects of different loss functions and data augmentation techniques.
The findings contribute to the advancement of sketch-to-portrait conversion systems, pushing the boundaries of realism and detail in generated
portrait images. We finally reached FID value of 0.2184, the fourth in
the CGI-PSG2023 leaderboard as of September 21st. The dataset can
be found on CGI-PSG2023 webpage. All code is open-source and can be
found in https://github.com/KKK-Liu/Portrait.git

Keywords: GAN · Portrait · Image translation

1 Introduction

Sketch to portrait conversion, the process of transforming rough facial line
sketches into highly detailed and realistic portrait images, has garnered significant interest in recent years. This task finds applications in various fields
such as digital art, character design, and entertainment industries [7]. With the
advancement of deep learning techniques, computer vision researchers have made
notable progress in achieving more accurate and visually appealing conversions.

The primary goal of sketch to portrait conversion is to bridge the gap between
the abstract representation of a sketch and the intricate details present in a
portrait image. Traditional methods relied on manual techniques and extensive

B. Sheng et al. (Eds.): CGI 2023, LNCS 14495, pp. 270–281, 2024.
https://doi.org/10.1007/978-3-031-50069-5_23

human intervention, which were time-consuming and subjective. However, with the emergence of deep learning and generative models, researchers have been able to automate and improve the conversion process.

In this paper, we aim to explore and analyze the impact of different loss functions and data augmentation techniques on the quality of sketch to portrait conversion. We focus on the widely adopted U-Net256 network architecture, which has shown remarkable performance in various image-to-image translation tasks. By leveraging this architecture, we investigate the effects of Mean Squared Error (MSE) loss, L1 loss, Generative Adversarial Network (GAN) loss [3], and the number of parameters on the generated portrait images' fidelity and level of detail (Fig. 1).

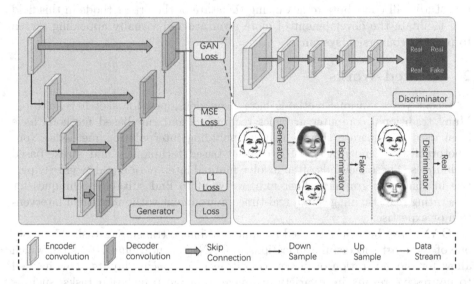

Fig. 1. The whole pipeline of the proposed model. The whole model has two models: the generator model and the discriminator model. The generator takes the line image as input and outputs the exquisite portrait sketching. The discriminator tries to identify the input image to real-world ground truth or the generated image with the line image as a reference. The generator follows the U-Net [17] structure while the generator follows the patch-discriminator structure.

The choice of loss function plays a crucial role in the optimization process, as it guides the network to minimize the discrepancy between the generated portraits and the ground truth images. MSE loss emphasizes pixel-level accuracy, while L1 loss promotes a more robust representation of the overall structure. GAN loss, on the other hand, introduces an adversarial component to encourage the generation of realistic and high-fidelity details [1,16].

Furthermore, we explore the relationship between the number of parameters in the network and the resulting image quality. By varying the network's complexity, we investigate the trade-off between computational efficiency and the ability to capture fine details in the generated portraits.

In addition to loss functions, we also investigate the importance of data augmentation techniques in improving the network's performance. Data augmentation, such as random rotations, random erasing, and scaling, can enhance the network's ability to handle variations in sketch quality and improve generalization. Moreover, the utilization of synthetic data generated from existing portrait images can further augment the training dataset and potentially boost the conversion quality.

By conducting comprehensive experiments and evaluations, we aim to provide insights into the strengths and limitations of different loss functions and data augmentation techniques for sketch to portrait conversion. The findings of this study will contribute to advancing the state-of-the-art methods in this field and facilitate the development of more accurate and visually appealing sketch to portrait conversion systems.

2 Related Works

In recent years, various methods have been developed for sketch generation. Many traditional computer graphics techniques and rule-based methods have been used to generate sketch images, including interpolation methods, Non-Photorealistic Rendering (NPR), contour-based techniques, and stroke-based techniques. These methods often involve manual intervention and require expertise in computer graphics. Therefore, we want to find suitable techniques for generating realistic images in a real-time environment without manual intervention or expertise.

GANs have been widely used for image-to-image translation tasks [7,14,24], one of the most successful applications of GANs is conditional GANs [8], which allow for the generation of images conditioned on specific inputs. This has led to impressive results in a variety of image-to-image translation tasks, such as style transfer [2], semantic image inpainting [22], and image super-resolution [20]. The adversarial loss is leveraged in our approach to guarantee the reality of the generated images.

Several works also focus on the sketch image transition. Naoki Nozawa [15] leveraged GAN and lazy learning to reconstruct 3D car shape by using a contour sketch image. Ping Li [11] used regularized broad learning system to synthesis sketch face image with the real image as input. Sifei Li [12] proposed PLDGAN to generate high quality portrait line drawing using the real human picture as input. Takato Yoshikawa [23] focus more on generating diverse, photorealistic image from a single portrait sketch and controlling the details and appearance.

One particular style of conditional GANs that has gained recent attention is pix2pixGAN [10]. This technique has the potential for multiple deep learning tasks, including image to image translation [13], semantic segmentation [19], and image compression [18].

This technique is able to generate realistic sketch images from simple lines, allowing designers and artists to quickly create visual concepts without the need for complex image editing software, and has the potential to revolutionize the way that designers and artists create visual concepts.

3 Methodology

3.1 Network

Generator. The generator is a crucial component in the sketch to portrait conversion system, responsible for transforming rough facial line sketches into detailed and realistic portrait images. In this paper, we adopt the U-Net256 network architecture as our generator, which has demonstrated exceptional performance in various image-to-image translation tasks.

The U-Net256 architecture is an extension of the original U-Net model, specifically designed to handle high-resolution images [17]. It consists of an encoder-decoder structure with skip connections [4] that allow for both local and global information fusion. The skip connections facilitate the direct flow of low-level features from the encoder to the decoder, enabling the generator to capture fine-grained details while preserving the overall structure of the input sketch.

Let $G(x)$ represent the generator network, which takes an input sketch x and generates a corresponding portrait image $G(x)$. The generator aims to minimize the discrepancy between the generated portrait and the ground truth portrait, effectively mapping the input sketch to a realistic and visually appealing image.

The generator architecture can be formulated as follows:

$$
\begin{aligned}
&Encoder: &&Decoder: \\
&E = ConvBlock(x) &&D = UpconvBlock(\text{Concat}(E, D_1)) \\
&E_1 = Downsample(E) &&D_1 = Upsample(\text{Concat}(E_1, D_2)) \\
&E_2 = Downsample(E_1) &&D_2 = Upsample(\text{Concat}(E_2, D_3)) \\
&\quad \cdots &&\quad \cdots
\end{aligned} \tag{1}
$$

where ConvBlock represents a series of convolutional layers, Downsample denotes downsampling operations (such as max-pooling or strided convolutions), UpconvBlock represents a series of transposed convolutional layers, and Upsample denotes upsampling operations (such as bilinear interpolation or transposed convolution).

To enhance the generator's ability to capture fine details and texture, we incorporate residual blocks within the network architecture [4]. The residual blocks consist of multiple convolutional layers, and the residual connections enable the network to learn residual mappings, focusing on the difference between the input and output. This mechanism facilitates the generation of more detailed and realistic portrait images.

During the training process, we utilize a combination of loss functions to guide the generator's optimization. Let y_{real} represent the ground truth portrait image corresponding to the input sketch x. We experiment with different loss functions, including Mean Squared Error (MSE) loss, L1 loss, and Generative Adversarial Network (GAN) loss [3].

The MSE loss (L_{MSE}) measures the pixel-level differences between the generated portrait $G(x)$ and the ground truth portrait y_{real}. It is calculated as:

$$L_{MSE} = ||G(x) - y_{real}||_2 \tag{2}$$

The L1 loss (L_{L1}) promotes a more robust representation of the overall structure and is computed as:

$$L_{L1} = ||G(x) - y_{real}||_1 \tag{3}$$

The GAN loss (L_{GAN}) compares the discriminator's output for the generated portrait $D(G(x))$ with the target label of "real". It encourages the generator to produce more visually pleasing and realistic results. The GAN loss is formulated as:

$$L_{GAN} = -\log(D(G(x))) \tag{4}$$

The overall loss for the generator (L_G) is a combination of these individual losses, weighted by hyperparameters λ_{MSE}, λ_{L1}, and λ_{GAN}:

$$L_G = \lambda_{MSE}L_{MSE} + \lambda_{L1}L_{L1} + \lambda_{GAN}L_{GAN} \tag{5}$$

By optimizing this combined loss function, the generator learns to minimize the discrepancy between the generated portraits and the ground truth images, resulting in high-quality and visually appealing conversions.

In summary, the generator in our sketch to portrait conversion system is implemented using the U-Net256 architecture. It consists of an encoder-decoder structure with skip connections, enabling the fusion of local and global information. The inclusion of residual blocks enhances the network's ability to capture fine details. Through the combination of different loss functions, the generator

Discriminator. In addition to the generator, the sketch to portrait conversion system incorporates a discriminator network to assess the realism and quality of the generated portrait images. The discriminator plays a crucial role in the implementation of the Generative Adversarial Network (GAN) framework, enabling adversarial training and promoting the generation of more realistic portraits [3].

For our sketch to portrait conversion system, we employ a PatchGAN discriminator, which evaluates the local image patches rather than the entire image [7]. This approach allows for a more fine-grained assessment of the generated portraits. The PatchGAN discriminator consists of multiple convolutional layers followed by downsampling operations, which progressively reduce the spatial dimensions while increasing the number of channels. These layers enable the discriminator to extract discriminative features from the input images.

Let $D(x)$ represent the discriminator network, which takes an input image x and outputs a probability score indicating the likelihood of x being a real portrait image. The discriminator aims to distinguish between real and fake images by assigning high probabilities to real portraits and low probabilities to generated ones.

During the training process, the discriminator receives pairs of real portrait images (x_{real}) and corresponding generated portraits (x_{fake}) from the generator. The discriminator aims to maximize the probability of assigning the correct label to real portraits and minimize the probability of misclassifying the generated portraits. This objective can be formulated as follows:

$$\max_{\Theta_D} \quad D(x_{real}) + (1 - D(x_{fake})) \tag{6}$$

To train the discriminator, we employ the binary cross-entropy loss function, which measures the discrepancy between the predicted probability and the ground truth label (real or fake). The binary cross-entropy loss (L_D) can be calculated as follows:

$$L_D = -\log(D(x_{real})) - \log(1 - D(x_{fake})) \tag{7}$$

By optimizing this loss function, the discriminator learns to differentiate between real and generated portraits effectively.

The training process of the sketch-to-portrait conversion system follows a min-max game between the generator and the discriminator. The generator aims to generate portraits (x_{fake}) that the discriminator classifies as real, while the discriminator strives to accurately distinguish between real and generated portraits. This adversarial training process iteratively updates both networks, with the generator attempting to improve its performance based on the feedback from the discriminator.

By incorporating the discriminator into the system, we introduce a competitive dynamic that pushes the generator to generate more visually pleasing and realistic portraits. The discriminator acts as a critical component in the overall optimization process, guiding the generator's learning and facilitating the convergence toward high-quality conversions.

In summary, the sketch-to-portrait conversion system includes a PatchGAN discriminator to evaluate the realism and quality of the generated portrait images. The discriminator employs multiple convolutional layers to extract discriminative features from local image patches. Through adversarial training using the binary cross-entropy loss, the discriminator learns to differentiate between real and generated portraits. This competitive dynamic between the generator and discriminator enhances the overall performance of the system, leading to the generation of more realistic and visually appealing portrait images.

3.2   Objective

The objective function of the sketch-to-portrait conversion system combines multiple loss terms to guide the training process and optimize the generator network. The objective is to minimize the discrepancy between the generated portraits and the corresponding ground truth images while promoting the generation of visually pleasing and realistic results.

Let $G(x)$ represent the generator network, which takes an input sketch x and generates a corresponding portrait image $G(x)$. The objective function for the sketch to portrait conversion system can be formulated as follows:

$$\min_{\Theta_G} \quad \lambda_{MSE} L_{MSE}(x, y_{real}) + \lambda_{L1} L_{L1}(x, y_{real})$$
$$+ \lambda_{GAN} L_{GAN}(x) \tag{8}$$

where Θ_G represents the parameters of the generator network, x denotes the input sketch, and y_{real} represents the ground truth portrait image corresponding to the input sketch.

The Mean Squared Error (MSE) loss term in Eq. 8, $L_{MSE}(x, y_{real})$, measures the pixel-level differences between the generated portrait $G(x)$ and the ground truth portrait y_{real}. It encourages the generator to produce portraits that closely resemble ground truth images. The L1 loss term, $L_{L1}(x, y_{real})$, promotes a more robust representation of the overall structure by measuring the absolute differences between the generated portrait and the ground truth. This loss term ensures that the generated portraits capture the essential features and maintain the overall structure of the input sketch. The Generative Adversarial Network (GAN) loss term, $L_{GAN}(x)$, leverages the discriminator network to assess the realism of the generated portrait. It encourages the generator to produce portraits that are indistinguishable from real portraits. The GAN loss is calculated based on the discriminator's output for the generated portrait, aiming to minimize the discriminator's ability to differentiate between real and generated portraits.

The hyperparameters λ_{MSE}, λ_{L1}, and λ_{GAN} control the relative importance of each loss term in the objective function. By adjusting these hyperparameters, the trade-off between fidelity to the ground truth, preservation of the structure, and visual realism can be customized to achieve the desired results.

In summary, the objective function of the sketch-to-portrait conversion system combines the MSE, L1, and GAN loss terms to guide the training of the generator network. By minimizing this objective function, the generator network learns to generate high-quality portraits that accurately capture the characteristics of the input sketches while exhibiting visual realism. We novelly explored the effect of each loss term on the training process and the visual result and the influence of the number of parameters of the generator network.

4   Experiment Results and Discussion

4.1   Dataset

To train and evaluate the sketch-to-portrait conversion system, we utilize a diverse dataset of CGI-PSG2023, which consists of paired rough facial line sketches and corresponding high-quality portrait images. The dataset comprises 420 train samples to ensure the model's ability to generalize to various facial features, and expressions and 180 test samples to test the model's generalization ability. Some images are shown in Fig. 2.

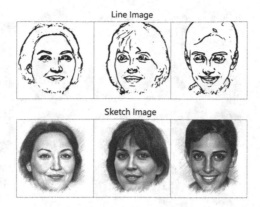

Fig. 2. Dataset of CGI-PSG2023. Our model takes the line image as input and outputs the sketch image.

4.2 Experiment Settings

The hyper-parameters are set as follows: The learning rate is set to 0.0002 and holds for 100 epochs and linear decline to 0 in 100 epochs. We use Adam [9] optimizer to update the parameters of generator and discriminator with beta1 set to 0.5 and beta2 set to 0.999. The batch size is set to 8 when the number of filters is 64, 4 when 128, and 2 when 256. As for the normalization method, we use the batch norm method [6]. Normal initialization is used for model initialization.

We employ quantitative evaluation metrics to assess the performance of the sketch-to-portrait conversion system. For quantitative evaluation, we calculate metrics such as FID [5] and Structural Similarity Index (SSIM) [21] to measure the fidelity of the generated portraits compared to the ground truth images.

4.3 Implementation

All experiments are performed on one NVIDIA GeForce A10 with 24GiB memory. Our proposed framework and compared methods are all implemented on Pytorch (version 2.0.0+cu117) in Python (3.9.16) environment.

4.4 Results and Discussion

We initially employ only the Mean Squared Error (MSE) loss function, disregarding the L1 and Generative Adversarial Network (GAN) losses. However, the generated images produced by the generator lack visual appeal and only present a basic outline of the line images. To enhance the quality, we introduce the L1 loss, leading to improved feature edges. Subsequently, the GAN loss is integrated, resulting in a significant improvement in the detailed features of human faces.

Figure 3 illustrates the visualization of different models or settings on the test set (without available ground truth). Furthermore, we present quantitative results in Table 1.

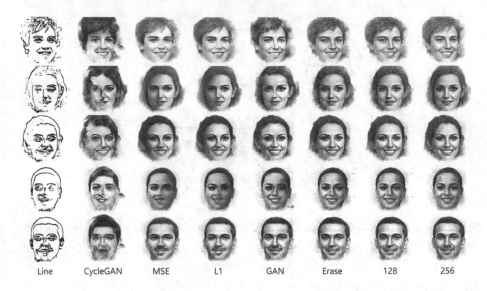

Line   CycleGAN   MSE   L1   GAN   Erase   128   256

Fig. 3. The visualization of different models or different settings.

As depicted in Fig. 3, the use of MSE loss tends to generate color lumps, while the incorporation of L1 loss mitigates this issue. This discrepancy arises from the optimization process, where the MSE loss relies on the Gaussian prior distribution, resulting in smoother outputs, while the L1 loss operates based on the Laplace prior distribution, producing sharper outputs, as shown in Fig. 4.

Both loss functions focus on the global feature distribution, but the L1 loss places greater emphasis on preserving edge information. Consequently, the MSE loss achieves a FID value of 0.671, while the L1 loss yields an improved FID value of 0.358. In contrast, the GAN loss leverages the discriminator network to identify abnormal pixels, enhancing the reproduction of fine-grained details. When both L1 and GAN losses are considered, the FID value improves further, reaching 0.319, surpassing the individual contributions of L1 or MSE loss.

We also conducted experiments with CycleGAN, which utilizes only GAN loss and cycle loss, resulting in a FID value of 0.427. The inclusion of CycleGAN loss is necessary for ensuring fairness during training, as using only GAN loss might not directly exploit the ground truth information. Despite these attempts, the combination of L1 and GAN losses remains superior in achieving better compatibility and overall performance.

Table 1. FID and SSIM of different models or different Settings.

Models	CycleGAN	Ours					
		MSE	L1	GAN+L1	Erase	128 Filter	256 Filter
FID	0.427	0.671	0.358	0.319	0.274	0.270	**0.218**
SSIM	0.697	0.780	0.718	0.770	0.769	0.766	**0.792**

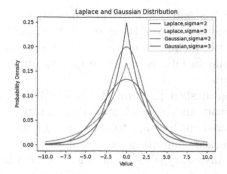

Fig. 4. Laplace and Gaussian Distribution with different sigma values.

Moreover, we have observed that certain critical lines are missing in the line image, making it challenging to produce the sketch image accurately. To address this issue, we introduced the random-erase augmentation technique during data pre-processing, resulting in a slight improvement in the output quality.

Additionally, we explored scaling up the generator model to a larger size. Specifically, we increased the number of generator filters in the last convolution layer to 128 and 256. This modification yielded significant improvements in the FID metric, achieving values of 0.270 and 0.218, respectively. We further attempted to set the maximum number of generator filters in the last convolution layer to 256, as this aligns with the limitations of the available 24GB video storage, which restricts the support for larger models.

Fortunately, we did not encounter any performance saturation within the experimental scope, even with the increased model size. This scaling strategy effectively enhanced the generation quality without reaching the storage-related limitations.

5   Conclusion

In this paper, we conducted a comprehensive investigation on the sketch to portrait conversion task, with a focus on exploring the impact of different loss functions and data augmentation techniques using the U-Net256 network architecture. Our primary objective was to enhance the transformation of rough facial line sketches into highly detailed and realistic portrait images.

Through extensive experimentation, we gained valuable insights into the effects of various loss functions on the quality and fidelity of the generated portraits. The Mean Squared Error (MSE) loss and L1 loss were found to be instrumental in capturing the overall structure of the portraits, while the Generative Adversarial Network (GAN) loss played a crucial role in enhancing the generation of fine-grained details and texture. By judiciously selecting and combining these loss functions, we were able to achieve more accurate and visually appealing conversions.

Additionally, we delved into the impact of data augmentation techniques on the robustness and generalization of the network. Specifically, random rotations and random erasing were identified as effective methods for improving the network's ability to handle variations in sketch quality and generate diverse and realistic portrait images.

Our experiments also shed light on the trade-off between the number of parameters in the network and the quality of the generated images. While higher parameter counts allowed the network to capture more intricate details, it came at the expense of increased computational complexity. Hence, careful consideration of this trade-off is necessary when designing the sketch to portrait conversion system, depending on the available computational resources and the desired level of detail.

Overall, our study provides valuable insights into the factors influencing the performance of the sketch-to-portrait conversion system, making important contributions to the development of more advanced and effective methods in this field. By optimizing the choice of loss functions, leveraging data augmentation techniques, and thoughtfully considering the model complexity, remarkable results can be achieved in transforming rough facial line sketches into highly detailed and realistic portrait images.

For future research, we suggest exploring additional loss functions, such as perceptual loss or style loss, to further improve the visual quality and artistic style transfer in the generated portraits. Investigating advanced data augmentation strategies and exploring the use of generative models, such as conditional variational autoencoders or transformer-based architectures, could also open up promising avenues for enhancing the sketch-to-portrait conversion task.

In conclusion, the study presented in this paper advances the field of sketch-to-portrait conversion systems, pushing the boundaries of realism and detail in generated portrait images. The insights gained from this research can guide future developments and inspire innovative approaches in the realm of computer vision and digital art.

References

1. Choi, Y., Choi, M., Kim, M., Ha, J., Kim, S., Choo, J.: StarGAN: Unified generative adversarial networks for multi-domain image-to-image translation (2017). CoRR abs/1711.09020, http://arxiv.org/abs/1711.09020
2. Gatys, L.A., Ecker, A.S., Bethge, M.: Image style transfer using convolutional neural networks. In: 2016 IEEE Conference on Computer Vision and Pattern Recognition (CVPR), pp. 2414–2423 (2016). https://doi.org/10.1109/CVPR.2016.265
3. Goodfellow, I.J., et al.: Generative adversarial networks (2014)
4. He, K., Zhang, X., Ren, S., Sun, J.: Deep residual learning for image recognition (2015)
5. Heusel, M., Ramsauer, H., Unterthiner, T., Nessler, B., Hochreiter, S.: GANs trained by a two time-scale update rule converge to a local Nash equilibrium (2018)
6. Ioffe, S., Szegedy, C.: Batch normalization: Accelerating deep network training by reducing internal covariate shift (2015)

7. Isola, P., Zhu, J.Y., Zhou, T., Efros, A.A.: Image-to-image translation with conditional adversarial networks. In: 2017 IEEE Conference on Computer Vision and Pattern Recognition (CVPR), pp. 5967–5976 (2017). https://doi.org/10.1109/CVPR.2017.632

8. Isola, P., Zhu, J.Y., Zhou, T., Efros, A.A.: Image-to-image translation with conditional adversarial networks (2018)

9. Kingma, D.P., Ba, J.: Adam: A method for stochastic optimization (2017)

10. Lata, K., Dave, M., Nishanth, K.N.: Image-to-image translation using generative adversarial network. In: 2019 3rd International conference on Electronics, Communication and Aerospace Technology (ICECA), pp. 186–189 (2019). https://doi.org/10.1109/ICECA.2019.8822195

11. Li, P., Sheng, B., Chen, C.L.P.: Face sketch synthesis using regularized broad learning system. IEEE Trans. Neural Netw. Learn. Syst. 33(10), 5346–5360 (2022). https://doi.org/10.1109/TNNLS.2021.3070463

12. Li, S., Wu, F., fan, Y., Song, X., Dong, W.: PLDGAN: portrait line drawing generation with prior knowledge and conditioning target. Vis. Comput. 39(8), 3507–3518 (2023). https://doi.org/10.1007/s00371-023-02956-1

13. Li, Z., Togo, R., Ogawa, T., Haseyama, M.: Semantic-aware unpaired image-to-image translation for urban scene images. In: ICASSP 2021–2021 IEEE International Conference on Acoustics, Speech and Signal Processing (ICASSP), pp. 2150–2154 (2021). https://doi.org/10.1109/ICASSP39728.2021.9414192

14. Liu, M.Y., Huang, X., Mallya, A., Karras, T., Aila, T., Lehtinen, J., Kautz, J.: Few-shot unsupervised image-to-image translation (2019)

15. Nozawa, N., Shum, H.P.H., Feng, Q., Ho, E.S.L., Morishima, S.: 3D car shape reconstruction from a contour sketch using GAN and lazy learning. Vis. Comput. 38(4), 1317–1330 (2022). https://doi.org/10.1007/s00371-020-02024-y

16. Park, T., Liu, M., Wang, T., Zhu, J.: Semantic image synthesis with spatially-adaptive normalization (2019). CoRR abs/1903.07291, http://arxiv.org/abs/1903.07291

17. Ronneberger, O., Fischer, P., Brox, T.: U-Net: Convolutional networks for biomedical image segmentation (2015)

18. Tschannen, M., Agustsson, E., Lucic, M.: Deep generative models for distribution-preserving lossy compression (2018)

19. Tsuda, H., Hotta, K.: Cell image segmentation by integrating pix2pixs for each class. In: 2019 IEEE/CVF Conference on Computer Vision and Pattern Recognition Workshops (CVPRW), pp. 1065–1073 (2019). https://doi.org/10.1109/CVPRW.2019.00139

20. Uzunova, H., Ehrhardt, J., Jacob, F., Frydrychowicz, A., Handels, H.: Multi-scale GANs for memory-efficient generation of high resolution medical images (2019)

21. Wang, Z., Bovik, A., Sheikh, H., Simoncelli, E.: Image quality assessment: from error visibility to structural similarity. IEEE Trans. Image Process. 13(4), 600–612 (2004). https://doi.org/10.1109/TIP.2003.819861

22. Yeh, R.A., Chen, C., Lim, T.Y., Schwing, A.G., Hasegawa-Johnson, M., Do, M.N.: Semantic image inpainting with deep generative models (2017)

23. Yoshikawa, T., Endo, Y., Kanamori, Y.: Diversifying detail and appearance in sketch-based face image synthesis. The Visual Computer (Proc. of Computer Graphics Internatinal 2022) (2022)

24. Zhu, J.Y., Park, T., Isola, P., Efros, A.A.: Unpaired image-to-image translation using cycle-consistent adversarial networks (2020)

EAID: An Eye-Tracking Based Advertising Image Dataset with Personalized Affective Tags

Song Liang[1], Ruihang Liu[2], and Jiansheng Qian[3]([✉])

[1] School of Mines, China University of Mining and Technology, Xuzhou, China
[2] Xuhai College, China University of Mining and Technology, Xuzhou, China
[3] School of Information and Control Engineering, China University of Mining and Technology, Xuzhou, China
qianzhangiqa@126.com

Abstract. Contrary to natural images with randomized content, advertisements contain abundant emotion-eliciting manufactured scenes and multi-modal visual elements with highly related semantics. However, little research has evaluated the interrelationships of advertising vision and affective perception. The absence of advertising data sets with affective labels and visual attention benchmarks is one of the most pressing issues that have to be addressed. Meanwhile, growing evidence indicates that eye movements can reveal the internal states of human minds. Inspired by these, we use a high-precision eye tracker to record the eye-moving data of 57 subjects when they observe 1000 advertising images. 7-score opinion ratings for the five advertising attributes (i.e., ad liking, emotional, aesthetic, functional, and brand liking) are then collected. We further make a preliminary analysis of the correlation among advertising attributes, subjects' visual attention, eye movement characteristics, and personality traits, obtaining a series of enlightening conclusions. To our best knowledge, the proposed dataset is the largest advertising image dataset based on eye tracking and with multiple personalized affective tags. It provides a new exploration space and data foundation for multimedia visual analysis and affection computing community. The data are available at: https://github.com/lscumt/EAID.

Keywords: Advertising · Affective computing · Eye movement analysis

1 Introduction

At present, advertisement related research focuses on the recommendation system and one central task is the user response prediction [18]. The realization of this task tightly depends on the establishment of user portrait model and the analysis of user behavior [5,7]. Although these methods have achieved good results in various applications, they are all recommended based on the way of big data mining. Moreover, although consumers finally buy the products promoted by the advertisement, it can not be completely explained that the advertising

B. Sheng et al. (Eds.): CGI 2023, LNCS 14495, pp. 282–294, 2024.
https://doi.org/10.1007/978-3-031-50069-5_24

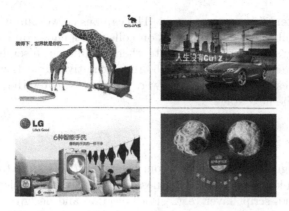

Fig. 1. Advertising samples display.

design is effective, perhaps it is only caused by the life needs of users. Therefore, the study on whether the audience increases their favorable impression for the product or brand is from advertising charm itself is greatly beneficial to advertising design and recommendation.

Compared with natural scenes, advertising scenes are mostly artificial and have more visual elements, deeper semantic information, and richer genre styles. Furthermore, advertisement incorporates abundant strategies and tricks of cognitive psychology, as shown in Fig. 1. Hence, they are often persuasive, seductive and purposive. However, it is unknown how these characteristics affect the visual attention, psychological motivation, emotional bias and behavioral decision of the observer. And also, the audiences' impression and feeling on advertisements are influenced by numerous factors, such as subjects' cultural background, social status, age, gender, region, brand preference, and even their internal factors like expectations, memories, intentions [6, 13]. These potential influencing factors are difficult to be fully counted and measured in one model, or to characterize with one or several single indicators. There is also a lack of relevant advertising data sets to solve similar problems. Inspired by this, we return the advertisement to the visual stimulation level and analyze the affective traceability from the perspective of visual perception.

2   Creating Dataset

2.1   Subject Selection

Big-Five (BF) personality trait is one of the most stable models describing human personality characteristics in psychological research, which is widely adopted by the computer vision community [2]. The BF personality traits include: Neuroticism (N), Extraversion (E), Openness (O), Agreeableness (A) and Conscientiousness (C). In the process of selecting the subjects, we adopted the BF personality scale with 60 questions. There are five grades, from very inconsistent

1 to very consistent 5 for each question. The campus crowdsourcing was adopted for collection. Subjects mainly focuses on college students, covering undergraduate students, graduate students and teachers of different disciplines. 381 valid questionnaires were collected. Finally, 57 representative subjects with high main personality scores and good eyesight were selected to enter the eye movement experiment in the next stage.

2.2   Stimulus Selection

Advertising design usually consists of four layers from bottom to top: vision layer (e.g., element color, shape and brightness), space layer (e.g., element position, size and number), script layer (e.g., style selection and design), and aesthetics layer (e.g., layout management, aesthetic rendering and quantification). Inspired by this, we elaborately selected 1000 advertising images focusing on four pairs of perspectives with eight attributes, namely (Calming, Exciting), (Retro, Fashional), (Aesthetic, Utilitarian) and (Emotional, Rational). Finally, the authors, along with an economics professor, handpicked about 125 representative ads from the Internet for each attribute category, totally 1000 advertising images with different sizes. The 1000 ads contain alcohol, tea, home appliance, vehicle, food, toiletry, beverage, tourism, electronic product, real estate, clothing, and other abundant themes.

2.3   Eye Tracking Experiment

We used a high-precision eye tracker, the EyeLink 1000 Plus, for eye tracking data collection in a lab with stable light. The 57 participants were asked to take part in eight experiments, each looking at 125 advertising samples. The interval between each observation experiment was more than three days, and each observation lasted an average of half an hour.

Unlike the seminal work [14] on eye movement reasoning, in which it is hypothesized that the eye-moving patterns of observers change with respect to the tasks. However, the scenes of watching advertisements in our lives are usually unprepared and unexpected, without any task assignment. Therefore, in our eye movement study, no task was set in the observation process. Different from these experiments [4,8], the authors proposed the normal viewing time should be unstinted, since the commodity diversity, scene complexity, variable size of the ad images and the different individuals' observation habits. For more detail eye-tracking experimental settings, please refer to our previous work [9].

2.4   Ad Liking Label Collection

For advertisement, the visual attention on advertisement significantly affects consumers' decision-making action, it is important to investigate the factors influencing human visual behavior and preference [3,11]. In order to explore the clues that the eye movement characteristics imply users' emotional preferences,

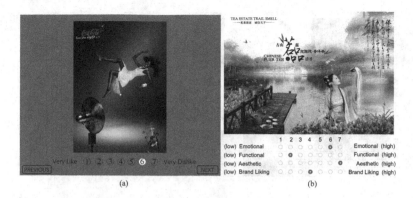

Fig. 2. Rating interface for advetising labels collection.

we further quantified the audience's preference into a specific advertising liking score. The human-computer interaction interface is shown in Fig. 2(a), where "1" means very dislike and "7" means very like. The larger the value, the greater the degree of ad liking.

2.5   Other Label Designs

We further collected the score of 57 subjects on the four labels as showen in Fig. 2(b). 7-score options were available for selection. The higher the value, the stronger the corresponding attribute.

Emotional. Emotional attribute refers to the degree of emotion released by advertising, including family affection, friendship, love, social care, patriotic feelings, etc., and also refers to the emotion intensity perceived by observers, such as moved, excited, sad, angry, anxious, obnoxious and so on.

Aesthetic. Aesthetic is a kind of non-utilitarianism and humans' universal abstract emotional expression. It represents people's expectations for beautiful things, and has strong subjectivity [21]. For advertising, beautiful visual design can undoubtedly increase the goodwill of consumers.

Functional. Functional attribute denotes the effectiveness, usefulness, or practicability of a product or brand in an advertisement. Conveying the product practicability is one of the most important functions of advertising. Hence, the functional lable is collected.

Brand Liking. Brand is also a non-negligible factor affecting consumers' visual attention. Generally, we tend to pay more attention to the advertisements with the brand we like. In tourism advertising, the tourism location is regarded as the advertising brand.

Fig. 3. Samples presentation of different scores for five attributes.

3   Data Statistics and Processing

- Subject Personality Statistics: Among the 57 subjects with prominent main personalities screened by the Big Five Personality Scale, there are about 11 people in each personality.
- Eye Movement Feature: We collected the eye movement data of 57 subjects when observing 1000 advertisements. After excluding 22 blank data caused by equipment failure and deviation data caused by inaccurate eye calibration, 56978 valid data were kept.
- Advertising Visual Saliency: By visualizing the fixation, duration and location features of the eye movement features, the personalized visual attention distribution can be obtained, and the general saliency groundtruth can be generated by averaging the 57 personalized saliency maps.
- Advertising Attribute Groundtruth: We took the 57 subjects' ratings of the five ad attributes as the personalized groundtruth. In addition, we averaged the 57 opinion scores separately as the general groundtruth for each advertisement. Figure 3 shows advertising samples with different scores under different attributes. For each attribute, the histogram probability distribution of the opinion scores are shown in Fig. 4. It indicates that the subjective score values cover the whole range with different estimation levels for advertising samples.

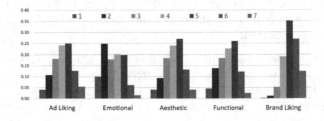

Fig. 4. 1–7 subjective scores statistics for five attributes.

4   Data Analysis and Discussion

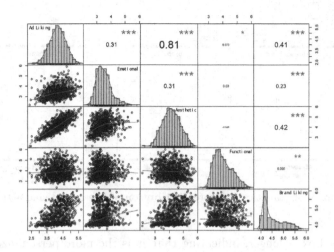

Fig. 5. Correlation analysis of advertising attributes.

4.1   Correlation Analysis of Advertising Attributes

In Fig. 5, we performed correlation analysis on the average score distribution of 1000 ads on five attributes. It indicates that advertising aesthetics can largely affect ad liking perception, with the highest Pearson Linear Correlation Coefficient (PLCC) value 0.81. Comprehensive analysis of significance level index p and PLCC correlation coefficient shows that brand liking is also positively correlated with advertising liking and advertising aesthetic evaluation. However, the emotional attribute has a weak correlation with ad liking and aesthetic attribute. Except for the functional attribute, which has the strongest independence, the other attributes have different degrees of correlation with each other, and the specific mutual influence relationship needs to be further explored. The correlation less than 0.5 indicates that the two attributes present more heterogeneity of their own, representing different aspects of advertisements severally.

The variances of five attributes are visualized in Fig. 6. In the box subplot (a), the boxes are located at different score levels, which indicates that the five attributes measure the different dimensions of the advertisement. Moreover, each box extends over a long score range. It indicates that the subjective score distribution of each attribute has a certain dispersion, and verifies that the selected ad samples have the characteristics of diversity. Among them, the boxes of ad liking and aesthetic are in a similar position, reflecting the high correlation between these two attributes. It is consistent with the above analysis results. However,

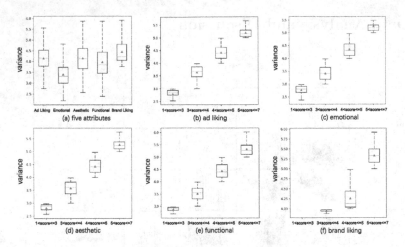

Fig. 6. Box plot statistics for score distribution of five advertising attributes.

the aesthetic box is longer, indicating that it is the more personalized dimension than ad liking. From the box subplots (b), (c), (d) and (e), each attribute has a flatter box in the higher and lower score range than in the middle score range, showing that the subjects have more subjective consistency when perceiving the extreme affective dimension. The subgraph (f) reveals that among the acquainted advertising brands, and there is no particular dislike ($score \leq 3$). Moreover, the subjective rating for "very like" brands is more uniform than the "little like" brand. It also implies that non-mainstream brands present stronger instability in the space favored by the audience than mainstream brands.

4.2   Advertising Attributes and Visual Attention

In computer vision, visual attention or visual saliency have been considered in many visual emotion analysis tasks [12,17,19], but they are used as auxiliary cues. The relationship between visual attention and human emotion has always been vague and difficult to be quantified. In order to quantify the intensity of vision attention for every sample, we introduce a scalar index Saliency Intensity Factor (SIF) inspired by an adaptive threshold in [1]. That is the average saliency per pixel in the whole visual field region, calculated as follows:

$$\text{SIF} = \frac{1}{M \times N} \sum_{i=0}^{M-1} \sum_{j=0}^{N-1} S_{gt}(i, j), \tag{1}$$

where M and N are respectively the width and height of advertising saliency groundtruth and S_{gt} (i, j) denotes the gray value in pixel location (i, j). SIF ranges from 0 to 255.

In Fig. 7(a), we further give the average SIF distribution of the five advertising attributes on the 7 score scales. Apparently, subjects have an unexpectedly

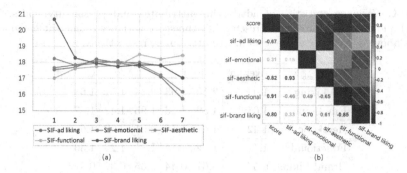

Fig. 7. SIF distribution and correlation analysis between SIF and ad attributes.

high SIF for the extremely dislike ads (brand liking score $= 1$). Through inspecting such advertisements, we find that most of them belong to unpopular brands or have complicated logos. This indicates that advertisements with higher brand awareness are more likely to gain goodwill. In addition, advertising brands are generally composed of text, numbers and special symbols, which have special attraction to the human eye, especially in the case of low familiarity. The lower the brand liking score, the higher the SIF value, which is consistent with the above analysis. The overall observation shows that the SIF distributions in the middle range (3–5 scores) is relatively concentrated and similar, while the distribution of the two ends tends to be more heterogeneous and dispersive. The authors infer that stimuli with extreme attribute performance induce unstable heterogeneous visual attention, and visual stimuli with moderate attributes are accompanied by stable visual attention.

In Fig. 7(b), we calculate the correlation coefficient PLCC between the SIF distribution of each advertising attribute and 1–7 opinion scores. We find that the three subjective dimensions of ad liking, aesthetic and brand liking have a strong negative correlation with SIF, and the correlation coefficients were -0.67, -0.82 and -0.80, respectively. This indicates that the average visual attention intensity given by the human eye is less when the more like or beautiful visual stimuli are perceived. It is consistent with the fact that we tend to focus on our favorite targets and ignore other objects in the entire visual field. In addition, SIF showed a weak correlation with emotional attribute, but an extremely strong positive correlation with functional attribute (PLCC $= 0.91$). The authors analyzed that the functionality are mainly described through text, and understanding text information could take relatively more time, which leads to the more output of visual attention. This is consistent with the conclusion in our previous work [9].

4.3   Advertising Attributes and Personality Traits

We calculate the variance of subjective scores for every personality dimension and every advertising attribute, as shown in Table 1. Through horizontal observation, the subjective scores of N and O personalities have larger variance values in all

Table 1. Variance statistics of advertising attributes and personality traits. The upward and downward arrows represent that the score variance of current personality trait is above or below average level in five attributes, respectively.

	Average	N ↑	E ↓	O ↑	A ↓	C
Ad Liking	1.94	2.10	1.93	2.34	1.71	1.68
Emotional	1.65	1.89	1.23	1.95	1.42	1.77
Aesthetic	1.42	1.47	1.15	2.01	0.92	1.62
Functional	1.41	1.52	1.14	1.81	1.23	1.30
Brand Liking	0.54	0.61	0.44	0.65	0.37	0.57

advertising attributes and are both larger than the average. This indicates that the subjective opinions of subjects in these two personalities are more discrete and unstable than those of other personalities. Especially, the performance of type O is the most obvious. Through longitudinal observation, both N and O (E and A) types showed larger (smaller) variance than the average level in all attributes, showing that in these four types of personality, subjects with the same personality tended to make the consistent subjective choices, and this consistency hold a certain stability and do not transfer with different evaluation tasks.

The reason for the higher score variance of (N, O) and lower score variance of (E, A) perhaps is related to the characteristics of their respective personalities. For example, Neuroticism has the characteristics of sensitivity and instability, and Openness has the characteristics of curiosity and imagination. These characteristics could induce the uncertainty in decision making. While the positive and confidence factors in Extraversion, or the kindness and tolerance factors in Agreeableness could stimulate the subjects' stable emotional output and behavioral decision-making. Unfortunately, the Conscientiousness subjects do not show such regular tendency according to Table 1, but this also reflects the fact that there are heterogeneities in subjective choices among different personalities and the personalized analysis is needed.

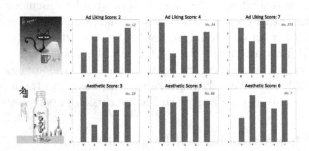

Fig. 8. Different personalities and different subjective choices.

For intuitive observation, we show the personality traits of different subjects together with their subjective judgements for advertising attributes (e.g. ad liking and aesthetic) in Fig. 8. It is easy to observe that subjects with different personality traits have different affective tastes.

4.4 Advertising Attributes and Eye Movements

Different from the visual attention in Sect. 4.3, which tends to indicate the gaze result, the eye movement features emphasize the process of gaze [20]. It should be pointed out that among the five attributes, only the ad liking was collected simultaneously with the eye movement experiment. Therefore, when analyzing the relationship between the other four attributes and eye movement behaviors, the interference factor of subject heterogeneity caused by time transformation cannot be excluded. Nevertheless, the authors consider that the observation habit of human is stable and not be distorted in short time. Hence, eye movement data can still provide important visual information in the understanding and analysis of these properties.

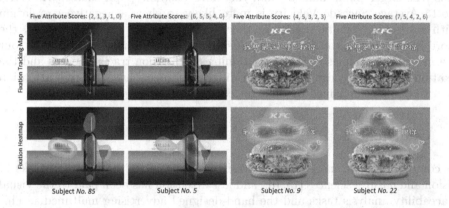

Fig. 9. Samples of eye-tracking maps and the fixation heatmaps. Five attribute are orderly denoted as (ad liking, emotional, aesthetic, functional, brand liking). Score 0 indicates that the subject did not recognize the advertising brand.

The analysis of eye movement behavior mainly involves two basic fixation and saccade indexes and their synthetic indexes [10]. Table 2 shows the correlation performance between 18 statistics-based eye movement indicators and the scores of five advertising attributes. Three evaluation metrics were used, PLCC, spearman rank-order correlation coefficient (SRCC) and kendall rank-order correlation coefficient (KRCC). It can be seen that the correlation in different subjective assessment tasks is significantly different. Compared with the non-affectivity functional attribute, the affectivity related attributes are more closely related to eye movement behavior. Moreover, the correlation values between pupil diameter and emotional attribute are all more than 0.9 in the three statistical methods of

Table 2. Correlation of advertising attributes and eye movement indicators. The symbols *, **, and *** represent the sum, average, and variance statistics, respectively. Correlation metric values greater than 0.6 are bold black.

Eye-moving Index	Ad Liking			Emotional			Aesthetic			Functional			Brand Liking		
	PLCC	SRCC	KRCC	PLCC	SRCC	KRCC	PLCC	SRCC	KRCC	PLCC	SRCC	KRCC	PLCC	SRCC	KRCC
1 Viewing Time **	0.370	0.429	0.429	**0.703**	**0.607**	0.524	**0.613**	**0.714**	0.524	−0.082	−0.143	−0.048	**0.666**	**0.607**	0.524
2 Fixation Number **	0.350	0.250	0.238	**0.701**	**0.607**	0.524	0.313	0.286	0.238	0.574	0.429	0.333	**0.768**	**0.750**	**0.619**
3 FIX Pupil Diameter *	0.302	0.393	0.238	**0.941**	**0.964**	**0.905**	**0.879**	**0.857**	**0.714**	0.192	0.179	0.143	**0.721**	**0.714**	**0.619**
4 FIX Pupil Diameter **	0.237	0.357	0.143	**0.914**	**0.929**	**0.810**	**0.851**	**0.786**	**0.619**	−0.044	0.036	0.048	**0.719**	0.571	0.429
5 FIX Pupil Diameter ***	0.289	0.393	0.238	**0.931**	**0.929**	**0.810**	**0.790**	**0.750**	0.524	0.325	0.250	0.143	**0.849**	**0.857**	**0.714**
6 FIX Duration *	0.446	**0.607**	0.524	**0.764**	**0.857**	**0.714**	**0.675**	**0.714**	0.524	−0.083	−0.143	−0.048	**0.626**	0.500	0.429
7 FIX Duration **	**0.796**	**0.857**	**0.714**	−0.313	−0.036	−0.048	**0.719**	**0.679**	0.524	**−0.670**	−0.500	−0.333	**−0.825**	**−0.857**	**−0.714**
8 FIX Duration ***	0.289	0.393	0.238	**0.931**	**0.929**	**0.810**	**0.790**	**0.750**	0.524	0.325	0.250	0.143	**0.849**	**0.857**	**0.714**
9 SAC Amplitude *	0.410	0.357	0.333	**0.899**	**0.857**	**0.714**	**0.609**	0.536	0.429	0.500	**0.643**	0.524	0.569	0.321	0.238
10 SAC Amplitude **	−0.194	0.000	−0.048	0.508	0.357	0.333	**0.613**	0.464	0.429	−0.517	−0.214	−0.143	−0.568	**−0.714**	−0.524
11 SAC Amplitude ***	**0.821**	**0.786**	**0.714**	**0.947**	**0.964**	**0.905**	**0.912**	**0.893**	**0.810**	−0.277	0.018	0.098	0.435	0.000	−0.048
12 SAC Average Velocity *	0.127	0.214	0.143	0.311	0.357	0.333	0.270	0.250	0.238	0.210	0.000	−0.048	**0.705**	**0.607**	0.524
13 SAC Average Velocity **	**−0.729**	**−0.750**	**−0.619**	**−0.762**	**−0.714**	**−0.619**	−0.150	−0.071	−0.048	**−0.744**	**−0.821**	**−0.619**	0.228	0.286	0.238
14 SAC Average Velocity ***	−0.567	−0.429	−0.429	**−0.681**	**−0.643**	−0.524	0.118	0.000	−0.048	−0.582	**−0.679**	−0.524	**0.608**	0.536	0.429
15 SAC Duration *	−0.058	−0.071	−0.048	0.302	0.143	0.238	0.037	0.000	0.048	0.002	0.214	0.143	**0.799**	**0.857**	**0.714**
16 SAC Duration **	**−0.845**	**−0.893**	**−0.810**	−0.458	−0.179	−0.143	**−0.736**	**−0.714**	−0.429	−0.474	−0.393	−0.238	**0.653**	**0.607**	0.524
17 SAC Duration ***	**−0.833**	**−0.786**	**−0.714**	−0.278	−0.143	−0.048	**−0.705**	**−0.643**	−0.429	−0.097	−0.143	−0.048	0.430	0.393	0.333
18 SAC Angle ***	**−0.859**	**−0.857**	**−0.714**	0.265	−0.071	−0.143	**−0.803**	**−0.750**	**−0.619**	0.303	0.179	0.143	**0.636**	0.536	0.429

sum, mean and variance. It indicates that the more emotional advertising stimulus, the larger pupil diameter and the more unstable pupil change. However, No.13 Average Saccade Velocity is more likely to show a negative correlation with subjective cognition, that is, the faster the visual attention switch, the more likely it is to lead to a negative subjective evaluation. We visualize four eye movement samples in Fig. 9, containing the fixation tracking maps and the fixation heatmaps. It can be seen that different subjects have different attention distribution, accompanied by different cognitive results.

5   Conclusions

In computer vision, more efforts have been made in the downstream tasks of vision and natural sciences [15,16], and less attention has been paid to the visual traceability analysis tasks and the hand-designed advertising multimedia. This paper presents an advertising image database based on eye tracking, which contains 1000 advertising samples, 57 observers' personalized information, and their subjective cognitive labels of five advertising attributes. This dataset provides a reliable data basis for the community of visual perception and affective computing in advertising. Moreover, we give a preliminary correlation analysis and discussion between advertising attributes and human visual features. We hope that this work could be helpful to advertising practices such as ad design and ad recommendation, as well as the affection analysis in other visual scenes.

Acknowledgements. This research did not receive any specific grant from funding agencies in the public, commercial, or not-for-profit sectors.

References

1. Achanta, R., Hemami, S., Estrada, F., Susstrunk, S.: Frequency-tuned salient region detection. In: 2009 IEEE Conference on Computer Vision and Pattern Recognition, pp. 1597–1604. IEEE (2009)
2. Barnett, T., Pearson, A.W., Pearson, R., Kellermanns, F.W.: Five-factor model personality traits as predictors of perceived and actual usage of technology. Eur. J. Inf. Syst. **24**, 374–390 (2015)
3. Chen, Z., Song, W.: Factors affecting human visual behavior and preference for sneakers: an eye-tracking study. Front. Psychol. **13**, 914321 (2022)
4. Jeck, D.M., Qin, M., Egeth, H., Niebur, E.: Attentive pointing in natural scenes correlates with other measures of attention. Vision. Res. **135**, 54–64 (2017)
5. Jiang, H., Hu, Z., Zhao, X., Yang, L., Yang, Z.: Exploring the users' preference pattern of application services between different mobile phone brands. IEEE Trans. Comput. Soc. Syst. **5**(4), 1163–1173 (2018)
6. Jiang, H., Liang, J., Wang, H., Sun, P.: The interplay of emotions, elaboration, and ambivalence on attitude-behavior consistency. J. Consum. Behav. **15**(2), 126–135 (2016)
7. Jiang, N., Sheng, B., Li, P., Lee, T.Y.: Photohelper: portrait photographing guidance via deep feature retrieval and fusion. IEEE Trans. Multimedia **25**, 2226–2238 (2023)
8. Judd, T., Ehinger, K., Durand, F., Torralba, A.: Learning to predict where humans look. In: 2009 IEEE 12th International Conference on Computer Vision, pp. 2106–2113. IEEE (2009)
9. Liang, S., Liu, R., Qian, J.: Fixation prediction for advertising images: dataset and benchmark. J. Vis. Commun. Image Represent. **81**, 103356 (2021)
10. Melcher, D., Morrone, M.C.: Spatiotopic temporal integration of visual motion across saccadic eye movements. Nat. Neurosci. **6**(8), 877–881 (2003)
11. Milosavljevic, M., Cerf, M.: First attention then intention: Insights from computational neuroscience of vision. Int. J. Advert. **27**(3), 381–398 (2008)
12. Peng, K.C., Sadovnik, A., Gallagher, A., Chen, T.: Where do emotions come from? Predicting the emotion stimuli map. In: 2016 IEEE International Conference on Image Processing (ICIP), pp. 614–618. IEEE (2016)
13. Rayner, K., Castelhano, M.S.: Eye movements during reading, scene perception, visual search, and while looking at print advertisements (2008)
14. Tatler, B.W., Wade, N.J., Kwan, H., Findlay, J.M., Velichkovsky, B.M.: Yarbus, eye movements, and vision. i-Perception **1**(1), 7–27 (2010)
15. Wen, Y.: Structure-aware motion deblurring using multi-adversarial optimized cyclegan. IEEE Trans. Image Process. **30**, 6142–6155 (2021)
16. Xia, H., Lu, L., Song, S.: Feature fusion of multi-granularity and multi-scale for facial expression recognition. Vis. Comput. pp. 1–13 (2023)
17. Yang, J., She, D., Lai, Y.K., Rosin, P.L., Yang, M.H.: Weakly supervised coupled networks for visual sentiment analysis. In: Proceedings of the IEEE Conference on Computer Vision and Pattern Recognition, pp. 7584–7592 (2018)
18. Yang, Y., Xu, B., Shen, S., Shen, F., Zhao, J.: Operation-aware neural networks for user response prediction. Neural Netw. **121**, 161–168 (2020)
19. You, Q., Jin, H., Luo, J.: Visual sentiment analysis by attending on local image regions. In: Proceedings of the AAAI conference on artificial intelligence, vol. 31 (2017)

20. Zhang, J., Hou, W., Zhu, X., Wei, Y.: Analysis of situation map user cognitive characteristics based on eye movement data. In: Yamamoto, S., Mori, H. (eds.) HCII 2022, LNCS, vol. 13305, pp. 282–294. Springer, Cham (2022). https://doi.org/10.1007/978-3-031-06424-1_21
21. Zhu, H., Zhou, Y., Li, L., Li, Y., Guo, Y.: Learning personalized image aesthetics from subjective and objective attributes. IEEE Trans. Multimedia **25**, 179–190 (2021)

Image Restoration and Enhancement

Controllable Deep Learning Denoising Model for Ultrasound Images Using Synthetic Noisy Image

Mingfu Jiang[1,5], Chenzhi You[2], Mingwei Wang[3], Heye Zhang[4], Zhifan Gao[4], Dawei Wu[2(✉)], and Tao Tan[1(✉)]

[1] Faculty of Applied Sciences, Macao Polytechnic University, Macao 999078, China
taotan@mpu.edu.mo

[2] State Key Laboratory of Mechanics and Control for Aerospace Structures, Nanjing University of Aeronautics and Astronautics, Nanjing 210016, China
dwu@nuaa.edu.cn

[3] Department of Dardiovascular Medicine, Affiliated Hospital of Hangzhou Normal University, Hangzhou 311121, China

[4] School of Biomedical Engineering, Sun Yat-Sen University, Shenzhen 518107, China

[5] College of Information Engineering, Xinyang Agriculture and Forestry University, Xinyang 464000, China

Abstract. Medical ultrasound imaging has gained widespread prevalence in human muscle and internal organ diagnosis. Nevertheless, various factors such as the interference effect of ultrasonic echoes, mutual interference between scattered beams, inhomogeneity and uncertainty in the spatial distribution of human body tissue, inappropriate operation, and imaging signal transmission processes, can lead to noise and distortion in ultrasound images. These factors make it difficult to obtain clean and accurate ultrasound images, which may adversely affect medical diagnosis and treatment processes. While traditional denoising methods are time-consuming, they are also not effective in removing speckle noise while retaining image details, leading to potential misdiagnosis. Therefore, there is a significant need to accurately and quickly denoise medical ultrasound images to enhance image quality. In this paper, we propose a flexible and lightweight deep learning denoising method for ultrasound images. Initially, we utilize a considerable number of natural images to train the convolutional neural network for acquiring a pre-trained denoising model. Next, we employ the plane-wave imaging technique to generate simulated noisy ultrasound images for further transfer learning of the pre-trained model. As a result, we obtain a non-blind, lightweight, fast, and accurate denoiser. Experimental results demonstrate the superiority of our proposed method in terms of denoising speed, flexibility, and effectiveness compared to conventional convolutional neural network denoisers for ultrasound images.

Keywords: Plane-wave Imaging · Noise Transfer Learning · Non-blind Ultrasound Image Denoising · Lightweight Model

---

M. Jiang and C. You—Contribute equally.

B. Sheng et al. (Eds.): CGI 2023, LNCS 14495, pp. 297–308, 2024.
https://doi.org/10.1007/978-3-031-50069-5_25

1 Introduction

Ultrasound imaging has become a widely used medical imaging modality due to its relative safety, affordability, and portability [1]. Unfortunately, hardware acquisition and ultrasound scattering can introduce severe noise into the signal, leading to corrupt textural structure and image details and impeding the clinician's accurate diagnosis and assessment. The difficulty of reducing the above-mentioned noise arises due to its tissue-dependent and non-uniform modeling. The generation of noise in medical ultrasound images is a complex phenomenon, attributable to the interaction of backscattered coherent waves from multiple fundamental scatterers with varying phases, resulting in random and constructive or destructive disturbances. This interference is labeled as speckle noise, a granular texture pattern that may potentially provide useful diagnostic information [2]. Speckle noise affects all coherent imaging systems, including medical ultrasound [3], and exhibits multiplicative behavior that is strongly associated with non-Gaussian statistics. Conventional filtering techniques are not suitable for addressing speckle noise due to their primary design to suppress additive noise. Although several advanced processing methods have been developed by researchers to eliminate or reduce speckle noise, they do not consider preserving important details such as edges and lines in the image [4, 5]. Consequently, eliminating speckle noise from medical ultra-sound images while preserving pertinent details remains a "classical challenge" for researchers.

Most current deep learning-based ultrasound denoising methods are constrained by the scarcity of training images and clean images. G. Sobhan, et al. [6] proposed a novel beamforming method based on deep learning that accurately maps pre-beamformed channel data to the output image by leveraging a sufficient number of ground-truth echogenicity maps obtained from the transformation of real photographic images. Their method successfully improved resolution and contrast of plane-wave imaging while preserving frame rate, addressed the scarceness of training and labeled data, and removed background speckle noise in ultrasound images. Nonetheless, their model did not employ the Dirac delta function as the point-spread function (PSF) for ultrasound image formation, thus only reducing background speckle noise without considering other interfering clutter embedded in the actual ultrasound images such as side lobes and grating lobes. All the existing learning methods have the challenge of obtain the ground truth of clean ultrasound image.

In stead of working on the imaging end, this paper presents a deep learning-based denoising model for ultrasound images as a post-processing step. We utilize synthetic noisy images to achieve precise control. The proposed approach is capable of efficiently eliminating various noises such as speckle noise, while preserving image details. Code is available at: https://github.com/daming876/image-denoise.

2 Related Work

2.1 Deep Learning Network Denoiser

The denoising methods can be divided into three categories: filter-based, model-based, and machine learning and deep learning algorithm. Dabov, Kostadin et al. proposed BM3D [7], which utilizes sparse representation in the transform domain, non-local image similarity, and a 3D filtering method based on block matching to achieve strong image denoising performance, and small mean squared error. Gu [8] used different weighting characteristics of the WNNM algorithm and image non-local self-similarity to obtain better model-based image denoising results. However, these traditional methods are difficult to deal with the non-smooth part of the image, and the texture information of the image can not be effectively preserved while denoising, generally the image is blurred after denoising. With the development of deep learning technology, many researchers put forward the method of using deep learning to denoise images. Sil et al. [9] proposed a method that utilizes convolutional neural network transfer learning for image classification and denoising. This method can accurately predict the noise model and is particularly effective for blind image denoising. Zhang et al. [10] introduced a method which is Residual Learning of Deep CNN for Image Denoising (DnCNN), which employs the residual algorithm for gradual improvement of CNN models. However, these methods tend to be limited in their effectiveness for specific noise levels, thus restricting their versatility. As a solution, Zhang Kai et al. developed an fast and flexible denoising network (FFDNet) [11] for denoising, based on DnCNN. The FFDNet method downsamples the input image and divides it into four sub-images, each sub-image acquiring an eigenvalue, followed by the addition of noise generated through the Additive White Gaussian Noise (AWGN) method. After CNN processing, upsampling is performed to regain the overall output image. The resulting image is denoised through the successful FFDNet method, which manifests improved denoising effects on images with varying noise levels.

2.2 Transfer Learning

The insufficiency of data sets is a prevalent issue faced by deep learning networks. Due to the sensitive nature of medical ultrasound images with respect to patient privacy, a similar lack of data sets is prevalent in this domain. Furthermore, even if abundant data sets were available, training a neural network from scratch would incur prohibitive costs. Consequently, most models aim to simplify the network to reduce data requirements. As a viable alternative, transfer learning can overcome these challenges effectively. In this paper, we adopt the definition of transfer learning by most researchers [12], which involves transferring pre-trained model parameters to enable new model training. Since most data or tasks are related in some way, transfer learning allows us to share the previously acquired model parameters with the new model, thereby accelerating and optimizing learning efficiency without the need to start from scratch [13].

3 Proposed Method

3.1 Plane-Wave Imaging Technique

In the clinical setting, acquiring a sizeable corpus of clear ultrasound images alongside noisy counterparts proves arduous. In addition, it is imperative to preserve the unaltered fine structure of the denoised image owing to the unique attributes of medical images. To tackle this predicament, we leverage the plane-wave imaging technique to simulate a vast number of noisy ultrasound images that align with clean natural images, thus constituting the training dataset. Plane-wave imaging improves imaging frame rates significantly by concurrently activating the entire aperture of the array, thereby generating images of the complete region in a single emission [14, 15]. To enhance the quality of plane-wave imaging, coherent plane wave compounding (CPWC) was proposed [16]. A uniform linear transducer array comprising N elements is used for transmission and reception. The received delayed echo signals from the aperture are delay-compensated based on their distances from the imaging point P (x_p, z_p). The delay-compensated signals are then coherently summed to create the output of a single plane wave imaging (PWI) as expressed by Eq. (1):

$$Y_{PWI}(p) = \sum_{i=0}^{N-1} \omega_i x_i(p) \tag{1}$$

where ω is the weighting factor of length N, and $x_i(p)$ is defined as a vector containing the RF data recorded by the i-th element, corresponding to each pixel P (x_p, z_p) in the imaging field. Assuming that the transmit beam is steered in M different angles θ_m, then the final output of CPWC imaging can be obtained by coherently summing the values obtained from each plane wave for the imaging point P (x_p, z_p), and can be defined as Eq. (2):

$$Y_{CPWCI}(p) = \frac{1}{M} \sum_{m=1}^{M} Y(p, \theta_m) \tag{2}$$

The collected backscattered ultrasound signal $x_i(p)$ in Eq. 1 can be expressed as the convolution of the tissue reflectivity function (TRF) and the point spread function (PSF) of the imaging system. The TRF represents the pixel information of the pristine natural image, it accounts for the position and size of the pixels and replaces the position and scattering intensity of the scatterers, respectively. Nevertheless, due to various assumptions of the ultrasound imaging system, the observed signal $x_i(p)$ can only signify an approximation of the real signal, more specifically, the collected ultrasonic signal consists the original signal as well as various noise and interference items, in which case the signal model in Eq. (1) can be modified into:

$$x_i(p) = o_i(p)m_i(p) + a_i(p) \tag{3}$$

where $m_i(p)$ and $a_i(p)$ represent the components of the multiplicative and additive noise respectively, and $o_i(p)$ and $x_i(p)$, the original and observed signal respectively.

Consequently, the evaluated ultrasound noise level can be expressed as the difference between the acquired signal and the real signal, it can be expressed by the Eq. 4:

$$N(p) = Y(p) - O(p) \tag{4}$$

where N(x, y), Y(x, y), and O(x, y) indicate the noisy image, the transferred ultrasound image, and the natural image, respectively.

3.2 Denoiser Analysis

We use FFDNet as our basic network which utilizes a flexible and efficient network architecture for image denoising. It can handle varying noise levels and spatially transformed noise by taking a controllable noise level map as input. The input clean image (IM_i) has a size of c × h × w. To improve processing speed, IM_i is sliced into c × h/2 × w/2 patches using a downsampling technique. The patches are grouped into different channels based on their colors, resulting in a total of 4 channels, each with a size of c × h/2 × w/2. . Consequently, the image pixels become 1/4 of their original size. In FFDNet, Additive White Gaussian Noise (AWGN) is used to emulate camera noise. AWGN follows the Gaussian distribution and is added to IM_i to produce a noisy image (NM_i).

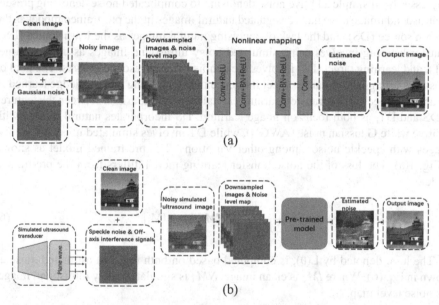

Fig. 1. (a) Architecture of Pre-trained Model for Noisy Natural Image Denoising, (b) Architecture of Deep Learning with Noise Transfer Learning for Simulated Noisy Ultrasound Image Denoising.

The different AWGN are generated according to different noise levels (σ) and combined with the four downsampled submaps to form a five-channel noisy image. The first layer comprises Conv+Relu, The intermediate layer assumes a convolution form, employing multiple Conv+BN+Relu operations. BN has the ability to enhance the convergence of the neural network model and improve the generalization of the model. The ultimate layer is Conv, which executes convolution using a filter of size n × f × f. The loss is determined as Eq. (5),

$$L(\theta) = \frac{1}{2m} \sum\nolimits_{i=1}^{m} \left\| F(NM_{i}, \sigma; \theta) - IM_{i} \right\|^2 \tag{5}$$

Adam is a first-order optimization algorithm that facilitates iterative updates to the weight of a neural network by utilizing training data. Specifically, when Adam is utilized to compute the minimum value of the loss, the loss gradually decreases during the training process at different epochs.

3.3 Noise Transfer Learning Model

Transfer learning entails transferring the trained parameters of a pre-existing model to aid in the training of a new model [17]. The pre-trained and newly trained models are affiliated in terms of the majority of the data or tasks. Specifically, the pre-trained model is trained using natural images that include additive noise, whereas the transfer learning model is trained using ultrasound images that encompass speckle noise, and other forms of clutter noise. The transfer learning technique utilized in this paper gradually progresses from simple additive noise denoising to complicated noise denoising present in ultrasound images. We have designated natural images in the pre-trained model as the domain source (DS), and the task of denoising natural images as the learn source (LS). Transfer learning involves using simulated noisy ultrasound images as domain target (DT), and learning target (LT) involves the denoising of ultrasound images. The goal of transfer learning is to enhance object inference in DT, drawing on knowledge learned in DS and LS. Specifically, transfer learning capitalizes on similarities between the features of DS and DT, as both focus on image learning. DS incorporates natural images with additive white Gaussian noise (AWGN), while DT involves simulated noisy ultrasound images with speckle noise, among other variations. The pre-trained model as shown in Fig. 1(a). The loss of the noise transfer learning model differs from the pre-trained model.

$$L\theta = \frac{1}{2m} \sum_{i=1}^{m} \|F(NM_i; \theta) - IM_i\|^2 \tag{6}$$

The loss, denoted by $L(\theta)$, is computed based on both real and estimated noise as shown in Eq. (6). Where IM_i is clean image, NM_i is simulated noisy ultrasound image, θ is noise level map.

3.4 Downsampled Images

In this study, for improving the execution efficiency of the model, we leverage a reversible down-sampling layer that shapes the input image into a series of smaller sub-images. Specifically, we set the down-sampling factor to 2, which substantially enhances speed without reducing modeling ability. The down-sampled sub-image is presented to the CNN for feature extraction, which consequently extends the receptive field. Finally, the image is restored by upsampling.

3.5 Noise Level Map and Model Without Noise Transfer Learning

To enable flexible adjustment of image denoising intensity, a noise level map can be employed to regulate the denoising level of the denoiser. In [18], the technique of adjusting the noise level map is applied to add noise to the image, which bears resemblance to the approach presented in this study. Figures 1 demonstrate the integration of the noise level map with the input image in a Convolutional Neural Network (CNN). The input image is segmented into patches, and the obtained noise level map is joined with the input image to create a new channel. In Fig. 1(a), σ represents the noise level, which is randomly selected from a uniform distribution. Different from the pre-trained model, in Fig. 1(b) actual noise is measured initially. The standard deviation (STD) of the noise is estimated using Eq. (7).

$$\sigma = \sqrt{\frac{\sum_{i=1}^{n} (x_i - \bar{x})^2}{n - 1}} \tag{7}$$

σ represents the noise level of an ultrasound image, where $\bar{x}$ denotes the image's average noise level and x_i represents the pixel value of the noisy image. As STD is a real number and cannot be applied to a batch of images, we formulate a batchsize noise level map by combining the noise across the batch of images. The degree of denoising and preservation of image details varies with different noise level map. A high σ value indicates a greater degree of denoising, but a lower retention of image details.

This paper proposes denoisers for transfer learning and non-transfer learning that incorporate controllable noise level maps to accommodate different noise levels in denoising images, thereby enhancing the flexibility of our denoising model. In Eq. (6), using noise = $NM_i - IM_i$, we can obtain the noise of each image in the training set, and then use Eq. (7), we obtain the STD of noise, use Eq. (6) to construct a loss, which can make our model flexible and controllable for non-blind denoising. For model without noise transfer learning, we use data set C to train CNN, σ value and loss in the same way as model with noise transfer learning.

4 Experimental Results

- **Dataset A**: The Waterloo Exploration Dataset (WED) [19] includes rich natural image information such as houses, cars, people, fruits, animals, etc. In order to facilitate the generation of simulated noisy ultrasound images and train model, we convert 4744 RGB natural images into gray.
- **Dataset B**: The Berkeley Segmentation Dataset (BSD400) [20] as validation dataset, it contains 400 grayscale images of size 180×180.
- **Dataset C**: 300 clean images which sourced from the WED and their corresponding simulated noisy ultrasound images as training dataset.
- **Dataset D**: The Berkeley Segmentation Dataset (BSD68) [21] as validation dataset, it contains 400 grayscale images of size 256×256.
- **Dataset E**: 50 breast ultrasound images for testing, obtained from the cooperative hospital (Table 1).

4.1 Obtaining Simulated Noisy Ultrasound Image

The natural images datasets A, B, C, and D are transferred to the ultrasound image domain using the Field II simulator [22, 23]. The datasets are simulated using a standard

Table 1. Datasets in this paper.

Dataset A	Dataset B	Dataset C	Dataset D	Dataset E
WED	BSD400	WED	BSD68	Breast ultrasound images
4744 images	400 images	300 images	68 images	50 images
RGB to gray	gray	RGB to gray	gray	gray
Not-fixed	180×180 (size)	Not-fixed	256×256 (size)	Not-fixed

L11-4v probe (Verasonics Inc., Redmond, WA). The probe settings as shown in Table 2, and the dataset used for model training was simulated using a 5.208 MHz transmission with a bandwidth of 77% and a sampling frequency of 30.4 MHz. Use dataset A, B, C, and D create 2-D distribution of scatterers whose depth is 10 cm based on the pixel information of the original image.

Table 2. Full parameters used in Field II simulator.

Parameter	Value	Parameter	Value
Center frequency f_c	7.6 MHz	Sampling frequency f_s	$4f_c$
Element width	0.27 mm	Element kerf	0.03 mm
Number of elements	128	Pitch	0.3
Fractional bandwidth	77%	Element height	5 mm
Speed of sound c	1540 m/s	Focal depth	18 mm

4.2 Experiments on Pre-trained Model and Transfer Learning Model

The pre-trained model needs to be obtained by training it on Dataset A and validating it on Dataset B. As per the assumptions made in references [24], the noise in the camera can be considered as AWGN. To avoid introducing visual artifacts caused by the tradeoff between noise reduction, noise level adjustment, and image detail preservation, we employ the orthogonal initialization method for convolution filters. The results in Fig. 2(c) demonstrate that the pre-trained model yields superior denoising efficacy in natural image AWGN at different change spaces. Specifically, Fig. 2(f) indicates that the pre-trained model's denoising efficacy for ultrasound images is general. Therefore, further noise transfer learning is necessary to enhance the pre-trained model's capacity for denoising ultrasound images. The subsequent procedure involves an experiment in noise transfer learning.

The simulated noisy ultrasound images corresponding to Dataset c are fed into the pre-training model to continue training and then fine-tune the model parameters. To achieve non-blind denoising and enhance the denoising performance for images with varying noise levels using the noise transfer learning model, we initially calculated the standard deviation of the noise to determine the noise level. Based on this, we constructed a noise level map containing the noise levels for a batch of images. The model was trained using simulated noisy ultrasound images and their corresponding noise level maps. Figure 2(h) shows that our noise transfer learning model achieved state-of-the-art performance in denoising ultrasound images, and exhibited strong ability in denoising images with varying noise levels.

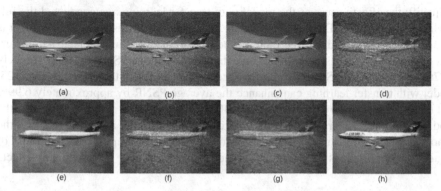

Fig. 2. Result of image denoising using different model. For natural image: (a) clean natural image, (b) AWGN noisy image, (c) denoising with Pre-trained Model. For simulated noisy ultrasound image: (d) simulated noisy ultrasound image, (e) denoising with CGAN, (f) denoising with Pre-trained Model, (g) denoising without transfer learning model, (h) denoising with transfer learning model. Denoising with transfer learning model achieves state-of-the-art.

Table 3. The results of PSNR、SSIM obtained from the other model for denoising simulated noisy ultrasound images. Pix2pixGAN denoising does not need Sigma adjustment.

Model	Sigma = 25		Sigma = 40		Sigma = 55	
	PSNR (dB)	SSIM	PSNR (dB)	SSIM	PSNR (dB)	SSIM
pix2pixGAN	23.51	0.7352	\	\	\	\
CNN Pre-trained model	21.93	0.7230	21.21	0.7115	19.61	0.6236

4.3 Experiments Without Transfer Learning and Other Model

We use the CNN model for image denoising is discussed in Sect. 3.2 which is non-transfer learning, then we use Dataset D for testing. Results as shown in Table 3, the PSNR and SSIM performance are not as impressive as those with noise transfer learning method, and as Fig. 2(g) illustrates, the model without transfer learning is less effective than the noise transfer learning model. Then, the experiment is compared with other denoising methods. In recent years, there are several studies on image denoising using pix2pix Generative Adversarial Network (pix2pixGAN) [25, 26]. For the pix2pixGAN, we take the simulated ultrasound image as the input image and the clean image as the limiting condition, the denoised image was compared with the clean image, leading a PSNR of 23.51 and SSIM of 0.7352, as shown in Table 3. The denoised image had distortion and contour distortion, as shown in Fig. 2(e).

4.4 Ablation Study

To justify the effectiveness of the model with transfer learning, we conducted the following experiments on Dataset D for testing. The detailed process of the experiment is described in Sect. 4.2 and 4.3. See Table 4, when the noise level (our denoising parameter) was 40, model with transfer learning can enhance the average PSNR by approximately 3.17% and the average SSIM by approximately 10.84%. When the noise level was 25, model with transfer learning can enhance the average PSNR by approximately 6.99% and the average SSIM by approximately 9.40%. Obviously, the denoising effect of the model with transfer learning has been improved. When Sigma is greater than 25, the denoised image is too smooth, causing serious problems of blurred edges and loss of detail, so when Sigma is 25, the proposed model can achieve the best denoising effect.

Table 4. The results of PSNR, SSIM obtained from the proposed model with and without transfer learning for denoising simulated noisy ultrasound images.

Model	Sigma = 25		Sigma = 40		Sigma = 55	
	PSNR (dB)	SSIM	PSNR (dB)	SSIM	PSNR (dB)	SSIM
Proposed model without transfer learning	23.15	0.8232	23.01	0.8035	20.15	0.6010
Proposed model with transfer learning	**24.77**	**0.9006**	**23.74**	**0.8906**	**20.88**	**0.6565**

4.5 Experiments on Real Ultrasound Images

Using dataset E, we fed real breast ultrasound images into pix2pixGAN and our noise transfer learning models. The denoising time of pix2pixGAN is 0.1572 s, the time of our proposed model is 0.1090 s, and the denoising time is reduced by 44%, As shown in Fig. 3, we found that non-transfer learning will distort the ultrasound image and cause the loss of the details of the ultrasound image when the same noise level is employed. It is evident that the implementation of transfer learning for ultrasound image denoising purposes is substantially more effective than non-transfer learning.

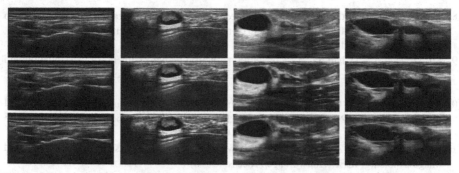

Fig. 3. From top to bottom: real breast ultrasound image, denoised image without transfer learning, denoised image with transfer learning.

5 Conclusion

This paper proposes a novel approach to denoise ultrasound images using a deep learning model, which incorporates a noise generation synthetic for fast and lightweight denoising. The model design and training involve the utilization of plane-wave imaging technique, CNN, transfer learning. However, using our proposed method to denoise the real ultrasound image, a small amount of speckle noise is still retained in the lesion area, and there is a slight distortion in the image. In the future, we will use the downstream task to verify the benefits from denoising, and invite clinicians to score images by observation, to verify the impact of the ultrasound image denoising model on clinical diagnosis.

Acknowledgment. This work was supported by Research Fund of Macao Polytechnic University (RP/FCA-05/2022), and Science and Technology Development Fund of Macao (0105/2022/A).

References

1. Quien, M., Saric, M.: Ultrasound imaging artifacts: how to recognize them and how to avoid them. Echocardiography **35**(9), 1388–1401 (2018)
2. Dainty, J.: Some statistical properties of random speckle patterns in coherent and partially coherent illumination. Optica Acta Int. J. Opt. **17**(10), 761–772 (1970)
3. Sudha, S., Suresh, G.R., Sukanesh, R.: Speckle noise reduction in ultrasound images by wavelet thresholding based on weighted variance. Int. J. Comput. Theory Eng. **1**(1), 7 (2009)
4. Duarte-Salazar, C.A., Castro-Ospina, A.E., Becerra, M.A., Delgado-Trejos, E.: Speckle noise reduction in ultrasound images for improving the metrological evaluation of biomedical applications: an overview. IEEE Access **8**, 15983–15999 (2020)
5. Geng, M., Meng, X., Yu, J., Zhu, L., Jin, L., Jiang, Z.: Content-noise complementary learning for medical image denoising. IEEE Trans. Med. Imaging **41**(2), 407–419 (2022)
6. Goudarzi, S., Rivaz, H.: Deep reconstruction of high-quality ultrasound images from raw plane-wave data: a simulation and in vivo study. Ultrasonics **125**, 106778 (2022)
7. Dabov, K., Foi, A., Katkovnik, V., Egiazarian, K.: Image denoising by sparse 3-D transform-domain collaborative filtering. IEEE Trans. Image Process. **16**(8), 2080–2095 (2007)

8. Gu, S., Zhang, L., Zuo, W., Feng, X.: Weighted nuclear norm minimization with application to image denoising. In: IEEE Conference on Computer Vision and Pattern Recognition (CVPR), pp. 2862–2869 (2014)

9. Sil, D., Dutta, A., Chandra, A.: Convolutional neural networks for noise classification and denoising of images. In: TENCON 2019 IEEE Region 10 Conference (TENCON). IEEE (2019)

10. Zhang, K., Zuo, W., Chen, Y., Meng, D., Zhang, L.: Beyond a Gaussian denoiser: residual learning of deep CNN for image denoising. IEEE Trans. Image Process. 26(7), 3142–3155 (2017)

11. Zhang, K., Zuo, W., Zhang, L.: FFDNet: toward a fast and flexible solution for CNN-based image denoising. IEEE Trans. Image Process. (2018)

12. Ribani, R., Marengoni, M.: A survey of transfer learning for convolutional neural networks. In: 2019 32nd SIBGRAPI Conference on Graphics, Patterns and Images Tutorials (SIBGRAPI-T), pp. 47–57. IEEE (2019)

13. Mishkin, D., Matas, J.: All you need is a good init. arXiv preprint:1511.06422 (2015)

14. Couture, O., Fink, M., Tanter, M.: Ultrasound contrast plane wave imaging. IEEE Trans. Ultrason. Ferroelectr. Freq. Control 59(12), 2676–2683 (2012)

15. Tanter, M., Fink, M.: Ultrafast imaging in biomedical ultrasound. IEEE Trans. Ultrason. Ferroelectr. Freq. Control 61(1), 102–119 (2014)

16. Montaldo, G., Tanter, M., Bercoff, J., Benech, N., Fink, M.: Coherent plane-wave compounding for very high frame rate ultrasonography and transient elastography. IEEE Trans. Ultrason. Ferroelectr. Freq. Control 56(3), 489–506 (2009)

17. Pan, S.J., Yang, Q.: A survey on transfer learning. IEEE Trans. Knowl. Data Eng. 22(10), 1345–1359 (2010)

18. Yao, H., Wang, S., Zhang, X., Qin, C., Wang, J.: Detecting image splicing based on noise level inconsistency. Multimedia Tools Appl. 76, 12457–12479 (2017)

19. Ma, K., et al.: Waterloo exploration database: new challenges for image quality assessment models. IEEE Trans. Image Process. 26(2), 1004–1016 (2016)

20. Martin, D., Fowlkes, C., Tal, D., Malik, J.: A database of human segmented natural images and its application to evaluating segmentation algorithms and measuring ecological statistics. In: International Conference on Computer Vision, pp. 416–423 (2001)

21. Roth, S., Black, M.J.: Fields of experts. Int. J. Comput. Vis. 82(2), 205–229 (2009). https://doi.org/10.1007/s11263-008-0197-6

22. Jensen, J.A., Svendsen, N.B.: Calculation of pressure fields from arbitrarily shaped, apodized, and excited ultrasound transducers. IEEE Trans. Ultrason. Ferroelectr. Freq. Control 39(2), 262–267 (1992)

23. Jensen, J.A.: FIELD: a program for simulating ultrasound systems. In: 10th Nordic-Baltic Conference on Biomedical Imaging, vol. 4, pp. 351–353 (1996)

24. Luisier, F., Blu, T., Unser, M.: Image denoising in mixed Poisson–Gaussian noise. IEEE Trans. Image Process. 20(3), 696–708 (2011)

25. Isola, P., Zhu, J.Y., Zhou, T.: Image-to-image translation with conditional adversarial networks. IEEE (2016)

26. Alsaiari, A., Rustagi, R., Alhakamy, A., Thomas, M.M., Forbes, A.G.: Image denoising using a generative adversarial network. In: IEEE 2nd International Conference on Information and Computer Technologies (ICICT), pp. 126–132 (2019)

Degradation-Aware Blind Face Restoration via High-Quality VQ Codebook

Yuzhou Sun, Sen Wang, Hao Li, Zhifeng Xie, Mengtian Li, and Youdong Ding[✉]

Shanghai University, Shanghai 200072, China
ydding@shu.edu.cn

Abstract. Blind face restoration, as a kind of face restoration method dealing with complex degradation, has been a challenging research hotspot recently. However, due to the influence of a variety of degradation in low-quality images, artifacts commonly exist in the low fidelity results of existing methods, resulting in a lack of natural and realistic texture details. In this paper, we propose a degradation-aware blind face restoration method based on a high-quality vector quantization (VQ) codebook to improve the degradation-aware capability and texture quality. The overall framework consists of Degradation-aware Module (DAM), Texture Refinement Module (TRM) and Global Restoration Module (GRM). DAM adopts the channel attention mechanism to adjust the weight of feature components in different channels, so that it has the ability to perceive complex degradation from redundant information. In TRM, continuous vectors are quantized and replaced with high-quality discretized vectors in the VQ codebook to add texture details. GRM adopts the reverse diffusion process of the pre-trained diffusion model to restore the image globally. Experiments show that our method outperforms state-of-the-art methods on synthetic and real-world datasets.

Keywords: Blind face restoration · Degradation-aware · VQ codebook · Image restoration

1 Introduction

In the real world, face images often suffer from degradation problems such as downsampling, blur, noise and compression. Blind face restoration aims to remove such complex degradation, and restore natural and realistic faces. In real-world scenarios, the challenge of this task is that it is difficult to completely remove various types of degradation and restore facial texture details.

In recent years, existing blind face restoration methods usually rely on different kinds of facial priors such as geometric priors [1,8], generative priors [18,24,27] and reference priors [5,10,19,26]. Geometric priors are directly estimated from degraded images, so it is difficult to extract high-quality texture features. The generation quality of methods based on generative priors depends on whether the degraded face can be accurately projected to the required latent code, and artifacts are likely to occur. Methods based on the reference priors have great advantages in generating texture details, but it also brings the problem that restored facial features are inconsistent with the ground-truth.

To address the above-mentioned problems, we propose a new blind face restoration method based on high-quality VQ codebook. As shown in Fig. 1, the framework consists of three main components: Degradation-aware Module (DAM), Texture Refinement Module (TRM) and Global Restoration Module (GRM). Our method centers on the VQ codebook comprising high-quality facial features in TRM to address the challenge of blurry facial details. Firstly, DAM adjusts the weight of deep features in different channels with the Channel Attention Degradation-aware Block (CADAB) to remove perceived degradation, and then a smooth image that only contains critical facial information is generated. Secondly, to further refine the facial texture details, TRM quantizes the smooth image into high-quality discrete vectors with VQ codebook [4]. When discrete vectors are decoded as high-quality texture features, the smooth facial features are also obtained after the smooth image is fed into a convolution. The proposed Multi-scale Feature Fusion Block (MSFFB) then integrates them to restore the pseudo high-quality image. Finally, GRM leverages the transition distribution [25] to make the data distribution of pseudo high-quality images approximate to the ground-truth, thereby further realizing the degradation elimination of the whole image. Moreover, our method is evaluated on the synthetic and real-world datasets, and extensive experiments demonstrate the effectiveness of our method for degradation awareness and texture refinement.

In summary, our contributions are as follows:

(1) We propose a degradation-aware blind face restoration method based on high-quality VQ codebook, which can restore face images with fine texture details under severe degradation conditions.
(2) The design of the Channel Attention Degradation-aware Block in DAM enables the network to perceive complex degradation. By adjusting the weight of deep features with channel attention, the adaptive suppression of degradation is achieved and the facial features are better preserved.
(3) We construct TRM to combine the high-quality face information in the VQ codebook with the smooth face information, which effectively improves the texture quality of the restored image.

2   Related Work

2.1   Blind Face Restoration

Traditional blind face restoration methods [1,8] mainly use geometric priors, and are more inclined to use the limited information of the low-quality image itself. However, it is difficult to remove complex degradation only by using the limited information. Recently, some methods [21,22] have attempted to strengthen

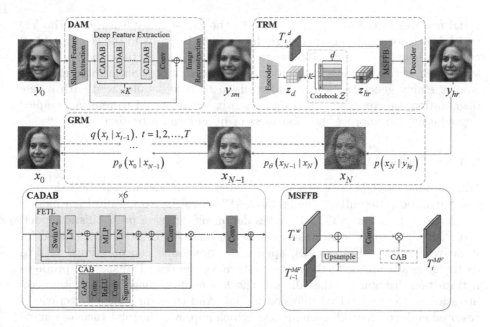

Fig. 1. Overview of our method. Our method consists of three modules: Degradation-aware Module (Sect. 3.2), Texture Refinement Module (Sect. 3.3) and Global Restoration Module (Sect. 3.4).

feature representation utilizing frequency information and contextual information. The methods based on generative priors [18,24,27] and reference priors [5,10,19,26] have achieved excellent performance in terms of clarity and fidelity. To achieve coarse-to-fine restoration, some methods [10,11,19] refer to the most similar facial features from the dictionary, and others [3,5,26] try to refer to the discretized feature libraries. GPEN [24] and GFP-GAN [18] leverage generative priors encapsulated in the pre-trained generative adversarial net to generate high-quality images. However, the size of the dataset used in pre-training limits the diversity and richness of facial textures. Although some methods [7,9,20] have been proposed to solve problems such as colorization and deblurring, they still cannot completely eliminate complex degradation. In terms of such problems, our method can effectively solve the artifact problem under severe degradation conditions and improve the quality of generated facial features.

2.2 Vector Quantization Codebook

The vector quantized variational autoencoder (VQVAE) model [17] combines the idea of vector quantization to learn a discrete codebook. In VQVAE2 [14], large-scale image generation is completed by the multi-layer quantized representation. VQGAN [4] achieves megapixel-level image generation, and the patch-based discriminator used in it introduces adversarial loss to improve the perceptual quality of the codebook. However, existing methods [5,26] only directly match the facial features in the low-quality image to the high-quality features in the VQ codebook, ignoring the effect of degradation, which results in the generated features not being consistent with the ground-truth. Besides, these methods often suffer from artifacts under severe degradation conditions. Since these methods cannot stably generate natural and realistic texture details faced with severe degradation, we construct TRM and place it behind DAM to remove complex degradation and improve the robustness of blind face restoration.

2.3 Diffusion Model

Diffusion model (DM) [16] is a kind of generative model with a solid theoretical foundation. Recently, some methods [13,15,25] try to use diffusion models for image restoration. SR3 [15] applies denoising diffusion probabilistic models (DDPM) [6] to conditional image generation, and the U-Net model is used for iterative denoising. RePaint [13] applies the pre-trained unconditional DDPM as the generative prior to the image restoration process. DifFace [25] proposes a transition distribution that diffuses the low-quality image to the intermediate state of the pre-trained diffusion model. And then the image is iteratively restored in the reverse diffusion process, which improves the robustness of removing degradation. In general, diffusion models can provide powerful prior knowledge for image generation. However, fine texture details are still absent in the results. To take full advantage of the powerful generative capability of the diffusion model, we combine it with the VQ codebook, and leverage high-quality facial features in the codebook to make up for the lack of texture details.

3   Method

3.1   Overview

The specific blind face restoration process is shown in Fig. 1. First, the original low-quality image y_0 is input to DAM, and the smooth result y_{sm} without degradation information is obtained. TRM then uses the discretized feature vectors in the pre-trained VQ codebook to add fine texture details to y_{sm}, and then a pseudo high-quality result y'_{hr} is achieved. Finally, y'_{hr} is diffused to the intermediate state $x_N \sim P\left(x_N | y'_{hr}\right)$ of the diffusion model, and the high-quality image x_0 is obtained by iterative restoration from x_N through the reverse diffusion process [25], which ensures the rationality of the global face structure and further optimizes the facial details in y'_{hr}.

3.2   Degradation-Aware Module

When faced with severely degraded images, existing models are difficult to completely remove all kinds of degradation because of the lack of degradation-aware ability. Inspired by SwinTransformer [12], we construct DAM to perceive various types of degradation.

DAM is mainly divided into three stages: shallow feature extraction, deep feature extraction and image reconstruction. In the shallow feature extraction stage, the low-quality face image $y_0 \in \mathbb{R}^{C \times H \times W}$ (C, H and W represent the channel number, height and width of the image respectively) is input into a 3×3 convolution to extract the shallow feature $F_{sh} \in \mathbb{R}^{C \times H \times W}$. Then, in the deep feature extraction stage, we design a Channel Attention Degradation-aware Block (CADAB) inspired by RSTCA [23] and Swin2SR [2]. Each CADAB consists of six improved Feature Enhancement Transformer Layers (FETL), six Channel Attention Blocks (CAB), a 3×3 convolution and a residual connection. Fusion convolution and residual connection are added to FETL, which realizes feature complementarity across layers. For each FETL, CAB is composed of adaptive average pooling, downsampling, upsampling and sigmoid function. The output feature X_ℓ of the ℓ-th FETL can be expressed as:

$$X_\ell' = LN\left(SwinV2\left(X_{\ell-1}\right)\right) + X_{\ell-1}, \tag{1}$$

$$X_\ell = Fuse\left(\left[LN\left(MLP\left(X_\ell'\right)\right) + X_\ell'\right] + X_{\ell-1}\right), \tag{2}$$

where $SwinV2$ represents SwinV2 Attention, LN represents Layer Norm, MLP represents multilayer perceptron, and $Fuse$ represents fusion convolution. Then, channel statistics generated by CAB are multiplied with the output of the FETL. After the feature components are reweighted in different channels, the 3×3 convolutional layer and residual connection are used to obtain the intermediate feature F_i of the i-th CADAB. Deep feature F_{dp} can be obtained by K CADABs. Finally, in the image reconstruction stage, shallow features and deep features are element-wise summed, and then input into a 3×3 convolution to reconstruct the smooth image y_{sm}.

3.3 Texture Refinement Module

Limited information extracted only from low-quality images often lacks texture features, so we construct TRM based on the VQ codebook, which is meticulously trained on the high-definition face dataset FFHQ, encompassing high-quality facial features, [4] to generate pseudo high-quality face images y_{hr}. Leveraging the fine facial details available in the VQ codebook, facilitates further refinement of the face, distinguishing our approach from restoring natural images. To achieve texture refinement under the premise of consistent fidelity, we further design the Multi-scale Feature Fusion Block (MSFFB). It fuses different scales of smooth facial features and high-quality texture features via residual connections.

TRM consists of encoder, dual-branching decoder and high-quality VQ codebook $\mathcal{Z} = \{z_k\}_{k=1}^{K} \in \mathbb{R}^{K \times d}$ (K and d respectively represent the size and dimension of the codebook). First, the smooth image $y_{sm} \in \mathbb{R}^{C \times H \times W}$ is input into the encoder $E\left(\cdot\right)$ to obtain a continuous vector sequence $z_d = E\left(y_{sm}\right)$. Then, it is mapped to a discrete vector space by the following mapping rules, and the vector quantized representation z_{hr} containing only high-quality textures can be obtained:

$$z_{hr} = q\left(z_d\right) := \left(\underset{z_k \in Z}{\arg\min} \|z_{ij} - z_k\|\right) \in \mathbb{R}^{c_z \times h \times w}, \tag{3}$$

where $q(\cdot)$ denotes quantification of elements, z_{ij} denotes continuous vectors, z_k denotes discrete vectors, and c_z denotes the dimensions of latent vectors. To update the codebook during training, the vector quantization loss function $\mathcal{L}_{vq}$ in Eq. (7) is used. Then, z_{hr} is decoded by the texture branch decoder [5] to obtain the texture features $T^{hr} = \{T_i^{hr}\}$. Meanwhile, y_{sm} is fed into a 3×3 convolution and downsampled to obtain the smooth features $T^d = \{T_i^d\}$. To make T_i^{hr} consistent with the original face structure, according to the texture warping module TWM in [5], the warped feature T_i^w can be obtained. MSFFB consists of upsampling, fusion convolution and channel attention, which effectively promotes the fusion of texture feature T^{hr} and smooth facial feature T^d. The output fusion feature T_i^{MF} of layer i in it can be expressed as follows:

$$T_i^{MF} = Fuse\left(Cat\left[T_i^w, Up\left(T_{i-1}^{MF}\right)\right]\right) \otimes CA\left(T_{i-1}^{MF}\right), i = 1, 2, 3, \qquad (4)$$

where Up represents upsampling, Cat represents concat, $\otimes$ represents element-wise product, and CA represents the Channel Attention Block. The output feature T_{i-1}^{MF} of layer $i-1$ in MSFFB is concated with the warped feature T_i^w of layer i after being upsampled. Smooth facial features contained in T_{i-1}^{MF} and high-quality texture features contained in T_i^w are fully fused by fusion convolution. Finally, T^{MF} and T^{hr} are element-wise summed, and then are sequentially input to group normalization layer, SiLU activation function and 3×3 convolution to generate a pseudo high-quality image y_{hr}' with realistic details.

3.4   Global Restoration Module

Although DAM preliminarily removes part of degradation in the low-quality image y_0, the degradation that cannot be approximated by the neural network is still retained in y_{hr}'. To solve such problem, inspired by the image restoration method based on diffusion models [25], we construct GRM to restore y_{hr}' globally.

As shown in Fig. 1, x_0 is the real high-quality image corresponding to the low-quality image y_0. For the discrete time step T, it is iteratively added noise according to the predefined noise variance table $\beta = \{\beta_t\}_{t=1}^T$:

$$q(x_N|x_0) = \mathcal{N}\left(x_N; \sqrt{\alpha_N}x_0, (1 - \alpha_N)I\right), \qquad (5)$$

where $\alpha_N = \prod_{l=1}^N (1 - \beta_l)$, $x_N \sim q(x_N|x_0)$ represents the diffusion state of x_0 at time step $N \in [1, T]$. By constructing the transition distribution $p\left(x_N|y_{hr}'\right)$ similar to $q(x_N|x_0)$, the pseudo high-quality image y_{hr}' can also be diffused to the intermediate state x_N at time step N:

$$x_N = \sqrt{\alpha_N}y_{hr}' + \sqrt{1 - \alpha_N}\zeta = \sqrt{\alpha_N}x_0 - \sqrt{\alpha_N}e + \sqrt{1 - \alpha_N}\zeta, \qquad (6)$$

where $e = x_0 - y_{hr}'$ represents the predicted error, and $\zeta \sim \mathcal{N}(\zeta|0, I)$ represents the variable that obeys the standard normal distribution. The principle of GRM is that the factor $\sqrt{\alpha_N} < 1$ in Eq. (6) reduces the predicted error e between y_{hr}' and x_0. Therefore, the removed degradation is no longer limited to the fixed degradation model used during training, but is the actual degradation involved in the whole image. In the end, x_N is iteratively restored by the reverse diffusion process $p_\theta(x_{N-1}|x_N)$, and the high-quality image similar to x_0 is obtained.

3.5 Optimization Objectives

To learn a high-quality VQ codebook, the quantization loss $\mathcal{L}_{vq}$ [4] is used:

$$\mathcal{L}_{vq} = \|I_{HQ} - I_{RQ}\|_1 + \|sg[E(I_{HQ}) - z_q]\|_2^2 + \beta\|sg[z_q] - E(I_{HQ})\|_2^2, \quad (7)$$

where $\|I_{HQ} - I_{RQ}\|_1$ is the pixel reconstruction loss, I_{RQ} is the reconstructed image, I_{HQ} is the real high-quality image, $sg[\cdot]$ represents stop gradient operation, $\beta\|sg[z_q] - E(I_{HQ})\|_2^2$ is the commitment loss [17].

Pixel reconstruction loss $\mathcal{L}_{pix}$ defined in Eq. (7) is used to train DAM.

As for TRM, the code alignment loss $\mathcal{L}_{code}$ is used to measure the distance between z_d and z_{hr} (z_d and z_{hr} are defined in Sect. 3.3):

$$\mathcal{L}_{code} = \|z_d - z_{hr}\|_2^2. \quad (8)$$

Perceptual loss $\mathcal{L}_{per}$ is as follows:

$$\mathcal{L}_{per} = \gamma\|Gram(\phi(I_{RQ})) - Gram(\phi(I_{HQ}))\|_1 + \|\phi(I_{RQ}) - \phi(I_{HQ})\|_1, \quad (9)$$

where ϕ represents the VGG-16 network, and $Gram$ represents the Gram matrix. The adversarial loss $\mathcal{L}_{adv}^{global}$ and $\mathcal{L}_{adv}^{local}$ are respectively expressed as follows:

$$\mathcal{L}_{adv}^{global} = -\mathbb{E}_{I_{RQ}}[softplus(D_g(I_{RQ}))], \quad (10)$$

$$\mathcal{L}_{adv}^{local} = \mathbb{E}_{I_{RQ}}[\log D_l(I_{HQ}) + \log(1 - D_l(I_{HQ}))], \quad (11)$$

where D_g and D_l respectively represent the global and local discriminator. The total loss of TRM [5] is as follows:

$$\mathcal{L}_{total} = \lambda_1\mathcal{L}_{pix} + \lambda_2\mathcal{L}_{code} + \lambda_3\mathcal{L}_{per} + \lambda_4\mathcal{L}_{adv}^{global} + \lambda_5\mathcal{L}_{adv}^{local}, \quad (12)$$

where $\lambda_1, \lambda_2, \lambda_3, \lambda_4, \lambda_5$ are scare factors of $\mathcal{L}_{pix}, \mathcal{L}_{code}, \mathcal{L}_{per}, \mathcal{L}_{adv}^{global}$ and $\mathcal{L}_{adv}^{local}$.

GRM is trained by establishing the Kullback-Leibler (KL) divergence [25] between the transition distribution $p\left(x_N|y_{hr}'\right)$ and the target distribution $q(x_N|x_0)$.

4 Experiments

4.1 Implementation Details

The proposed three modules are trained one-by-one, and $2\times$RTX-3090ti GPUs are used. AdamW optimizer is used in DAM and GRM. β_1 and β_2 are 0.9 and 0.999 respectively, and the learning rate is 0.0001. DAM takes about 3000k

Table 1. Quantitative results on CelebA-Test dataset. Bold and underlined indicate best and second best performance.

Method	PSNR	SSIM	FID	LPIPS	NIQE
DFDNet	21.067	0.593	83.490	0.489	5.680
GPEN	**21.372**	0.603	71.611	0.448	6.247
GFP-GAN	21.272	0.594	74.715	0.418	6.197
VQFR	20.981	0.601	24.077	0.342	4.759
DifFace	21.080	0.616	23.739	0.363	5.094
Ours	21.175	**0.619**	**18.135**	**0.337**	**4.551**

Table 2. Quantitative results on real-world datasets in terms of FID. Bold and underlined indicate best and second best performance.

Method	LFW-Test	CelebChild-Test	WebPhoto-Test
DFDNet	100.692	73.440	111.547
GPEN	85.321	53.987	**107.611**
GFP-GAN	100.159	47.978	119.496
VQFR	82.984	50.323	112.127
DifFace	84.845	46.022	110.338
Ours	**80.902**	**44.090**	109.771

iterations, and GRM takes about 800k iterations. The VQ codebook is trained with Adam optimizer. β_1 and β_2 are respectively 0.9 and 0.96. It takes around 800k iterations, and the learning rate is 0.0001. TRM is trained with Adam optimizer. When training the encoder, β_1 and β_2 are 0.9 and 0.96 respectively and the learning rate is 0.0001. When training the decoder, β_1 and β_2 are 0.5 and 0.9 respectively and the learning rate is 0.00002. It takes around 500k iterations. β_1 governs the decay rate of the gradient's first moment estimate, while β_2 controls the decay rate of the gradient's second moment estimate. Due to the significant noise in our training dataset, we increase the values of β_1 and β_2 to enhance the smoothness of the historical gradients.

4.2 Datasets and Metrics

Datasets. Our training dataset is based on the FFHQ dataset. High-quality images I_h are input to the degradation model $I_d = \left\{ [(I_h * k_l) \downarrow_s + n_\sigma]_{JPEG_q} \right\} \uparrow_s$ [18] to synthesize low-quality images I_d. Our parameter settings are consistent with DifFace [25]. Our testing dataset is based on one synthetic dataset CelebA-Test and three real-world datasets LFW-Test, CelebChild-Test, WebPhoto-Test [5]. CelebA-Test is processed by the degradation model above. The kernel width l, the scale of sampling s, the standard deviation σ and the quality factor q are sampled from [0.1, 18], [0.8, 36], [0, 25], and [20, 120] respectively.

Evaluation Metrics. Two pixel metrics: PSNR, SSIM, one perceptual metric: LPIPS and two no-reference metrics: FID, NIQE are used to evaluate restored images. However, PSNR and SSIM cannot reflect the texture quality of images, so we adopt FID, LPIPS and NIQE to measure the quality of restored images. Since real images corresponding to the CelebA-Test are accessible, FID is calculated between restored images and real images. As for the real-world datasets, FID is calculated based on the FFHQ dataset.

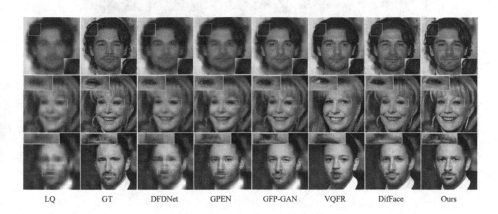

LQ   GT   DFDNet   GPEN   GFP-GAN   VQFR   DifFace   Ours

Fig. 2. Qualitative results of facial details

4.3   Comparison with State-of-the-Art Methods

Quantitative Evaluation. The comparison results on CelebA-Test are shown in Table 1. It can be seen that our method is superior to the five compared methods in terms of SSIM, FID, LPIPS, and NIQE. Compared with DifFace [25], FID decreases by 5.604. Compared with VQFR [5], our method reduces LPIPS by 0.005 and NIQE by 0.208. The results of FID on real-world datasets are shown in Table 2. It can be seen that our method is superior to existing methods and second only to GPEN [24] on the Celeb Child-Test dataset. While compared with GPEN [24], our results have better texture quality.

Qualitative Evaluation. The visual results of the six methods are shown in Fig. 2. It can be observed that DFDNet [10] cannot restore the texture features such as hair and beard, and facial details of GPEN [24] and GFP-GAN [18] are very blurred. The texture details of VQFR [5] lack realism, since the hair cannot appear in a natural state. DifFace [25] cannot restore facial details as fine as VQFR [5]. Compared with them, our method can restore a face image faithful to the ground-truth and have fine texture details under severe degradation conditions. It can be clearly seen that the hair in our results is more natural and realistic, the wrinkle lines are more complex, and the beard is clearer.

4.4   Ablation Study

To analyze the effectiveness of our method, this section conducts ablation study on the CelebA-Test dataset. Since the baseline method has proved the effectiveness of the Global Restoration Module (GRM), it does not need to be compared separately in the ablation study.

LQ   w/o both   w/o TRM   w/o DAM   Ours

Fig. 3. Ablation study on effects of DAM and TRM

Table 3. Ablation study on CelebA-Test dataset. Bold and underlined indicate best and second best performance.

SwinIR	DAM	VQFR	TRM	FID	LPIPS	NIQE
✓				23.739	0.363	5.094
	✓			22.164	0.353	5.100
✓		✓		18.216	0.345	4.606
✓			✓	<u>18.148</u>	0.344	4.573
	✓	✓		18.150	<u>0.339</u>	<u>4.557</u>
	✓		✓	**18.135**	**0.337**	**4.551**

Visual Comparisons. As shown in Fig. 3, obvious artifacts can be observed in the results of the baseline method. When only DAM is included in our model, the artifact problem can be effectively resolved. This illustrates that DAM plays an important role in the awareness of degradation. In terms of texture details, when only TRM is adopted, facial components can be represented more clearly. This shows that TRM can refine blurred facial components with high-quality facial features in VQ codebook. By taking full advantage of both DAM and TRM, face images with natural and realistic textures can be restored.

Quantitative Comparisons. In Table 3, we add CADAB on the basis of SwinIR [12] to construct DAM. When only DAM is added, FID and LPIPS are reduced by 1.575 and 0.01 respectively. MSFFB is added to construct TRM on the basis of VQFR [5]. Comparative analysis against a baseline where VQFR [5] is directly incorporated reveals that our constructed TRM achieves notable reductions in all evaluation indicators. Finally, adding both DAM and TRM to the baseline method, FID is reduced by 5.604, LPIPS is reduced by 0.026, and NIQE is reduced by 0.543. Results show that both DAM and TRM can effectively improve the texture quality and the fidelity of the image.

5   Conclusion

We propose a degradation-aware blind face restoration method based on the high-quality VQ codebook. Under severe degradation conditions, Degradation-aware Module realizes degradation awareness and effectively suppresses the influence of degradation. Texture Refinement Module makes full use of the high-quality facial features in the VQ codebook to add more texture details. Global Restoration Module reduces the global error. However, our method also has certain limitations. 1) Since the three modules need to be trained separately, training takes a long time. 2) Faced with slight degradation, our method cannot fully exploit the advantages of Degradation-aware Module. Therefore, in future work, we can try to build an end-to-end network that can simultaneously perform the degradation-aware task and the texture refinement task.

References

1. Chen, C., Li, X., Yang, L., Lin, X., Zhang, L., Wong, K.Y.K.: Progressive semantic-aware style transformation for blind face restoration. In: Proceedings of the IEEE/CVF Conference on Computer Vision and Pattern Recognition, pp. 11896–11905 (2021)
2. Conde, M.V., Choi, U.J., Burchi, M., Timofte, R.: Swin2sr: swinv2 transformer for compressed image super-resolution and restoration. In: Karlinsky, L., Michaeli, T., Nishino, K. (eds.) ECCV 2022. LNCS, vol. 13802, pp. 669–687. Springer, Cham (2022). https://doi.org/10.1007/978-3-031-25063-7_42
3. Ding, H., Wang, S., Xie, Z., Li, M., Ma, L.: A fine-grained vision and language representation framework with graph-based fashion semantic knowledge. Comput. Graphics (2023)
4. Esser, P., Rombach, R., Ommer, B.: Taming transformers for high-resolution image synthesis. In: Proceedings of the IEEE/CVF Conference on Computer Vision and Pattern Recognition, pp. 12873–12883 (2021)
5. Gu, Y., et al.: VQFR: blind face restoration with vector-quantized dictionary and parallel decoder. In: Avidan, S., Brostow, G., Cissé, M., Farinella, G.M., Hassner, T. (eds.) ECCV 2022. LNCS, vol. 13678, pp. 126–143. Springer, Cham (2022). https://doi.org/10.1007/978-3-031-19797-0_8
6. Ho, J., Jain, A., Abbeel, P.: Denoising diffusion probabilistic models. Adv. Neural. Inf. Process. Syst. **33**, 6840–6851 (2020)

7. Jung, M.: Correction: saturation-value based higher-order regularization for color image restoration. Multidimension. Syst. Signal Process. **34**(2), 395–395 (2023)
8. Kouno, M., Nakae, K., Oba, S., Ishii, S.: Microscopic image restoration based on tensor factorization of rotated patches. Artif. Life Robot. **17**, 417–425 (2013)
9. Li, H., Sheng, B., Li, P., Ali, R., Chen, C.P.: Globally and locally semantic colorization via exemplar-based broad-GAN. IEEE Trans. Image Process. **30**, 8526–8539 (2021)
10. Li, X., Chen, C., Zhou, S., Lin, X., Zuo, W., Zhang, L.: Blind face restoration via deep multi-scale component dictionaries. In: Vedaldi, A., Bischof, H., Brox, T., Frahm, J.-M. (eds.) ECCV 2020. LNCS, vol. 12354, pp. 399–415. Springer, Cham (2020). https://doi.org/10.1007/978-3-030-58545-7_23
11. Li, X., Zhang, S., Zhou, S., Zhang, L., Zuo, W.: Learning dual memory dictionaries for blind face restoration. IEEE Trans. Pattern Anal. Mach. Intell. **45**(5), 5904–5917 (2023). https://doi.org/10.1109/TPAMI.2022.3215251
12. Liang, J., Cao, J., Sun, G., Zhang, K., Van Gool, L., Timofte, R.: SwinIR: image restoration using swin transformer. In: Proceedings of the IEEE/CVF International Conference on Computer Vision, pp. 1833–1844 (2021)
13. Lugmayr, A., Danelljan, M., Romero, A., Yu, F., Timofte, R., Van Gool, L.: Repaint: inpainting using denoising diffusion probabilistic models. In: Proceedings of the IEEE/CVF Conference on Computer Vision and Pattern Recognition, pp. 11461–11471 (2022)
14. Razavi, A., van den Oord, A., Vinyals, O.: Generating diverse high-fidelity images with VQ-VAE-2. In: Advances in Neural Information Processing Systems 32: Annual Conference on Neural Information Processing Systems 2019, NeurIPS 2019, December 8–14, 2019, Vancouver, BC, Canada, pp. 14837–14847 (2019)
15. Saharia, C., Ho, J., Chan, W., Salimans, T., Fleet, D.J., Norouzi, M.: Image super-resolution via iterative refinement. IEEE Trans. Pattern Anal. Mach. Intell. **45**(4), 4713–4726 (2023). https://doi.org/10.1109/TPAMI.2022.3204461
16. Sohl-Dickstein, J., Weiss, E., Maheswaranathan, N., Ganguli, S.: Deep unsupervised learning using nonequilibrium thermodynamics. In: International Conference on Machine Learning, pp. 2256–2265. PMLR (2015)
17. Van Den Oord, A., Vinyals, O., et al.: Neural discrete representation learning. Advances in Neural Information Processing Systems, vol. 30 (2017)
18. Wang, X., Li, Y., Zhang, H., Shan, Y.: Towards real-world blind face restoration with generative facial prior. In: Proceedings of the IEEE/CVF Conference on Computer Vision and Pattern Recognition, pp. 9168–9178 (2021)
19. Wang, Z., Zhang, J., Chen, R., Wang, W., Luo, P.: Restoreformer: high-quality blind face restoration from undegraded key-value pairs. In: Proceedings of the IEEE/CVF Conference on Computer Vision and Pattern Recognition, pp. 17512–17521 (2022)
20. Wen, Y., et al.: Structure-aware motion deblurring using multi-adversarial optimized cyclegan. IEEE Trans. Image Process. **30**, 6142–6155 (2021)
21. Xie, Z., et al.: Boosting night-time scene parsing with learnable frequency. IEEE Trans. Image Process. **32**, 2386–2398 (2023)
22. Xie, Z., Zhang, W., Sheng, B., Li, P., Chen, C.P.: BAGFN: broad attentive graph fusion network for high-order feature interactions. IEEE Trans. Neural Networks Learn. Syst. (2021)
23. Xing, W., Egiazarian, K.: Residual swin transformer channel attention network for image demosaicing. In: 2022 10th European Workshop on Visual Information Processing (EUVIP), pp. 1–6. IEEE (2022)

24. Yang, T., Ren, P., Xie, X., Zhang, L.: Gan prior embedded network for blind face restoration in the wild. In: Proceedings of the IEEE/CVF Conference on Computer Vision and Pattern Recognition, pp. 672–681 (2021)
25. Yue, Z., Loy, C.C.: Difface: blind face restoration with diffused error contraction. arXiv preprint arXiv:2212.06512 (2022)
26. Zhou, S., Chan, K., Li, C., Loy, C.C.: Towards robust blind face restoration with codebook lookup transformer. Adv. Neural. Inf. Process. Syst. **35**, 30599–30611 (2022)
27. Zhu, F., et al.: Blind face restoration via integrating face shape and generative priors. In: Proceedings of the IEEE/CVF Conference on Computer Vision and Pattern Recognition, pp. 7662–7671 (2022)

Seamless Image Editing for Perceptual Size Restoration Based on Seam Carving

Naohiko Ishikawa[1,2], Zhenyang Zhu[1], Jong-nam Kim[2], Wan-Young Chung[2],
Kentaro Go[1], and Xiaoyang Mao[1(✉)]

[1] University of Yamanashi, 4-3-11, Kofu, Yamanashi 400-8511, Japan
{g22tk004,zzhu,go,mao}@yamanashi.ac.jp
[2] Pukyong National University, 45, Yongso-ro Nam-gu, Busan, Republic of Korea
wychung@pknu.ac.kr

Abstract. Thing of interest (ToI) in a photograph may be perceived as smaller than being perceived from the real scene due to the discrepancy between the imaging principles in the camera and human perception. When using existing image resizing approaches to enlarge the ToI in the input image, the resulting image may have problems, such as loss of distance sense, composition collapse, failure to preserve salient object shapes, etc. In this study, we propose a ToI resizing method based on seam carving method. The proposed method adopts an energy function, which takes image composition preservation into consideration. Furthermore, to prevent salient objects from being edited, the state-of-the-art deep learning model for salient object detection (SOD) has been adopted in the proposed method. To confirm the performance of the proposed method, a subjective evaluation experiment was conducted in this study. The experimental result shows that the effectiveness of the proposed method in terms of the preservation of perceptual size and perceptual distance of the ToI.

Keywords: Thing of interest · Perceptual size · Seam carving · Compositional energy · Salient object energy

1 Introduction

Standing in front of grand natural object amid landscape, one may be touched by its magnificence and tend to take a photo to commemorate. However, people are usually disappointed when they find that the object, such as Mt. Fuji, in other words, thing of interest (ToI), in the photograph is much smaller than that being perceived from the original one in the real scene. This situation is caused by the discrepancy between imaging principles of camera and human perception. Photographs are rendered following the principle of perspective projection, while human's perception is more complex, and psychological factors may also affect perceptual size of ToI. Figure 1 depicts a situation that a user took a photo of Mt. Fuji. Figure 1(a) shows the image captured by camera. Noticing that the Mt. Fuji in Fig. 1(a) seems too small, the user may manually zoom in the photo, i.e., enlarging the photo centering on ToI (Fig. 1(b)); despite the enlarged ToI, features distributed in boundaries of the original photo, especially those in front of the user, become invisible, which may collapse the shooting contents intended by the user, for example, the bottom part of the tower in Fig. 1(a) is invisible in Fig. 1(b). Moreover, it can affect user's distance sense to ToI; in Fig. 1(b), the Mountain seems closer than that in Fig. 1(a). Enlarging the ToI segmented from the original photo and pasting it back to the photo can be another option (Segment-Enlarge-Paste, SEP); however, this approach may produce weird results, such as Fig. 1(c), that is, the enlarged mountain occludes the tower.

| (a) Input Image | (b) UU | (c) SEP | (d) Our |

Fig. 1. Comparison of enlarged images.

Content aware image retargeting (CAIR) studies can be deemed to a high-related research field to aforementioned problem. Seam carving (SC) method proposed in [1] is a pioneering work of the CAIR studies; these techniques aim to adapt the input image to different devices, which are with varying aspect ratios, rather than individually rescale a specific object or area. SC [1] allows a user to specify a certain area using binary mask, which indicates the corresponding area should not be edited. A naïve approach that introducing SC [1] to solve the ToI size problem is illustrated in Fig. 4, which 1) downsize the input image while keeping its original aspect ratio and preserving the ToI area by a user-input mask (Fig. 4(b)), and then 2) restore the original image size by uniformly upscaling (UU) for the downsized image (Fig. 4(c)). By this, the size of ToI in the processed image (Fig. 4(c)) can be enlarged. However, such approach may cause the shift of the ToI in the result image, which can lead to collapse of photograph composition designated by the user. At the same time, without taking the preservation of the salient object, the structure of the tower in Fig. 4(c) has been distorted. Nevertheless, the concept of seam operation, that is, inserting or deleting seams of the original image is referable to this study; here, seam refers to a combination of contiguous pixels cross through the image vertically or horizontally, and each seam is assigned with an energy value. In this study, we aim to enlarge the size of ToI in the input image to make its perceptual size be consistent with that perceived from the real scene by the user. At the same time, preservations of photograph composition and salient objects [2, 3] are two important objectives of this study. One example of editing result by the proposed method is depicted in Fig. 1(d). With the detection of salient object, the outstanding tower in the front of Fig. 1(a) is preserved well in Fig. 1(d).

In this paper, we propose an image editing method for enlarging the ToI size based on SC [1]. To uniformly scale up the ToI specified by the user, a mask-originated seam inserting mechanism is introduced in this paper. To keep the position of the ToI in the image before and after editing, an composition constraint is adopted to the calculation of energy value for each seam. Moreover, to preserve the appearance of salient objects in the original image, the state-of-the-art deep learning model [2] for salient object detection

(SOD) is introduced into this study. To validate the effectiveness of the proposed method, a subjective experiment was conducted. The experimental result show that the proposed method is efficient in restoring the perceptual size of ToI while preserving the perceptual distance of ToI.

2 Related Work

2.1 Discrete CAIR Methods

Discrete CAIR methods directly manipulate pixels in the original image. SC method [1] is one of pioneer work for discrete CAIR methods. In [5], constraints were added to prevent Seams from overlapping or intersecting a region to prevent Seams from passing through and affecting the appearance of a local region. Considering that it will destroy the characteristics of symmetric images when applying the original SC method [1], in [6], a method was proposed to solve this problem. Specifically, when deleting a seam crossing a region which is symmetry to another region, the modified SC method [6] seeks for a seam locating in the opposite region of the axis of symmetry and deletes new found seam at the same time.

The SC-based CAIR technique searches for the optimal seam based on an energy map, a map that quantifies the importance of each pixel. Some methods use depth maps [7–10] or shadow maps [11] for energy maps, but most of them use gradient maps or saliency maps, which are calculated from gradients, as shown in [4]. Su et al. addressed the issue of image distortion caused by the concentration of seams by dynamically adjusting the energy map after seam removal [12]. In [13], performance of image editing approaches, which are based on SC [1], was compared.

2.2 Continuous CAIR Methods

CAIR methods based on image distortion are classified as continuous methods [14–16]. These methods resize the image by minimizing the distortion of salient regions in the image. Specifically, these methods adopt optimization functions for warping or mapping. Discrete methods completely remove pixels that are deemed insignificant, whereas continuous methods preserve these regions in a distorted manner.

In [17], a mesh is overlaid on the image and positions of its controlling points are transformed non-uniformly when resizing the image. Distortions in regions of high importance are required to be minimized, while other regions are allowed to be deformed with a larger scale. In addition to the gradient map, the energy map is combined with the saliency map from [18]. The problem with the continuous method is that distortions occur in the image due to the nature of the processing.

In this paper, we aim to enlarge the ToI in the input image while preserving its internal structure via the proposed mask-originated seam inserting mechanism. At the same time, the original image composition is supposed to be preserved by composition and salient object constraints.

3 Proposed Method

In this paper, the usage of the proposed method is depicted in the Fig. 2. Facing the real scene (Fig. 2(a)), which contains the grand landscape, the user takes a photo (Fig. 2(b)) of it and specifies the ToI within the photo; then, the image as well as the ToI information ToIs sent to a remote server (Fig. 2(c)) via network, and the server generates the ToI enlarged result (Fig. 2(d)) and sends it back to the user.

In this study, the flowchart of the proposed method is illustrated in Fig. 3. Given an input photograph I (Fig. 3(a)), the user is required to specify the ToI in the image by a binary mask UM (Fig. 3(b)); in parallel, the input photograph is sent to a server deployed with the SOD model, which is proposed in [2], and the SOD Mask SM (Fig. 3(c)) can be obtained. With the input image I and two masks, the proposed method firstly enlarges the ToI area utilizing the technique, which will be elaborated in Section "Mask-Originated Seam Inserting", and the intermediate result I' (Fig. 3(d)) can be obtained; finally, given the I', the postprocess component outputs the result image O (Fig. 3(e)), whose size is restored to the original one. In this paper, we only demonstrate the case of enlarging the ToI in horizontal direction; to enlarge the ToI in vertical direction, we only need to rotate the image by 90° and apply the same procedures, and then rotate it back.

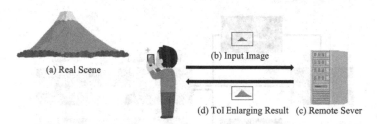

(a) Real Scene

(b) Input Image

(d) ToI Enlarging Result   (c) Remote Sever

Fig. 2. Usage of the proposed method.

3.1 Background

Same with SC [1], the proposed method achieves the ToI enlargement by seam manipulation, each of which is composed by a combination of pixels that horizontally or vertically cross through the image. By inserting vertical seams one by one, the width of the image can be enlarged gradually; if horizontal seams are deleted one by one, the height of the image can be reduced by step. In this paper, we take vertical seams as example for explanation, which can horizontally resize the ToI area as well as the whole image.

In [1], each pixel has been granted with an energy value, and the algorithm is to find a path, that is, a seam, which passing through the whole image with a minimal sum of the energy value of the pixels. Dynamic programming method is adopted to calculate seams efficiently. In [1], the energy of a seam, E_{sc}, is composed by a gradient energy e_g and a user mask energy e_m, which is utilized to specify the ToI by the user. And the E_{sc} of a seam is calculated as follows:

$$E_{sc}(S^t) = \sum_{i=1}^{h} \left(e_g(s_i^t) + e_m(s_i^t) \right), \tag{1}$$

where S^t indicates t^{th} seam found by the Seam generation method, and s_i^t denotes the ith pixels in S^t; h stands for the number of pixels in a seam, i.e., the height of the input or the current immediate image. The gradient energy e_g of each pixel p is calculated as follows:

$$e_g(p) = \left|\frac{\partial}{\partial x}p\right| + \left|\frac{\partial}{\partial y}p\right|, \qquad (2)$$

where ∂x, ∂y indicate x and y direction gradient of p, respectively. If a user intends to preserve contents of a specific region, then the user can specify it by inputting a binary mask UM, whose size is same with that of the input image; and value "1" in UM representing that the corresponding pixel is specified by the user. And the user mask energy e_m is calculated as follows:

$$e_m(s_i^t) = \begin{cases} 5 * 10^7, & UM(s_i^t) = 1 \\ 0, & \text{otherwise} \end{cases}. \qquad (3)$$

The seam with the lowest energy E_{sc} is defined as the optimal seam that should be deleted, or duplicated and inserted into the image.

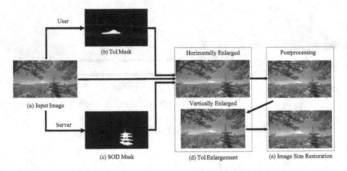

Fig. 3. Framework of the proposed method.

Since there is no mechanism for SC [1] to enlarge the ToI by inserting seams that passing through the ToI, a possible way of utilizing SC is to reduce the size of image by deleting those seams that do not pass through ToI, and then uniformly upscaling the image using interpolation. At the same time, a magnification r of the ToI should be specified by the user, and the number of seams that should be removed, N, can be calculated as follows:

$$N = \left(1 - \frac{1}{r}\right) * W, \qquad (4)$$

where W is the width of the input image. Figure 4 shows an image created using above approach.

Mt. Fuji in Fig. 4(a) is specified as the ToI (Fig. 4(b)), and the user intends to enlarge the ToI by $r = 1.5$ times. The SC method [1] was used to reduce the entire image except for the ToI region, and then the entire image was uniformly upscaled to produce the image shown in Fig. 4(c). Figure 4(c) shows that the blue sky in Fig. 4(a) has been cropped out, and the composition of the entire photo is changed significantly. For detail, the Mt. Fuji locates near the center line in Fig. 4(a), while it was shifted to the top region in Fig. 4(c). In addition, the tower in front of the user is prominent in the input image (Fig. 4(a)); while in the generated image (Fig. 4(c)), those seams passing through the tower had been selected as optimal ones and being removed, which leads to the appearance of tower in Fig. 4(c) becomes very strange. Another problem is that the entire image is enlarged, so areas other than the ToI are also enlarged. On the other hand, the result of the proposed method is shown in Fig. 4(d). In Fig. 4(d), the position of the ToI (the mountain) is kept as same as that in the original image (Fig. 4(a)), while the appearance of the SOD (the tower) is preserved.

In this study, in addition to the gradient energy calculated from the image, we take the ToI mask image, composition energy, and salient object energy into consideration when generating seams.

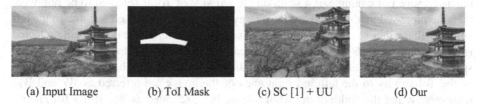

   (a) Input Image   (b) ToI Mask   (c) SC [1] + UU   (d) Our

Fig. 4. Result of generating ToI enlarged images by seam carving [1] and the proposed method.

3.2 Mask-Originated Seam Inserting

To enlarge the ToI area, we utilize the same image upscaling scheme proposed in SC [1], that is, selecting optimal seams one by one and inserting the duplication of them to the image. Therefore, in this study, it is necessary to select those seams that passing through ToI area UM. To preserve the inner struct of the ToI, we add a constraint on the seam generation procedure, that is, the part of the seam that passing through the ToI area is required to be straight. However, such goal is difficult to achieve by utilizing the seam creation strategy in SC [1]. As a result, we introduce a new mask-originated seam generation strategy into the proposed method, which is illustrated in Fig. 5. As Fig. 5(a) illustrates, a seam S for ToI enlargement is composed by three parts: s^u, l^m, and s^l.

Selecting a pair of pixels on the upper border p^u and the lower border p^l of the ToI mask that have the same x coordinate, the proposed seam generation strategy connects these two pixels using a straight line l^m, and all pixels on the line l^m are selected as a part of the seam S. Then, starting from the upper border pixel p^u and the lower border pixel p^l, rest parts s^u, s^l of the seam S is generated using the searching algorithm in SC [1]. At the same time, to uniformly enlarge the ToI area, the interval between two adjacent seams is evenly. As Fig. 5(b) and Fig. 5(c) showing, the seams inside the ToI lined up like a fence, while the parts of seams outside the ToI are in irregular shapes.

| (a) Seam Passing | (b) Seams Passing | (c) Enlarged View for (b) |

Fig. 5. Seam insertion for ToI enlargement.

3.3 Compositional Energy

To deal with the issue of ToI shift problem in SC (e.g., the mountain in Fig. 4(c) has been shifted upwards due to the intensive removal of seam in the upper region), the proposed method gradually increases the energy value of those seams that make the ToI shift. In this study, we introduce a compositional energy term when we calculate the energy of seam. The compositional energy aims to distribute seams to both sides of the ToI in a balanced way. For example, if a seam on the left side of ToI is selected to be removed, then the proposed method increase the energy of those seams that cross through the left side of ToI; in other words, the possibility of seams on the right side of ToI being selected is increased. As Fig. 6(a) shows, the mountain is the ToI of the input image (Fig. 6(a)) specified by the user, and the yellow dot indicates the gravity of the ToI. The distances of the ToI gravity to the left and right ends of the image are referred as W_L and W_R, respectively, and the width of the whole image is represented as W_o. If the ToI gravity is shifted towards left side or right side of the image, then, the ratio of W_L to W_R will change, and new distances to left and right ends of the intermediate image (Fig. 6(b)) are represented as W_L' and W_R', respectively, and the width of the intermediate image is denoted as W_0'. To prevent ToI from being shifted, it is necessary to minimize the difference between ratios W_L'/W_0' and W_L/W_0 during the seam removing. In this study, the compositional energy term is denoted as e_c.

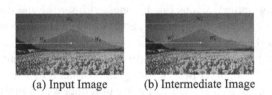

| (a) Input Image | (b) Intermediate Image |

Fig. 6. Symbolic explanation of compositional energy formula.

On the other hand, two cases should be considered, that is, seams on the left or right side of ToI will lead to different ways to calculate e_c. Here, we calculate the compositional energy by defining the compositional energy of the seam locates at the left side as *ECL*, and that locates at the right side as *ECR*. And the compositional energy is calculated as follows:

$$e_c(S^t) = \begin{cases} ECL, \ Cox(s_j^t) < W_L' \\ ECR, \ otherwise \end{cases}, \tag{5}$$

$$ECL(S^t) = \left| \frac{W'_L - 1}{W'_0 - 1} - \frac{W_L}{W_0} \right| + \left| \frac{W'_R}{W'_0 - 1} - \frac{W_R}{W_0} \right|, \qquad (6)$$

$$ECR(S^t) = \left| \frac{W'_L}{W'_0 - 1} - \frac{W_L}{W_0} \right| + \left| \frac{W'_R - 1}{W'_0 - 1} - \frac{W_R}{W_0} \right|, \qquad (7)$$

where $Cox()$ function returns the x coordinate of the pixel within t^{th} seam S^t, whose y coordinate is same with that of ToI gravity.

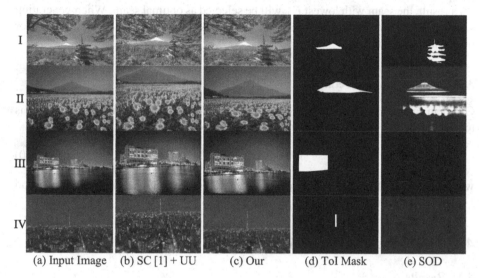

(a) Input Image   (b) SC [1] + UU   (c) Our   (d) ToI Mask   (e) SOD

Fig. 7. Input images and result images by the proposed method.

3.4 Salient Object Energy

The preservation of salient objects is realized by introducing the state-of-the-art SOD method [2]. Given an input image, the SOD method outputs a mask indicating the pixels of salient objects. Figure 3(c) shows the results of detecting salient object regions using the SOD technique on the input image (Fig. 3(a)). The region marked white indicates the salient object region.

To avoid those seams that passing through SOD area to be selected, high energy value is assigned to pixels within SOD area.

In this study, salient object energy is introduced as e_s. The salient object energy e_s is defined as follows:

$$e_s(p) = \begin{cases} 5 * 10^5, & p \in SM \\ 0, & \text{otherwise} \end{cases}, \qquad (8)$$

where p stands for arbitrary pixel in the image. The energy should be set to a value sufficiently larger than the value shown in (1). Considering that the region of ToI should have the highest priority, we set the value of e_s of pixels lower than that set to ToI mask energy e_m.

Finally, the energy $E_{sc}(S^t)$ of a seam in the proposed method can be rewritten as below:

$$E_{sc}(S^t) = \sum_{i=1}^{h} \left(e_g(s_i^t) + \alpha e_m(s_i^t) + e_s(s_i^t) \right) + \alpha e_c(S^t), \tag{9}$$

where h denotes the height of the image; α is the parameter to control the different energy components. In this paper, seam generation method [19] is utilized to generate seams. As a result, the seam with lowest E_{sc} will be selected as optimal seam. When generating seams for ToI enlargement, α is set to 0; while α is set to 1 when generating seam for postprocessing part.

3.5 Implementation Detail

Given an enlargement factor σ ($1 < \sigma \leq 2$) specified by the user, the number N^s of seams to enlarge the ToI is calculated using the following equation:

$$N^s = \lfloor (\sigma - 1) \cdot L^u \rfloor, \tag{10}$$

where L^u denotes the length of the projection result of the ToI mask onto the x-axis, and $\lfloor \bullet \rfloor$ is round down operation.

4   Results and Evaluation Experiments

4.1   Results

Figure 7 shows 4 result images produced by the proposed method. Each line contains the input image (Fig. 7(a)), the SC [1] + uniformly upscaling (Fig. 7(b)), the proposed method (Fig. 7(c)), the ToI Mask (Fig. 7(d)), and the SOD detection result (Fig. 7(e)). The magnification for ToI is set to 1.5.

For the example I, the mountain was enlarged well and the position and the salient object (the tower) were preserved well. For examples II–IV, the mountain and buildings were enlarged while the content as well as the photo composition were preserved well.

To further evaluate the effectiveness of the proposed method, objective and subjective experiments were conducted in this study.

4.2   Objective Experiment

To evaluate the effectiveness of the proposed method in ToI composition preservation, we calculated the distance between the ToI gravities of the input image and the result image. The average distance of 4 result images produced by the proposed method is shown in Table 1; the result of SC [1] is also contained in Table 1. The experimental result shows that the preserve the ToI composition. Euclidean metric was used to calculate the deviation from the gravity of the input ToI and that of the ToI of the images created by each method. δ_1 and δ_2 in the table are defined by the following equations.

$$\delta_1 = \sqrt{(g_x - g_x^{sc})^2 + (g_y - g_y^{sc})^2}, \tag{11}$$

$$\delta_2 = \sqrt{(g_x - g_x^{our})^2 + (g_y - g_y^{our})^2}, \tag{12}$$

where g_x, g_y indicate the x and y coordinates of the gravity of ToI in the input image, g_x^{sc}, and g_y^{sc} indicate the x and y coordinates of the gravity of ToI in the SC [1] + upscaling image, g_x^{our} and g_y^{our} indicate the x and y coordinates of the gravity of ToI in the result image by the proposed method. The evaluation result is shown in Table 1. In Table 1, the mean deviation of ToI in the result image by the proposed method is distinctly smaller that by the SC [1] + uniformly upscaling approach. It shows that the effectiveness of the proposed method in the preservation of image composition.

Table 1. Results of objective evaluation.

Image	Input Gravity		SC [1] + UU			Our		
	g_x	g_y	g_x^{sc}	g_y^{sc}	δ_1	g_x^{our}	g_y^{our}	δ_2
I	226	176	228	151	25	225	176	1
II	260	109	189	32	104	259	109	1
III	119	174	140	132	46	125	174	6
IV	249	146	259	65	81	248	146	1
Mean	–	–	–	–	64	–	–	2

4.3 Subjective Experiment

To evaluate whether the perceptual size of ToI in the result images generated by the proposed method is consistent with that in the real scene, subjective evaluation experiments were conducted in this study. The experiment was conducted at two locations. A total of 8 volunteers (21–28 years old, 8 males) were invited and taken to above locations in-person (Location A: 4 volunteers, Location B: 4 volunteers); and the mountain was set as ToI for both locations. The distances from the ToI to both observation points were 38 km. The device used in the experiment was Dell Inspiron 7300 laptop installed with CPU Intel® Core(TM) i7-1165G7 2.80 GHz, RAM 16 GB, and a 13.3-in. screen, which is for both the algorithm execution and result image display. The server for executing the SOD model is installed with Nvidia GeForce RTX 3080 GPU. Socket communication was adopted to data transfer between the server and laptop. The subjects were first shown with a picture capture by a camera, and then were required to specify a magnification by comparing the photo and the real scene. Then, the magnification was used to generate the result image. Next, the participants were asked to evaluate the generated image from aspects of perceptual size and distance sense (DS), comparing the result image and the real scene. For both evaluation aspects, the scale was a numerical value [%] ranging from 0 to 100, and the score "100" indicates that the perceptual size of ToI or the perceptual distance to ToI is totally same with those from the real scene. For reference, the result image generated using uniform upscaling were also shown to the participants. The results of the subjective evaluation experiment are shown in Table 2. Table 2 shows that the average sizes of ToI in images generated by the proposed method at both locations were slightly lower than those of the uniformly upscaled images, while uniform upscaling method resulted in loss of distance information. And results of both locations show that the distance sense with the proposed method was significantly higher than that of the uniform upscaled image. A t-test was conducted at the 5% level of significance for perceptual size and distance; for the Location A, there was no significant difference found for size, but a significant difference was found for the distance aspect. The same test was conducted on the Location B, and significant differences were found for both size and distance. The reason for the decrease in the with respect to size can result from the fact that the upper enlargement limit of the proposed method is 200%, and the enlargement required by the subjects exceeded the limit. However, the preservation of distance from the ToI was significantly improved compared to the result image with uniform scaling.

Table 2. Results of subjective evaluation.

Location A						Location B					
		UU		Our				UU		Our	
Part	Mag	Size	DS	Size	DS	Part	Mag	Size	DS	Size	DS
A	200	90	50	90	90	E	300	90	25	90	60
B	300	100	5	90	95	F	250	80	40	60	80
C	200	100	20	95	100	G	150	85	70	70	70
D	220	85	50	90	80	H	210	90	30	80	95
Mean	230	93	31	91	91		227	86	41	75	76

5 Discussion

Before the evaluation experiments of this study were conducted, a preliminary experiment was conducted to determine whether the ToI in the result image with uniform upscaling is consistent with the perceived size.

The experiment shows that there are individual differences in perceived size. The participants in this experiment included international students, and the magnification set by international students was lower than that of home country students. Even among home country students, there were differences depending on their birthplace. How to quantify the individual differences caused by such factors is still a matter of debate.

In this study, ToI masks were manually created in the evaluation experiment. Although SOD technology has the potential of generating ToI mask, its accuracy cannot satisfy the requirement of this study. Automation of ToI Mask generation is necessary to realize practical application of the proposed method.

6 Conclusion

Based on the SC method [1], we proposed a method of ToI upscaling to reflect the perceptual size in the generated image. The proposed method introduces compositional energy and salient object energy. The evaluation experiments shows that the distance to ToI was maintained well in the result image, and the preservation to size of ToI in the edited image was comparable to the result of the uniformly upscaling method. In the future, the proposed method should be extended to arbitrary scaling factors. Automatic generation of ToI masks is also needed.

Acknowledgment. This work is supported by JSPS Grants-in-Aid for Scientific Research (Grant No. 20K20408). We would like to thank volunteers for evaluating the proposed method.

References

1. Avidan, S., Shamir, A.: Seam carving for content-aware image resizing. ACM Trans. Graph. **26**(3), 10-es, Article no. 10 (2007)
2. Lee, M.S., Shin, W., Han, S.W.: TRACER: extreme attention guided salient object tracing network. In: AAAI, vol. 36, no. 11, pp. 12993–12994 (2022)
3. Liu, J.-J., Hou, Q., Cheng, M.-M., Feng, J., Jiang, J.: A simple pooling-based design for real-time salient object detection. In: CVPR, pp. 3917–3926 (2019)
4. Asheghi, B., Salehpour, P., Khiavi, A.M., Hashemzadeh, M.: A comprehensive review on content-aware image retargeting: from classical to state-of- the-art methods. Signal Process. **195**, 108496 (2022)
5. Garg, A., Negi, A., Jindal, P.: Structure preservation of image using an efficient content-aware image retargeting technique. Signal Image Video Process. **15**(1), 185–193 (2021)
6. Patel, D., Nagar, R., Raman, S.: Reflection symmetry aware image retargeting. Pattern Recognit. Lett. **125**, 179–186 (2019)
7. Shen, J., Wang, D., Li, X.: Depth-aware image seam carving. IEEE Trans. Cybern. **43**, 1453–1461 (2013)
8. Chen, Y., Pan, Y., Song, M., Wang, M.: Image retargeting with a 3D saliency model. Signal Process. **112**, 53–63 (2015)
9. Chen, Y., Pan, Y., Song, M., Wang, M.: Improved seam carving combining with 3D saliency for image retargeting. Neurocomputing **151**, 645–653 (2015)
10. Cui, J., Cai, Q., Lu, H., Jia, Z., Tang, M.: Distortion-aware image retargeting based on continuous seam carving model. Signal Process. **166**, 107242 (2020)
11. Hashemzadeh, M., Asheghi, B., Farajzadeh, N.: Content-aware image resizing: an improved and shadow-preserving seam carving method. Signal Process. **155**, 233–246 (2019)
12. Su, H., Ye, Z., Liu, Y., Yu, S.: Seam carving based on dynamic energy regulation. Multimedia Tools Appl. **82**, 25795–25810 (2023)

13. Sharma, S., Piplani, Y.: Comparative analysis of seam carving in images. In: Proceedings of the Second International Conference on Information Management and Machine Intelligence, pp. 139–146 (2021)
14. Jiang, W., Haifeng, X., Chen, G., Zhao, W., Wei, X.: An improved edge-adaptive image scaling algorithm. In: 2009 IEEE 8th International Conference on ASIC, pp. 895–897 (2009)
15. Liu, F., Gleicher, M.: Automatic image retargeting with fisheye-view warping. In: Proceedings of the 18th Annual ACM Symposium on User Interface Software and Technology, Seattle, WA, USA, pp. 153–162. ACM (2005)
16. Ren, T., Liu, Y., Wu, G.: Image retargeting based on global energy optimization. In: 2009 IEEE International Conference on Multimedia and Expo, pp. 406–409. IEEE (2009)
17. Wang, Y.S., Tai, C.L., Sorkine, O., Lee, T.Y.: Optimized scale-and-stretch for image resizing. In: ACM SIGGRAPH Asia, pp. 1–8 (2008)
18. Itti, L., Koch, C., Niebur, E.: A model of saliency-based visual attention for rapid scene analysis. IEEE Trans. Pattern Anal. Mach. Intell. 20(11), 1254–1259 (1998)
19. Rubinstein, M., Shamir, A., Avidan, S.: Improved seam carving for video retargeting. ACM Trans. Graph. 27(3), 1–9 (2008)

Underwater Image Enhancement Based on the Fusion of PUIENet and NAFNet

Chao Li and Bo Yang[✉]

School of Computer Science, Inner Mongolia University, Hohhot 010000, China
csyb@imu.edu.cn

Abstract. Due to light absorption and scattering in the ocean, underwater images suffer from blur and color bias, and the colors tend to be biased towards blue or green. To enhance underwater images, many underwater image enhancement (UIE) methods have been developed. Probabilistic Network for UIE (PUIENet) is a neural network model that produces good results in processing underwater images. However, it cannot handle underwater images with motion blur, which is caused by camera or object motion. Nonlinear Activation Free Network (NAFNet) is a network model designed to remove image blur by simplifying everything. Inspired by NAFNet, we simplified the convolution, activation function, and channel attention module of PUIENet, resulting in Probabilistic and Nonlinear Activation Hybrid for UIE (PNAH_UIE), which reduced training time by approximately 19% and also reduced loss. In this paper, we propose a deep learning-based method for underwater image enhancement, called Probabilistic and Nonlinear Activation Hybrid Network for UIE (PNAHNet_UIE), which integrates the two most advanced network structures, PNAH_UIE and NAFNet, to improve overall image clarity and remove motion blur. The URPC2022 dataset was used in the experiments, which comes from the "CHINA UNDERWATER ROBOT PROFESSIONAL CONTEST." PNAH_UIE was used to enhance the URPC2022 dataset, and the processed images were checked for motion blur. If the variance of an image was below a certain threshold, the NAFNet network was used to process the image, thus reducing computational pressure.

Keywords: Underwater image enhancement · Motion blur · PUIENet · NAFNet

1 Introduction

Due to intensive ocean exploitation, underwater images have become increasingly important. However, the attenuation and scattering of light in seawater result in severe color distortion and blurring of underwater images. Therefore, techniques for processing underwater images have emerged. Although underwater image enhancement is a low-level visual task, it can provide better support for underwater operations, marine research, and other applications. Hence, a

© The Author(s), under exclusive license to Springer Nature Switzerland AG 2024
B. Sheng et al. (Eds.): CGI 2023, LNCS 14495, pp. 335–347, 2024.
https://doi.org/10.1007/978-3-031-50069-5_28

good underwater image processing technique is of great significance for ocean development.

In the early stages, special hardware, such as polarization filtering, was used to restore blurred underwater images. Later, as technology continued to develop, researchers utilized various methods to calculate and estimate different parameters for the restoration of underwater images based on the underwater image formation model (IFM).

Recently, deep learning technology has made remarkable progress in the field of computer vision, and the PUIENet [10] network has surpassed many previous methods in restoring underwater images. When collecting underwater image datasets, image blur due to motion is inevitable. However, neither the PUIENet network nor previous methods can handle motion blur. The NAFNet [7] network model performs well in processing images with motion blur. Now many network models are constantly developing towards complexity and high computational requirements. The recent ChatGPT is a super large model. However, the NAFNet network model simplifies the network model. Even though the model is simplified, its performance remains unchanged or even surpasses previous methods. Therefore, we propose the Probabilistic and Nonlinear Activation Hybrid Network for UIE, namely the PNAHNet_UIE network model, which integrates the PNAH_UIE and NAFNet network models and surpasses previous methods. PNAH_UIE is a modified version of PUIENet, where some network structures use activation functions, while others replace the convolution and activation functions and modify the attention mechanism. The detailed structural modifications are described in Sect. 3. After modifying the network structure, the training time is reduced and the loss is also decreased. We use the URPC2022 dataset to evaluate the PNAHNet_UIE network model.

The main contributions of this paper are summarized as follows:

- We propose the PNAHNet_UIE network model, which solves the problem of motion blur in underwater images that previous methods were unable to remove, making underwater images clearer.
- We modify the PUIENet network model by using multiplication operations instead of convolution and activation functions in some of its structures. We also modify the channel attention module of PUIENet. The modified network model has reduced training time and loss.
- We used the PNAH_UIE network model to process underwater images on the URPC2022 dataset, and sampled images with motion blur to calculate their variance. Finally, we performed statistical analysis on the data to obtain the final threshold. If the Laplacian variance of an image is less than this threshold, we used the NAFNet model for processing to reduce computational complexity.

2   Related Work

In recent years, many methods for enhancing underwater images have been developed and can be broadly categorized into three types.

2.1   Traditional Methods

The first type is traditional methods, where researchers typically use special hardware equipment such as polarization filtering, range-gated imaging, and fluorescence imaging to restore degraded underwater images. However, this method is costly, making it unsuitable for most people. As an alternative, researchers tend to prefer single underwater image enhancement methods that improve image clarity by modifying pixel values. For example, Iqbal et al. [17] used an unsupervised color correction method (UCM) for enhancing degraded underwater images by stretching their histograms. References [2,11] employed a histogram-based approach to achieve image enhancement.

2.2   Physical Models

The second type refers to underwater image enhancement methods based on physical models. He et al. [12] proposed the famous dark channel prior (DCP) method, which is effective for defogging outdoor images as most fog-free outdoor images have low pixel values in some channel. However, directly using the DCP method for enhancing underwater images yields unsatisfactory results. Chiang and Chen [8] enhanced underwater images through wavelength compensation and defogging (WCID), which is based on the DCP method to judge whether there is artificial light compensation for wavelength attenuation. Li et al. [21] proposed a mixed underwater image correction method for color correction and underwater image defogging. After a series of algorithms, the degraded underwater images are finally restored.

2.3   Deep Learning Methods

The third type of underwater image enhancement method is based on deep learning. Previously, traditional and physics-based methods for underwater image enhancement showed better results than deep learning. However, with the continuous enrichment and development of datasets, deep learning has also demonstrated good performance. Ding et al. [9] used convolutional neural networks (CNN) to extract features of corrected underwater images to predict scene depth, which successfully improved the quality of underwater images. Li et al. [22] adopted a deep learning-based underwater image enhancement method, namely WaterGAN, to generate a dataset of simulated underwater images, and then restored degraded underwater images through two steps: depth estimation and color restoration. The biggest feature of this method is introducing GAN into image restoration. Li et al. [20] constructed an Underwater Image Enhancement Benchmark (UIEB) dataset and proposed a CNN model, namely Water-Net, trained on UIEB for underwater image enhancement. The biggest innovation of this method is the fusion of multiple algorithms for the input image.

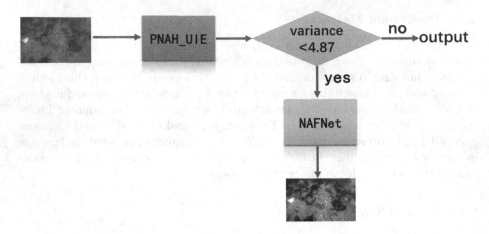

Fig. 1. The flowchart of the PNAHNet_UIE model.

3   Proposed Method

We propose a Probabilistic and Nonlinear Activation Hybrid Network for Underwater Image Enhancement (PNAHNet_UIE), which integrates the most advanced network structures, PNAH_UIE(a modified version of the PUIENet) and NAFNet. The flowchart of the PNAHNet_UIE model is shown in Fig. 1, and the algorithm is presented in Algorithm 1. We continue to use the loss functions of PUIENet and NAFNet. NAFNet uses PSNR loss as its experimental results are better.

Inspired by NAFNet, we simplified the PUIENet network structure while ensuring efficiency. The feature extraction network is based on a combination of the UNet structure proposed in [26] and the residual structure proposed by He [13]. We modified the Conv+LeakyReLU and SE-ResNet Block. We replaced the Conv+LeakyReLU modules of the Decoder module with element-wise multiplication, as shown in Fig. 2. First, we split the number of channels in the feature map in half and then perform element-wise multiplication to obtain a feature map with half the number of channels. Here, C represents the number of channels, and W and H represent the width and height of the feature map, respectively, and $\odot$ represents element-wise multiplication.

We also modified the attention mechanism of the SE-ResNet module as shown in Fig. 3. Firstly, AdaptiveAvgPool2d was applied, followed by 1×1 convolution, and then each channel was multiplied to obtain the final feature layer. The symbol $*$ denotes channel-wise multiplication. In order to alleviate the computational pressure, it is not necessary to input all underwater images processed by PNAH_UIE into NAFNet. Even if all underwater images are input into NAFNet, there is little difference between the results obtained by NAFNet and those obtained by PNAH_UIE, if there is no motion blur in the underwater images. Therefore, we use PNAH_UIE to process underwater images in the URPC2022 dataset. If the calculated value of the image is less than a certain threshold,

---

Algorithm 1. Restoration of Underwater Images

Require:
  Input: input image I^c.
  Output: output image O^c.
  1: **function** PNAH_UIE(I^c)
  2:     Underwater Image Feature Extraction Network: Modified UNet
  3:     PAdaIN model
  4:     Output block
  5: **return** output
  6: **end function**
  7:
  8: **function** NAFNET($Output^c$)
  9:     UNet Architecture
10: **return** Deblurring images
11: **end function**
12:
13: **if** PNAH_UIE(I^c) <4.87 **then**
14:     NAFNet($Output^c$)
15: **else**
16:     **return** PNAH_UIE(I^c)
17: **end if**
18:

---

the image is sent to the NAFNet network for processing. We used Python, as described in Algorithm 2, based on [5], to detect whether the processed underwater images have motion blur. Firstly, we used the cv2 package in Python to process the images. Then, the images were converted to grayscale and a Gaussian blur was applied, which reduces noise and image details, while preserving the edges and overall structure of the image. Next, the Laplace of the image was computed by convolution operation, and the variance of the Laplace was calculated to obtain the result. We statistically analyzed 9000 underwater images in the URPC2022 dataset and manually judged whether the images had motion blur, using subjective human perception as the evaluation standard. Finally, the threshold was determined based on the statistical analysis.

We also applied Dynamic Region-Aware Convolution (DRConv) [6] to modify the PUIENet. This structure utilizes an adaptive mechanism to adjust the size of convolution kernels, enabling better feature capturing of different regions. As reported in [6], DRConv exhibits superior performance in computer vision tasks. However, when used in the PUIENet network model, it did not show satisfactory results. Please refer to Sect. 4 for detailed experimental results.

4   Experiments

In this section, we will provide a detailed introduction and analysis of the experimental results and data. We conducted experiments to verify the efficiency of PNAHNet_UIE, and then performed comparative experiments on the UIEB [20]

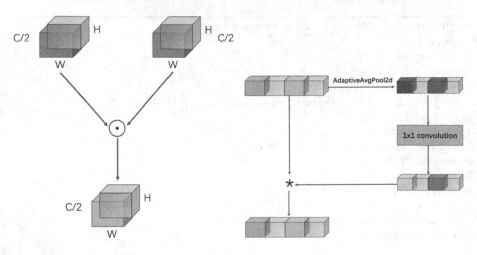

Fig. 2. Multiplying Element By Element.

Fig. 3. Modified Channel Attention.

Algorithm 2. Calculating the variance of image

Require:

  Input: input image I^c.

  Output: variance of the Laplacian.

1: **function** VARIANCE(I^c)

2:     Cv2 read the image

3:     Convert the image to grayscale

4:     Apply a Gaussian blur to the image

5:     Compute the Laplacian of the image

6:     Compute the variance of the Laplacian

7:     **return** variance

8: **end function**

---

test dataset. We used both full-reference image quality assessment (FR-IQA) and no-reference image quality assessment (NR-IQA) to evaluate the images, such as MSE [24], PSNR [16], SSIM [14], UCIQE [28], and UIQM [25]. Since the UIEB dataset did not contain underwater images with motion blur, we only used the network structure of PNAH_UIE. However, the URPC2022 dataset contained some underwater images with motion blur that PNAH_UIE could not handle. Therefore, we used the entire network model of PNAHNet_UIE to process these images. Some of the programs used in this experiment were obtained from references [27], [3,11,23], and [2].

Table 1. The total training time and loss of PUIENet, PUIE_Feature, PUIE_Conv, and PNAH_UIE. The best results are highlighted in bold red.

Network Model	Total Training Time	Average loss	Minimum loss
PUIENet	10580.60	**0.0620**	0.0529
PUIE _Feature	8689.28	0.0660	0.0496
PUIE_Conv	31560.65	0.1450	0.1037
PNAH_UIE(ours)	**8593.90**	0.0637	**0.0491**

Table 2. Full-reference image quality assessment. The best results are highlighted in bold red, while the second-best results are highlighted in bold blue.

Methods/Metrics	MSE ↓	PSNR ↑	SSIM ↑
Retinex [29]	100.00	28.14	0.77
GC	102.83	28.02	0.76
ICM [18]	**84.06**	**29.10**	0.82
RGHS [15]	85.25	28.92	0.81
RayleighDistribution [1]	97.23	28.27	0.73
Histogram prior [19]	91.25	28.87	0.77
Fusion [4]	**76.22**	**29.47**	0.82
WCID [8]	102.72	28.02	0.31
PUIENet(MC) [10]	89.21	28.70	**0.86**
PNAH_UIE(ours)	89.74	28.66	**0.85**

Table 3. Non-reference image quality assessment. The best results are highlighted in bold red, while the second-best results are highlighted in bold blue.

Methods/Metrics	UCIQE ↑	UIQM ↑
Retinex [29]	0.59	1.39
GC	0.51	1.12
ICM [18]	0.58	1.30
RGHS [15]	0.62	1.40
RayleighDistribution [1]	**0.67**	**1.55**
Histogram prior [19]	**0.66**	**1.48**
Fusion [4]	0.63	1.42
WCID [8]	0.61	1.45
PUIENet(MC) [10]	0.58	1.24
PNAH_UIE(ours)	0.57	1.23

Raw   Fusion   PUIENet(MC)**PNAH_UIE** reference

PSNR   28.73   28.52   27.71   \

Fig. 4. PSNR of Fusion, PUIENet, and PNAH_UIE.

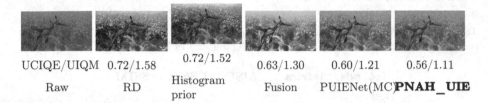

UCIQE/UIQM 0.72/1.58   0.72/1.52   0.63/1.30   0.60/1.21   0.56/1.11

Raw   RD   Histogram   Fusion   PUIENet(MC)**PNAH_UIE**
                        prior

Fig. 5. Comparison of UCIQE and UIQM metrics.The Rayleigh distribution [1](RD).

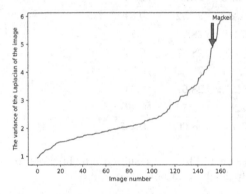

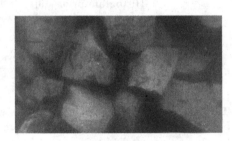

Fig. 6. Selection of threshold values. The x-axis represents the image number, and the y-axis represents the variance of the Laplacian of the images.

Fig. 7. Variance (1.70)

4.1   Comparison of Network Structures

We compared different network structures by evaluating their performance on the UIEB training dataset through experiments and analyzing the results in detail. To ensure the accuracy of the results, all experiments were conducted on a 32GB graphics card for 500 epochs.

The total training time and loss for PUIENet, PUIE_Feature, PUIE_Conv, and PNAH_UIE are presented in Table 1. PUIENet has the same architecture as the original paper [10] and was not modified. PUIE_Feature modifies the feature extractor from the original paper by replacing some activation functions in the encoder's Conv+LeakyReLU modules with element-wise multiplication. Similarly, in the decoder, the Conv+LeakyReLU modules are replaced

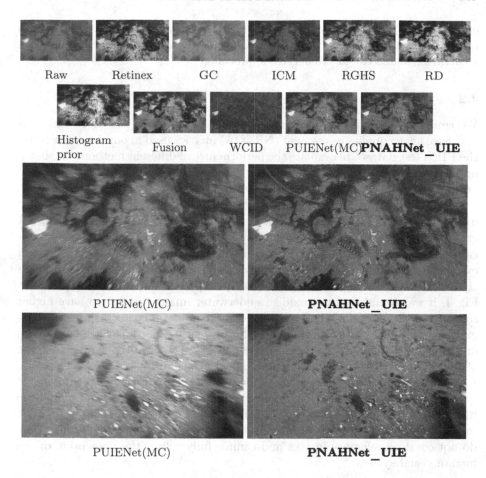

Fig. 8. Underwater images processed by different methods. The Rayleigh distribution [1] (RD)

with element-wise multiplication. Furthermore, the attention mechanism of the SE-ResNet module is replaced with a modified channel attention mechanism. PUIE_Conv replaced the Convolution layers of the Encoder and Decoder modules with DRConv [6]. PNAH_UIE modified the feature extractor of the original paper by replacing the Conv+ LeakyReLU modules of the Decoder module with Multiplying Element By Element, and replacing the attention mechanism of the SE-ResNet module with Modified Channel Attention.

After observing Table 1, our PNAH_UIE network structure shows a significant decrease in overall training time, approximately 19% less than PUIENet and approximately 73% less than PUIE_Conv. The use of the Dynamic Region-Aware Convolution network structure did not yield optimal results in this experiment. Since the source code for DRConv has not been made publicly available, the experimental results for the PUIE_Conv network structure are provided for reference only. The experimental results demonstrate that modifying the attention mechanism and replacing convolution and activation functions in the network structure remains the most effective approach.

4.2 FR-IQA and NR-IQA

We compared the full-reference image quality assessment (FR-IQA) and non-reference image quality assessment (NR-IQA) metrics used in our experiments on the UIEB test dataset to evaluate the performance of different methods, as shown in Table 2 and Table 3. We analyzed the experimental results and discussed the performance of each metric in detail.

In general, lower MSE and higher PSNR and SSIM values indicate better image quality. In this experiment, the Fusion method achieved the highest PSNR value, which is due to the drawback of the PSNR evaluation metric. The numerical value of PSNR is inconsistent with the image quality perceived by the human eye because the human perception is affected by the surrounding pixels. Although the PSNR value is high, the image quality is poor. From the observations in Fig. 4, it was found that the reddish underwater images tended to have higher scores, and the Fusion method introduced more noise and a reddish hue. In this experiment, SSIM was found to be a better evaluation metric, as it focuses more on the details differences between images. Overall, the results showed that the PUIENet and PNAH_UIE methods produced better results.

Generally, the higher the values of UCIQE and UIQM, the better the image quality. In Fig. 5, we found that the RayleighDistribution [1] method scored the highest in terms of UCIQE and UIQM metrics. It is worth noting that NR-IQA metrics have limitations in accurately evaluating image quality because they do not consider reference images and cannot fully reflect the perception of the human visual system.

4.3 PNAHNet_UIE

We used the PNAH_UIE network to process underwater images from the URPC-2022 dataset, while sampling images with motion blur. We calculated the variance of the Laplacian of the images with motion blur using Algorithm 2 and sorted the variance in ascending order. To prevent misjudgment, we selected the maximum value of the top 95% of the data, which was 4.87, as the final threshold, as shown in Fig. 6. As a comparison, we processed images with motion blur using different methods, as shown in Fig. 8.

Through experimental comparisons, although we simplified our proposed network PNAHNet_UIE, it still showed good performance, with the shortest time and lowest loss during network training. Methods such as Retinex, GC, ICM, RGHS, RayleighDistribution, Histogram prior, Fusion, WCID, and PUIENet were all ineffective in removing motion-blurred underwater images. The PUIENet network model restored the underwater images with good overall results but still failed to solve the motion blur problem. Our proposed PNAH-Net_UIE network model addresses the limitations of the above methods and removes motion blur from underwater images. Through experiments, our results show that our method is still the best.

5   Conclusion

In this paper, we propose a network, PNAHNet_UIE, which mainly consists of two sub-networks: PNAH_UIE and NAFNet. Among them, the training time of the PNAH_UIE network is reduced by approximately 19% compared to PUIENet. Our network model addresses the limitation of PUIENet in processing underwater images with motion blur. We calculated the variance of the Laplacian of underwater images with motion blur using an algorithm. Finally, we performed statistical analysis and obtained a threshold value of 4.87. If the variance of an image is below 4.87, it is processed by the NAFNet network, thereby reducing the computational resource burden.

In this paper, the use of Laplacian-calculated variance for identifying underwater images with motion blur is relatively accurate, but there are still limitations as shown in Fig. 7, where this type of blur is also considered as motion blur in underwater images.

Our future work will involve accurately detecting and counting underwater images with motion blur using certain algorithms. We will optimize the loss function of the network and explore and discover a more accurate image evaluation metric. Finally, we hope that our work can make a certain contribution to the development of marine information technology!

References

1. Abdul Ghani, A.S., Mat Isa, N.A.: Underwater image quality enhancement through composition of dual-intensity images and rayleigh-stretching. Springerplus **3**(1), 1–14 (2014)
2. Acharya, U.K., Kumar, S.: Image enhancement using exposure and standard deviation-based sub-image histogram equalization for night-time images. In: Bansal, P., Tushir, M., Balas, V.E., Srivastava, R. (eds.) Proceedings of International Conference on Artificial Intelligence and Applications. AISC, vol. 1164, pp. 607–615. Springer, Singapore (2021). https://doi.org/10.1007/978-981-15-4992-2_57
3. Al-Jebrni, A.H., et al.: Sthy-net: a feature fusion-enhanced dense-branched modules network for small thyroid nodule classification from ultrasound images. Vis. Comput. 1–15 (2023)
4. Ancuti, C., Ancuti, C.O., Haber, T., Bekaert, P.: Enhancing underwater images and videos by fusion. In: 2012 IEEE Conference on Computer Vision and Pattern Recognition, pp. 81–88. IEEE (2012)
5. Bansal, R., Raj, G., Choudhury, T.: Blur image detection using laplacian operator and open-cv. In: 2016 International Conference System Modeling & Advancement in Research Trends (SMART), pp. 63–67. IEEE (2016)
6. Chen, J., Wang, X., Guo, Z., Zhang, X., Sun, J.: Dynamic region-aware convolution. In: Proceedings of the IEEE/CVF Conference on Computer Vision and Pattern Recognition, pp. 8064–8073 (2021)

7. Chen, L., Chu, X., Zhang, X., Sun, J.: Simple baselines for image restoration. In: Avidan, S., Brostow, G., Cissé, M., Farinella, G.M., Hassner, T. (eds.) ECCV 2022, Part VII. LNCS, vol. 13667, pp. 17–33. Springer, Cham (2022). https://doi.org/ 10.1007/978-3-031-20071-7_2

8. Chiang, J.Y., Chen, Y.C.: Underwater image enhancement by wavelength compensation and dehazing. IEEE Trans. Image Process. **21**(4), 1756–1769 (2011)

9. Ding, X., Wang, Y., Zhang, J., Fu, X.: Underwater image dehaze using scene depth estimation with adaptive color correction. In: OCEANS 2017-Aberdeen, pp. 1–5. IEEE (2017)

10. Fu, Z., Wang, W., Huang, Y., Ding, X., Ma, K.K.: Uncertainty inspired underwater image enhancement. In: Avidan, S., Brostow, G., Cissé, M., Farinella, G.M., Hassner, T. (eds.) Computer Vision-ECCV 2022, Part XVIII. LNCS, vol. 13678, pp. 465–482. Springer, Chm (2022). https://doi.org/10.1007/978-3-031-19797-0_27

11. Goyal, V., Shukla, A.: An enhancement of underwater images based on contrast restricted adaptive histogram equalization for image enhancement. In: Tiwari, S., Trivedi, M.C., Mishra, K.K., Misra, A.K., Kumar, K.K., Suryani, E. (eds.) Smart Innovations in Communication and Computational Sciences. AISC, vol. 1168, pp. 275–285. Springer, Singapore (2021). https://doi.org/10.1007/978-981-15-5345-5_25

12. He, K., Sun, J., Tang, X.: Single image haze removal using dark channel prior. IEEE Trans. Pattern Anal. Mach. Intell. **33**(12), 2341–2353 (2010)

13. He, K., Zhang, X., Ren, S., Sun, J.: Deep residual learning for image recognition. In: Proceedings of the IEEE Conference on Computer Vision and Pattern Recognition, pp. 770–778 (2016)

14. Hore, A., Ziou, D.: Image quality metrics: PSNR vs. SSIM. In: 2010 20th International Conference on Pattern Recognition, pp. 2366–2369. IEEE (2010)

15. Huang, D., Wang, Y., Song, W., Sequeira, J., Mavromatis, S.: Shallow-water image enhancement using relative global histogram stretching based on adaptive parameter acquisition. In: Schoeffmann, K., et al. (eds.) MMM 2018. LNCS, vol. 10704, pp. 453–465. Springer, Cham (2018). https://doi.org/10.1007/978-3-319-73603-7_37

16. Huynh-Thu, Q., Ghanbari, M.: Scope of validity of PSNR in image/video quality assessment. Electron. Lett. **44**(13), 800–801 (2008)

17. Iqbal, K., Odetayo, M., James, A., Salam, R.A., Talib, A.Z.H.: Enhancing the low quality images using unsupervised colour correction method. In: 2010 IEEE International Conference on Systems, Man and Cybernetics, pp. 1703–1709. IEEE (2010)

18. Iqbal, K., Salam, R.A., Osman, A., Talib, A.Z.: Underwater image enhancement using an integrated colour model. IAENG Int. J. Comput. Sci. **34**(2) (2007)

19. Li, C.Y., Guo, J.C., Cong, R.M., Pang, Y.W., Wang, B.: Underwater image enhancement by dehazing with minimum information loss and histogram distribution prior. IEEE Trans. Image Process. **25**(12), 5664–5677 (2016)

20. Li, C., et al.: An underwater image enhancement benchmark dataset and beyond. IEEE Trans. Image Process. **29**, 4376–4389 (2019)

21. Li, C., Guo, J., Guo, C., Cong, R., Gong, J.: A hybrid method for underwater image correction. Pattern Recogn. Lett. **94**, 62–67 (2017)

22. Li, J., Skinner, K.A., Eustice, R.M., Johnson-Roberson, M.: Watergan: unsupervised generative network to enable real-time color correction of monocular underwater images. IEEE Robot. Autom. Lett. **3**(1), 387–394 (2017)

23. Li, L., Tang, J., Ye, Z., Sheng, B., Mao, L., Ma, L.: Unsupervised face superresolution via gradient enhancement and semantic guidance. Vis. Comput. **37**, 2855–2867 (2021)

24. Marmolin, H.: Subjective MSE measures. IEEE Trans. Syst. Man Cybern. **16**(3), 486–489 (1986)
25. Panetta, K., Gao, C., Agaian, S.: Human-visual-system-inspired underwater image quality measures. IEEE J. Oceanic Eng. **41**(3), 541–551 (2015)
26. Ronneberger, O., Fischer, P., Brox, T.: U-Net: convolutional networks for biomedical image segmentation. In: Navab, N., Hornegger, J., Wells, W.M., Frangi, A.F. (eds.) MICCAI 2015, Part III. LNCS, vol. 9351, pp. 234–241. Springer, Cham (2015). https://doi.org/10.1007/978-3-319-24574-4_28
27. Wang, Y., Song, W., Fortino, G., Qi, L.Z., Zhang, W., Liotta, A.: An experimental-based review of image enhancement and image restoration methods for underwater imaging. IEEE access **7**, 140233–140251 (2019)
28. Yang, M., Sowmya, A.: An underwater color image quality evaluation metric. IEEE Trans. Image Process. **24**(12), 6062–6071 (2015)
29. Zhang, S., Wang, T., Dong, J., Yu, H.: Underwater image enhancement via extended multi-scale retinex. Neurocomputing **245**, 1–9 (2017)

Infrared Image Enhancement for Photovoltaic Panels Based on Improved Homomorphic Filtering and CLAHE

Wanchang Jiang[✉] and Dongdong Xue

School of Computer Science, Northeast Electric Power University, Jilin 132012, China
jwchang84@163.com

Abstract. To address the problems of low contrast and low illumination of infrared images of photovoltaic panels, an infrared image enhancement for photovoltaic panels is proposed. Firstly, in order to improve the overall brightness and contrast of the infrared image, a homomorphic filtering algorithm based on improved transfer function is designed, which constructs a transfer function with a similar structure to the homomorphic filtering profile. Secondly, using the contrast limited adaptive histogram equalization (CLAHE) algorithm fused with gamma correction to further process the image, which not only overcomes the defects of weak details and uneven brightness of the image enhanced by homomorphic filtering, but also improves the clarity and anti-interference of the image. The experimental results show that the proposed algorithm can effectively enhance the visual effect of infrared images, and then improve the integrity of photovoltaic panels in manually labeled images and the detection accuracy of photovoltaic panels.

Keywords: Image enhancement · Infrared image of photovoltaic panels · Homomorphic filtering · CLAHE algorithm · Gamma correction

1   Introduction

Infrared images can be get by equipped drones of photovoltaic (PV) power plants [1], which can be used to analyze abnormal situation of the PV panel. However, infrared images are easily affected by external factors during the imaging process. This will result in low illuminance, clarity and contrast of the captured images, making it difficult to distinguish the PV panels from the background, which will affect follow-up detection experiments. It is urgent to design an algorithm to enhance the infrared image of low-contrast PV panels. At present, the enhancement algorithms of infrared images are mainly divided into two categories: spatial domain method and frequency domain method [2].

The representative algorithms in the spatial domain include histogram equalization (HE) [3] and adaptive histogram equalization (AHE) [4]. Among them,

B. Sheng et al. (Eds.): CGI 2023, LNCS 14495, pp. 348–361, 2024.
https://doi.org/10.1007/978-3-031-50069-5_29

AHE optimizes HE, which realizes the brightness redistribution of the image through the local histogram, thereby changing the image contrast. However, when this method reduces noise in the later stage, the amplification of contrast will be limited. Reference [5] proposes the CLAHE method to solve this problem, which uses contrast to control the enhancement of background noise. At the same time, each area of the image is individually histogram equalized, and then use the obtained local information to enhance the image.

To make the enhanced image have higher quality, the frequency domain method is usually used to further process the image. It mainly includes low-pass filtering, high-pass filtering and homomorphic filtering. Among them, homomorphic filtering [6] is widely used in various fields because of its small amount of calculation and better image processing effect than other algorithms. But it has many parameters and is difficult to control, so Feng [7] and Zhang [8] proposed two improved single-parameter homomorphic filtering algorithms. However, the infrared images of PV panels processed by these two algorithms are dark, which does not conform to the human visual characteristics, and is not conducive to the subsequent manual labeling of the image.

In the end, this paper proposes an infrared image enhancement for photovoltaic panels based on improved homomorphic filtering and CLAHE. To improve the effect of image enhancement, the algorithm constructs a single-parameter transfer function with a similar structure to the homomorphic filter profile. Then a CLAHE algorithm fused with gamma correction is designed to improve the details and contrast of the edge profile of PV panels and darken the noise in the interference area.

2   Infrared Image Enhancement for Photovoltaic Panels Based on Improved Homomorphic Filtering and CLAHE

To improve the overall contrast and edge contour detais of infrared images of PV panels, an infrared image enhancement for photovoltaic panels based on improved homomorphic filtering and CLAHE(IHFC) is proposed.

Firstly, a homomorphic filtering algorithm based on improved transfer function is proposed. By analyzing the structure of the homomorphic filter, a new single-parameter homomorphic filtering transfer function is constructed, which effectively improves the overall brightness and details of the infrared image.

Then, the pixels in the filtered infrared image are adjusted by using the CLAHE algorithm fused with gamma correction. This algorithm can effectively darken the interference area of the image and improve the contrast of the edge contour of the PV panel. The infrared images of PV panels enhanced by the proposed algorithm are helpful for subsequent manual labeling dataset, thereby improving the accuracy of subsequent PV panel detection.

2.1   Homomorphic Filtering Algorithm Based on Improved Transfer Function

Homomorphic Filtering Algorithm. Homomorphic filtering uses the illuminat-ion-reflection model [9] of infrared images as the basis for frequency domain processing. It improves the quality of the image by compressing the brightness range and increasing the contrast. Therefore, an infrared image of PV panels can be regarded as composed of two parts, namely:

$$f(x,y) = f_i(x,y) \times f_r(x,y) \tag{1}$$

where (x,y) represents a two-dimensional spatial plane coordinate of the infrared image $f(x,y)$. $f_i(x,y)$ is the illumination component of the image, which is concentrated in the low-frequency part of the image. $f_r(x,y)$ is the reflection component of the PV panel reflected to the human eye, including various details of the PV panel, mainly distributed in the high-frequency part of the image.

To separate the illumination component and the reflection component of the $f(x,y)$, the nonlinear logarithmic transformation ln is performed on Eq. (1):

$$\ln f(x,y) = \ln f_i(x,y) + \ln f_r(x,y) \tag{2}$$

Subsequently, the fourier transform is applied to Eq. (2) to obtain the frequency domain expression corresponding to the logarithmic image $\ln f(x,y)$:

$$F(u,v) = I(u,v) + R(u,v) \tag{3}$$

where $F(u,v)$, $I(u,v)$, $R(u,v)$ are fourier transform of $\ln f(x,y)$, $\ln f_i(x,y)$, $\ln f_r(x,y)$ respectively. u,v are the spatial frequencies of fourier transform.

To enhance the details of the image, the transfer function $H(u,v)$ is used to filter the image in the frequency domain:

$$H(u,v) \times F(u,v) = H(u,v) \times (I(u,v) + R(u,v)) \tag{4}$$

After filtering, the inverse fourier transform of Eq. (4) is simplified as:

$$h_f(x,y) = h_i(x,y) + h_r(x,y) \tag{5}$$

where $h_f(x,y)$, $h_i(x,y)$, $h_r(x,y)$ are inverse fourier transform of $H(u,v) \times F(u,v)$, $H(u,v) \times I(u,v)$, $H(u,v) \times R(u,v)$ respectively.

Finally, Eq. (5) is transformed exponentially. The light intensity component and the reflection component of the image are merged to obtain the image $g(x,y)$ enhanced by the homomorphic filtering algorithm.

$$g(x,y) = e^{h_f(x,y)} \tag{6}$$

In the homomorphic filtering algorithm, the selection of the transfer function $H(u,v)$ determines the enhancement effect of the infrared image of PV panels.

Design of Transfer Function. In order to improve the contrast and details of the edge profile of the PV panel in the infrared image, it is necessary to suppress the low-frequency part of the transfer function and increase the high-frequency part. This characteristic is similar to a homomorphic filter, while the traditional homomorphic filter has many parameters and is difficult to control.

To solve the above problems, this paper designs a single-parameter transfer function for enhancing low-contrast infrared images of PV panels by studying the characteristics of homomorphic filters. The basic function model is:

$$y = \ln(x + a) \times k^{-1} \tag{7}$$

where the selection of the hyperparameter a is an empirical value obtained through multiple experiments. When the value of a is greater than 48 or less than 48, it may cause partial images distortion in subsequent experiments. Therefore, in order to ensure that the transfer function is applicable to the enhancement of all infrared images, the hyperparameter a is set to 48.

When $a = 48, k = 77$, the transfer function curve is shown in Fig. 1.

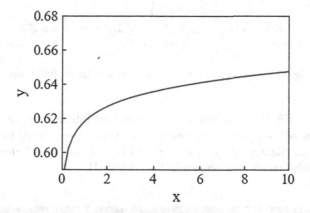

Fig. 1. Transfer function curve.

According to the structure of the curve is similar to that of the homomorphic filter, a new transfer function is constructed as follows:

$$H(u, v) = \ln[D(u, v) + 48] \times k^{-1} \tag{8}$$

where $D(u, v)$ is the distance from frequency (u, v) to center frequency (u_0, v_0). The transfer function only needs to control the parameter k, and its three-dimensional structure is shown in Fig. 2(a).

Reference [7] and reference [8], which have similar improvement measures to this section, respectively proposed a single-parameter homomorphic filter image enhancement, and their transfer function equations are expressed as follows:

$$H(u,v) = \frac{1}{1 + e^{-k \times D(u,v)}} \tag{9}$$

$$H(u,v) = e^{e^{1-k \times D(u,v)}} \tag{10}$$

The parameters in above equations have the same meaning as Eq. (8).

The three-dimensional structure figures corresponding to the transfer function (9) and (10) are shown in Fig. 2(b) and Fig. 2(c), respectively. The minimum value of the newly constructed transfer function in this section is 0.08 higher than that in [7]. The improvement shows that the algorithm in this section has a better effect on contrast stretching. On the other hand, by comparing Fig. 2(a), Fig. 2(b) and Fig. 2(c), it can be seen that the newly constructed transfer function in this section has the smallest slope when it transits from the center frequency to the high frequency part, indicating that the filtering will be more uniform.

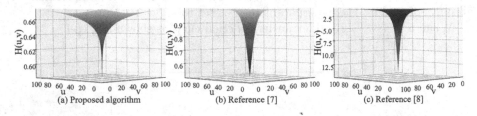

(a) Proposed algorithm   (b) Reference [7]   (c) Reference [8]

Fig. 2. Three dimensional structure of transfer functions.

To further verify this conclusion, a low-contrast infrared image of PV panels (Fig. 3(a)) was selected for experimentation. Apply the algorithm proposed in this section and the algorithms proposed in [7] and [8] to enhance the image. The experimental results are shown in Fig. 3(b)–(d).

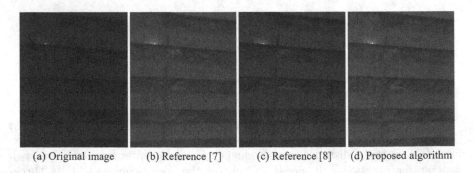

(a) Original image   (b) Reference [7]   (c) Reference [8]   (d) Proposed algorithm

Fig. 3. Experimental results of infrared image of photovoltaic panels.

It can be seen from Fig. 3 that the image processed by the algorithm proposed in [7] and this section is obviously superior to [8] in terms of illumination.

The average gradient(AG) [10] and contrast [11] are used to objectively evaluate the experimental results. Among them, the AG and contrast reflect the details and illumination of the infrared image, respectively. The objective evaluation index values of the original and enhanced images are shown in Table 1.

Table 1. Parameters and evaluation indexes.

Algorithm	Parameter	AG	Contrast
Original image	/	0.5506	0.2383
Reference [7]	$k = 0.5$	1.1423	2.5315
Reference [8]	$k = 0.1$	0.8754	1.5793
Proposed algorithm	$k = 77$	**1.2533**	**3.0389**

As shown in Table 1, the AG and contrast of the image enhanced by the proposed algorithm are 0.7 and 2.8 higher than those of the original image, indicating that the proposed algorithm can effectively improve the brightness and details of the infrared image of PV panels. In addition, the indexes of the image enhanced by the proposed algorithm is better than that of [7] and [8]. It indicates that the proposed algorithm is more suitable for enhancing the infrared image of PV panels. However, the enhanced image (Fig. 3(d)) still has the defects of low contrast and unobvious details, and there is still room for optimization.

2.2 CLAHE Algorithm Fused with Gamma Correction

The overall infrared image enhanced by the algorithm in Subsect. 2.1 is dark, and the edge contour details of PV panels in the image are weak. Therefore, this paper proposes an improved CLAHE algorithm fused with gamma correction to enhance the contrast of the edge contour of the PV panel and weaken the influence of the interference area, so as to improve the visual effect.

CLAHE Algorithm. The CLAHE algorithm is an optimization algorithm for AHE [12,13]. By introducing a method of limiting histogram distribution, the contrast of the edge profile of the PV panel is improved on the basis of effectively suppressing the noise of the infrared image of PV panels.

Firstly, the infrared image is divide into $M \times N$ rectangular block subgraphs of the same size, continuous and non-overlapping. The division result is shown in Fig. 4(a), where $M \times N = 16$.

Secondly, calculate the clipping threshold σ of the infrared image:

$$\sigma = \frac{C_{clip} \times M \times N}{S} \tag{11}$$

where C_{clip} is the clipping limit of CLAHE. Where M and N represent the number of pixels in the x-axis and y-axis directions of the rectangular block, respectively. Where S is the brightness level of the rectangular block.

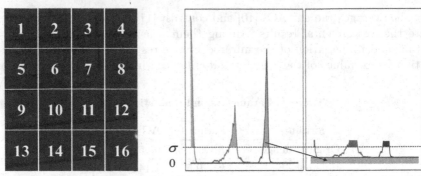

(a) Rectangular block segmentation (b) Pixel redistribution of rectangular block 1

Fig. 4. Histogram clipping and pixel redistribution.

Then, use the obtained threshold σ to clip the histogram of each rectangular block subgraph. And evenly distribute the parts exceeding the σ in the original histogram to ensure that no pixels are lost. Taking the rectangular block 1 as an example, the pixel allocation process is shown in Fig. 4(b). It can be seen from the figure that once the pixels are redistributed, the cut area will exceeds σ again. So the histogram corresponding to each rectangular block subgraph needs to be cropped multiple times separately until the exceeded pixels are negligible.

Finally, bilinear interpolation [14] is used to solve the problem of unnatural transition between rectangular block subgraphs, and the infrared image of the PV panel enhanced by the CLAHE algorithm is obtained.

Introduction of Gamma Correction. Since CLAHE only improves the contrast of the infrared image, it has weak anti-interference ability in areas such as the ground and the shadow of the PV panel. Therefore, the CLAHE are fused with the gamma correction [15]. By automatically selecting the appropriate γ, the dynamic range of the brightness of the interference area is expanded, so as to achieve the effect of reducing the brightness of the interference area.

Generally, gamma correction is done by manually adjusting the γ, but considering the large number of infrared images in the dataset, this section will use automatic gamma correction.

Firstly, calculate the gray mean of the infrared image of PV panels. Then, calculate the γ:

$$\gamma = \frac{\ln midrange}{\ln(mean/255)} \tag{12}$$

where *mean* represents the gray mean of the greyed input image, *midrange* is the intermediate value 0.5 of the normalized range 0 to 1.

Finally, the γ is used to establish the mapping table, and the gamma correction of the image is realized by looking up this table. The output image is the final image enhanced by the algorithm proposed in this paper.

3   Experiment

3.1   Experimental Environment and Dataset

The experiment is completed under the Windows 11. The hardware CPU configuration is i7-12700H, the GPU is Geforce RTX 3060, the memory is 16G, the hard disk is 512G.

The experimental dataset contains 1097 infrared images of PV panels. The dataset is an open source dataset obtained from the website on October 11, 2022 (https://universe.roboflow.com/surshri280-gmail-com/drone-ylaj1). The resolution of all images in the dataset was 512 × 640, and the image format was jpg.

3.2   Enhancement Effect Analysis

Subjective Visual Evaluation. Three low-contrast infrared images of PV panels obtained from different locations were selected from the dataset as the experimental objects of experiments 1–3. Then, the experiments were carried out using the contrast adjustment algorithm suitable for enhancing the image of PV panels in [16] (CA), the improved exponential single-parameter homomorphic filtering image enhancement algorithm(ESHF) in [7], the infrared image enhancement algorithm combined with single-parameter homomorphic filtering and CLAHE(SHFC) in [8], and the IHFC algorithm proposed in this paper.

The original image was compared with the enhanced image, and the experimental results are shown in Fig. 5, Fig. 6 and Fig. 7. The parameter of the IHFC, ESHF and SHFC is set according to Eq. (8), Eq. (9) and Eq. (10) respectively. And the parameter of CA is set based on the contrast adjustment equation in [14]. These four algorithms only need to set one parameter, and the parameter setting is different for different images.

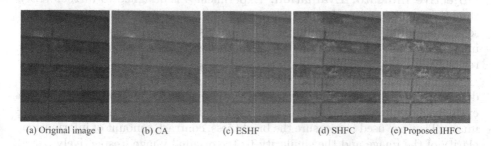

(a) Original image 1   (b) CA   (c) ESHF   (d) SHFC   (e) Proposed IHFC

Fig. 5. Results of Experiment 1.

(a) Original image 2   (b) CA   (c) ESHF   (d) SHFC   (e) Proposed IHFC

Fig. 6. Results of Experiment 2.

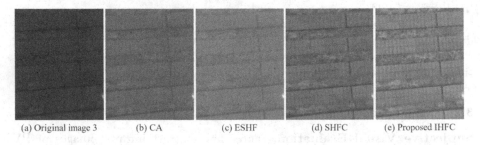

(a) Original image 3   (b) CA   (c) ESHF   (d) SHFC   (e) Proposed IHFC

Fig. 7. Results of Experiment 3.

Combining the three sets of experimental results, it can be seen that the brightness and contrast of the image enhanced by the CA and ESHF have been improved, but there is still a lack of details. Moreover, the image details after SHFC processing have increased, but there is still space to improve. Meanwhile, the IHFC significantly improves the illumination, contrast and clarity of the image. The edge contour details of the PV panel are obviously prominent, and the background noise is suppressed to a certain extent. The overall visual effect of the image is better than other algorithms. Thus, the proposed IHFC is more suitable for the enhancement of low-contrast infrared images of PV panels.

Objective Indicator Evaluation. Experiment 4 is designed to further verify the effectiveness and performance stability of the proposed IHFC. It randomly select 150 different infrared images of PV panels from the dataset as the experimental objects, and apply the above four algorithms to enhance the images respectively.

Mean, information entropy (IE) [17], average gradient (AG) [10], standard deviation (SD) [18] and mean structural similarity (MSSIM) [19,20] are used to evaluate the enhancement effect of each algorithm in experiments on the infrared image. They are used to measure the brightness, contrast, amount of information, clarity of the image and the similarity to the original image, respectively.

The fourth group of experiments has a large amount of calculated data. In order to make the enhancement effect of each algorithm more intuitive, Eq. (13)

is used to normalize the above five objective evaluation indexes to obtain the comprehensive evaluation index value (CEI) [21].

$$CEI = \sum_{j=1}^{s} w_j \frac{Z_j - Z_{min}}{Z_{max} - Z_{min}} \tag{13}$$

where $j = 1, 2, ..., S$, S is the number of evaluation indexes. This paper set $S = 5$. In addition, w_j denotes the weight of the jth evaluation index. Z_j is the jth evaluation index value. Z_{min} and Z_{max} represent the minimum and maximum values of the jth evaluation index, respectively.

The weights of the evaluation indexes are set according to the weighted average method. On account of AG and SD are positively correlated, while the mean, IE and MSSIM are independent. Therefore, the weight of mean, IE, and MSSIM is set to 0.25, and the weight of AG and SD is set to 0.125.

The CEI values of the experiments are shown in Table 2, where the MSSIM of the original image is set to 1.

Table 2. Comprehensive evaluation indicators.

Experiment	Original image	CA	ESHF	SHFC	IHFC
1	0.25	0.46	0.50	0.58	**0.75**
2	0.25	0.52	0.58	0.62	**0.75**
3	0.25	0.52	0.60	0.62	**0.75**
4	0.25	0.50	0.61	0.63	**0.75**

Combined with the Fig. 5, Fig. 6, Fig. 7 and the Table 2, it can be seen that the CEI of the image enhanced by the CA is better than the original image. However, the visual effect of the processed image is still not good. ESHF-enhanced images and SHFC-enhanced images have better visual effects than CA, and their CEI is similar. But the images processed by these two algorithms, one lacks detailed features and the other has low brightness. The IHFC-enhanced images have the best visual effect, and its CEI value is the highest, maintaining around 0.75. This shows that the proposed IHFC has the best enhancement effect and robustness.

According to the CEI of Experiment 4 in Table 2, the relative improvement of the proposed IHFC compared with other algorithms is calculated. Its corresponding histogram is shown in Fig. 8. It can be seen from the figure that the CEI of the proposed algorithm is 50%, 25%, 14% and 12% higher than that of the original image, CA, ESHF, and SHFC, respectively.

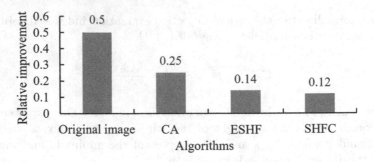

Fig. 8. Relative improvement of the CEI value.

3.3 Detection Effect Analysis

To verify the proposed IHFC can effectively improve the accuracy of PV panel detection, the YOLOX-s model is used to conduct experiments on the original dataset and the IHFC-enhanced dataset.

The whole experimental dataset is divided into training set (1215 sheets), validation set (135 sheets) and test set (150 sheets). The batch size is set to 4, the training epoch is set to 150, and the initial learning rate is 0.001.

The P-R curves of the model is shown in Fig. 9. The area between the P-R curve and the two coordinate axes represents the average precision, which is used to measure the accuracy of detection model. It can be seen from the figure that when the IHFC-enhanced dataset is used for detection, the area is larger, indicating that the average precision is higher.

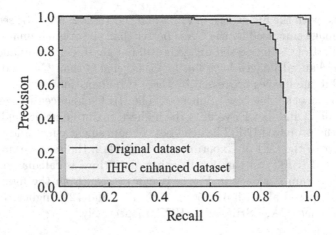

Fig. 9. P-R curve of photovoltaic panel detection.

The detection results of the YOLOX-s model are analyzed using the evaluation indexes of precision, recall, F1-score [22] and average precision (AP) [23]. The experimental detection results are shown in Table 3.

Table 3. The detection results of the model on different datasets.

Dataset	Precision	Recall	F1-score	AP
Original dataset	0.854	0.857	0.86	0.872
IHFC-enhanced dataset	**0.990**	**0.967**	**0.98**	**0.996**

It can be seen from Table 3 that the AP of IHFC-enhanced dataset is higher, as high as 99.6%. Compared with using the original dataset, the AP, precision and recall increased by 12.4%, 13.6% and 11%, respectively. It has a good detection effect and basically solves the phenomenon of missed detection of photovoltaic panels caused by unclear boundary contours. The F1-score is the weighted harmonic mean of the precision and recall. It can be used here to evaluate the quality of the dataset. As can be seen from the table, when the model uses the IHFC-enhanced dataset, the F1-value increased by 12%, indicating that the dataset is more suitable for the detection of PV panels.

4   Conclusion

This paper proposes an infrared image enhancement for PV panels based on improved homomorphic filtering and CLAHE. Firstly, in order to improve the overall brightness and contrast of the image, a homomorphic filtering algorithm based on the improved transfer function is proposed. Then, the CLAHE algorithm is used to adjust the pixels in the image to improve the details and visual effects of the image. Finally, automatic gamma correction is adopted to reduce the brightness of interference areas such as the ground, and improve the anti-interference of the image. The experimental results show that the proposed IHFC can effectively improve the contrast, clarity and brightness of infrared images of PV panels. The enhanced image can obtain better visual effects, which is helpful for the manual labeling of the dataset during the PV panel detection, thereby indirectly improving the accuracy of the detection model. Moreover, the accuracy of the model is higher while using the IHFC-enhanced dataset for detection.

References

1. Liao, K.C., Lu, J.H.: Using UAV to detect solar module fault conditions of a solar power farm with IR and visual image analysis. Appl. Sci. **11**(4), 1835 (2021)
2. Rao, Y., Zhao, W., Zhu, Z., et al.: Global filter networks for image classification. Adv. Neural. Inf. Process. Syst. **34**, 980–993 (2021)

3. Dhal, K.G., Das, A., Ray, S., et al.: Histogram equalization variants as optimization problems: a review. Arch. Comput. Methods Eng. **28**, 1471–1496 (2021)
4. Acharya, U.K., Kumar, S.: Genetic algorithm based adaptive histogram equalization (GAAHE) technique for medical image enhancement. Optik **230**, 166273 (2021)
5. Ulutas, G., Ustubioglu, B.: Underwater image enhancement using contrast limited adaptive histogram equalization and layered difference representation. Multimedia Tools Appl. **80**(10), 15067–15091 (2021). https://doi.org/10.1007/s11042-020-10426-2
6. Pullagura, R., Valasani, U.S., Kesari, P.P.: Hybrid wavelet-based aerial image enhancement using georectification and homomorphic filtering. Arab. J. Geosci. **14**(13), 1–13 (2021). https://doi.org/10.1007/s12517-021-07551-z
7. Feng, X.H.: An improved homomorphic filtering image enhancement algorithm. J. Chongqing Univ. Posts Telecommun. Nat. Sci. Ed. **32**(1), 138–145 (2020)
8. Zhang, K., Liao, Y.R., Luo, Y.L., et al.: Infrared image enhancement algorithm based on improved homomorphic filtering. Laser Optoelectron. Progress. **60**(10), 63–69 (2023)
9. Fan, W., Huo, Y., Li, X.: Degraded image enhancement using dual-domain-adaptive wavelet and improved fuzzy transform. Math. Probl. Eng. **2021**, 1–12 (2021)
10. Ma, B., Zhu, Y., Yin, X., et al.: Sesf-fuse: an unsupervised deep model for multi-focus image fusion. Neural Comput. Appl. **33**, 5793–5804 (2021)
11. Wang, Y., Jiang, Z., Liu, C., et al.: Shedding light on images: multi-level image brightness enhancement guided by arbitrary references. Pattern Recogn. **131**, 108867 (2022)
12. Ying, L.L., Shu, T.J., Ye, Z., et al.: Unsupervised face super-resolution via gradient enhancement and semantic guidance. Vis. Comput. **37**(9–11), 2855–2867 (2021)
13. Acharya, U.K., Kumar, S.: Image enhancement using exposure and standard deviation-based sub-image histogram equalization for night-time images. In: Bansal, P., Tushir, M., Balas, V.E., Srivastava, R. (eds.) Proceedings of International Conference on Artificial Intelligence and Applications. AISC, vol. 1164, pp. 607–615. Springer, Singapore (2021). https://doi.org/10.1007/978-981-15-4992-2_57
14. Yan, F., Zhao, S., Venegas-Andraca, S.E., et al.: Implementing bilinear interpolation with quantum images. Digital Signal Process. **117**, 103149 (2021)
15. Ye, H., Su, K., Huang, S.: Image enhancement method based on bilinear interpolating and wavelet transform. Electron. Autom. Control Conf. **5**, 1147–1150 (2021)
16. Xu, W., Zhang, K.J.: Research on indentification of PV module strings based on image processing. Inf. Technol. Inform. **238**(1), 187–190 (2020)
17. Omar, Y.M., Plapper, P.: A survey of information entropy metrics for complex networks. Entropy **22**(12), 1417 (2020)
18. Kim, J.H., Yoon, H.J., Lee, E., et al.: Validation of deep-learning image reconstruction for low-dose chest computed tomography scan: emphasis on image quality and noise. Korean J. Radiol. **22**(1), 131 (2021)
19. Setiadi, D.R.I.M.: PSNR vs SSIM: imperceptibility quality assessment for image steganography. Multimedia Tools Appl. **80**(6), 8423–8444 (2021)
20. Li, L., Tang, J., Ye, Z., et al.: Unsupervised face super-resolution via gradient enhancement and semantic guidance. Vis. Comput. **37**, 2855–2867 (2021)
21. Zhang, Y.L., Li, W.Y., Li, C.L., et al.: Method for enhancement of the multi-scale low-light image by combining an attention guidance. J. Xidian Univ. **50**(1), 129–136 (2023)

22. DeVries, Z., Locke, E., Hoda, M., et al.: Using a national surgical database to predict complications following posterior lumbar surgery and comparing the area under the curve and F1-score for the assessment of prognostic capability. Spine J. **21**(7), 1135–1142 (2021)
23. Maxwell, A.E., Pourmohammadi, P., Poyner, J.D.: Mapping the topographic features of mining-related valley fills using mask R-CNN deep learning and digital elevation data. Remote Sens. **12**(3), 547 (2020)

An Efficient and Lightweight Structure for Spatial-Temporal Feature Extraction in Video Super Resolution

Xiaonan He[1], Yukun Xia[2], Yuansong Qiao[1], Brian Lee[1], and Yuhang Ye[1(✉)]

[1] Technological University of the Shannon, Athlone N37HD68, Ireland
A00268945@student.tus.ie, {Ysqiao,Yye}@research.ait.ie, Brian.Lee@tus.ie
[2] Jiangxi University of Finance and Economics, Nanchang 330032, China
https://www.ait.ie/

Abstract. Video Super Resolution (VSR) model based on deep convolutional neural network (CNN) uses multiple Low-Resolution (LR) frames as input and has a strong ability to recover High-Resolution (HR) frames and maintain video temporal information. However, to realize the above advantages, VSR must consider both spatial and temporal information to improve the perceived quality of the output video, leading to expensive operations such as cross-frame convolution. Therefore, how to balance the output video quality and computational cost is a worthy issue to be studied. To address the above problem, we propose an efficient and lightweight multi-scale 3D video super-resolution scheme that arranges 3D convolution features extraction blocks using a U-Net structure to achieve multi-scale feature extraction in both spatial and temporal dimensions. Quantitative and qualitative evaluation results on public video datasets show that compared to other simple cascaded spatial-temporal feature extraction structures, an U-Net structure achieves comparable texture details and temporal consistency while with a significant reduction in computation costs and latency.

Keywords: Video Super Resolution · U-Net · 3D convolution · Efficiency

1 Introduction

Super-resolution (SR) technology, utilized to refine low-resolution images or videos by restoring lost detail during high-resolution compression, has been applied widely in computer vision sectors like video surveillance [5], panorama video super-resolution [12], and high-definition video playback [9]. Its advanced variant, VSR considers the temporal dynamics of videos, necessitating the reconstruction of time relevance between frames. Recent VSR techniques, using deep neural networks, focus on enhancing video frame quality by optimizing CNN-based structures and integrating novel strategies such as a 2-stage feature extraction framework [18,23] (Fig. 1). This includes the first stage of spatial-temporal

© The Author(s), under exclusive license to Springer Nature Switzerland AG 2024
B. Sheng et al. (Eds.): CGI 2023, LNCS 14495, pp. 362–374, 2024.
https://doi.org/10.1007/978-3-031-50069-5_30

feature extraction, employing rule-based or temporal neural network models [1,3,16], and the second stage of refining these features using neural networks or attention mechanisms [23]. Despite the potential for higher-quality frame reconstruction, these stages pose challenges due to high computational costs, particularly in the spatial-temporal feature extraction stage. Processing multiple frames and extracting combined features are resource-intensive due to the high spatial and temporal dimensions of videos, compounded by additional complexities with techniques like deformable convolution [23]. Efficient computational management is therefore vital to progress in video super-resolution.

This paper addresses this efficiency issue in VSR spatial-temporal processing by identifying a general structure to link feature extraction blocks, specifically a U-Net-like structure as a substitute to the traditionally linear cascaded structure. U-Net architectures, by downsampling feature maps multiple times for extraction, decrease computational load significantly, each $/2$ downsample reducing the feature map to a quarter and cutting required convolution computations by about 75%. Though downsampling could potentially compromise feature quality, our modified U-Net has proven through experimentation to boost both feature extraction efficiency and quality. Thus, it enhances the final video output and signifies the U-Net as a potential tool for improving spatial-temporal processing in VSR. The key contributions of this paper include: **1)** an efficient U-Net-based spatial-temporal feature extraction structure for VSR that reduces computational cost without sacrificing video quality, and **2)** the implementation of Deformable 3D Convolution (D3D) and Non-deformable 3D Convolution (C3D) using this structure, leading to improved performance on Vid4 and REDS datasets while keeping computational costs low and slightly enhancing video quality.

2   Related Work

A proliferation of research focusing on deep learning-based Single Image Super-Resolution (SISR) has emerged [8]. Early work such as SRCNN [7] utilized a combination of patch extraction, non-linear mapping, and reconstruction for SR, driving substantial progress in the field. The introduction of Generative Adversarial Networks (GANs) in SISR [11], employing 16 residual blocks in the Generator and 8 convolution operations with 2 skip connections in the Discriminator, marked a significant advancement. Most recently, TTSR [22] merged the transformer architecture with SISR, using a feature fusion mechanism and upsampling to achieve multi-level feature fusion.

Deep learning-based VSR techniques have made significant strides in enhancing SISR by leveraging the additional information present in neighboring low-resolution frames. The utilization of inter-frame information in the feature extraction module leads to the classification of VSR methods into two categories - those employing alignment techniques and that without [13]. Motion Estimation and Motion Compensation (MEMC) [1] and Deformable Convolution [6] represent the two main approaches to achieve alignment, both of which have proven to be effective methods in the field of VSR. VESPCN [2] represents a typical approach that is based on Motion Estimation and Motion Compensation. It utilizes a spatial motion compensation transformer that employs a coarse-to-fine approach to compute the optical flow between two frames. By combining coarse and fine optical flow, the transformer can generate a warped frame, which is then used to align the neighboring frame with the target frame. This is achieved by warping the previously warped frame with the estimated fine optical flow. The use of this approach allows VESPCN to achieve high-quality video super-resolution results. Regarding Deformable Convolution, [18] introduced EDVR, which employs cascading deformable convolutions to enrich the aligned information needed to handle complex and long-range motion within the Deformable Alignment Unit (PCD). The use of deformable convolution has garnered significant attention due to its adaptable receptive field and implicit incorporation of motion information. However, while the unstable training phenomenon can be alleviated to some degree by [4], overcoming the heavy computational burdens remains a challenge.

3   U-Net and Motivation

U-Net's capacity for analyzing feature maps at diverse scales, capturing both local and global features, has rendered it a favored choice for image segmentation tasks in scholarly literature [10]. especially in the area of medical imaging. For example, the U-Net enables ECSU-Net [15] to efficiently perform intervertebral disc segmentation and classification, while consuming reduced time and computational resources. The SAUnet++ [20] can make segmentation easier while facing the variety of lesions and small regions of early lesion, which utilizes U-Net++ to obtain context information by atrous convolution using various sampling rates. Its application in VSR e.g., (EDVR [18] uses it for multi-scale MEMC) is well-documented. Nevertheless, U-Net's potential as a universal structure for temporal-spatial feature extraction modules aimed at reducing computational complexity in VSR remains unexplored. Although the downsampling operation in U-Net cuts down the size of the feature map and convolutional cost, the effect on the video quality is uncertain. This paper endeavors to scrutinize the performance of VSR videos derived from U-Net structured spatial-temporal feature extraction blocks, juxtaposing it with a linear cascaded structure to ascertain if the output video quality is maintained.

4   Reference Architecture for VSR

The comparative study conducted in this paper is based on a reference architecture as shown in Fig. 1. It is composed of 4 parts, which the first stage and the third stage relate to feature extraction:

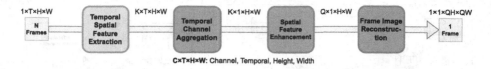

Fig. 1. Four Stage VSR, with 2 Stage Feature Extraction

- **Spatial-Temporal Feature Extraction** leverages 3D convolution models. This enables the extraction of features that combine spatial and temporal information, allowing missing details of a reference frame to be found in neighboring frames.
- **Temporal Channel Aggregation** combines (via convolution) feature maps across the temporal channel, which means merging multiple frames into a single frame. This allows the model to embed contextual information from neighboring frames into a single frame. A Conv2D layer is used.
- **Spatial Feature Enhancement** further processes the single-frame feature map output from the previous step so as to utilize the aggregated features to obtain the high-level image super-resolution features. For simplicity, Six cascaded Resblock modules are used.
- **Frame Image Reconstruction** maps the image super-resolution features to sub-pixel images and then rearranges them using a pixel shuffle layer to generate a higher-resolution image. A Conv2D layer and a PixelShuffle layer are used.

This paper focuses on the efficiency of "Spatial-Temporal Feature Extraction". Two structures, linear cascaded and U-Net, are examined. For a broader comparative study, we use two 3D convolutional modules for feature extraction: D3D and C3D. Thus, four experimental comparisons are conducted: cascaded D3D, U-net D3D, cascaded C3D, and U-Net C3D.

5   Design Details

This section will present additional details about the model design including the conventional linear cascaded structure and U-Net structure and a description of the 3D feature extraction blocks. In a linear cascaded structure, inputs are sequentially processed through N feature extraction blocks arranged in a linear way, which enables capturing spatial-temporal features.

5.1   U-Net Structure

To mitigate additional complexity, our proposed U-Net structure deviates from the original in two distinct ways. Firstly, we employ a simple addition operator rather than concatenation for the fusion of residual links between same-layer features. This approach avoids the augmentation of feature map channels, which directly impacts computational complexity. Secondly, we append a residual link

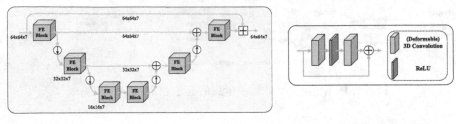

(a) Proposed U-Net Structure

(b) Residual Feature Extraction (FE) Block

Fig. 2. Proposed U-Net Architecture

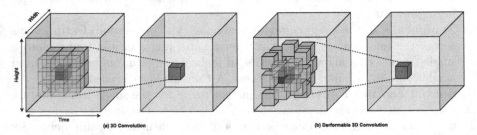

(a) 3D Convolution

(b) Deformable 3D Convolution

Fig. 3. 3D Convolution and Deformable 3D Convolution.

outside the U-Net module to clearly establish an identity mapping, reducing the risk of overfitting and potentially enhancing the module's capability. As depicted in Fig. 2, our proposed U-Net architecture sequentially connects six feature extraction blocks across three different scales, bolstering the model's proficiency in extracting multi-resolution features within frames. The computation process of the proposed U-Net is given as follows:

$$h = x + f_2(x)r$$
$$f_k(x) = g(x) + \psi_2(f_{k-1}(\phi_2(g(x)))) \quad \forall k > 1 \tag{1}$$
$$f_0(x) = g(g(x))$$

where h represents the final output feature maps of the whole U-Net structure. f denotes a layer of U-Net function written in a recursive form; g denotes the temporal-spatial feature extraction module; ψ_2 denotes the $\times 2$ upsampling function, ϕ_2 denotes the $\times 2$ downsampling function. In our example, we only use a 3-layer U-net, and for the bottom layer, the feature map is processed via two cascaded feature extraction modules g.

For the feature extraction function g, we examine two structures: D3D and convention 3-D convolution (C3D). In the case of C3D, the receptive field per filter kernel is of a fixed size and compact without dilation. This means that the input pixels are sampled in a predetermined pattern. The functionality of the 3D convolution, as seen in the C3D methodology, can be explained through the following two stages: initially, the input features 'a' are subjected to 3D convolution kernel sampling, subsequently followed by a weighted sum of these sampled values, using the function 'w'. More explicitly, the process involving these features passing through a conventional $3 \times 3 \times 3$ convolution kernel with a dilation factor of 1 can be formulated as follows:

$$y(p_0) = \sum_{d \in G} w(d) \cdot x(p_0 + d) \tag{2}$$

where p_0 denotes the center of the filter kernel that corresponds to the reference position of the feature in the output map, while d represents the nth value in the $3 \times 3 \times 3$ convolution sampling grid $G = (-1, -1, -1), ...,(1, 1, 1)$ of size $N = 27$. As illustrated in Fig. 3 (a), the plain C3D sampling grid can be visualized as the $3 \times 3 \times 3$ cubes in the input feature. Compared with C3D, a deformable filter in D3D enlarges the filter's receptive field without additional parameters. It enhances the model modeling capabilities of large patterns. According to the original paper, D3D version [23], the deformed only along the height and width dimensions. Subsequently, the learned offsets are used to guide the deformation of the plain C3D sampling grid to produce a D3D sampling grid. Finally, the D3D sampling grid is utilized to generate the output temporal-spatial feature. To summarize, D3D can be expressed as follows:

$$y(p_0) = \sum_{n=1}^{N} w(p_n) \cdot x(p_0 + p_n + \Delta p_n) \tag{3}$$

where Δp_n denotes the offset that corresponds to the nth value in the $3 \times 3 \times 3$ convolution kernel. The offsets Δp_n may be fractional, therefore, a bilinear interpolation is used to generate approximated values for a fractional offset.

6   Experimental Results

6.1   Experiment Settings

The model was trained on the Vimeo-90K dataset [21], using a 64×64 pixel patch size. It was evaluated on Vid4 [2] and REDS [14] datasets, utilizing the Adam optimizer and Mean Square Error (MSE) loss function. The learning rate started at $4e-4$ and halved every six epochs with a batch size of 10. Training was conducted for 40 epochs on the Nvidia A100 platform via PyTorch.

6.2   Experimental Analysis

We compared the effectiveness of U-Net and linear structures on two benchmark datasets, Vid4 and REDS, using either C3D or D3D as the temporal-spatial feature extraction block to demonstrate the generalizability of our experiments. The structure that cascades D3D blocks is named "D3Dnet", and D3Dblocks with U-Net structure is "U-Net-D3Dnet". Similarly, the cascaded-C3D block

Table 1. Objective results in 2 datasets. **BOLD** font presents the best.

Dataset	Model	PSNR↑	SSIM↑	S-MOVIE↓	T-MOVIE↓	MOVIE↓
vid4	D3Dnet	25.843	0.761	31.318	17.424	4.056
	U-Net-D3Dnet	**25.901**	**0.764**	**31.026**	**17.061**	**4.003**
	C3Dnet	25.367	0.738	32.993	21.480	4.824
	U-Net-C3Dnet	**25.509**	**0.746**	**31.942**	**20.504**	**4.549**
REDS	D3Dnet	29.288	**0.820**	32.553	**5.133**	2.524
	U-Net-D3Dnet	**29.294**	**0.820**	**32.499**	6.091	**2.508**
	C3Dnet	28.780	0.802	29.548	6.773	2.414
	U-Net-C3Dnet	**28.937**	**0.807**	**29.109**	**6.679**	**2.361**

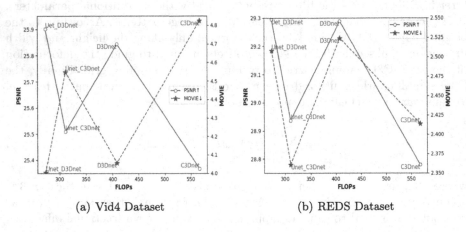

(a) Vid4 Dataset   (b) REDS Dataset

Fig. 4. Computation and performance on the Vid4 and REDS datasets.

structure is "C3Dnet", the combination of C3D and U-Net is called "U-Net-C3Dnet". We evaluated the performance of each structure using objective metrics such as Peak Signal-to-Noise Ratio (PSNR), Structural Similarity Index (SSIM) [19], Temporal-MOVIE (T-MOVIE) [17], Spatial-MOVIE (S-MOVIE) [17], and MOtion-based Video Integrity Evaluation index (MOVIE) [17]. All the metrics were calculated using the luminance channel. The results of the analysis can be found in Table 1, while Table 2 records the computational cost of the methods, measured in Floating-Point operations (FLOPs).

Efficiency. On U-Net-based structures, the number of features at each layer is reduced by $3/4$ with each downsampling, theoretically shortening computation time. If the computation time for a single feature extraction block is 1 unit, then cascading 5 linear blocks without changing channel numbers or image size would require 5 units. Using the same feature module, the computation time required for a three-layer U-Net structure (3 layers) is $(1 + 0.25 + 0.0625) \times 2 = 2.625$.

(a) The left is from D3Dnet, the right is from U-Net-D3Dnet

(b) The left is from D3Dnet, the right is from U-Net-D3Dnet

Fig. 5. The SR results comparison between D3Dnet and U-Net-D3Dnet on Vid4 dataset "calendar" and REDS dataset "011"

(a) The left is from C3Dnet, the right is from U-Net-C3Dnet

(b) The left is from C3Dnet, the right is from U-Net-C3Dnet

Fig. 6. The SR results comparison between C3Dnet and U-Net-C3Dnet on Vid4 dataset file "calendar" and REDS dataset file "011"

However, sampling and U-Net's skip connection operations bring additional computational costs, so the final computation time is not simply $2.625/5=0.525$. In our experiments, we sampled the delays and conducted a simple mean analysis. The computation latency results are presented in Table 2. As we can see, for the models that apply D3D blocks, the time cost of feature extraction of U-Net-D3Dnet is nearly 0.56 times of D3Dnet. And the efficiency of U-Net-C3Dnet is much higher than C3Dnet in the aspect of models using C3D blocks with only 46.7% time-consuming.

Table 2. Computation Efficiency of methods. "time" is time-consuming on the feature extraction module and "FLOPS" is the computational cost. All the results are computed based on source frames with a resolution of 320×180. **BOLD** font presents the best.

Model	Frames	Time	FLOPs
D3Dnet	7	189.64 ms	408.38G
U-Net-D3Dnet	7	**106.27 ms**	**274.26G**
C3Dnet	7	24.995 ms	567.23G
U-Net-C3Dnet	7	**11.674 ms**	**310.83G**

Table 3. The parameter(M) and FLOPs(G) of models in different numbers of layers and Residual Feature Extraction Blocks. For example, D3D-Layer4Block2 means this structure consists of a 4-layer U-Net structure and each layer has two D3D blocks for downsampling and two for upsampling

	D3D		C3D	
	1 Block	2 Blocks	1 Block	2 Blocks
3 Layers	3.10M	5.55M	1.98M	3.30M
	274.26G	471.78G	310.83G	544.94G
4 Layers	3.91M	7.18M	2.42M	4.19M
	276.56G	476.38G	313.56G	550.39G
5 Layers	4.73M	8.81M	2.86M	5.07M
	277.13G	477.53G	314.24G	551.75G

Video Quality. To highlight, we also drew the line graphs Fig. 4 to demonstrate the differences in the performance of these four structures on PSNR and MOVIE on the Vid4 and REDS datasets respectively, since these two objective metrics are representative.

As Tables 1, 2 and Fig. 4 are shown, the models that apply the U-Net structure both outperform the "cascading" models in both datasets. In the Vid4 dataset, U-Net with D3D blocks can achieve slightly better quality in all objective indicators than D3Dnet, and with the FLOPs 134.12G smaller, which means we can gain roughly the same result with D3Dnet, but the computation cost is only around two-thirds of D3Dnet. Especially, the proposed structure integrates 6 ResD3D blocks, however, D3Dnet only uses 5 blocks for feature extraction. Seen from Fig. 5, the subjective results are much clear, the results of D3Dnet have serious artifact and edge blur problems. While comparing the two C3D-based models, all the results that U-Net with C3D blocks generated are much better than cascaded C3D blocks in the REDS dataset with only approx half the computational cost. Also, Fig. 6 shows the SR results of cascaded C3D blocks have a jagged edge that contains much noise and the content is relatively blurred. This demonstrates that SR performance and spatial-temporal consistency gains are not due to the use of large capacity models.

7   Ablation Studies

This section presents a series of ablation studies to probe the efficacy of the proposed structure, specifically examining the U-Net depth and the number of Residual blocks. These studies are performed on the Vid4 and REDS datasets.

7.1 Architecture Depth of U-Net

The proposed U-Net model comprises three layers, designed with an emphasis on maximizing overall structural efficiency. In order to substantiate this three-layered design, it was compared against four-layer and five-layer architectures by evaluating several objective metrics. Given identical input feature map dimensions, the minimum sizes for four-layer and five-layer structures were $8 \times 8 \times 7$ and $4 \times 4 \times 7$, respectively. The comparative results are presented in Tables 4 and 5, which utilize D3D and C3D blocks respectively. Despite the superior performance of the five-layer U-Net architecture in some metrics, an examination of Table 3 reveals that its parameter value is approximately 1.5 times larger than ours. This underlines the high effectiveness of our three-layer U-Net architecture.

7.2 Count of Residual Feature Extraction Blocks

The Residual FE block functions as the cornerstone of the feature extraction module, and its quantity undeniably impacts performance. For the purposes of this study, comparisons were drawn between architectures employing one block and two blocks per layer for the downsampling/upsampling procedures, constrained by GPU capabilities. Table 3 displays the computational burden associated with the structure utilizing two blocks. The floating point operations per second (FLOPs) of this structure are significantly high, even surpassing linear cascaded modules. As such, structures with two FE blocks are not regarded as capable of significantly diminishing computational costs and latency.

Table 4. D3D blocks ablation of different U-Net layers. **BOLD** denotes the best.

Dataset	Model	PSNR↑	SSIM↑	S-MOVIE↓	T-MOVIE↓	MOVIE↓
Vid4	Ours	25.901	0.764	**31.026**	**17.061**	4.003
	4-layer	25.894	0.764	31.069	17.103	3.994
	5-layer	**25.904**	**0.765**	30.896	17.083	**3.96**
REDS	Ours	**29.294**	**0.82**	**32.499**	6.091	2.508
	4-layer	29.24	0.819	32.573	**6.043**	**2.506**
	5-layer	29.262	0.819	32.608	6.081	2.518

Table 5. C3D blocks ablation of different U-Net layers. **BOLD** denotes the best.

Dataset	Model	PSNR↑	SSIM↑	S-MOVIE↓	T-MOVIE↓	MOVIE↓
Vid4	Ours	**25.509**	**0.746**	**31.942**	20.504	**4.549**
	4-layer	25.385	0.738	33.137	20.251	4.691
	5-layer	25.466	0.745	32.927	**20.072**	4.634
REDS	Ours	**28.937**	**0.807**	**29.109**	6.679	**2.361**
	4-layer	28.863	0.804	34.142	**6.43**	2.715
	5-layer	28.891	0.806	33.886	6.485	2.702

8   Limitation and Discussion

The wider applicability of U-Net structures warrants further investigation. However, the study already offers valuable insights by evaluating Linear Cascaded and U-Net structures on specific spatial-temporal feature extraction blocks, such as C3D and D3D. These findings, which include methods like temporal and deformable convolution used for optical flow estimation [18], may prove useful for future work with similar feature extraction blocks, like attention mechanisms or recurrent CNN structures.

9   Conclusion

Recent studies on video super-resolution (VSR) have shown that 3D convolutions outperform 2D convolutions in preserving temporal continuity. However, the high computational cost of 3D convolutions is a major challenge in achieving high-performance VSR. To address this issue, we conducted a comparative study aiming to enhance the efficiency of 3D convolutions in VSR without compromising the output video quality. Our proposed study combines the U-Net architecture with 3D feature extraction blocks to strike a balance between computational cost and model performance. The resulting U-Net model demonstrates not only effectiveness but also efficiency i.e., the U-Net structure achieves the improved VSR performance for both deformable and conventional 3D convolutional blocks, with a significant reduction of computational requirements.

Acknowledgements. This work was supported by the President Doctoral Scholarship at the Technological University of Shannon.

Contribution Statement. Xiaonan He and Yukun Xia contributed equally to this work.

References

1. Bao, W., Lai, W.S., Zhang, X., Gao, Z., Yang, M.H.: MEMC-Net: motion estimation and motion compensation driven neural network for video interpolation and enhancement. IEEE Trans. Pattern Anal. Mach. Intell. **43**(3), 933–948 (2019)
2. Caballero, J., et al.: Real-time video super-resolution with spatio-temporal networks and motion compensation. In: Proceedings of the IEEE Conference on Computer Vision and Pattern Recognition, pp. 4778–4787 (2017)
3. Cao, J., et al.: Towards interpretable video super-resolution via alternating optimization. In: Avidan, S., Brostow, G., Cissé, M., Farinella, G.M., Hassner, T. (eds.) Computer Vision – ECCV 2022. ECCV 2022. Lecture Notes in Computer Science, vol. 13678, pp. 393–411. Springer, Cham (2022). https://doi.org/10.1007/978-3-031-19797-0_23

4. Chan, K.C., Wang, X., Yu, K., Dong, C., Loy, C.C.: Understanding deformable alignment in video super-resolution. In: Proceedings of the AAAI conference on artificial intelligence, vol. 35, pp. 973–981 (2021)
5. Chiche, B.N., Woiselle, A., Frontera-Pons, J., Starck, J.L.: Stable long-term recurrent video super-resolution. In: Proceedings of the IEEE/CVF Conference on Computer Vision and Pattern Recognition, pp. 837–846 (2022)
6. Dai, J., et al.: Deformable convolutional networks. In: Proceedings of the IEEE International Conference on Computer Vision, pp. 764–773 (2017)
7. Dong, C., Loy, C.C., Tang, X.: Accelerating the super-resolution convolutional neural network. In: Leibe, B., Matas, J., Sebe, N., Welling, M. (eds.) ECCV 2016. LNCS, vol. 9906, pp. 391–407. Springer, Cham (2016). https://doi.org/10.1007/978-3-319-46475-6_25
8. Kim, J., Lee, J.K., Lee, K.M.: Accurate image super-resolution using very deep convolutional networks. In: Proceedings of the IEEE Conference on Computer Vision and Pattern Recognition, pp. 1646–1654 (2016)
9. Kim, S.Y., Oh, J., Kim, M.: Deep SR-ITM: joint learning of super-resolution and inverse tone-mapping for 4K UHD HDR applications. In: Proceedings of the IEEE/CVF International Conference on Computer Vision, pp. 3116–3125 (2019)
10. Kiran, I., Raza, B., Ijaz, A., Khan, M.A.: DenseRes-Unet: segmentation of overlapped/clustered nuclei from multi organ histopathology images. Comput. Biol. Med. **143**, 105267 (2022)
11. Ledig, C., et al.: Photo-realistic single image super-resolution using a generative adversarial network. In: Proceedings of the IEEE Conference on Computer Vision and Pattern Recognition, pp. 4681–4690 (2017)
12. Liu, H., et al.: A single frame and multi-frame joint network for 360-degree panorama video super-resolution. arXiv preprint arXiv:2008.10320 (2020)
13. Liu, H., et al.: Video super-resolution based on deep learning: a comprehensive survey. Artif. Intell. Rev. **55**(8), 5981–6035 (2022)
14. Nah, S., et al.: Ntire 2019 challenge on video deblurring and super-resolution: dataset and study. In: Proceedings of the IEEE/CVF Conference on Computer Vision and Pattern Recognition Workshops, pp. 0–0 (2019)
15. Nazir, A., et al.: ECSU-Net: an embedded clustering sliced u-net coupled with fusing strategy for efficient intervertebral disc segmentation and classification. IEEE Trans. Image Process. **31**, 880–893 (2021)
16. Sajjadi, M.S., Vemulapalli, R., Brown, M.: Frame-recurrent video super-resolution. In: Proceedings of the IEEE Conference on Computer Vision and Pattern Recognition, pp. 6626–6634 (2018)
17. Seshadrinathan, K., Bovik, A.C.: Motion tuned spatio-temporal quality assessment of natural videos. IEEE Trans. Image Process. **19**(2), 335–350 (2009)
18. Wang, X., Chan, K.C., Yu, K., Dong, C., Change Loy, C.: EDVR: video restoration with enhanced deformable convolutional networks. In: Proceedings of the IEEE/CVF Conference on Computer Vision and Pattern Recognition Workshops, pp. 0–0 (2019)
19. Wang, Z., Bovik, A.C., Sheikh, H.R., Simoncelli, E.P.: Image quality assessment: from error visibility to structural similarity. IEEE Trans. Image Process. **13**(4), 600–612 (2004)
20. Xiao, H., Ran, Z., Mabu, S., Li, Y., Li, L.: Saunet++: an automatic segmentation model of COVID-19 lesion from CT slices. Vis. Comput. **39**(6), 2291–2304 (2023)
21. Xue, T., Chen, B., Wu, J., Wei, D., Freeman, W.T.: Video enhancement with task-oriented flow. Int. J. Comput. Vision **127**, 1106–1125 (2019)

22. Yang, F., Yang, H., Fu, J., Lu, H., Guo, B.: Learning texture transformer network for image super-resolution. In: Proceedings of the IEEE/CVF Conference on Computer Vision and Pattern Recognition, pp. 5791–5800 (2020)
23. Ying, X., Wang, L., Wang, Y., Sheng, W., An, W., Guo, Y.: Deformable 3D convolution for video super-resolution. IEEE Signal Process. Lett. **27**, 1500–1504 (2020)

Specular Highlight Detection and Removal Based on Dynamic Association Learning

Jinyao Shen[1], Huanmei Guan[2], Shuohan Tao[3], Kang Yan[4], Fu Zhou[2], and Fei Luo[2(✉)]

[1] School of Cyber Science and Engineering, Wuhan University, Wuhan, China
[2] School of Computer Science, Wuhan University, Wuhan, China
{hmguan,zhoufu,luofei}@whu.edu.cn
[3] Selwyn College, Cambridge, UK
[4] Faculty of Mathematics and Statistics, Hubei University, Wuhan, China

Abstract. Specular highlight widely exists in daily life. Its strong brightness influences the recognition of text and graphic patterns in images, especially for documents and cards. In this paper, we propose a coarse-to-fine dynamic association learning method for specular highlight detection and removal. Specifically, based on the dichromatic reflection model, we first use a sub-network to separate the specular highlight layer and locate the regions of the highlight. Instead of directly subtracting the estimated specular highlight component from the raw image to get the highlight removal result, we design an associated learning module (ALM) together with a second-stage sub-network to restore the color distortion of the specular highlight layer removal. Our ALM respectively extracts features from the specular highlight part and non-specular highlight part to improve the color restoration. We conducted extensive evaluation experiments and the ablation study on the synthetic dataset and the real-world dataset. Our method achieved 36.09 PSNR and 97% SSIM on SHIQ dataset, along with 28.90 PSNR and 94% SSIM on SD1 dataset, which outperformed the SOTA methods.

Keywords: Highlight Detection and Removal · Color Restoration · Dynamic Association Learning

1 Introduction

Specular highlight is a common phenomenon of light reflection in daily life, where the sourced light shines on smooth and glossy surfaces, such as metals, polished wooden goods and printed materials, to form a bright spot or regions with higher light intensity than the surrounding areas. Its size and position vary depending on the shape of the reflecting surface, the angle of the incident light, and the properties of the material [18]. Specular highlights can also affect the visual perception and information recognition of objects like ID cards, plastic

---

J. Shen and H. Guan—Contribute equally to this work.

© The Author(s), under exclusive license to Springer Nature Switzerland AG 2024
B. Sheng et al. (Eds.): CGI 2023, LNCS 14495, pp. 375–387, 2024.
https://doi.org/10.1007/978-3-031-50069-5_31

licenses and human organs in medical imaging [2]. Therefore, it is necessary to detect and deal with such a negative impact of specular highlights.

Phong model [20] describes the combination of ambient light, diffuse reflection, and specular reflection under a single light source. Dichromatic Reflection model [22] considers a pixel as a linear combination of body reflection and surface reflection and is more suitable for computation. Most traditional methods for highlight detection and removal took effect only in the labs or the ideal scenarios. Their generalization is poor. Deep learning based methods [5,6,17,24] could learn the features of specular highlights and the principles to repair their influencing regions from a large amount of data. Thus they have good generalization. However, the specular highlights always occur in irregular regions of a single image and their intensity varies much in different conditions. It is challenging to accurately locate their positions and alleviate color inconsistency after specular highlight removal.

To address the above issues, we propose a coarse-to-fine dynamic association learning network to jointly tackle the detection and removal of a single image with specular highlights. Based on the Dichromatic Reflection model, we first use a sub-network to separate the specular highlight layer of the Dichromatic Reflection model and locate the regions of the specular highlights. Instead of directly subtracting the estimated specular highlight layer from the raw image to get the highlight removal result, we design an associated learning module (ALM) to separately extract features from the specular highlight part and the non-specular highlight part. Finally, another sub-network uses features from ALM to restore the color distortion caused by directly removing the specular highlight layer. The overall pipeline is shown in Fig. 1. We conduct extensive experiments and the ablation study. Our method achieves satisfactory performance on both detection and removal. It restores better colors and appearances after removing specular highlights. To sum up, our contributions are as follows:

- We propose a specular highlight detection and removal method based on coarse-to-fine dynamic association learning.
- We design a two-stage network consisting of two U-Nets for highlight detection and color restoration. Meanwhile, we introduce an Associated Learning Module between two U-Nets to further extract features, which helps to generate better highlight-free results.

2   Related Work

Traditional Methods. Traditional methods just worked under specific lighting conditions. They could not deal with complex illumination and objects with color textures in images. He *et al.* [7] used the dark channel for highlight removal. Tan *et al.* [12] proposed to estimate the reflection model of the highlights based on texture analysis and subtract it from the image to remove the highlights. Liu *et al.* [16] estimated the ratio of highlight reflection and adjusted the saturation of the input image based on this ratio to remove the highlights.

Deep Learning Methods. Fu *et al.* [4] created a dataset of 16K real images to fill in the domain gap between synthetic training samples and real test images. They used a single neural network to sequentially fulfill highlight detection and removal. Especially, a multi-scale contextual module named DSCFA was proposed to exploit contextual information from multiple receptive fields at varied scales, which aimed to deal with the issue of highlights with a wide range. Focusing on specific objects of documents and cards, Hou *et al.* [8] not only created two important synthetic datasets but also proposed a text-aware single-image highlight removal method. They used the pre-trained text detection and recognition models to provide supervision on text recovery and introduced a patch-based discriminator to enhance the visual realism of results. Hu *et al.* [9] converted the highlight removal problem to image-to-image translation and proposed a highlight mask-guided Cycle-GAN network. Based on the observation that specular highlights mainly had characteristics in lightness, they first trained a module only on the luminance channel and then adopted the training results to guide the subsequent highlight removal. Wang *et al.* [23] proposed a fully convolutional network with feature loss and region loss for single image highlight removal, using pseudo specular-free images. Huang *et al.* [11] proposed a unified multi-scene highlight removal framework, which was capable of handling synthetic images, face images, text images, and natural images. They used a contextual feature attention mechanism to detect highlight locations.

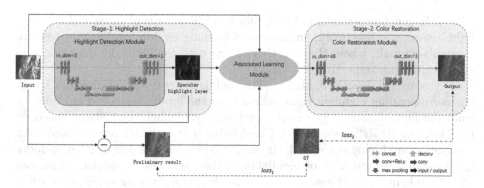

Fig. 1. Pipeline of our two-stage dynamic association learning method. It consists of a highlight detection sub-network, an ALM, and a color restoration sub-network. The highlight detection sub-network and the color restoration sub-network have the same U-Net structure with different input and output dimensions. $loss_1$ and $loss_2$ use the same calculation method on different objects. The preliminary result is obtained by subtracting the detected specular highlight layer from the input image.

3   Methodology

The image enhancing strategy is more suitable for restoring residual contents in highlight regions. We also use the Dichromatic Reflection model as the illumination formation basis. In this model, an image with highlights is considered as an additive model of two independent layers, described by the equation below,

$$I = D + S \tag{1}$$

where I is the color image with highlights, D is the diffuse reflection layer (i.e., body reflectance), representing the object's properties, and S is the specular reflection layer (i.e., the highlights), representing the illuminant color properties.

The Dichromatic Reflection model usually takes effect in scenarios where there is a unique lighting source or the color of objects covered by highlights is monochromatic. When the textures in images are complex or their color is quite similar to the illuminant color, the results of highlight removal always have color distortion, which is mainly caused by inaccurate specular reflection layer estimation and improperly removing the specular reflection layer without non-linear post-processing. Therefore, we propose a specular highlight detection and removal method based on coarse-to-fine dynamic association learning.

3.1   Pipeline

The entire pipeline is shown in Fig. 1. Our method consists of three parts, a highlight detection sub-network, an associated learning module, and a color restoration sub-network, where the two U-Nets are used for highlight detection and color restoration respectively.

Given an image with highlights, The highlight detection sub-network learns the corresponding highlight distribution from the input image and subtracts it from the input image to generate a preliminary highlight-free image based on the Dichromatic Reflection model. Considering that highlight removal and color restoration are highly correlated, the predicted specular highlight layer includes the location and intensity of highlights in the background regions, which can effectively help repair the residual content. Before performing color restoration, a module called ALM is used, which takes the predicted highlight distribution as input to learn the mask image, and further extracts valuable color information from the input highlight image to assist in accurate color restoration. The color restoration sub-network uses the output of the ALM module to recover the nonlinear changes of the highlight regions, thereby generating an improved highlight-free image.

3.2   U-Net Based Sub-network

Both sub-networks have the same structure with different input and output dimensions based on U-Net because of its simple but effective structure with high precision in processing small objects or complex details. We adopt the classical U-Net with an encoder-decoder cascade structure, where the encoder gradually compresses information into a lower-dimensional representation. Then the decoder decodes this information back to the original image dimension. The encoder includes two convolutional layers and a max pooling layer, while the last level has no max pooling layer. The decoder has the same structure with a deconvolutional layer, a concatenation operation, and two convolutional layers.

For the highlight detection sub-network, the input is a 3D RGB image with highlights, and the output is the specular highlight layer, a 1D grayscale image representing the position and intensity of detected highlight regions. For the color restoration sub-network, the input is the 48D output of the ALM, and the output is the ultimate RGB highlight-free image.

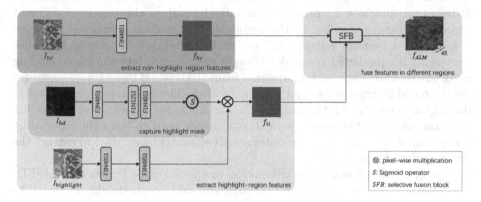

Fig. 2. Diagram of ALM. $I_{highlight}$: input highlight image, I_{hd}: the output of highlight detection sub-network, I_{hr}: the preliminary highlight-free image after coarse highlight removal, f_{hr}: feature information of I_{hr}, f_{ti}: texture information in highlight regions, f_{ALM}: enhanced global background feature representation, $\otimes$: pixel-wise multiplication, S: Sigmoid operator to perform feature mapping and normalization, SFB: operation of selective fusion block to fuse features of highlight and non-highlight.

3.3 Associated Learning Module

We introduce the dynamic learning strategy into our method, which can adapt the structure or parameters to changes in its input during the inference process, thus having significant advantages in the accuracy and adaptability of the model. The highlight regions in an image may be sparsely distributed, and a dynamic learning strategy based on feature selection provides a feasible solution for accurate highlight detection and color restoration. Figure 2 shows the detailed structure of the ALM module, which uses two branches to learn texture features f_{hr} of highlight-free regions and f_{ti} of highlight regions, and selectively fuses them to obtain an enhanced global background feature expression f_{ALM}. In the first branch, the input is the preliminary highlight-free image to extract non-highlight-region features. In the second branch, the input is the original highlight image and the grayscale highlight detection result to extract highlight-region features. Then the two features are selectively fused to get enhanced global features, thus offering the color restoration sub-network more detailed color and texture information.

$$f_{ti} = F_M(I_{hd}) \otimes F_R(I_{highlight})$$
$$f_{hr} = F_B(I_{hr}) \qquad (2)$$
$$f_{ALM} = F_{SFB}(f_{ti}, f_{hr})$$

Equation 2 represents the calculation approach for f_{ALM} output by the ALM module, where F_M is the mask generation function, consisting of an initial convolutional layer and a bottleneck unit, used to learn the predicted highlight-distribution matrices. In order to dynamically adjust the fusion of different regional features according to the highlight distribution, a Sigmoid operator is followed to perform feature mapping and normalize them into [0,1.0], thus converting the predicted grayscale highlight distribution into the corresponding mask to extract background information from the original highlight image to get the degraded distribution weight mask map of the highlight region, expressed as the degraded position and intensity of the highlight. F_R is the feature embedding function, which includes two convolutional layers, used to learn the embedding expression of $I_{highlight}$. $F_B(\cdot)$ includes a convolutional layer, used to extract the feature information f_{hr} of I_{hr}.

$F_{SFB}(\cdot)$ represents the fusion function in the Selective Fusion Block (SFB) [13], which is used to fuse features of highlight and non-highlight regions. The SFB consists of depth-wise separable convolutions and the channel attention layer to fuse multi-source features in different dimensions and remove redundancy, thus achieving more efficient and high-quality feature expressions. It has been proved to be significant in the texture restoration operation by [13].

3.4   Loss Function

To jointly optimize the two sub-networks, the loss function during training includes image content loss and structural similarity loss between the highlight-free images output by the two sub-networks and the ground truth highlight-free images, guiding the network to maintain similarity in both image content and texture structure. The former is measured using the Charbonnier penalty function, while the latter is evaluated with the Structural Similarity Index Measure (SSIM) function. The Charbonnier function is defined as follows:

$$Charb(x,y) = \sqrt{(x-y)^2 + \epsilon^2} \qquad (3)$$

and the penalty coefficient ϵ is empirically set to 10^{-6}. The final **loss** is:

$$loss_1 = Charb(I_1, I_{gt}) + \lambda \cdot SSIM(I_1, I_{gt})$$
$$loss_2 = Charb(I_2, I_{gt}) + \lambda \cdot SSIM(I_2, I_{gt}) \qquad (4)$$
$$loss = loss_1 + \alpha * loss_2$$

$loss_1$ and $loss_2$ are respectively the loss functions of the highlight detection sub-network and color restoration sub-network. I_{gt} is the ground truth highlight-free image, λ is the weight coefficient between the Charb function and SSIM function, set to -1 in the experiments, and α is the weight coefficient between $loss_1$ and $loss_2$. For the highlight detection sub-network, I_1 is obtained by subtracting its output highlight layer from the input highlight image (i.e., considering only the dichromatic reflection model); for the color restoration sub-network, I_2 is directly the output of this network. In general, $loss_1$ is used in the highlight detection stage, calculated with the GT and the preliminary highlight-free image to improve detection accuracy. $loss_2$ is used in the color restoration stage, calculated with the GT and the final highlight-free result to optimize the restoration.

4   Experiment

4.1   Datasets

SD1. Hou *et al.* [8] artificially synthesized the text highlight dataset SD1 based on document materials. To demonstrate the effectiveness of our method on document-type images with highlights, we choose the SD1 dataset, which includes 12,000 pairs of training data, 650 pairs of validation data, and 2,000 pairs of testing data, with a resolution of 512*512. We resized them to 128*128 in the experiments.

SHIQ. Fu *et al.* [4] proposed a semi-automatic method to construct a large-scale real dataset SHIQ by leveraging multi-illumination sequences to produce ground truth. To demonstrate the effectiveness of our method in diverse real-world highlight scenes, we also choose the natural scene highlight dataset SHIQ, which includes 9,825 pairs of training data and 1,000 pairs of testing data, with a resolution of 200*200.

4.2   Specular Highlight Detection

After obtaining the grayscale specular highlight layer in stage 1, we empirically set a threshold of the pixel value to 40, thus converting the grayscale highlight layer to a binary highlight mask image to evaluate the accuracy of highlight detection. We compared our method with the state-of-the-art highlight detection methods. To quantitatively evaluate the highlight detection performance, we used Balanced Error Rate (BER) [10] and accuracy, $accuracy = (TP+TN)/(N_p+N_n)$, where TP, TN, N_P and N_n are true positives, true negatives, number of highlight pixels and number of non-highlight pixels. Higher accuracy and lower BER represent better detection performance.

Table 1 illustrates the accuracy and BER results of our highlight detection against SOTA methods on SHIQ. Note that SD1 is a synthetic dataset with no highlight GT mask in the test set, which makes it difficult to determine a precise threshold. Thus we only use SHIQ to evaluate highlight detection performance.

Table 1. Quantitative comparison results of our method in highlight detection against other methods on SHIQ.

Metric	Li [14]	Zhang [27]	Fu [3]	Fu [4]	**Ours**
accuracy↑	0.70	0.71	0.91	0.93	**0.97**
BER↓	18.8	24.4	6.18	5.92	**5.37**

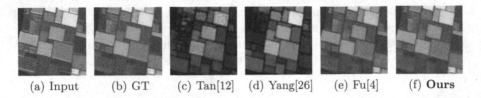

  (a) Input   (b) GT   (c) Tan[12]   (d) Yang[26]   (e) Fu[4]   (f) **Ours**

Fig. 3. Visual comparison of our method against state-of-the-art highlight removal methods on the testing set of SHIQ.

  (a)   (b)   (c)   (d)   (e)   (f)

Fig. 4. Visual results of our method on SD1. From left to right are (a) GTs, (b) input images, (c) detected specular highlight layer, (d) our highlight removal without color restoration, (e) highlight removal with color restoration, and (f) results of TASHR [8].

4.3 Specular Highlight Removal

Figure 3 illustrates the highlight removal effects of different methods on the real highlight dataset SHIQ. From the results, traditional highlight removal methods mistakenly recover the color and texture of non-highlight regions, thus decreasing the overall quality of the restored image. SHIQ is created by Fu [4]. Our color results of highlight removal are closer to the GT image than Fu's method.

Figures 4 and 5 are the quantitative comparison results on SD1. SPEC [19] and JSHDR [4] methods have obvious color distortion and broken textural details. Although the color distortion problem of the M2Net [11] method has been alleviated, broken textures still exist.

Table 2 represents the PSNR and SSIM values of different methods on the SHIQ and SD1 datasets respectively. Here, larger PSNR and SSIM values indicate better highlight removal effects. From the table, it can be seen that our method exceeds the traditional highlight removal methods and outperforms state-of-the-art deep learning-based highlight removal methods on both synthesized and natural highlight images.

(a)   (b)   (c)   (d)   (e)   (f)

Fig. 5. Visual comparison of our method against state-of-the-art highlight removal methods on the testing set of SD1. From left to right are (a) Inputs, (b) results of SPEC [19], (c) results of JSHDR [4], (d) results of M2Net [11] (**psnr=29.75, ssim=0.926**), (e) our results (**psnr=32.20, ssim=0.968**) and (f) GTs.

Table 2. Quantitative results of comparison between our method and other highlight removal methods on SHIQ and SD1.

Dataset	SHIQ		SD1	
Metric	PSNR↑	SSIM↑	PSNR↑	SSIM↑
Tan [12]	14.12	0.47	–	–
Yang [26]	23.26	0.77	–	–
Shen [21]	12.21	0.45	–	–
Akashi [1]	22.09	0.63	–	–
Yama. [25]	12.20	0.45	–	–
Hu [9]	30.94	0.97	–	–
Multi-class [15]	–	–	26.29	0.89
SPEC [19]	–	–	15.61	0.69
TASHR [8]	–	–	22.65	0.88
M2Net [11]	35.72	0.91	–	–
Fu [4]	34.13	0.86	24.59	0.85
Ours	**36.09**	**0.97**	**29.45**	**0.94**

Table 3. Metrics of our method's two stages on Masked SD1 and Masked SHIQ.

Dataset		PSNR↑	SSIM↑
Masked SD1	Stage 1	28.52	0.957
	Stage 1+2	**31.19**	**0.962**
Masked SHIQ	Stage 1	40.01	0.986
	Stage 1+2	**40.41**	**0.987**

Table 4. Quantitative comparison results of the ablation study on SHIQ and SD1.

Dataset	Model	PSNR↑	SSIM↑
SD1	w/o ALM	28.90	0.932
	Ours	**29.45**	**0.937**
SHIQ	w/o ALM	32.28	0.952
	Ours	**36.09**	**0.970**

4.4 Ablation Study

Firstly, we validate the color restoration of the second stage. The second stage can obviously improve the visual quality of highlight removal for both natural scenes and document-type highlight images. On the SHIQ dataset, we used a threshold to select significant highlight regions according to the output of the highlight detection sub-network to avoid the influence of non-specular-highlight factors. We called this subgroup of SHIQ as Masked SHIQ. The same procedure was carried out on SD1 and obtained Masked SD1. We quantitatively evaluated how the second stage further improved highlight removal results. Table 3 shows the PSNR and SSIM metrics of the two stages. The data in the table demonstrates that the second stage has improved highlight removal performance on both datasets. Note that we limited quantitative evaluation into the masked highlight regions only when validating stage 2 validation (black parts are not taken into account), so the evaluation metric values are higher than those in Table 2. We calculated metrics in the whole image scale in the other comparisons.

Secondly, we conducted an ablation study of ALM on SHIQ and SD1 to verify the importance of the ALM module in highlight removal and color restoration. We excluded the ALM module from the network structure and just modified the input channel number of the color restoration sub-network in the remaining two U-Nets to ensure the normal operation of the network. Figure 6 shows the highlight removal results of the network without the ALM module, and Table 4 shows the quantitative evaluation metrics of highlight removal under modified network components. Without the help of ALM in color restoration, the highlight regions have problems with broken texture details and abnormal color restoration. By comparing the outputs of the network **with** and **without** the ALM module, it can be seen that the ALM module plays an important role in the highlight removal process, which helps a lot in color and texture restoration, and especially improves the ability when dealing with images with texts.

5   Limitation

Our method shows excellent results in highlight removal and color restoration, but it has some limitations. When it comes to large region highlights or too intensive highlights, our method can hardly handle them. As shown in the bottom row of Fig. 5(e), the reconstructed character lost part of its structure information.

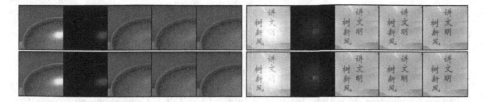

Fig. 6. Visual results of ablation study on SHIQ and SD1. The top line shows the results without ALM, and the bottom line shows the results with ALM. For every 5 columns, from left to right are input images, detected specular highlight layer, highlight removal without color restoration, highlight removal with color restoration, and GTs.

6   Conclusion

We proposed a deep learning-based two-stage highlight detection and removal method for a single image based on the Dichromatic Reflection model. The network structure includes two simple but effective U-Nets, which work as the highlight detection sub-network and the color restoration sub-network, and the ALM module, which is fused between two stages to enhance the network. Compared to state-of-the-art methods, our method got better performance.

Acknowledgement. This research is supported by the National Natural Science Foundation of China (No. 62172309).

References

1. Akashi, Y., Okatani, T.: Separation of reflection components by sparse non-negative matrix factorization. In: Cremers, D., Reid, I., Saito, H., Yang, M.-H. (eds.) ACCV 2014. LNCS, vol. 9007, pp. 611–625. Springer, Cham (2015). https://doi.org/10.1007/978-3-319-16814-2_40
2. Ali, S.G., et al.: Experimental protocol designed to employ nd: YAG laser surgery for anterior chamber glaucoma detection via UBM. IET Image Proc. **16**(8), 2171–2179 (2022)
3. Fu, G., Zhang, Q., Lin, Q., Zhu, L., Xiao, C.: Learning to detect specular highlights from real-world images. In: Proceedings of the 28th ACM International Conference on Multimedia, pp. 1873–1881 (2020)
4. Fu, G., Zhang, Q., Zhu, L., Li, P., Xiao, C.: A multi-task network for joint specular highlight detection and removal. In: Proceedings of the IEEE/CVF Conference on Computer Vision and Pattern Recognition, pp. 7752–7761 (2021)
5. Fu, G., Zhang, Q., Zhu, L., Lin, Q., Wang, Y., Fan, S., Xiao, C.: Towards high-resolution specular highlight detection. Int. J. Comput. Vis. 1–23 (2023)
6. Funke, I., Bodenstedt, S., Riediger, C., Weitz, J., Speidel, S.: Generative adversarial networks for specular highlight removal in endoscopic images. In: Medical Imaging 2018: Image-Guided Procedures, Robotic Interventions, and Modeling, vol. 10576, pp. 8–16. SPIE (2018)
7. He, K., Sun, J., Tang, X.: Single image haze removal using dark channel prior. IEEE Trans. Pattern Anal. Mach. Intell. **33**(12), 2341–2353 (2010)

8. Hou, S., Wang, C., Quan, W., Jiang, J., Yan, D.-M.: Text-aware single image specular highlight removal. In: Ma, H., et al. (eds.) PRCV 2021. LNCS, vol. 13022, pp. 115–127. Springer, Cham (2021). https://doi.org/10.1007/978-3-030-88013-2_10

9. Hu, G., Zheng, Y., Yan, H., Hua, G., Yan, Y.: Mask-guided cycle-GAN for specular highlight removal. Pattern Recogn. Lett. **161**, 108–114 (2022)

10. Hu, X., Zhu, L., Fu, C.W., Qin, J., Heng, P.A.: Direction-aware spatial context features for shadow detection. In: Proceedings of the IEEE Conference on Computer Vision and Pattern Recognition, pp. 7454–7462 (2018)

11. Huang, Z., Hu, K., Wang, X.: M2-Net: multi-stages specular highlight detection and removal in multi-scenes. arXiv preprint arXiv:2207.09965 (2022)

12. Ikeuchi, K., Miyazaki, D., Tan, R.T., Ikeuchi, K.: Separating reflection components of textured surfaces using a single image. In: Digitally Archiving Cultural Objects, pp. 353–384. Springer, Boston, MA (2008). https://doi.org/10.1007/978-0-387-75807_17

13. Jiang, K., et al.: Multi-scale progressive fusion network for single image deraining. In: Proceedings of the IEEE/CVF Conference on Computer Vision and Pattern Recognition, pp. 8346–8355 (2020)

14. Li, R., Pan, J., Si, Y., Yan, B., Hu, Y., Qin, H.: Specular reflections removal for endoscopic image sequences with adaptive-RPCA decomposition. IEEE Trans. Med. Imaging **39**(2), 328–340 (2019)

15. Lin, J., El Amine Seddik, M., Tamaazousti, M., Tamaazousti, Y., Bartoli, A.: Deep multi-class adversarial specularity removal. In: Felsberg, M., Forssén, P.-E., Sintorn, I.-M., Unger, J. (eds.) SCIA 2019. LNCS, vol. 11482, pp. 3–15. Springer, Cham (2019). https://doi.org/10.1007/978-3-030-20205-7_1

16. Liu, Y., Yuan, Z., Zheng, N., Wu, Y.: Saturation-preserving specular reflection separation. In: Proceedings of the IEEE Conference on Computer Vision and Pattern Recognition, pp. 3725–3733 (2015)

17. Madessa, A.H., Dong, J., Gan, Y., Gao, F.: A deep learning approach for specular highlight removal from transmissive materials. Expert. Syst. **40**(2), e12598 (2023)

18. Meka, A., Maximov, M., Zollhoefer, M., Chatterjee, A., Theobalt, C.: Live Intrinsic Material Estimation. IEEE (2018)

19. Muhammad, S., Dailey, M.N., Farooq, M., Majeed, M.F., Ekpanyapong, M.: Spec-Net and spec-CGAN: Deep learning models for specularity removal from faces. Image Vis. Comput. **93**, 103823 (2020)

20. Phong, B.T.: Illumination for computer generated pictures. Commun. ACM **18**(6), 311–317 (1975)

21. Shen, H.L., Zheng, Z.H.: Real-time highlight removal using intensity ratio. Appl. Opt. **52**(19), 4483–4493 (2013)

22. Tominaga, S.: Dichromatic reflection models for a variety of materials. Color Res. Appl. **19**(4), 277–285 (1994)

23. Wang, X., Tao, C., Tao, X., Zheng, Z.: SIHRNET: a fully convolutional network for single image highlight removal with a real-world dataset. J. Electron. Imaging **31**(3), 033013–033013 (2022)

24. Xu, J., Liu, S., Chen, G., Liu, Q.: Highlight detection and removal method based on bifurcated-CNN. In: Liu, H., et al. Intelligent Robotics and Applications. ICIRA 2022. Lecture Notes in Computer Science, vol. 13458, pp. 307–318. Springer, Cham (2022). https://doi.org/10.1007/978-3-031-13841-6_29

25. Yamamoto, T., Nakazawa, A.: General improvement method of specular component separation using high-emphasis filter and similarity function. ITE Trans. Media Technol. Appl. **7**(2), 92–102 (2019)

26. Yang, Q., Tang, J., Ahuja, N.: Efficient and robust specular highlight removal. IEEE Trans. Pattern Anal. Mach. Intell. **37**(6), 1304–1311 (2014)
27. Zhang, W., Zhao, X., Morvan, J.M., Chen, L.: Improving shadow suppression for illumination robust face recognition. IEEE Trans. Pattern Anal. Mach. Intell. **41**(3), 611–624 (2018)

Highlight Removal from a Single Image Based on a Prior Knowledge Guided Unsupervised CycleGAN

Yongkang Ma[1] , Li Li[1,2,3(✉)] , Hao Chen[1] , Xian Li[1], Junchao Chen[1] ,
Ping Zhu[1,2,3], Tao Peng[1,2,3], and Xiong Pan[1,2,3]

[1] School of Computer Science and Artificial Intelligence, Wuhan Textile University,
Wuhan 430200, China
lli@wtu.edu.cn
[2] Engineering Research Center of Hubei Province for Clothing Information, Wuhan 430200,
China
[3] Hubei Provincial Engineering Research Center for Intelligent Textile and Fashion,
Wuhan 430200, China

Abstract. Highlights widely exist in many objects, such as the optical images of high-gloss leather, glass, plastic, metal parts, and other mirror-reflective objects. It is difficult to directly apply optical measurement techniques, such as object detection, intrinsic image decomposition, and tracking which are suitable for objects with diffuse reflection characteristics. In this paper, we proposed a specular-to-diffuse-reflection image conversion network based on improved CycleGAN to automatically remove image highlights. It does not require paired training data, and the experimental results verify the effectiveness of our method. There are two main contributions for this framework. On one hand, we proposed a confidence map based on independent average values as the initial value to solve the slow convergence problem of the network due to the lack of a strict mathematical definition for distinguishing specular reflection components from diffuse reflection components. On the other hand, we designed a logarithm-based transformation method generator which made the specular reflection and diffuse reflection components comparable. It could solve the anisotropy problem in the optimization process. This problem was caused by the fact that the peak specular reflection on the surface of a specular object was much larger than the value of the off-peak diffuse reflection. We also compared our method with the latest methods. It was found that the SSIM and PSNR values of our proposed algorithm were significantly improved, and the comparative experimental results showed that the proposed algorithm significantly improves the image conversion quality.

Keywords: CycleGAN · Confidence map · Highlight removal · logarithm-based transformation method generator

B. Sheng et al. (Eds.): CGI 2023, LNCS 14495, pp. 388–399, 2024.
https://doi.org/10.1007/978-3-031-50069-5_32

1 Introduction

The single-image method is based on chromaticity space analysis and used to analyze the specular reflection and diffuse reflection components in the color space. Lu et al. [1] designed an efficient highlight removal method based on a bilateral filter. This method utilizes the local smoothness of the maximum diffuse reflection chromaticity, and uses a bilateral filter to propagate and diffuse the maximum value of the chromaticity, thereby completing a single Image highlight removal. Akashi et al. [2] separated diffuse and specular reflection components by using a sparse nonnegative matrix decomposition model. Guo et al. [3] proposed a sparse low-rank highlight removal reflection model that transformed the highlight removal task into a constrained kernel norm and l1-norm minimization problem. Using the frequency domain analysis to treat highlights as noise, Yang et al. [4] developed a low-pass filter to smooth the maximum part of the color component in the original image to remove specular highlights by comparing and analyzing the difference in spectral distribution between diffuse and highlight light bars. Gao et al. [5] obtained the conversion relationship between the specular reflection component and the maximum diffuse reflection chromaticity through the transformation of the two-color reflection model, and it used a threshold to classify the image pixels into pixels with only diffuse reflection and pixels with specular reflection. In addition, they used the maximum chromaticity map of the image as the guide map for the bilateral filter to perform edge-preserving de-noising. Traditional methods have two main limitations: they cannot distinguish the material with high brightness from the highlight area in the scene, and different thresholds need to be set to deal with highlight problems in different scenes.

In recent years, deep CNNs as a general function mapping relationship fitter have been extensively employed in the research field of image data processing. The rendering parameters of the material are obtained based on deep neural network learning to automatically remove the highlights on the surface of the object. Xiao et al.[6] constructed the first real large dataset (4310 sheets), wherein the highlight regions were finely hand-labeled; using this dataset, they proposed a supervised multi-task convolutional network for joint highlight detection and removal, using a coding structure with DSCFA to extract highlight features from the input highlight image and predict Mask, specular, diffuse for joint Highlight detection and removal. Wu et al. [7] proposed an efficient end-to-end deep learning model for automatic detection and removal of highlights in a single image, using an encoder-decoder network to detect highlight regions, and a novel Unet-Transformer network for highlight removal. Wu et al. [8] proposed a CycleGAN-based S2D Net method, which is an unsupervised generative confrontation network, which is used to convert multiple views of objects with specular reflections into diffuse objects, by converting unsupervised images apply to image conversion to multi-view "specular to diffuse" conversion for highlight removal.

In fact, the natural intrinsic map and highlight map corresponding to a given image can be obtained by intrinsic image decomposition. The decomposition process of intrinsic images can be regarded as the problem of image-to-image translation, which aims to learn the mapping relationship between two visual domains by training a CNN to obtain the rendering parameters, such as the materials, [9–12] reflectance maps, [13–15] and lighting [16, 17]. However, it is still faced some difficulties during training. Generative Adversarial Networks(GAN) and improved network based on it can effectively solve these problems [18]. The network using Pix2Pix GAN was the first attempted at image-to-image translation using GANs. By training a large number of labeled paired images, night photos can be converted into day photos, but the network requires paired (paired data) training sets to supervise the processing of one-to-one images. However, for many practical problems, obtaining a large number of paired images are difficult. But dual learning can fully use unlabeled data so that the models automatically learn from unlabeled data. It can improve the performance of the models in the pairwise task. The most commonly used dual learning networks are CycleGAN, [19] DualGAN, [20] and DiscoGAN, [21] Inspired by this, we regard the correspondence between diffuse and specular domains as a closed-loop dual learning task, and use dual learning to convert specular and diffuse materials to each other for highlight removal.

Currently, the main problems encountered when employing unsupervised generation countermeasure networks for specular image highlights removal were as follows: (1) There is no strict mathematical definition available at present to distinguish between specular reflection and diffuse reflection, which leads to the problem of slow convergence of the network. Therefore, we proposed a confidence map of independent means. It can guide our network for quickly determining the initial values. (2) The generators of S2D-NET network based on CycleGAN algorithm are prone to lose the feature information of images. To overcome this problem, we improve the generator by replacing ResNet with Denes-Net and adding a U-Net structure between the encoder and decoder to improve the detail information of the generated images. (3) The S2D-NET network based on the CycleGAN algorithm adopts the conventional distance metric. By comparing the specular object surface material data in the MERL dataset, we found that for a typical high-gloss metal ball, the diffuse reflection of the non-peak part component is approximately 0.1, whereas the specular reflection component of the peak part can reach 100. Thus, we introduce a logarithmic transformation which can make the highlight and non-highlight parts comparable.

2   Methods

In this section, we first briefly reviewed the basic framework of the CycleGAN model for specular to diffuse image style transfer networks. And then we improved the generator by replacing ResNet with Denes-Net and adding a U-Net structure between the encoder and decoder to improve the detail information of the generated images. In addition, we introduced an independent mean confidence map to solve the problem of slow convergence of the network without a strict mathematical definition for distinguishing between specular and diffuse components. Finally, we presented the logarithm-based metric to make the specular and diffuse reflection components comparable. The whole architecture is shown in Fig. 1.

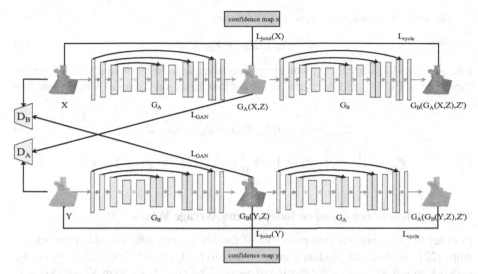

Fig. 1. The whole structure of our proposed specular highlight removal framework.

2.1 Unsupervised S2D-NET Based on CycleGAN

The core algorithm is the framework of dual learning GANs which is used to achieve the translation from specular to diffuse reflection domains. Figure 1 shows the framework of image translation. There are two generators and two discriminators. The first G_A generator translates the image of specular material (X) to the image of diffuse reflection material (Y) · $G_A(X, Z)$, where Z is noise, and passes this translated image to the second generator G_B, which translates the diffuse reflection material to specular reflection material and yields $G_B\Big(G_A(X, Z), Z'\Big)$ as a result, which is a reconstruction of the original specular reflection image, where Z' is also noise. Next, we consider the dual process. First, the image Y is translated to a specular reflection map $G_B(Y, Z)$ by using the generator G_B. Then, the generated specular material map is translated by using the generator G_A to obtain $G_A\Big(G_B(Y, Z), Z'\Big)$. The discriminator D_A corresponding to the generator G_A is used to determine whether a diffuse reflection-material image resembles a diffuse reflection material, and the discriminator D_B corresponding to the generator G_B determines whether a specular-material image resembles a specular material.

The image modeling is shown as follows:

$$I = (1 - M) \odot B + R \tag{1}$$

$$M(x) = \begin{cases} 1, Highlight\ area \\ 0, Non - Highlight\ area \end{cases} \tag{2}$$

where M represents the binary mask, I represents the input image, B represents the background texture, R is the highlight area, and the symbol $\odot$ indicates pixel-by-pixel multiplication.

The loss function can be expressed as follows:

$$L = \lambda_{adv}\mathcal{L}_{adv} + \lambda_{cyc}\mathcal{L}_{cyc} \tag{3}$$

where λ_{adv} and λ_{cyc} are hyperparameters. The adversarial loss function of GAN can be expressed as Eq. (4), and the cycle consistent loss based on CycleGAN can be written as Eq. (5):

$$\mathcal{L}_{adv} = \mathcal{L}_{GAN}(G_A, D_A) + \mathcal{L}_{GAN}(G_B, D_B) \tag{4}$$

$$\mathcal{L}_{cyc} = \left\| \left(G_B(Y, Z), Z' \right) - Y \right\| + \left\| G_B\left(G_A(X, Z), Z' \right) - X \right\| \tag{5}$$

2.2 Confidence Map Based on Independent Average Values

In order to overcome the two problems of the above methods, we added confidence maps [22] based on independent average values to the CycleGAN network to guide the network to quickly search for the initial value. The confidence map X^* proposed in this paper is used to perform normalization calculation of the input image. It is shown in Eq. (6), where X^{mean} is subtracted from X and then point-by-point division by the standard deviation X^σ is performed, X is the input image, X^{mean} is the mean, and X^σ is the standard deviation:

$$X^* = \frac{X - X^{mean}}{X^\sigma + 10^{-4}} \tag{6}$$

$$X^{mean} = blur(X) \tag{7}$$

$$X^\sigma = \sqrt{blur((X - X^{mean})^2)} \tag{8}$$

$$confidence\ mapx = X^* \tag{9}$$

Based on the proposed confidence map x, we proposed a joint loss function between $G_A(X)$ and the confidence map $L_{joint}(X)$:

$$\mathcal{L}_{joint}(X) = E\big[|X^* - G_A(X, Z)|_1\big] \tag{10}$$

2.3 Improved Generator Network

The generator of traditional CycleGAN network adopts ResNet (residual neural network) [23], The generator is full convolution connection type [24], which is composed of encoder, converter and decoder. In this paper, we improve the traditional CycleGAN network, the generator adopts Denes-Net (dense convolutional network) [25, 26] and the residual blocks in the converter are replaced by densely connected blocks with deeper levels and fewer parameters to improve the texture clarity of the generated images. At the same time, we add U-Net structure between the encoder and decoder, which enables the decoder to extract shallow-level features and allows the network to better retain detailed information. As shown in Fig. 2.

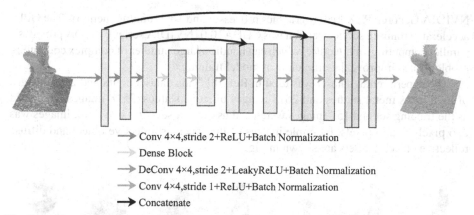

   → Conv 4×4,stride 2+ReLU+Batch Normalization
   → Dense Block
   → DeConv 4×4,stride 2+LeakyReLU+Batch Normalization
   → Conv 4×4,stride 1+ReLU+Batch Normalization
   → Concatenate

Fig. 2. Generator structure. We replace the feature extraction network in the middle from ResNet to Dense-Net, and then add the idea of U-Net to connect the feature maps of the same size in the deep layer and the shallow layer.

2.4 Logarithm-Based Distance Metric

Matusik et al. [27] built the MERL dataset by intensive sampling. For this dataset, it was found that for a typical high-gloss metal sphere, the diffuse reflection component of the non-peak portion of the measurement is approximately 0.1, whereas the specular reflection component of the peak portion can reach 100 [28]. The use of a simple distance metric generates anisotropy in the process of network optimization. To overcome this problem, we introduced a logarithmic transformation to eliminate the anisotropy and it could make the highlight and non-highlight components comparable. Furthermore, In order to train the unpaired image samples better, this paper introduces the perceptual loss function based on the original loss function. Equation (11) shows the representation of the loss function $L_d(X)$ obtained by performing the corresponding logarithmic transformation on the loss function $L_{joint}(X)$ Eq. (12) is the overall loss function of the improved CycleGAN network, where the hyperparameters λ_1, λ_2 and λ_3 control the relative importance of each object.

$$\mathcal{L}_d(X) = \mathbb{E}\big[|log2(X^*) - G_A(X, Z)|_1\big] \tag{11}$$

$$\mathcal{L}_{full} = \mathcal{L}_{GAN}(G_A, D_A) + \mathcal{L}_{GAN}(G_B, D_B) + \lambda_1 \mathcal{L}_{cyc} + \lambda_2 \mathcal{L}_d(X) + \lambda_3 \mathcal{L}_d(Y) \tag{12}$$

3 Datasets and Main Results

3.1 Experimental Environment and Datasets

The experiment was performed in the Ubuntu 18.04 operating system. The programming language was python 3.7, the development tool was Anaconda, and the development framework and version were TensorFlow-GPU1.15. The computer was equipped with an

NVIDIA GeForce RTX3080Ti graphics processor and 16G running memory. The GPU-accelerated running service version was CUDA10.0 (NVIDIA series); CUDA provides a parallel computing architecture, which can handle a large number of complex computing problems and improve the efficiency of model training.

The experimental dataset was used in Ref. [8]. This dataset contained 2675 images of high-gloss metal statues and 2675 images of stone statues. 2518 images were used as the training set and 157 images were used as the test set. The size of all images was 256 pixels × 256 pixels. Example images of the specular reflective object and diffuse reflective object datasets are shown in Fig. 3.

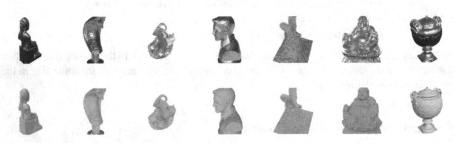

Fig. 3. Examples of datasets: images of specular-reflection objects (top); images of diffuse-reflection objects (bottom).

3.2 Qualitative Comparison

Under the same experimental environment and settings, we performed de-highlighting experiments on the dataset by using different methods. The experimental results are shown in Fig. 4, Each row shows the input image, Ours, CycleGAN + Confidence Map (named CM1), CycleGAN + Confidence Map + (log2) (named CM2), CycleGAN, DRIT [29], and Pix2pix, respectively. The surface of the image generated by Pix2pix is not smooth, with obvious depressions. It can be seen from the figure that the image generated by the CycleGAN has the problem of loss of contour information and the background of its generated image has partial shadows. The image generated by DRIT recovers the details relatively well, but the contour information is not recovered correctly. The image generated by CM1 and CM2 recovers the image details and contours to some extent. The second row shows an improvement in the quality of the images generated by our method, which generates images with better details.

Furthermore, experiments from diffuse reflection to specular reflection were performed, and the results were shown in Fig. 5. As shown in the figures, comparing with CycleGAN, DRIT and Pix2pix, the highlight image generated by CycleGAN + confidence map (columns 3 and 4) has less loss of detail and more contour information. The highlight image generated by our method not only has less loss of detail and contour information but also can better recover the highlight metallic luster state of the statue.

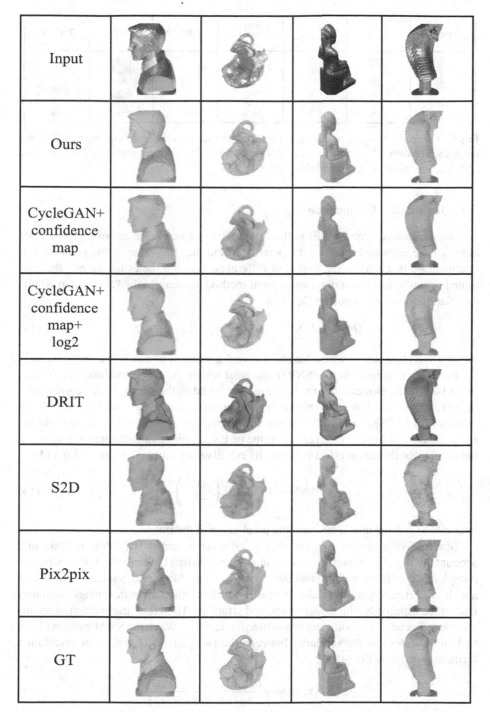

Fig. 4. Specular images generated using different method models to diffuse converted images, the last row is ground truth.

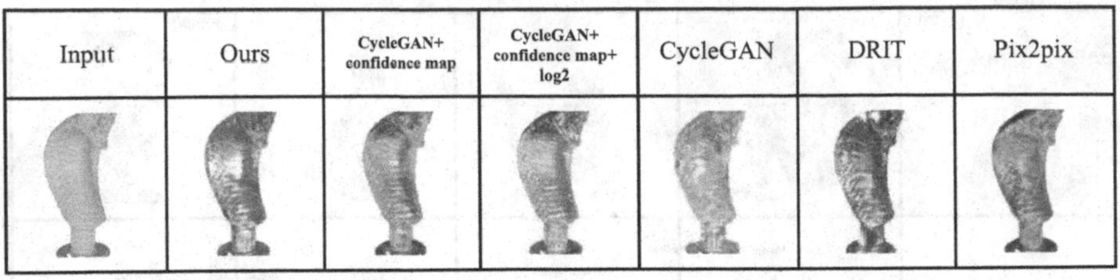

Input	Ours	CycleGAN+ confidence map	CycleGAN+ confidence map+ log2	CycleGAN	DRIT	Pix2pix

Fig. 5. Comparison of generated images for diffuse to specular reflection conversion by different methods. The fifth column is the CycleGAN method [8]. The sixth column is the DRIT method [29]. The seventh column is the Pix2pix method [18].

3.3 Quantitative Comparison

The mean squared error (MSE) is the expected value of the square of the difference between the estimated value of the parameter and the true value of the parameter. It is a measure that reflects the degree of difference between the estimator and the estimated quantity, and it is a more convenient method to measure the "average error". Its calculation formula is given by Eq. (13):

$$MSE = \frac{1}{mn} \sum_{i=0}^{m-1} \sum_{j=0}^{n-1} \left[I(i,j) - K(i,j) \right]^2 \tag{13}$$

where I is a clean image with a length of m and a width of n, and K is a noisy image.

Peak signal-to-noise ratio (PSNR) is the most widely used objective image evaluation index because it helps evaluate the image quality based on the error between corresponding pixels (i.e., based on error sensitivity) without considering the visual characteristics of human eyes. PSNR and MSE are essentially the same, and PSNR is the logarithmic representation of MSE. The larger the value of PSNR, the smaller the image distortion, indicating that the image effect is better. Its calculation formula is given by Eq. (14):

$$PSNR = 10 \cdot \log_{10} \left(\frac{MAX_I^2}{MSE} \right) \tag{14}$$

where MAX_I^2 is the maximum possible pixel value of the image.

Since PSNR evaluates image quality based on error sensitivity, it does not take into account the visual characteristics of the human eye, so that the evaluation results are not completely consistent with human subjective feelings. Structural Similarity (SSIM) is also a full-reference image quality evaluation index, which measures image similarity from three aspects: brightness, contrast, and structure. Therefore, the evaluation results are basically consistent with people's subjective feelings. When the SSIM value is closer to 1, it indicates that the similarity between the two pictures is higher. Its calculation formula is given by Eq. (15):

$$SSIM(x, y) = \frac{(2\mu_x \mu_y + C_1)(2\sigma_{xy} + C_2)}{\left(\mu_x^2 + \mu_y^2 + C_1\right)\left(\sigma_x^2 + \sigma_y^2 + C_2\right)} \tag{15}$$

where x and y represent the two given images; μ_x and μ_y represent the mean of x and y, respectively; σ_x^2 and σ_y^2 represent the variance of x and y, respectively; σ_{xy} represents the covariance of x and y; $C_1 = (k_1L)^2$ and $C_2 = (k_2L)^2$ are constants used to maintain stability, and L is the dynamic range of pixel values. $k_1 = 0.01$, $k_2 = 0.03$.

In this study, PSNR and SSIM were used to evaluate the experimental results. The larger their values, the greater the similarity. Table 1 shows the SSIM and PSNR data of the de-highlighted images generated using different methods.

Table 1. A comparison with the state-of-the-art unsupervised network and supervised network methods on the task of highlight removal.

METHOD	SSIM	PSNR
CycleGAN [8]	0.8705	25.2072
DRIT [29]	0.8430	21.6584
Pix2pix [18]	0.8934	**29.8443**
CycleGAN + confidence map	0.8992	26.4116
CycleGAN + confidence map + log2	0.9025	27.2009
Ours	**0.9156**	29.6548

From the comparison results of SSIM and PSNR, it can be seen that the SSIM values of our proposed algorithm are higher than those of other methods after improving the generator and adding the confidence map and adopting the logarithm-based distance metric. The PSNR value of our proposed method is also almost higher than others except the Pix2pix which is due to the fact that the method in this paper is unsupervised while Pix2pix is supervised, so it is reasonable that the PSNR is lower than the latter. In a word, the image generated by using our proposed algorithm is better than that generated by using other methods.

For the highlight recovery, our method are also better than the other methods. It can be seen from the results generated in Fig. 5. Just like highlight removal, the SSIM and PSNR values were calculated for evaluation. From Table 2, it can be seen that the SSIM and PSNR values of the images generated by using the algorithm proposed in this paper are better.

Table 2. A comparison with the state-of-the-art unsupervised network and supervised network methods on the task of highlight recovery.

METHOD	SSIM	PSNR
CycleGAN [8]	0.7150	16.8847
DRIT [29]	0.7366	16.7983
Pix2pix [18]	0.8001	**21.9131**
CycleGAN + confidence map	0.7716	18.1264
CycleGAN + confidence map + log2	0.7920	18.9581
Ours	**0.8015**	19.6548

4 Conclusion

In this article, we proposed a confidence map based on independent average values to guide the network to converge quickly. Furthermore, we improved the generator by replacing ResNet with Denes-Net and adding U-Net structure between the encoder and decoder to enhance the detail information of the generated images. Subsequently, we introduced a logarithmic transformation to ensure that the specular reflection component and diffuse reflection component were comparable, thus addressing the heteroscedasticity issue that arose during network optimization. Extensive experiments demonstrated that our method effectively removed the specular highlights on the image surface compared to previous approaches.

In the forthcoming time, we plan to incorporate additional prior knowledge, such as the variation in highlight position with the change in incidence angle of light, while the diffuse reflection position remains constant, to enhance the efficacy of our approach and conduct further experimentation.

Acknowledgment. This research was made possible by the financial support of the Educational Commission of Hubei Province of China (Grant No. D20211701).

References

1. Guirong, L., Jingfan, T., Ming, J.: Research on image highlight removal based on fast bilateral filtering. Comput. Eng. Appl. **10**, 176–179 (2014)
2. Yasuhiro, A., Okatani, T.: Separation of reflection components by sparse non-negative matrix factorization. Computer Vision–ACCV 2014: 12th Asian Conference on Computer Vision, Singapore, Singapore, November 1–5, 2014, Revised Selected Papers, Part V 12. Springer, Cham (2015)
3. Jie, G., Zhou, Z., Wang, L.: Single image highlight removal with a sparse and low-rank reflection model. In: Proceedings of the European Conference on Computer Vision (ECCV) (2018)
4. Yang, Q., Tang, J., Ahuja, N.: Efficient and robust specular highlight removal. IEEE Trans. Pattern Anal. Mach. Intell. **37**(6), 1304–1311 (2014)
5. Duan, G., et al.: Deep inverse rendering for high-resolution SVBRDF estimation from an arbitrary number of images. ACM Trans. Graph. **38.4**, 134–1 (2019)
6. Gang, F., et al.: A multi-task network for joint specular highlight detection and removal. In: Proceedings of the IEEE/CVF Conference on Computer Vision and Pattern Recognition (2021)
7. Wu, Z., et al.: Joint specular highlight detection and removal in single images via Unet-Transformer. Comput. Visual Media **9.1**, 141–154 (2023)
8. Wu, S., et al.: Specular-to-diffuse translation for multi-view reconstruction. In: Proceedings of the European conference on computer vision (ECCV) (2018)
9. Yang, J., et al.: Using deep learning to detect defects in manufacturing: a comprehensive survey and current challenges. Materials **13.24**, 5755 (2020)
10. Tamás, C., et al.: Visual-based defect detection and classification approaches for industrial applications—a survey. Sensors **20.5**, 1459 (2020)
11. Kahraman, Y., Durmuşoğlu, A.: Deep learning-based fabric defect detection: a review. Text. Res. J. **93**(5–6), 1485–1503 (2023)

12. Niu, S., et al.: Defect image sample generation with GAN for improving defect recognition. IEEE Trans. Autom. Sci. Eng. **17.3**, 1611–1622 (2020)
13. Mark, B., et al.: Nerd: neural reflectance decomposition from image collections. In: Proceedings of the IEEE/CVF International Conference on Computer Vision (2021)
14. Partha, D., Karaoglu, S., Gevers, T.: PIE-Net: photometric invariant edge guided network for intrinsic image decomposition. In: Proceedings of the IEEE/CVF Conference on Computer Vision and Pattern Recognition (2022)
15. Stamatios, G., et al.: Delight-net: Decomposing reflectance maps into specular materials and natural illumination. arXiv preprint arXiv:1603.08240 (2016)
16. Song, S., Funkhouser, T.: Neural illumination: lighting prediction for indoor environments. In: Proceedings of the IEEE/CVF Conference on Computer Vision and Pattern Recognition (2019)
17. Li, Z., et al.: Inverse rendering for complex indoor scenes: Shape, spatially-varying lighting and svbrdf from a single image. In: Proceedings of the IEEE/CVF Conference on Computer Vision and Pattern Recognition (2020)
18. Guo, Z., Shao, M., Li, S.: Image-to-image translation using an offset-based multi-scale codes GAN encoder. Visual Comput. 1–17 (2023)
19. Chen, M., et al.: Cycle-attention-derain: unsupervised rain removal with CycleGAN. Visual Comput. 1–13 (2023)
20. Yi, Z., et al.: Dualgan: unsupervised dual learning for image-to-image translation. In: Proceedings of the IEEE International Conference on Computer Vision (2017)
21. Kim, T., et al.: Learning to discover cross-domain relations with generative adversarial networks. In: International Conference on Machine Learning. PMLR (2017)
22. Zhao, Y., et al.: Joint SVBRDF Recovery and Synthesis From a Single Image using an Unsupervised Generative Adversarial Network. EGSR (DL) (2020)
23. He, K., et al.: Deep residual learning for image recognition. In: Proceedings of the IEEE Conference on Computer Vision and Pattern Recognition (2016)
24. Long, J., Evan, S., Trevor, D.: Fully convolutional networks for semantic segmentation. In: Proceedings of the IEEE Conference on Computer Vision and Pattern Recognition (2015)
25. Huang, G., et al.: Densely connected convolutional networks. In: Proceedings of the IEEE Conference on Computer Vision and Pattern Recognition (2017)
26. Zhang, Z., et al. "A sparse-view CT reconstruction method based on combination of DenseNet and deconvolution. IEEE Trans. Med. Imag. **37.6**, 1407–1417 (2018)
27. Wojciech, M.: A data-driven reflectance model. Diss. Massachusetts Institute of Technology (2003)
28. Sun, T., Jensen, H.W., Ramamoorthi, R.: Connecting measured brdfs to analytic brdfs by data-driven diffuse-specular separation. ACM Trans. Graph. (TOG) **37.6**, 1–15 (2018)
29. Lee, H.-Y., et al.: Diverse image-to-image translation via disentangled representations. In: Proceedings of the European conference on computer vision (ECCV) (2018)

Image Attention and Perception

Facial Expression Recognition with Global Multiscale and Local Attention Network

Shukai Zheng, Miao Liu$^{(\boxtimes)}$, Ligang Zheng, and Wenbin Chen

School of Computer Science and Cyber Engineering, Guangzhou University,
Guangzhou Higher Education Mega Center, Guangzhou 510006, China
liumiao@gzhu.edu.cn

Abstract. Due to problems such as occlusion and pose variation, facial expression recognition (FER) in the wild is a challenging classification task. This paper proposes a global multiscale and local attention network (GL-VGG) based on the VGG structure, which consists of four modules: a VGG base module, a dropblock module, a global multiscale module, and a local attention module. The base module pre-extracts features, the dropblock module prevents overfitting in the convolutional layers, the global multiscale module is used to learn different receptive field features in the global perception domain, which reduces the susceptibility of deeper convolution towards occlusion and variant pose, and the local attention module guides the network to focus on local rich features, which releases the interference of occlusion on FER in the wild. Experiments on two public wild FER datasets show that our GL-VGG approach outperforms the baseline and other state-of-the-art methods with 88.33% on RAF-DB and 74.17% on FER2013.

Keywords: Facial expression recognition · Convolutional neural networks · Deep learning · Local attention

1 Introduction

Facial expression, the most intuitive signal for humans to convey emotions, is essential for nonverbal communication in daily social interactions. FER has been widely used in many fields, such as driver fatigue monitoring, medical diagnosis, and so on. In computer vision, FER has become a critical recognition technology that is receiving more and more attention.

In recent years, with the development of Convolutional Neural Networks (CNN), FER has made incredible advances in computer vision. FER has many laboratory-controlled datasets, such as JAFER [15] and MMI [20], which the faces are frontal without any occlusion. When the recognition scene is transferred from the laboratory to the wild, occlusion and pose variation bring challenges to FER. Datasets collected in the wild, such as RAF-DB [12] and FER2013 [1], perform considerably worse than those controlled by the laboratory when using the same FER method.

© The Author(s), under exclusive license to Springer Nature Switzerland AG 2024
B. Sheng et al. (Eds.): CGI 2023, LNCS 14495, pp. 403–414, 2024.
https://doi.org/10.1007/978-3-031-50069-5_33

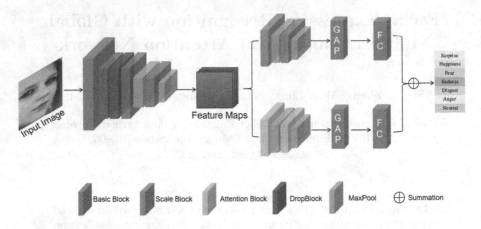

Fig. 1. The structure of the proposed network. The network consists of four components, including a VGG base module, a dropblock module, a global multiscale module, and a local attention module. GAP denotes global average pooling, and FC denotes a fully-connected network.

To deal with the problems caused by uncertainties such as occlusion and pose changes, researchers have proposed many deep learning-based FER methods. For the occlusion problem, patch-based methods are effective. Li et al. [13] proposed ACNNs to shift the attention from the occluded patches to other related but unobstructed ones, it improves the recognition accuracy on both the non-occluded faces and occluded faces. To suppress the uncertainty of expression recognition, Wang et al. [22] proposed an adversarial feature learning method to address pose variation and identity bias. Peng et al. [21] proposed a regional attention network (RAN) to adaptively capture the importance of facial regions for occlusion and pose variant FER. Due to the significant intra-class variations and inter-class similarities, equally supervising all features may reduce the generalization ability of the learning algorithm. Qi et al. [3] proposed a Deep Attentive Center Loss (DACL) method to adaptively select a subset of significant feature elements for enhanced discrimination. Due to the large variations of individuals and the lack of consistent annotated samples, Lei et al. [10] proposed a representation swapping procedure (SwER) to disentangle facial representations into expression-specific representations and expression-unrelated representations. Li et al. [11] proposed a new heuristic objective function based on the domain knowledge so as to better optimize deep neural networks for facial expression recognition.

Despite the improved performance of the above methods, occlusion and pose variation still remain a great challenge. For this reason, we propose a global multiscale and local attention network (GL-VGG), which achieves better performance by learning both holistic and local features of the face. In CNNs, deep convolution has a wider receptive field and is susceptible to occlusion and pose changes, while shallow convolution has a narrower receptive field but is rich in geometric features. Adding shallow geometric features to deep convolution can effectively reduce its susceptibility, thus allow the network to learn a more comprehensive set of features. Therefore, we introduce a global multiscale module in the VGG13 [19] network. Inspired by Res2Net [4], we design the basic block of VGG13 as a global multiscale block to extract multiscale features. Meanwhile, the local attention module is designed to extract local salient features, thus reduces the interference of occlusion and non-frontal pose situations. Figure 1 illustrates the main idea of the proposed network.

The contributions of our work can be summarized as follows:

– We propose a global multiscale and local attention network (GL-VGG) based on the VGG13 structure, which can address the issues of occlusion and pose variation well for FER in the wild.
– We design a global multiscale module that extracts multiscale features, which reduces the susceptibility of deeper convolution in occlusion and variant pose.
– We design a local attention module that extracts the local salient facial region features, which releases the interference of occlusion and non-frontal pose problems.
– We conduct a series of experiments on two wild FER datasets, RAF-DB and FER2013, to demonstrate the advantages of our GL-VGG over other methods.

2 Proposed Method

2.1 Overview

As shown in Fig. 1, our proposed GL-VGG consists of a VGG base module, a dropblock [5] module, a global multiscale module and a local attention module. We also set the number of fully connected layers in the VGG structure to one in order to reduce the number of network parameters. The basic block structure shown in Fig. 2(a) is the basic building block used in VGG13. First, to speed up the network convergence, we design to let the feature map go through the dropblock module. Then, a two-branch network is designed to process the extracted feature maps, with one branch using the multiscale module to learn global multiscale features, and the other branch using the local attention module to learn local significant features. Then the two feature maps are passed into the global average pooling layer and the fully connected network respectively. Finally, the recognition results are obtained using decision-level fusion.

2.2 Dropblock Module

Due to the elements at adjacent positions in the output feature map of the convolution layer sharing semantic information in space, adding dropout in the convolutional layer has no obvious effect. To achieve regularization in the convolutional layer, prevent overfitting and improve the generalization ability of the model, we add the dropblock strategy. Dropblock enables the network to learn more useful information by randomly inactivating the units in the convolutional layer (as shown in Fig. 1), and outperforms dropout in optimizing the convolutional layer.

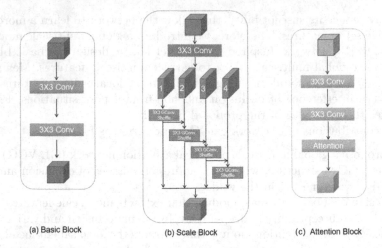

(a) Basic Block   (b) Scale Block   (c) Attention Block

Fig. 2. Three types of the block are employed in GL-VGG. The basic block pre-extracts features, the scale block is used to fuse features with different receptive fields, where Gconv denotes group convolution and Shuffle denotes channel reorganization. The attention block guides the network to focus on local rich features.

Block_size and γ are two important parameters of dropblock. Block_size indicates the size of the blocks to be dropped, and γ controls the number of active units to be dropped. The value of γ is not set explicitly, but can be calculated as:

$$\gamma = \frac{1 - keep\_prob}{block\_size^2} \frac{feat\_size^2}{(feat\_size - block\_size + 1)^2} \tag{1}$$

where $keep\_prob$ can be understood as the probability that a cell in a traditional dropout is reserved. The size of the effective seed region is $(feat\_size - block\_size + 1)^2$, where $feat\_size$ is the size of the feature map.

As shown in Fig. 1, we add the dropblock module after the first basic module, and can achieve very good performance by setting $block\_size$ to 7 and $keep\_prob$ to 0.1 through several controlled experiments.

2.3   Global Mutilscale Module

In CNNs, most methods obtain multiscale features in a layer-by-layer manner, such as object detection [14], facial analysis [18], and so on. Inspired by Res2Net, we design a multiscale block that can represent multiscale features at the granularity level, and increase the receptive field of each network layer. Since the multiscale convolution considers both deeper semantic and shallower geometric features, the learned multiscale features not only enhance the diversity and robustness of global features, but also reduce the sensitivity of deeper convolution to occlusion and variant pose, and thus allow the network to learn a more comprehensive set of features.

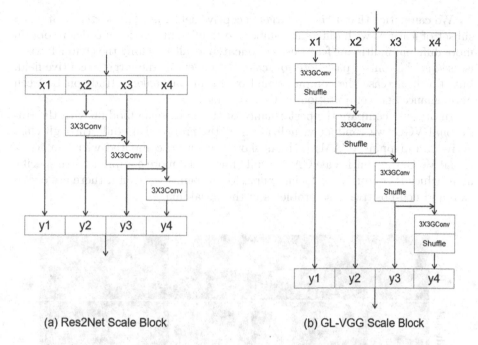

(a) Res2Net Scale Block (b) GL-VGG Scale Block

Fig. 3. The structure of Res2net multi-scale block and the improved structure of GL-VGG.

The structure shown in Fig. 3(a) is a multiscale processing method designed by Res2Net. On this basis, we add 3 × 3 convolutional layers for the first line, then replace the convolutional layers of all lines using the idea of group convolution [6], inspired by ShuffleNet [24], to reorganize the channels of the extracted feature maps respectively. Grouping is to reduce the number of parameters of the network, while channel reorganization can establish the connection between the features of different groups, and improve the performance of the network. The structure is shown in Fig. 3(b).

As shown in Fig. 2(b), we replace the second 3×3 convolution layer in the basic block with the designed multiscale processing method. Specifically, after the first 3×3 convolution, the feature maps X are obtained. We divide the feature maps X with channel number n into s feature map subsets uniformly, denoted by X_i, where i ∈ {1, 2, ..., s}. Each feature map subset X_i has the same spatial size compared to the feature maps X, and the number of channels is n/s. Then, each X_i is subjected to the corresponding 3 × 3 group convolution and channel reorganization process, denoted by $K_i(\cdot)$. Y_i denotes the output of $K_i(\cdot)$. Thus, Y_i can be written as:

$$Y_i = \begin{cases} K_i(X_i), & i = 1 \\ K_i(X_i + Y_{i-1}), & 1 < i \leq s \end{cases} \quad (2)$$

We can notice that Y_i has a larger receptive field than $\{Y_k, k <i\}$, contains a subset of features with different numbers and different scales. In order to obtain more different multiscale features, we concatenate all Y_is along the channel axis. s is used as the control parameter of scale, the larger s is the larger receptive field, but it will increase the computational overhead, we make a trade-off between performance and computation and set s = 4.

In order to compare the performance of the multi-scale module with the traditional VGG, we conduct visualization of the proposed module through class activation mapping (CAM) [25]. As shown in Fig. 4, compared with the traditional VGG, the multi-scale CAM results focus on a more comprehensive specific area, which is conducive to facial expression recognition, even if there are occlusion and non-positive pose problems in the facial image.

Fig. 4. The comparison of CAM between the multiscale module and traditional VGG.

2.4   Local Attention Module

Focusing the network on non-occlusion and local salient regions through the attention mechanism enhances the significance of local features, which is essential for enhancing robustness to occlusion and non-frontal facial expression conditions.

The channel attention module (SE) [8] considers the channel information, but ignores the importance of location information. The CBAM module [23] tries to invoke location information by adding global maximum pooling on the channels, but this approach can only capture local information, it cannot obtain information about long range dependencies. To obtain the remote dependencies and location information of the feature maps, we invoke the attention module Coordinate Attention (CA) [7]. As shown in Fig. 2(c), in the basic block, we add the CA module after the second 3 × 3 convolution. The CA module decomposes channel attention into two 1-dimensional features encoding processes that aggregate features along 2 spatial directions respectively. In this way, remote dependencies can be captured along one spatial direction, while accurate location information can be retained along the other spatial direction. The generated pair of weighted feature maps are then applied complementarily to the input feature maps, thus enhances the representation of the object of interest. The output of the CA module can be written as:

$$y_c(i,j) = x_c(i,j) \times g_c^h(i) \times g_c^w(j) \tag{3}$$

where $x_c(i,j)$ denotes the value of coordinate (i,j) in the feature map of Channel C, $g_c^h(i)$ is the weight value of row i in the vertical direction of Channel C, $g_c^w(j)$ denotes the weight value of column j in the horizontal direction of Channel C, and $y_c(i,j)$ denotes the value of coordinate (i,j) in the feature map of Channel C after applying the weight.

Analogously, to better explain the effect of the local attention module, we also conduct visualization of CAM to validate the performance of the local attention module as well as the tradition VGG. As shown in Fig. 5, the images in the first and second rows are visualization consequences of the tradition VGG and the local attention module respectively. We can see that the basic model focuses on a relatively small area, with many important facial regions not being noticed. However, the local attention module can pay good attention to the facial regions with high relevance to the judgment of the expression, such as the eyes, the nose, and the mouth, and at the same time pay attention to a wider range of areas, which indicates that the local attention module can really help the model to capture the important feature information in the expression image, and to highlight the key feature regions, so as to have a better recognition effect.

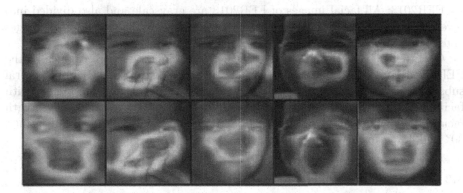

Fig. 5. The comparison of CAM between the local attention module and traditional VGG.

2.5 Fusion Loss

We use a decision-level fusion strategy to merge the recognition results of the two branches. The feature maps are transformed to two feature vectors of size 512 after two GAP layers, denoted by $x^{(m)}$, where $m \in \{local, global\}$ denotes branch. We use two cross-entropy losses to form the loss function, which can be formulated as:

$$\mathcal{L}_m = -\frac{1}{N}\sum_{i=1}^{N}\log\frac{e^{W_{y_i}^{(m)T}x_i^{(m)}+b_{y_i}^{(m)}}}{\sum_{j=1}^{C}e^{W_j^{(m)T}x_i^{(m)}+b_j^{(m)}}} \tag{4}$$

where N is the number of samples; C is the number of expression categories; $W^{(m)}$ is the weight matrix of the FC layer; $b^{(m)}$ is the bias term of the FC layer; $x_i^{(m)}$ is the FC input of sample i and y_i is its category label.

The final loss function is as follows:

$$\mathcal{L} = \lambda\mathcal{L}_{local} + (1 - \lambda)\mathcal{L}_{global} \tag{5}$$

where λ is a hyper-parameter to balance two parts.

3   Experiments

3.1   Datasets

We conduct experiments on two public wild facial expression datasets to validate the effectiveness of our network.

RAF-DB: The dataset is a real-world database of emotional faces, contains seven basic emotion categories annotated by 40 people with basic or compound expressions. In our experiments, only images with basic emotions are used, where the number of training and test images is 12,271 and 3,068 respectively.

FER2013: All facial images of FER2013 are grayscale and also divided into seven basic categories. It contains 28709 training images, 3589 validation images and 3589 test images.

Occlusion-RAF-DB & Pose-RAF-DB: To examine the performance of the FER model under occlusion and variant poses, Wang et al. [21] built several subsets from the test set of RAF-DB. Occlusion-RAF-DB collects images with facial occlusions and includes 735 images. Pose-RAF-DB collects images with facial-pose changes and contains 1,248 and 558 faces with an angle larger than 30° and 45° respectively in total.

3.2   Implementation

During train time, we randomly crop the RAFDB dataset with the original size of 100×100 and the FER2013 dataset with the original size of 48×48 to 90×90 and 40×40 respectively, then both perform a random horizontal flip. Due to the single channel of the FER2013 datasets, we duplicate the channel of each image twice. When testing, a ten-fold cropped data enhancement approach is performed on both datasets. We use a stochastic gradient descent (SGD) optimizer with momentum and weight decay values set to 0.9 and 5×10^{-4} respectively. 250 epoch training is performed on both RAFDB and FER2013, and the batchsize is set to 64. The learning rate is initialized to 0.01, and we adopt the cosine annealing learning rate decay strategy (CosineAnnealingLR).

3.3   Ablation Experiments

To verify the effectiveness of each component, we conduct ablation experiments on RAF-DB and FER2013 respectively. Specifically, we add the dropblock module after the first basic block of VGG13, and replace the last two basic blocks of VGG13 with the multiscale block of Res2Net, the improved multiscale block and the local attention module respectively. The results of each module are shown in Table 1.

Table 1. Evaluation of each component in GL-VGG on RAF-DB, FER2013.

Methods	RAF-DB	FER2013
Baseline(VGG13)	86.734	73.252
+ Dropblock	86.930	73.307
+ Dropblock + Attention	87.810	73.502
+ Dropblock + Res2net-Scale	87.516	73.502
+ Dropblock + GL-VGG-Scale	87.777	73.670

3.4   The Hyper-parameter λ

λ is a hyper-parameter that balances the two parts of the loss function. To explore the effect of weight on GL-VGG, we investigate different values from 0.1 to 0.9. Figure 6 shows the results on the RAF-DB and FER2013 datasets respectively.

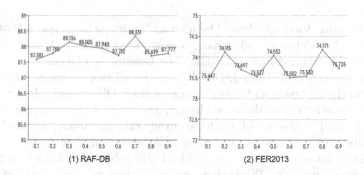

Fig. 6. Evaluation of different λ values on RAF-DB and FER2013 dataset.

3.5　Comparison with State-of-the-Art Methods

Real-World Datasets. We compare the best results with the current state-of-the-art FER methods. As shown in Table 2, we show the wild FER results for RAF-DB and FER2013. Our GL-VGG outperforms other methods, achieving 88.33% accuracy on RAF-DB and 74.17% accuracy on FER2013.

The proposed GL-VGG is an improvement on the basic model VGG. These modules have been designed to enhance the original model's ability to extract specific features. Through ablation experiments, it can be seen that each module has played an excellent role in improving. After combining the multiscale module and local attention module, the model has further improved, indicating that the model has the ability to extract both multiscale and local attention features. And the relationship between these two features is complementary, their combination does not have a negative effect on the model.

Table 2. Classification results on RAF-DB and FER2013.

Methods	Years	RAF-DB	FER2013
gACNN [13]	2019	85.07	
RAN [21]	2020	86.90	
DACL [3]	2021	87.78	
DeepEmotion [17]	2021		70.02
ResNet18 With Tricks [9]	2021		73.70
Ad-Corre [2]	2022	86.96	72.03
Ours	2023	88.33	74.17

Occlusion and Variant-Pose Datasets. To investigate the robustness of GL-VGG under occlusion and variant poses, we compare its best results with Occlusion-RAF-DB and Pose-RAF-DB. The baseline is VGG13.

As can be seen from Table 3, GL-VGG achieved more advanced recognition accuracy in the occlusion and pose changes of RAF-DB datasets. In general, the greater the magnitude of the pose change, the more limited the features that can be extracted by the model, so the accuracy rate for larger magnitudes tends to be smaller than for smaller magnitudes. As shown in Table 3, most methods reflect this situation. However, our method still achieved a higher accuracy in the same position of 45°. While there are individual methods that outperform us in this regard, the results under occlusion and posture of 30° are not as good as ours, suggesting that our method is more adapted to the general situations.

The experimental results verified the superiority of GL-VGG network in processing occlusion and posture changes of facial expression images in natural scenes, and it is more suitable for facial expression recognition tasks in natural scenes.

Table 3. Classification results on Occlusion-RAFDB and Pose-RAFDB.

Methods	Occlusion	Pose(30)	Pose(45)
Baseline	82.31	85.94	84.96
RAN [21]	82.72	86.74	85.20
ASF [16]	83.95	87.97	88.35
Ours	84.21	88.53	87.17

4   Conclusion

In this paper, we propose a global multi-scale and local attention network (GL-VGG). The dropblock module is added to the convolutional layer to prevent the network from overfitting, the global multiscale module reduces the susceptibility of deeper convolution towards occlusion and variant pose, and the local attention module releases the interference of occlusion and non-frontal pose situations. Through these improvements, GL-VGG can obtain powerful global and local features. The results show that our GL-VGG outperforms the baseline method and other FER methods on two wild datasets.

Acknowledgements. The paper's work is supported by 2022 Guangzhou education scientific research project 202214086 (Research on evaluation of children's development based on artificial intelligence technology) and the Joint Project of University and City in Guangzhou Science and Technology Bureau under Grant No. SL2022A03J00903.

References

1. Barsoum, E., Zhang, C., Ferrer, C.C., Zhang, Z.: Training deep networks for facial expression recognition with crowd-sourced label distribution. In: Proceedings of the 18th ACM International Conference on Multimodal Interaction, pp. 279–283 (2016)
2. Fard, A.P., Mahoor, M.H.: Ad-Corre: adaptive correlation-based loss for facial expression recognition in the wild. IEEE Access **10**, 26756–26768 (2022)
3. Farzaneh, A.H., Qi, X.: Facial expression recognition in the wild via deep attentive center loss. In: Proceedings of the IEEE/CVF Winter Conference on Applications of Computer Vision, pp. 2402–2411 (2021)
4. Gao, S.H., Cheng, M.M., Zhao, K., Zhang, X.Y., Yang, M.H., Torr, P.: Res2net: a new multi-scale backbone architecture. IEEE Trans. Pattern Anal. Mach. Intell. **43**(2), 652–662 (2021)
5. Ghiasi, G., Lin, T.Y., Le, Q.V.: Dropblock: a regularization method for convolutional networks. In: Advances in Neural Information Processing Systems, vol. 31 (2018)
6. Hinton, G.E., Krizhevsky, A., Sutskever, I.: ImageNet classification with deep convolutional neural networks. Adv. Neural. Inf. Process. Syst. **25**(1106–1114), 1 (2012)
7. Hou, Q., Zhou, D., Feng, J.: Coordinate attention for efficient mobile network design. In: Proceedings of the IEEE/CVF Conference on Computer Vision and Pattern Recognition, pp. 13713–13722 (2021)

8. Hu, J., Shen, L., Sun, G.: Squeeze-and-excitation networks. In: Proceedings of the IEEE Conference on Computer Vision and Pattern Recognition, pp. 7132–7141 (2018)
9. Khaireddin, Y., Chen, Z.: Facial emotion recognition: state of the art performance on fer2013. arXiv preprint arXiv:2105.03588 (2021)
10. Lei, J., et al.: Facial expression recognition by expression-specific representation swapping. In: Farkaš, I., Masulli, P., Otte, S., Wermter, S. (eds.) ICANN 2021. LNCS, vol. 12892, pp. 80–91. Springer, Cham (2021). https://doi.org/10.1007/978-3-030-86340-1_7
11. Li, H., Xiao, X., Liu, X., Guo, J., Wen, G., Liang, P.: Heuristic objective for facial expression recognition. Vis. Comput. **39**, 4709–4720 (2022)
12. Li, S., Deng, W., Du, J.: Reliable crowdsourcing and deep locality-preserving learning for expression recognition in the wild. In: Proceedings of the IEEE Conference on Computer Vision and Pattern Recognition, pp. 2852–2861 (2017)
13. Li, Y., Zeng, J., Shan, S., Chen, X.: Occlusion aware facial expression recognition using CNN with attention mechanism. IEEE Trans. Image Process. **28**(5), 2439–2450 (2018)
14. Liu, W., et al.: SSD: single shot multibox detector. In: Leibe, B., Matas, J., Sebe, N., Welling, M. (eds.) ECCV 2016. LNCS, vol. 9905, pp. 21–37. Springer, Cham (2016). https://doi.org/10.1007/978-3-319-46448-0_2
15. Lyons, M., Akamatsu, S., Kamachi, M., Gyoba, J.: Coding facial expressions with Gabor wavelets. In: Proceedings Third IEEE International Conference on Automatic Face and Gesture Recognition, pp. 200–205. IEEE (1998)
16. Ma, F., Sun, B., Li, S.: Facial expression recognition with visual transformers and attentional selective fusion. IEEE Trans. Affect. Comput. **14**, 1236–1248 (2021)
17. Minaee, S., Minaei, M., Abdolrashidi, A.: Deep-emotion: facial expression recognition using attentional convolutional network. Sensors **21**(9), 3046 (2021)
18. Najibi, M., Samangouei, P., Chellappa, R., Davis, L.: SSH: single stage headless face detector. In: 2017 IEEE International Conference on Computer Vision (ICCV) (2017)
19. Simonyan, K., Zisserman, A.: Very deep convolutional networks for large-scale image recognition. Computer Science (2014)
20. Valstar, M., Pantic, M., et al.: Induced disgust, happiness and surprise: an addition to the mmi facial expression database. In: Proceedings of the 3rd International Workshop on EMOTION (satellite of LREC): Corpora for Research on Emotion and Affect, p. 65. Paris, France. (2010)
21. Wang, K., Peng, X., Yang, J., Meng, D., Qiao, Y.: Region attention networks for pose and occlusion robust facial expression recognition. IEEE Trans. Image Process. **29**, 4057–4069 (2020)
22. Wang, K., Peng, X., Yang, J., Lu, S., Qiao, Y.: Suppressing uncertainties for large-scale facial expression recognition. In: Proceedings of the IEEE/CVF Conference on Computer Vision and Pattern Recognition, pp. 6897–6906 (2020)
23. Woo, S., Park, J., Lee, J.Y., Kweon, I.S.: CBAM: convolutional block attention module. In: Proceedings of the European conference on computer vision (ECCV), pp. 3–19 (2018)
24. Zhang, X., Zhou, X., Lin, M., Sun, J.: ShuffleNet: an extremely efficient convolutional neural network for mobile devices. In: Proceedings of the IEEE Conference on Computer Vision and Pattern Recognition, pp. 6848–6856 (2018)
25. Zhou, B., Khosla, A., Lapedriza, A., Oliva, A., Torralba, A.: Learning deep features for discriminative localization. In: 2016 IEEE Conference on Computer Vision and Pattern Recognition (CVPR), pp. 2921–2929 (2016)

MARANet: Multi-scale Adaptive Region Attention Network for Few-Shot Learning

Jia Chen[1,2], Xiyang Li[1], Yangjun Ou[1,2]([✉]), Xinrong Hu[1,2], and Tao Peng[1,2]

[1] Wuhan Textile University, Wuhan 430200, Hubei, China
yjou@wtu.edu.cn
[2] Engineering Research Center of Hubei Province for Clothing Information, Wuhan 430200, Hubei, China

Abstract. Few-shot learning, which aims to classify unknown categories with fewer label samples, has become a research hotspot in computer vision because of its wide application. Objects will present different regional locations in nature, and the existing few-shot learning only focuses on the overall location information, while ignoring the impact of local key information on classification tasks. To solve this problem, (1) we propose a new multi-scale adaptive region attention network (MARANet), which makes use of the semantic similarity between images to make the model pay more attention to the areas that are beneficial to the classification task. (2) MARANet mainly includes two modules—the multi-scale feature generation module uses low-level features (LF) of different scales to solve the problem of different target scales in nature; the adaptive region metric module selects the LF of key regions by assigning masks to each classification task. We have conducted experiments on three common data sets (*i.e.* miniImageNet, CUB-200, and Stanford Cars). The experimental results show that the new category classification task of MARANet is 1.1% ∼ 4.9% higher than the existing methods.

Keywords: Few-shot learning · Multi-scale · Adaptive · low-level features · Classification

1 Introduction

Few-shot learning aims to build an accurate machine-learning model with a small amount of training data. It can be used in the fields of computer vision, natural language processing, acoustic signal processing, and so on. Because the input data dimension determines the resource cost (such as time cost, computational cost, etc.), we need to use few-shot learning to reduce the cost of data analysis. However, the sparsity of sample data and the particularity of sampling mean that the few-shot model does not play a sufficient role in feature extraction, and effective data features are the key for the model to approach real data

Supplementary Information The online version contains supplementary material available at https://doi.org/10.1007/978-3-031-50069-5_34.

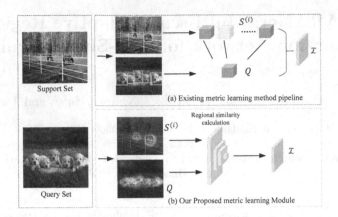

Fig. 1. (a) The existing metric-based learning method is to compare the similarity between the overall features of each task and the query set features. (b) The proposed method is to calculate the similarity between the local key features of each task and the query features.

distribution and achieve better results. This makes it difficult for few-shot learning to break through in various fields.

The existing few-shot methods are roughly divided into two categories. One is the meta-learning method [4,17], which is a method of learning to learn, and its purpose is to hope that the model can acquire a kind of ability of "learning to learn" so that it can quickly learn new tasks based on acquiring existing "knowledge". Although this method has achieved satisfactory results in few-shot learning, it still has some defects in the definition of hyperparameters and loss functions [30]. One is the metric learning method [19,23], which calculates the distance between the samples to be classified and the known samples, and finds the adjacent categories to determine the classification results of the samples to be classified. This kind of method usually depends on the design of the distance function, but the current few-shot method based on the distance function is difficult to improve the detection accuracy [30].

In few-shot learning, some researchers [1,14] have proposed a metric learning method based on depth neural networks to achieve few-shot detection. These methods look at each supporting class as a whole, and then extract different categories of features separately, as shown in Fig. 1 (a). Although this method can improve the accuracy of small shot detection, it ignores the possible local key semantic similarity between the query set and all support classes, as shown in Fig. 1 (b). Therefore, driven by this idea, after the feature extraction of the model, we introduce the adaptive region attention module to assign the region attention mask to each task and weigh the regions with high similarity, to make the model pay more attention to the most discriminant features. This method can effectively improve the accuracy of small sample detection and reduce the amount of calculation of the model.

In this work, we propose a new multi-scale adaptive regional attention network (MARANet), which is mainly composed of a multi-scale feature generation module and an adaptive region metric module. Specifically, the multi-scale feature generation module includes five-scale feature generation functions, which are used to generate low-level features of different scales. The adaptive region metric module includes a region relation matrix, a region attention module, and a region attention mask. The region relation matrix is used to calculate the regional relationship between query sets and support sets and to measure the regional correlation of low-level features at different scales. The regional attention module is used to select key areas by adaptively considering the regional priorities of different tasks. The regional attention mask consists of all regional attention scores and is used to strengthen the regional relationship with the task. To sum up, we first use the multi-scale feature generator to generate multiple low-level features on different scales. Then, we use the adaptive region metric module to select the low-level features (LF) of the key regions in the classification task. After that, the joint multi-scale similarity between the query image and the support set is calculated by using the region similarity module and the fusion layer. Finally, the similarity score is used to determine the category, and the classification results are obtained.

To sum up, the main contributions are summarized as follows:

- We propose a multi-scale adaptive regional attention network (MARANet) for few-shot learning classification tasks.
- We design a multi-scale feature generator that can capture rich multi-scale information through different levels of local feature representation.
- We propose an adaptive region metric module that uses regional attention to generate a region mask to enhance the correlation between multi-layer regions.

2   Related Work

The main idea of the meta-learning method [4,8] is how to make rational use of existing experience or knowledge to achieve rapid learning when facing new tasks. Sebastian et al. [8] proposed that meta-learning guides a goal and then optimizes the meta-learning by minimizing the distance from the object under the selected (pseudo) metric. Metric learning-based methods [2,32] aim to optimize task-related features by calculating the similarity between the query set and support set. Wu et al. [27] proposed an object-aware long-and short-range spatial alignment network to maintain the spatial consistency between supporting features and query features. Li et al. [12] try to find the task-related features of few-shot learning through category traversal. Although these methods have achieved excellent results in small sample learning tasks, they can only measure the similarity between query images and support sets on a single scale, which may reduce the accuracy of classification when the scales of objects are different.

On the contrary, our proposed MARANet is good at using a multi-scale feature generator to represent all images as LF sets of different scales to calculate the similarity between images, to enhance the feature representation of different categories. And it can be trained in an end-to-end way, which can effectively reduce the training difficulty of the model.

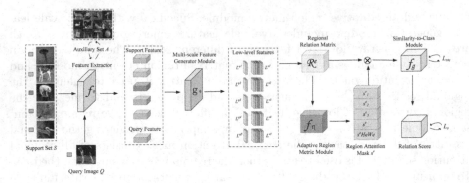

Fig. 2. The MARANet consists of four modules: the feature extractor f_θ to learn local representations, the multi-scale feature generator g_θ to generate multiple features at different scales, the adaptive region metric module f_η generates adaptive region attention masks, and the region similarity-to-class module f_g obtains similarity scores.

3   Proposed Method

3.1   Overview

In Few-shot Learning, there are three datasets: query set Q, support set S, and auxiliary set A. We aim to determine which category the samples in the query set Q belong to through auxiliary set A and support set S. Our model is trained by the scene training mechanism, and in each scene, the auxiliary set A will create a new task with the mechanism. Each task consists of two subsets: auxiliary support set A_S and auxiliary query set A_Q, in which N tag samples are in A_S and the rest are in A_Q. We use hundreds of tasks to train the model during the training phase.

As shown in Fig. 2, our MARANet consists of four main modules: a feature extraction module, a multi-scale feature generation module, an adaptive region metric module, and a similarity-to-class module. First, we send all the samples of the image set into the feature extractor to obtain feature embedding and rich low-level features (LF). Then, the features of different scales are generated by the multi-scale feature generation module, and the regional correlation of query set Q and support set S on each scale is measured by calculating the region relation matrix. After that, the adaptive region metric module assigns a region attention mask to each small classification task according to the region correlation, and the mask adaptively calculates the importance of each LF in the current classification task. The purpose of using the area attention mask is to weight the region relation matrix to highlight the elements related to the classification task. Then, the weighted region relation matrix is processed by the class similarity module f_g to determine which supporting class the query image belongs to. Finally, the similarity of different scale features is adaptively fused by learning vectors. Note that all of our modules can be jointly trained end-to-end.

3.2   Multi-scale Feature Generator Model

Recent studies on Few-shot learning [13] show that low-level features (LFs) can show richer representation ability, and can effectively alleviate the problem of sample scarcity in few-shot learning. Therefore, we use LF to represent the characteristics of each image. By comparing with the actual results, we find that the LF formed by involution instead of convolution has a better representation ability. We first extract the query set A_Q^q through the feature extractor, and get the three-dimensional vector $F_A = f_\theta(A_Q^q) \in \mathbb{R}^{C \times H \times W}$. In the case of several times of learning, there are N images for each supporting class in the task. Through feature extraction, we can get the 4-dimensional vector of the support set S, which is marked as $F_S = f_\theta(S) \in \mathbb{R}^{NK \times C \times H \times W}$.

In this paper, an effective and novel multi-scale feature generator is formed by combining an involution set with a feature generator. For details on the specific network model of the feature generator, see the supporting materials. With the multi-scale feature generator, we can obtain 3D features $LFs \in \mathbb{R}^{C_e \times H_e \times W_e}, e \in 1, 2, 3, 4, 5$, which can be viewed as a set of H×W×C-dimensional LFs,

$$L^{qe} = [x_1, ..., x_{H_e W_e}] \in \mathbb{R}^{C_e \times H_e \times W_e}, \tag{1}$$

where x_i is the ith LF, and by using the multiscale generator, we can also obtain the LFs of the support set S,

$$L^{Se} = [x_1, ..., x_{NKH_e W_e}] \in \mathbb{R}^{C_e \times NKH_e \times W_e}. \tag{2}$$

3.3   Adaptive Region Metric Module

In the case of few-shot learning in K-way N-shot, the region correlation is measured by calculating the region relation matrix R^e between the query image A_Q^q and the support set S. We try Euclidean distance, Manhattan distance, and Pinch cosine as functions of the regional correlation matrix. Finally, the actual test shows that the performance of the pinch cosine function is the best and the absolute value is not sensitive. From the point of view of the calculation method and measurement characteristics, it is more suitable to be used as the region correlation matrix. R^e is calculated as follows:

$$R_{i,j}^e = cos(L_i^{qe}, L_j^{Se}), \tag{3}$$

$$cos(L_i^{qe}, L_j^{Se}) = \frac{(L_i^{qe})^T L_j^{Se}}{||L_i^{qe}|| \cdot ||L_j^{Se}||}, \tag{4}$$

where $R_{i,j}^e$ is the distance between the element R^e of (i,j) reflecting the ith LF of the query image A_Q^q and the jth LF of the support set at the eth scale. R^e can be decomposed into N submatrices R^{en}, $n \in \{1, 2, ..., N\}$ according to columns, representing the semantic relation between the query image and each supported class.

Considering the need for adaptive regions for different tasks and the need to think about the prioritization of regions. We take the whole image information as the whole region, defined as Ω_i^l, such that messages from less task-relevant regions are computed from the coarse level, while messages from highly relevant regions are computed under the fine level. Partial information Reg_i is calculated as follows:

$$Reg_i = \sum_{j \in \Omega_i^l} s_{i,j}^l v_j^l, \tag{5}$$

where Reg_i denotes the information in the evaluation section of level $l (1 \leq l \leq L)$. $s_{i,j}^l$ is the attention score between the lth level query and the key token. The attention scores are calculated recursively as follows:

$$s_{i,j}^l = s_{i,j}^{l-1} t_{i,j}^l, \tag{6}$$

where $s_{i,j}^{l-1}$ is the attention score corresponding to the parent query and the key token, $s_{i,j}^l = 1$, and $t_{i,j}^l$ is the tentative attention score used for the evaluation in the first parent query token at the very beginning.

We know the semantic relationship between the query image and each support class at different scales, and also the regions that are highly relevant to the task. We compute the region attention score for each element of the current task R^e,

$$s_i^e = \frac{\sum_{j=1}^{NKH_eW_e} R_{i,j}^e s_{i,j}^l}{\sqrt{\sum_{i=1}^{H_eW_e} \sum_{j=1}^{NKH_eW_e} R_{i,j}^e}}, \tag{7}$$

the region attention mask s^e consists of all region attention fractions $s_i^e, i \in \{1, ..., H_eW_e\}$. Afterwards, we use dot-product to weight R_i^e by s_i^e,

$$M_i^e = s_i^e \cdot R_i^e, \tag{8}$$

where M_i^e is the i-th row of the weighted region relation matrix. This gives us the weighted region relation matrix M^e, which can be decomposed into N submatrices $M^e n$ by columns, $n \in \{1, ..., N\}$. And the task-irrelevant region relations are suppressed; meanwhile, the task-relevant region relations are enhanced.

3.4   Similarity-to-Class Module and Loss Function

The similarly-to-class module aims to determine which supported class the query image belongs to. In this module, for each LF of the query image, we find the k most similar LFs among all supported LFs for class n. Then, we sum the LFs chosen by kH_eW_e as the similarity score between the query image and the n-th supported class at the e-th scale,

$$Pro^{en} = \sum_{i=1}^{kH_eW_e} Maxk(M_i^{en}), \tag{9}$$

where Pro^{en} denotes the similarity between the query image and the support class n at scale z, and $Maxk(\cdot)$ denotes the selection of the k largest elements in each row of the weighted semantic relation matrix M^{en}.

We obtain five scales of relational scores integrated with adaptive learnable five-dimensional vectors. The final fusion similarity can be defined as:

$$Pro^q = w_1 \cdot Pro^1 + w_2 \cdot Pro^2 + w_3 \cdot Pro^3 + w_4 \cdot Pro^4 + w_5 \cdot Pro^5, \quad (10)$$

Finally, in loss learning, we use dice loss and cross-entropy loss function together for optimization, considering that oscillation may occur in training due to the problem of few targets. The joint loss function is as follows:

$$L = \frac{2|X_{i,j} \cap Y_{i,j}|}{|X_{i,j}| + |Y_{i,j}|} - \sum_{j=1}^{c} y_{i,j} log(Pro_{i,j}), \quad (11)$$

where $y_{i,j}$ is a one-hot vector defined as:

$$y_{i,j} = \begin{cases} 1 & same - category \\ 0 & otherwise \end{cases}, \quad (12)$$

where $Pro_{i,j}$ denotes the probability that the i-th sample belongs to category j. In this paper, the softmax function is used to obtain the probability that the sample belongs to each category. The final five-dimensional vector is used for the final classification.

4   Experiments

4.1   Datasets

MiniImageNet. As a mini-version of ImageNet [21], this dataset [25] contains 100 classes with 600 images per class, and has a resolution of 84 × 84 for each image. Following the splits used in [6], we take 64, 16, and 20 classes for training (auxiliary), validation, and test, respectively.

CUB-200. This dataset [26] contains 6033 images from 200 bird species. Similarly, we select 130, 20, and 50 classes for training (auxiliary), validation, and testing.

Stanford Cars. This dataset [10] is also a benchmark dataset for fine-grained classification tasks, which consists of 196 classes of cars with a total number of 16, 185 images. Similarly, 130, 17, and 49 classes in this dataset are split for training (auxiliary), validation, and testing.

4.2   Implementation Details

Experiment Settings. Our framework was performed on Ubuntu-18.04 and NVIDIA-V100 (50G) which was made by NVIDIA Corporation in Santa Clara,

USA. This work exploited the current popular deep neural frameworks, such as Python (3.6.13), PyTorch (1.8.1), and torch-vision (0.9.1).

Our experiments are conducted in K-way N-shot settings for three datasets. All images in the three datasets are tuned to 84×84. In the training phase, we randomly construct $250, 000$ episodes to train our MARANet for miniImageNet and Stanford Car, and train 300,000 for other datasets via the episode training mechanism. In each episode, we select 15 or 10 query images from each category for the 1-shot or 5-shot setup, respectively. We use the Adam algorithm [9] with cross-entropy (CE) loss to train the network. In addition, the initial learning rate is set to 0.001, which is reduced by half every 50,000 episodes. In the testing phase, 600 episodes are constructed from the test set and this testing process will be repeated five times. Both the average accuracy and the 95% confidence interval will then be reported.

Evaluation Protocol. We use the Accurate Recognition Rate (Acc), which reflects the performance evaluation criteria under the recoding of small sample data. After random sampling, the number of samples used in each classification task is very small, typically only about 10 or 30. Therefore, instead of continuously importing the original image labels for each training session, a simpler recording of each class of samples is performed before the data samples are trained.

4.3   Ablation Study

Influence of Each Module in MARANet. To further validate the effectiveness of the multiscale feature generator, the adaptive region metric module, and the class similarity module, we conducted an ablation study on miniImageNet. We remove g_θ, f_η, and f_g from MARANet separately to confirm that each part of the model is indispensable. We remove both the g_θ, f_η, and f_g class similarity modules as a baseline, as shown in Table 1, with the main improvement coming from the adaptive region metric module f_η. If we remove f_η, the performance of the 1-shot and 5-shot tasks will be reduced by 2.7% and 3.8%, respectively. This empirical study demonstrates that discriminative f_η improves performance and brings more discriminative features to the classification. Similarly, if we delete the g_θ and f_g modules respectively, it will degrade the performance of task classification to some extent.

Influence of Metric Function. Table 2 reports the results for the different metric functions used in the adaptive region metric module. To measure the region relationship between feature descriptors, the appropriate metric function is the key factor. From Table 2, it can be seen that the best metric function is Cosine Similarity.

Table 1. The influence of each module in MARANet. The table represents the experimental results without a separate modules.

Model	5-Way Accuracy(%)	
	1-shot	5-shot
baseline	50.97 ± 0.77	67.84 ± 0.64
g_θ	52.14 ± 0.67	71.54 ± 0.57
f_η	51.46 ± 0.74	69.48 ± 0.67
f_g	53.45 ± 0.81	71.59 ± 0.81
MARANet(ours)	**59.15 ± 0.88**	**78.24 ± 0.78**

Table 2. The influence of metric function.Experimental results of MARANet on mini-ImageNet using different metric functions.

Metric Function	5-Way Accuracy(%)	
	1-shot	5-shot
Euclidean Distance	51.16 ± 0.88	70.55 ± 0.78
Manhattan Distance	52.22 ± 0.83	71.26 ± 0.74
Chebyshev Distance	52.67 ± 0.81	72.14 ± 0.72
Mahalanobis Distance	53.45 ± 0.83	72.35 ± 0.75
Cosine Similarity	**58.23 ± 0.85**	**76.18 ± 0.76**

4.4 Performance Results

Results on MiniImageNet Datasets. The experimental results on miniImageNet are reported in Table 3. It can be observed that our method significantly outperforms the other methods in both 5-way 1-shot and 5-shot settings. With the 5-way 1-shot setting, we outperform EASE [33] by 3.9%, with an accuracy of 82.54%. Similarly, we achieve 89.48% in the 5-way 5-shot setting, which is 3.7% better than RSSPP [18]. Note that our model improves 11.7% and 13.3% over the most relevant work CovaMNet [13] on 1-shot and 5-shot, respectively. This verifies the effectiveness of our model, which adaptively selects the most discriminative local features on multiple scales in a given task.

Results on Stanford Cars and CUB-200 Datasets. As can be seen from Table 4, the proposed MARANet outperforms most other state-of-the-art methods in the 5-way 1-shot and 5-way 5-shot few-shot learning settings. In particular, for the 5-way 1-shot task, our approach improved returns on Stanford cars and CUB-200 by 3.4% and 4.5%, respectively, compared with OLSA [27]. For the 5-way 5-shot task, the performance of our method is 4.9%, and 4.1% higher than that of OLSA [27] on two datasets, respectively. We can achieve these state-of-the-art performances because MARANet can adaptively select region-related LF for classification on multiple scales.

Table 3. Comparison results on miniImageNet. The confidence interval was set at 95%. The best experimental data are shown in bold.

Method	Backbone	5-way 1-shot	5-way 5-shot
SNAIL [16]	Conv-32F	63.96 ± 0.41	69.18 ± 0.37
TPN [15]	Conv-32F	67.52 ± 0.33	75.49 ± 0.56
MAML+L2F [3]	Conv-32F	70.29 ± 0.46	81.73 ± 0.49
Transductive tuing [5]	Conv-32F	69.62 ± 0.34	82.31 ± 0.52
HT [31]	Conv-32F	54.0 ± 0.33	70.2 ± 0.43
SEGA [28]	Conv-32F	71.67 ± 0.23	82.57 ± 0.18
Relation Nets [24]	Conv-64F	60.46 ± 0.74	72.45 ± 0.46
CovaMNet [13]	Conv-64F	64.13 ± 0.67	73.57 ± 0.51
MetaOpt [11]	Conv-64F	65.84 ± 0.74	74.48 ± 0.37
DSN [22]	Conv-64F	70.16 ± 0.73	79.45 ± 0.52
DeepEMD [29]	Conv-64F	72.49 ± 0.76	81.51 ± 0.47
MIAN [20]	Conv-64F	73.32 ± 0.42	82.24 ± 0.23
RSSPP [18]	Conv-64F	76.63 ± 0.75	85.74 ± 0.38
EASE [33]	Conv-64F	78.59 ± 0.37	85.32 ± 0.13
MARANet	Conv-64F	**82.54 ± 0.49**	**89.48 ± 0.49**

Table 4. Comparison results on Stanford Cars and CUB-200. The best experimental data are shown in bold.

Model	5-Way Accuracy(%)			
	Stanford Cars		CUB-200	
	1-shot	5-shot	1-shot	5-shot
MAML [7]	48.22 ± 0.43	62.57 ± 0.94	61.43 ± 0.68	73.71 ± 0.39
Relation Nets [24]	48.51 ± 0.38	61.92 ± 0.73	63.58 ± 0.39	78.51 ± 0.92
CovaMNet [13]	57.48 ± 0.37	73.71 ± 0.64	64.37 ± 0.67	83.69 ± 0.83
DN4 [23]	56.37 ± 0.63	76.94 ± 0.81	62.76 ± 0.64	81.73 ± 0.97
DSN [22]	72.33 ± 0.54	82.78 ± 0.83	78.47 ± 0.55	85.44 ± 0.88
DeepEMD [29]	71.99 ± 0.67	83.66 ± 0.91	79.44 ± 0.72	86.92 ± 0.77
RSSPP [18]	75.48 ± 0.88	83.46 ± 0.67	81.69 ± 0.79	90.48 ± 0.68
MAML+L2F [3]	69.72 ± 0.55	79.57 ± 0.62	76.33 ± 0.29	83.29 ± 0.55
MsKPRN [1]	76.64 ± 0.84	89.88 ± 0.46	69.49 ± 0.95	82.94 ± 0.65
OLSA [27]	77.03 ± 0.46	88.85 ± 0.46	77.77 ± 0.44	89.77 ± 0.47
MARANet	**80.46 ± 0.53**	**93.78 ± 0.46**	**86.19 ± 0.51**	**95.67 ± 0.48**

5   Conclusions

In this paper, we revisit local representation-based metric learning and propose a novel multi-scale adaptive region attention network (MARANet) for few-sample learning that aims to learn multiple features at different scales by generating regionally relevant and more discriminative local representations at different scales and viewing the entire task in context. By looking at the whole task, our method can adaptively select the most discriminative local representation in the current task at different scales, which can effectively solve the problem of few-shot learning with few features. Extensive experiments on three benchmark datasets demonstrate the effectiveness and advantages of the proposed MARANet.

Acknowledgments. Chen's research was supported by the National Natural Science Foundation of China(Grant No.62202345).

References

1. Abdelaziz, M., Zhang, Z.: Multi-scale Kronecker-product relation networks for few-shot learning. Multimed. Tools. Appl. **81**(5), 6703–6722 (2022)
2. Afrasiyabi, A., Lalonde, J.-F., Gagné, C.: Mixture-based feature space learning for few-shot image classification. In: ICCV, pp. 9041–9051 (2021)
3. Baik, S., Hong, S., Lee, K.M.: Learning to forget for meta-learning. In: CVPR, pp. 2379–2387 (2020)
4. Deleu, T., et al.: Continuous-time meta-learning with forward mode differentiation. arXiv preprint arXiv:2203.01443 (2022)
5. Dhillon, G.S., Chaudhari, P., Ravichandran, A., Soatto, S.: A baseline for few-shot image classification. arXiv preprint arXiv:1909.02729 (2019)
6. Finn, C., Abbeel, P., Levine, S.: Model-agnostic meta-learning for fast adaptation of deep networks. In: ICML, pp. 1126–1135 (2017)
7. Finn, C., Abbeel, P., Levine, S.: Model-agnostic meta-learning for fast adaptation of deep networks. In: ICLR, pp. 1126–1135 (2017)
8. Flennerhag, S., Schroecker, Y., Zahavy, T., van Hasselt, H., Silver, D., Singh, S.: Bootstrapped meta-learning. arXiv preprint arXiv:2109.04504 (2021)
9. Kingma, D.P., Ba, J.: Adam: a method for stochastic optimization. arXiv preprint arXiv:1412.6980 (2014)
10. Krause, J., Stark, M., Deng, J., Fei-Fei, L.: 3D object representations for fine-grained categorization. In: ICCVW, pp. 554–561 (2013)
11. Lee, K., Maji, S., Ravichandran, A., Soatto, S.: Meta-learning with differentiable convex optimization. In: CVPR, pp. 10657–10665 (2019)
12. Li, H., Eigen, D., Dodge, S., Zeiler, M., Wang, X.: Finding task-relevant features for few-shot learning by category traversal. In: CVPR, pp. 1–10 (2019)
13. Li, W., Jinglin, X., Huo, J., Wang, L., Gao, Y., Luo, J.: Distribution consistency based covariance metric networks for few-shot learning. Proc. AAAI Conf. Artif. Intell. **33**, 8642–8649 (2019)
14. Lin, X., Sun, S., Huang, W., Sheng, B., Li, P., Feng, D.D.: EAPT: efficient attention pyramid transformer for image processing. IEEE Trans. Multimedia **25**, 50–61 (2021)
15. Liu, Y., et al.: Learning to propagate labels: transductive propagation network for few-shot learning. arXiv preprint arXiv:1805.10002 (2018)
16. Mishra, N., Rohaninejad, M., Chen, X., Abbeel, P.: A simple neural attentive meta-learner. arXiv preprint arXiv:1707.03141 (2017)

17. Phaphuangwittayakul, A., Ying, F., Guo, Y., Zhou, L., Chakpitak, N.: Few-shot image generation based on contrastive meta-learning generative adversarial network. Vis. Comput. **39**(9), 4015–4028 (2023)
18. Qi, G., Yu, H., Lu, Z., Li, S.: Transductive few-shot classification on the oblique manifold. In: ICCV, pp. 8412–8422 (2021)
19. Qian, K., Wen, X., Song, A.: Hybrid neural network model for large-scale heterogeneous classification tasks in few-shot learning. Vis. Comput. **38**, 719–728 (2022)
20. Qin, Z., et al.: Multi-instance attention network for few-shot learning. Inf. Sci. **611**, 464–475 (2022)
21. Russakovsky, O., et al.: ImageNet large scale visual recognition challenge. Int. J. Comput. Vis. **115**, 211–252 (2015)
22. Simon, C., Koniusz, P., Nock, R., Harandi, M.: Adaptive subspaces for few-shot learning. In: CVPR, pp. 4136–4145 (2020)
23. Sung, F., Yang, Y., Zhang, L., Xiang, T., Torr, P.H.S., Hospedales, T.M.: Learning to compare: relation network for few-shot learning. In: CVPR, pp. 1199–1208 (2018)
24. Sung, F., Yang, Y., Zhang, L., Xiang, T., Torr, P.H.S., Hospedales, T.M.: Learning to compare: relation network for few-shot learning. In: CVPR, pp. 1199–1208 (2018)
25. Vinyals, O., Blundell, C., Lillicrap, T., Wierstra, D., et al.: Matching networks for one shot learning. In: NIPS 2016: Proceedings of the 30th International Conference on Neural Information Processing Systems, vol. 29, pp. 3637–3645 (2016)
26. Wah, C., Branson, S., Welinder, P., Perona, P., Belongie, S.: The caltech-UCSD birds-200-2011 dataset (2011)
27. Wu, Y., et al.: Object-aware long-short-range spatial alignment for few-shot fine-grained image classification. arXiv preprint arXiv:2108.13098 (2021)
28. Yang, F., Wang, R., Chen, X.: Sega: semantic guided attention on visual prototype for few-shot learning. In: WACV, pp. 1056–1066 (2022)
29. Zhang, C., Cai, Y., Lin, G., Shen, C.: DeepEMD: few-shot image classification with differentiable earth mover's distance and structured classifiers. In: CVPR, pp. 12203–12213 (2020)
30. Zhao, K., Jin, X., Wang, Y.: Survey on few-shot learning. J. Softw. Eng. **32**(2), 349–369 (2021)
31. Zhmoginov, A., Sandler, M., Vladymyrov, M.: HyperTransformer: model generation for supervised and semi-supervised few-shot learning. In: ICML, pages 27075–27098 (2022)
32. Zhou, Yu., Chen, Z., Sheng, B., Li, P., Kim, J., Enhua, W.: AFF-Dehazing: attention-based feature fusion network for low-light image dehazing. Comput. Animat. Virtual Worlds **32**(3–4), e2011 (2021)
33. Zhu, H., Koniusz, P.: Ease: unsupervised discriminant subspace learning for transductive few-shot learning. In: CVPR, pp. 9078–9088 (2022)

Enhancing Image Rescaling Using High Frequency Guidance and Attentions in Downscaling and Upscaling Network

Yan Gui[1,2]($\boxtimes$), Yan Xie[1,2], Lidan Kuang[1,2], Zhihua Chen[3], and Jin Zhang[1,2]

[1] School of Computer and Communication Engineering, Changsha University of Science and Technology, Changsha 410114, Hunan, China
guiyan@csust.edu.cn
[2] Hunan Provincial Key Laboratory of Intelligent Processing of Big Data on Transportation, Changsha University of Science and Technology, Changsha 410114, Hunan, China
[3] Department of Computer Science and Engineering, East China University of Science and Technology, Shanghai 200237, China

Abstract. Recent image rescaling methods adopt invertible bijective transformations to model downscaling and upscaling simultaneously, where the high-frequency information learned in the downscaling process is used to recover the high-resolution image by inversely passing the model. However, less attention has been paid to exploiting the high-frequency information when upscaling. In this paper, an efficient end-to-end learning model for image rescaling, based on a newly designed neural network, is developed. The network consists of a downscaling generation sub-network (DSNet) and a super-resolution sub-network (SRNet), and learns to recover high-frequency signals. Concretely, we introduce dense attention blocks to the DSNet to produce the visually-pleasing low resolution (LR) image and model the distribution of the high-frequency information using a latent variable following a specified distribution. For the SRNet, we adapt an enhanced deep residual network by using residual attention blocks and adding a long skip connection, which transforms the predicted LR image and the random samples of the latent variable back during upscaling. Finally, we define a joint loss and adopt a multi-stage training strategy to optimize the whole network. Experimental results demonstrate that the superior performance of our model over existing methods in terms of both quantitative metrics and visual quality.

Keywords: Image rescaling · High-frequency information · Channel and spatial attentions · Multi-stage training strategy

Supplementary Information The online version contains supplementary material available at https://doi.org/10.1007/978-3-031-50069-5_35.

1   Introduction

With the significant progress of network technology and hardware devices, the number of high-resolution (HR) images has exploded. They are usually reduced to fit the screen of different mobile devices or save the cost of storage and bandwidth [1] while maintaining visually valid information [2–4]. Thus, it is desirable to develop efficient image downscaling and upscaling methods to make such applications more practical and resources saving. Most image downscaling methods are divided into several different domains: reducing the resolution for image compression [5] and display device [6], image retargeting [7], and perceptual quality-oriented downscaling [8]. According to the Nyquist-Shannon sampling theorem [9], it is inevitable that the high-frequency information will be lost during image downscaling. Additionally, the traditional super-resolution (SR) methods [10–13] can be categorized into interpolation-based methods, reconstruction-based model methods and learning-based methods. Recently, several researchers have applied convolutional neural networks (CNNs) to gain features with higher-level understanding for image to improve the performance of SR [14–21]. In above-mentioned works, image downscaling and upscaling are two separate and independent tasks.

In recent years, many efforts [2–4] attempt to model the image downscaling and upscaling as a single unified task. Since these methods link two processes only through the training losses, and any feature of the lost high-frequency information cannot be captured, these methods thus did not tackle much on the ill-posedness. More recently, Xiao et al. [22] employed an invertible neural network to model image downscaling and upscaling. FGRN [23] proposed an additional invertible flow guidance module. HCFlow [24] proposed a hierarchical conditional mechanism to make the high-frequency components conditional on LR image hierarchically. DLV-IRN [25] introduced a dual latent variable in the image scaling process. Although these methods can obtain the reconstructed images with good quality, the high-frequency information is not fully and reasonably leveraged for reconstruction.

In this paper, we devise a unified, end-to-end trainable neural network architecture for image rescaling. As shown in Fig. 1, the network contains two main modules: a down-scaling generation sub-network (DSNet) and a super-resolution sub-network (SRNet). More specifically, the DSNet is responsible for generating a low resolution version of a given HR original image and learning the high-frequency information in image downscaling process. Here, the learned high-frequency information can be modeled as a simple specified distribution using an auxiliary latent variable, in which we force it to obey an isotropic Gaussian distribution. During the image upscaling process, we employ an enhanced EDSR network as the SRNet by introducing residual attention blocks and a long skip connection (LSC) for feature aggregation. Furthermore, the SRNet uses a concatenation of the LR image and the learned high-frequency information from the pre-specified distribution as an input, which holds the rich information and then uses it to reconstruct the HR image. For network training, we use three losses on massive data to jointly train for image scaling. To this end, we

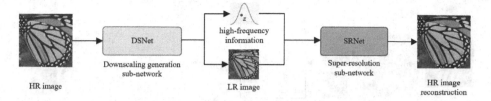

Fig. 1. Illustration of our framework. The high-frequency information and the LR image learned from the DSNet are used to produce a reconstructed HR image through the SRNet.

adopt a multi-stage training strategy, which makes our learned model get very good reconstruction results. We also conduct comprehensive experiments on five benchmark datasets to demonstrate the effectiveness of our proposed method.

The main contributions of this work are summarized as follows: 1) We propose to reuse an image super-resolution network as the upscaling sub-network, instead of directly performing the inverse upscaling process. In this case, the SR network not only works in backward upscaling to implicitly recover missing details, but also takes the high-frequency information captured in the downscaling process as the input, which effectively enhance the HR image quality. 2) We develop the DSNet based on dense attention blocks and the SRNet based on residual attention blocks, which adaptively focuses on the high-frequency information and establishes associations between features, to maximize the HR reconstruction performance. 3) Our model achieves a new state-of-the-art performance on the image rescaling task, for example, with the PSNR of 35.57 dB and SSIM of 0.9368 on DIV2K validation set with scale 4×. Codes are available at https://github.com/guiyan2018/Image_Rescaling.

2   Image Rescaling Network

2.1   Downscaling Generation Sub-network

The DSNet converts an input HR image x to an LR image y_{down} and meanwhile models a distribution of high-frequency information by a latent variable z, which we force it to be case-agnostic (i.e., $z \sim p(z)$) and obey an isotropic Gaussian distribution. As shown in Fig. 2(a), it is made up of several Downscaling Modules, each of which includes a Haar Transformation Block and some stacked DownBlocks. One Downscaling Module is used to reduce the spatial resolution by 2×.

In order to keep high-frequency information, we apply the Haar Transformation Block as the first layer of the Downscaling Module to effectively separate low-frequency and high-frequency information. Specifically, given an input HR image or a group of feature maps with the size of $H \times W \times C$, the output of the Haar Transformation Block is a $H/2 \times W/2 \times 4C$ feature tensor. The first C slice of the output tensor approximately is a low-frequency information equivalent to

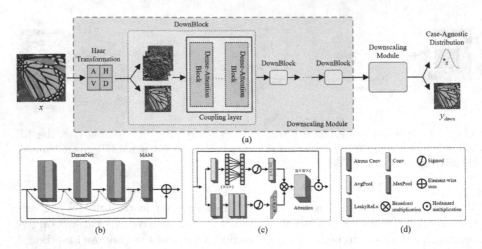

Fig. 2. Detailed architecture of the Downscaling generation network. (a) DSNet structure, (b) Dense-Attention Block (DAB), (c) Mixed attention module (MAM), (d) Legend. Here, the DSNet is designed for scale 4×.

the bilinear interpolation downsampling. The rest $3C$ slices contain residual components in the vertical, horizontal and diagonal directions respectively, which are the high-frequency information of the input HR image.

The DownBlock is composed of a stack of dense attention blocks (DABs), which is referred as the coupling layer in [22,26]. As shown in Figs. 2(b) and 2(c), a DAB includes two parts: a dense convolutional network (DenseNet) [27] and a mixed attention module (MAM). The DenseNet is a 3-layer dense block with a growth rate of 4, where each layer takes all preceding features as input and atrous convolution in each layer is used to learn and capture high-frequency information with a large receptive field. The residual structure is used to avoid missing meaningful information. The MAM contains parallel channel and spatial sub-modules, as shown in Fig. 2(c), where the channel attention is adopted to suppress meaningless feature channels and highlight meaningful ones, and the spatial attention is used to enhance high-frequency features. In our implementation, we set the number of DownBlock to 8, and the number of Downscaling Module to 1 or 2 for the scales 2× or 4×. Finally, we train the DSNet by minimizing a LR guidance loss and a distribution matching loss, which will be detailed in Sect. 2.3. Additionally, to ensure that the DSNet can be optimized during training, we simply use rounding operation to store output LR images by PNG format and use it in the subsequent upscaling process.

2.2   The Super-Resolution Sub-network

The SRNet takes the resulting downscaled LR image y_{down} and random sampling of high-frequency information z from the case-agnostic $p(z)$ as inputs, and tries to restore the HR image x_{up}. As shown in Fig. 3(a), the SRNet includes two parts:

a backbone network and a long skip connection (LSC). We take an enhanced EDSR as the backbone, where the original residual block is replaced with a residual attention block (RAB). As shown in Fig. 3(b), the RAB is composed of a multi-scale residual block (MSRB) and a mixed attention module (Fig. 2 (c)). For the MSRB, its basic module is a multi-scale fusion module (MSFM), where we connect the atrous convolutions with different rates (i.e., $r = 1, 2, 5$) in parallel and series, as shown in Fig. 3(c). The MSFM is used to extract more fine-grained multi-scale features and improve the perceptive field of the RAB. The RAB uses attention mechanism to obtain the correlation between low frequency features and high frequency features and further guides image reconstruction. Note that, we set the number of channels of filters in the first convolutional layer of the network to four, due to that the low-resolution image y_{down} and the information z from the pre-specified distribution learned by the DSNet are used as the inputs of the SRNet. In our implementation, the number of the RAB is set as 64. We show the effect of the number of RABs of the SRNet on the reconstructed results in the supplementary materials.

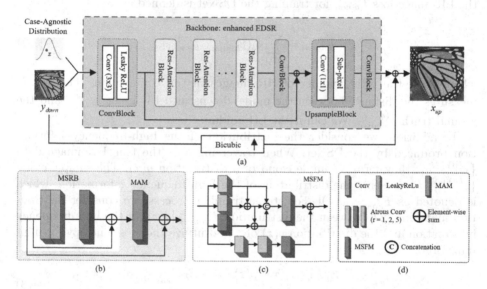

Fig. 3. Detailed architecture of the super-resolution sub-network. (a)SRNet structure, (b) Residual attention block (RAB), (c) Multi-scale fusion module (MSFM), (d) Legend.

For the long skip connection (LSC) shown in Fig. 3(a), a bicubic linear interpolation is performed on the input LR image y_{down}, and the upscaled image is then directly combined with the output of the backbone to produce the reconstructed SR image x_{up}. With the use of LSC, we explicitly reformulate the enhanced EDSR as learning a residual function with reference to the LR image input. It is worth noting that SRNet can be of any one of SR network, even the differentiable bilinear or bicubic upscaling operations, as will be shown in the ablation study in Sect. 3.2. To achieve this, we train the SRNet by minimizing the reconstruction loss.

2.3 Training Loss

The whole image rescaling network is optimized via a joint loss function L_{total} during the training stage:

$$L_{total} = \omega_1 \times L_{down} + \omega_2 \times L_{distr} + \omega_3 \times L_{recon}, \tag{1}$$

where L_{down}, L_{distr} and L_{recon} represent the LR guidance loss, distribution matching loss and reconstruction loss, respectively. ω_1, ω_2 and ω_3 are the weights to balance different loss terms. The three losses are detailed below.

As described in Sect. 2.1, given HR image data $\{x^{(n)}\}_{n=1}^N$, the DSNet outputs a LR image $y_{down}^{(n)}$ for each $x^{(n)}$. Let $y_{bicubic}^{(n)}$ be the ground truth LR image corresponding to the HR image $x^{(n)}$, which is produced by the Bicubic method, the LR-image loss L_{down} for training the DSNet is defined as:

$$L_{down} = \sum_{n=1}^N l_2(y_{bicubic}^{(n)}, y_{down}^{(n)}), \tag{2}$$

where N is the total number of HR images in the training set. The loss l_2 measures the distance between the model-downscaled LR image $y_{down}^{(n)}$ and the ground truth $y_{bicubic}^{(n)}$. We call it the LR guidance loss.

In addition, we consider the distribution of the high-frequency information produced by the DSNet. When traversing over the true HR image data $\{x^{(n)}\}_{n=1}^N$, they form a sample cloud of a distribution $q(x)$. The sample cloud $\{z^{(n)}\}_{n=1}^N$ represents the distribution of the high-frequency information, which is denoted as $F_{down\#}^z[q(x)]$. For stable training process, we consider distribution matching [22] between the distribution $F_{down\#}^z[q(x)]$ of the high-frequency information and the distribution $p(z)$ of z and utilize the cross entropy for minimization:

$$
\begin{aligned}
L_{distr} &= CE(F_{dowm\#}^z[q(x)], p(z)) = -E_{F_{down\#}^z[q(x)]}[\log p(z)], \\
&= -E_{q(x)}[\log p(z = F_{down}^z(x))].
\end{aligned} \tag{3}
$$

The distribution matching loss encourages the DSNet to learn the distribution of the high-frequency information, and ensure that the SRNet can do a perfect reconstruction by passing a randomly-drawn latent variable from the learned distribution with the low-resolution image. Moreover, we traverse over all the HR images and minimize the expected difference between reconstructed SR image $x_{up}^{(n)}$ and the original one $x^{(n)}$ using the reconstruction loss L_{recon}:

$$L_{recon} = \sum_{n=1}^N E_{p(z)}[l_1(x^{(n)}, x_{up}^{(n)})] = \sum_{n=1}^N E_{p(z)}[l_1(x^{(n)}, F_{SR}(y_{down}^{(n)}, z))], \tag{4}$$

where l_1 is a difference metric. With this loss, we train the SRNet to make the reconstructed SR images appear more realistic.

We implement a multi-stage training strategy consisting of three optimization steps to train the proposed image rescaling network. First, we try to seek a good initialization through training the DSNet separately. We do hope to use a HR image as input and get a visually pleasing LR image and the learned high-frequency information using the LR guidance loss and the distribution matching loss, respectively. Then, we fix the parameters of the DSNet and train the SRNet using the HR reconstruction loss. Finally, we relax all parameters of the trained DSNet and SRNet, and fine-tune the whole network. With such progressive training, the DSNet refines its distribution of high frequency information by the reconstructed HR results, and the SRNet is updated according the new distribution results, achieving a converged model.

3   Experiments and Comparisons

3.1   Implementation Details

We employ the widely used DIV2K dataset [28] for network training, which contains 800 HR training images. For quantitative evaluation, we use HR images of four commonly used benchmark datasets, including the Set5 [29], Set14 [30], BSD100 [31] and Urban100 [32], plus 100 HR images from the DIV2K validation set. And, we adopt the peak noise-signal ratio (PSNR) and the structural similarity index SSIM as the evaluation metrics to measure image reconstruction quality under the upscaling factors of 2× and 4×.

During training, we consider random horizontally and vertically flipping and crop the images randomly to a size of 144×144 for data augmentation. The entire network is trained on the DIV2K training set using Adam optimizer with the PyTorch library on two NVIDIA RTX 3090 GPUs with 24 GB memory. The total number of iterations is 50k. The mini-batch size is set to 16 and the learning rate is initialized as 2×10^{-4} where halved at $[10\,k, 20\,k, 30\,k, 40\,k]$ mini-batch updates. In our experiment, the hyper-parameters in (1) are set to $\omega_1 = 4$, $\omega_2 = 1$ and $\omega_3 = 1$ for scale 2×, and $\omega_1 = 16$ for scale 4×.

3.2   Evaluation of Proposed Method

Study on the Upscaling Network. Table 1 shows the PSNR results of our network and multiple variants without and with high-frequency contents on five benchmark datasets. In lines 1–4, we perform the HR image reconstruction from the predicted LR images generated by DSNet, and replace the SRNet of our network with other three classic SR networks, including shallow SRCNN [14] and VDSR [15] and a deeper EDSR [16]. It can be seen that our network has the best performance, and boost the PSNR with 4–6 dB against DSNet_SRCNN, which is the worst performing on each benchmark dataset. This is because we adapt the enhanced EDSR by using the residual attention block (RAB) and adding a long skip connection (LSC), significantly improves the reconstructed results. In lines 5–8, we combine the LR image with the learned high-frequency information for HR image reconstruction. The results indicate that using the high-frequency information for HR image reconstruction is important for achieving good results. For training the variants and our networks, the iteration numbers are set to 5 k, 10 k, 50 k and 50 k respectively.

Table 1. PNSR results of our network with different upscaling networks, without/with the high-frequency information, on Set5, Set14, BSD100, Urban100 and DIV2K validation sets with scale 2×. HfI: High-frequency information.

	Variants	HfI	Set5	Set14	BSD100	Urban100	DIV2K	# of iterations
1	DSNet_SRCNN	×	41.18	37.66	37.51	35.47	40.41	5 k
2	DSNet_VDSR		42.87	39.52	40.00	38.39	42.91	10 k
3	DSNet_EDSR		44.44	41.42	41.80	40.85	44.92	50 k
4	DSNet_SRNet (our network)		45.86	42.94	43.49	42.15	46.19	
5	DSNet_SRCNN	✓	41.62	38.25	38.15	36.51	41.13	5 k
6	DSNet_VDSR		43.29	39.91	40.45	38.74	43.41	10 k
7	DSNet_EDSR		45.61	42.59	43.22	41.84	45.99	50 k
8	DSNet_SRNet (our network)		**46.14**	**43.26**	**43.73**	**42.74**	**46.49**	

Effect of the Amount of High-Frequency Information. Different from invertible neural networks [22,23,25], the SRNet in our model is not the inverse function of the DSNet. And, the main difference between our model and the existing encoder-decoder models [3,4] is that the SRNet take the learned high-frequency information by the DSNet as input during the upscaling procedure. Here, the learned high-frequency information of an image can be randomly selected from the learned distribution $z \sim p(z)$ by the DSNet and is represented as a feature embedding with 9 channels. We randomly sample c feature channel as the input to the SRNet of our network for HR image reconstruction. The comparison results are reported in Table 2. In line 3 and line 6, when we follow the IRN [22] (i.e., $c = 9$) and the CAR & EDSR [4] (i.e., $c = 0$), we gain average 1.5 dB and 7.5 dB improvement of PSNR, respectively. In line 4, we randomly sample one feature channel of the high-frequency information in the vertical, horizontal and diagonal directions and set $c = 3$. In this case, there is a slight performance improvement. In line 5, when we set $c = 1$, our model achieves better results on the five benchmark datasets compared to line 3. In summary, we use a combination of the predicted LR image and one randomly selected feature channel of the high-frequency information to produce the reconstructed results.

Table 2. Reconstruction quality (PSNR) of our network using different amounts of high-frequency information, on Set5, Set14, BSD100, Urban100 and DIV2K validation sets with scale 2×.

	# of channels	Set5	Set14	BSD100	Urban100	DIV2K
1	IRN (c = 9) [22]	43.99	40.78	41.32	39.91	44.32
2	CAR & EDSR [4]	38.94	35.61	33.83	35.24	38.26
3	$c = 9$	45.44	42.38	42.72	41.40	45.72
4	$c = 3$	45.77	42.74	43.32	41.96	46.06
5	$c = 1$ (our)	**46.14**	**43.26**	**43.73**	**42.74**	**46.49**
6	$c = 0$	45.67	42.66	43.13	41.93	46.03

Analysis on the Losses. In Table 3, we show the performance comparison with different loss function. Overall, our model performs the best when the L2 loss is used for the LR guidance loss (L_{down}) and the L1 loss is used the HR reconstruction loss (L_{recon}), as shown in line 3. It can be seen that we observe about 2–10 dB improvements in PSNR over the other cases. The reason is that the L1 loss encourages more pixel-wise similarity, while the L2 loss is less sensitive to minor changes. During downscaling process, the L_{down} loss only acts as a constraint to maintain visually pleasing downscaling images, so the L2 loss is more suitable. In the upscaling process, our aim is to reconstruct the ground truth image accurately, so the L1 loss is more appropriate. In line 5, we also shows the necessity of the distribution matching loss (L_{distr}), which restricts the distribution on z and benefits the forward distribution learning.

Table 3. Analysis results (PSNR) of training our network with L1 or L2 LR-guidance loss and reconstruction loss, with/without distribution matching loss, on Set5, Set14, BSD100, Urban100 and DIV2K validation sets with scale 2×.

	L_{down}	L_{recon}	L_{distr}	Set5	Set14	BSD100	Urban100	DIV2K
1	L_1	L_1	✓	41.56	38.58	38.57	37.84	41.53
2	L_1	L_2	✓	38.35	34.99	33.95	34.02	37.30
3	L_2	L_1	✓	**46.14**	**43.26**	**43.73**	**42.74**	**46.49**
4	L_2	L_2	✓	43.77	40.81	41.09	40.05	43.80
5	L_2	L_1	✗	45.67	42.66	43.13	41.93	46.03

3.3 Comparison with State-of-the-Arts

We compare our method with ten state-of-the-art image scaling methods [4, 14–18, 22–25], which can be categorized into two main groups: I) the downscaling module is the bicubic interpolation and the upscaling is the state-of-the-art SR methods; II) the downscaling module is jointly optimized with the upscaling module. Table 4 summarizes the quantitative results of each method with scales 2× and 4×. We evaluate them on five benchmark datasets. In overall comparison, our method achieves a higher PSNR and SSIM metrics and significantly outperforms the other methods. We also compare our model with all of the above models in 4× scale. The performance of all models is inferior to that of the models of the scale 2×, as a large amount of information is lost in the 4× scaling networks. In addition, the network parameters of our model are 3.03M at 2× and 7.05M at 4×, which is lower than those of traditional super-resolution networks belonging to type I models, but slightly higher compared to the latest image scaling models [22–25]. Figure 4 presents the qualitative upscaled results of 4× scale on the six challenging images. Overall, HR images reconstructed by our model significantly outperform those of previous state-of-the-art methods in visual quality and similarity to original images.

Table 4. Quantitative evaluation results on five validation sets with scales 2× and 4×. Red color indicates the best performance and blue color refers the second best.

	Downscaling & Upscaling	Scale	Param	Set5 PNSR/SSIM	Set14 PNSR/SSIM	BSD100 PNSR/SSIM	Urban100 PNSR/SSIM	DIV2K PNSR/SSIM
I	Bicubic & SRCNN [14]	2×	57.3K	36.66/0.9542	32.42/0.9063	31.36/0.8897	29.5/0.8946	33.05/0.9581
	Bicubic & VDSR [15]		666K	37.53/0.9587	33.03/0.9213	31.90/0.8986	30.76/0.9140	33.66/0.9625
	Bicubic & EDSR [16]		40.7M	38.06/0.9615	33.88/0.9202	32.31/0.9202	32.92/0.9359	35.12/0.9482
	Bicubic & RCAN [18]		15.4M	38.27/0.9614	34.12/0.9216	32.41/0.9027	33.34/0.9384	-/-
II	CAR & EDSR [4]	2×	51.5M	38.94/0.9658	35.61/0.9404	33.83/0.9262	35.24/0.9572	38.26/0.9599
	IRN [22]		1.66M	43.99/0.9870	40.78/0.9777	41.32/0.9875	39.91/0.9865	44.32/0.9908
	FGRN [23]		1.33M	44.15/0.9902	42.28/0.9840	41.87/0.9887	41.71/0.9904	45.08/0.9917
	DLV-IRN [25]		1.89M	45.42/0.9910	42.16/0.9839	42.91/0.9916	41.29/0.9904	45.58/0.9934
	Our		3.03M	46.14/0.9921	43.26/0.9863	43.73/0.9927	42.74/0.9918	46.49/0.9944
I	Bicubic & SRCNN [14]	4×	57.3K	30.48/0.8628	27.48/0.7503	26.90/0.7101	24.52/0.77221	27.78/0.8753
	Bicubic & VDSR [15]		666K	31.35/0.8838	28.01/0.7674	27.29/0.7251	25.18/0.7524	28.17/0.8841
	Bicubic & EDSR [16]		43.1M	32.35/0.8981	28.64/0.7885	27.71/0.7432	26.62/0.8041	31.04/0.8452
	Bicubic & RCAN [18]		15.6M	32.63/0.9002	28.87/0.7889	27.77/0.7436	26.82/0.8087	30.77/0.8459
	Bicubic & ESRGAN [17]		16.3M	32.74/0.9012	29.00/0.7915	27.84/0.7455	27.03/0.8152	30.92/0.8486
II	CAR & EDSR [4]	4×	52.8M	33.88/0.9174	30.31/0.8382	29.15/0.8001	29.23/0.8710	32.82/0.8837
	IRN [22]		4.35M	36.19/0.9451	32.66/0.9015	31.63/0.8825	31.40/0.9156	35.07/0.9318
	FGRN [23]		3.35M	36.97/0.9505	33.77/0.9168	31.83/0.8907	31.91/0.9253	35.15/0.9322
	HCFlow [24]		4.40M	36.29/0.9468	33.02/0.9065	31.74/0.8864	31.62/0.9206	35.23/0.9346
	DLV-IRN [25]		5.49M	36.62/0.9484	33.26/0.9093	32.05/0.8893	32.26/0.9253	35.55/0.9363
	Our		7.05M	36.98/0.9518	33.83/0.9195	32.25/0.8908	32.86/0.9307	35.57/0.9368

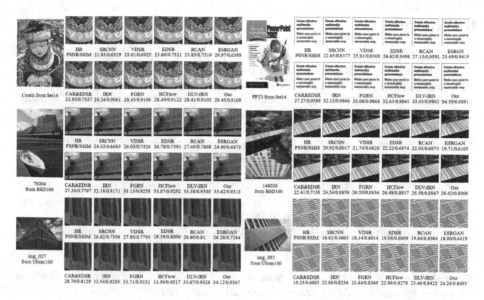

Fig. 4. More qualitative results of upscaling the downscaled images on Set14, BSD100 and Urban100 validation sets with scale 4×.

4   Conclusion

We have proposed a learning approach for bidirectional image rescaling using new defined deep convolutional neural network. Our method adopted a differentiable downscaling network to learn a mapping between HR and LR images by modeling the LR image and the distribution of the high-frequency information simultaneously. This allows the downscaling model to learn to keep essential information in a more optimal way. And, a key difference from prior method lies in that we performed the upscaling process using a SR network, which receives a latent variable that models the variations of high-frequency information and combine with the LR image to learn to recover missing details in image upscaling. Such enhancement is capable of further improving reconstructed HR image quality. Comprehensive experimental analyses and comparisons on five challenging datasets show that our method outperforms state-of-the-art rescaling methods with a noticeable margin in PSNR, SSIM, and perceptual quality metrics.

Acknowledgements. This work was supported by the National Natural Science Foundation of China (Project Nos. 62272164, 61402053), the Hunan Provincial Natural Science Foundation of China (Grant No. 2023JJ30050) and the Scientific Research Fund of Education Department of Hunan Province (Grant No. 21B0287).

References

1. Zhang, Y., Zhao, D., Zhang, J., Xiong, R., Gao, W.: Interpolation-dependent image downsampling. IEEE Trans. Image Process. **20**(11), 3291–3296 (2011)
2. Kim, H., Choi, M., Lim, B., Lee, K.M.: Task-aware image downscaling. In: Proceedings of the 15th European Conference Computer Vision, Munich, Germany, 8–14 September, Part IV, vol. 11208, pp. 419–434 (2018)
3. Li, Y., Liu, D., Li, H., Li, L., Li, Z., Wu, F.: Learning a convolutional neural network for image compactresolution. IEEE Trans. Image Process. **28**(3), 1092–1107 (2019)
4. Sun, W., Chen, Z.: Learned image downscaling for upscaling using content adaptive resampler. IEEE Trans. Image Process. **29**, 4027–4040 (2020)
5. Jiang, F., Tao, W., Liu, S., Ren, J., Guo, X., Zhao, D.: An end-to-end compression framework based on convolutional neural networks. IEEE Trans. Circuits Syst. Video Technol. **28**(10), 3007–3018 (2018)
6. Fang, L., Au, O.C., Tang, K., Wen, X., Wang, H.: Novel 2-d MMSE subpixel-based image down-sampling. IEEE Trans. Circuits Syst. Video Technol. **22**(5), 740–753 (2012)
7. Rubinstein, M., Gutierrez, D., Sorkine, O., Shamir, A.: A comparative study of image retargeting. ACM Trans. Graph. **29**(6), 160 (2010)
8. Liu, J., He, S., Lau, R.W.H.: L0-regularized image downscaling. IEEE Trans. Image Process. **27**(3), 1076–1085 (2018)
9. Shannon, C.E.: Communication in the presence of noise. Proc. IEEE **86**(2), 447–457 (1998)
10. Mitchell, D.P., Netravali, A.N.: Reconstruction filters in computer-graphics. In: Proceedings of the 15th Annual Conference on Computer Graphics and Interactive Techniques, Atlanta, Georgia, USA, 1–5 August, pp. 221–228 (1988)
11. Schultz, R.R., Stevenson, R.L.: A Bayesian approach to image expansion for improved definition. IEEE Trans. Image Process. **3**(3), 233–242 (1994)
12. Glasner, D., Bagon, S., Irani, M.: Super-resolution from a single image. In: Proceedings of the IEEE 12th International Conference on Computer Vision, Kyoto, Japan, 27 September–4 October, pp. 349–356 (2009)
13. Yang, J., Wright, J., Huang, T.S., Ma, Y.: Image super-resolution via sparse representation. IEEE Trans. Image Process. **19**(11), 2861–2873 (2010)
14. Dong, C., Loy, C.C., He, K., Tang, X.: Image super-resolution using deep convolutional networks. IEEE Trans. Pattern Anal. Mach. Intell. **38**(2), 295–307 (2016)
15. Kim, J., Lee, J.K., Lee, K.M.: Accurate image super-resolution using very deep convolutional networks. In: Proceedings of the IEEE Conference on Computer Vision and Pattern Recognition, Las Vegas, NV, USA, 27–30 June, pp. 1646–1654 (2016)
16. Lim, B., Son, S., Kim, H., Nah, S., Lee, K.M.: Enhanced deep residual networks for single image super-resolution. In: Proceedings of the IEEE Conference on Computer Vision and Pattern Recognition Workshops, Honolulu, HI, USA, 21–26 July, pp. 1132–1140 (2017)
17. Wang, X., et al.: ESRGAN: enhanced super-resolution generative adversarial networks. In: Leal-Taixé, L., Roth, S. (eds.) ECCV 2018, Part V. LNCS, vol. 11133, pp. 63–79. Springer, Cham (2019). https://doi.org/10.1007/978-3-030-11021-5_5
18. Zhang, Y., Li, K., Li, K., Wang, L., Zhong, B., Fu, Y.: Image super-resolution using very deep residual channel attention networks. In: Ferrari, V., Hebert, M., Sminchisescu, C., Weiss, Y. (eds.) ECCV 2018, Part VII. LNCS, vol. 11211, pp. 294–310. Springer, Cham (2018). https://doi.org/10.1007/978-3-030-01234-2_18

19. Hashemzadeh, M., Asheghi, B., Farajzadeh, N.: Content-aware image resizing: an improved and shadow-preserving seam carving method. Sig. Process. **155**, 233–246 (2019)
20. Li, L., Tang, J., Ye, Z., Sheng, B., Mao, L., Ma, L.: Unsupervised face super-resolution via gradient enhancement and semantic guidance. Vis. Comput. **37**(9–11), 2855–2867 (2021)
21. Liu, Y., Yang, D., Zhang, F., Xie, Q., Zhang, C.: Deep recurrent residual channel attention network for single image super-resolution. Vis. Comput. (2023)
22. Xiao, M., et al.: Invertible image rescaling. In: Vedaldi, A., Bischof, H., Brox, T., Frahm, J.-M. (eds.) ECCV 2020, Part I. LNCS, vol. 12346, pp. 126–144. Springer, Cham (2020). https://doi.org/10.1007/978-3-030-58452-8_8
23. Li, S., Zhang, G., Luo, Z., Liu, J., Zeng, Z., Zhang, S.: Approaching the limit of image rescaling via flow guidance. In: Proceedings of 32nd British Machine Vision Conference, Online, 22–25 November, p. 13 (2021)
24. Liang, J., Lugmayr, A., Zhang, K., Danelljan, M., Gool, L.V., Timofte, R.: Hierarchical conditional flow: a unified framework for image super-resolution and image rescaling. In: Proceedings of IEEE/CVF International Conference on Computer Vision, Montreal, QC, Canada, 10–17 October, pp. 4056–4065 (2021)
25. Zhang, M., Pan, Z., Zhou, X., Kuo, C.J.: Enhancing image rescaling using dual latent variables in invertible neural network. CoRR abs/2207.11844 (2022)
26. Dinh, L., Sohl-Dickstein, J., Bengio, S.: Density estimation using real NVP. In: Proceedings of 5th International Conference on Learning Representations, Toulon, France, 24–26 April (2017)
27. Huang, G., Liu, Z., van der Maaten, L., Weinberger, K.Q.: Densely connected convolutional networks. In: Proceedings of IEEE Conference on Computer Vision and Pattern Recognition Honolulu, HI, USA, 21–26 July, pp. 2261–2269 (2017)
28. Agustsson, E., Timofte, R.: NTIRE 2017 challenge on single image super-resolution: dataset and study. In: Proceedings of the IEEE Conference on Computer Vision and Pattern Recognition Workshops, Honolulu, HI, USA, 21–26 July, pp. 1122–1131 (2017)
29. Bevilacqua, M., Roumy, A., Guillemot, C., Alberi-Morel, M.: Low-complexity single-image super-resolution based on nonnegative neighbor embedding. In: Proceedings of British Machine Vision Conference, Surrey, UK, 3–7 September, pp. 1–10 (2012)
30. Zeyde, R., Elad, M., Protter, M.: On single image scaleup using sparse-representations. In: Proceedings of the 7th International Conference on Curves and Surfaces, Avignon, France, 24–30 June, vol. 6920, pp. 711–730 (2010)
31. Martin, D.R., Fowlkes, C.C., Tal, D., Malik, J.: A database of human segmented natural images and its application to evaluating segmentation algorithms and measuring ecological statistics. In: Proceedings of the Eighth International Conference on Computer Vision, Vancouver, British Columbia, Canada, 7–14 July, vol. 2, pp. 416–425 (2001)
32. Huang, J., Singh, A., Ahuja, N.: Single image super-resolution from transformed self-exemplars. In: Proceedings of the IEEE Conference on Computer Vision and Pattern Recognition, Boston, MA, USA, 7–12 June, pp. 5197–5206 (2015)

Convolutional Neural Networks and Vision Transformers in Product GS1 GPC Brick Code Recognition

Maciej Szymkowski[1,2]([⊠]), Maciej Niemir[1,3], Beata Mrugalska[3], and Khalid Saeed[2]

[1] Computer Science Research Group, Łukasiewicz –Poznań Institute of Technology, Poznań, Poland
{maciej.szymkowski,maciej.niemir}@pit.lukasiewicz.gov.pl
[2] Faculty of Computer Science, Bialystok University of Technology, Bialystok, Poland
k.saeed@pb.edu.pl
[3] Faculty of Engineering Management, Poznań University of Technology, Poznań, Poland

Abstract. Online stores and auctions are commonly used nowadays. It means that we buy much more on the Internet than in traditional stores. It leads to the case that during looking for the products we need to have precise categories assigned to each of them (to find only records that can be of interest for a consumer). Sometimes it is hard, users make simple mistakes by assigning wrong categories to the product they sell. In this paper, we propose an approach to the analysis of product images and their real categories assignment. The proposed algorithm is based on Convolutional Neural Networks (CNNs). Vision Transformers were also tested and compared with CNNs. Products categories were represented by GS1 GPC brick codes. The maximum accuracy reached around 80%. Based on the discussions with e-commerce experts, it was claimed that such precision is acceptable, as the differences between real and assigned categories were effectively small (change in the class does not segment or family).

Keywords: GPC codes · artificial intelligence · machine learning · ResNet-50 · VGG-16 · InceptionV4 · product data quality

1 Introduction

Nowadays, in the sales sector, it is extremely important to appropriately present the product we would like to sell. We do not think about presentation 'on a shelf', but rather in online stores. This means that the image needs to fulfil some rules. One of them is related to the GS1 GPC (Global Product Classification) segment, family, class, and brick codes. These are the codes that appropriately classify products by grouping them into categories and subcategories [1]. For example, let us classify milk – the correct classification will be as follows: Segment – "Food, beverages and tobacco"; Family – "Milk, butter, cream, yoghurts, cheese, eggs, and substitutes"; Class – "Milk and milk substitutes"; Brick – "Milk". The general question is – why is it important? The answer is very simple – because in online stores we need to assign products to specific categories and classes. We do not wish to observe, for example, a car in the category of milk and yoghurt. Based on our analysis (especially in the on-line auctions portals) such situation (incorrect assignment of the category) is often observed. It is why there is a need to propose a precise solution to automatically assign the classification of an object in an image.

How is it used to be done? In most cases, the user who prepares the auction is also responsible for assigning the category and subcategories. However, it is sometimes extremely difficult to determine them correctly. There are products that can be classified into different categories based on their details. As a vital example, we can mention the bottle. If it is filled with drink, we can classify it as products based on water (e.g., juice, tea, coffee), if it is filled with paint or solvent, we will assign it to the category of chemicals, and if it is empty, then it can be classified as a product based on glass. As we can see, there are plenty of possibilities and it is the reason we can easily make a mistake and assign the product an inappropriate category.

To improve the whole process, we propose an automatic algorithm for the recognition of product categories. It is based on Convolutional Neural Networks [2] and compared to the approach using Vision Transformers [3]. The main goal of the worked-out approach is to determine the classification code (brick code) – not the product itself. We are interested in the brick (e.g., drink) rather than specific product (e.g., coffee). It means that we tackle the problem with GS1 GPC brick codes (not a segment or family). Within this paper, we also present different approaches to Convolutional Neural Networks - diversified architectures and settings of this soft computing algorithm is compared. As conclusions, we are pointing out the most precise architecture and its settings.

The work is organised as follows: In the second chapter, we are mentioning diversified works that are related to the problem we are analysing in this paper. Especially, we are checking approaches based on Machine and Deep Learning. In the third section the proposed approach is presented – all details are given. The fourth chapter is related to the experiments. Diversified algorithms and their settings are checked and compared. Especially, we concentrate on Convolutional Neural Networks which seems to provide more precise results. Finally, conclusions and future work are given in the last section of the paper.

2 Related Works

Object detection and recognition is one of the well-known topics in the world-wide literature (papers, conferences). There are a couple of approaches to this problem that can be claimed as traditional – e.g., YOLO [4, 5], SSD [6] or RetinaNet [7]. Especially interesting algorithm is the first of above mentioned – as it is still developed, and new versions are created on a regular basis. The latest version of YOLO is number 8 (it was shared with the community in December 2022). Moreover, this algorithm has one huge advantage – it can be retrained (to detect only specific objects) as well as transfer learning can be applied to it (so we will recognize not only general objects but also the specific ones that are of interest for creators of the new approach). What is interesting, in the literature we can also find papers in which all these networks are combined – it means that for the aim of object detection and classification, multimodel neural networks are used. The well prepared paper related to this topic is [23].

On the other hand, it also needs to be pointed out that solutions based on soft computing are also consumed for object detection and recognition. Such papers are printed in the top ranked conference proceedings and journals. For example, one of the commonly used approaches is based on Convolutional Neural Networks. The interesting idea based on this solution was described in [8]. The Authors proposed a real-time system for object detection and recognition. At the very beginning, the object is detected with Faster R-CNN, then the label for the object is assigned with traditional CNN. It was claimed that a couple of images represent each potential object in the database. Another interesting approach based on CNNs was described in [9]. In this case, the Authors proposed their own Residual Attention Network for the task of image classification. It means that the model is built with stacked Attention modules – each of them generate attention-aware features that are further consumed for description of the object. It needs to be claimed that in this approach the Authors did not introduce any specific object detection procedure, they simply classify images with their own idea. CNNs and algorithms like them for object detection and recognition can also be observed in different papers [10–12]. In [10] the survey about recent approaches to CNNs for object detection was presented. Paper [11] consumes solutions such as Faster R-CNN and DCGAN for object recognition. What is interesting is that the night scenes are analysed. The authors did not consider any other types of scenes. Such an approach can be useful – especially when the light conditions are not sufficient (we mean that not only in night conditions that approach can be used). In [12] the Authors consumed Transfer Learning technique for object detection. They also claimed their approach reach 97% of Mean Squared Error on the whole dataset – however, it was claimed that this dataset consisted only of 175 images. It is why these results are hard to be evaluated and further deployed in real life solutions.

In the literature, we can also find different methodologies connected with object detection and recognition. For example, one of the papers [13] uses genetic algorithms, another one [14] consumes Support Vector Machines (SVM), whilst [15] proposed an approach based on Generative Adversarial Networks (GAN). However, the same methodologies can be consumed in completely different areas – e.g., Convolutional Neural Networks proved their efficiency in the area of image denoising [24] as well as they can be successfully consumed for detection of defects and anomalies [25].

It is also important to note that, in our approach, objects are labelled with GS1 GPC brick codes. Right now, we would like to present the rationale behind that selection as well as where and how these codes are consumed. The Global Product Classification (GPC) by GS1 is a standardised classification system for products in different sectors. It plays a vital role in facilitating efficient communication, data management, and trade in a wide range of sectors worldwide. It provides a common language for everyone involved in an organisation's supply chain, facilitating communication between different departments, stakeholders, and even different companies, allows companies to organise, manage, and catalogue their products in a more efficient way, supports e-commerce by enabling efficient and precise product searches, and allows customers to filter and compare products across different websites and platforms. Finally, it is an essential attribute of a product [16] that must be completed in the global register maintained by the GS1 organization if it is to receive a GTIN (Global Trade Item Number) which is then represented by a barcode on the label. This is what led us to use the GPC as a benchmark for our research, being aware of many other classifications and approaches in e-Commerce. Importantly, the methodology itself can be applied regardless of the classification adopted, making it universal.

3 Proposed Approach

Recently, we can observe that Machine and Deep Learning are one of the trends in automated recognition of the objects. Such statement was proven in the state-of-the-art analysis (in chapter number 2). It is why, we also would like to apply such an app-roach to our problem. Moreover, Artificial Intelligence-based approaches can guarantee higher precision and can provide results in shorter time (we are not mentioning the time needed to train the models but rather classification process itself). We selected two classes of algorithms that were trained during experiments – these are: Convolutional Neural Networks (with architectures: ResNet-50, VGG-16 and InceptionV4) and Vision Transformer. These two solutions were considered as it was proven they can guarantee high accuracy in the object recognition problem. The selected architectures are given in Fig. 1.

Our models were trained on the database collected with GS1 Poland (each of them was placed within online stores – and obtained from them with the agreement of the owner). It consists of 30000 samples of diversified products – from bread to nails. An example of the product is shown in Fig. 2. In the database we placed 100 GPC codes (each product has one GS1 GPC brick code assigned). During training of the models, we split the dataset into training and testing. We checked different splits, but the highest accuracy and precision was obtained when 70% of the set was assigned as a training set and 30% as a testing set. We also established that each GPC brick code was represented in both datasets (70% of specific code samples were taken into training dataset whilst 30% were in the testing set).

It is also important to mention that all models were trained on a pre-processed data. The pipeline was simple – as it consists of three general stages. At the very beginning, the image was loaded (we used local files instead of cloud resources). In the next step, the background of the image was removed – it was done based on the process of segmen-tation. For this aim, we checked traditional algorithms – like the Watershed algorithm [19] or simple binarization, but also more advanced ideas (based on Machine Learn-ing and Artificial Intelligence) were considered. It should be noted that for the purpose of segmentation, we selected the RemBG model [20] that was placed in the Hugging-Face repository [21]. This approach enabled us to appropriately process the image – the object was clearly separated from the background (it was observed that the colour of the background was of no importance). Finally, after background removal, we binarized the image (it was done with traditional approach – Otsu binarization algorithm) – so that only the general shape is observable – no additional information was given to the algorithm. This step improves the general representation of the image – we would like to develop an algorithm that will be based on shape only rather than any additional details. The initial image and the image after pre-processing are presented in Fig. 3.

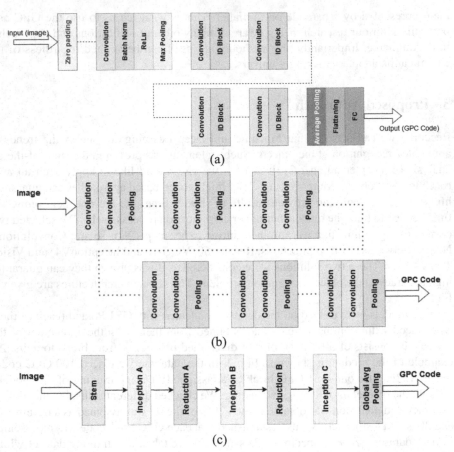

Fig. 1. Selected architectures for Convolutional Neural Network – ResNet-50 (a), VGG-16 (b) and InceptionV4 (c).

Fig. 2. Sample image from GS1 Poland dataset – with clear background (a) and with the non-white background.

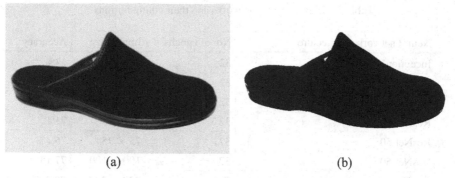

(a)   (b)

Fig. 3. Initial image (a) and image after pre-processing (b).

4 Experiments

The experiments performed were mostly related to the general research question: Is it possible to precisely recognize GS1 GPC brick code of the product on the basis of image outline (without additional details, as shown in Fig. 3b)? To deal with that problem, we selected two approaches that can guarantee precise results that can be then collected effectively – these are: Convolutional Neural Networks (CNNs) and Vision Transformers (VT). Both were chosen based on literature review (we considered not only top-ranked JCR journals, but also well-known conferences, such as MICCAI or NeurIPS, ICML).

In the experimental phase related to the CNNs different neural networks architectures and their configurations were considered. From one side, we trained models based on traditional architectures as ResNet-50 and VGG-16 whilst also novel ideas as InceptionV4 were taken into consideration. On the other hand, we also considered simple multi-layered neural network – it was done to observe how well it will perform with images and GPC brick codes. Its architecture is given in Fig. 4. It needs to be claimed that traditional approach provided much more satisfying results – it means that higher accuracy and precision was obtained (precision was calculated as in 1)). Moreover, as stated before, we analysed how well the network performs with different parameters (we think here about the number of epochs and the initial size of the sample – in one source [22] it was claimed that the best results can be obtained when the image size equals 224x224px). For each configuration we created figures presenting the changes in accuracy and loss. These images can simplify the analysis of the results and provide a general view of the results. All configurations and their parameters are given in Table 1. Figures 5, 6, 7 and 8 present changes in accuracy and loss for different configurations (in the Figures we presented only the best results for each architecture).

$$\frac{TC}{TC + FC} \tag{1}$$

where TC – means True Classification (in our case, it means that the algorithm correctly classified GPC code of the object in image) whilst FC is related to False Classification (it is related to all these objects which GPC code was not appropriately assigned.

It also needs to be claimed that we performed experiments with Vision Transformers. This algorithm was selected because we would like to check whether embeddings (that

Table 1. Trained neural networks and their configurations

#	Neural network architecture	No. of epochs	Image size	Accuracy
1	InceptionV4	32	40×40	13%
2	VGG-16	32	40×40	69.9%
3	VGG-16	32	75×75	75.67%
4	ResNet-50	32	40×40	71%
5	ResNet-50	32	75×75	76.4%
6	ResNet-50	32	100×100	77.15%
7	*ResNet-50*	*8*	224×224	*79.34%*
8	Multilayered Simple Neural Network	32	40×40	60%

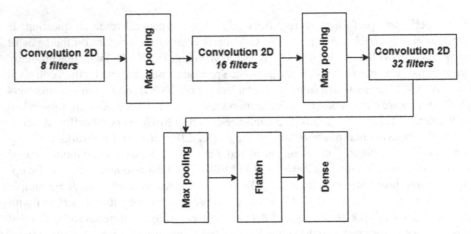

Fig. 4. Architecture of simple multilayered neural network

are performed within VT) can increase the accuracy and efficiency of product GS1 GPC brick code recognition. The training of the model was done as in the case of convolutional neural network – we did not change any procedure when it comes to the data. We tested, one general Vision Transformer (based on the weights of google/vit-base-patch16-224-in21k). This one configuration was selected as in the literature it was mentioned, it can guarantee satisfactory results in his original area. It means that we performed transfer learning. The result of evaluated precision was quite satisfactory. It reached **67,94%**. It also leads to the conclusion that this path still needs to be carefully explored in the next stages of our work. At that moment, Convolutional Neural Networks can guarantee much higher precision than trained Vision Transformer.

The results of all the performed experiments provided evidence that the proposed approach can be applied in real circumstances. It means that the accuracy of the algorithm is satisfactory and can effectively classify the object into the appropriate category. It is

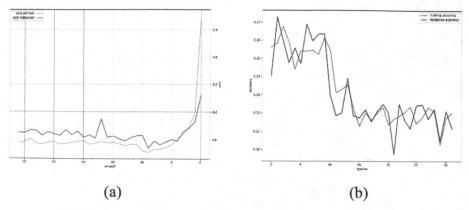

(a)   (b)

Fig. 5. Loss (a) and accuracy (b) functions for InceptionV4 architecture

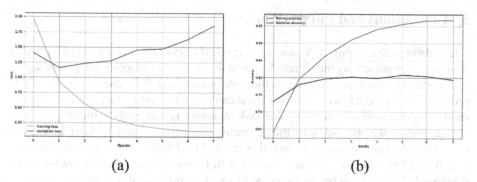

(a)   (b)

Fig. 6. Loss (a) and accuracy (b) functions for ResNet-50 architecture

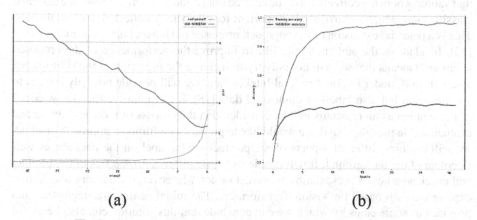

(a)   (b)

Fig. 7. Loss (a) and accuracy (b) functions for VGG-16 architecture

especially true in the case of CNNs – ResNet-50 guarantees around 80% of precision (only one image in the set of five can be classified with an inappropriate brick code).

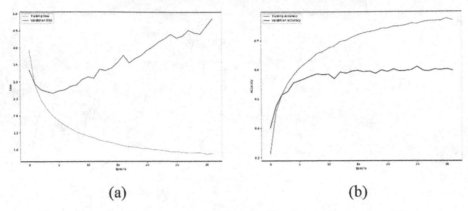

Fig. 8. Loss (a) and accuracy (b) functions for Simple neural network architecture

5   Conclusions and Future Work

The main objective of this work was to recognise the GS1 GPC brick code of a product from an image presenting the object. As stated, it is crucial to properly assign a category to a product (as this affects searches in the store or auctions). If we don't take care of this properly, some products won't be found (and can't be sold - so the impact is also directly on the manufacturer). Performing this task manually is extremely difficult and time-consuming - so we proposed an artificial intelligence-based approach. After analysis of the collected results, we can conclude that product GS1 GPC brick code recognition is clearly possible - this is especially evident with Convolutional Neural Networks. The developed algorithm can be implemented in a real auction portal or store.

As the future work, there is a chance to use this algorithm retroactively, as a system that validates both the correctness of the entered image and the correctness of the assigned classification, which is particularly important for all socially collected data catalogues. This is a potential extension of the approach proposed in Human Factors in Engineering [17]. In addition, the authors would like to improve the performance of the proposed solution. It means that we will not only try to increase the precision of the solution but also will work under hybrid Artificial Intelligence. We will provide not only images to the algorithm but also labels or contextual data [18]. It can improve the "knowledge" of the solution as more details will be considered in the process of models training and evaluation. On the other hand, we would like to prepare a multimodal approach in which we will combine different aspects of the product – e.g., label on the package as well as colour of the background. It will enable us to rate different properties of the product and check whether its presentation is correct or not. Moreover, the authors will further explore the path based on Vision Transformers. The initial results are interesting and provided us some clues by which we can conclude that this solution can also be useful (can provide satisfactory precision) in our problem.

Acknowledgment. This work was partially supported by funds provided by Łukasiewicz Research Network – Poznan Institute of Technology and by grant WI/WI-IIT/4/2022 from Białystok University of Technology, funded with resources for research by the Ministry of Science and Higher Education in Poland.

References

1. Sean, L.: The Global Data Synchronisation Network (GDSN): tchnology and standards improving supply chain efficiency. In: First International Technology Management Conference, pp. 630–637. IEEE (2011)
2. O'Shea, K., Nash, R.: An Introduction to Convolutional Neural Networks. arXiv: 1511.08458 [cs.NE] (2015)
3. Dosovitskiy, A., Beyer, L., Kolesnikov, A., et. al.: An Image is worth 16x16 words: Transformers for image recognition at scale. In: 2021 International Conference on Learning Representation, ICLR 2021, Proceedings
4. https://www.section.io/engineering-education/introduction-to-yolo-algorithm-for-object-detection/. Accessed 29th May 2023
5. https://medium.com/cord-tech/yolov8-for-object-detection-explained-practical-example-23920f77f66a. Accessed 29th May 2023
6. Liu, W., Anguelov, D., Erhan, D., et. al.: SSD: Single Shot MultiBox Detector. arXiv: 1512.02325 [cs.CV] (2016)
7. Lin, T.-Y., Goyal, P., Girshick, R., et. al.: Focal Loss for Dense Object Detection. arXiv: 1708.02002 [cs.CV] (2018)
8. Kumar, A., Srivastava, S.: Object detection system based on convolution neural networks using single shot multi-box detector. Procedia Comput. Sci. **171**, 2610–2617 (2020)
9. Wang, F., Jiang, M., Qian, C., et. al.: Residual attention network for image classification. In: 2017 IEEE Conference on Computer Vision and Pattern Recognition (CVPR), 21–26 July 2017, Honolulu, USA, Proceedings, pp. 3156–3164 (2017)
10. Hakim, H., Fadhil, A.: Survey: convolution neural networks in object detection. J. Phys. Conf. Ser. **2020**, 012095 (1804)
11. Wang, K., Liu, M.: Object recognition at night scene based on DCGAN and faster R-CNN. IEEE Access (2020). https://doi.org/10.1109/ACCESS.2020.3032981
12. Emmanuel, S., Onuodu, F.E.: Object detection using convolutional neural network transfer learning. Int. J. Innov. Res. Eng. Multidiscipl. Phys. Sci. **10**(3), 49–59 (2022)
13. Mezzadri Centeno, T., Silverio Lopes, H., Kleber Felisberto, M., et al.: Object detection for computer vision using a robust genetic algorithm. In: Rothlauf, F., et. al. (eds.) Applications of Evolutionary Computing", EvoWorkkshops 2005, Lausanne, Switzerland, March/April 2005, Proceedings, pp. 284–293 (2005)
14. Wasala, M., Kryjak, T.: Real-time HOG+SVM based object detection using SoC FPGA for a UHD video stream. arXiv: 2204.10619 [cs.CV] (2022)
15. Prakash, C., Karam, L.: It GAN DO Better: GAN-based Detection of Objects on Images with Varying Quality. arXiv: 1912.01707 [cs.CV] (2019)
16. Niemir, M., Mrugalska, B.: Basic Product Data in E-Commerce: Specifications and Problems of Data Exchange. ERSJ, vol. XXIV, no. Special Issue 5, pp. 317–329 (2021). https://doi.org/10.35808/ersj/2735
17. Niemir, M., Mrugalska, B.: Monitoring and improvement of data quality in product catalogs using defined normalizers and validation patterns. In: Human Factors in Engineering, pp. 173–187. CRC Press (2023). https://doi.org/10.1201/9781003383444

18. Muszyński, K., Niemir, M., Skwarek, S.: Searching for Ai solutions to improve the quality of master data affecting consumer safety. In: Business Logistics in Modern Management, Osijek, Croatia: Faculty of Economics in Osijek, pp. 121–140 (2022). http://blmm-conference.com/wp-content/uploads/BLMM2022_Conference_Proceedings.pdf. Accessed 10 Jan 2023

19. Zhang, W., Jiang, D.: The marker-based watershed segmentation algorithm of ore image. In: 2011 IEEE 3rd International Conference on Communication Software and Networks (2011). https://doi.org/10.1109/ICCSN.2011.6014611

20. https://github.com/danielgatis/rembg. Accessed 10th May 2023

21. https://huggingface.co/. Accessed 10th May 2023

22. Wightman, R., Touvron, H., Jegou, H.: "ResNet strikes back: An improved training procedure in timm", arXiv: 2110.00476 [cs.CV], 2021

23. Li, J., Chen, J., Sheng, B., et. al.: Automatic detection and classification system of domestic waste via multimodel cascaded convolutional neural network. IEEE Trans. Indust. Inform. **18**(1), 163–173 (2022)

24. Shi, J., Li, T., Xu, J.: Recursive lightweight convolutional neural networks that make noisy images purer and purer. Vis. Comput. (2022). https://doi.org/10.1007/s00371-022-02749-y

25. Yang, T., Zhang, T., Huang, L.: Detection of defects in voltage-dependent resistors using stacked-block-based convolutional neural networks. Vis. Comput. **37**, 1559–1567 (2021)

Multi-source Information Perception and Prediction for Panoramic Videos

Chenxin Qu, Kexin Li, Xiaoping Che$^{(\boxtimes)}$, Enyao Chang, and Zhongwei Zhang

School of Software Engineering, Beijing Jiaotong University,
Beijing 100044, China
{21112201,19281042,xpche,22121749,23121592}@bjtu.edu.cn

Abstract. With the popularization and development of virtual reality technology, panoramic video has gradually become one of the mainstream forms of VR technology in various fields. However, the research on the information perception of panoramic video in different media is insufficient. And shortcomings still exist in building information perception and prediction models owing to small samples. This work focuses on users' perception of multi-source information in panoramic videos with different media. We conducted the experiment (N = 40) to analyze the differences of users' perception level when viewing panoramic videos using different media (i.e. VR and traditional media). We also studied the correlation between user characteristics and information reception effectiveness. The results show that users' perception of multi-source information in VR is better than in traditional media, except for sound information. Besides, there is a positive correlation between observational ability, memory, concentration, and spatial perception, whether playing computer games frequently and multi-source information perception.

Keywords: Panoramic Videos · Virtual Reality · Information Perception

1 Introduction

Panoramic video, a brand-new way of communication, allows users to watch videos in 720° [1]. During capture, panoramic video is shot from many cameras at multiple angles covering all directions of space, so that all scenes within the panoramic range can be recorded. After that, computer technology is used to stitch and process the captured videos from various perspectives. After mapping calculation, each pixel in each frame is mapped to the corresponding surface of a sphere, and finally, a 720° video of a sphere is synthesized. When using players to play panoramic video, the viewing angle is located in the center of the sphere, and the viewer can change the viewing angle by dragging the sphere to see various local videos, to achieve an all-round viewing experience.

C. Qu and K. Li—These authors contributed equally to this work and considered as co-first authors.

© The Author(s), under exclusive license to Springer Nature Switzerland AG 2024
B. Sheng et al. (Eds.): CGI 2023, LNCS 14495, pp. 451–462, 2024.
https://doi.org/10.1007/978-3-031-50069-5_37

At present, there are two main viewing methods for panoramic video. Traditional mobile devices for viewing, such as smartphones and tablets, which have built-in gyroscopes that allow viewers to change their viewing angle by moving the screen direction. Or watch the panoramic video in a VR environment. Viewers can change their viewing angle solely by rotating their heads, which is more similar to the observed behavior in the real world. However, the disadvantage is that additional costly VR equipment needs to be purchased. Moreover, due to the heavy weight of VR displays, prolonged wear may lead to eye fatigue and other discomfort [2].

Based on the above differences in viewing methods, user information perception and reception when using different devices have become the focus of scholars. According to the existing research, compared with traditional media (such as mobile phones, computers, etc.), the user experience of watching the panoramic video in a VR environment is better, which is reflected in the user's better enjoyment and space perception. However, there is limited research on the perceptual effects of multi-source information (such as visual and auditory information), and no further research has been conducted to explore the correlation between different characteristics of users and VR video reception performance.

Therefore, the aim of our work is to explore the specific differences in user perception in different media and identify the target users of VR content based on user characteristics. This paper provides optimization solutions and development directions for future VR-related content production and promotes the progress of the VR industry. Therefore, the following two questions are raised:

- RQ1: What are the differences in users' perception of multi-source information between traditional media and VR environments?
- RQ2: Is there a correlation between the users' perception of multi-source information effects and characteristics?

To address the above questions, this paper designed experiments to collect different user characteristics and perception effects in different media, and analyzed the collected data through various analysis methods. The detailed process and conclusions can be found in subsequent sections.

2   Related Work

Many research has shown that when viewing panoramic video using different media (traditional media and VR head display), the user experience in a VR environment is better than other media. As early as 2002, Moreno R et al. [3] studied the methods of learning science in VR environments and the role of media. The results show that students have higher scores of sense of presence when using VR. Albert Rizzo et al. [4] proposed a method for memory assessment using virtual environments. The researchers used the virtual environment based on graphics and 360° video to compare the difference in users' memory effect. It can be found that the instant memory effect using single frame images is superior to VR head display and flat screen. MacQuarrie et al. [5] studied the impact of different display types on the viewing experience of panoramic video. The results show that users have significant advantages in enjoyment and spatial perception in VR environments. Q. W. Qu et al. [6] studied the relationship between information perception and presence and believed that due to the fact that VR environments make it easier for users to enter scenes in videos, which deepens their memory, users' information reception performance in VR environments is better than in traditional media. B. Sarune et al. [8] studied the reading in different environments. It is indicated that VR environments can make learners more focused and engaged, and improve the effectiveness of reading. Similarly, other studies [9,10] have also demonstrated that in VR environments, users have better learning outcomes than in traditional media.

Much research was also conducted on user experience and learning effects specifically in VR environments [11,12], most of which indicate that VR environments can bring positive experiences to users. By designing a VR game, Liang improved children's cognitive ability of multi-source information [16]. Morelot et al. [14] also conducted similar experiments to compare the effects of different levels of immersion and presence on the learning effectiveness in fire safety training scenarios. By using the user's perception of sound to adjust the route in time, Weller et al. realized effective path manipulation [15].

Although there are studies on panoramic video at present, the above studies do not dig deeply into the user's reception of multi-source information in panoramic video using different media. In this paper, we will refer to existing research to design and conduct our research on panoramic video and further experiments.

3   Proposed Method

3.1   Participants and Equipment

A total of 40 volunteers (20 males and 20 females) were recruited. The volunteers are all undergraduate students, ranging in age from 19 to 22 years old. Before the experiment, it was confirmed that none of the experimenters had seen the experimental video. 40 volunteers fully participated in the entire process. In the experiment, two playback media were selected, VR Head Display Pico 4 and traditional display device tablet iPad Pro 2018. Considering that the specific parameters of the two devices are slightly different, the screen Refresh rate, screen resolution, screen brightness, and sound size will be set in advance to keep them consistent. And we have confirmed in advance that both devices play videos smoothly and completely without any delay or missing frames.

3.2   Scenario Design

When selecting suitable experimental scenarios, we hope that there will be some differences between the content to cover all video types comprehensively. Therefore, we divide scenarios into four categories.

- Category 1: Videos with distinct themes, strong storytelling, and frequent occurrences.
- Category 2: Videos with no characters and rich background and environmental details.
- Category 3: Films with a large number of characters, actions, interactions between characters, and content information.
- Category 4: Films with rich sound effects, strong sensory stimulation, and a strong sense of mainline substitution.

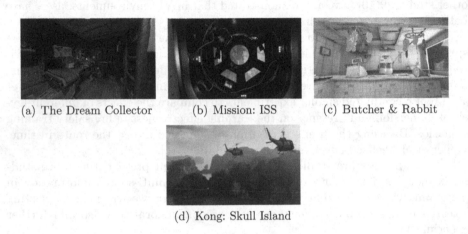

(a) The Dream Collector   (b) Mission: ISS   (c) Butcher & Rabbit

(d) Kong: Skull Island

Fig. 1. Selected Videos in Experiment

At the same time, to ensure the accuracy and reliability of subsequent experimental results, we also control the video variables such as the duration and quality. According to the above rules, four videos were selected for the experiment, each with a duration of about 2 min and a resolution of 1080p.

The first video A, corresponding to category 1, is an excerpt from the VR film The Dream Collector (in Fig. 1(a)), whose main events are relatively rich. The excerpt is taken from the movie 2'49" to 4'25", which takes place in the old man's house, and describes the process of the old man's refurbishment of the guitar and Baseball glove he picked up.

The second video B, corresponding to category 2, is a VR live video Mission: ISS (in Fig. 1(b)), with a total duration of 1'45". The video takes place inside the International Space Station, depicting the process of astronauts exploring the space station module. Its main feature is that there are no characters or interactions, but the background environment has many details.

The third video C, corresponding to category 3, is an excerpt from the VR humorous animated film The Butcher and the Rabbit(in Fig. 1(c)). The excerpt is taken from the movie's 0'0" to 1'53", which includes many events, characters, frequent interaction between characters, and a large amount of content information.

The fourth video D, corresponding to category 4, is the entire segment of the VR 3D film Kong: Skull Island, with a total duration of 1'58" (in Fig. 1(d)). The main events are intense and the sound effects are quite rich.

Questionnaire Design. This work will explore the correlation between user characteristics and the perceived effect of multi-source information in different media. Therefore, the pre-test information of users is needed to extract user characteristics. The questionnaire includes conventional questions such as gender and personality, and learning ability-related questions, such as observation ability, concentration, and spatial perception. The questionnaire is in the form of a 5-point Likert scale. For each question, five options are given to express the degree of approval. And a score of 1 to 5 is used to score each answer, with "strongly disagree" being the lowest score of 1 point and "strongly agree" being the highest score of 5 points.

3.3   Experimental Procedure

After signing the informed consent and filling out the pre-test questionnaire, participants will be randomly divided into four groups. The first and second groups watch both video A and video B. The first group first watches video A using a VR head display and then uses an iPad to watch video B. The second group first watched video A on the iPad and then watched video B with the VR head display. Similarly, the third group first watched video C in a VR environment while the fourth group watched video C using iPad, and then for video D the third group uses iPad while the fourth group uses VR. During the experiment, after watching each video, the participants are asked to recall and retell the video content. Notably, the leading questions can be used to help the participants recall various information, i.e., the main line information, action information, background information, and sound information. The retelling of each participant will be recorded for subsequent statistics, especially for the number of all kinds of memory information.

4   Results

4.1   Data Process

By questionnaire and experiment, we obtained data on the user characteristics, as well as information memory data on information perception effects. In the data processing stage, we conducted perceptual quantification and data augmentation.

In the video selection stage, we counted the number of mainline information n_{main} for all videos, taking Video A as an example.

- The old man entered the house, took out a guitar and sat down.
- The old man repaired the guitar.

- The old man sprayed new paint on the guitar.
- The old man sent the guitar away.
- The old man took out a Baseball glove and sat back at the table.
- The old man repaired the Baseball glove.

The other three types of information, namely action information, background information, and sound information, have not been quantified. In addition, we define m_{main}, m_{act}, m_{back}, and m_{sound} as the number of memories a participant has of mainline information, action information, background information, and sound information.

When quantifying the perception of mainline information, we define $\mu = m_{main}/n_{main}$, the larger the μ, the better the perception of the mainline information. For the other three perceptual effects, we directly use m as the perception score. The higher the m, the better the perceptual effect of information.

In the data augmentation phase, we amplified the data for each type of information by a factor of 20 using the SMOTE algorithm. Notably, for the information perception of actions, backgrounds, and sounds, there are extreme data in the collected samples. Which need to be removed. And the perception of mainline information μ is decimal between 0 and 1, so there is no need to delete extreme data. The augmented data is used to draw the probability distribution maps below, which fully characterize the sample distribution by increasing sample diversity. Besides, in the machine learning phase, augmented data is used to prevent over-fitting problems.

4.2 Statistical Analysis of User's Perception of Multi-source Information

To address RQ1, we analyze the scores of multi-source information perception in VR environments and traditional iPad environments.

Analysis of the Perception of Mainline Information. According to participants' mainline information perception data, probability distribution maps are drawn for four videos (Fig. 2). The vertical axis represents the normalized number of participants, the horizontal axis represents the mainline information perception score μ, the red represents the distribution when using VR media, and the blue represents the iPad media.

From Fig. 2, it can be seen that there are significant differences in the scores and user distributions of the four videos with both media. The user distribution when using VR media is significantly concentrated on higher scores than when using iPad.

Statistical analysis is further conducted. One-way ANOVA was conducted on the mainline perception data of four videos (Fig. 3), and the dependent variable was the mainline information perception score to explore whether different media had an impact on the score. Considering that the augmented data may introduce noise, real samples are still used for variance analysis. As shown in Fig. 3, in video A, the average score of the VR group (0.866) is higher than that of the iPad group

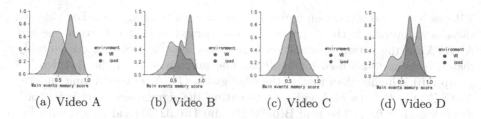

| (a) Video A | (b) Video B | (c) Video C | (d) Video D |

Fig. 2. Mainline Information Probability Distribution

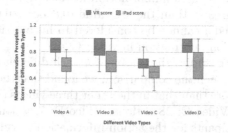

Fig. 3. The scores of mainline information perception

(0.6), and the P is 0.00074, which is much less than 0.01. The average score of the VR group in video B (0.875) is higher than that of the iPad group (0.65), and P (0.02874) is less than 0.05. The data analysis of videos C and D is consistent with A and B. Based on the above statistical analysis, it can be found that there are significant differences in user perception of mainline information when using different media, and the perception in the VR environment is generally better than that with an iPad.

Analysis of the Perception of Action Information. According to participants' action information perception data, probability distribution maps are drawn for four videos (Fig. 4).

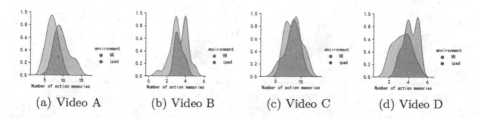

| (a) Video A | (b) Video B | (c) Video C | (d) Video D |

Fig. 4. Action information probability distribution

In Fig. 4, it can be seen that there are significant differences in the distribution of videos A, B, and D in the two media. The probability distribution when using

VR media is concentrated on higher scores than when using iPad. For video C, there is an overlap in the distribution when using two media. Further one-way ANOVA on the action information perception data was conducted. Notably, real samples are also used for analysis. The average score of the A video VR group (10) is higher than that of the iPad group (7). After conducting one-way ANOVA, the P-value of A video representing the significance level is 0.00661, much less than 0.01. The P of B(0.03443) and D(0.02151) videos are both less than 0.05. Therefore, it is believed that different media have a significant impact on the perception score of action information in videos A, B, and D. The P-value of C video is much greater than the set value (0.80608 > 0.05), indicating that different playback media cannot be considered to have a significant impact on the perception of action information in video C.

This paper further studies the reasons for such differences between video C and other videos. Through the comparison, we found that the action information in video C is much more than that in the other three videos (Video A: 16 actions, Video B: 4 actions, Video C: 28 actions, Video D: 7 actions), but the average memory of the participants for the action information in video C is actually less than that of video A with less total action information.

According to the Cognitive Load Theory, the capacity of working memory is limited in the process of learning, so when the amount of information is too much, the cognitive load will be overloaded, which will affect learners' learning efficiency. The large amount of action information in video C resulted in the participants being unable to remember more action information in a short period of time, leading to statistically different results compared to other videos.

Based on the above, it can still be determined that there are indeed differences in the perception of action information when using different media, and the perception level in VR environment is better than that using an iPad.

Analysis of the Perception of Background Information. According to participants' background information perception data, probability distribution maps are drawn for four videos (Fig. 5).

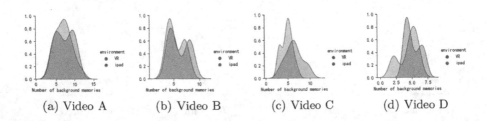

(a) Video A	(b) Video B	(c) Video C	(d) Video D

Fig. 5. Background information probability distribution

For video C, there are significant differences in the perception of background information when using different media, and the probability distribution when using VR media is concentrated on higher scores than when using iPad. However, for A, B, and D, there is an overlap in the score distribution obviously when using the two media. Then, a one-way ANOVA on the background information perception scores for four videos was conducted.

The P-values of A, B, and D videos (0.86248, 0.40748, 0.19215) are greater than the set value of 0.05. Therefore, it cannot be considered that different playback media have a significant impact on the perception scores of background information in videos A, B, and D. The average score of the C video VR group (6.5) is significantly higher than that of the iPad group (4.7), and the P-value (0.04164) is less than 0.05. Therefore, it can be considered that different playback media have a significant impact on the perception effect score of video C background information.

Therefore, this paper explores the reasons for this difference. After comparison, we ultimately found that much background information in video C often requires the viewer to move their perspective to see it, that is, there are more non-front perspectives in video C. And it is hypothesized that when using VR media, non-front information is perceived better than using traditional media.

In summary, when there is a lot of front background information in the video, there is no significant difference in the perception of background information using different media. When there is a large amount of non-front background information, VR media has better information reception performance than traditional media.

Analysis of the Perception of Sound Information. According to participants' sound information perception data, probability distribution maps are drawn for four videos (Fig. 6).

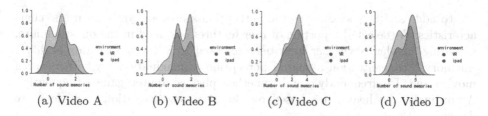

|(a) Video A|(b) Video B|(c) Video C|(d) Video D|

Fig. 6. Sound information probability distribution

There is an obvious overlap in the score distribution of all videos using two different media, and the difference in distribution is not significant. And a one-way ANOVA on the sound information perception scores for four videos was further conducted.

There is no obvious difference in the scores of the VR and iPad groups for the four videos (A: 1.1, 0.7, B: 1.5, 1.3, C: 2.3, 2.4, D: 3.6, 2.5), and the P-values are all much greater than 0.05 (0.22204, 0.46970, 0.85015, 0.18345). Therefore, a unified conclusion can be drawn that there is no significant difference in the perceptual effects of user sound information when using different media.

At this point, this paper has answered RQ1 about the differences in user perception of multi-source information using different media.

4.3 Analysis of the Impact of User Characteristics on Information Perception

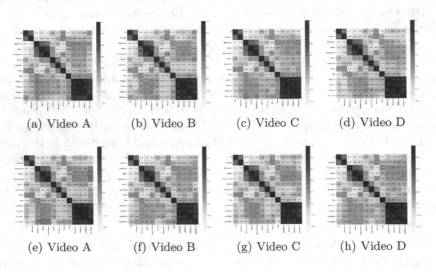

(a) Video A   (b) Video B   (c) Video C   (d) Video D

(e) Video A   (f) Video B   (g) Video C   (h) Video D

Fig. 7. Heat map in the VR (a–d) & iPad (e–h) environment

To address RQ2, we analyze the perception scores and data on users' characteristics. We selected a portion of user features obtained in the questionnaire, including "gender", "whether have been exposed to VR", "observation ability", "memory", "concentration", "spatial perception", "imagination", "whether watch movies and TV frequently", and "whether play computer games frequently". Accordingly, the heat maps based on the Pearson correlation coefficient are drawn.

Figure 7 (a–d) shows the user characteristics and information perception effects of four videos in a VR environment. The linear correlation between different characteristics and information perception can be observed. The larger the score and the darker the color, the greater of linear correlation. In the above four images, it can be seen that the colors of grids that intersect the five user characteristics (i.e., "observation ability", "memory ability", "concentration", "spatial perception", and "whether play computer games frequently") with the effect of information perception are deeper, with values close to or greater than 0.2. According to the judging criteria, it can be determined that there is a weak correlation between these five user characteristics and the perceived effect of multiple information in the VR environment. The Pearson correlation coefficient between other user characteristics and the information perception effect is generally close to 0, so it is believed that there is no correlation.

Figure 7 (e–h) shows the user characteristics and information perception effects of four videos on traditional iPad media. It can be found that the colors of grids that intersect with the effects of multi-source information perception and the above five characteristics are darker. Their values are all close to 0.2, with the largest correlation coefficient value (0.39) appearing between memory and the sound perception of video A. It can be determined that there is a weak correlation between these five user characteristics and the perceived effect of multi-source information in the iPad environment. The Pearson correlation coefficient between other user characteristics and information perception is still generally close to 0, so it is believed that there is no correlation between other user characteristics and information perception.

In summary, it can be concluded that, regardless of the media environment, there is a weak correlation between the five user characteristics of "observation ability", "memory ability", "concentration", "spatial perception", and "whether play computer games frequently" and the user's perception of multi-source information. And RQ2 is basically answered.

5   Conclusion

Our work mainly studies the perception and reception performance of users towards panoramic video information, identifies the differences in perception performance when using different playback media (VR environment and traditional iPad), and further explores the correlation between user characteristics and information perception performance. We aim to help VR content developers find target user groups, improve video content, and promote the development of the VR industry.

We divide video information into mainline information, action information, background information, and sound information. To cover all video types, we select four representative videos for experiments (N = 40). The main contributions are as follows. Firstly, for mainline information, action information, and background information, the user perception using VR media is better than traditional media. For sound information, there is no significant difference between the two media. The results also indicate that for non-front information, the perception using VR media is better. Secondly, there is a positive correlation between user characteristics of observation ability, memory, concentration, spatial perception, whether play computer games frequently, and information perception. The higher the quantification score of these characteristics, the better the information perception of the corresponding user.

There also exist limitations in the paper. Such as, the collected experimental sample size is relatively small. Even with data augmentation, noise may still be introduced, resulting in inaccurate prediction results. Therefore, more sample data will be collected in the future.

References

1. Gaddam, V.R., et al.: Tiling in interactive panoramic video: approaches and evaluation. In: IEEE Transactions on Multimedia, vol. 18, no. 9, pp. 1819–1831 (2016)
2. Ziang, L., et al.: Prediction of motion sickness degree of stereoscopic panoramic videos based on content perception and binocular characteristics. Digit. Sig. Process. **132**, 103787 (2023)
3. Moreno, R., Mayer, R.E.: Learning science in virtual reality multimedia environments: role of methods and media. J. Educ. Psychol. **94**(3), 598–610 (2002)
4. Rizzo, A., Pryor, L., Matheis, R., et al.: Memory assessment using graphics-based and panoramic video virtual environments. In: Proceedings of 5th International Conference on Disability Virtual Reality and Association and Technology (2004)
5. MacQuarrie, A., Steed, A.: Cinematic virtual reality: Evaluating the effect of display type on the viewing experience for panoramic video. In: 2017 IEEE Virtual Reality (VR), pp. 45–54. IEEE (2017)
6. Qu, Q.W., et al.: Research on virtual reality user presence based on information perception. Comput. Sci. **49**(09), 146–154 (2022)
7. Wu, Y.: Immersive virtual reality news: a study of user experience and media effects. Int. J. Hum Comput Stud. **147**(1), 102576 (2021)
8. Sarune, B., et al.: Remediating learning from non-immersive to immersive media: using EEG to investigate the effects of environmental embeddedness on reading in virtual reality. Comput. Educ. **164**(Apr.), 104122.1–104122.15 (2021)
9. Buttussi, F., Chittaro, L.: Effects of different types of virtual reality display on presence and learning in a safety training scenario. IEEE Trans. Visual. Comput. Graph. **24**(2), 1063–1076 (2018)
10. Selzer, M.N., Gazcon, N.F., Larrea, M.L.: Effects of virtual presence and learning outcome using low-end virtual reality systems. Displays **59**(4), 9–15 (2019)
11. Lee, W.Y., et al.: Do curious students learn more science in an immersive virtual reality environment? Exploring the impact of advance organizers and epistemic curiosity. Comput. Educ. **182**(Jun.), 104456.1–104456.16 (2022)
12. Lui, M., Mcewen, R., Mullally, M.: Immersive virtual reality for supporting complex scientific knowledge: augmenting our understanding with physiological monitoring. Br. J. Edu. Technol. **51**(6), 2181–2199 (2020)
13. Ahn, S.J., Nowak, K.L., Bailenson, J.N.: Unintended consequences of spatial presence on learning in virtual reality. Comput. Educ. **186**(2), 104532 (2022)
14. Henríquez, F.J.S., Quintana, M.: Measuring stimulation and cognitive reactions in middle schoolers after using immersive technology: design and validation of the TINMER questionnaire. Comput. Educ. **166**(2), 104157 (2021)
15. Coxon, M., Kelly, N., Page, S.: Individual differences in virtual reality: are spatial presence and spatial ability linked? Virtual Real. **20**(4), 203–212 (2016)
16. Liang, H., Dong, X.: Enhancing cognitive ability through a VR serious game training model mixing Piaget's epistemological methodology and Lumosity concept. Vis. Comput. **38**, 3487–3498 (2022)
17. Weller, R., Brennecke, B., Zachmann, G.: Redirected walking in virtual reality with auditory step feedback. Vis. Comput. **38**, 3475–3486 (2022)

Multi-scale Attention Conditional GAN for Underwater Image Enhancement

Yiming Li[1,2], Fei Li[1,2], and Zhenbo Li[1,2,3(✉)]

[1] College of Information and Electrical Engineering, China Agricultural University,
Beijing 100083, People's Republic of China
`lizb@cau.edu.cn`
[2] National Innovation Center for Digital Fishery, Ministry of Agriculture and Rural Affairs,
Beijing 100083, People's Republic of China
[3] Key Laboratory of Agricultural Information Acquisition Technology, Ministry of Agriculture
and Rural Affairs, Beijing, People's Republic of China

Abstract. Underwater image enhancement (UIE) has achieved impressive achievements in various marine tasks, such as aquaculture and biological monitoring. However, complex underwater scenarios impede current UIE method application development. Some UIE methods utilize convolutional neural network (CNN) based models to improve the quality of degradation images, but these methods fail to capture multi-scale high-level features, leading to sub-optimal results. To address these issues, we propose a multi-scale attention conditional generative adversarial network (GAN), dubbed Mac-GAN, to recover the degraded underwater images by utilizing an encoder-decoder structure. Concretely, a novel multi-scale conditional GAN architecture is utilized to aggregate the multi-scale features and reconstruct the high-quality underwater images with high perceptual information. Different from the reference model, a novel attention module (AMU) is designed to integrate associated features among the channels for the UIE tasks and embedded after the down sampling layer, effectively suppressing non-significant features to improve the extraction effect of multi-scale features. Meanwhile, perceptual loss and total variation loss are utilized to enhance smoothness and suppress artifacts. Extensive experiments demonstrate that our proposed model achieves remarkable results in terms of qualitative and quantitative metrics, such as 0.7dB improvement in PSNR metrics and 0.8dB improvement in UIQM metrics. Moreover, Mac-GAN can generate a pleasing visual result without obvious over-enhancement and over-saturation over the comparison of UIE methods. A detailed set of ablation experiments analyzes core components' contribution to the proposed approach.

Keywords: Conditional Generative Adversarial Network · Underwater Image Enhancement · Attention Module

1 Introduction

Underwater image enhancement (UIE) methods are widely used in marine resource exploration, underwater biological monitoring, and aquaculture [1, 2]. However, the light is absorbed and scattered underwater, which leads to the color deviation. Meanwhile, the

B. Sheng et al. (Eds.): CGI 2023, LNCS 14495, pp. 463–475, 2024.
https://doi.org/10.1007/978-3-031-50069-5_38

suspended particles make underwater images have noise and blur [3]. Due to these issues, degraded images present significant challenges for various underwater applications.

Traditional UIE methods utilized fixed parameters and physical model to enhance the degraded images. They may work well in certain scenarios [4–7]. However, the above methods are unfit for complex underwater scenarios. Recently, the deep learning model achieves a great success in various vision tasks. It is a potential solution to utilize a CNN-based model for the UIE community. Some researchers elaborate on the UIE network to recover clean underwater images. For instance, Wang et al. [8] proposed an end-to-end framework, UIE-Net, to extract the inherent features in local patches, which correct color cast and haze removal. Hou et al. [9] proposed an underwater residual CNN with jointly performed residual learning. Another line of research involves employing the generative adversarial network (GAN) to reconstruct the degradation of underwater images. For example, Guo et al. [10] proposed a multi-scale dense GAN to improve image details by removing over-enhancement and blur. However, existing methods failed to capture the various high-level features and preserve the structure and perceptual information.

| Input | UDCP | MLFcGAN | Mac-GAN |

Fig. 1. Visual comparison of real images. The results of our Mac-GAN have more favorable color balance and contrast compared with UDCP [7] and MLFcGAN [11].

To solve above issues, we propose a novel UIE method, Mac-GAN, that utilize the multi-scale information to reconstruct clean underwater images. Moreover, Mac-GAN leverages the advantages of conditional GAN and attention mechanisms to effectively preserve the structure and perceptual information. Specifically, we first utilized a feature fusion module to aggregate multi-scale local and global features, which learns fine-grained features to recover the details of input images. In order to improve the feature information aggregation effect of the reference model, we designed a novel attention module (AMU) to improve UIE network representation and focus on contextual infor-mation. Moreover, for better practicality, we introduce the perceptual loss and total variation loss to improve the model performance. Qualitative and quantitative experi-ments demonstrate that Mac-GAN can achieve impressive performance on synthetic and real underwater datasets. Besides, the ablation analysis can indicate the effectiveness of the proposed components. Figure 1 shows a typical example by our Mac-GAN against other UIE methods including UDCP and MLFcGAN. In contrast, the proposed model achieves more pleasing visual results than the existed methods.

We emphasize the core contributions of this paper as follows:

- A UIE method (Mac-GAN) is proposed to utilize the multi-scale feature with a novel attention mechanism to reconstruct high-quality underwater images.
- A novel attention module is designed to make the model highly expressive.
- Extensive experiments show that the proposed Mac-GAN achieves pleasing visual results and the best evaluation metrics.

2 Method

In this section, we introduce the detailed structure of the proposed method, including generator, discriminator, attention module for underwater, and objective function.

2.1 Generator and Discriminator

The overall of the generator structure is shown in Fig. 2, it consists of two core components: an encoder-decoder network and a global-local feature fusion block. We refer to the classic U-Net [16] and build the generator on the basis of encoder-decoder structure.

Global features have the long-range dependence of the image. In the encoder network, there are 7 downsampling layers to extract local and global features from multi-scales. Compared with the features from single scale, multi scale features contain more detailed information of the image. In addition, multiple convolutional layers are utilized to enrich the semantic information. This strategy can deliver crucial improvement in the extraction effects of features to ensure that the generated images have more details. Moreover, a novel attention module AMU is used after each downsampling layer to aggregate key features effectively. The decoder network is used to recover the low-resolution image.

Mac-GAN utilizes the global and local feature fusion modules before the skip layer connection. The process of fusion module is as the following. Firstly, a 1×1 convolutional layer is utilized to adjust the number of channels c_g of the global feature f_g same as local feature map f_l. This operator defined as: $f_{g1} = F_{conv}(f_g, W)$, where F_{conv} denotes the convolution layer, and W is the learnable weight. Subsequently, f_{g1} is duplicated as $h_i \times w_i$, h_i and w_i denote the height and width of f_l at scale i, it is defined as: $f_{g2} = F_{dup}(f_{g1}, num = h_i \times w_i)$. Then, f_{g2} is reshaped to the same dimension as $h_i \times w_i \times c_i$ of f_l: $f_{g3} = F_{re}(f_{g2}, size = h_i \times w_i \times c_i)$, where F_{re} is the reshape operation. After that, f_{g3} is concatenated with f_l, which is defined as: $f_{out} = Concat(f_l, f_{g3})$. Finally, f_{out} is concatenated with the corresponding upsampling layers.

To discriminate the generated images more comprehensively, PatchGAN [17] is adopted as the discriminator. Benefitting from this module, the generator can produce high-quality images more efficiently.

2.2 Attention Module for Underwater

Mac-GAN is designed to capture pixel interactions and suppress noise signal during feature extract processing. This is incompatible directly using the local and global feature extraction. Thus, a novel attention module dubbed AMU is designed as a task-specific module focusing on the detailed and context information to improve the feature extract

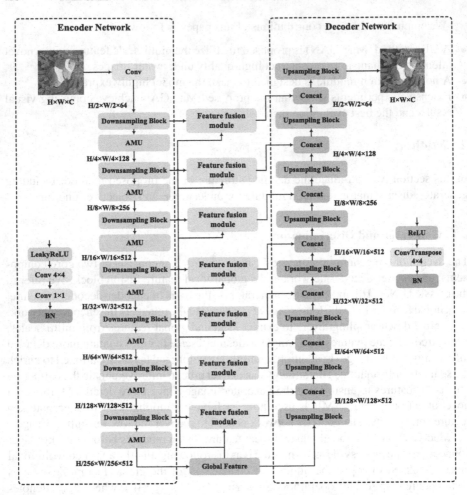

Fig. 2. The overall architecture of the generator.

effect and ensure the global feature has sufficient effective information. It utilizes the trained model weight difference measure to highlight key features and imposing a weight sparsity penalty. The AUM refers to the structure of SENet [15] and normalization-based attention module [18]. The scaling factor from Batch Normalization (BN) [19] is applied, and the formula can be presented as:

$$B_{out} = BN(B_{in}) = \gamma \frac{B_{in} - \mu_B}{\sqrt{\sigma_B^2 + \epsilon}} + \beta \tag{1}$$

where γ and β denote the trainable transformation parameters, μ_B and σ_B are the mean and standard deviation of the mini-batch B, B_{out} and B_{in} are output and input, ϵ represents a constant for numerical stability. The structure of the AMU and SE is shown in Fig. 3.

Different from SE block, the AMU replaces the GAP module of SE with the scaling factor of BN to improve the effect of suppressing insignificant features and add a

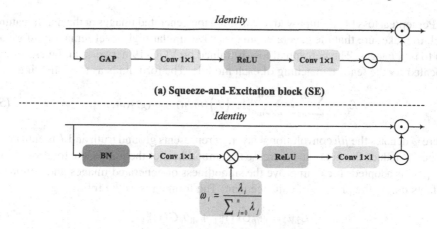

(a) Squeeze-and-Excitation block (SE)

(b) Attention module for Underwater (AMU)

Fig. 3. The structure of (a) Squeeze-and-Excitation block (SE) and (b) Attention module for underwater (AMU).

multiplication with weight parameter between 1×1 convolution and ReLU activation function. In AMU, the input feature map is scaled by the BN layer. Then it is multiplied with the weight parameter ω after a 1×1 convolution. Subsequently, it is processed by a ReLU activation function, a 1×1 convolution and finally multiplied with the input features after the sigmoid activation function. The formula of the weight parameter ω is defined as:

$$\omega_i = \frac{\lambda_i}{\sum_{j=0}^{n} \lambda_j} \tag{2}$$

where i, j denote the number of channels, λ represents the scaling factor of each channel, and n is the sum of channels.

2.3 Objective Function

GAN is difficult to converge during the training process, resulting in gradient explosion or gradient disappearance. To stabilize the network training, the loss function of WGAN-GP [20] is adopted, which utilizes gradient penalty on the basis of WGAN to replace weight clipping. The formula is as the following:

$$\mathcal{L}_{WGAN-GP} = E_{x,y}\big[D(x, y)\big] - E_x[D(x, G(x))] + \lambda E_{\hat{x}}[(\|\nabla_{\hat{x}} D(\hat{x})\|_2 - 1)^2] \tag{3}$$

where x denotes the degraded underwater image, y denotes the reference image, $\hat{x}$ is the uniform sampling between the generated image $G(x)$ and y, λ denotes the weight factor. $\mathcal{L}_1$ loss is utilized to reconstruct the clean image, which promotes the generator to produce less blur than the $\mathcal{L}_2$ loss, the formula is expressed as:

$$\mathcal{L}_1 = E_{x,y}[\|gt - G(x)\|] \tag{4}$$

where gt represents ground truth, $G(x)$ is generated image.

Perceptual loss [4] is employed to constrain the generated images at the depth feature level, to make sure that the generated images have similar high-level semantic information to real images. The perceptual loss is trained on VGG-19 network, and weights are allocated for the feature matching of each module. The formula is as the following:

$$\mathcal{L}_p = \sum_{m=1}^{H} \sum_{n=1}^{W} \left| \varphi_j\left(\hat{J}\right)(m, n) - \varphi_j(gt)(m, n) \right| \tag{5}$$

where φ denotes the jth convolutional layer, gt represents ground truth and $\hat{J}$ is enhanced image. To reduce the noise and increase the smoothness of the image, the total variation loss [21] is adopted. It can improve the smoothness of generated images and eliminate artifacts during the process of enhancement. The formula is as the following:

$$\mathcal{L}_{TV} = \|\theta_h G(x)\|_1 + \|\theta_v G(x)\|_1 \tag{6}$$

where θ_h denotes the horizontal gradient operator, and θ_v is the vertical gradient operator. The overall objective function is defined as the following:

$$\mathcal{L} = \min_{G} \max_{D} \mathcal{L}_{WGAN-GP} + \lambda_1 \mathcal{L}_1 + \lambda_2 \mathcal{L}_p + \lambda_3 \mathcal{L}_{TV} \tag{7}$$

where $\lambda_1, \lambda_2, \lambda_3$ denote the weight parameter.

3 Results

3.1 Experimental Settings

Dataset. We select the paired underwater image dataset made in [1]. Among them, 6000 pairs of images are set as the training set and the remaining 128 pairs of images are set as the validation set. To evaluate the enhancement effects of our method more comprehensively, we use RUIE [26] dataset and randomly select 100 underwater images that do not have ground truth including marine and aquaculture environment from the Internet for further testing. All images are resized to the size of 256×256 before training or testing.

Experimental Environment and Parameter Settings. The training is performed on Pytorch 1.5 framework and a workstation with Intel(R) Xeon(R) E5–2630 v4, NVIDIA GTX 1080. The weight parameter of the loss function is set to $\lambda = 10, \lambda_1 = 10^{-1}, \lambda_2 = 10^{-2}, \lambda_3 = 10^{-3}$. The Adam optimizer is utilized, and the initial learning rate is set to $1e^{-4}, \beta_1 = 0.5, \beta_2 = 0.99$. The batch size is set to 16, and the model is trained for 200 epochs.

Compared Methods. Some state of art methods in UIE are selected for comparing, all of them have good enhancement effects. These methods are divided into two categories: traditional methods including Fusion [4], IBLA [5], UDCP [7], ULAP [6]; learning-based methods: UGAN [1], FunieGAN [14], WaterNet [12], Style-Transfer [13], UWCNN [2], MLFcGAN [11], Ucolor [27]. All methods are tested with the pre-trained model provided by the author. Due to UWCNN provides 10 pre-trained models, UWCNN-type I is selected as the test model after comparison.

Evaluation Metrics. To evaluate the quality of the results, two types of image evaluation metrics are adopted: the full-reference quality evaluation metrics including peak signal-to-noise ratio (PSNR) [22] and structural similarity (SSIM) [23]. For the real underwater images without corresponding ground truth, no-reference evaluation metrics are utilized, including Underwater Image Evaluation Metric (UIQM) [24] and Underwater Color Image Quality Evaluation Metric (UCIQE) [25]. UIQM indicator is based on color measurement indicator (UICM), sharpness measurement indicator (UISM), and contrast measurement indicator (UIConM).

3.2 Experimental Results Analysis

Qualitative Comparison. The comparison results of the enhanced images in UGAN dataset are shown in Fig. 4. The results indicate that the learning-based methods can achieve better performance than those of traditional methods. Most results of traditional methods have over-saturation, such as UDCP, IBLA and ULAP. For Fusion, its results have low degree of saturation. In learning-based methods, the results of GAN-based methods like UGAN, FunieGAN and Style-Transfer loss some texture information. Meanwhile, the results of CNN-based methods including WaterNet and UWCNN are lack of detail information, the results of Ucolor have low color saturation. Different from results above, the effect of MLFcGAN is like more natural. Compared with MLFcGAN, the results of our method have been further optimized in terms of color saturation.

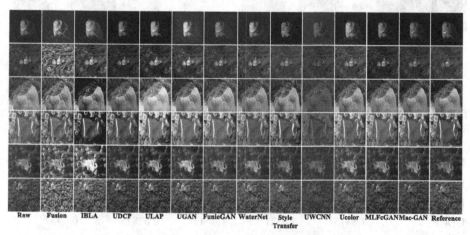

Raw Fusion IBLA UDCP ULAP UGAN FunieGAN WaterNet Style UWCNN Ucolor MLFcGAN Mac-GAN Reference
Transfer

Fig. 4. Qualitative comparison of UGAN dataset.

To evaluate the robustness of our method, we choose the RUIE dataset and randomly select 100 underwater images from the Internet for comparative experiment, and the qualitative comparison results are shown in Figs. 5, 6 and 7. In traditional methods, the enhancement effect of IBLA and UDCP is not obvious. Fusion whitens degraded images, and the results of ULAP have color cast. In learning-based methods, the enhancement effects of FunieGAN, WaterNet are similar. For Style-Transfer, its results are whitish.

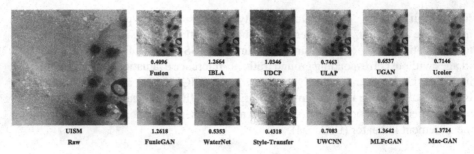

Fig. 5. Qualitative comparison of RUIE dataset. The value is UISM

Some results of UWCNN have low brightness. UGAN works well. Ucolor has limited ability to correct blue color bias. Some results of MLFcGAN have uneven halos and color smears. Mac-GAN is more effective in correcting the color. Cast of degraded images, and maintaining the color coherence of the image.

Fig. 6. Qualitative comparison of Internet images. The value is UIQM

Table 1. Comparison of quality evaluation indicators of real images. The better results will be with the increase of scores (↑) and suboptimal results are underlined.

Methods	UIQM↑	UICM↑	UISM↑	UIConM↑	UCIQE↑
Fusion	1.5422	3.7886	1.0999	0.0618	0.0463
IBLA	1.7239	4.7481	**2.1639**	**0.1133**	0.0824
UDCP	1.5315	3.6321	1.4647	0.0287	0.0457
ULAP	2.1199	5.0534	2.0366	0.1062	0.0861
UGAN	1.3103	2.7545	0.9974	0.0668	0.0558
FunieGAN	2.6549	5.1722	0.9853	0.0928	**0.1033**
WaterNet	1.1734	2.7473	1.2181	0.0875	0.0484
Style-Transfer	0.3717	0.6804	0.7672	0.0291	0.0124

(continued)

Table 1. (*continued*)

Methods	UIQM↑	UICM↑	UISM↑	UIConM↑	UCIQE↑
UWCNN	1.0221	2.1237	1.0252	0.0288	0.0427
Ucolor	2.4516	3.5727	1.0296	0.0409	0.0592
MLFcGAN	2.5574	4.5872	1.2087	0.0903	0.0911
Mac-GAN	**3.1529**	**5.6902**	1.1985	0.0969	<u>1.1001</u>

Quantitative Comparison. Due to the lack of ground truth of real images from the Internet and RUIE dataset, we only select no-reference indicators to evaluate the quality of the enhancement results. The comparison results are shown in Tables 1 and 2. In Table 1, Mac-GAN achieves optimal results in UIQM, UICM and sub-optimal results in UCIQE, indicating that our results have good color density and clarity. In no-reference metrics, some of traditional methods are superior to few learning-based methods. It is possible that the enhanced results of traditional methods have relatively good saturated colors, but these images with high saturation may not be directly applied for subsequent tasks like detection and segmentation. The results also show that Mac-GAN can be applied to a variety of underwater environments. In Table 2, Mac-GAN achieves optimal results in UISM and UCIQE and suboptimal results in UIQM. It is worth noting that the UIQM of UDCP and the UICM of Fusion are highest among all methods, and in qualitative comparison, their results have excessive saturation and brightness.

Table 2. Comparison of quality evaluation indicators of RUIE dataset. The better results will be with the increase of scores (↑) and suboptimal results are underlined.

Methods	UIQM↑	UICM↑	UISM↑	UIConM↑	UCIQE↑
Fusion	1.5541	**3.2424**	0.4096	0.0571	0.0392
IBLA	3.3425	<u>1.8991</u>	1.2664	**0.0966**	0.0642
UDCP	**4.8658**	1.6409	1.0346	0.0518	0.0709
ULAP	2.4075	1.7266	0.7463	<u>0.0816</u>	0.0658
UGAN	2.0604	1.2396	0.6537	0.0246	0.0335
FunieGAN	2.7475	1.4263	1.2618	0.0486	<u>0.0801</u>
WaterNet	2.1072	1.8274	0.5353	0.0273	0.0431
Style-Transfer	1.4928	0.4002	0.4318	0.0258	0.0093
UWCNN	1.7231	1.0647	0.7083	0.0235	0.0418
Ucolor	1.8831	1.4261	0.7146	0.0211	0.0291
MLFcGAN	3.3762	1.1588	<u>1.3642</u>	0.0429	0.0735
Mac-GAN	<u>3.5189</u>	1.4041	**1.3724**	0.0419	**0.0817**

Table 3. Comparison of quality evaluation indicators of UGAN dataset. The better results will be with the increase of scores (↑) and suboptimal results are underlined.

Methods	PSNR↑	SSIM↑	UIQM↑	UCIQE↑
Fusion	18.2647	0.6437	2.7266	0.0625
IBLA	20.2019	0.6059	3.1725	0.0523
UDCP	18.6979	0.6171	3.5883	0.0415
ULAP	20.6336	0.6535	3.3515	0.0533
UGAN	23.3311	0.7497	2.8354	0.0392
FunieGAN	22.8422	0.7248	3.1934	**0.0788**
WaterNet	23.5637	0.7491	2.4786	0.0393
Style-Transfer	24.2179	0.7714	2.9364	<u>0.0695</u>
UWCNN	17.2855	0.6332	2.3561	0.0452
Ucolor	21.9421	0.7378	1.7704	0.0341
MLFcGAN	<u>25.1974</u>	<u>0.7982</u>	<u>4.1145</u>	0.0533
Mac-GAN	**26.1698**	**0.8281**	**5.0935**	0.0638

The comparison of evaluation indicators in UGAN dataset is shown in Table 3. Mac-GAN has obvious advantages in PSNR and SSIM. It is worth noting that the scores of traditional methods are generally lower than those of learning-based methods, which also reflects the advantages of learning-based methods. In no-reference indicators, Mac-GAN has an obvious advantage in UIQM, which means that the images enhanced by our method are at good level in terms of color balance, sharpness, and contrast.

In quantitative comparison, Mac-GAN failed to achieve optimal results in some evaluation indicators, like UISM in Table1, UICM in Table2 and UCIQE in Table3, and there is a large gap between our indicator values and the optimal results. The reason may be that Mac-GAN loses part of the global information when performing multi-scale feature fusion and upsampling, resulting in decreasing in the sharpness and color of some generated images. Besides, Mac-GAN is capable of global color correction for underwater images, but has poor ability to separate foreground objects from background, resulting in a decrease in sharpness and contrast of some results. In addition, the high saturation enhancement results of some methods may lead to a significant increase in the value of some color-focused no reference indicators. However, these images are difficult to apply to underwater vision tasks directly.

Ablation Study. The ablation experiment indicates the effect of each proposed component in Mac-GAN. [11] is set as a baseline and gradually insert the following contents:

(1) SE: add SE module at the end of feature extraction network based on baseline; (2) AMU: add AMU to extract more key information of the image based on baseline; (3)$\mathcal{L}_p$: utilize perceptual loss based on (2); (4)$\mathcal{L}_{TV}$: use total variation loss based on (2); (5) Mac-GAN: apply AMU, $\mathcal{L}_p$, $\mathcal{L}_{TV}$. The methods above are trained on the UGAN dataset

for 200 epochs, with batch size set to 16, and the comparison of evaluation indicators is shown in Table 4.

Table 4. Comparison of quality evaluation indicators of different improvement structures. The better results will be with the increase of scores (↑) and suboptimal results are underlined.

Methods	PSNR↑	SSIM↑	UIQM↑	UCIQE↑
Baseline	25.3861	0.8012	4.2183	0.0561
SE	25.5836	0.8125	4.3921	0.0583
AMU	26.0934	0.8272	4.7608	**0.0639**
$\mathcal{L}_p$	26.0209	0.8236	3.5008	0.0563
$\mathcal{L}_{TV}$	26.0995	0.8235	4.6202	0.0628
Mac-GAN	**26.1698**	**0.8281**	**5.0935**	0.0638

From the Table 4, the results indicate that the application of AMU and SE has an improvement effect on various evaluation indicators. While the improvement of AMU is larger. It is not difficult to see that only utilizing the perceptual loss or the total variation loss based on AMU does not improve the indicators, even causing the indicators to decline. In $\mathcal{L}_p$, the UIQM has decreased by about 1.2. This may be related to the failure of using the perceptual loss alone to fit the network structure well. After adding all contents, each metric has improved. It maybe that the noise reduction effect of the total variation loss improves the understanding of the semantic information of perceptual loss, thereby improving the overall enhancement effect.

4 Conclusion

This paper proposes a novel UIE method, dubbed Mac-GAN, to correct color distortion and reconstruct high-quality underwater images. The generator uses the encoder-decoder structure to produce clear images by fusing multi-scale local and global features. Specifically, a multi-scale UIE architecture is employed to extract the local- and global-feature, which effectively recovers the details of degradation images. Moreover, a novel attention module is designed in the Mac-GAN to suppress insignificant features and improve the model's representation. Experiments demonstrate that the proposed model achieves impressive results in terms of qualitative and quantitative metrics. And the ablation study analyzed the contribution of the core components in the Mac-GAN. Mac-GAN has improved by 3% in the PSNR metric compared to the baseline. In the future, we will first extend the proposed model to more challenging scenarios, such as low-light and dynamic underwater scenarios. In addition, since the training process of the GAN-based method is time-consuming and the number of parameters is large, we will focus on exploring the lightweight UIE method. Besides, we will adopt other backbones types in UIE, such as transformer and diffusion models. Finally, we will introduce other impressive image enhancement method [29–31] and generation method [28] and attention modules to improve the underwater image enhancement effect. We hope this work can inspire future work in UIE.

Acknowledgments. This study is supported by Key-Area Research and Development Program of Guangdong Province - Ecological engineering breeding technology and model in seawater ponds (2020B0202010009). We thank editor and the anonymous reviewers who reviewed this paper for their valuable suggestions.

References

1. Fabbri, C., Islam, M.J., Sattar, J.: Enhancing underwater imagery using generative adversarial networks. In: 2018 IEEE International Conference on Robotics and Automation (ICRA), pp. 7159–7165(2018)
2. Li, C., Anwar, S., Porikli, F.: Underwater scene prior inspired deep underwater image and video enhancement. Pattern Recogn. **98**, 107038 (2020)
3. Li, C., Anwar, S., Hou, J., et al.: Underwater image enhancement via medium transmission-guided multi-color space embedding. In: 2021 IEEE Transactions on Image Processing, vol. 30, pp. 4985–5000 (2021)
4. Cosmin, A., et al.: Enhancing underwater images and videos by fusion. In: 2012 IEEE Conference on Computer Vision and Pattern Recognition (CVPR), pp. 81–88 (2012)
5. Peng, Y.-T., Cosman, P.C., et al.: Underwater image restoration based on image blurriness and light absorption. In: 2017 IEEE Transactions on Image Processing, vol. 26, pp. 1579–1594 (2017)
6. Jian, S., Wen, W.: Study on underwater image denoising algorithm based on wavelet transform. J. Phys. Conf. Ser. **806**, 012006 (2017)
7. Drews, P., Nascimento, E., Moraes, F., et al.: Transmission estimation in underwater single images. In: 2013 IEEE Conference on Computer Vision and Pattern Recognition (CVPR) Workshops, pp. 825–830 (2013)
8. Wang, Y., Zhang, J., Cao, Y., et al.: A deep CNN method for underwater image enhancement. In: 2017 IEEE International Conference on Image Processing (ICIP), pp. 1382–1386 (2017)
9. Hou, M., Liu, R., Fan, X., et al.: Joint residual learning for underwater image enhancement. In: 2018 IEEE International Conference on Image Processing (ICIP), pp. 4043–4047 (2018)
10. Guo, Y., Li, H., Zhuang, P.: Underwater image enhancement using a multiscale dense generative adversarial network. IEEE J. Oceanic Eng. **45**, 862–870 (2019)
11. Liu, X., Gao, Z., Chen, B.M.: MLFcGAN: multilevel feature fusion-based conditional GAN for underwater image color correction. IEEE Geosci. Remote Sens. Lett. **17**, 1488–1492 (2019)
12. Li, C., Guo, C., Ren, W., et al.: An underwater image enhancement benchmark dataset and beyond. In: 2019 IEEE Transactions on Image Processing, vol. 29, pp. 4376–4389 (2019)
13. Jamadandi, A., Mudenagudi, U.: Exemplar-based underwater image enhancement augmented by wavelet corrected transforms. In: 2019 IEEE Conference on Computer Vision and Pattern Recognition (CVPR) workshops, pp. 11–17 (2019)
14. Islam, M.J., Xia, Y., Sattar, J.: Fast underwater image enhancement for improved visual perception. IEEE Robot. Autom. Let. **5**, 3227–3234 (2020)
15. Hu, J., Shen, L., Sun, G.: Squeeze-and-excitation networks. In: 2018 IEEE Conference on Computer Vision and Pattern Recognition (CVPR), vol. 42, pp. 7132–7141 (2018)
16. Ronneberger, O., Fischer, P., Brox, T.: U-net: convolutional networks for biomedical image segmentation. In: 2015 International Conference on Medical Image Computing and Computer-Assisted Intervention, vol. 9351, pp. 234–241 (2015)

17. Isola, P., Zhu, J.Y., Zhou, T., et al.: Image-to-image translation with conditional adversarial networks. In: 2017 IEEE Conference on Computer Vision and Pattern Recognition (CVPR), pp. 1125–1134 (2017)
18. Liu, Y., Shao, Z., Teng, Y., et al.: NAM: normalization-based attention module. In: 2021 Conference on Neural Information Processing Systems (NeurIPS) Workshops (2021)
19. Ioffe, S., Szegedy, C.: Batch normalization: accelerating deep network training by reducing internal covariate shift. In: 2015 International Conference on Machine Learning (ICML), vol. 37 (2015)
20. Gulrajani, I., Ahmed, F., Arjovsky, M., et al.: Improved training of wasserstein gans. In: 2017 Advances in Neural Information Processing Systems (NIPS), vol. 30 (2017)
21. Shao, Y., Li, L., Ren, W., et al.: Domain adaptation for image dehazing, in 2020 IEEE Conference on Computer Vision and Pattern Recognition (CVPR), pp. 2808–2817 (2020)
22. Sheikh, H.R., Sabir, M.F., Bovik, A.C.: A statistical evaluation of recent full reference image quality assessment algorithms. IEEE Trans. Image Process. **15**, 3440–3451 (2006)
23. Wang, Z., Bovik, A.C., Sheikh, H.R., et al.: Image quality assessment: from error visibility to structural similarity. IEEE Trans. Image Process. **13** (2004)
24. Panetta, K., Gao, C., Agaian, S.: Human-visual-system-inspired underwater image quality measures. IEEE J. Oceanic Eng. **41**(3), 541–551 (2016). https://doi.org/10.1109/JOE.2015.2469915
25. Yang, M., Sowmya, A.: An underwater color image quality evaluation metric. IEEE J. Oceanic Eng. 246062–246071(2015)
26. Liu, R., Fan, X., Zhu, M., Hou, M., Luo, Z.: Real-world underwater enhancement: challenges, benchmarks, and solutions under natural light. IEEE Trans. Circuits Syst. Video Technol. **30**, 4861–4875 (2020)
27. Li, C., Anwar, S., Hou, J., et al.: Underwater image enhancement via medium transmission-guided multi-color space embedding. IEEE Trans. Image Process. **30**, 4985–5000 (2021)
28. Lin, X., Sun, S., Huang, W., et al.: EAPT: efficient attention pyramid transformer for image processing. IEEE Trans. Multimedia **25**, 50–61 (2023)
29. Li, L., Tang, J., Ye, Z., et al.: Unsupervised face super-resolution via gradient enhancement and semantic guidance. Vis. Comput. **37**, 2855–2867 (2021)
30. Guo, Z., Shao, M., Li, S.: Image-to-image translation using an offset-based multi-scale codes GAN encoder. Visual Comput. 1–17 (2023)
31. Zhang, Y., Han, S., Zhang, Z., et al.: CF-GAN: cross-domain feature fusion generative adversarial network for text-to-image synthesis. Vis. Comput. **39**(4), 1283–1293 (2023)

MANet: Multi-level Attention Network for 3D Human Shape and Pose Estimation

Chenhao Yao, Guiqing Li$^{(\boxtimes)}$, Juncheng Zeng, Yongwei Nie, and Chuhua Xian

South China University of Technology, Guangzhou 510006, China
ligq@scut.edu.cn

Abstract. Although there has been some progress in 3D human pose and shape estimation, accurately predicting complex human poses is still challenging. To tackle this issue and improve the accuracy of the human mesh reconstruction, we propose an end-to-end framework called Multi-level Attention Network (MANet). MANet consists of three modules: Intra Part Attention Network (IntraPA-Net), Inter Part Attention Network (InterPA-Net), and Hierarchical Pose Regressor (HPR), which model attention at various levels. IntraPA-Net utilizes pixel attention and aggregates pixel-level features for each body part, InterPA-Net establishes attention between different body parts, and HPR implicitly captures the attention of different joints in a hierarchical structure. Experimental results demonstrate that MANet achieves high accuracy in reconstructing the human mesh and aligning well with images that contain flexible human motion.

Keywords: 3D human pose · Human body reconstruction · Self-attention · 2D to 3D

1 Introduction

Recovering 3D human pose and shape from monocular images is a fundamental and challenging task in computer vision. Due to flexible body motions, complex intersections with the environment, and inherent ambiguities in lifting 2D observations to 3D space, it is difficult to estimate 3D human pose and shape accurately. Deep learning has been utilized to tackle this task and have made significant progress [4,5,11,14,15,30]. However, current DNN-based methods often struggle with challenging scenarios involving flexible human motion.

METRO [18] and MAED [29] employ self-attention mechanisms to improve the accuracy of regression. However, both methods have limitations. As shown in Fig. 1, METRO's attention mechanism requires interaction with a large number of vertices, leading to computational intensity. And MAED's MSA-S is affected by low resolution, leading to redundant feature information. Additionally, high-resolution feature maps contribute to the enhanced accuracy of regression [16].

Inspired by PARE [14], which effectively generates high-resolution attention maps as demonstrated in Fig. 1, we suggest incorporating pixel-level attention to

© The Author(s), under exclusive license to Springer Nature Switzerland AG 2024
B. Sheng et al. (Eds.): CGI 2023, LNCS 14495, pp. 476–488, 2024.
https://doi.org/10.1007/978-3-031-50069-5_39

Fig. 1. Different attention visualizations. We visualize the attention on the right wrist in the given image (a). (b) METRO [18] generates vertex-vertex attention, represented by brighter lines indicating higher attention. (c) MSA-S [29] generates attention at the feature map level. The redder the color, the higher the attention, as do (d) and (e). (d) PARE [14] generates attention at pixel level for body parts. (e) Attention generated by our method is used to fuse features from multiple body parts.

extract feature information of each body part more effectively. However, PARE does feature pixel-level attention for each body part (intra part attention), it does not adequately utilize the associations between different body parts (inter part attention) due to a lack of explicit modeling for inter part information. Intuitively, different body parts are closely related and it is essential to consider their interactions and incorporate their relationships into body part features. We can use the Transformer structure to model the inter part attention.

In this paper, we have developed a unified framework for image-based 3D human shape and pose estimation called Multi-level Attention Network (MANet). MANet leverages multiple attention mechanisms, including Intra Part Attention Network (IntraPA-Net) for pixel-level attention, Inter Part Attention Network (InterPA-Net) for establishing attention between different body part features, and Hierarchical Pose Regressor (HPR) for implicitly capturing the attention of different joints. Our key contributions are as follows.

- We present MANet, an end-to-end framework that utilizes multi-level attention to accurately estimate 3D human shape and pose from images.
- To improve the accuracy of regression, we incorporate InterPA-Net and HPR into the framework.
- Experimental results demonstrate that MANet is highly accurate in human mesh reconstruction and is well-aligned with images.
- Compared to other Transformer-based methods, MANet achieves higher accuracy while maintaining a smaller parameter count and faster speed.

2   Related Work

2.1   3D Human Pose and Shape Estimation

In recent years, more and more works has made great progress in 3D pose and shape estimation due to the pre-trained parametric human models [22]. Previous methods for estimating body pose and shape can be divided into two categories: optimization-based approaches and regression-based approaches.

The optimization-based methods fit parametric human models to pseudo labels, such as 2D keypoints [2]. They often require long iterations, which is why current optimization methods are often combined with regression methods [10].

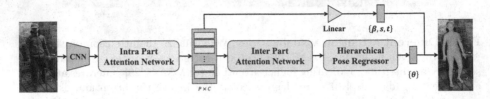

Fig. 2. Overview of the proposed Multi-level Attention Network (MANet).

Regression-based approaches mainly utilize deep neural networks to process pixels. Most human mesh recovery methods [6,11,14,17,29,32] select parameters for direct regression. This representation is highly abstract and embedded in the latent space, so the network only needs to output a low-dimensional vector that corresponds to a mesh with a specific pose and shape. These methods heavily rely on the parametric model and can sometimes become limited by the predefined space, making it challenging in some sports scenes. Instead of predicting the parameters of the human model, some methods directly regress the body shape in the form of 3D positions of mesh vertices [4,19,24]. However, such methods often result in mesh distortion.

2.2   Attention and Transformer

Transformer [27] was first proposed in the field of NLP, using Multi-Head Self-Attention mechanism. Inspired by the achievements of Transformer in the field of NLP, there is growing interest in exploring the use of Transformer architectures for various computer vision tasks [3,6,18,21,29]. Several works in 3D human mesh reconstruction have employed Transformer structure [4,18,19,29]. Most of these are non-parametric methods [4,18,19] that directly regress the 3D coordinates of coarse human meshes. While such methods can improve accuracy, the generated meshes are often non-smooth and distorted. Additionally, using the Transformer structure directly leads to a large number of parameters in the model, high computational demands, and inadequate memory during training and inference stages. Alternatively, there is a video-based parametric method called MAED [29] that combines temporal and spatial attention. However, this approach suffers from low resolution in the spatial attention map, which leads to redundant feature information and makes it susceptible to background noise.

3   Method

As depicted in Fig. 2, MANet comprises: Intra Part Attention Network (IntraPA-Net), Inter Part Attention Network (InterPA-Net), and Hierarchical Pose Regressor (HPR). The following subsections will provide more details.

Preliminaries: SMPL. SMPL [22] is a parametric human body model controlled by pose $\theta \in \mathbb{R}^{72}$ and shape $\beta \in \mathbb{R}^{10}$. Given θ and β, the SMPL model outputs a posed 3D mesh $M(\theta, \beta)$ with $N = 6890$ vertices and $K = 24$ joints. The 3D joint locations can be calculated by a linear regressor W_{reg}, i.e., $\mathcal{J}_{3D} \in \mathbb{R}^{K \times 3} = W_{reg}M$. We segment the SMPL mesh into $P = 24$ parts [22].

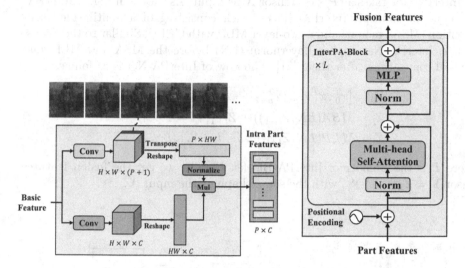

Fig. 3. Details of IntraPA-Net.   **Fig. 4.** Details of InterPA-Net.

3.1 Intra Part Attention Network

IntraPA-Net adopts the design of PARE [14]. Given an input image, a CNN backbone extracts the basic feature. As shown in Fig. 3, the basic feature is fed into two separate branches. The 2D segment branch result is denoted as $S \in \mathbb{R}^{H \times W \times (P+1)}$, where H and W represent the height and width of the feature maps. Each pixel $S_{h,w}$ contains the likelihood of belonging to a body part or background. The 3D feature branch result is denoted by $F \in \mathbb{R}^{H \times W \times C}$.

Let $S_i = S_{...,i} \in \mathbb{R}^{H \times W}$ and $F_j = F_{...,j} \in \mathbb{R}^{H \times W}$ represent the i-th and j-th channel of S and F, where $i \in \{1, \cdots, P\}$ and $j \in \{1, \cdots, C\}$. We denote $X \in \mathbb{R}^{P \times C}$ as the body part features. The element at location (i, j) in X is computed as: $X_{i,j} = \sum_{h,w} \sigma(S_i) \odot F_j$, where σ is spatial softmax operation and $\odot$ is the Hadamard product. Each element in F_j contributes proportionally to $X_{i,j}$ according to the corresponding element in $\sigma(S_i)$.

Body Shape and Camera Parameters. We flatten the feature tensor X and pass it through two separate linear regressors to estimate the body shape parameters β and the weak perspective camera parameters, consisting of scale and translation $[s, t], t \in \mathbb{R}^2$.

3.2   Inter Part Attention Network

In this subsection, we introduce InterPA-Net, which is a module that utilizes a Transformer encoder. Compared to MSA-S [29], InterPA-Net employs a higher level of spatial attention, specifically focusing on the connections between regions of different body parts.

InterPA-Net takes a $(P \times C)$ tensor X as input. As shown in Fig. 4, InterPA-Net contains multiple InterPA-Blocks, each consisting of a multiheaded self-attention (MSA) module and a two-layer MLP with GELU. Similar to the Transformer, InterPA-Net applies Layernorm (LN) before the MSA and MLP, and residual connections after them [31]. The flow of InterPA-Net is as follows:

$$Z_0 = \left[x_0^T; x_1^T; \ldots; x_{p-1}^T \right] + E_{pos}, \ E_{pos} \in \mathbb{R}^{P \times C} \tag{1}$$

$$Z_l' = MSA(LN(Z_{l-1})) + Z_{l-1}, \ l = 1 \ldots L \tag{2}$$

$$Z_l = MLP(LN(Z_l')) + Z_l', \ l = 1 \ldots L \tag{3}$$

where L is the number of InterPA-Blocks. Finally, we get the fusion features tensor $Y = Z_L \in \mathbb{R}^{P \times C}$, with the same shape as the input X.

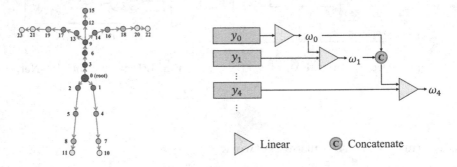

Fig. 5. SMPL skeleton structure.   **Fig. 6.** Display of the regression process of HPR.

3.3   Hierarchical Pose Regressor

HPR is inspired by KTD [29], which also utilizes a hierarchical structure. However, instead of using a global feature as input, HPR takes the features of each body part separately. Each row of the tensor $Y = \{y_0^T, y_1^T, \ldots, y_{p-1}^T\}$ is passed through a separate MLP to predict the rotation of corresponding joint ω_i. The rotations of each joint are generated in order, following the SMPL skeleton defined in Fig. 5. Fig. 6 illustrates the regression process for joints $\{0, 1, 4\}$. HPR first uses a learnable matrix $W_0 \in \mathbb{R}^{6 \times C}$ for joint 0, and calculates $\omega_0 = W_0 \cdot y_0$. Then, for joint 1, HPR takes the feature y_1 and previous ω_0 as input and uses another matrix $W_1 \in \mathbb{R}^{6 \times (C+6)}$ to compute $\omega_1 = W_1 \cdot Concat(y_1, \omega_0)$, where $Concat(\cdot)$ denotes the concatenation. Finally, the calculation of joint 4 uses the results of the ancestor joints: $\omega_4 = W_4 \cdot Concat(y_4, \omega_0, \omega_1)$, where $W_4 \in \mathbb{R}^{6 \times (C+6 \times 2)}$.

HPR implicitly amplifies the importance of ancestor joints, thus effectively reducing the cumulative error caused by small disturbances in the ancestor joints.

3.4 Loss Function

To train the network, we minimize the errors between predictions and ground truths. Using predicted SMPL parameter θ and β, we can get the predicted meshes and 3D joint locations $\mathcal{J}_{3D}$. As for 2D joint locations $\mathcal{J}_{2D}$, we compute it with the 3D joints and the predicted weak-perspective camera. 3D joint loss $\mathcal{L}_{3D} = \left\| \mathcal{J}_{3D} - \hat{\mathcal{J}}_{3D} \right\|_2^2$, 2D projection loss $\mathcal{L}_{2D} = \left\| \mathcal{J}_{2D} - \hat{\mathcal{J}}_{2D} \right\|_2^2$, pose loss $\mathcal{L}_\theta = \left\| \theta - \hat{\theta} \right\|_2^2$ and shape loss $\mathcal{L}_\beta = \left\| \beta - \hat{\beta} \right\|_2^2$ of SMPL are as follows, where $\hat{x}$ represents the ground truth for the corresponding x.

We denote $S_{h,w} = S_{h,w,1...P+1} \in \mathbb{R}^{P+1}$ as the fiber of S at the location (h, w). $\hat{S}_{h,w} \in \{0,1\}^{(P+1)}$ represents the ground-truth. We normalize $S_{h,w}$ using softmax operation $\sigma(\cdot)$ and apply cross-entropy loss $\mathcal{L}_S$.

$$\mathcal{L}_S = \frac{1}{HW} \sum_{h,w} CrossEntropy\left(\sigma\left(S_{h,w}\right), \hat{S}_{h,w} \right) \tag{4}$$

The overall loss function is defined as $\mathcal{L}$, where λ is a set of scalar weights used to balance the effects of losses.

$$\mathcal{L} = \lambda_{3D}\mathcal{L}_{3D} + \lambda_{2D}\mathcal{L}_{2D} + \lambda_\theta \mathcal{L}_\theta + \lambda_\beta \mathcal{L}_\beta + \lambda_S \mathcal{L}_S \tag{5}$$

3.5 Implementation Details

We use HRNet-W32 [26] as the backbone. There are two 3×3 convolutional layers with 128 kernels in both branches. Batch-norm and ReLU are applied. We apply a 1×1 convolutional layer with $P + 1$ kernels to get segmentation maps. For InterPA-Blocks, each block has 8 heads and hidden dimension is 128. We train our network using Adam optimizer with a learning rate of 5×10^{-5} and the batch size of 64 on an NVIDIA 1080Ti GPU. The scalar weights of loss are $\lambda_{3D} = 300$, $\lambda_{2D} = 300$, $\lambda_\theta = 60$, $\lambda_\beta = 0.06$, $\lambda_S = 60$. We have segmentation supervision via $\mathcal{L}_S$ throughout the training period.

4 Experiments

4.1 Datasets and Evaluation Metrics

Datasets. We use mixed datasets for training, including COCO [20], MPII [1], LSPET [9], Human3.6M [8] and MPI-INF-3DHP [23]. For COCO, MPII and

LSPET, we use pseudo-ground-truth provided by EFT [10]. We also use 3DPW [28] training data. To ensure consistency, we use fixed data sampling rates, as done in previous works [10,14,15]. For all experiments, the image size is 224×224. Our segmentation ground-truth is obtained by rendering ground-truth meshes using Neural Mesh Renderer [12].

Evaluation. We present our experimental results on 3DPW test set, Human3.6M validation set, COCO validation set, and LSPET test set. Three evaluation metrics are used: the Procrustes-Aligned Mean Per Joint Position Error (PA-MPJPE) [33], Mean Per Joint Position Error (MPJPE) [8], and Per Vertex Error (PVE) [25], all in millimeters. Additionally, we use Percentage of Correct Keypoints (PCK) [1] to evaluate the 2D alignment of results.

Table 1. Comparison with some previous methods on 3DPW and Human3.6M.

Method		3DPW			Human3.6M	
		PA-MPJPE ↓	MPJPE ↓	PVE ↓	PA-MPJPE ↓	MPJPE ↓
video	VIBE [13]	51.9	82.9	99.1	41.1	65.9
	TCMR [5]	52.7	86.5	103.2	52.0	76.6
	MAED [29]	45.7	79.1	92.6	38.7	56.4
image	HMR [11]	55.8	99.6	118.1	56.8	88.0
	SPIN [15]	54.2	96.1	112.6	41.3	62.9
	CLIFF [17]	47.3	76.0	89.0	**38.1**	**54.5**
	PyMAF [32]	46.8	76.8	88.7	40.2	58.8
	PARE [14]	46.5	76.5	89.6	44.1	63.1
	MANet	**44.6**	**72.6**	**86.0**	39.1	57.6

4.2 Comparisons with Parametric Regression Methods

Quantitative Results. We compare MANet with prior arts that use parametric models, all of which use ResNet-50 (R50) [7] or HRNet-W32 (H32) [26] as their backbones. These competitors include video-based methods [5,13,29] and image-based methods [11,14,15,17,32]. As shown in Table 1, MANet outperforms all other methods on 3DPW. While our method falls slightly behind CLIFF on Human3.6M, we have still made significant progress when compared to PARE. This result confirms our hypothesis that incorporating attention on different aspects significantly contributes to more accurate estimation.

Qualitative Results. Figure 7 shows the qualitative results of MANet on COCO dataset. Notably, the results reveal that MANet can generate well-aligned and plausible poses for diverse individuals, as well as situations involving complex scenes and flexible human movements. In Fig. 8, we compare MANet with CLIFF [17] on 3DPW test set, which is one of the best image-based methods.

Fig. 7. Qualitative results on COCO.

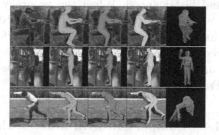

Fig. 8. Qualitative results on 3DPW. From left to right: input images, MANet, CLIFF, FastMETRO, and their visualizations from novel views (green for ground-truth, blue for MANet, red for CLIFF, and purple for FastMETRO). (Color figure online)

Table 3. Comparison with some previous methods on the LSPET dataset.

Method	PCK ↑	PA-MPJPE ↓
PARE [14]	0.57	96.5
HMR [11]	0.33	103.9
SPIN [15]	0.58	92.7
PyMAF [32]	0.62	86.1
MAED [29]	0.56	96.4
FastMETRO [4]	0.55	99.7
CLIFF [17]	0.60	88.6
MANet	**0.66**	**81.4**

Table 2. Comparison with vertex regression methods.

Model	Params	Time	error
METRO [18]	230.4M	262.8	47.9
Graphormer [19]	226.5M	264.3	45.7
FastMETRO [4]	153.0M	251.2	44.8
MANet	**33.2M**	**44.1**	**44.6**

When using CLIFF, we can observe clear pixel misalignment. From novel viewpoints, we can see that the predicted meshes by MANet have better alignment with the ground truth when compared to those generated by CLIFF, thanks to its more accurate estimation of articulated poses.

4.3   Comparison with Vertex Regression Methods

We compare MANet with the leading vertex regression methods on 3DPW, using PA-MPJPE metric. We measure the inference time with a batch size of 1, and the time unit is milliseconds. As shown in Table 2, MANet has fewer parameters and faster speed. When the accuracy is nearly identical, MANet's parameter count is 21.7% of that of FastMETRO [4], and the speed is 5.7 times faster than it. Furthermore, MANet outperforms FastMETRO in terms of alignment accuracy and generated mesh quality in Fig. 8. These results demonstrate that our multi-level attention method outperforms the direct application of the entire Transformer structure.

4.4   Comparison with State-of-the-art Methods on LSPET Dataset

In this subsection, we utilize LSPET [9], a dataset containing a large number of complex motions, to evaluate our method.

Quantitative Results. We evaluate the performance using both 2D and 3D alignment metrics, namely PCK and PA-MPJPE. As ground truth 3D keypoints are not available in LSPET, we use the data generated by EFT [10] as pseudo ground truth. To ensure fairness, all methods are only provided with a single image as input. As illustrated in Table 3, MANet shows significant improvement over PARE [14], with improvements in both 2D and 3D alignment exceeding 15%. Compared to PyMAF [32], MANet also demonstrates a 6% improvement in 2D alignment. When compared to MAED [29] and FastMETRO [3], which also utilize Transformer structures, MANet outperforms them by significant margins in all metrics. These results demonstrate the effectiveness of MANet in handling scenes with complex human motions.

Fig. 9. Qualitative results on LSPET. From left to right: input images, PARE, HMR, SPIN, PyMAF, MAED, FastMETRO, CLIFF, and MANet.

Qualitative Results. Figure 9 presents a qualitative comparison of MANet and prior arts. It is evident that MANet is better aligned with images, and the pose results are more natural. Compared to PARE, CLIFF, and PyMAF, MANet produces results that are better aligned with 2D images, particularly in terms of limb alignment. Likewise, MAED struggles with complex motion and noisy backgrounds due to its low-resolution spatial self-attention. Additionally, it is worth noting that FastMETRO is highly susceptible to mesh distortion. In contrast, our method achieves good alignment and generates smooth meshes.

4.5 Ablation Study

We conduct an ablation study using 3DPW to investigate MANet's capability. In Table 4, we use PA-MPJPE as the evaluation metric. The training sets comprise Human3.6M, MPI-INF-3DHP, and COCO-EFT. For network architectures without HPR, we use a simple linear regressor for each joint instead. To compare with KTD [29], we concatenate the fused features as the input. In Table 5, we show the parameter amount and running time of each component of MANet.

Table 4. Ablation study of different model architectures.

Architecture	PA-MPJPE ↓
PARE	50.9
IntraPA-Net	51.3
+ InterPA-Net	50.3
+ HPR	50.7
+ KTD	51.2
MANet	48.8

Table 5. Run time and parameter amount of different modules.

Module	Time	Params
CNN backbone	37.9	28.5M
IntraPA-Net	5.6	4.3M
InterPA-Net	0.4	0.3M
HPR	0.2	0.1M

Comparison of IntraPA-Net and PARE. PARE does not have segmentation supervision in the final stage, which allows it to gather information from farther regions. However, IntraPA-Net only focuses on intra part features. Based on the result, PARE slightly outperforms IntraPA-Net (50.9 < 51.3), which supports our speculation on the role of inter part information.

Effectiveness of InterPA-Net. The result demonstrates a significant 1.0 PA-MPJPE improvement compared to using only IntraPA-Net, indicating that incorporating inter part attention can help enhance regression accuracy. Moreover, the architecture outperforms PARE (50.3 < 50.9), which suggests that our method leverages inter part attention more effectively.

Effectiveness of HPR. This architecture achieves a modest improvement of 0.6 PA-MPJPE, smaller than PARE (50.7 < 50.9). This outcome demonstrates the effectiveness of HPR in reducing the error of joint pose regression.

Comparison of HPR and KTD. It can be observed that HPR performs better than KTD ($50.7 < 51.2$). This suggests that HPR is more suitable for MANet. HPR employs segmented features instead of global features, leading to reduced computation and improved learning of body part features.

Relationship Between InterPA-Net and HPR. We observe a significant improvement of 2.5 PA-MPJPE (51.3–48.8), which is greater than the sum of the individual improvements obtained by incorporating InterPA-Net and HPR ($1.0+$ 0.6). The result demonstrates that InterPA-Net and HPR effectively complement rather than conflict. We believe that HPR serves as a helpful guide for InterPA-Net, enabling it to establish more accurate associations between body parts.

Run Time and Parameter Amount. Table 5 displays parameter count and running time of each component of MANet. Parameter amount and running time of the backbone account for more than 85% of the total. Additionally, based on the result presented in Table 4, both InterPA-Net and HPR can improve performance with very few parameters, demonstrating their effectiveness.

5   Conclusion

We introduce MANet, a novel method that uses multi-level attention for accurate 3D human pose and shape estimation. MANet comprises three components: IntraPA-Net, InterPA-Net, and HPR, which model attention at different levels. Experimental results demonstrate that our approach achieves outstanding performance on 3DPW, COCO, and LSPET datasets.

References

1. Andriluka, M., Pishchulin, L., Gehler, P., Schiele, B.: 2D human pose estimation: new benchmark and state of the art analysis. In: Proceedings of the IEEE Conference on Computer Vision and Pattern Recognition, pp. 3686–3693 (2014)
2. Bogo, F., Kanazawa, A., Lassner, C., Gehler, P., Romero, J., Black, M.J.: Keep it SMPL: automatic estimation of 3D human pose and shape from a single image. In: Proceedings of the European Conference on Computer Vision, pp. 561–578 (2016)
3. Cho, J., Yoon, Y., Kwak, S.: Collaborative transformers for grounded situation recognition. In: Proceedings of the IEEE Conference on Computer Vision and Pattern Recognition, pp. 19659–19668 (2022)
4. Cho, J., Youwang, K., Oh, T.H.: Cross-attention of disentangled modalities for 3D human mesh recovery with transformers. In: Avidan, S., Brostow, G., Cissé, M., Farinella, G.M., Hassner, T. (eds.) ECCV 2022, Part I. LNCS, vol. 13661, pp. 342–359. Springer, Cham (2022). https://doi.org/10.1007/978-3-031-19769-7_20
5. Choi, H., Moon, G., Chang, J.Y., Lee, K.M.: Beyond static features for temporally consistent 3D human pose and shape from a video. In: Proceedings of the IEEE Conference on Computer Vision and Pattern Recognition, pp. 1964–1973 (2021)
6. Diaz-Arias, A., Shin, D.: Convformer: parameter reduction in transformer models for 3D human pose estimation by leveraging dynamic multi-headed convolutional attention. arXiv preprint arXiv:2304.02147 (2023)

7. He, K., Zhang, X., Ren, S., Sun, J.: Deep residual learning for image recognition. In: Proceedings of the IEEE Conference on Computer Vision and Pattern Recognition, pp. 770–778 (2016)

8. Ionescu, C., Papava, D., Olaru, V., Sminchisescu, C.: Human3. 6m: large scale datasets and predictive methods for 3D human sensing in natural environments. IEEE Trans. Pattern Anal. Mach. Intell. **36**(7), 1325–1339 (2013)

9. Johnson, S., Everingham, M.: Learning effective human pose estimation from inaccurate annotation. In: Proceedings of the IEEE Conference on Computer Vision and Pattern Recognition, pp. 1465–1472 (2011)

10. Joo, H., Neverova, N., Vedaldi, A.: Exemplar fine-tuning for 3D human pose fitting towards in-the-wild 3D human pose estimation. In: International Conference on 3D Vision (2020)

11. Kanazawa, A., Black, M.J., Jacobs, D.W., Malik, J.: End-to-end recovery of human shape and pose. In: Proceedings of the IEEE Conference on Computer Vision and Pattern Recognition, pp. 7122–7131 (2018)

12. Kato, H., Ushiku, Y., Harada, T.: Neural 3D mesh renderer. In: Proceedings of the IEEE Conference on Computer Vision and Pattern Recognition (2018)

13. Kocabas, M., Athanasiou, N., Black, M.J.: Vibe: Video inference for human body pose and shape estimation. In: Proceedings of the IEEE Conference on Computer Vision and Pattern Recognition, pp. 5253–5263 (2020)

14. Kocabas, M., Huang, C.H.P., Hilliges, O., Black, M.J.: Pare: part attention regressor for 3D human body estimation. In: Proceedings of the IEEE International Conference on Computer Vision, pp. 11127–11137 (2021)

15. Kolotouros, N., Pavlakos, G., Black, M.J., Daniilidis, K.: Learning to reconstruct 3D human pose and shape via model-fitting in the loop. In: Proceedings of the IEEE International Conference on Computer Vision, pp. 2252–2261 (2019)

16. Li, L., Tang, J., Ye, Z., Sheng, B., Mao, L., Ma, L.: Unsupervised face super-resolution via gradient enhancement and semantic guidance. Vis. Comput. **37**, 2855–2867 (2021)

17. Li, Z., Liu, J., Zhang, Z., Xu, S., Yan, Y.: Cliff: carrying location information in full frames into human pose and shape estimation. arXiv preprint arXiv:2208.00571 (2022)

18. Lin, K., Wang, L., Liu, Z.: End-to-end human pose and mesh reconstruction with transformers. In: Proceedings of the IEEE Conference on Computer Vision and Pattern Recognition, pp. 1954–1963 (2021)

19. Lin, K., Wang, L., Liu, Z.: Mesh graphormer. In: Proceedings of the IEEE International Conference on Computer Vision, pp. 12939–12948 (2021)

20. Lin, T.-Y., et al.: Microsoft COCO: common objects in context. In: Fleet, D., Pajdla, T., Schiele, B., Tuytelaars, T. (eds.) ECCV 2014. LNCS, vol. 8693, pp. 740–755. Springer, Cham (2014). https://doi.org/10.1007/978-3-319-10602-1_48

21. Lin, X., Sun, S., Huang, W., Sheng, B., Li, P., Feng, D.D.: EAPT: efficient attention pyramid transformer for image processing. IEEE Trans. Multimedia **25**, 50–61 (2023). https://doi.org/10.1109/TMM.2021.3120873

22. Loper, M., Mahmood, N., Romero, J., Pons-Moll, G., Black, M.J.: SMPL: a skinned multi-person linear model. ACM Trans. Graph. **34**(6), 1–16 (2015)

23. Mehta, D., et al.: Monocular 3D human pose estimation in the wild using improved CNN supervision. In: International Conference on 3D Vision, pp. 506–516 (2017)

24. Moon, G., Lee, K.M.: I2L-MeshNet: image-to-lixel prediction network for accurate 3D human pose and mesh estimation from a single RGB image. In: Vedaldi, A., Bischof, H., Brox, T., Frahm, J.-M. (eds.) ECCV 2020. LNCS, vol. 12352, pp. 752–768. Springer, Cham (2020). https://doi.org/10.1007/978-3-030-58571-6_44

25. Pavlakos, G., Zhu, L., Zhou, X., Daniilidis, K.: Learning to estimate 3D human pose and shape from a single color image. In: Proceedings of the IEEE Conference on Computer Vision and Pattern Recognition, pp. 459–468 (2018)
26. Sun, K., Xiao, B., Liu, D., Wang, J.: Deep high-resolution representation learning for human pose estimation. In: Proceedings of the IEEE Conference on Computer Vision and Pattern Recognition, pp. 5693–5703 (2019)
27. Vaswani, A., et al.: Attention is all you need. In: Advances in Neural Information Processing Systems, vol. 30 (2017)
28. von Marcard, T., Henschel, R., Black, M.J., Rosenhahn, B., Pons-Moll, G.: Recovering accurate 3D human pose in the wild using IMUs and a moving camera. In: Ferrari, V., Hebert, M., Sminchisescu, C., Weiss, Y. (eds.) ECCV 2018. LNCS, vol. 11214, pp. 614–631. Springer, Cham (2018). https://doi.org/10.1007/978-3-030-01249-6_37
29. Wan, Z., Li, Z., Tian, M., Liu, J., Yi, S., Li, H.: Encoder-decoder with multi-level attention for 3D human shape and pose estimation. In: Proceedings of the IEEE International Conference on Computer Vision, pp. 13033–13042 (2021)
30. Wang, K., Zhang, G., Yang, J.: 3D human pose and shape estimation with dense correspondence from a single depth image. Vis. Comput. 1–13 (2023)
31. Wang, Q., et al.: Learning deep transformer models for machine translation. arXiv preprint arXiv:1906.01787 (2019)
32. Zhang, H., et al.: Pymaf: 3D human pose and shape regression with pyramidal mesh alignment feedback loop. In: Proceedings of the IEEE International Conference on Computer Vision, pp. 11446–11456 (2021)
33. Zhou, X., Zhu, M., Pavlakos, G., Leonardos, S., Derpanis, K.G., Daniilidis, K.: MonoCap: monocular human motion capture using a CNN coupled with a geometric prior. IEEE Trans. Pattern Anal. Mach. Intell. 41(4), 901–914 (2019)

LIELFormer: Low-Light Image Enhancement with a Lightweight Transformer

Wei Zhao[1]([✉]), Zhaoyang Xie[2], and Lina Huang[1]

[1] Qingdao City University, Qingdao 266106, China
zhaowei00801@163.com
[2] Anhui University, Hefei 230601, China

Abstract. Images captured under low-light conditions often suffer from (partially) poor visibility. One of the challenges of low-light enhancement, in addition to inadequate lighting, is noise and color distortion due to the limited quality of the cameras. Previous researchers have typically used paired data (low-light and high-definition images) for training to solve single-image enhancement problems. However, those approaches have two disadvantages. One is the difficulty of collecting data in pairs, which wastes time and computational resources. Secondly, such models tend to be poorly generalizable and perform poorly on multiple datasets. Due to the consistent distribution of noise and low light intensity in specific datasets, models often perform poorly when faced with more adverse conditions. This paper proposes a simple but accurate single image enhancement network to solve this problem. Our network consists of the light estimation module and the color correction module. The light estimation module is based on the Retinex principle and uses CNN to enhance illumination. The color correction module uses a global prediction module (transformer block) to obtain the actual color distribution. This module extracts the image's original colors to make it more realistic. Our network structure is simple and does not require any paired or unpaired data for auxiliary training. It allows a single image enhancement task to be performed using only iterations of the image itself. Our approach outperforms current state-of-the-art methods in qualitative and quantitative experiments. We will release our code after publication.

Keywords: Low-Light enhancement · Image processing · Computer Vision for Computer Graphics

1 Introduction

It is a challenging task to capture high-quality images in low-light conditions. Although high ISO, long exposure, and flash can sometimes solve these problems, they suffer from different drawbacks. For example, a high ISO setting increases the sensitivity of an image sensor to light, but it also increases the noise, resulting

INPUT   Zero-DCE   RUAS

SCI   Ours   Ground Truth

Fig. 1. Visual comparison with a recent low-light enhancement method.

in a low signal-to-noise ratio (SNR). Some researchers should only use long exposure for static sense. Otherwise, the image may become blurred and impair the visual effect. The use of flash is also a great way to brighten up the surroundings, but this can often result in unexpected highlights and uneven lighting. That's why finding a stable, accurate way to enhance is essential.

Deep learning provides an effective solution, particularly through the use of deep convolutional neural networks (CNNs). These methods typically do not require the design of complex priors; instead, they directly estimate clear images from low-light images using deep end-to-end trainable networks [8,11,14,19,20,22]. As stated in [7], deep learning-based methods achieve better robustness, accuracy, and visual effects compared to traditional methods. However, these approaches are often trained on specific datasets and exhibit inconsistent performance on multiple data types. Additionally, some researchers have observed that most existing deep CNN-based methods heavily rely on local invariant convolution for image restoration feature extraction, without effectively modeling global information. Exploring global information for low-light image enhancement is crucial since global image regions contain valuable information.

In response to this state of research, several articles have attempted to apply zero-shot ways to achieve enhancement tasks. These models do not have any paired and unpaired data to train and complete a pleasing visual effect. Figure 1 shows some well-known zero-shot methods. including Zero-DCE(2020) [4], RUAS(2021) [10], and SCI(2022) [12], compared with our model. As the diagram shows, these methods exhibit overexposure and color distortion. This is primarily due to the need for effective loss function design and color correction, which adversely affect the image quality.

Recently, the Transformer architecture has shown remarkable success in various computer vision domains. In order to leverage global information and capture useful image structures for single image low-light enhancement, SPGAT [15] introduced a generator based on a U-shaped Transformer with skip connections.

This approach effectively explores global information for clear image restoration. Similarly, Xu et al. [18] proposed a Signal-to-Noise-Ratio-aware Transformer and convolutional model to dynamically enhance pixels, resulting in impressive visual effects. However, these models often suffer from high computational requirements, making real-time enhancement tasks impractical.

Based on this, in this paper, we design a zero-reference enhancement network inspired by Retinex theory to achieve real-time low-light enhancement tasks. Our network has two-stage. One is based on Retinex theory to implement the light enhancement module, which includes two parts: feature extraction and illumination estimation. We implemented feature extraction by CNN and obtained an enhanced image by illumination estimation module. The other is the image correction module, which is responsible for the color matrix transformation of the enhanced image so that the enhanced image has a more realistic visual effect. This also effectively prevents overexposure or color variation of the enhancement image.

Our contribution could be summarised as follow:

- We have proposed a lightweight network combining CNN and Transformer to achieve low-light image enhancement. This network does not require any training data and can obtain visually better enhanced images with only a single image and self-iteration. Moreover, it is very friendly for some real-time enhancement tasks.
- Compared to the previous zero-reference method, our model utilizes a global prediction module to generate enhanced images with colors closer to real images. The double-branch structure of the network does not cause additional computational pressure. Our method can achieve stable enhancement effects through self-iteration, and its speed is faster than the latest SCI [12] method. Both qualitative and quantitative experiments demonstrate the superiority of our model.

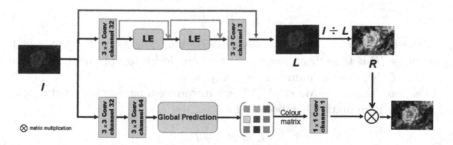

Fig. 2. Overview of proposed network architecture.

2 Method

2.1 Overview

Our enhancement network includes illumination enhancement and image correction module. As show in Fig. 2, the illumination enhancement module divided the feature extraction and illumination estimation blocks. The feature extraction module use the CNNs blocks to obtain approximate light component values. Then we obtain a great enhancement images through the retinex theory. For the image correction module, we obtain the color matrix of the input image through a global prediction module, which allows for better visualisation of enhanced images.

2.2 Illumination Enhancement Module

First, we use a 3×3 convolution to extract the basic features X from the input image:

$$X = F_{conv}^{3 \times 3}(I) \tag{1}$$

where $F_{conv}^{3 \times 3}$ is a 3×3 convolution operation, and I is the low-light image.

Then, we introduce the light estimation (LE) block to extract more accurate features, which consists of 3×3 convolutional network, BatchNorm block and Relu block. As shown in Fig. 3 (a):

$$\begin{aligned} T &= F_T(X) \\ f &= F_{Sigmod}(F_{Conv}(F_{Conv+BN+RELU}(x) + X)) \end{aligned} \tag{2}$$

where $F_{Conv+BN+RELU}$ is the LE module, and F_{Sigmod} is the $Sigmod$ function.

Second, according to retinex [17] theory, the image can be divided into two parts: the reflectance image R and the illuminated component L.

$$I = R \otimes L. \tag{3}$$

Here, the operator $\otimes$ represents elementwise multiplication. I represents the input image. R is the reflectance image that we desire to obtain by this framework, and L denotes the illumination component.

Therefore, similar to Ma et al. [12], we introduce a parametric operator φ to estimate the illumination component L.

$$\begin{aligned} L &= \varphi(f + I) \\ R &= I \oslash L. \end{aligned} \tag{4}$$

where I is the input image. In addition, to avoid data overflow errors, we truncate R between 0 and 1.

2.3 Image Correction Module

Inspired by DETR [1], we design global component queries to predict the color matrix of the input image. This module can capture the global interaction between individual pixels, thus effectively extracting the key features of the image.

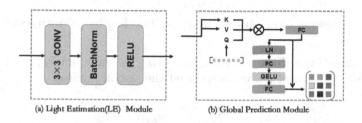

(a) Light Estimation(LE) Module (b) Global Prediction Module

Fig. 3. Overview of proposed network architecture.

As shown in Fig. 2, we first use a two-layer convolutional network superimposed as a lightweight encoder, which encodes the high-dimensional features of the image through a simpler structure. On the one hand, this lightweight approach can effectively save computational resources, and on the other hand, this facilitates the extraction of global features of the image. Then, the output features are passed to the global prediction block to obtain accurate color matrix. In particular, we set the initial values for helping maintain a stable training process. Finally, we combine R to obtain a visually pleasing enhanced image.

$$F_{Output} = R \otimes F_{Color}. \tag{5}$$

where F_{Color} is the color matrix and the F_{Output} is the output image.

Figure 3 shows the detailed structure of global prediction module, different from the DETR model, our global component queries Q are initialised as zeros without extra multi-head self-attention, which is a global component learnable feature. This operation can accelerate the model convergence process and reduce the running time. The positional encoding for K and V are from a deep convolutional networks, which is friendly with different input resolutions. After feed forward network with a linear layers, a GELU block and two FC block, which obtain accurate color matrix.

2.4 Loss

The loss function includes temporal consistency loss, spatial consistency loss and illumination smoothness loss:

$$\mathcal{L}_{Total} = \alpha\mathcal{L}_{ISL} + \beta\mathcal{L}_{SCL} \tag{6}$$

where L_{SCL} is the spatial consistency loss, and L_{ISL} is the illumination smoothness loss. With $\alpha = 1.5$ and $\beta = 1$.

Spatial Consistency Loss: To make the enhanced image have better visual effects, we added the spatial consistency loss, which guarantees the pixel-level consistency between the estimated illumination components L and the input I during each iteration. This function can be formulated as

$$\mathcal{L}_{SCL} = \sum_{t=1}^{T} ||I_t - L_t||^2 \qquad (7)$$

where T denotes the total iteration number. This loss keeps the recovered image more realistic.

Illumination Smoothness Loss. Considering the smoothness property of the illumination component [3], we introduced the smoothing loss:

$$\mathcal{L}_{ISL} = \sum_{i=1}^{T} \sum_{j \in \mathcal{N}(i)} w_{i,j} |L_i - L_j| \qquad (8)$$

where T is the total number of pixels. i is the i-th pixel. $\mathcal{N}(i)$ denotes the adjacent pixels of i in its 5×5 window. $w_{i,j}$ is the weight, whose formula is $w_{i,j} = exp(-\frac{(I_i - I_j)^2}{2\sigma^2})$. $\sigma = 0.1$ is the standard deviation for the Gaussian kernels (Table 1).

Table 1. Quantitative comparison results of low-light images.

Method (Year)	GladNet-Medium		GladNet-Extreme		LOL-V2		Time (8G-GPU)
	PSNR	SSIM	PSNR	SSIM	PSNR	SSIM	
EnlightGAN(20) [6]	18.01	0.74	17.96	0.70	17.95	0.65	1.6253 s
RUAS(21) [10]	16.05	0.63	14.39	0.61	16.50	0.55	0.0309 s
KinD(21) [20]	18.41	0.76	17.25	0.69	17.94	0.78	2.1340 s
SCL-LLE(22) [9]	16.26	0.64	16.54	0.72	16.20	0.63	1.8423 s
IAT(22) [2]	17.38	0.71	16	0.68	21.24	0.86	0.8652 s
FLW-Net(23) [21]	18.02	0.74	18.41	0.74	21.36	0.85	1.0251 s
R2RNet(23) [5]	17.64	0.68	17.62	0.71	19.64	0.71	1.6543 s
Ours	18.95	0.80	18.51	0.76	21.42	0.87	0.0201 s

3 Experiment

3.1 Implementation Details

We used ADAM optimizer with parameters $\beta_1 = 0.9$, $\beta_2 = 0.999$ and $\epsilon = 10^{-8}$ for model optimization. The learning rate was set at 10^{-4}. We mainly use four datasets for our experiments, first we select fifty medium-light and extreme-light images from the GladNet dataset [16] and twenty LOL-V2 dataset [13] for comparison, and then to further verify the performance, we further test on the Darkface dataset.

3.2 Quantitative Evaluation

Our comparison method uses the best model provided by them, and the selection of the dataset follows randomness, thus ensuring the fairness of the comparison experiment. In the comparison process, our method uses the best results within twenty rounds for the comparison. Since our model does not rely on training data, it only requires a few iterations to achieve superior results, thereby enhancing the competitive capabilities of our network effectively. Our classification test based on light intensity focuses on two main aspects. Firstly, none of the methods have been trained on this specific dataset, ensuring a fair comparison. Secondly, certain methods tend to exhibit varying performance under extreme illumination conditions, whereas our method can easily adapt to various scenarios, highlighting the excellent generalization ability of our model.

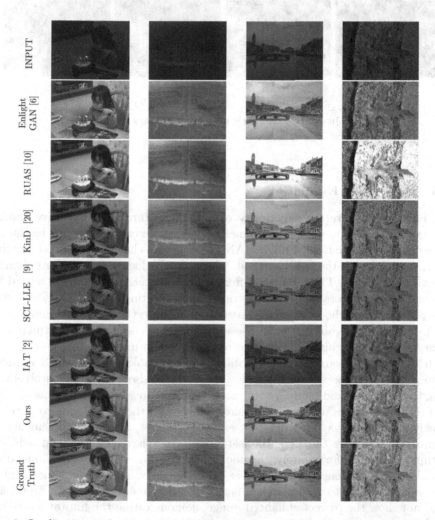

Fig. 4. Qualitative evaluation results of low-light images. GlatNet-extreme on the left and GlatNet-medium on the right.

Our model firstly does not need any dataset training to achieve better image enhancement effect, thus getting rid of the limitation of the dataset in supervised learning to make the model have better ability to adapt to the scene, and secondly our model has exposure control and color control modules to make the enhanced image of the model more realistic, thus making the model have faster and more stable performance and higher test index.

INPUT   RUAS   SCI   Ours

Fig. 5. Qualitative comparison results on Dark face dateset.

3.3   Qualitative Evaluation

We further illustrate the superiority of our model through qualitative experiments. Figure 4 shows the enhancement effect at different exposure levels. As shown in Fig. 4-2 and 4-5, EnlightGAN shows severe chromatic aberrations due to the instability of the GAN method, which clearly does not meet our enhancement requirements. Then, RUAS suffers from overexposure, which is caused by the lack of a good loss function constraint, thus affecting the visual effect. From the above two methods it can be seen that unsupervised methods often suffer from some instability. Unlike the above methods, supervised learning uses a large number of paired datasets to obtain a stable model. KinD uses images with different exposure levels to obtain a more stable model, which is much better than the above two methods. However, it also brings the problem of long training time and increases the computational pressure. Furthermore, SCL-LLE is trained using only one exposure image, and therefore tends to perform poorly when tested against different exposure images. IAT also implements an improved model for the LOL dataset using supervised learning and achieves optimal results. Unfortunately, the poor generalisation ability of the model does not show a consistent advantage over other datasets, and the enhancement is not as effective as it could be when faced with extreme illumination. Figure 4-4 does not show the correct enhanced image, demonstrating the limitations of the model.

Unlike the above, our model does not require any data for stable augmentation and has better generalization capability, thus demonstrating excellent performance on different datasets. Furthermore, our model has a color correction module to make the enhanced image more realistic, thus reducing overexposure and color differences. Figure 4-4 and 4-5 demonstrates more realistic enhanced color and texture compared to the above methods.

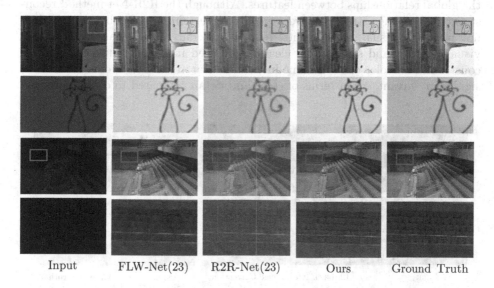

| Input | FLW-Net(23) | R2R-Net(23) | Ours | Ground Truth |

Fig. 6. Qualitative comparison results on LOL dateset.

3.4   Dark Face Recognition

Night face detection is known to be challenging. Fortunately, if we enhance the image and re-detect it, its recognition rate will increase substantially. Based on this, to further illustrate the performance of our model, we conduct further experiments on the darkface dataset. We chose the more advanced methods on this dataset, including RUAS [10] and SCI [12]. As many ways perform well on this dataset, we have decided to compare only the two most recent top-performing methods for convenience. As shown in Fig. 5-2, RUAS still shows its overexposure flaws, which blurs some image details. Furthermore, SCI is visually superior to RUAS. However, it does not enhance the actual color of some images. (Fig. 5-2 and -3) Unlike the above, our model iterates through the test image and has good color correction and loss function constraints, resulting in a more realistic and detailed image. For example, Fig. 5-1 has clearer text and the colours of the clothes in Fig. 5-3 are more realistic.

3.5   Visual Comparison with the Recently Methods

To further demonstrate the effectiveness of our approach, we conducted a visual comparison of our method with recently published methods on the LOL test set. The enhanced images are shown in Fig. 6. From the figure, it can be seen that the FLW-Net method has poor detail reconstruction, failing to reproduce the sharpness of the seat clearly due to the model's failure to effectively capture the global relationships between features. Although the R2R-Net method reconstructed the image structure, overexposure in certain areas is obvious and does not meet our visual requirements. In contrast, our method can easily obtain visually better and structurally clearer enhanced images through the Retinex constraint and color correction module. As shown in the figure, our method has significant advantages in terms of color and detail compared to other methods.

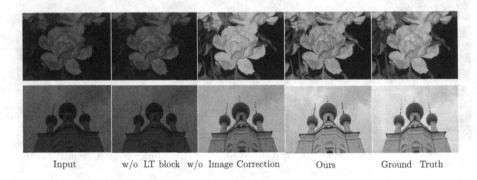

Input   w/o LT block w/o Image Correction   Ours   Ground Truth

Fig. 7. Visual results of ablation study.

3.6   Ablation Study

In this section, we analyze the impact of each component of our model in detail. We compare each experiment over only twenty iterations to better represent the real-time nature of our model. Table 2 quantitatively reveals the role of each component. When the LT block is laking, the model cannot achieve real-time enhancement, resulting in low test indicators. Subsequently, when the image correction module does not exist, the enhanced image often produces some problems of high exposure or color confusion, which leads to unsatisfactory PSNR indicators. However, our model can make the enhanced image have true color and normal lighting, thus improving the visual effect and the PSNR and SSIM indicators reached their peak at this time.

In order to further illustrate the experimental effect, we select some images for visual comparison. Figure 7-2 shows that when the LT block module is lacking, the model cannot achieve fast enhancement effect in a few iterations, thus the enhanced image is dark and fuzzy. Then, Fig. 7-3 illustrates the overexposure that occurs in the absence of the image correction module, resulting in a loss of original colour and an uncomfortable visual perception. Finally, our model is not only enhanced in near real time, but the colours are also very close to the real image.

Table 2. Ablation study on low-light dataset.

Base	LT block	Image Correction	PSNR	SSIM
✓	✗	✓	10.46	0.72
✓	✓	✗	16.47	0.88
✓	✓	✓	20.76	0.91

4 Conclusion

In this paper, we proposed a zero-reference enhancement network for single image enhancement tasks. Our network fully uses the advantages of CNN and Transformer to effectively obtain image information and achieves a better enhancement effect based on Retinex theory. Therefore, our enhanced images are not only more fully detailed but also have more realistic color distribution. In addition, our model has a lightweight structure and no required training data, allowing faster enhancement with fewer computational resources. At the same time, qualitative and quantitative experiments can demonstrate the robust adaptability of our model. A simple fine-tuning of parameters can show stable enhancement over a wide range of light conditions and data sets.

References

1. Carion, N., Massa, F., Synnaeve, G., Usunier, N., Kirillov, A., Zagoruyko, S.: End-to-end object detection with transformers. In: Vedaldi, A., Bischof, H., Brox, T., Frahm, J.-M. (eds.) ECCV 2020. LNCS, vol. 12346, pp. 213–229. Springer, Cham (2020). https://doi.org/10.1007/978-3-030-58452-8_13
2. Cui, Z., et al.: Illumination adaptive transformer. arXiv preprint arXiv:2205.14871 (2022)
3. Fan, Q., Yang, J., Wipf, D., Chen, B., Tong, X.: Image smoothing via unsupervised learning. ACM Trans. Graph. (TOG) **37**(6), 1–14 (2018)
4. Guo, C., et al.: Zero-reference deep curve estimation for low-light image enhancement. In: Proceedings of the IEEE/CVF Conference on Computer Vision and Pattern Recognition, pp. 1780–1789 (2020)
5. Hai, J., et al.: R2rnet: low-light image enhancement via real-low to real-normal network. J. Vis. Commun. Image Represent. **90**, 103712 (2023)
6. Jiang, Y., et al.: EnlightenGAN: deep light enhancement without paired supervision. IEEE Trans. Image Process. **30**, 2340–2349 (2021)

7. Li, C., et al.: Low-light image and video enhancement using deep learning: a survey. IEEE Trans. Pattern Anal. Mach. Intell. **44**(12), 9396–9416 (2021)

8. Li, M., Liu, J., Yang, W., Sun, X., Guo, Z.: Structure-revealing low-light image enhancement via robust retinex model. IEEE Trans. Image Process. **27**(6), 2828–2841 (2018)

9. Liang, D., et al.: Semantically contrastive learning for low-light image enhancement. In: Proceedings of the AAAI Conference on Artificial Intelligence, vol. 36, pp. 1555–1563 (2022)

10. Liu, R., Ma, L., Zhang, J., Fan, X., Luo, Z.: Retinex-inspired unrolling with cooperative prior architecture search for low-light image enhancement. In: Proceedings of the IEEE/CVF Conference on Computer Vision and Pattern Recognition, p. 10561–10570 (2021)

11. Lore, K.G., Akintayo, A., Sarkar, S.: Llnet: a deep autoencoder approach to natural low-light image enhancement. Pattern Recogn. **61**, 650–662 (2017)

12. Ma, L., Ma, T., Liu, R., Fan, X., Luo, Z.: Toward fast, flexible, and robust low-light image enhancement. In: Proceedings of the IEEE/CVF Conference on Computer Vision and Pattern Recognition, pp. 5637–5646 (2022)

13. Qiao, Z., Xu, W., Sun, L., Qiu, S., Guo, H.: Deep semi-supervised learning for low-light image enhancement. In: 2021 14th International Congress on Image and Signal Processing, BioMedical Engineering and Informatics (CISP-BMEI), pp. 1–6. IEEE (2021)

14. Shen, L., Yue, Z., Feng, F., Chen, Q., Liu, S., Ma, J.: MSR-net: low-light image enhancement using deep convolutional network. arXiv preprint arXiv:1711.02488 (2017)

15. Wang, C., Pan, J., Wu, X.-M.: Structural prior guided generative adversarial transformers for low-light image enhancement. arXiv preprint arXiv:2207.07828 (2022)

16. Wang, W., Wei, C., Yang, W., Liu, J.: Gladnet: low-light enhancement network with global awareness. In: 2018 13th IEEE International Conference on Automatic Face & Gesture Recognition (FG 2018), pp. 751–755. IEEE (2018)

17. Wei, C., Wang, W., Yang, W., Liu, J.: Deep retinex decomposition for low-light enhancement. arXiv preprint arXiv:1808.04560 (2018)

18. Xu, X., Wang, R., Fu, C.-W., Jia, J.: SNR-aware low-light image enhancement. In: Proceedings of the IEEE/CVF Conference on Computer Vision and Pattern Recognition, pp. 17714–17724 (2022)

19. Yang, W., Wang, S., Fang, Y., Wang, Y., Liu, J.: Band representation-based semi-supervised low-light image enhancement: bridging the gap between signal fidelity and perceptual quality. IEEE Trans. Image Process. **30**, 3461–3473 (2021)

20. Zhang, Y., Guo, X., Ma, J., Liu, W., Zhang, J.: Beyond brightening low-light images. Int. J. Comput. Vision **129**(4), 1013–1037 (2021)

21. Zhang, Y., et al.: A fast and lightweight network for low-light image enhancement. arXiv preprint arXiv:2304.02978 (2023)

22. Zhao, Z., Xiong, B., Wang, L., Qiaofeng, O., Lei, Yu., Kuang, F.: Retinexdip: a unified deep framework for low-light image enhancement. IEEE Trans. Circuits Syst. Video Technol. **32**(3), 1076–1088 (2021)

Author Index

Printed in the United States
by Baker & Taylor Publisher Services